THE FIFTEENTH (SCOTTISH) DIVIS.

MONUMENT TO 15TH (SCOTTISH) DIVISION AT BUZANCY.

“Ici fleurira Toujours le glorieux chardon d’Ecosse
Parmi les roses de France.”
“La 17 D. Française. La 15 D. Ecossaise.”

THE FIFTEENTH (SCOTTISH) DIVISION

1914-1919

BY LIEUT.-COLONEL J. STEWART, D.S.O.
AND JOHN BUCHAN

WITH

NINE ILLUSTRATIONS
AND EIGHTEEN MAPS

WILLIAM BLACKWOOD AND SONS
EDINBURGH AND LONDON
1926

This Book is Dedicated to the Glorious Memory of those who, whilst serving in the 15th (Scottish) Division, gave their lives for their King and their Country, 1915–1919

NOTE

ON behalf of old members of the Fifteenth (Scottish) Division, it is desired by the few mainly responsible for the production of this book to thank—

(*a*) The authors: Lieut.-Colonel J. Stewart, D.S.O., late The Black Watch, has expended much time and labour on study, research, and correspondence to enable him to compile and write the narrative and appendices, with the assistance of Lieut.-Colonel John Buchan, whose work has been a labour of love in memory of his gallant brother Alastair, who fell in action at Arras, 1917, while serving with the Division in the 6/7th Royal Scots Fusiliers.

(*b*) Lieut.-Colonel D. A. Foulis, D.S.O., late 10th Scottish Rifles, for his expert advice and material assistance.

(*c*) Major G. P. Geddes, D.S.O., late 8/10th Gordon Highlanders, and W. Storey Wilson, M.C., late 9th Black Watch: the former's offer of help of a material kind was accepted; the latter expended much time and labour in correspondence in connection with the work.

(*d*) Brig.-General J. E. Edmonds, C.B., C.M.G., and his staff of the Historical Section Committee of Imperial Defence, for unfailing courtesy and assistance to Lieut.-Colonel Stewart in affording access to records and documents in their possession.

(*e*) Private soldiers, N.C.O.'s, and officers, who have assisted the authors by lending diaries, letters, &c.

(*f*) All those who, when it appeared that it might be necessary to form a guarantee fund in order to ensure the publication of the history, came forward and generously gave guarantees of money, which now happily will not be required.

THE DIVISIONAL SIGN

The sign of the Fifteenth (Scottish) Division, shown on the cover of this book, consisted of the letter "O," the "fifteenth" letter of the alphabet, enclosing a "scotch" (i.e., *a wedge for jamming wheels). This sign was the distinguishing mark of the Division throughout the war.*

CONTENTS

ILLUSTRATIONS

MAPS

(In Pocket at End of Volume)

History of
The Fifteenth (Scottish) Division.

CHAPTER I.

FORMATION AND TRAINING.

WHEN in earlier days war was proclaimed at the Cross of Edinburgh and all enemies were ordered furth of the kingdom, the decent citizen of Scotland listened to the fanfaronade and went about his business. War was no concern of his since our ancient foes of England had ceased from troubling. To find a parallel to the summons of August 1914, we must go back to the time when old and young were called to man the walls after Flodden; and that was but a local affray after all, for the news of it scarcely penetrated beyond the Highland line. But in that sunny and confused month of destiny there was a stirring to the uttermost islands. The answer came quick, and after four bitter years we can judge the greatness of it.

The declaration of war against Germany found Britain ill prepared for the conflict. Battalions of the small Regular Army serving at home, the Reserve, Special Reserve, and Territorials constituted her available Army. The Territorials could not be sent abroad without their consent, and the despatch of the Expeditionary Force left her with few reserves with which to replace casualties. The problem to be faced was to find the best method of increasing the Army. Fortunately for the country Lord Kitchener's services were available. His powers of organisation were well known, and it was not surprising that on August 5 he was appointed Secretary of State for War.

August 1914.

August 1914.

The new Secretary for War did not take long to decide on his course of action. The day after he was appointed he produced his scheme. Written on half a sheet of foolscap, this historic document contains the primary instructions for the raising of those formations now familiarly known as "The New Armies"—"K. 1," "K. 2," &c. Realising that the Territorial Force was primarily required for home defence and that Parliamentary sanction would be necessary before it could be sent abroad,[1] Lord Kitchener decided to augment the Regular Army at once by 100,000 men. His scheme was not to raise new armies, but to duplicate those already existing. Stress was laid on this point, and thus every man enlisted under his scheme became at once a Regular soldier. Army Order 382, dated August 31, 1914, officially authorised the enlistment of the First Hundred Thousand.

Formation of Division.

The answer to this appeal must have astonished the War Minister himself. Every depot and recruiting office was besieged by men clamouring to enlist, and on August 24 he was able to inform the House of Lords that the men had been secured. At the same time he warned the country that the war would be long and arduous, and would require hitherto undreamt-of sacrifices on the part of all classes. Directly success was assured a second 100,000 were called for, followed two days later by a third. It is to the Second Hundred Thousand that the Fifteenth (Scottish) Division belongs.[2]

The scenes in regimental depots in August 1914 will not be readily forgotten by those whose duty took them there. An officer writing of this time says: "During this period we had great difficulties to contend with. We had to house and feed all recruits; they came in so fast that it was impossible for us to deal with them and despatch them to their units on the same day. It sometimes happened too that, although we had practically cleared the barracks one evening, there would be some 400 recruits on parade the following morning, these having come in during the night." A Cameron Diary contains

[1] It is only fair to state that at the declaration of war all ranks of the Territorial Army flocked to enlist. Whole units volunteered for service abroad. Many were sent at once, and others later: but no serving Territorial was permitted to enlist in either "K. 1" or "K. 2."

[2] See Appendix A: "Composition of Fifteenth (Scottish) Division."

the following: "The glamour of the kilt was irresistible. In Glasgow and the West of Scotland hundreds flocked to enlist in the famous regiment. The Glasgow Stock Exchange had, in an incredibly short time, raised a special company of its own, and, not to be outdone, the students of the University followed suit. Then for a few days every north-bound train carried its complement of recruits to the Cameron depot. Soon the barracks were crowded out, and for a few nights men had to sleep where they could. Even the distillery at Inverness (already with an insect population of its own) was brought into use. Drills there were practically none, for it was impossible to handle the ever-increasing swarms of men who poured in. We were all civilians then, and from a military point of view had nothing to recommend us save our enthusiasm."

Aldershot, 1914.

By September 12 the first six divisions of "K. 1" were up to strength. The formation of the second six then commenced. Numbered from 15 to 20, they made up the second "K." Army.

The Fifteenth, with the exception of a battalion of the Leicester Regiment and another of the Bedfordshire Regiment,[1] was entirely Scottish. The Division was raised at Aldershot. The nucleus was formed by those men from the 9th (Scottish) Division of "K. 1" who were surplus to establishment. Drafts to complete to war strength were sent from the various Scottish depots, and on September 15 the ranks of the Division were filled. Scarcely a battalion, however, had more than four officers, including the Commanding Officer, Adjutant, and Quartermaster. One battalion (7th Royal Scots Fusiliers) consisted of one officer (just commissioned from Quartermaster-Sergeant, R.G.A.) and 900 men. Units of the first 100,000 had been fortunate in each obtaining the services of a few Regular officers and N.C.O.'s from regimental depots. Not so their successors, who were only allowed one serving officer each to act as adjutant. At no time were there more than five Regular officers in any one brigade, including the staff, the seniors being retired Regulars, Militia officers, or Territorials. Major-General A. Wallace, C.B., was appointed as Divisional Commander, the Brigade Commanders being: 44th, Brig.-General M. G.

[1] As army troops. The Leicesters and Bedfords were line-of-communication troops, and never formed part of the Division.

Wilkinson, M.V.O.; 45th, Brig.-General F. E. Wallerston; 46th, Brig.-General E. J. Cooper, C.B., M.V.O., D.S.O.

As they arrived at Aldershot men were sent to their units and drafted into companies. Amongst them were a number of ex-Regular N.C.O.'s, pensioners, many wearing the ribbons of Egypt and Afghanistan. These were at once given acting rank, but it was difficult to select the remainder. In many instances the best-dressed men were chosen, solely on account of their smart appearance, and in nearly every instance the choice was justified. One fact was apparent from the commencement—every man was in deadly earnest. Knowing nothing of soldiering they were all keen—desperately keen—to learn, and gave no trouble to the small number of officers then available for dealing with them. Military Police had an easy task, and it is greatly to the credit of these thousands of embryo soldiers that perfect orderliness prevailed in the town. Men were too eager to make themselves soldiers to waste time in public-houses and other places of questionable reputation, with the result that there was practically no crime in the Division.

With the influx of such numbers of men accommodation soon became strained, and barracks designed to hold one unit had to suffice for two. Still recruits arrived, and the overflow were accommodated in tents. It was the same with the Headquarter Staffs. The 9th and the Fifteenth Divisions shared Headquarters with two Brigade Staffs in a building originally intended to house that of a single brigade.

Officers now flocked in—youngsters from public schools, business men, medical students. Every profession was represented, all as keen as the men, but few with more than the most elementary knowledge of soldiering. The seniors who knew the ropes had an arduous task, but the anxiety of all to learn quickly and to impart the knowledge to their subordinates made it pleasant work. From the commencement it was the custom to give lectures to officers and N.C.O.'s after the day's work, and often the budding officer instructed his platoon the following day on subjects he himself had only learnt the night before. Many mistakes were, very naturally, made, but keenness carried every one through, and soon the discerning eye of the ex-Regular glistened with pride at the sight of the machine he had helped to fashion.

At first the discomfort was appalling. Crowded into quarters far too small for them, with one blanket or a piece of tweed apiece to cover them, without mattresses or even the bare necessities of life, the men never grumbled; they knew that those in authority were doing their best, and were content. Luckily the weather was fine and no sickness broke out, but the first six weeks were anxious ones for the medical officers of the Division. In addition to overcrowding, the feeding of the men left much to be desired. These and many other drawbacks, however, did not damp the enthusiasm of the new force. No praise can be too high for these young soldiers at this the very commencement of their career. Every hardship was more than cheerfully borne. A jest carried things through on the blackest day. The predominant feeling was that they had a task to do and meant to do it.

From the beginning, order and the strictest discipline were features of the Division. True, one unit states in its diary: "In the early stages of training the men continually smoked on parade, even on Church Parade when service was going on. An attack practice was once completely stopped because the men fell out to eat blackberries." This, however, was in the very earliest stages of its existence.

Never before have recruits of the British Army been worked as were those of the new formations in 1914. For ten hours a day, including Sundays, all ranks were on parade, and long after they had been dismissed it was a common thing to find groups of young officers or N.C.O.'s studying their Drill-books and teaching one another the rudiments of their new profession. In spite of this intensive training, few men broke down. A brigadier writes: "After a certain amount of weeding out—owing to lax medical inspection on enlistment—the men were splendid. Quite the pick of the new forces. The finest material I ever saw. One company (6th Camerons, 45th Brigade) was entirely composed of men from the Glasgow University and High Schools, a shocking waste of good officer material." Another says: "Yes. I think the Second Army was better physically than their predecessors. The first 100,000 were greedily accepted, as there was such necessity for them. When the authorities found men were coming in, conditions altered, the standard all round was raised, the medical examination was stiffer, and yet they came in. Men rejected by us were ultimately taken by later formations."

By the end of September all units were more or less complete and had settled down, the 44th and 46th Brigades occupying barracks at Aldershot, the 45th being under canvas at Rushmoor, during which period Brig.-General A. G. Duff succeeded Brig.-General Cooper in command of the 46th Brigade. Divisional Artillery, under Brig.-General E. Lambart, were in barracks at Bordon.

Inspection by His Majesty, Sept. 26, 1914.

On September 26 the Division paraded for the first time as a formed unit for inspection by His Majesty. Drawn up in close column it was a curious sight. With the exception of Staff and a few senior officers, the whole Division was in plain clothes. Some wore straw hats, others caps and bowlers. Men clad in well-cut serge suits stood next others in workmen's clothes, but never did a body of recruits, small or large, with so little training to their credit, stand as steadily as did the Fifteenth Division on that occasion. The King, who was accompanied by the Queen, Lord Kitchener, and Sir Archibald Hunter, was obviously delighted, and expressed himself as much impressed with the bearing and physique of the men.

It was not long before the question of clothing became acute. Naturally the First Hundred Thousand had to be fitted out before the Second, and in doing this the Army Clothing Department had been denuded of its stock. Civilian clothes and boots are not designed to withstand the wear and tear of military training, and very soon the hardest-working platoons resembled Falstaff's ragged army. To relieve the situation the men were asked to obtain good suits, boots, and greatcoats from home, an allowance of 10s. per man being promised to those who produced these articles in good condition. This magnificent sum, however, did not help matters greatly. In these early days it was quite a common occurrence for men to be excused parade either because the state of their boots would not allow them to march or because their garments were not sufficiently decent to warrant their leaving camp or barracks.

Towards the end of the month the first consignment of army clothing made its appearance. It came as a distinct shock to the senior officers and a very considerable one to the men themselves. The garments consisted of English-pattern trousers and red serge jackets of every sort and description, some of which had been manufactured as far back as 1893. There were a few pairs of tartan trews, but these were nearly all snapped up by N.C.O.'s, and the men had to content themselves with what was left. One man was heard to remark that he had come down to be a Gordon Highlander and not a —— postman! A Cameron diarist writes as follows: "Who can recall our first uniforms without a shudder? The startling red of the tunics, the postmen's trousers with their red stripes, and, crowning absurdity, the cap comforters we wore in lieu of better head-dress. A few of us made the best of a bad job by purchasing glengarries and badges to show that we belonged to a Highland regiment and not to a Red Alsatian Band."

In spite of all drawbacks the Division quickly settled down. The effect of physical training and squad drill, hard and monotonous as they were, was soon apparent, and men became hard, fit, and inured to the trying conditions. Early in October a few obsolete rifles were issued for drill purposes, followed shortly afterwards by 100 modern rifles for the use of the "Service Companies,"[1] which were of great use on the miniature ranges.

Following the rifles came obsolete leather equipment, "Brodrick" head-dress, and a curious collection of civilian boots. By the end of October civilian clothing had—outwardly—vanished, and the Division took on the appearance of a military formation, but even then it was certainly more suggestive of comic opera than of His Majesty's Army.

The months which followed the birth of the Division cannot be passed over without some allusion to the quartermaster's branch. Never has a body of officers and men, from the Divisional Staff downwards, worked harder to obtain the hundred and one articles demanded of them. Using every method known to them—some more devious than the Regulations usually permit,—clothing, necessaries, and equipment of all kinds were obtained. It was a case of "every man for himself, &c." One commanding officer was heard to remark to a colleague that his quartermaster was the finest thief in the British Army—a compliment well deserved, as that battalion was certainly

[1] These companies consisted of 100 men from each infantry unit, and were held in readiness to proceed anywhere in case of emergency.

fitted out completely some time before the remainder of the brigade. A pleasant and persuasive manner, coupled with a lifelong experience of Staff and Ordnance methods, carried that particular quartermaster a long way, not only in England but later in France.

On October 16 Major-General Wallace left the Division on appointment to the Command of the Egyptian Expeditionary Force, and was succeeded by Major-General C. J. Mackenzie, C.B., from France.

Move to Liphook, Bramshott, and Bordon, Nov. 1914.

Between November 16 and the end of the month the Division left Aldershot to make room for its successors, the Third Hundred Thousand, the 44th Brigade moving to billets in Liphook and the neighbouring villages, the 45th and 46th to huts at Bramshott and and Bordon respectively, with Divisional Headquarters and artillery at Bordon. Although provided for by law, and carefully explained in Training Regulations, billeting was then a new experience in England. The villagers eyed the Highlanders with suspicion. They did not like being compelled to house and feed a number of men about whom they knew nothing, and whose speech they could scarcely understand. Here again a joke often carried things through, and when, as a last resort, a woman would be asked how she would like having a dozen Germans quartered on her, she invariably gave way with good grace and billeting officers had no further trouble. In this manner, with the help of willing but somewhat vague village constables, the 44th Brigade was soon comfortably housed.

As time wore on and the 45th and 46th Brigades left their huts at Bramshott and Bordon for billets, they too experienced the same treatment. Once the inhabitants found that the Scotsmen were not the barbarians they had feared, a real affection sprang up between hosts and guests, a feeling existing to this day. When the news of Loos and later engagements became known, the sorrow and pride at the losses and glory of the Fifteenth Division were almost as great in its billeting areas in England as in its native country.

In the move the 45th and 46th Brigades were not so fortunate as the 44th. True, the former had roofs to cover them at Bramshott, but they exchanged the cold comfort of tents for the doubtful benefits of half-finished huts, whilst the latter only moved to quarters similar to those vacated at Aldershot. Bramshott Camp then consisted of a number of wooden huts built on a wind-swept moor. No heating apparatus had been provided. Walls and roofs were not weatherproof, and the water supply, cooking arrangements, &c., were conspicuous by their absence. No roads or paths had been constructed through the camp; the ground was peaty moorland and speedily became a quagmire. The 45th Brigade certainly had the worst experience during this period. The inhabitants of Grayshott, Haslemere, and Hindhead, however, rendered what help they could. Buildings were set aside as recreation rooms, teas and suppers were provided, and baths fitted up. These and many other acts of kindness did much to lessen the deplorable conditions, and were much appreciated by all.

In billets, Nov.-Dec. 1914.

Training now was less monotonous than at Aldershot. Miniature ranges were erected, and shooting competitions added zest to musketry. Night work, entrenching, &c., varied the ordinary work, and, in spite of the lack of sufficient trained instructors and the scarcity of official manuals, the Division steadily improved, gaining generous praise from those who at various times inspected it.

Christmas 1914 brought with it leave for all ranks, and by half-battalions the men proceeded to their homes. Some journeying to Wick and Stornoway were only able to spend a few hours with their families before returning, but all agreed that the holiday was worth having, and, short as it was, this break certainly did much good. It was a bitter disappointment to the men to have to wear on leave the ludicrous garments provided by Government, but there was no help for it, and every one knew the reason.

Inspection by French War Minister, Jan. 1915.

The middle of January 1915 found units once more intact, and work continued steadily. On the 22nd the Division assembled for inspection by M. Millerand, the French War Minister. The only arms carried by the Division on this occasion were the obsolete drill rifles and the few modern ones provided for the Service Companies. These were only sufficient to arm the front ranks of battalions, a fact that did not escape the notice of the French Minister, who remarked to Lord Kitchener, "I see they have very few rifles."

None who took part in that inspection will ever forget it. Frensham Common was chosen for the parade ground, presumably as being equidistant from the areas occupied by the brigades. Weather conditions could not have been worse. Starting between 7 and 8 A.M., the march had hardly began before snow fell, which continued steadily for two hours. All ranks were soaked to the skin long before reaching the Common, where they had to wait some time before the inspecting party made its appearance. Standing in snow-covered heather, in a biting wind, wet through, would have proved a trying ordeal even for old soldiers. At last M. Millerand, Lord Kitchener, and Staff arrived. The ceremony occupied barely ten minutes, and, half-frozen, the Division returned to its camps and billets. It speaks well for the physical condition of the men, and for the way they were looked after by their medical officers, that little illness resulted from this trying experience. One brigade had thoughtfully provided a tot of rum for each man on their return to camp, thus undoubtedly saving much sickness. The correspondence as to who should pay for the luxury was still going on when the Division left England, and may be possibly still wending its way through " the usual official channels."

This occasion was the first on which any Highland unit of the Division appeared in the kilt. In October Government had offered to provide drab material for battalions willing to make up their own kilts, the sum of one shilling and sixpence to be allowed for the manufacture of each garment. This did not suit the Highlanders, who wisely waited till their correct tartans could be obtained. Even to the untrained eye the appearance of the men on parade was extraordinary. The uniform consisted of " Brodrick " head-dress, red or blue serge jackets, tartan kilts, and khaki hosetops, the latter provided through the generosity of friends and not by Government.

In January 1915 the 9th Battalion Gordon Highlanders, from the 44th Brigade, were formed into a Pioneer Battalion for the Division, their place in the Brigade being taken by the 7th Battalion Cameron Highlanders from the Third Hundred Thousand. The battalions of the Leicester and Bedfordshire Regiments then left the Division, which thus became, as far as the infantry was concerned, a purely Scottish Division, containing battalions of every Scottish regiment of the line.

February brought with it a change of both quarters and command. On the 20th the whole Division moved from the Aldershot to the Southern Command, with Headquarters at Cholderton. Artillery moved to Bulford Camp, the 44th Brigade to Draycott (camp) and Cirencester (billets), the 45th to Basingstoke (billets), the 46th to Winchester and Romsey (billets), and 9th Battalion Gordon Highlanders (Pioneers) to Perham Down Camp, where they remained until they embarked for France. The country was ideal for training, which now became more strenuous than ever. Battalion and elementary brigade training added to the variety, and with the issue of rifles musketry went on apace.

Move to Southern Command Area, Feb. 1915.

By the end of March the result of six months' hard work became apparent. Weaklings had been weeded out, and all ranks were as fit as fresh air, hard work, and good food could make them. There were still many deficiencies in equipment and necessaries, but when any particular article became essential there was generally some competent individual in the Division able to devise an efficient makeshift. This specially applied to musketry. Targets and appliances were well-nigh impossible to obtain, but the ingenuity of the new soldiers soon produced something as good if not better than the articles required. The new force held officers and men of all trades and professions, from miners to medical students, from lawyers to labourers; a request for any professional man or skilled artisan invariably produced many more than the number asked for.

Training of specialists had kept pace with that of the remainder, but under even greater difficulties. All equipment that could be spared necessarily went to fit out the First Hundred Thousand or the Territorials now being despatched to France and elsewhere. Little was therefore available for the Fifteenth Division. Lewis-gunners learnt their drill with the help of wooden models, signallers their work with anything they could manufacture in the shape of a telephone or telegraph instrument. It is only fair to the men of the new force to point this out, and to show how each difficulty was met and coped with as it arose.

On March 22 Major-General Colin Mackenzie, on appointment to the War Office, handed over command to Major-General F. W. N. McCracken. Destined to command the Division for over two years, it was not long before its new leader emphasised the point on which the fame of the Division eventually rested—namely, discipline. Good

Major-Gen. F. W. N. McCracken assumes command, March 1915.

as it had been before, General McCracken tried and succeeded in making it even better. An officer writing of the training period says: "Looking back on those days in England I cannot tell you how we did it. It seems impossible even now that such a magnificent fighting machine could have been turned out in ten short months. I am inclined to think that McCracken's first lecture to the Division, which formed the subject of many others to the men, had a good deal to do with it. He said that three things went to make a good soldier. The first was Discipline, the second was *Discipline*, and the third was DISCIPLINE. That lecture was never forgotten by those who heard it."

Between April 18 and 28 a general reshuffle of units took place. Division Headquarters moved to Marlborough, the 44th Brigade to Chisledon Camp, the 45th to Draycott Camp, and the 46th to Parkhouse Camp near Bulford. Billets were things of the past, and the final instruction in musketry, brigade, and divisional training commenced. Long and arduous marches put finishing touches to the previous work. Spring and early summer of 1915 were ideal for training, and as the days lengthened more and more work was accomplished in the twenty-four hours. By this time real Lewis-guns had taken the place of the wooden dummies. New leather equipment had been issued, and units were completely fitted out. Inspecting officers of all branches, from the War Minister downwards, visited the Division during this period, and, without exception, had nothing but praise to bestow.

Inspection by His Majesty, June 21, 1915.

June 21 was a red-letter day in the diary of the Division. Assembled at Sidbury Hill, it was inspected for the second and last time by His Majesty before it left England. The smart well-set-up units, not an unfit man amongst them, were very different from the crowd of civilians he had reviewed at Aldershot nine months before. It was certainly a proud day when commanders led their steady ranks of trained men past the King. The performance was all the more remarkable from the fact that, according to the diaries of certain units, they had never even practised a ceremonial march-past before this occasion.

In May, as the training drew to a close, arrangements were made to allow a certain number of all ranks to proceed on leave, a privilege much appreciated and well deserved after the arduous training of the past months. During the few remaining weeks in England parties of men were daily despatched to their homes. When the order to mobilise arrived about 2000 were on leave, but not a single man was absent when the Division embarked.

Early in July the Division was considered fit to take its place in France. Busy enough at all times, "Q" branch now had its work increased one-hundred-fold. All deficiencies were made up. Articles unobtainable a few weeks before now made their appearance in vast quantities. Clothing and equipment were carefully overhauled, and everything considered in the least unserviceable was replaced with a lavish hand. The final gift to every man from a paternal Government was a new pair of boots issued two days previous to embarkation. The result of this well-meant but belated present will be seen later.

In reviewing the work of the Division in England it seems extraordinary now how the men stood the strain. Seventy hours a week had been the programme at Aldershot, and although this was somewhat curtailed later, Sunday was the only rest-day in the week for many months. At the commencement, provided only with the clothes they stood up in, without greatcoats or change of clothing of any kind, living in muddy camps and verminous barracks, and often wet to the skin, not a murmur was heard from the ranks. Many men were miners from Fife, Lanarkshire, and elsewhere, who voluntarily gave up the comfortable conditions of home life and from £2 to £3 a week in wages to serve their country at a shilling a day. The vast majority of recruits knew nothing of soldiering or military discipline. Volunteers in the truest sense of the word, they cheerfully and uncomplainingly endured a state of affairs that would have produced something more than discontent in pre-war days. They surprised all who saw them, and especially the officers privileged to lead and train them. Although their progress satisfied those in higher authority, formations never quite came up to that standard of excellence looked for by their own commanders. One particular brigade, as good as any in the Division, will not readily forget its feelings when told by its brigadier, on the conclusion of a particularly long field-day, that it would never be fit for anything but to bury the dead! But it is certain that, in the above case, no man was really more proud of his command than was that particular brigadier.

When Germany first heard of the new divisions she scoffed at the idea of turning out well-trained and disciplined troops in a few months. She was soon to learn, and acknowledge, that she was wrong. Inheriting *esprit de corps* from the regiments whose names they bore, every unit in the Division showed by its conduct during training, and later in France, that hard work and willingness to learn can, in a short space of time, turn out troops better in war than those to whom discipline is only another word for slavery and *esprit de corps* is unknown. The men of the new formations did not enlist from mercenary motives, or to make the Army their profession, neither were they conscripts. Patriotism alone influenced them, and they submitted themselves willingly and unquestioningly to vigorous discipline and rule solely in order to serve their country. Here lies the secret of the success, not only of the Fifteenth Division but also of the remainder of the Empire's new formations.

If the training of the infantry came as a surprise, what can be said of the Artillery and Engineers? It had been generally conceded that it took three years to produce a well-trained artilleryman, and longer to train a sapper. No such time was available in 1914-15, and moreover, like the infantry, substitutes for training purposes had to be made from the best material available. In August 1914 the Divisional Artillery consisted of some 2000 men under Colonel, now Brig.-General, E. Lambart, C.B., and one other officer. For equipment, a dummy gun, made from a pine log and mounted on the funeral gun-carriage at Bordon, served as a start. An old victoria discovered in some stable was cut in two to represent carriage and limber. With these, and stones laid out on the ground, training commenced. Shortly afterwards Colonel Lambart "annexed" an obsolete 9-pr. brass Armstrong gun which adorned the grounds of the Ordnance Officers' Mess at Aldershot. Dragged from its peaceful resting-place, in spite of the protests of its owners, this ancient weapon was pressed into service. Makeshifts such as these lasted for some months. They were replaced by guns dating back to the Boer War, some still older, and a number of French pieces dated 1890. It was some time before guns of the latest pattern reached the Division.

Horses arrived soon after the Division had been formed, but, as headstalls only accompanied them, little instruction could be given in riding. To commence with, the recruit started on a wooden horse, passing later to the live animal when saddlery became available. In March the artillery moved to Bulford Camp to complete their training and gun practice, but it was the middle of June before they received their proper gun-sights. Labouring under such disadvantages, it is marvellous that this scientific arm could have been brought to such a pitch of perfection in a few short months. The first days of practice with live ammunition were nervous ones for all concerned. Shells burst at all ranges, and onlookers speculated somewhat uneasily on the fate of infantry in action supported by such artillery. Two months later these same gunners were making excellent practice on the German trenches in front of Loos; high-explosive shells burst with deadly accuracy on the enemy front line, whilst shrapnel searched the communication trenches.

Apart from work, the general conduct of the men had been excellent throughout the training. There were few even of the usual minor military offences. Thus the Division, by its correct conduct in England, laid the foundation of the fair name it held later in the villages of France and Flanders.

Receipt of orders to mobilise, July 4, 1915.

Although rumours of a move overseas had long been circulating in the Division, it was not until July 4 that the order "Mobilise" was actually received. All ranks were at once recalled from leave, the necessary equipment and stores required to complete units to the authorised scale were issued, and three days later advanced parties left for France.

R.E. TRAINING.

Headquarters R.E. and two (73rd and 74th) Field Companies R.E. were raised at Aldershot in September, under Colonel G. S. Cartwright, R.E., the 3rd, the 91st, joining them at Bordon the following January, whither the others had gone in October. The dismounted men were drafted from Chatham, whilst the mounted personnel came from the R.E. depot at Aldershot. Like the remainder of the Division, these drafts were composed of magnificent material. Nearly every man was a skilled tradesman, many having thrown up their own businesses to enlist. From Bordon all three companies and Headquarters moved to Bulford early in February, and the following month to Highcliffe and Muddiford, near Christchurch, to complete their technical training in bridging, &c. As was the case with artillery and infantry, improvisation of all kinds was necessary. It was only by hard work on the part of all, but especially by that of Captain Graeme, R.E., that some ten pontoons and twenty-six boats were collected from Portsmouth, Poole, and other places, and with these, and a collection of spars, planks, &c., found in Muddiford, training was carried out. The results were excellent. At the mouth of the river Avon the tide ran strong, and, in consequence, men learnt to think and act quickly, especially when working at night. In April the companies returned to Bulford, and the following month the 73rd and 74th Companies moved to Chisledon Camp, the 91st remaining at Bulford, whilst Headquarters R.E. joined Divisional Headquarters at Marlborough. It was from these stations that the companies went overseas with the Division in July 1915.

Major-General Sir F. W. N. McCRACKEN, K.C.B., D.S.O.

CHAPTER II.

LOOS.[1]

Departure for France, July 7-10, 1915.

BATTALION transport and machine-gun sections of infantry units were the first to leave. Commencing with the 44th Brigade and followed by those of the 45th and 46th, together with the Artillery, R.E., Field Ambulances, &c., they crossed from Southampton to Havre. The infantry travelled *viâ* Folkestone and Boulogne, meeting their advanced parties at Pont de Briques the evening after landing. On detraining at Watten or Audricq stations late that same night, units marched from four to eight miles to billets. The area had not previously been occupied by British troops, and village "Maires" were very vague regarding the accommodation required. In some cases a building scarcely large enough for twenty men was expected to house an entire company. Here, as later, interpreters provided by the French Army were of great assistance. Finding many buildings which had been overlooked by easy-going authorities, they made short work of any inhabitant daring to object to their occupation.

Concentrated near St Omer, July 13, 1915.

By July 13 the whole Division was concentrated about seven miles north-west of St Omer, with Headquarters at Tilques, where it rested for two days before proceeding to join the IV. Corps (Lieut.-General Sir H. Rawlinson), then holding the line between Grenay and the La Bassée Canal. While at Tilques the Division was visited by the Commander-in-Chief, who rode round the billeting area and interviewed most of the commanding officers of units and brigades.

Starting on the 15th, the Division took three days to reach its Corps area. The first stage of over twenty miles tried men severely, and many fell out. This was due partly to the new boots issued before leaving England, and also to the unaccustomed paved roads and warm

[1] Map No. 1.

climate of France. Nearly all, however, rejoined their units that evening, and once the troops became accustomed to the conditions of the country, falling out on the march was a rare occurrence. That night, billeted in and around Hazebrouck, the constant flashes from shells bursting over the trenches (near Ploegsteert) could be clearly seen, and Véry lights lit up the horizon from north to south. These, and the never-ending sound of the guns, made men realise that they were at last within measurable distance of the enemy.

On the evening of the 16th the Division billeted north and east of Lillers, with Headquarters at Bourecq. The final march was accomplished at night, and on the 18th, Division Headquarters opened at Douvrin. The 44th Brigade was billeted in Houchin, the 45th in Hesdigneuil and Labeuvrière, and the 46th in Lozinghem and Allouagne. Artillery and Ammunition Column were in billets and bivouacs at Lapugnoy, whilst the remaining units found accommodation in the neighbouring hamlets, the pioneer battalion (9th Gordons) being billeted at Noeux-les-Mines.

The surrounding country proved very different from that through which the Division had just marched. Situated in the centre of the chief coal-mining district of France, it greatly resembled parts of southern Scotland. The numerous slag-heaps made excellent observation-posts, and were therefore objects of special attention from the enemy's guns. The villages, especially those in the front area, were merely rows of small cottages, whose occupants—miners—were not overpleased to see the Division.

Instruction in trench warfare, July 18-26, 1915.

The remainder of July was taken up in gaining experience of trench warfare. Parties of senior officers, N.C.O.'s, signallers, &c., were first sent up to spend a few days with units of corresponding formations then holding the line. Complete companies were next attached to battalions of the 47th (London) Division, and thus by August 1 (a few days only) all ranks had been given some slight experience of the work before them. During this period of instruction the Division suffered its first casualties. On July 15 Major Gordon Forbes, 7th K.O.S.B., who had been sent up during the march to IV. Corps area, was severely wounded, and died the next day in hospital. Six days later Colonel S. MacDougall of Lunga, commanding 10th Gordons, was instantaneously killed by shell-fire whilst on a visit to the trenches. In a letter written about this time an officer unconnected with his regiment said: "Yesterday Colonel MacDougall of Lunga was killed. . . . His death came as a great shock to the brigade. I did not know him very well, in fact had only met him a few times before we left England, but it did not take long to realise that in MacDougall we had a man of a rare stamp. A great Highlander and a splendid soldier, he will be sorely missed, not only by his regiment but by the whole brigade."

Fifteenth Division in the line, July 27, 1915.

On July 27 the Division received orders to relieve the 47th Division in the right sector of the IV. Corps front. Artillery and R.E. moved up first, followed by the infantry, and by the night of August 3 the relief had been completed. The sector held by the Division then ran from the Grenay-Cité St Jeanne d'Arc road on the right to the Le Rutoire-Loos road on the left, about 4200 yards in length. Divided into two sub-sectors, it was first held by the 44th Brigade (right) and 45th (left), each finding its own supports, with the 46th in Divisional reserve. On the right of the 15th the line was held by the 58th Territorial Division of the (French) XXI. Corps (General Maistre), and on the left by the British 1st Division. It thus found itself on the extreme right of the British battle line. On the right, lying in a valley between the ruins of Maroc and Cité St Jeanne d'Arc, the opposing trenches ran almost due north and south. Northwards they climbed to the crest of the rising ground between Loos and Philosophe. Following this crest line they ran east of Le Rutoire and west of Hulluch, and thence, still almost due north, to the La Bassée Canal. At this time British and German trenches were from 200 to 400 yards apart, and the sector had, in consequence, the reputation of being a quiet one. Good observation of the enemy's front line and Loos village was obtainable from the slag-heaps and ruined mine-buildings of Maroc, but on the left, where his front line followed the crest of the higher ground, nothing could be seen beyond his front wire, whilst farther north, between Le Rutoire and Hulluch, very little even of that could be distinguished.

Brigades had only been a few hours in the front line before they began to realise the amount of work necessary to keep it in good order. At first, to their inexperienced eyes, little improvement seemed pos-

August 1915. sible. Reports from their Field Companies, however, soon disillusioned them. They were told that the front-line wire was in a deplorable condition, more dug-outs were necessary, and nearly all trenches required immediate strengthening and revetting. To carry out this work miles of barbed wire, quantities of timber, and tens of thousands of sandbags were sent up, and units and sappers alike worked night and day to complete the tasks allotted to them.

In addition to these, and to the ordinary routine duties of the trenches, the Division found it still had much to learn. In England training had been more or less on the lines of field rather than of trench warfare. Little instruction in bombing had been possible, due, probably, to lack of material in sufficient quantities to meet the requirements of the forces in France and those training at home. Instruction also was necessary in the tactical handling of machine-guns. To teach these and certain other subjects, Brigade Schools were at once started, to which officers and men were sent from the trenches, and this added considerably to the labour and strain on all ranks. Although looked upon as quiet, the sector was subjected to constant shelling. Support companies in the ruined houses of Maroc suffered from this almost as much as did those in the front line,[1] but on the whole there were very few casualties.

The French Territorials of the 58th Division were of the greatest assistance on this first tour. Mostly men of middle age, and to British eyes looking far too old to withstand the rigours of trench warfare, they proved to be good soldiers, anxious to assist in every way, and soon made great friends with the Division.

A curious incident occurred during this tour. Early one morning, just as it was getting light, a woman was seen to climb through the German front wire and run across No Man's Land towards the junction of the French and British lines. She got about half-way before the enemy opened fire on her. Nothing daunted, she ran on, and finally reached the French wire under heavy fire. By this time both the French and British were alive to the situation, and, shouting to her to lie down, they opened rapid fire on the enemy trenches. Unfor-

[1] Lieut.-Colonel Allenby, 7th Royal Scots Fusiliers, and the Medical Officer of that unit were killed at Philosophe whilst the Battalion was in Brigade reserve.

tunately the poor woman either did not hear or by this time had completely lost her head. Taking no notice of the order, screaming with terror, she tried frantically to push her way through the wire, only to collapse a few seconds later riddled with German bullets. Had she lain down it would have been an easy task to bring her in. Her body was recovered that night, and from papers found on it she proved to be a native of Lens.

At this time the enemy had gained the ascendancy in No Man's Land, on occasion sending scouts right up to the British wire. Constant and vigorous patrolling was therefore necessary, and nightly units sent out strong parties to stop these practices. Encounters were of common occurrence, and in one of these Lieutenant Alexander, 12th H.L.I., was killed whilst attempting to capture a German who had succeeded in crawling up to the front wire.

Once settled down, and with plenty of work night and day, August passed quickly. Brigades occupied the trenches for ten days at a time, followed by four or five " resting " in Divisional reserve, during which they were employed in digging communication trenches, gun emplacements, dressing stations, &c., behind the front and support lines. All this lent colour to the rumours of pending operations which now commenced to circulate throughout the Division, rumours which became facts when preliminary operation orders were received on August 27.

Preliminary orders for Loos battle received, Aug. 27, 1915.

During the late summer Russia, who had been defeated earlier in the year, had turned on her enemies, causing them considerable anxiety regarding their Eastern Front. Bulgaria had not then taken any part in the quarrel, and, from the enemy's point of view, it was very necessary to impress her with the power and might of Germany. To do this the latter was compelled to send troops from the Western Front to reinforce her armies in Russia. Neither Germany nor Austria thought much of the new armies England was forming. They openly stated that troops with so little training could be of no use, and had shown their contempt in a practical way by transferring large formations from France to Russia between July and September 1915.

Both the British and the French commanders had long contemplated an attack on a large scale in France, but they could do nothing until the arrival of reinforcements. By July the First and Second Hundred Thousand of these had arrived, and, the situation thus changed, it was decided to take the offensive. In this offensive the following Armies were to take part: east and west of Rheims, the Fourth, Ninth, Third, and Fifth French Armies; north and south of Arras, the First British and Tenth French Armies. The First British Army (General Sir Douglas Haig) then consisted of the III. (Indian), I., and IV. Corps, and at this period held the line from Grenay to Festubert. In addition to the main effort, demonstrations were to be carried out simultaneously on all parts of the line to prevent the enemy from reinforcing the principal point of attack.

Plan of coming attack.

The main British attack was to be carried out by the Ist and IVth Corps between Grenay and the La Bassée Canal, the dividing line between the Corps being the Vermelles-Hulluch road. South of this road the 1st Division was to capture Hulluch and Vendin-le-Vieil, and make good the crossings of the Haute Deule Canal at Pont-à-Vendin. On its right, and in the centre of the IV. Corps front, the Fifteenth Division had as its final objective the high ground north of Loisons-sous-Lens. The 47th (London) Division, on its right, was to capture the Double Crassier, immediately east of Maroc, and form a defensive flank facing south. Farther south the French, attacking from Souchez, were to push forward clear of Lens. That town and the outlying villages to the west and south of it were to be left to fall automatically when the advance of the French from the direction of Souchez and the British from Loos and Pont-à-Vendin rendered them untenable by the enemy. To the north of the Vermelles-Hulluch road the Ist Corps was to take Cité St Elie, the Quarries, Hohenzollern Redoubt, and "the dump" behind it, Haisnes, and Douvrin, and form a defensive flank to the north. In reserve the Commander-in-Chief had the XI. Corps, consisting of the Guards, the 21st, and 24th Divisions. In addition, the 3rd Cavalry Division, less the 7th Cavalry Brigade, was to be ready to move forward if and when the enemy's line was broken. This reserve was most necessary, not only on account of the length of line to be attacked (six or seven miles), but because of the gap that would be formed between the British and French forces before they could join hands east of Lens, should the operation be entirely successful.

Artillery preparation for Loos.

To prepare for and support the attack, the IV. Corps had at its disposal 253 guns of all calibres, including 36 howitzers of 8 inches or over. Expenditure of ammunition was based on the assumption of four days' deliberate bombardment, two days' battle, and four days' subsequent fighting, and was on a liberal scale considering the shortage of shell in 1915. In addition to the British artillery, certain batteries of French heavy guns co-operated throughout the bombardment on the IV. Corps front.

Until the capture of the German front trenches, all guns on the Corps front were under the command of Brig.-General Budworth, M.V.O., reverting then to their respective Division commanders. In order to exploit fully any success on the part of the infantry, it was arranged that, if called for, certain batteries would be attached to infantry brigades, and would follow up their advance after Hill 70 had been captured; and minute instructions on this point were given in both Corps and Division orders regarding the action of artillery during the actual assault.

Gas arrangements.

Taking "o" to denote the moment of the discharge of gas, or "zero hour," the lines on Map 1 show the different phases into which the artillery attack was divided. For the first forty minutes—*i.e.*, until 0.40—nearly all guns were allotted targets either in the German front and support lines or between them and the 0.40 line. The guns then "lifted," and for the next ten minutes—that is, until 0.50—engaged targets between that and the 0.50 line. Fire at targets in the next phase was for longer duration. It was expected that Loos village might give considerable trouble to the attacking forces, and also that the enemy resistance might have then stiffened. It was therefore subjected to artillery fire for twenty-five minutes, or until one hour and fifteen minutes after the commencement of the gas attack. From that time the targets were all east of the 1.15 line, and if the advance was to be continued eastward it would then be necessary to move the guns farther forward.[1]

[1] An enormous amount of work was necessary to prepare for the coming operations. Large infantry working-parties, averaging 2000 nightly, were employed under the 73rd

When operations of such magnitude are being undertaken it is scarcely possible to keep all preparations entirely dark. With a good intelligence service the enemy is certain to find out sooner or later some details of what is coming. This was so in September 1915. The operations, originally planned to commence on the 10th, were postponed first to the 20th, and again to the 25th; and during the interval the enemy frequently exhibited notices in his front trenches inquiring when the expected attack would take place.

There was one secret, however, that the Germans did not find out, namely, that poison gas—the barbarous method of warfare inaugurated by them at Ypres in April 1915—was to be used against them for the first time. It was now expected to cause them as much damage as it did the British and French troops on that occasion, and, by shaking their morale, act as a strong advance-guard to the assault. The gas was contained in metal cylinders, each weighing about 140 lb. Fifteen hundred of these were allotted to the Division, and had to

and 91st Field Companies between the 1st and 17th of September, and, in addition to other work, they accomplished the following:—

(1) 13,400 yards of communication trenches dug (no allowance in this is made for traverses).

(2) 83 recesses cut for gas cylinders.

(3) 3 covered saps, each 60 yards in length, pushed out from the front line.

(4) Bomb stores constructed in the front line. It is interesting to note that in September 1915 the supply of bombs for a whole brigade, in addition to those held by battalions, was 500. Large receptacles were therefore unnecessary.

(5) Advanced report centres for two divisional and three brigade headquarters built and made splinter-proof.

(6) Wooden tramway laid from Mazingarbe to Quality Street. 3650 yards of line laid and 50 trolleys constructed, the wheels being obtained from mine trolleys. They were constructed to take either stores or wounded, each trolley taking five stretchers.

(7) Advanced dressing-stations for 250 men, with splinter-proof protection, constructed at Fosse 7 and at Mazingarbe.

(8) Electric light installed at the brewery, Mazingarbe.

(9) 26 bridges constructed over front-line trenches, the majority fit for heavy traffic, the remainder for field guns only.

(10) Water supply arranged for by placing ten 200-gallon tanks in front-line trenches. Tanks were also provided for the dressing stations.

(11) Wells cleared behind Fosse 7 and provided with pumps. These were made from parts of old pumps found in the mines and neighbourhood, and delivered over two thousand gallons of water per hour.

(12) 10 first-aid posts constructed.

(13) S.A.A. stores provided.

(14) Ladders made and issued to facilitate exit of assaulting troops from the trenches.

(15) Additional splinter-proof protection provided in the front and support trenches.

Sept. 1915. Preparations continued.

be in position in the front line by dawn on September 21. The first consignment—500—arrived on the night of the 18/19th, and the remainder at the same rate on the two following nights. Brought up after dark as far as Fosse 7, south of the Lens-Philosophe road, they were carried from there to their destination. Parties were waiting behind the Fosse, and as the cylinders were unloaded each was slung on a pole and taken charge of by two men. When six had been thus prepared, the party of twelve men, under an officer with an N.C.O. and two extra men in case of accidents, left for the front line. Progress down the long communication trenches was slow and difficult, on account of the weight and dangerous nature of these "Special Stores," as they were called. Some parties took many hours to reach their allotted positions in the front line, but arrangements had been so well made by the Division staff that not one single party missed its way, nor did they cross one another in the maze of trenches through which they had to pass. Over 1000 men, to say nothing of officers, N.C.O.'s, and spare men, were employed each night, and, with only one exception, no party failed to complete its task according to the programme laid down. On arrival in the front line the cylinders were taken charge of by men specially detailed to deal with them on the day of attack, and were built into recesses already dug to receive them. It was a great relief to all concerned when this difficult and somewhat dangerous work was satisfactorily completed, and all ranks thoroughly deserved the thanks and congratulations they received the following day from General McCracken.

To supplement the gas on the morning of assault a supply of smoke candles was issued. These were to be lit alternately with the discharge of the gas, primarily to deceive the enemy, but more especially to act as a screen for the assaulting troops, and give the gas time to get well ahead of them over the enemy's trenches. The discharge of smoke and gas was to occupy forty minutes :—

12 minutes gas, followed by
8 minutes smoke, followed by
12 minutes gas, followed by
8 minutes smoke.

The last discharge of smoke was to be thickened for the final two

Sept. 1915. Preparations continued.

minutes to provide the above-mentioned screen, after which the infantry were to advance.

Another preparation, not the least important, was that of communications. The Divisional Signal Company laid duplicate wires to all advanced battle headquarters, and arrangements were made to carry these forward in close touch with the advancing troops. A wireless set was also available, but during the battle it proved of little use, being soon "jammed" by the enemy. To assist artillery and air observers, yellow flags were carried by the infantry to denote the position of forward troops. Divisions on the right and left carried flags of different colours. "Vermoral Sprayers" were to be carried forward by the sanitary squads. These sprayers contained a chemical solution with which to clear any poison gas likely to lurk in enemy trenches or dug-outs. The rear company of each battalion carried twenty-five picks and fifty shovels for entrenching purposes. Blankets and packs were stored under battalion arrangements, the men carrying their haversacks slung on their backs. On going into action, battalions left a proportion of officers behind to replace casualties; these included the second senior officer of each company and such others as were detailed for special duty under Brigade or Divisional arrangements. Lastly, and as a precaution against any ill-effects likely to result from the employment of gas, all ranks wore their gas-helmets rolled up instead of their ordinary head-dress.

Fifteenth Division plan of attack.

With a frontage of about 1500 yards, General McCracken decided to attack on a two-brigade front, with the 44th on the right and the 46th on the left, keeping the 45th as Division reserve. Each brigade was to attack in two columns, each column consisting of one battalion with a section of R.E. and one platoon of pioneers, leaving one battalion in brigade support and another in reserve. A fifth column was detailed later from the 46th Brigade for a special purpose.

The disposition and composition of these columns were as follows (see Map A):—

On the right, 44th Brigade (Brig.-General M. G. Wilkinson, M.V.O.):—

No. 1 Column (Lieut.-Colonel T. O. Lloyd)—9th Battalion Black Watch;

No. 2 Section 73rd Field Company Royal Engineers; and one platoon "G" Company 9th Battalion Gordon Highlanders (Pioneers).

No. 2 *Column* (Lieut.-Colonel N. A. Thomson)—8th Battalion Seaforth Highlanders; No. 3 Section 73rd Field Company Royal Engineers; and one platoon "G" Company 9th Battalion Gordon Highlanders (Pioneers).

In support of these columns were—

10th Battalion Gordon Highlanders (Lieut.-Colonel H. Wallace); 7th Battalion Cameron Highlanders (Lieut.-Colonel J. Sandilands); 73rd Field Company Royal Engineers (Major S. Mildred), less two sections; "G" Company 9th Battalion Gordon Highlanders, less two platoons.

On the left, 46th Brigade (Brig.-General T. G. Matheson):—

No. 3 *Column* (Lieut.-Colonel A. V. Ussher)—10th Battalion Scottish Rifles; No. 1 Section 91st Field Company Royal Engineers (Lieut. Davenport, R.E.); and one platoon "H" Company 9th Battalion Gordon Highlanders (Pioneers).

No. 4 *Column* (Lieut.-Colonel G. de W. Verner)—7th Battalion King's Own Scottish Borderers; No. 2 Section 91st Field Company Royal Engineers (Lieut. M'Court, R.E.); and one platoon "H" Company 9th Battalion Gordon Highlanders (Pioneers).

No. 5 *Column* (Captain P. W. Torrance, 12th Battalion Highland Light Infantry)—Two companies 12th Battalion Highland Light Infantry, and the Machine-Gun Section of that battalion, assisted by No. 63 Trench Mortar Battery.

In support of Columns 3, 4, and 5 were the 8th Battalion King's Own Scottish Borderers (Lieut.-Colonel T. B. Sellar), and in reserve were the 12th Battalion Highland Light Infantry (Lieut.-Colonel J. H. Purvis), less two companies and Machine-Gun Section; the 91st Field Company Royal Engineers (Major H. Pollard Lowsley), less two sections; and "H" Company 9th Battalion Gordon Highlanders, less two platoons.

The task of No. 5 Column was to bomb up Southern Sap, and clear it and the enemy front trenches in its immediate vicinity; it was then to rejoin its unit when the assaulting lines of the Fifteenth and 1st Divisions had gone forward.

In Divisional reserve were the 45th Brigade (Brig.-General F. E. Wallerston) disposed between Fosse 3 and Mazingarbe, with orders to move into the front-line trenches as soon as they had been vacated by the assaulting columns—the 7th Battalion Royal Scots Fusiliers (Lieut.-Colonel Henning) to occupy those of the 44th Brigade, with the 13th Battalion Royal Scots (Lieut.-Colonel Maclear) behind them; whilst the 6th Battalion Cameron Highlanders (Lieut.-Colonel A. F. Douglas Hamilton) occupied the 46th Brigade trenches, with the 11th Battalion A. & S. Highlanders (Lieut.-Colonel Malcolm McNeale)

Sept. 1915. Preparations continued.

behind him. At Mazingarbe were the 9th Battalion Gordon Highlanders, Pioneers (Colonel Scott), less two companies, the 11th Motor Machine-Gun Battery (Major C. B. Hall), and the Divisional mounted troops and cyclists. The 74th Field Company worked under the orders of the C.R.E., Fifteenth Division.

On the right the objectives of the 44th Brigade were: first, the German front-line trenches; second, the trenches from Loos cemetery northwards to the inter-brigade boundary as shown on Map 1; third, Loos village; fourth, Puits 15, just east of Loos; and fifth, the enemy redoubt on Hill 70. Those of the 46th Brigade on the left were: first and second, the German front trenches; third, the trench running north of Loos village; fourth, the road leading north from Puits 15; and fifth, the trenches from the redoubt on Hill 70 to Puits 14 *bis* exclusive.[1]

In the first instructions issued by the Fifteenth Division on August 30 the final objective was given as Hill 70. This was altered later by Division Operation Order No. 19, dated September 21, which gave as the sixth and seventh objectives the Cité St Auguste, and the high ground north of Loissons-sous-Lens (two miles farther on), these two being common to both brigades.[2]

Division and brigade boundaries are shown on Map 1. On the right of the 44th Brigade was the 1st Brigade (47th Division), its left battalion being the 19th Battalion London Regiment. On the left of the 46th Brigade were the 2nd Battalion King's Royal Rifle Corps (2nd Brigade, 1st Division).

From the above it will be seen that the Division was destined to take a leading, and by no means an easy, part in the forthcoming battle. It had to advance nearly five miles, taking two villages and at least three well-fortified trench systems on its way—a difficult task even for well-seasoned troops; and in order that there should be no doubt whatever in the minds of any one as to how this was to be done, General McCracken's final operation order contained the following sentence: "It is the intention of the Divisional Commander to push on to these objectives with all the offensive power of the

[1] For Fifteenth Division "Draft Instructions for Attack," see Appendix E.

[2] This disposes of statements which have appeared in some publications to the effect that the troops exceeded their orders and went too far on September 25.

Division." The spirit of the men may be judged from what an officer wrote: "I heard —— —— say to another N.C.O. at the end of the lecture (at which the operations had been explained), 'Wi' a' oor offensive power, indeed! We'll gang straight tae Berlin if we use a' that force.' Poor fellow! *his* offensive power carried him no farther than the German front line; but they were all like that."

When the two farther objectives were given, brigade commanders were told that there would be *at least* a corps in rear of the Division, which would push on when the final objective had been reached. Fifteenth Division Operation Order No. 9, dated September 17, Para 4, stated: "The XI. Corps will be in reserve behind the IV. Corps with its leading troops about Noeux-les-Mines," and in addition to this Corps the 3rd Cavalry Division was to be ready to move forward if and when the German line was broken.

The country between La Bassée Canal and Grenay over which the attack took place was, generally speaking, open, cultivated, and undulating. There were no hedges or ditches and few fences, except in the vicinity of villages.

The chief natural features were:—

(1) The high ground east and south of Loos, including Hill 70.
(2) A spur running north-east from Grenay to the Vermelles-Hulluch road.
(3) The valley between (1) and (2), in which lay the village of Loos.

In September 1915, following a line almost due north and south, the opposing trenches crossed the above-mentioned spur at its highest point on the Lens-Philosophe road, and nothing could be seen from the British trenches of the German support line on the reverse slope. On the other hand, from the high ground east and south of Loos, and from Hill 70, the country to the north, south, and west was under direct observation, the spur hiding only part of the British front line from view.

Being in a mining and manufacturing district, the villages were mostly blocks of cottages of similar type known as "Corons," generally clustered in the immediate vicinity of the mines or factories them-

Sept. 1915.

selves. Behind the German lines there were many of these villages. All had been fortified, making excellent strong-points, whilst for observation purposes the slag-heaps or factory buildings adjoining them left nothing to be desired.

Four of these were of special tactical importance :—

(*a*) The Double Crassier. A double slag-heap running out in an easterly direction from the high ground south of Loos.

(*b*) The mine buildings—known as the Tower Bridge—at Loos.

(*c*) A slag-heap at Fosse 8—known as the Dump—south of Auchy-la-Bassée and west of Cité St Elie.

(*d*) The ruined mine buildings round Puits 14 *bis*.

Of these, the Double Crassier commanded the valley in which lay Loos. From the Dump, Loos was also visible, and, what was far more important, the whole of the back area between the British front line and Vermelles, as far south as the Lens-Philosophe road, was under observation from it. An observer on the Tower Bridge could see both the above points and could also overlook the spur immediately in front of him. Puits 14 *bis* commanded the village of Loos and the country between it and Fosse 8—the Dump.

Behind the British line there were few such good points from which to observe and assist the attack. From Fosse 3 at Maroc, Loos, part of the valley, and Hill 70 were under observation. Farther north, from Fosse 7 on the Lens-Philosophe road, the German front line and the chimneys of Loos behind it could be seen, but the spur hid the intervening ground. Still farther north, fairly good observation of the immediate front was obtainable from Vermelles, but here again a slight fold in the ground hid the German third line from view.

With such excellent view-points the advantage clearly lay with the enemy. So long as he held the Loos valley under observation no artillery could be brought up to assist a farther advance of the infantry. It was therefore of vital importance that the Double Crassier, Loos, Hill 70, and the Dump should be taken as quickly as possible.

PRELIMINARY BOMBARDMENT.

Battle of Loos. Preliminary bombardment.

At 8 A.M. on Tuesday, September 21, the preliminary bombardment commenced, and continued with varying intensity up to the moment of assault on the 25th. During these four days every battery on the Corps front had its area and tasks assigned to it. The most important work of the guns was that of wire-cutting. The German front-line wire defence was much stronger and thicker than that of the British, and it was essential that it should be damaged as much as possible before the actual assault. To do this effectively certain guns from each 18-pr. battery were directed to fire low-bursting shrapnel at the wire, the result being carefully noted and checked from posts in the front line. Where the opposing lines were close together, observation was easy, and the work was consequently well done all along the Fifteenth Division front. Farther north, however, the lines were some distance apart, and it was almost impossible to see the German wire from the British trenches. Here the wire was not well cut; in fact, in some places it was found to be intact when the assault took place, the result being that the attack was held up in its initial stages on a part of the 1st Division front.

When the wire was cut it was necessary to prevent the enemy repairing it at night. Certain batteries were therefore detailed to fire salvoes of high explosive and shrapnel at irregular intervals each night on the gap cut during the day. Bursts of fire from machine-guns in the front line also assisted in this work. Other guns systematically searched the enemy communication trenches and back areas throughout the period, and at stated times every gun on the Corps front concentrated on his front and support lines. With such a well-thought-out and well-executed programme, and with—for 1915—a sufficient supply of ammunition, life in the German line at this time must have been far from pleasant.[1]

[1] The following is part of a letter found on a dead German after the attack. It was apparently written on the morning of the assault:—

"*September* 25, 1915.—I cannot describe to you the reality. It is impossible. No one could believe what is passing here. It is perfectly horrible. In a few hours my company has lost 35 men, of whom 23 are killed. . . . Here in the first line we can get

THE ATTACK.

Battle of Loos, Sept. 25, 1915.

As the 25th grew nearer, weather and the direction of the wind were closely watched. For gas to be entirely successful it was necessary that the day should be fine, the wind west, and travelling at about three miles an hour. On the 24th atmospheric conditions could hardly have been worse. What little breeze there was died down completely before nightfall, and the weather—hitherto fine—showed signs of breaking. The attack had already been postponed twice, and now another delay seemed likely, or the gas—from which so much was expected—would have to be abandoned. So unfavourable were the conditions that all moves of troops to positions of assault were postponed. At 8 A.M., however, IV. Corps telephoned that the original programme would be adhered to, and units then commenced moving forward.

Owing to the number of batteries then in position between Mazingarbe, Philosophe, and the front line, movement above ground was impossible. Assaulting brigades had therefore to make their way down long communication trenches in order to reach their positions of attack. Encumbered with picks, shovels, and the impedimenta necessary for the assault and consolidation of captured positions, progress was difficult. It was 3 A.M. before General Wilkinson reported that the 44th Brigade was in position. The 46th were more fortunate, and reached their destination some time earlier.

All doubt regarding a postponement of the attack was set at rest at 3.35 A.M., when a message arrived from the IV. Corps stating that "zero hour" would be 5.50 A.M. Dawn broke dull and cloudy, with a slight wind from the south-south-west and south-west, which increased in strength towards zero hour, but was scarcely sufficient to do full justice to the gas, from which so much was expected.

Gas attack commences.

At 5.50 A.M. the gas attack commenced, and, to an onlooker,

nothing to drink or eat, and in reserve we are exposed to a still more terrible fire, and are unable to advance to reinforce the front line. If it were the end of the world it could not be worse. The great shells fall like drops of water. . . ."

—a striking testimonial to the accuracy of fire from those whose only weapon a few months before had been a pine log mounted on a broken-down victoria.

every gun on the Corps front appeared to redouble its fire. The effect of the white clouds of smoke rolling slowly towards the enemy trenches was extraordinary. It looked as if a curtain, stabbed here and there with the red bursts of shrapnel, had been drawn across the Division front. At first the enemy rifle and artillery fire was intense, but the gas made itself felt in a short time, for this fire decreased considerably after the first few minutes. As far as the Fifteenth Division was concerned, the gas was liberated without much trouble. Here and there a few cylinders leaked or were damaged by artillery fire, and great gallantry was shown by the troops in their neighbourhood. One case stood out conspicuously—namely, that of No. 15851 Piper Laidlaw, 7th K.O.S.B., who, prior to the actual assault, finding that the men of his battalion were nervous on account of the gas in their trenches, jumped on the parapet and piped away in spite of heavy rifle and machine-gun fire which swept that part of the line. For this deed Piper Laidlaw was awarded the Victoria Cross.[1]

Battle of Loos, 5.50 A.M.

On the whole, it is questionable whether the discharge of gas was a success, even on the Fifteenth Division front, where the wind was more favourable than it proved to be elsewhere. It was no doubt calculated to give the troops a feeling of confidence. On the other hand, its somewhat doubtful results, owing to the unfavourable direction and velocity of the wind, must have weakened the moral effect. The casualties it caused in the British ranks farther north were a debit account against it.

The assault, 6.30 A.M.

At 6.30 A.M. the leading lines of assaulting columns left their trenches. Gaps had been cut diagonally in the British wire, and men had no difficulty in getting through, but directly they left the shelter of the trenches and the enemy became aware of their approach, they encountered an extremely heavy rifle and machine-gun fire. This was particularly so on the right of the 44th Brigade, where an enemy redoubt on the Loos-Philosophe road, known as the "Jew's Nose," was responsible for at least half the casualties suffered by the 9th Black Watch on that day.

[1] See Appendix J.

The assault continued.

An officer who witnessed the assault of the Division wrote :—

" It was magnificent. I could not have imagined that troops with a bare twelvemonth's training behind them could have accomplished it. As the men reached our wire they made their way through it with perfect coolness and deliberation, in spite of the enemy's increasingly heavy rifle fire. Once in No Man's Land they took up their dressing and walked—yes, coolly walked—across towards the enemy trenches. There was no running or shouting ; here and there a man finding himself out of line would double for a pace or two, look to his right and left, take up his dressing and continue the advance at a steady walk. The effect of these seemingly unconcerned Highlanders advancing upon them must have had a considerable effect on the Germans. I saw one man whose kilt had got caught in our wire as he passed through a gap ; he did not attempt to tear it off, but, carefully disentangling it, doubled up to his correct position in the line and went on."

On the left the 46th Brigade met with much the same experience. Their left column (No. 5) suffered severely at first, as they found that Southern Sap, although shown clearly in aeroplane photographs, was merely a shallow dummy trench, and the column had to face heavy rifle and machine-gun fire from the enemy front line behind it. Another reason was that the 2nd Infantry Brigade on its left were unable to make any progress on account of uncut enemy wire in front of them. The result of this was that the 46th Brigade came under enfilade fire from the German front-line trenches opposite the 2nd Brigade, 1st Division, when it reached the trenches opposite its own front. No. 5 Column alone lost nine out of ten officers in the first few minutes. Regardless, however, of all resistance, the assaulting line swept on, and at 7.5 A.M. the whole of the 44th and 46th Brigades were over the German front-line trenches and pushing on towards Loos, with the exception of No. 5 Column, which was held up on the left.

7.5 A.M. Capture of enemy front and support lines.

On reaching the enemy trenches, the effect of the accurate and intense artillery fire was apparent. The front line was badly damaged—in fact, in some places was non-existent—and the communication trenches leading to Loos were filled with dead and dying men.

After the front-line German trenches were captured the assaulting columns swept down the slopes to Loos village, meeting with little opposition until they reached its western edge. Here they found uncut wire, and the 44th Brigade came under hot rifle and machine-gun fire from the houses in Loos itself.[1] Nothing, however, could by this time stop the impetus of the attack, and the remnants of the 9th Black Watch and 8th Seaforths, now reinforced by the 10th Gordons and 7th Camerons, forced their way into the village. Here fierce hand-to-hand and house-to-house fighting took place. Street barricades were stormed one by one, and many prisoners taken. A German battery of field-guns was captured by the Seaforths actually in the village, the battery commander being shot by Sergeant R. MacPhail of "D" Company. It was not possible to clear the village entirely, and many Germans were left in cellars and houses to be dealt with later. In spite of all opposition, using bombs freely, and never giving the enemy time to rally, the 44th Brigade penetrated the village, and at 8 A.M. its leading lines were reported advancing up the western slope of Hill 70.

Capture of Loos village, 7.30 A.M.

Advance to Hill 70.

On the left the 46th Brigade had progressed just as rapidly. Many men of the assaulting battalions—10th Scottish Rifles and 7th K.O.S.B.—had been gassed before leaving their own trenches. Both battalions had also lost heavily in the initial assault, but by 7 A.M. the whole of Nos. 3 and 4 Columns were across the German front lines and pushing on. No. 5 Column was also across, but was held up in the front German lines owing to the failure of the 2nd Brigade to advance. Nos. 3 and 4 Columns continued their advance steadily, in touch with Nos. 2 and 1 of the 44th Brigade, and by 8 A.M. their leading lines too were approaching the north-west slopes of Hill 70, opposite Puits 14 *bis*.

The attack so far had progressed rapidly, far more so than could have been anticipated, with the result that the leading brigades found themselves in advance of those on either flank, the left especially giving cause for anxiety.

At 8.30 A.M. the situation was as follows:—

Situation, 8.30 A.M.

On the right, the 47th Division had captured the German front-line system from the Double Crassier to Loos Cemetery, and were in touch with the 7th Cameron Highlanders, whose commanding officer, writing from Loos Church, reported the village full of men of the

[1] In addition, an enemy machine-gun, concealed in a grave in Loos Cemetery and difficult to locate, caused many casualties.

Attack on Hill 70.

44th and some of the 45th Brigades. The leading lines of the 44th and 46th Brigades were then advancing up the slopes of Hill 70, and the 45th Brigade in Divisional reserve occupied the original British front line, with the exception of two companies of the 7th Royal Scots Fusiliers, who, owing to a mistaken order, had followed the 44th Brigade into Loos. On the left, Captain Torrance's No. 5 Column was held up in the captured German front line, and the 2nd Infantry Brigade were still occupying their original front-line trenches, unable to advance.

From this it will be seen that the situation was somewhat disquieting. The Fifteenth Division had outstripped those on the right and the left, and both flanks were in the air, the left being in the worse case. No. 5 Column, however, was able to hold on until reinforced by 100 bombers of the 6th Camerons (45th Brigade) and a platoon of that battalion as a covering party. With these reinforcements Captain Torrance endeavoured to bomb northwards, along the German front-line trench, to assist the troops of the 2nd Brigade. He was only able to progress for about seventy yards, but his party prevented the enemy from getting behind the assaulting columns of the Fifteenth Division until the afternoon, when another brigade of the 1st Division was sent to attack the German trenches from the north-east, and succeeded in clearing the way for the 2nd Brigade. As will be seen later, the exposure of this left flank had a serious effect upon the whole operation.

8.45 A.M. Capture of Hill 70.

While this was taking place on the left, the 44th and 46th Brigades were still advancing, the former up the western slopes of Hill 70 and the latter straight on Puits 14 *bis*. The 46th had received orders to avoid entering the village itself, and therefore did not suffer so severely as the 44th. Once past Loos, however, Hill 70 had a sinister fascination for the troops of both brigades. The hill was reached with ease, so easily, in fact, that, without a pause, the leading lines of the 44th and the left of the 46th swept on, driving the Germans in front of them out of a half-finished redoubt on the top, and pursuing them into a group of houses on the southern slopes, known as the Dynamitière.

This proved their undoing. By the time the crest was reached all familiar landmarks had disappeared. Loos and its towers were behind the assaulting troops, who now found themselves on unfamiliar ground.

The trend of slope of Hill 70 follows a north and south-easterly direction, and the result was that the farther advance of the 44th Brigade, instead of being directed against the Cité St Auguste, was deflected towards the Dynamitière and the strongly wired salient formed by it and the Cité St Auguste, part of the German fourth line, the right of the 46th Brigade keeping touch and conforming with this deflection. From the enemy's point of view a more perfect defensive position could not be imagined. Once they had reached the shelter of the houses, the Germans, who by this time had recovered from their panic, opened a deadly fire with rifles and machine-guns from the upper storeys as the Highlanders raced down the slopes towards them.

Advance east of Hill 70.

Units had now become so mixed up that for the remainder of the day it is somewhat difficult to follow the progress of each individually. Some men of the 19th Londons had joined the 44th Brigade, and fought with it throughout the day, whilst, on the other hand, men of the 9th Black Watch joined a battalion of the 47th Division, and remained with it until relieved on the 28th.

Situation, 9 A.M.

At 9 A.M. the front line of the Division ran from the extreme eastern end of the Loos Crassier, round the east slope of Hill 70, thence to Puits 14 *bis* and the "Chalk Pit." This was almost the farthest point reached by the Division. The leading lines of the 44th Brigade, consisting of Black Watch, Seaforths, Gordons, and Camerons, all mixed up, certainly gained the houses of the Dynamitière. Some men actually entered them, but all were either killed or taken prisoners, and the remainder, with a few of the 46th Brigade who had followed them, took up a position 200 yards down the south-eastern slope of the hill, and there made what cover they could for themselves. Here they remained exposed to heavy rifle, machine-gun, and artillery fire until all were either killed or wounded. Very few came back to tell the story; fewer still were taken prisoners. It was one of these—Sergeant J. M. Cavers, 10th Gordons—who, whilst interned in Holland, was able to clear up the fate of those leading lines, and to establish the farthest point reached that day by the 44th Brigade.

In the initial stages of the advance, and the taking of Loos village, nearly all company and platoon commanders of assaulting battalions had either been killed or wounded before the hill was reached.

Loos, 9 A.M.-10 A.M.

On gaining the crest, units had become so mixed up that it was impossible to reorganise. The Scotsmen's blood was up; they only saw the flying enemy and remembered their task, "with all the offensive power of the Division." It is not to be wondered at that they endeavoured to follow up their phenomenal success to the uttermost. Many men of the support battalions had joined the leading lines in the advance on the Dynamitière, and the remainder endeavoured to hold on to the redoubt on the hill. The Germans, however, knew its value full well, and were determined it should not fall into British hands. Redoubling their efforts, the enemy swept the crest of the hill with artillery, rifle, and machine-gun fire. Time after time did men of the 44th and 46th Brigades enter the redoubt only to be driven back, and about 11 A.M., finding it an impossible task, what was left of both brigades began to retire.

Rallied, however, by Lieutenant Johnson (R.E.) and Captain D. P. W. Strang—by this time the sole surviving unwounded officer of the Seaforths—and one or two other infantry and Engineer officers (mostly wounded), they still attempted to hold the hill. Further attempts were made to enter the redoubt, but without success. Nothing could live in the intense fire that now swept the crest. By this time Colonel Sandilands (7th Camerons), accompanied by the two companies of the 7th Royal Scots Fusiliers, under Major R. Campbell, who had followed the 44th Brigade into Loos, arrived on the scene. Seeing that all attempts to hold the redoubt had failed, he gave orders to consolidate and dig in on a line just below the western crest of the hill.[1] The mixture of units made this a difficult matter, but with the help of Colonel H. Wallace (10th Gordons) and the remaining officers and a few sappers left of those who had accompanied the assaulting columns, the task was begun, and by noon the remnants of the 44th and 46th Brigades, with some of the 45th Brigade, were constructing a trench with their entrenching tools and a few shovels taken from a German store in Loos.

On the right of the line, shortly before 10 A.M., the enemy brought up machine-guns to the railway embankment, north of the Dyna-

[1] In the work of getting back those men remaining exposed on the top of the hill, Major Barron, 7th Camerons, did particularly good service. He was badly wounded and taken prisoner, finally dying from his wounds in Germany.

mitière, at the extreme eastern end of the Loos Crassier, with which they enfiladed the whole Division front, more especially the left of the 46th Brigade. To counter this move Colonel Lloyd (9th Black Watch) threw back his right flank slightly, and from that position a party of twenty men of the Black Watch effectively kept down the machine-gun fire, and prevented the enemy from making progress on the flank. Owing to the height of the Loos Crassier and the absence of definite news regarding the progress of the 47th Division, the situation on this flank was obscure for the rest of the day. Several messages were sent back asking for information, but no reply was received, and, until late in the afternoon this flank, like the left, was in the air.

Loos, 12 noon. 45th Brigade sent up.

About noon General McCracken ordered the 45th Brigade to Loos to hold it. By noon all troops of the Division were engaged, and the only reserves at General McCracken's disposal were the 9th Gordons (Pioneers), less two companies, and machine-gun sections (who had accompanied the assaulting columns), and the Divisional mounted troops (B Squadron Westmoreland and Cumberland Yeomanry). Of these, at 1 P.M., he ordered Colonel W. A. Scott, 9th Gordons (Pioneers), to take his two remaining companies into Loos, and place it in a state of defence.

While this was going on, the left of the 46th Brigade was still in the air. The 7th K.O.S.B. had sent out numerous patrols to ascertain the whereabouts of the 2nd Brigade. No trace of it could be found, and at 10.15 A.M., in response to requests for reinforcements, General McCracken sent up the 6th Camerons (Lieut.-Colonel Douglas Hamilton) from the 45th Brigade to cover the left of the 46th. He also ordered the 7th Royal Scots Fusiliers (45th Brigade) to move into the third German trench line. It was then discovered that they had already gone forward. They were therefore told not to proceed farther than Hill 70, and put under the orders of General Wilkinson (44th Brigade). In place of them the 11th Argylls were ordered to occupy the German third-line trenches west of Loos; and the remaining battalion of the 45th Brigade—13th Royal Scots—was sent forward to hold the German front-line trench from Lens Road Redoubt to Loos Road Redoubt. At 12.20 P.M. General McCracken sent 11th Motor Machine-Gun Battery (Major C. B. Hall) to report to General

Loos.

Wilkinson (44th Brigade) at Quality Street, and ordered the Division Cyclist Company to send two platoons to Loos to report to G.O.C. 46th Brigade, and Divisional mounted troops to move to Mazingarbe.

So far all had gone well; the losses had certainly been heavy, but if fresh troops arrived, there was no reason why the victorious career of the Fifteenth Division should not have continued. General McCracken explained the situation to Corps, and pressed for the forward movement of Army reserves. According to IV. Corps Operation Order No. 35, dated September 20, 1915, the 3rd Cavalry Division and XI. Corps were in Army reserve, and "would be brought forward in support as occasion demanded." At 11.25 A.M. General McCracken explained the situation to IV. Corps by telephone, and suggested that the Corps reserve be moved up "in readiness."

On the left flank the situation had become no better. Colonel Purvis (12th H.L.I.) had sent out numerous patrols throughout the morning to endeavour to gain touch with the 2nd Brigade without result. Many of his men, too, had been attracted by the redoubt on Hill 70 and had swung too much to the right. His left had captured Puits 14 *bis* and a part of Bois Hugo beyond it, but when the centre of the attack retired from the crest his right was compelled to follow suit. He retained his hold, however, on Puits 14 *bis*.

Situation, 2 P.M.

At 2 P.M. General McCracken was informed by IV. Corps that the 21st Division (XI. Corps) had been ordered to advance on Loos *viâ* Fosse 7, and that the 62nd Brigade of that Division was placed at his disposal. Shortly after, General McCracken saw the G.O.C. 62nd Brigade, and explained the situation to him. Verbal orders were given to him to move his brigade by Quality Street to Loos to get in touch with Brig.-Generals Wilkinson and Wallerston (44th and 45th Brigades). If Hill 70 were lost, he was to retake it; if held, to relieve our troops on it; and if the situation favoured a further advance on Cité St Auguste, he was to act accordingly in co-operation with the 44th and 45th Brigades. These orders were afterwards confirmed in writing.

At 2 P.M. Major C. B. Hall (Motor Machine-Gun Battery, with six guns), unable to find General Matheson (46th Brigade), reported to Colonel Lloyd (9th Black Watch) at the eastern end of Loos. He was told to send two guns to assist the party of the Black Watch on the right flank, and to take the other four to Colonel Sandilands on Hill 70. This he did, and undoubtedly gave very valuable support at an exceedingly critical time.

Loos.

The situation remained unchanged until 4 P.M., when the 1st Division announced the capture of the Germans who till then had been holding them up. Half an hour later the 2nd Brigade moved forward, and at dusk were in line with the 45th, from Puits 14 *bis* northwards, thus making safe the left flank of the Fifteenth Division.

Situation, 4 P.M.

At 5 P.M. the O.C. of a battalion of the East Yorks (62nd Brigade) reported to the G.O.C. 44th Brigade in Loos. He informed General Wilkinson that the remainder of the brigade were just arriving, but nothing was seen of them till some time later. About now troops of the 47th Division commenced crossing the eastern end of Loos Crassier, and joined hands with the 9th Black Watch. They had been held up till now at the Cemetery and " Enclosure " south of the Crassier.

At 6 P.M. what remained of the 44th and 46th Brigades were well-nigh exhausted. They had fought continuously for twelve hours, had penetrated four German lines to a depth of over 3000 yards, and had lost about 75 per cent of their fighting strength. General McCracken decided to withdraw the 44th Brigade into Divisional reserve behind Loos, and instructed the 62nd Brigade to place one battalion at the disposal of General Matheson (46th Brigade), and to hold the remainder in support of the 45th and 46th Brigades about Puits 15, just east of Loos. He directed the 45th to take over the defence of Hill 70 from the 44th, and placed Lieut.-Colonel MacLear (13th Royal Scots) in command of all the troops on Hill 70. At 7 P.M. General Matheson went forward himself to the Chalk Pit Wood, and there, with the G.O.C. 2nd Brigade, arranged the details for night defence, the latter brigade being responsible for the line northwards from Puits 14 *bis* inclusive. The situation at dusk was therefore as follows: The crest of Hill 70 and the redoubt on it were in the hands of the enemy. A mixture of troops of the 44th, 45th, and 46th Brigades were entrenching themselves just below the crest. The line ran from the Loos Crassier to Puits 14 *bis*, now held by troops of the 2nd Brigade.

Situation, 6 P.M.

At 8.45 P.M. General Matheson informed General McCracken that he considered it imperative to relieve the worn-out units with fresh

Loos, 9.45 P.M. 45th Brigade take over defence of Hill 70.

troops that night if complete success was to be expected from a farther advance, adding that although the 62nd Brigade were round Loos, the location of its headquarters could not yet be found. An hour later General Wallerston reported he had taken over the defence of Hill 70, and was in touch with the 47th Division on his right. The 44th Brigade then moved into Divisional reserve.

The 45th Brigade was now disposed as follows: 7th Battalion Royal Scots Fusiliers on the right; 13th Battalion Royal Scots, centre; and 11th Battalion A. & S. Highlanders on the left, in touch with the 2nd Brigade, the 6th Battalion Cameron Highlanders being still under the 46th Brigade. In addition, and reinforcing them, were the remnant of the 46th Brigade, and on the right, a few men of the 19th Battalion London Regiment. Regrouping was impossible, and under cover of darkness the troops proceeded to improve the trenches dug during the day.

Meanwhile, at 9 P.M., General McCracken received orders from IV. Corps to be prepared to resume the offensive the next morning, the 2nd Brigade (1st Division) being placed under his orders for this purpose. This latter provision, however, was cancelled two hours afterwards. Knowing the state of affairs on Hill 70 and round Loos, General McCracken telephoned the Corps Commander his doubts as to the fitness of his Division to resume the offensive. At 11.30 P.M., however, he received a message to the effect that the Division, assisted by the 62nd Brigade, would attack Hill 70 at 9 A.M. on the 26th, after one hour's intense bombardment. Orders were accordingly at once issued for this attack by the 45th and 62nd Brigades.

Midnight, Sept. 25. 62nd Division ordered to attack Hill 70.

Until midnight the enemy actively shelled Hill 70, its western slopes, and Loos village, and at 12.30 A.M. delivered a counter-attack against the 7th Royal Scots Fusiliers on the right of the line. This was easily repulsed, and for the remainder of the night fire slackened on both sides. About 11 P.M. the 13th Northumberland Fusiliers (62nd Brigade) was sent up to relieve the 46th. It lost its way, but, fortunately, was met by Colonel Purvis (12th H.L.I.) in Loos, and, knowing the orders, he guided it into its allotted position.

Throughout the night rain fell heavily, making communication exceedingly difficult. Telephone instruments had got thoroughly soaked, and nearly all were rendered useless. General Wallerston, however, was able to issue orders for the forthcoming attack to be carried out by the 45th Brigade, followed by three battalions of the 62nd in close support, with what remained of the 46th Brigade in reserve in Loos. About 5.30 A.M. the enemy delivered another, and very heavy, counter-attack against the right of the line, which also was repulsed.

Loos, Sept. 26, 1915.

At 8 A.M. the bombardment of Hill 70 by every available British gun commenced, and continued for one hour, when at 9 A.M. the assault was delivered. It was unfortunate that, both during the bombardment and assault, parts of the Divisional line were shelled by its own guns, but, on the whole, the artillery fire was extremely accurate, especially when the weather conditions—thick mist—are taken into consideration.

9 A.M. Assault of Hill 70 by 62nd Brigade.

The assault failed, was resumed, and failed again. The 62nd Brigade, worn out by its march from Army reserve area and the long and trying night of the 25th/26th, was incapable of giving much assistance. The attack died away, and the front line took up a position a few yards only in advance of the trenches from which it had advanced. All reports agree that it required but little more pressure to have captured the hill, as at one time the enemy actually evacuated the redoubt on the top. The few men remaining of the Fifteenth Division were insufficient to accomplish the task by themselves, and as the brigade sent up to help had not the requisite energy, the crest remained in German hands.

Assault fails.

Seeing what had occurred, and recognising that by now the situation had become critical, General Wallerston asked for assistance, and General McCracken requested the 47th Division to send him one battalion. This assistance, however, never came. About 10 A.M. matters became worse. The retirement of the 62nd Brigade began to affect men of the Fifteenth Division. General Matheson (46th Brigade) shortly before this had arrived in Loos, and, ably assisted by Captain A. P. Sayer (91st Field Company R.E.), personally rallied these men, led them back, and placed them in position along the Loos-Benefontaine road, sending Captain Sayer forward to stop others who might be coming back. On arrival in the front line, Captain Sayer saw the enemy retiring hurriedly from the redoubt, and at once called

Situation, 10 A.M.

Attack on Redoubt by 6th Camerons.

on the troops near him to charge. The men of the Fifteenth Division responded gallantly to this call, but the assault was met by such heavy rifle and machine-gun fire that they were compelled to regain the cover of their own trenches. On the left, another and final effort was being made by the 6th Camerons, most gallantly led by Lieut.-Colonel A. F. Douglas Hamilton in person. The story of this charge is told as follows in a Cameron Journal:—

Death of Colonel Douglas Hamilton, V.C.

"The magnificent dash of the Fifteenth Division was spent, and adequate supports were nowhere forthcoming. It was left to scattered groups of men and to the initiative of stray officers to hold and consolidate part of the ground so gloriously gained. Of these officers, Lieut.-Colonel Douglas Hamilton was the most conspicuous.

"Four times he led the poor remnant of his battalion and some 100 others who had rallied round him against the ever-increasing enemy now holding Hill 70. Then he sank to the ground with the quiet natural words, 'Colquhoun, I'm done!' 'Of course,' said Captain Colquhoun to himself, 'of course he's done. He has had the whole thirty hours of cold, hunger, and anxiety, and he has been doubling all these times ten yards in front of us up Hill 70.' Then, perceiving the facts, the two officers still with him bandaged his wounds, but twenty minutes later, with the words 'I must get up, I must get up!' he passed away."

Colonel Douglas Hamilton's sublime quixotry, which had an immense practical as well as an incalculable moral value, was recognised by the highest honour which can fall to a soldier of the King.[1]

Sept. 26, 1915, 11 A.M.

At 11 A.M. two battalions of the brigade on the left of the Fifteenth Division retired, leaving the flank of the 45th Brigade again exposed, and for the remainder of the morning the whole of the Fifteenth Division line suffered from flanking fire from that direction, which caused heavy casualties in its already depleted ranks. Once more the situation became critical, and General Wallerston again asked for reinforcements. It was about this time, too, that the brigade on the left of the Fifteenth Division evacuated Puits 14 *bis*, and it seemed as if it would not be long before the Fifteenth Division would be compelled to give up all ground east of Loos in consequence.

Failure of 21st Division attack.

At noon the remaining brigades of the 21st Division, which had come up during the night, attacked the Cité St Auguste. They made no progress, and when shelled by the enemy retired. The Germans now commenced to advance from Bois Hugo, and the 45th Brigade

[1] See Appendix J.

were then obliged to withdraw down the slopes of Hill 70 to Loos, where they were told to hold out at all costs. Ammunition was running short, not only because carriers were shot down, but also on account of the difficulty of sparing men from the already thin front line to carry it up. No reinforcements arrived, and the enemy, about 1 P.M., were slowly but steadily working round the left flank of the Division. Orders were then given that if forced to do so, battalions would retire to the old German front-line trenches. Opinions differed regarding this order; some considered it unnecessary, and others thought the position was untenable. At all events, battalions were so mixed up that the order, in its proper form, did not reach commanding officers. The result was that some units retired whilst others remained, the last being the 7th Royal Scots Fusiliers, who, at 4.30 P.M., retired most reluctantly, only to find that by this time the 6th Cavalry Brigade had been sent up, and were occupying Loos village. At 3.40 P.M. Brig.-General Campbell (6th Cavalry Brigade) had been placed in command of Loos and Hill 70. He had under him his own brigade and all troops of the Fifteenth Division then in Loos, the latter to be relieved by a cavalry regiment later in the day.

Sept. 26, 12 noon to 4.30 P.M.

4.30 P.M. Arrival of 6th Cavalry Brigade.

No further attempt on the part of the enemy was made that day to retake the ground he had lost. Apparently he was just as exhausted as were his opponents, and for the moment his reinforcements were not available.

Whilst this was taking place at Loos, General Wilkinson, whose headquarters were then at Quality Street, saw to his astonishment, at 9 A.M. on the 26th, large numbers of British troops of another division streaming down the Loos-Philosophe road towards him. They had neither equipment, rifles, nor gas-helmets, and gave out that the Germans were in Loos, and that they had been told to come back. This, of course, was untrue. The only reason for the panic seems to have been that the enemy were then shelling the ground between Loos and the original British lines with lachrymatory shells in retaliation for the bombardment prior to the second assault that morning. The new and untried troops of this division—a division which later in the war was to win the highest honours—had never experienced anything of this kind before, and moreover were utterly famished and exhausted.

44th Brigade sent up to man O.B. line.

In view of what he saw, General Wilkinson at once ordered his brigade to move to the original British support line east of Mazingarbe, and shortly afterwards from there up to the old German front-line trenches, where for the remainder of the day it was engaged in reversing the parapet in case that line eventually had to be held.

Sept. 26, 1915. 46th Brigade.

About 1 P.M. General Matheson, knowing there were some men of his brigade still in Loos, proceeded thither. On the way he met the remaining men of No. 5 Column under Captain Torrance (H.L.I.), with a few of the 6th Camerons who had been sent to assist him the day before. The general asked this party for volunteers to go to the assistance of their comrades in Loos. The whole party at once responded, although by this time they had been fighting for over thirty hours. They arrived on the western slopes of the hill at 4.30 P.M., just as the 7th Royal Scots Fusiliers were leaving, and, together with that battalion and some men of the Royal Dragoons, they reoccupied the hill without opposition.

Sept. 27. 15th Division relieved.

Nothing further took place for the remainder of the day, the enemy being content to shell Loos village and its approaches. At midnight orders were received from IV. Corps to withdraw the Fifteenth Division, less artillery, to billets in Mazingarbe. The 44th and 46th Brigades complied at once, the 45th at dawn on the 27th, and by noon the whole Division had left the scene of action, and were billeted in Mazingarbe, Houchin, and adjoining villages, the Divisional Artillery remaining in the line.

On September 28 the following message was received by all units :—

15th Division G/167.

SPECIAL DIVISIONAL ORDER.

The following message has been received from Sir Henry Rawlinson :—

"The Corps Commander is anxious that you should communicate to all ranks of the Fifteenth Division his high appreciation of the admirable fighting spirit which they displayed in the attack and capture of Loos village and Hill 70.

"Sir Douglas Haig has also desired the Corps Commander to convey his congratulations to the Division."

The Major-General wishes to say that he is very proud of his Command.

(Sgd.) J. T. BURNETT-STUART,
Lieut.-Colonel, General Staff.

27th September 1915.

Sept. 28. After the battle.

Thus, as far as the Fifteenth Division was concerned, closed the battle of Loos. Words are but a poor medium in which to chronicle the deeds of the Scottish troops. Pages might be written concerning actions of individuals on those memorable two days. The best and shortest commentary upon them all is contained in a certain official report of the operations: "When all did so well it would be invidious to make distinctions. It was difficult to say which had the best right to be proudest, the officers of their men or the men of their officers."

Another brigadier at the conclusion of his report of the battle writes as follows:—

"This brief summary cannot be closed without some slight testimony to the extraordinary fighting spirit displayed by all ranks. Every single officer and man was doing his utmost, and nothing would have stopped them getting through. Nothing could have surpassed the dash and fury with which the brigades captured the German front trenches. This is a fact well worth recording when it is remembered that a year before the profession of arms was foreign to most of the men."

Action of R.A. and R.E.

Throughout the action the Corps and Divisional Artillery, under Brig.-Generals Budworth and Alexander respectively, were magnificent. During the assault their barrage was exceptionally good, and materially assisted the advance. Artillery and infantry worked together in the closest co-operation, and the bold manner in which the guns were handled was beyond all praise. At 10 A.M. on the 25th "C" Battery, 73rd R.F.A. Brigade (Lieut.-Colonel A. M'Micking), actually marched into Loos as far as the Tower Bridge, hoping to take up a position on the eastern side of the village, but, finding none, the battery commander withdrew his guns, and came into action 800 yards north-east of Quality Street, on the forward slope, and in full view of the enemy. Later, it was found impossible to remain even there or for any guns to come into action east of the original German front line.

The 73rd, 74th, and 91st Field Companies R.E., 9th Gordons (Pioneers), together with the 108th (Tunnelling) and 187th Companies R.E. (attached), played a great part throughout the battle. To a large extent they joined in the actual fighting, yet, when required,

Loos.

carried out such R.E. and pioneer work as was called for—*e.g.*, digging communication trenches between the British and German front systems, crossings for artillery, repairs to roads, and, most important of all, assisting in the consolidation of the ground won. In this service 2nd Lieutenant F. H. Johnson, 73rd Field Company R.E., rendered inestimable service, for which he was subsequently awarded the V.C.[1]

Signal Company.

The Fifteenth Divisional Signal Company deserves the greatest credit for the way in which communications were maintained throughout. Telephone wires were constantly cut by artillery fire, and in many instances by British troops mistaking the lines in Loos for German wires, all of which they promptly cut; but in every case, no matter how heavy the artillery or machine-gun fire might be, the lines were repaired and communications kept up throughout.

M.M.G. Battery.

Allusion has already been made to the 11th Motor Machine-Gun Battery (Major C. B. Hall) and Fifteenth Divisional Cyclist Company (Captain J. C. Cooke). Exceptionally good work was done by 2nd Lieutenant R. N. Chubb of the latter unit. During the evening and night of the 25th this officer made numerous journeys through Loos, bringing up ammunition to the firing line. The timely arrival of Major Hall with his guns on the afternoon of the 25th undoubtedly relieved the whole front of the Division. In order to get his guns into Loos he had to cross unbridged trenches, man-handle his motorcycles over shell-swept roads, and finally, abandoning his cycles and cars, brought his guns and ammunition into Loos and up to Hill 70 in hand-carts.

R.A.M.C.

Before the action every arrangement humanly possible had been made for the reception and evacuation of the wounded. Special trenches were dug and carefully marked, down which none but wounded men were allowed. Advance dressing stations, collecting stations, and main dressing stations were constructed. Accommodation was provided in these for the reception of 3600 lying and 2690 sitting cases. The total number of wounded that passed through these Divisional stations was 4763. Some of these were men of other divisions, but the work none the less fell on the Field Ambulances, the total staff of which was only 423. With the exception of about 100 cases,

[1] See Appendix J.

Lieut.-Colonel A. F. DOUGLAS HAMILTON, V.C.

6th Battalion Cameron Highlanders.

all the casualties admitted to the Fifteenth Divisional Field Ambulances (45th, 46th, and 47th Field Ambulances, R.A.M.C.), which meant 4600 cases, had been collected, their wounds dressed, and all ranks fed and housed by midnight on the 26th. The scheme for removing the wounded worked admirably. Evacuation by No. 8 Motor Ambulance Convoy from September 27 was rapid, and by the 29th all cases had been sent to Casualty Clearing Stations. The report by Colonel Rawnsley, A.D.M.S., Fifteenth Division, concluded: "I should like to place on record the heroism displayed by the wounded, which lightened the task of those who had to minister to them. No murmur or groan was heard among this vast assembly of stricken heroes, many with grievous wounds joking and making light of them, thus cheering up their wounded comrades. It was an honour appreciated by all ranks of the medical service to serve such men."

Loos.

The Casualty List (Appendix I) shows the devotion and determination with which General McCracken's orders were obeyed. 6606 men out of the total fighting strength of 19,212 died or were wounded in pushing forward to their given objective "with all the offensive power of the Division."

The following is taken from a letter from Major-General Thuillier, who at Loos was at first C.R.E. of the 1st Division, and later commanded the 2nd Infantry Brigade of the same division:—

"A day or two after the first attack I had occasion to pass over the ground where the Fifteenth Division had assaulted the German trenches. In front of the remains of the work known as the 'Lens Road Redoubt' (Jew's Nose) the dead Highlanders in Black Watch tartan lay very thick. In one place, about forty yards square, on the very crest of the ridge, and just in front of the enemy's wire, they lay so close that it was difficult to step between them. Nevertheless the survivors had swept on and through the German line.

"As I looked on the smashed and riven ground, the tangled belt of wire still not completely cut, and the thick swathes of dead, every man lying as he had fallen, face to the enemy, I was amazed when I thought of the unconquerable irresistible spirit which those newly raised units of the 'New Armies' must possess to have enabled them to continue their advance after sustaining such losses.

"Returning from Loos along the straight Lens road I met a sergeant and six or eight men of the 7th K.O.S.B. near the top of the ridge where the old German front line had been. I warned the sergeant that he would be exposed to enemy machine-gun fire farther along the road, and advised him to take his men across country. He thanked me, and asked how he could get to Hill 70. I replied that he couldn't get there at all, as it was now in the enemy's hands. He evidently doubted this statement, for he said, 'How can that be, sir? The regiment took the hill and got over the other side.' I answered that there had been a lot of fighting since then, and that the Germans were on the top of it now, and inquired why he wanted to go there so particularly. He said that his colonel had sent him up to bury two officers of the regiment who had been killed on the top of the hill. I again told him that it was out of the question, but his reply was that he knew exactly where the officers had fallen, and that he and his party proposed to get as near the spot as possible by daylight, creep out at night, and bring in the bodies. I explained, or tried to, the utter impossibility of such a proceeding. His answer was, 'Well, sir, we couldn't go back and face the regiment when we hadn't even tried to bury the officers, so we'll be getting along and make the best try we can. Thank you kindly for warning us all the same.' At these words his men, who had been listening intently throughout, gave unmistakable murmurs of assent, and the party prepared to move off. Knowing the futility of their errand, I then said, 'Now, look here, sergeant, it's really quite useless. You'll only lose your lives, and we cannot afford to lose men like you. Your spirit does you and your regiment credit, but I'm not going to allow you to go to certain death. I therefore take it on myself to forbid you to go, and order you back to your regiment.' To this the N.C.O. replied, rather obstinately and evidently very disappointed, 'Well, sir, if you *order* me to go back I must go, but I can't face the colonel and say I haven't carried out his orders unless I show him in writing the order you've given me. I must also ask you, sir, if you will excuse me, to give me a note with your name, rank, and regiment on it.' I gave him the necessary documents, and saw him and his party, very reluctantly, turn about and go down the road towards Mazingarbe.

"I do not think I have ever been more impressed with the soldierly bearing and spirit of any men than I was with that of those eight or nine Scotsmen. The N.C.O. appeared to be an old Regular soldier, but his men were all youngsters.

"The above account does not show the real difficulty I had in turning them from their purpose. It is a weak description of the true spirit of discipline, determination, and courage, combined with loyalty and affection towards their officers, which positively shone in their words and looks. I thought at the time what a splendid battalion it must be, of which a small detachment, far from its own officers, could carry with it such a manifestation of the true regimental spirit. Later, in 1917, when I had the great privilege of commanding the Fifteenth (Scottish) Division, I learnt that every battalion was the same. I found the same spirit undestroyed by two years of hard and stubborn fighting, or by the losses which every unit had suffered in the great battles of 1915, '16, and '17."

The battle of Loos was, it may now fairly be said, neither a strategic nor a tactical success. It taught the Germans one lesson—that the new formations of the British Army, when properly handled, were not to be despised. The Fifteenth Division, unsupported by adequate reserves, had nobly done their duty, and had made the farthest advance of any British division in a day's battle between the outbreak of war and the battle of Cambrai in November 1917. The last paragraphs of General McCracken's report may be quoted :—

" My orders to push on to the full extent of the power of the Division were clear and definite, and were carried out to the full in the confident assurance that the promised flow of reinforcements behind me would be maintained. In the event, I consider that nothing but the highest soldierly qualities displayed by officers and men of my Division averted a disastrous retreat from the position won."

The Allied command learned much from Loos, and returned forthwith to a more cautious battle plan. Yet in that little Highland spearhead, broken off at Cité St Auguste in the September mist, there was a forecast of victory. For it was the "infiltration" of bodies of highly disciplined troops which was the essence of the German tactics in their great attack of March 1918, and it was the same tactics on the Allied side, as perfected by the hand of Foch, that six months later brought Germany to her knees.

No account of Loos would be complete without reference to Mlle. Emilienne Moreau, the " Lady of Loos."

Living with her mother, brother, and small sister, she and her family had remained in Loos throughout the German occupation. On September 25, after the 44th Brigade had stormed the village, she attached herself to the dressing-station of Captain Bearn, M.O. to the 9th Black Watch. Throughout the day she and her mother supplied the wounded with coffee made in the cellar of their ruined home, and rendered what assistance she could to Captain Bearn. Three times the dressing-station had to be changed on account of shell-fire, but on each occasion Mlle. Moreau accompanied it. Whilst occupying the third, Captain Bearn and his party found they were being sniped from some houses opposite, but they could not make out from which particular house the fire came. Snatching up a revolver lying on a table in the dressing-station, Mlle. Moreau ran out, and disappeared behind the opposite houses. A few seconds afterwards two shots, and two only, were heard, and almost immediately the girl returned, laid down the revolver, quietly remarking "C'est fini," and continued her work of attending to the wounded as if nothing had happened. Although the firing from the houses stopped, Captain Bearn could hardly believe its cessation was due to any action of Mlle. Moreau's. Later in the day, when there came a lull in the stream of wounded, he questioned her, and was taken by her round the back of the houses, through some gardens, up a flight of stairs, and there in the front room lay the bodies of two Germans she had shot. Asked why she had gone by herself, she replied that she knew the way, and others might have found it difficult. She made no fuss about what she had done, and by no means looked on her action as anything out of the ordinary. A few days later, after the Fifteenth Division had left Loos, the exploit was officially reported to General McCracken. A car was sent for Captain Bearn, and he was told to go and find this gallant Frenchwoman. With a good deal of trouble, as by this time all civilian inhabitants of Loos had been evacuated to the neighbouring villages, Captain Bearn managed to find first the mother, then the brother and sister, and lastly, Mlle. Moreau herself, and conveyed them to Divisional Headquarters. After some difficulty Mlle. Moreau was persuaded to give an account of her exploit, and very shortly afterwards she received the British Military Medal as an immediate reward. Later she also received the Croix de Guerre with palms, and shortly afterwards the medals of the British Red Cross and St John Ambulance Society. "Only 17½ years of age at the time," said the citation, "Mlle. Moreau displayed the courage of the bravest of the brave."

CHAPTER III.

WINTER AND SPRING, 1915-16.[1]

Fifteenth Division to IV. Corps Reserve at Lillers, Oct. 3, 1915.

AFTER Loos it was imperative that the Division should be given time to reorganise and rest. Conditions did not permit of this being done at once. The enemy, furious at having been driven back, brought up large reserves—the 2nd Guard Reserve Division,—and heavy fighting took place along the whole line from La Bassée to Maroc. The situation was relieved somewhat on the 30th, when the French took over the defence of Loos village and Hill 70, but it was not until October 3 that the Division marched to Lillers and became IV. Corps reserve. The 44th and 46th Brigades were billeted in the town, the 45th at Allouagne, 9th Gordons at Haute Rieux, Divisional mounted troops and 70th and 71st Brigades, R.F.A., at La Pugnoy, with Divisional Headquarters at La Boeuvrière. Here the work of reorganisation was carried out. All deficiencies were made good, and large drafts, amounting to some 4000 men, arrived from the base. By October 12 most units were almost up to strength, classes of instruction were started, and training carried out.

Back to the line, Oct. 12-15.

The period of rest allowed to the Division was not long. The enemy was still endeavouring to retake the ground he had lost on September 25, and the situation was somewhat disquieting. On October 10 the Division was ordered to proceed to the Nœux-les-Mines area, and two days later the infantry, field ambulances, and field companies R.E. moved up by train (the transport going by road), while the rest of the Division remained in and around Lillers. At the conclusion of the move the 44th and 46th Brigades were billeted in Nœux-les-Mines; the 45th Brigade, with the 74th Field Company R.E. and 45th Field Ambulance, at Houchin and Haillicourt; the 47th

[1] Maps 2 and 3.

Field Ambulance at Lozinghem; Divisional Train at La Buissière, with Divisional Headquarters at Nœux-les-Mines—all under orders to move at half an hour's notice.

On October 15 Division Headquarters moved to Douvrin and 45th Brigade to Mazingarbe, 11th M.M.G. Battery and Divisional M.G. School to Haillicourt, and mounted troops to Houchin. The 3rd and 63rd Trench-Mortar Batteries were temporarily transferred to the XI. Corps (Guards Division). For the next few days infantry, R.E., and pioneers furnished large working-parties to assist in consolidating the recently captured ground. It was quite a common occurrence for an infantry battalion to find 300 to 350 men each night, with the result that the new drafts did not get as much training and instruction as was necessary before they took their place in the front line. Weather, too, made things more difficult. Fine till now, it broke on October 10, torrents of rain fell, and the ground speedily became a quagmire.

In the line, Quarries sector, Oct. 19.

On the 18th orders were received that the Division would take over the front-line trenches then held by the 12th Division. In accordance with these orders, on the night of the 19th the 45th Brigade took over the Quarries sector from the 35th. There was some delay owing to an enemy attack on the Quarries, which broke down completely, however, and the relief was finished by 10 A.M. on the 20th.

The Division found the new sector very different from that which it had occupied in August and September. The heavy fighting that had taken place in the area had made it impossible to do much in the construction of proper defences. The trench system was extensive, but, with the exception of those dug by the Germans before they retired, most trenches were only a few feet deep, and afforded next to no cover either from fire or view.

Owing to the failure to capture Hohenzollern Redoubt and Puits 14 *bis* east of Loos, the whole of the British area between these points was under direct observation by the enemy. No movement could be made above ground during the day, and long communication trenches as far back as Vermelles (2½ miles) were necessary. The task of putting these into and keeping them in proper order meant an additional strain on the Division. No attempt had been made to drain any of the trenches, and continual rain soon made them almost impassable; inter-battalion and brigade reliefs which, under ordinary circumstances, would have taken only a few hours, now occupied the whole night. Many of the front-line trenches were not even provided with fire-steps or properly traversed, and in addition an enormous amount of equipment, S.A.A., and bombs had to be salved, and a considerable number of British and German dead buried.

In the line, Oct. 1915.

This work of consolidation, carried out under most adverse conditions, spoke well for the moral of the Division. Every man did his utmost, and matters gradually improved. "Up" and "down" trenches were dug, gratings laid down, and trenches properly finished, traversed, and drained. Telephone wires, which were found to be in chaotic confusion, were relaid, and long before the Division handed over this sector the whole system was in first-class order. On October 28 His Majesty the King inspected detachments of the Division at La Buissière. It was a disappointment to all that, as the Division was then in the line, His Majesty was unable to see it as a whole.

His Majesty inspects detachments of Fifteenth Division, Oct. 28, 1915.

Beyond the usual inter-brigade reliefs no event of special importance occurred on the Divisional front whilst occupying this sector. Brigades held the front system for twelve to fourteen days at a time, then going into Divisional reserve for six to eight days at Nœux-les-Mines for rest, training, and reorganisation. Throughout the period October 19 to December 15 the enemy systematically shelled the area, especially the front line south of Hohenzollern Redoubt, and retaliatory fire did not stop his activity.

No enemy attack took place during the tour. On several occasions messages were received, some emanating from "a reliable source," to the effect that the enemy was preparing to attack in the Lens area, but nothing materialised. Raids had not then become fashionable, and enemy mining activities, although suspected, did not trouble the Division. On November 16 the 1/4th Black Watch, 1/4th Seaforths, and 1/4th Suffolk Regiment from the Indian Corps joined the Division. The first was posted to the 44th Brigade and the other two to the 46th, as that brigade was numerically much weaker than either the 44th or 45th.

At all times the Divisional Artillery rendered loyal and unfailing

In the line.

support to the infantry whenever called upon. Cut down to a few rounds per gun per day, they could not do much in the way of retaliation; but whenever the enemy showed signs of restlessness, or of an inclination to attack, the gunners gave all assistance in their power. On October 11 the Victoria Cross was earned by No. 36830 A/Sergeant John Crawshay Raynes, A/71st Brigade, R.F.A., "For most conspicuous bravery and devotion at Fosse 7 under very heavy shell-fire on October 11, 1915, and at Quality Street on the 12th, when, though himself wounded, he assisted to rescue four men buried by the fall of a house, and afterwards reported for duty at his battery." [1]

It is not often that a gleam of humour lights up the pages of an official Diary. The following entry is therefore worth quoting: "On December 9, at 3 P.M., B/73 Battery demolished an enemy saphead, causing a bomb store to explode. Much débris was blown into our lines, including portions of Germans, AND A DOG WHICH ANSWERED TO THE NAME OF FRITZ."

The entries in the Engineer diaries do scant justice to the enormous amount of work which the Corps accomplished during these three months. Amongst other things, they sank wells in the support line, thus obviating the long "carry" of water from Vermelles to the front line; existing dug-outs were improved, and many built; wire defences were strengthened and erected; strong posts were constructed in and behind the line, and much other work accomplished before the Division left that part of the line.

During this tour the Divisional mounted troops were employed as observers in the front line, and furnished trench patrols to regulate the traffic in the long "up" and "down" communication trenches.

It is somewhat difficult to chronicle the doings of either the R.A.S.C., R.A.O.C., or R.A.M.C. Their diaries are one continuous story of laborious, unobtrusive, and well-carried-out work. The historian cannot make much out of a Diary in which the entry day after day reads, "Supply work as usual." Under that dull and uninteresting heading lies a story of long journeys over vile roads in all kinds of weather, often under artillery and machine-gun fire, with stores, rations, and ammunition up to forward areas. Those four

[1] Appendix J.

words occur day after day in the R.A.S.C. diary. It is all that The Corps says of its work, but the men of the Division know how well they were served on every occasion.

In the line, Nov. 1915.

As regards ordnance. Amongst the numberless articles issued from time to time came one which eventually proved of inestimable value. Towards the end of October the first issue of steel helmets was made, on the scale of 50 per infantry unit. This ugly, but very necessary, head-dress did not at first appeal to the Scotsmen, who thought rightly that it did not add to their personal appearance, and some difficulty was experienced at first in getting even the sentries to wear them in the front line. It was not until the full number had been received, and officers themselves wore them, that they came into general use. Even then the staff, probably for the same reasons as the men, were often to be seen in the front line wearing the well-known " brass " and not the regulation " steel " hat. At first these helmets were put to all sorts of unauthorised uses. The writer well remembers finding one of his men using his steel helmet as a washing-basin one morning just after " Stand to." Cleanliness is certainly next to Godliness, but in the front-line trenches " protection " comes a d—d long way first.

Steel helmets first issued.

Before the commencement of the tour, arrangements had been made to continue the various schools of instruction whilst the Division was in the line. Parties of officers, N.C.O.'s, and men were sent to them from each unit throughout the period, and systematic and thorough training was carried out. This was the commencement of that intensive training which was to reach such vast proportions later in the war. It was realised that instruction could be better carried out in France, where conditions were known, and any necessary alteration could be made immediately. A Divisional Trench-Mortar School was opened on November 16. At first these weapons were somewhat primitive and uncertain in their action ; the supply of them was small, and they were looked upon with grave suspicion by the infantry whose sector their owners chose for their operations on account of their invariably drawing retaliatory fire from the enemy. One morning an enthusiastic trench-mortar officer was sent down by a certain brigadier to the front line with orders to select the best position pos-

Nov. 1915. A trench-mortar story.

sible in the brigade line. He reported to a certain Highland C.O., who sent him down to the front line, he himself following shortly afterwards. On arrival, the C.O. found his two company commanders having a somewhat heated argument as to which of their sub-sectors was best fitted for the trench-mortar battery, Captain S. recommending that of Captain B., who, on the other hand, pointed out that the ground behind Captain S.'s line was far more suitable than that behind his own. On carefully going over the whole of his area with the trench-mortar expert, the C.O. came to the conclusion that even a better site could be obtained some 100 yards to the right of his line, and still in the brigade area. To this spot the trench-mortar expert betook himself, where he set to work with the usual result, much to the discomfort of the battalion in whose area he operated.

On the 11th the suspicions that the enemy was engaged in mining operations became a certainty. His miners could be distinctly heard tunnelling in the vicinity of the Hairpin trench south of the Quarries. Steps were at once taken to counter-mine from a shaft originally made as a trial. Fortunately the Germans were not ready to "blow" their mine while the Division was in the sector, but it was far from pleasant to know that sooner or later that particular part of the trench would be demolished. This mine was "blown" two days after the Division left, causing a considerable number of casualties to the battalion holding that part of the line.

Dec. 1915. To Corps reserve.

Early in December it became known that the Division would shortly be withdrawn to Corps reserve for a well-earned rest. On the 13th the move commenced, the 46th Brigade being relieved by a brigade of the 47th Division, and moving to billets in Raimbert. On the two following days the relief of the 44th and 45th Brigades took place, the former moving to Allouagne and the latter to Lillers, Divisional Headquarters opening at the Chateau Philomel, Lillers, on the afternoon of the 15th.

Most of the Divisional artillery was relieved by that of the 47th Division about the same time, and was billeted in Marles-les-Mines and Auchel, but the 72nd Brigade and C/73rd Battery did not leave the line until relieved by batteries from the 16th Divisional Artillery on the night of the 27/28th, only to be sent up again the following day.

The R.E. moved back on the 12/13th as follows: 73rd Field Company to Lillers, 74th to Lapugnoy, and 91st to Lozinghem. Divisional cavalry and cyclists were billeted at Hurionville, 9th Gordons (Pioneers) at Lapugnoy, and the remainder of Divisional troops at Lillers, Raimbert, and Hesdigneuil.

Dec. 1915.

The first few days in Corps reserve were spent in cleaning up and reorganisation. Owing to the wet weather and bad trenches it had not been possible to keep units up to that pitch of perfection required by General McCracken, but it was not long before the Division resumed its usual smart appearance. Intensive training commenced at once. Carried out first by companies, then by battalions and brigades, it culminated in a Divisional exercise lasting three days, from January 5 to 7. This was held in the area west of Lillers, and, in spite of bad weather, considerable instruction was derived from it. In view of the conditions of trench warfare, the marching of the troops on this occasion was remarkably good.

In addition to the Schools of Instruction already in progress, others were commenced. On December 16 eighteen officers joined a Divisional Officers' Training School, under Major A. G. Taylor, Suffolk Regiment. The same day a Signal Course started. These and others were of the greatest value. Lecturers came from other schools, and the future efficiency of the Division was largely due to the training and instruction received by all ranks attending them.

The first T.-M. Battery.

During the month the first Divisional trench-mortar battery was formed. Numbered 46/1, it consisted of 25 officers, N.C.O.'s and men, and was armed with four 3.7-in. howitzers, Woolwich pattern. Unfortunately the diaries of this and other trench-mortar batteries from December 1915 to July 1916 are missing from the official records, and what little information is contained in this history regarding their doings has been taken from the few extracts found in the G.S. Diary, supplemented by information supplied by individuals who served in the various batteries.

Between the time the Division landed in France and the end of 1915 several changes had taken place in the Division staff. In September Brig.-General Lambart, R.A., left the Division, his place as C.R.A. being taken by Brig.-General E. W. Alexander, V.C. The

Dec. 1915. Staff changes.

same month Major E. G. Wace, R.E., succeeded Major E. G. Henderson, R.E., as G.S.O. 2. In November Colonel G. T. Rawnsley, R.A.M.C., handed over the duties of A.D.M.S. to Colonel C. E. Pollock, R.A.M.C. Lieut.-Colonel J. Burnett-Stuart, G.S.O. 1, also left the Division that month, being succeeded by Lieut.-Colonel H. H. S. Knox, Northamptonshire Regiment. It was largely owing to Colonel Burnett-Stuart's efforts that the excellent relations existed between the Divisional staff and all other headquarters in the Division.

There had also been two changes in brigade commanders. In August, Brig.-General T. G. Matheson, Grenadier Guards, had succeeded Brig.-General A. G. Duff, the Black Watch, in command of the 46th Brigade; and in October Brig.-General E. W. B. Green, Royal Sussex Regiment, took over command of the 45th Brigade from Brig.-General F. E. Wallerston, K.O.S.B.

Both Christmas and New Year's Days were observed in the usual manner. In one battalion diary the following entry occurs: "January 1—The officers saw the New Year in, but as a whole the battalion slept it in."

On January 10, 1916, orders were issued for the relief of the 1st Division by the Fifteenth, and three days later the move to the forward area began. Brigades moved by train to Nœux-les-Mines in turn, commencing with the 45th, each as it arrived relieving a brigade of the 1st Division. The month's rest had done all ranks much good. The new drafts which had arrived during the past three months completed their training, and were absorbed in their various units. Special attention had been paid to discipline, ceremonial drill, and dress, with the result that by the time the Division left Lillers for the front line, it was, in every respect, up to the high standard it had attained before leaving England.

Jan. 1916. Loos sector taken over.

By 10 A.M. on the 16th the move had been completed, and at that hour General McCracken assumed command of the sector, with headquarters at the Chateau Mazingarbe. The Division now held the left sector of the IV. Corps front. On the right the 47th (London) Division held the line, and were responsible for the defence of Loos village, the dividing line between Divisions being the Loos-St Laurent road. "Devon Lane," just south of the Quarries, was the north boundary of the IV. Corps area. As before, two brigades occupied the line at a time, the dividing line being Vendin Alley (inclusive to the right brigade). The brigade in Divisional reserve occupied billets in Mazingarbe and Nœux-les-Mines.

Jan. 1916.

The Division found the trenches in its new area much better than those they had occupied previously. They had been thoroughly well looked after, were dry, and properly drained, and provided with fair dug-out accommodation. No Man's Land was wide along the whole of the Divisional front, and afforded good opportunities for scouting and patrol work.

Mining operations.

The start of the tour was comparatively quiet. Both sides were busily engaged upon mining operations, each trying to tunnel under the galleries of the other. During December the enemy had obtained the upper hand in this method of warfare, and special precautions were now necessary, not only to stop further activity in this direction, but also to destroy any new gallery that might be made in future. To do this, counter-galleries had been commenced at many places in the front line, and infantry and engineer units were called on to supply as many miners as possible to continue their construction. There was no lack of skilled miners in the ranks of the Division. Fife, Lanark, and the coal districts of Scotland were well represented, and there were scores of men willing and anxious to undertake this dangerous work, many for no other reason than to avoid the deadly monotony of life in the front line at this time.

As far as the Divisional sector was concerned, it was comparatively free from mining activity. The front line ran along the shallow valley between Hill 70 and west of Hulluch. Here the presence of water ten to twelve feet below the surface of the ground rendered mining operations impossible, and in consequence that part of the sector was fairly quiet. Farther north, and just on the Divisional boundary, things were different. From this point to Hohenzollern Redoubt the explosion of mines was of daily occurrence, and fierce fighting invariably took place for the possession of craters formed by these explosions.

Before it took over the section the Division had been warned that special precautions would have to be taken as regarded gas attacks.

Jan. 1916.
Gas precautions.

At that time of the year the wind generally blew from an easterly direction, and in consequence enemy gas attacks might be looked for. Gongs made from empty shell-cases were hung in each bay in the front line, and sentries had instructions to beat these should there be any sign or smell of gas. Farther back, in the support and reserve lines, Klaxon horns were installed, and when any of these were sounded, the signal was repeated up and down the line, and every man at once donned his gas-mask. Practice alarms were of constant occurrence, and the whole Division was well exercised in these very necessary precautions.

Nothing further of importance occurred during the month. The weather was fairly fine throughout, and made patrol work easier. Parties went out nightly to investigate the enemy's wire, and ascertain what work he was engaged on. These patrols were instrumental in recovering many bodies of men of the Division and others who had been killed on September 25, 1915. Amongst these was the body of Lieut.-Colonel Douglas Hamilton, V.C., 6th Camerons, which was recovered by a party of men from the 7th Battalion of that regiment.

By this time trench warfare had become more intensive, and gradually both sides made increasing use of grenades and trench-mortars. Bombing attacks were of nightly occurrence, and these served not only to harass the enemy considerably, but fostered a spirit of aggression and emulation between battalions. Throughout the tour many casualties were caused by enemy snipers, especially in the neighbourhood of the Quarries, one of these being Lieut.-Colonel Cruddas, 1/4th Battalion Suffolk Regiment, who was shot whilst reconnoitring a crater formed by an enemy mine. Snipers' sections were formed in each infantry unit, and as there were plenty of gamekeepers and good shots in the Division, it was not long before the enemy lost his superiority in this line.

On January 26 units of the 16th (Irish) Division were attached for instruction, and for two days assisted in holding the line. The following day, possibly to celebrate their ruler's birthday, the Germans endeavoured to carry out a local attack on that part of the line held by the 46th Brigade, north of Chalk Pit Wood. At 3 P.M. the trenches held by the 7th K.O.S.B. were heavily shelled, and almost flattened

A German attack.

Jan. 1916.

for several hundred yards. This was followed by heavy rifle and machine-gun fire, under which the enemy attempted to advance against the Borderers and the 10th Scottish Rifles on their left. The attack failed signally, but casualties were heavy, the Borderers losing some 100 men and the Scottish Rifles 28 killed and 33 wounded. The attack had been more or less anticipated, and the machine-guns of the 9th Black Watch and 6th Royal Irish Regiment—the latter then in the line for instruction—had been left at the disposal of General Matheson. These rendered great assistance in repulsing the attack, No. S/3982 Sergeant A. E. Bayne and No. S/6660 L/Cpl. A. Thomson, 9th Black Watch, being awarded the D.C.M. for their action on this occasion.

Formation of Machine-Gun Companies.

Early in February each infantry brigade received an important addition to its fighting efficiency in the shape of a machine-gun company, the 44th, 45th, and 46th Machine-Gun Companies being formed and joining their respective brigades on the 12th.

On February 4 General Sir C. C. Monro assumed command of the First Army, succeeding General Sir Douglas Haig. A fortnight later, on February 20, he visited the Division, accompanied by Lieut.-General Sir H. Rawlinson, and saw men of the Division who had been awarded the D.C.M.

At the end of the month the 1/4th Battalion Suffolk Regiment left the 46th Brigade for the 30th Division. After having been with the IV. Corps since its arrival in France, the Division now, on March 2, found itself transferred to the I. Corps, then commanded by Lieut.-General H. de la P. Gough. The other three Divisions in that Corps were the 1st, 12th, and 16th, and of these the 16th was then in Corps reserve at Lillers. It may be worth recording that on the same day on which this change came into force, another took place—the continental system of timing being adopted by the British Armies. It certainly tended to lessen confusion as regards orders, &c., but the Scotsmen found it rather difficult at first to grasp the fact that 23.59 hours meant one minute to midnight.

Continental time.

As time passed more and more attention was paid to the direction of the wind. Rude spirits in the front line made ribald remarks regarding the "vertical" instead of the "horizontal" position of the air in the minds of those behind the line, who so constantly ordered

Feb.-Mar. 1916.

the "alert" signal to be given. There is no doubt, however, that the constant practice in quickly donning their masks did all ranks much good, and undoubtedly saved many lives later on.

It was now noticed that the enemy was using a new and heavier type of trench-mortar. Those of the British were unable to deal effectually with them. A very much better gun—the "Stokes"—had been promised, but it did not appear until April, and for the remainder of the tour the Division was practically powerless to stop the enemy's trench-mortar activity.

Bad weather.

The weather at this time can only be described as vile. Constant snow, frost, and rain not only added considerably to the amount of work to be done, but greatly increased the rate of sickness, which at this time reached 200 to 240 cases per week. With weak battalions little new work was possible, for all hands were engaged in repairing their trenches; the Field Companies, R.E., were almost continuously in the line. Six weeks in and two weeks out of the line was the usual tour of each of the Division field companies at this time. To assist in dealing with these abnormal conditions, the Divisional Cyclist Company was pressed into service. Converted for the time being into a "Trench Maintenance" company, it did good work, and considerably relieved the pressure on the front-line troops.

To Corps reserve.

On March 24 the Division commenced moving into Ist Corps reserve at Lillers and the neighbouring villages, their place in the line being taken by the 16th. By the 27th the move had been completed, and the Division was disposed as follows :—

Divisional Headquarters, Chateau Philomel, Lillers.
44th Brigade, Allouagne.
45th Brigade, Lapugnoy; headquarters at Marles-les-Mines.
46th Brigade, Raimbert and Cauchy a la Tour.
9th Gordons (Pioneers), Lillers.
Artillery (not relieved till April 16 by 16th Divisional Artillery).
70th Brigade, Ecquedecques.
71st Brigade, Ames.
72nd Brigade, Bellemy.
73rd Brigade, Liers.
D.A.C., Les Perses.
Field Companies, R.E.—73rd, Burtrue; 74th, Cauchy a la Tour; 91st, to Lapugnoy.

Divisional Mounted Troops, Hurionville, thence to Coudette and St Omer.
Train, Lillers.
Divisional Troops, Lillers.

Mar.-April 1916.

Although there had been no engagements of importance during the last tour, casualties had been constant, and in the case of some units heavy. Sickness, too, had thinned the ranks of the Division, and once more intensive training was required to bring the new drafts up to the excellence of their predecessors, and to polish up the knowledge of the older hands. Training and reorganisation was commenced at once, and for the next four weeks was steadily carried out. Sports were arranged for, and, as the weather was fine the whole time, every one greatly enjoyed the work and recreation. Two days after it had come out of the line the 44th Brigade was inspected by General Sir C. C. Monro at Lillers. On this parade he presented medals to certain men of the Tunnelling Companies who had won them by actions during the past tour. Commencing on April 9, and lasting for three days, a Divisional exercise was carried out in the neighbourhood of Estrée Blanche, during which General Joffre watched the Division march past him.

To Hohenzollern sector.

On April 24 the Division again moved into the line—this time in relief of the 12th Division, then holding the Hohenzollern or left section of the I. Corps front. The move was completed by 10 A.M. on the 26th, when General McCracken assumed command, with headquarters at the Chateau Des Pres, Sailly Labourse. The same day the Divisional artillery returned to the line, being grouped as follows :—

Right Group (Lieut.-Colonel H. W. A. Christie, R.A.)—

72nd Brigade.
A/70th Brigade.
Composite Howitzer Battery, B/73 and 1/2 C/73.

Left Group (Lieut.-Colonel F. W. Heath, R.A.)—

71st Brigade.
B/70th Brigade.
C/70th Brigade.
Composite Howitzer Battery, D/73 and 1/2 C/73.

Each group covered the front of an infantry brigade.[1]

[1] D/70 remained in reserve area with 12th Divisional Artillery.

April 1916.

The sector extended from the Vermelles-Hulluch road on the right to Mud Trench on the Vermelles-Auchy road. It was subdivided into two sections, the one on the right being known as "the Quarries" and that on the left as the "Hohenzollern" sections respectively. At the start the 44th Brigade occupied the Quarries section, the 46th the Hohenzollern, with the 45th Brigade in Divisional reserve at Annequin, Sailly Labourse, and Bethune.

From its experience during the previous tour the Division knew well what to expect in this particular section. Along almost its entire length No Man's Land was a mass of mine craters, for the possession of which there was daily fighting. In several places the enemy had already tunnelled underneath portions of the British trenches, and it behoved units occupying such areas to take special measures for their defence, and for the protection of their garrisons. Listening-posts were established in the front line and on the near lips of the craters. In areas where enemy mining was known to exist the number of men occupying the front line was reduced to a minimum, the main garrison being kept in the support line a few yards in rear of the danger area.

Gas attacks.

It had not been twenty-four hours in the line before the Division experienced its first enemy gas attack. At 5.20 A.M. on April 27, after a somewhat heavy artillery bombardment, clouds of greenish gas were seen rolling towards the trenches held by the 44th Brigade, Quarries sector. On this occasion it was not followed up by any infantry attack, and "normal conditions" were resumed at 8.20 A.M. At the time no reason was apparent for this attempt on the part of the enemy, but in the light of what took place two days later it would seem that this particular effort was in the nature of a practice, or to ascertain whether the Division was alert and well prepared.

On the 29th another, and very different, gas attack took place. This time it was directed mainly against the line held by the 16th (Irish) Division on the south, the northern edge of the cloud only passing over the right battalion of the 44th Brigade (9th Black Watch). This time the gas was much stronger, and not mixed with smoke as it had been before. It was very difficult to see, and the Black Watch suffered a good many casualties from a change of wind which blew the gas back over their area after the men had removed their masks. In connection with these attacks a curious story may be told. During the night of the 26th a machine-gun N.C.O. in the Irish Division observed an extraordinary number of rats jumping into his front-line trench from No Man's Land. The man had been a seaman in civil life, and therefore, remembering that "rats leave a sinking ship," he warned his gun's crew that something might happen, and told them to wear their masks rolled up on their heads. Two hours later clouds of gas rolled over his line, but that particular crew were prepared, and consequently suffered no casualties.

April 1916.

The "Lone How."

Again no infantry attack took place on the Division front, the enemy confining his attention to the 16th Division, then in the neighbourhood of the Chalk Pit Wood, where at first he gained a small temporary success, only to be driven back to his trenches with considerable loss an hour later. The enemy actually gained possession of the Chalk Pit Wood, in which was hidden the celebrated "Lone How." This remarkable piece originally formed part of the equipment of the 43rd Brigade, R.F.A. In September it had assisted in supporting the attack of the 1st Division against Hulluch. Two months later, by a very fine piece of work on the part of Lieutenant F. Aitkens, R.F.A., it was taken up into the Chalk Pit Wood, and from there brought enfilade fire to bear on the German trenches north of the wood and west of Hulluch. Being so close to the front line, only forty yards behind, there was always a danger of the gun falling into enemy hands in the event of a successful attack. The officer in charge of the gun, therefore, had orders to destroy it if necessary. On the morning of April 27, 1916, the Germans attacked, and captured the Chalk Pit and the wood, then held by the 16th (Irish) Division. Before the gun's crew left the wood, however, the gun had been prepared for demolition, and the fuse lit. A few hours later, after the wood had been recaptured by the 48th Brigade, it was found that the gun was intact and undamaged, the fuse having gone out a few inches from the charge. Its position had been so well camouflaged that the enemy had not discovered it, and it was able to resume its work shortly afterwards. During the whole time it was in position the gun was never seriously damaged, although the enemy knew of

April-May 1916.

its existence, and made many attempts to silence it. From an infantryman's point of view, it was a doubtful asset, as it invariably drew retaliatory fire whenever it was used, but there is no doubt that it did very considerable damage to the enemy.[1]

In connection with this attack on the part of the enemy, it is interesting to note that in October 1918, at the commencement of the "Advance to Victory," an officer of the 15th Division saw, in the German cemetery at Pont-a-Vendin, the graves of 400 Germans killed on April 27 and 29, 1916, "gassed with their own gas."

Once units had settled down into the new section they found that the chief work demanded of them was to remove the soil dug out by the tunnelling companies. This, of course, could not remain in the vicinity of the galleries, as its presence would warn the enemy of what was going on, and also because it blocked all trenches in the neighbourhood. Every ounce had therefore to be carried away in sandbags for some distance and dumped above ground. Luckily, the weather was gloriously fine, and the upkeep of trenches did not entail as much work as it had done during the previous tour. Large parties were therefore available to assist the miners, and after some time more men were employed underground than in the defence of the sector.

Reorganisation of Brigades.

Several changes took place in the infantry brigades during this tour. On May 7 the 6th Battalion Royal Scots Fusiliers and 8th Battalion Gordon Highlanders joined the Fifteenth from the 9th Division. They were absorbed in the 7th Royal Scots Fusiliers and 10th Gordons respectively, which were then designated as 6/7th Royal Scots Fusiliers and 8/10th Gordon Highlanders. A week later, on May 13, the 10th and 11th H.L.I. also arrived from the 9th Division. They were amalgamated into one battalion, and joined the 46th Brigade. The 7th and 8th Battalions K.O.S.B. of the same battalion were also formed into one battalion on May 19 whilst still in the line.

Undoubtedly at this period of the war the Hohenzollern section had for its size by far the worst reputation of any on the British front

[1] The "Lone How." was withdrawn from its position in the latter part of 1916, and, after doing good work elsewhere, finally returned to England, and is now in the Imperial War Museum.

in almost every respect. The explosion of mines was of daily and nightly occurrence, and it was only by dogged perseverance and almost superhuman efforts that the sappers at last established superiority over the enemy. The whole section was overlooked by the enemy, either from mine craters in his possession, from the Hohenzollern Redoubt itself, or from Fosse 8 behind it. From all these points accurate observation could be obtained, and the fire of artillery and trench-mortars directed.

May 1916.

Bad as was the whole of this part of the line, the centre, known as "The Kink," and the trenches in its immediate vicinity, were decidedly the worst. Here the British line formed a slight salient, and was overlooked from both north and south by the enemy. This part of the line always received more than its share of enemy "frightfulness." The climax was reached on May 11, when the enemy attacked and captured nearly the whole of "The Kink," thereby straightening out the salient.

Loss of "The Kink."

Early in the morning of May 11 the enemy subjected the whole Divisional line to a considerable bombardment. This died down about 10 A.M., only to increase again at intervals during the day. Whilst these bombardments were going on, the 46th Brigade were relieving the 44th in the Quarries sector, the relief being completed by 2.30 P.M., when the latter brigade proceeded on its way to Divisional reserve at Sailly Labourse, Labourse, and Bethune.

The two brigades in the front line were then disposed as follows:—

Quarries, Right Sector, 46th Brigade—

Right Sub-Sector, 8th K.O.S.B.
Left Sub-Sector, 10th Scottish Rifles.
Brigade Support, 7th K.O.S.B.
Brigade Reserve, 12th H.L.I.
(At Vermelles and Noyelles.)

Hohenzollern, Left Sector, 45th Brigade—

Right Sub-Sector, 13th Royal Scots.
Left Sub-Sector, 11th A. & S. Highlanders.
Right Brigade Reserve, 6/7th Royal Scots Fusiliers.
Left Brigade Reserve, 6th Cameron Highlanders.

From the above disposition it will be seen that the 10th Scottish

May 1916.

Rifles, 46th Brigade, and the 13th Royal Scots, 45th Brigade, held the centre of the Divisional line. It was against these two battalions that the attack was directed. Throughout the morning and afternoon the craters in front of "The Kink," and particularly the trenches occupied by the 13th Royal Scots, were subjected to severe artillery and trench-mortar fire, the front line being almost obliterated in many places. A few mines had been blown by the enemy the night before, and he had been more than usually active with machine-gun fire during the darkness, in order to prevent the British from wiring the craters. There was therefore very little in the way of obstacles at this particular point to stop an enemy attack.

At 5.45 P.M. the enemy's artillery fire increased still further in violence, and at the same time began counter-battery fire on the Divisional artillery positions round Philosophe and Vermelles, battery positions round Annequin receiving particular attention. In reply the Fifteenth Divisional Artillery and 1st Corps Horse Artillery, ably assisted by the 33rd Divisional Artillery on the left, concentrated their fire on the enemy trenches opposite "The Kink." During the afternoon General McCracken, anticipating that the enemy attack might be on a large scale, ordered the 44th Brigade to be prepared to move up from Divisional reserve, and at the same time directed that all machine-gun posts in the "Village Line" round Vermelles should be manned.

German Infantry attack.

At 6 P.M. the enemy launched his attack on a narrow front, his flanks protected by machine-gun fire from Hohenzollern Redoubt and the craters near the Quarries, and succeeded in penetrating the British line at "The Kink" on a front of about 600 yards and to a maximum depth of 400 yards (from G. 5 d. 1 2 to G. 5 c. 2 3). That he was able to do as much as this was due to the fact that the 13th Royal Scots had suffered severely during the preliminary bombardment. Their commanding officer, Lieut.-Colonel R. B. C. Raban, his second-in-command, Major H. T. M. Worthington Wilmer, and the machine-gun officer had been killed, and the remainder of the headquarter staff wounded by one shell that penetrated the entrance of their dug-out, and killed or wounded every occupant. This was all the more unfortunate, as it had been decided to move battalion headquarters farther back that same afternoon. In addition, other officers had been killed; the adjutant, Captain Francis, and several more wounded; and about half the battalion either killed or wounded during the bombardment.

May 1916.

Counter-attacks.

At 6.30 P.M. Major Smith, commanding 6/7th Royal Scots Fusiliers, took over command of the right sub-section, and prepared to counter-attack. Bombing parties of the 6/7th Royal Scots Fusiliers up Gordon and Hulluch Alleys, assisted by others of the 10th Scottish Rifles over the open from Boyau 98, and 7th K.O.S.B. along Crown Trench, made no progress, the party of Scottish Rifles, under 2nd Lieutenant Smith, being mown down by machine-gun fire, whilst the other two suffered severely.

As these counter-attacks did not appear to progress, Brig.-General Allgood, commanding 45th Brigade, went forward himself about 8 P.M., and arranged with Major Smith that another counter-attack would be made across the open at 1.30 A.M., bombers of the 11th A. & S. Highlanders co-operating on the right. At 1.25 A.M. the 6/7th Royal Scots Fusiliers, led by Captain Paton, attacked, and were able to retake the western end of Hussar Horn, but beyond this farther progress could not be made. The attackers were caught by cross-fire from enemy machine-guns, and at 3 A.M. it was realised that all hope of retaking the lost trenches before daylight must be abandoned. General Allgood therefore issued orders to consolidate the new line between Boyau 98 and Kaiserin Trench during the remaining hours of darkness. This was carried out by troops in the line, assisted by No. 3 Section, 73rd Field Company, R.E., and 9th Gordon Highlanders (Pioneers). Before daylight much work had been done, and, in view of the fairly heavy enemy shelling, troops in the front line were thinned out, and as many as possible withdrawn to the support trenches.

Although the 44th Brigade had been ordered up from Divisional reserve, only two companies of the 9th Black Watch were required. These were sent into Lancashire Trench in support of the 45th Brigade, sending one of their platoons to relieve one of the 6/7th Royal Scots Fusiliers in Junction Keep.

Having thus straightened out his line south-east of the Hohenzollern Redoubt, the enemy contented himself for the next three

May 1916.

days in consolidating the ground won, and consequently the section was comparatively quiet. The casualties sustained by the Division

Casualties.

on this occasion were 11 officers killed, 14 wounded, and 2 missing; 97 other ranks were killed, 297 wounded, and 72 missing. Of the latter there is every reason to suppose that most, if not all, were buried during the bombardment. In addition, 61 men attached to the 170th Tunnelling Company were also missing. The chief reason why the enemy were not able to penetrate on a wider front was due to the fact that the 11th A. & S. Highlanders, who had not suffered as much from the bombardment as had others, had repulsed every attack made on their particular front.

Attack on Boyau 99.

On May 14 the 8th K.O.S.B., Lieut.-Colonel Sellar, were directed to retake Boyau 99, the attack to be preceded by an artillery bombardment. At 6.45 P.M. that evening the attackers, led by Captain Crawshaw, advanced across the open for 200 yards, and succeeded in reaching their objective. Owing, however, to intense enemy artillery and trench-mortar fire they were unable to maintain their ground, and returned to their original position shortly afterwards. Captain Crawshaw was wounded in four places, and 5 officers and 85 other ranks were either killed or wounded. None of the captured trenches were recovered. At 8.30 P.M. another attack was ordered. This did not mature at once, owing to the difficulty experienced in assembling fresh assaulting troops. Three hours later, just as the Borderers were ready to advance, orders were received cancelling those previously issued, and the enemy was thus left in possession of the ground he had taken.

The next day the following message was received by the 46th Brigade commander:—

"The G.O.C. directs me to inform you that he considers the organisation of the attack on the evening of May 14 on Boyau 99, and the dash and the gallantry with which it was carried out, are highly creditable to Lieut.-Colonel Sellar and the 8th K.O.S.B.

(Sgd.) H. KNOX, *Lieut.-Colonel, General Staff, Fifteenth Division.*"

About this time, in view of certain contemplated operations on the Somme, certain alterations were necessary in the line. Divisions were withdrawn at several points, and those remaining had to extend their lines and fill the gaps. One of these was the Fifteenth. On May 16 it extended its line southwards as far as Vendin Alley, taking over an additional 1400 yards of front. The new line was now subdivided into two sub-sections, known as the Hulluch (South) and Hohenzollern (North) respectively.

May 1916.

Extension of line.

During these two months heavy fighting was going on in other parts of the Allied front. In the south the battle of Verdun was at its height, whilst in the north the enemy was preparing to make a third attack on Ypres, and in consequence the Loos salient was comparatively quiet for the remainder of May and June. On June 21 the Divisional cyclists left to become part of the I. Corps Cyclist Battalion.

Raids.

Organised raids on portions of the enemy's line now began to take the place of the smaller patrol and bombing attacks which had been in vogue in the past. The first of these was carried out by a company of the 9th Black Watch under Captain Storey Wilson on June 27 against the enemy trenches east of the Quarries. Unfortunately, most of the raiders lost direction, one officer and two men only being able to enter the enemy trenches. The party suffered 15 casualties, all wounded and brought in. The following day the 11th A. & S. Highlanders, 45th Brigade, carried out a similar operation under cover of a gas and smoke attack. This party succeeded in entering the German trenches, and disposed of a number of the enemy. Although no prisoners were taken, this particular raid was an exceedingly good piece of work. It was carried out against one of the worst parts of the Hohenzollern section, and reflected great credit on Captain P. S. Wilson, who was largely instrumental in drawing up the scheme and making the necessary arrangements.

On the night of July 4th/5th a very successful raid was made by the 10/11th H.L.I., 46th Brigade, with a party of R.E. The enemy trenches east of Holly Lane and Vendin Alley were entered. A German officer and about 20 men were killed, and two men belonging to the 5th Bavarian Regiment were taken prisoners. Many dug-outs were bombed, including one blown up by the R.E., and much damage was done to the hostile trenches. The party suffered 14 casualties, of

July 1916. which 3 alone were serious. The whole operation only occupied fifteen minutes.

Raids. Another well-carried-out raid was made by " B " and " C " Companies, 8th Seaforth Highlanders, Captains Holmes and Hart, 44th Brigade, and a party of R.E. under 2nd Lieutenant Ware, R.E., all under the direction of Major G. W. Lumsden, on the extreme left of the Divisional front. On the night of July 10 two companies entered the enemy trenches, and remained there for half an hour. Dug-outs were destroyed, most of which contained Germans, a cadet officer of the 23rd Bavarian Regiment being taken prisoner. The enemy casualties were estimated at over 100. The raiders lost 2nd Lieutenant Ware, R.E., killed, 6 Seaforth officers wounded, 6 other ranks killed, and 57 wounded. Before returning to their own trenches the party left pamphlets detailing the British successes on the Somme in the enemy's trenches. This is the first occasion on which " propaganda " is mentioned in any of the Divisional diaries.

Requiring exceedingly careful organisation, practice, and attention to the smallest detail, the first raids were not very successful. As time went on, however, the lessons then learnt bore fruit, and the many excellent operations carried out later by troops of the Division were largely due to these initial efforts in the Loos salient.

By this time the Division had been three months in the line. Brigades occupied the front-line system for sixteen days at a time, after which eight were spent in Divisional reserve.

About the middle of July rumours commenced to circulate throughout the Division that it was destined to move southward in the near future. These were confirmed on the 20th, when orders were issued that the Division would be relieved by the 76th, and would withdraw

Into Reserve. into reserve area south-west of Bruay. The move began the following day, and by the 24th the whole Division, with its artillery, had left the forward area, and were billeted as follows :—

Division Headquarters, Chateau Bryas.
44th Brigade, Dieval.
45th Brigade, Tangry.
46th Brigade, Heuchin.

July 1916.

Artillery, Anvin, Monchy-Cayeux. Eps.
R.E., Heuclin, Conteville.
9th Gordons (Pioneers), Valhuon.
Field Ambulances, Pernes and Divion.
Divisional Ammunition Column, Wavrans.

Retrospect.

After twelve months in the vicinity of Loos and Bethune all ranks were not sorry to leave the district. From Grenay to Hohenzollern Redoubt and from Loos to Bethune every inch of the ground was familiar. The numberless crosses in the front line and cemeteries behind it were proof of what it had cost the Fifteenth Division, amongst others, to take and hold the salient. Although, with the exception of the battle of Loos, there had been only one operation of any size during the year, casualties had been heavy and continuous. At times battalions were so reduced in numbers that assistance had to be given by other formations, such as cyclists, Divisional cavalry, &c. On one occasion, in the winter of 1915, cavalrymen were dismounted and sent up to help in holding the front line.

March 1916. Visit of the sailors.

The writer well remembers an incident that occurred in February or March 1916, when infantry units were not up to strength, and when every man who could handle a rifle was required. Returning from Vermelles early one wet and windy day, he met a party of about twenty bluejackets in charge of a gunner N.C.O. proceeding to the front line on a visit. Not one of them had more than he stood up in—no rifles, gas or steel helmets,—but all were cheery and full of excitement over their coming trip. They asked if any British attack, in which they could join, was likely to take place, and were very disappointed when told that, with the exception of raids by either side, they were not likely to see much actual fighting. As it turned out, either this party or another similar one was actually in the trenches when the enemy made a raid in the neighbourhood of the Quarries. The sailors got hold of some spare rifles, bombs, &c., and very ably assisted in repelling the enemy. One, if not two, of the party were decorated for their services on this occasion.

Casualties.

It is not possible to give an accurate total of the casualties suffered by the Division during the twelve months. Official diaries vary on this point, and in some cases full lists have not been issued. The following is approximately correct for the period from April to July 1916 :—

Officers—	*Other Ranks*—
Killed, 49.	Killed, 522.
Wounded, 124.	Wounded, 2988.
Missing, 3.	Missing, 308.

Total, 3994.

CHAPTER IV.

THE BATTLE OF THE SOMME.[1]

July 1916. The move south.

THE first two days were spent, as usual, in cleaning up and refitting, and on the 26th the Division began its move, by road, southward. Space forbids mention of the various areas occupied by brigades, &c.; but the following were the various Divisional Headquarters and the dates on which they were occupied :—

22nd to 26th July, Chateau Bryas.
26th to 27th July, Chateau Flers.
27th to 28th July, Frohen le Grand.
28th to 31st July, Mairie, Bernaville.
31st July to 4th August, Vignacourt.
4th to 5th August, Chateau St Gratien.
5th to 8th August, Chateau Baizieux.

Incidents of the march.

The length of the march was sixty-four miles, and it was completed in six stages. At the start a considerable number of men fell out on account of sore feet and unaccustomed exercise after the long spell in the trenches. Such cases were brought on in motor omnibuses, rejoining the units at the first halt. Some difficulty, too, was experienced with heavily loaded transport waggons. Moreover, the weather was hot, and the hilly country through which the Division marched was different from the comparative flat country round Bethune. It was remarkable how quickly the Division regained its marching powers. After two days on the road march discipline was excellent, and all ranks enjoyed the change from the tedium of trench duty. The fighting value of the Division was increased 50 per cent by this march to the south.

In spite of these disadvantages the march was enjoyable. In

[1] Maps 4, 4A, 5, and 6.

July 1916.

some places accommodation was cramped, but, as the weather was gloriously fine, troops actually preferred to bivouac in the adjoining fields and orchards sooner than occupy ill-ventilated houses and dirty barns.

Preliminaries.

The Somme Battle.

The fighting in which the Division was about to take part is described in the official despatches as "The Opening of the wearing-out Battle." It was undertaken for three principal reasons: (*a*) To relieve the pressure on Verdun; (*b*) to stop the transfer of German troops from the west to Russia and elsewhere; (*c*) to wear down the strength of the enemy forces in France.

Beginning on July 1 with a Franco-British attack on a twenty-five mile front astride the Somme, the first two phases of the battle had already been reasonably successful. On the front with which the Fifteenth Division was concerned, the Germans had been driven back over three miles from Montauban, Mametz, and La Boiselle to the crest of the plateau running from Ginchy through Delville Wood to High Wood, and thence west, between Martinpuich and Pozières.

This plateau, about 500 feet in height, dominated the country to the north-east and south-west. Its possession was therefore of great importance to both sides. To the south the Allies found themselves in a desolate and devastated area, in which very little cover, either from the weather or shell-fire, was obtainable. The few roads leading to the front line were always crowded and constantly shelled by the enemy, whose observers on the plateau could detect every movement for some distance behind the line. On the other hand, the Germans knew that once the Allies gained entire possession of this plateau the position would be reversed; they in turn would suffer from being overlooked, and movement of troops behind the lines would be a target for the British guns.

The third phase of the battle was now about to commence—a phase which resolved itself into a series of engagements for the possession of the plateau and its attendant advantages.[1] The opera-

[1] See "Exploitation of Success," pp. 39-53, Sir Douglas Haig's Despatches.

tion had been planned on a grand scale. On a given date the French Army on the right, the Fourth British Army in the centre, and the right of the British Reserve Army on the left, were to seize Morval, Les Bœufs, Guudecourt, and Flers, thereby breaking through the third and last line of the main hostile system of trenches.

July-August 1916.

The plan of attack on the British front was that the Fourth Army should capture the German line between Morval and Le Sars, and in this effort the 50th, Fifteenth, and 2nd Canadian Divisions were to take part. On the front allotted to the Fifteenth Division the line ran just south of the high ground, almost due east and west from High Wood to the Albert-Bapaume road north of Pozières, and about 1200 yards south of Martinpuich, which lay on the reverse slope of the plateau.

Into the battle line.

On August 8 General McCracken, with headquarters just west of Albert Chateau, took over the left sector of the III. Corps (Fourth Army) front from the 23rd Division, the left being held by the 34th. The sector was divided into two sections, and was held as follows :—

Right Section—from the Bazentin le Petit-Martinpuich road to Gloucester Alley, 46th Brigade, Brig.-General Matheson.

Left Section—from Gloucester Alley to Munster Alley, 45th Brigade, Brig.-General Allgood.

Divisional reserve, 44th Brigade, Brig.-General Marshall.

The 73rd Field Company, R.E., was placed under the orders of the G.O.C. right section, the 91st under those of the left section commander, whilst the 74th remained directly under the C.R.E.

State of the trenches.

Owing to the recent fighting and the newly established line, the Division found their trenches in a deplorable condition. Many had practically ceased to exist, whilst others were merely series of shell-holes linked together by shallow ditches, giving little or no cover from either fire or view. The field companies, pioneers, and battalions actually holding the line worked like trojans to overcome these defects, but it was some considerable time before they were able to put it in anything like proper order.

In addition to improving their new quarters, battalions at once set about raiding and otherwise annoying the enemy. At this time considerable confusion existed amongst the Germans owing to their

August 1916.

set-backs. New formations had been brought up, and information was required regarding the composition of enemy forces on this part of the front, and to do this it was necessary to capture prisoners. On August 7, in Munster Alley, prisoners were captured belonging to four different German divisions, and between August 8 and September 15, when the advance was resumed, every infantry battalion carried out at least one raid. Most of these were successful, and much valuable information was obtained.[1]

Raids.

Orders for attack.

On August 10 orders were issued for an attack by the Division on the German trenches south of Martinpuich, in co-operation with another by the 34th Division against the Intermediate Line. This particular trench lay between the German front line and Cardiff Trench. Several attempts had already been made to take it, but without success. Flanked by the fire of machine-guns in High Wood, it was a formidable obstacle, and its capture was necessary before a farther advance could be made on Martinpuich.

Objectives.

The objectives of both divisions were strictly limited. The 34th were to take the Intermediate Line, while the Fifteenth had to capture that part of the German front known as the Switch Line, level with it, from the Bazentin-Martinpuich road to Munster Alley. On the right the 10th Scottish Rifles, 46th Brigade, was to assist the 34th Division by attacking the western end of the Intermediate Line.

The Divisional attack was carried out by three battalions as follows: *Right*—12th H.L.I., Lieut.-Colonel Heyman, 46th Brigade, with No. 3 Section, 73rd Field Company, R.E., under 2nd Lieutenant Swire, R.E. *Centre*—6/7th Royal Scots Fusiliers, Lieut.-Colonel Gordon. *Left*—6th Camerons, Lieut.-Colonel Russell, both of the 45th Brigade, with No. 2 Section, 73rd Field Company, R.E., under 2nd Lieutenant Howie.

It had been decided that the assault should take place at night, and, in order that there should be no confusion in forming up, tapes

[1] From these raids it was discovered that units of the following enemy divisions, all belonging to the IX. Reserve Corps, held the line from the Albert-Bapaume road to High Wood on August 12:—

162nd	Reserve	Regiment,	17th	Reserve	Division.
84th	"	"	18th	"	"
31st	"	"	"	"	"
75th	"	"	17th	"	"

2ND LIEUTENANT F. H. JOHNSON, V.C.

73rd Field Company Royal Engineers.

were laid down in No Man's Land by the 73rd Field Company, R.E., indicating the position of the attacking waves. This difficult work was exceedingly well done, and lessened the many difficulties attendant on forming up for an attack in the dark.

August 1916.

The bombardment.

For four days prior to the assault the enemy's trenches were subjected to a prolonged and heavy bombardment by every available gun of the Fifteenth Divisional Artillery, assisted by that of the 23rd and two brigades of the 34th, all under Brig.-General Fasson, in conjunction with III. Corps Heavy Artillery. So heavy was this fire that it was found, when the position was captured, to have obliterated many of the German trenches.

On the morning of the 11th a very smart piece of patrol work was done by a party of the 6/7th Royal Scots Fusiliers under 2nd Lieutenant Fairlie, who captured four prisoners of the 174th Regiment, 24th Saxon Division, in Munster Alley. Another patrol of the same battalion discovered that the Switch Line opposite them was unoccupied. Saps were at once pushed out from Butterworth Trench to within 30 yards of the Switch. These were of great value when the latter was captured, as it did not take long to link them up with the captured portion of the Switch Line, and turn them into communication trenches.

The assault launched, August 12.

At 10.32 P.M. on the 12th the assault was delivered. On the right it did not succeed, owing to the failure of the 34th Division to capture the Intermediate Trench. Unfortunately, too, the enemy had chosen the same hour at which to attack the line held by the 10th Scottish Rifles. This was easily repulsed, but the 12th H.L.I., who were then actually forming up on their tapes in No Man's Land, suffered severely from machine-gun fire from the right flank of the German advance. In a few minutes they lost two-thirds of their officers and a large proportion of men, and their advance stopped 50 yards from their original position.[1]

On learning what had happened, General Matheson ordered Colonel Heyman to push up his fourth company, which was still in reserve. He replied that one would not be sufficient, and asked leave to use

[1] On this occasion the 12th H.L.I. lost 4 officers killed, 10 wounded, and 1 missing; 30 other ranks killed, 147 wounded, and 26 missing.

Aug. 12, 1916. two companies of the 10/11th H.L.I., then in his area. By this time it was 2 A.M., and as it was found impossible to organise any further attack before daylight, General McCracken decided to make no further effort that night, and at 2.30 A.M. the H.L.I. returned to their original front line.

Success of 45th Brigade.

In the meantime the attack by the 45th Brigade had been more successful. Leaving their trenches at 10.15 P.M., the two leading waves of the Scots Fusiliers and Camerons formed up in succession on their tapes without trouble and with no casualties. At 10.30 P.M., accompanied by a heavy and accurate artillery barrage, they advanced to the attack, and two minutes later had occupied nearly the whole of their objective. As the 12th H.L.I. had been unable to advance, the right flank of the Fusiliers was exposed, and suffered somewhat severely from enemy machine-gun fire. To make this secure, Colonel Gordon reinforced his right with one company from Butterworth Trench, and proceeded to dig in on that portion of the Switch Line then occupied by his battalion.

On the left the Camerons had experienced difficulty in locating the Switch Line, as the heavy bombardment prior to the attack had almost obliterated all trace of it. One company in fact overshot its objective and had to be recalled, but by 11.30 P.M., an hour after the assault had been delivered, the battalion was not only in touch with the Australian division on its left, but had dug a continuous line of trench 2½ feet deep on the site of what had been the Switch Line. The ease with which the 45th Brigade was able to capture its objective was largely due to the super-excellence of the artillery barrage. "The leading wave advanced right under the barrage, and all ranks certify to its excellence. There was hardly a shot fired, and no casualties resulted from our artillery fire. All describe it as a 'wall of flame and steel, behind which we felt quite secure,' and are loud in their praise of it."

At 2 A.M. two platoons, 11th A. & S. Highlanders, were sent up to support the left flank of the Camerons in Munster Alley, and when dawn broke on the 13th the firing on both sides died down, and the situation became what is known officially as "normal." The following day the position was further consolidated. Communication trenches were completed between the Switch and Butterworth Trench, and the new front line wired and rendered secure.

Aug. 12, 1916.

Although the Division had not gained all its objectives, those won were of great importance. From the captured Switch Line an extensive view was obtained, and, on the night of August 13th/14th, observers in it were able to direct effective artillery and machine-gun fire on enemy troops advancing from Martinpuich, with the object of either delivering an attack or of relieving others in the front line. (See panorama sketch.)

Operations continued, Aug. 13-17.

On the 13th and 14th local operations were continued; bombing attacks were made by the 45th Brigade on that portion of the Switch Line still held by the enemy, but little progress was made. On the 14th the 10/11th H.L.I. actually got into the enemy's front line, and remained there for some time, but were obliged to withdraw owing to enemy machine-gun fire, which prevented reinforcements coming up.

For the next three days the weather was wet, and little could be done. The ground in front was almost impassable on account of numberless shell-holes, now full of water, there being scarcely a square foot of earth that had not been broken up by the shell-fire.

There was no intention, however, of giving the enemy time to consolidate the position to which he had been driven. On the 17th another attack was made by three companies of the 7th Camerons, Lieut.-Colonel Marsh, 44th Brigade. Leaving Highland Trench at 8.55 A.M., accompanied by the usual barrage, they easily entered the enemy's trenches. A number of Germans surrendered at once, and the work of consolidation was promptly begun. It had been intended to construct five strong-points in front of the line when captured, but work was stopped on account of heavy casualties amongst the working-parties caused by the enemy's artillery fire.

An hour later the Germans started a bombing attack against the Switch Elbow on the right. This was at first successful, and the enemy retook the Elbow. Their farther advance, however, was stopped by the energetic action of Captain McCrae, 7th Camerons, who, with 2nd Lieutenant Orr of that regiment, at once organised a vigorous counter-attack, and formed a block in the trench just east of the Elbow. When this attack was made, the Camerons had run out of

Aug. 17, 1916. bombs, and endeavoured to defend the captured trench with the only weapons at their disposal, the picks and shovels which they were using to consolidate it, and which, as a last resort, they threw at the advancing Germans. Luckily two platoons of the 9th Gordons were on the spot carrying up trench-boards. With their assistance and that of some men of the H.L.I., a chain was formed, and bombs passed up to the new front line. An hour later Captain McCrae managed to get up a Stokes' mortar, but unfortunately both the gun and its team were knocked out by artillery fire before they could do much.

Operations continued.

Gallantly and well did the Camerons hold on to their gains, and their efforts were not unavailing. At 2 P.M. a company of the 8th Seaforths, 44th Brigade, arrived on the scene, and with it and his own battalion Colonel Marsh proceeded to organise a further attack on the Switch Elbow. Launched about 4 o'clock, this was completely successful, the Elbow being retaken and consolidated with very little trouble. In this work a company of the 9th Black Watch, under Captain Binnie, did most excellent work in conjunction with the Seaforths and Camerons.

Seeing the troops of the 44th Brigade charging across the open eastwards along the Switch Line, 2nd Lieutenant Anderson and a dozen men of the 10/11th H.L.I. dashed across the open from H.L.I. Trench and joined in the struggle. They came upon a German machine-gun crew endeavouring to bring their gun into action; Private McGarvie of "D" Company, who was leading, knocked out the first German with his rifle, and the remainder were scattered by bombs when the rest of the party came up, the gun being sent back to the British lines. With this exception very little resistance was encountered, and a block was established and held by the H.L.I. 120 yards east of the Elbow. Consolidation then proceeded rapidly. Bombs, S.A.A., R.E. stores, and three Lewis-guns were brought up, and by 7.30 P.M. everything was satisfactorily organised, and the captured trench securely held by a mixed party of H.L.I. and Seaforths.

During the night all was quiet. Patrols from the 8th Seaforths covered the whole of the new front, and found nothing unusual. Several small parties of the enemy were seen cowering in shell-holes, but these invariably fled on the approach of the patrols. Aug. 18, 1916.

The following morning, at 6 A.M., Lance-Corporal Blackburn of "B" Company, 10/11th H.L.I., crossed over the block and reconnoitred the Switch Line eastward. He met with no opposition, and found the trench filled with dead and dying Germans. Shortly after he returned, a party of ten of the enemy approached the block, threw down their arms, and were taken prisoners.

Later in the morning Colonel Ussher moved a party of the 10th Scottish Rifles down the Switch eastward, where they constructed a strong-point close to the railway. About noon the Brigade-Major, 46th Brigade, ordered Lance-Corporal McDonald, 10/11th H.L.I., to put up a block still farther to the east to protect the Scottish Rifles party. McDonald and four men reconnoitred the Switch for a distance of 250 yards, and met a German officer and four men. The men ran away, but the officer was killed whilst attempting to resist. The party then returned, and put up their block east of the railway as ordered.

Aug. 19, 1916. Switch Line secured.

On the 19th the 45th Brigade relieved the 46th in the right section. The following day their patrols discovered that the Switch Line opposite them was empty. It was promptly occupied, and consolidated as far east as the Bazentin-Martinpuich road.

During the next few days things were comparatively quiet. A good deal of work was done in linking up the forward line with the old British front trench, now called Butterworth Trench. A chain of posts were established in front of the captured Switch Line, rechristened Cameron and Sanderson Trench. These were afterwards linked up, and known as Post Trench.

Whilst this fighting had been taking place on the left, the Intermediate Line still held out. The 1st Division had made good progress on the right in the neighbourhood of High Wood and the crests between it and Martinpuich, thereby making the position of the enemy in the Intermediate Line somewhat precarious. On the 24th another attempt was made by the 45th Brigade to capture it. This time the 6th Camerons, attacking at 4.45 A.M. from Sanderson Trench (old Switch Line) succeeded in seizing the north-west corner, but, owing to the

August 1916. explosion of their bomb store and consequent lack of bombs, they were unable to retain their hold on it, and returned to their own line two hours later.

Intermediate line taken.

The numerous attacks on this wretched trench having all failed, it was now decided to surround it and force the garrison to surrender. To do this a chain of posts was successfully established between Sanderson Trench on the west and Clarke's Trench on the east. This work was carried out on the night of August 29th/30th, in spite of exceedingly bad weather, and on the following afternoon the enemy, realising that they were surrounded, surrendered to the 45th Brigade. Four officers and 153 other ranks belonging to the 17th and 23rd Bavarian Regiments were taken prisoners. The trench was at once consolidated and linked up with Lancashire trench. Most of the work of digging this chain of posts was done by the 13th Royal Scots (Lieut.-Colonel Hannay). Unfortunately that battalion was relieved a few hours before the enemy surrendered, and therefore did not reap the reward of its labour.

Preparations for attack on Martinpuich.

As the result of these operations, the British line had been advanced just beyond the crest of the rising ground south of Martinpuich. From the new line the ground sloped gently downwards to the village, which was to be the next objective. Before this could be attacked, a good deal of preparation was necessary, and for the next three weeks little actual fighting took place except the ordinary trench warfare.

During the pause all enemy positions and communications in the neighbourhood of Martinpuich were subjected to a systematic bombardment by every available gun on the Corps front. To this the enemy replied with vigour, and as High Wood was still in his possession, his observers there were able to direct the fire of their guns with great accuracy on the new position, and on any working-parties near it. This greatly interfered with the preparations, but in spite of it an enormous amount of work was done. Four "jumping-off" trenches were dug in front of the line, bearing the homely names of "Egg," "Bacon," "Ham," and "Liver" respectively. Dumps of bombs, S.A.A., &c., dressing-stations, and advanced battalion headquarters were built, water supply was arranged for, and the most careful and minute instructions issued regarding the forthcoming attack.

August 1916.

To assist him in holding the line whilst preparing for the attack, the 103rd Infantry Brigade and the 18th Battalion Northumberland Fusiliers (Pioneers), both from the 34th Division, had been placed under General McCracken's orders. On the 7th the 45th and 46th Brigades were withdrawn to rest and train for the attack, whilst the 44th and 103rd [1] Brigades took their place in the front line.

Sept. 8, 1916. A local attack.

On September 8 "B" and "D" Companies, 9th Black Watch, under Captains Stirling and Bruce, made a very successful local attack from Bethell Sap on the enemy trench running from the north-west corner of High Wood in conjunction with an attack by the 1st Division on High Wood. Thirty prisoners of the 18th Bavarian Regiment and one of the 193rd Machine-Gun Company were captured, and a heavy enemy counter-attack was driven off; but the party were unable to retain possession of the enemy trench, and ultimately returned to their original trenches, as the 1st Division were unable to maintain their gains in High Wood. The casualties on this occasion were severe. Both company commanders were wounded, 1 officer, Lieutenant J. B. Ireland, was reported missing, 24 other ranks were killed, 59 wounded, and 14 missing.

Resting behind the line, the 45th and 46th Brigades spent eight days rehearsing the assault over ground marked out with flags representing the enemy trenches to be attacked. In this way every man knew exactly where to go and what to do when the day came. Three days before the operation the 8th and 9th Battalions York and Lancaster Regiment, 23rd Division, were attached to the Fifteenth to assist in the coming battle, if required.

The Taking of Martinpuich.

Operation orders.

Divisional Operation Orders, dated 12th, 13th, and 14th, contain the plan of attack on Martinpuich, which was carried out by the two brigades as follows (see Map 5):—

[1] The panorama sketch (Map 4A) is the work of one of their officers, and gives an exceedingly good idea of the ground over which the attack was made.

Sept. 1916. Preparations for attack on Martinpuich.

On the right the 45th Brigade was to attack with two battalions on the front line :—

Right battalion—11th A. & S. Highlanders.
Left battalion—13th Royal Scots.
Support battalions—Right, 6/7th Royal Scots Fusiliers.
Left, 6th Camerons.
Reserve battalion—8th York and Lancaster Regiment, in Gourlay Trench.

On the left the 46th Brigade had three battalions in the front line :—

Right battalion—10th Scottish Rifles.
Centre battalion—7/8th K.O.S.B.
Left battalion—10/11th H.L.I.
Support battalion—12th H.L.I.
Reserve battalion—9th York and Lancaster Regiment.

A section from the 91st and another from the 74th Field Companies were attached to the 45th and 46th Brigades respectively to assist in consolidation.

General McCracken kept the 44th Brigade in reserve in Contalmaison.

Four "tanks" were allotted to the Division. These came from "D" Company, Heavy Machine-Gun Corps, and were under the command of Captain Mann of that Corps. The greatest secrecy was to be observed regarding these new weapons of warfare. This was the first occasion on which they were tried, and in order that the enemy should have no inkling of their arrival, aeroplanes were specially detailed to fly over the hostile trenches whilst they were moving into position to drown the noise of their exhausts.

The artillery barrage was worked out with the utmost care by Brig.-General Fasson, who had under him—

Fifteenth Divisional Artillery (less 71st Brigade).
39th Brigade, 1st Divisional Artillery.
102nd Brigade, 23rd Divisional Artillery.
III. Corps Heavy Artillery.

Under this barrage the infantry were to advance at the rate of 50 yards per minute, and in order to allow the tanks to accompany them, a lane 100 yards wide was left in the barrage.

For several days prior to the actual assault the enemy trenches had as usual been subjected to a steady and continuous bombardment, but it had been decided on this occasion to discard the usual preliminary bombardment and rely on the barrage, backed by the material and moral effect of the new "tanks."

Sept. 1916.

The attack was to be carried out in three bounds, the final objective being the southern portion of Martinpuich village. As an after order, on September 14, instructions were issued to the effect that should the assault be successful, the attacking battalions should endeavour to gain more ground, and were, three hours after zero, to push forward strong patrols for this purpose.

During the night 14th/15th September the assaulting battalions moved into position in Liver, Ham, and Bacon Trenches.

Sept. 15, 1916. The assault launched.

At 6.20 A.M. on the 15th the assault took place. "The enemy," says the official report, "taken completely by surprise, surrendered freely. Many prisoners were taken, especially by the 46th Brigade." This particular brigade had an exceedingly difficult task to perform. Owing to the line taken by the barrage it was not possible for it to advance on a line parallel to its objective, as was the case with the 45th.[1] General Matheson's first objective was the "Sunken Road," which lay at an angle of roughly 45 degrees to the starting line. It was therefore necessary for the left battalion, 10/11th H.L.I., at once to change direction, and for the centre battalion, 7/8th K.O.S.B., to advance 500 yards, and then *for its left half* to change front half left, whilst its right half led straight on to the objective. The Borderers had also the additional task of clearing Bottom Trench *en route*, whilst the Scottish Rifles had to clear three-quarters of Bottom Trench and the whole of Tangle Trench in like manner. It will be admitted that this task was one which might have caused anxiety to the most highly trained troops of the British Army. It should further be mentioned that General Matheson had no opportunity of practising the above intricate movement, as the orders concerning it were only received a few hours before the actual assault.

At 6.45 A.M., having taken Bottom and Tangle Trenches and the "Sunken Road," the troops advanced against their final objective.

[1] This was due to the fact that the Fifteenth was the flank division of the Corps, and the Canadian Division on the left moved at a slower pace.

Sept. 15, 1916. So far casualties had been exceedingly few, but from now onwards they became more severe, many being caused by our own creeping barrage, which moved at the rate of 50 yards a minute. The men seem to have got excited with victory whilst moving from the first to the second objective, and to have come in contact with this barrage in more than one place.[1]

On the right the 45th Brigade had made as rapid an advance. The Cutting, the Tangle South, and Tangle Trench had been captured without much trouble, and a number of prisoners taken in them. Shortly after 7 A.M., forty-five minutes after zero, the final objective was reached. All positions were at once made good, stores brought up, and the work of consolidation begun by both brigades.

The line then ran as follows: from the Tangle South along Tangle Trench, southern portion of Martinpuich to the Factory Line, where the 10/11th H.L.I. joined hands with the 2nd Canadian Division. On the right the 45th Brigade were in touch with the left of the 50th Division.

Final objective gained.

The final objectives having been gained, there now fell a lull in the operations. On the right the 50th Division was progressing towards the Tangle North and Prue Trench. On the left General Matheson, realising that his leading battalions might require support in endeavouring to gain more ground, sent up two companies of the 12th H.L.I. to replace two from the assaulting battalions that had been left in the first objective, Bottom Trench and Sunken Road, to mop up.

Martinpuich entered.

In accordance with the order to push on if possible, strong patrols were sent out by Colonel Ussher, 10th Scottish Rifles, into Martinpuich at 9.20 A.M. These captured many prisoners, including several officers in a battalion headquarters. The patrols penetrated right through the village, returning an hour later with the news that the Germans appeared to be entirely demoralised, and had retired to a ridge about 600 yards east of the village. "The enemy behaved like a thoroughly beaten man, running out with hands up, crying *Kamerad*. In the opinion of those assaulting, the advance could have been carried

[1] In commenting on this battle General McCracken remarked to the Author: "Yes, in this case, as on other occasions, the Division overshot the objective according to the time-table, but *never* did it yield one single inch of ground it had once taken and consolidated."

on over the ridge in front (north-east) of Martinpuich. He had lost all his nerve." Sept. 15, 1916.

In the meantime the 7/8th K.O.S.B., Lieut.-Colonel T. B. Sellar, had sent out patrols round the north side of the village. These reached Gunpit Trench, where they captured 13 prisoners, 6 of them being officers, one of whom was a regimental commander, and another his adjutant.

Work of the tanks.

Before going further, it is necessary to record the doings of the tanks during the attack. Unfortunately there is no report in any diary from Captain Mann, O.C. Tanks. In the Divisional order four were allotted to assist in the assault, but only two materialised. One machine, the "female," broke down on its way to the position of assault; possibly its constitution was more highly strung than that of the "male." The "male" tank did not cross the British front line until after the infantry had started, and even then it does not seem to have been of much assistance. Eventually it reached the south-west corner of Martinpuich after the 46th Brigade had taken its final objective. It then returned to its base to refill. It is recorded that some Germans tried to surrender to it on its way up, but these must have been prisoners who had already surrendered to the infantry in front. About mid-day Brig.-General Matheson managed to get in touch with Captain Mann, and instructed him to take up ammunition and form a dump at the south-east end of the village, and then go to the assistance of the 45th Brigade, but it was not until 7 P.M., however, that the tank was seen approaching Martinpuich, then far too late to be of much assistance to the 45th Brigade.

Up till now few casualties had resulted from the somewhat feeble retaliatory fire brought to bear by the enemy. By this time, however, he had recovered from his surprise, and both artillery and machine-gun fire became more intense, with the result that losses became numerous, the front line of one battalion, the 10th Scottish Rifles, being reduced to 100 men and 2 officers.

Advance resumed.

At noon, on learning that Martinpuich as far as the church was clear of the enemy, General McCracken ordered the 45th and 46th Brigades to push forward, take the rest of the village, and establish a line of posts north of it west of the Martinpuich-Eaucourt-l'Abbaye

Sept. 15, 1916. road, along Push Alley, to connect with the right of the 2nd Canadian Division. This further attack started about 3 P.M., and an hour later the whole of Martinpuich had been captured. On the left the 46th Brigade met with practically no opposition, and occupied that part of Push Alley allotted to it. On the right the 45th Brigade swept through the north-east portion, reached the hill on the far side, and, after some bombing, forced the remainder of the garrison to surrender. This attack was carried out by the 6th Camerons, support battalion of the 45th Brigade. Moving forward from the right flank of the brigade, the battalion was skilfully led to an assembly position opposite and parallel to its objective. Such a movement in the turmoil of a battle reflects the greatest credit on all concerned. 189 prisoners were taken, and in addition an enormous amount of wire, wood, S.A.A., bombs, and R.E. material of all kinds was discovered in the village, all of which proved invaluable in the work of consolidation. A chain of posts was established from Gunpit Trench, thence eastward north of Martinpuich to Prue Trench, where the right of the Fifteenth Division should have linked up with the left of the 50th. Unfortunately, however, whilst the farther advance of the Fifteenth was being made, the troops of the 50th had been shelled out of Prue Trench, and the right flank of the 45th Brigade was consequently for some time in the air. It was made as secure as possible by the establishment of a post in Prue Trench, which was held until the 50th Division came up later.

Capture of Martinpuich.

Consolidation.

During the night of the 15th/16th the work of consolidation went on. A trench was dug connecting the new line north of Martinpuich with Prue Trench, and the whole front was wired with enemy material found in the village.

With the exception of two weak counter-attacks delivered early in the morning of the 16th, both of which were easily repulsed, the enemy made no attempt to regain the ground he had lost. Later in the morning the 46th Brigade extended its left as far as the Bapaume-Albert Road, and before dusk work had been started on a line of posts 200 yards in front of the new position. During the morning, in consequence of a report received from an artillery officer visiting the front line, to the effect that certain enemy trenches opposite were unoccupied, the 8/10th Gordon Highlanders[1] and 10/11th H.L.I. were ordered to send out patrols to verify the statement. They found the trenches occupied, and lost heavily before regaining their own line. The following is the comment of a C.O. on this unfortunate occurrence: "Inaccurate reports rendered by passenger-visitors to the front line are not worthy of forming the basis of offensive operations, and we have suffered severely in consequence." The brigadier added: "I am under the impression that the artillery officer had not read his map correctly."

Sept. 1916.

Such is the story of the capture of Martinpuich. A better conceived and better executed operation it would be difficult to find. Artillery, Engineers, and infantry worked together in a manner little short of marvellous; losses were not excessive,[2] and a serious blow had been dealt to the enemy.

Prisoners and guns taken.

The exact number of prisoners taken is not clear, as practically all those taken by the 46th Brigade failed to pass through the Divisional collecting station at Middle Wood, and many others were diverted to various fatigue duties, such as stretcher-bearers, &c. Those accounted for, however, numbered between 600 and 700, and belonged to the following regiments: 133rd Reserve; 211th Reserve; 17th, 18th, and 23rd Bavarian; 19th Foot Artillery; 49th Reserve Field Artillery Regiments; and the 167th Machine-Gun Company. In addition to the vast store of R.E. material taken in Martinpuich, 13 machine-guns, 3 heavy howitzers, 3 77 mm. guns, and 1 trench-mortar fell into the hands of the Division.

For the next two days the Division was employed in clearing the battlefield behind it, and completing the consolidation of its gains. For this purpose the area was divided up and allotted to units, and within that time, undisturbed by the enemy except for the usual artillery and machine-gun fire, the ground was cleared of British and German dead, communication trenches were dug, bomb and ammunition stores established, and work on dug-outs started.

[1] 44th Brigade, sent up from Divisional Reserve late in the afternoon of the 15th.

[2] Casualties on the 15th/16th were as follows:—

	Killed.	Wounded.	Missing.
Officers	15	74	...
Other Ranks . . .	206	1208	351
Total casualties . .		1854.	

Sept. 1916.

On the 18th the 23rd Division commenced taking over the line from the Fifteenth. The same day the following telegram was received by General McCracken, and communicated to all ranks.

" *From* G.O.C. Fourth Army *to* G.O.C. Fifteenth (Scottish) Division :—

" Please convey to my old friends in the Fifteenth Division my congratulations on their splendid performance the day before yesterday. To have captured Martinpuich after having been a month in the line is a very fine performance, and I greatly appreciate their gallantry and vigorous fighting spirit."

Relief of Division.

The relief was completed by noon on the 19th, and Divisional Headquarters opened at Baizieux Chateau. With the exception of the 70th and 71st Brigades, R.F.A., who were still in the line, the Division was now in Corps reserve, and billeted as follows :—

Divisional Troops, 9th Gordons (Pioneers), Baizieux.
44th Brigade, Lavieville.
45th Brigade, Baizieux Wood.
46th Brigade, Behencourt.
R.E., Franvillers, Baizieux, and Behencourt.
Divisional Train, Behencourt.
Divisional Signals, Montigny.

The following day Divisional Headquarters moved to Montigny, 44th Brigade to Franvillers, with the Fifteenth Divisional Artillery at St Gratien. As usual, the first few days of the rest were spent in refitting and reorganisation, after which training commenced in earnest.

Amiens, only a few miles away, proved a great attraction to all. Leave was freely granted, and full advantage taken of the many attractions to be found in the city. The following is rather an amusing tale of how some gunners managed to get out of what might have been an awkward situation resulting from one of these visits :—

" Some of these New Army soldiers are learning how to look after themselves. When we came out to rest I told my army that they would be allowed passes to go for the day into the local metropolis, a few at a time, but that if there was any trouble of any kind I should stop their leave at once. A few days ago a couple of sergeants and a few men went in, and one of the sergeants unfortunately ' looked on the wine when it was red,' was arrested by the military police, and clapped into the guard-room. Whereupon the other sergeant collected two men of his party, marched them up to the guard-room, and said he was the escort come for the prisoner. The police guard handed the prisoner over, and nothing more was heard of it (officially)." [1]

Sept. 1916.

On the whole, the following three weeks passed uneventfully. Billets were good, but the weather, generally fine, was now very cold, and straw for bedding was difficult to find; in consequence a certain amount of sickness prevailed. Early in October, in anticipation of an operation against the Butte de Warlencourt, brigades carried out practice attacks in the vicinity of Bresle, over a course marked out with flags.

Shortage of Scotsmen.

At this time the shortage of men in Scotland began most seriously to make itself felt. Units which up till now had been able to obtain sufficient men from their own districts now received drafts composed of men from all parts of England and Scotland. Amongst these were a number of "Bantams." These little men, though full of fight, were quite unfitted for service in an ordinary infantry battalion. Not only were they unable to keep up with their comrades on the march, but special arrangements had to be made in the trenches to enable them to look over the parapet. The mistake of sending them into the front line was soon apparent, and they were eventually drafted into Labour and other units.

Oct. 1916. Return to the line.

One unfortunate occurrence took place before the Division returned to the line. On October 7 Albert received more attention than usual from the German guns. One shell hit the building occupied by the headquarters of the 12th H.L.I., with the result that the commanding officer, Lord Rothes, the second in command, adjutant, medical officer, chaplain, and another officer were all wounded.

THE WINTER MONTHS.

On October 8th the Division commenced to relieve the 23rd in the left sector of the III. Corps front. By this time the weather had become really bad, and the operation was carried out in torrents of rain, a taste of what was to come. The following is an extract from

[1] From the diary of Major F. Graham, R.F.A., 24/9/16.

Oct. 1916.

a private diary, and gives some idea of the difficulty experienced during this relief :—

State of the trenches.

" This part of the front line was not like anything I had seen before. Previously we had had regular trench lines that had been in use for months with well-kept " up " and " down " communication trenches, all nicely duck-boarded and fairly dry. There every ruin and stump was well known, and even shell-holes were well-known landmarks. Here the whole countryside from Le Sars to Contalmaison was one mass of mud and shell-holes, with paths running all over the place, up and down over shell-holes, along the edge of an old trench, then along it for a yard or two ; then out again, till it was almost impossible to remember one's direction, especially when darkness blotted out the few landmarks there were. On moving to ' Crescent Alley,' B. was told to lead the company. Ye Gods ! what a follow-my-leader it was. At one time B. actually led the front of the company round and through the centre again like a musical ride. We spent twenty-four hours in Crescent Alley, during which time it rained continuously. Our only shelters were little shelves in the wall of the trench, in each of which one man slept covered by his ground-sheet. Every time a shell fell near the trench, parts of the sides fell in, and gradually, as it did not stop raining, the trench became two feet in liquid mud. The next evening we set off for the front line, then in the eastern gardens of Le Sars village. It was pitch-dark and raining hard. Some of the trenches were waist-deep in water, and even the surface of the ground was a sea of mud. It was useless to attempt to keep dry ; it was like wading in a muddy river with one's clothes on. I have heard it said that one man in the brigade was drowned during this relief, although I cannot vouch for it, but I know that we ourselves had to spend nearly an hour at one point digging three men out of the mud. Although it was only 500 yards long it took us till midnight to reach the top of 26th Avenue. We struck off north up Tangle Alley into Le Sars village, and, after crossing the Bapaume road, entered another horrible trench, " Jock's Alley," by means of which we reached our destination. It had taken us ten hours, and yet it was only 3000 yards from Crescent Alley to the front line. We arrived looking like nothing on earth, covered with mud from head to foot ; even the tartan of our kilts was quite unrecognisable. It was easily the worst relief I ever took part in."

Such were the conditions under which the relief was carried out. It was, however, completed by 9 A.M. on the 9th, at which hour General McCracken assumed command of the sector, with headquarters at Shelter Wood, the 44th Brigade occupying the right section, the 45th the left, with the 46th in reserve at Villa Wood.

Although an enormous amount of work was done, conditions remained bad for some time, so much so that it was found impossible to continue the operations which so far had been so successful. The position was described by Sir Douglas Haig in his despatch dated December 23, 1916 (p. 47) :—

Oct.-Nov. 1916.

"Unfortunately, at this juncture very unfavourable weather set in, and continued with scarcely a break during the remainder of October and the early part of November. Poor visibility seriously interfered with the work of our artillery, and constant rain turned the mass of hastily dug trenches for which we were fighting into channels of deep mud. The country roads, broken by numerous shell craters, that crossed the deep stretch of ground we had lately won, rapidly became almost impassable, making the supply of food, stores, and ammunition a serious problem. These conditions multiplied the difficulties of attack to such an extent that it was found impossible to exploit the situation with the rapidity necessary to enable us to reap the full benefits of the advantages we had gained. . . . The delay in our advance, however, though unavoidable, had given the enemy time to re-organise and rally his troops. His resistance became more stubborn, and he seized every favourable opportunity for counter-attacks. Trenches changed hands with great frequency, the conditions of ground making it difficult to renew exhausted supplies of bombs and ammunition, or to consolidate the ground won, and so rendering it an easier matter to take a battered trench than to hold it."

With the exception of the usual patrol activities, no actual fighting took place during this tour. Infantry, sappers, and pioneers alike had as much as they could do to keep the line in anything approaching proper order and free from water. Conditions could not have been worse, and towards the end of October frost added to the difficulties, with the result that a number of cases of "trench feet" occurred. Every precaution was taken to ward off this disease, but it was well-nigh impossible to keep the men's feet dry in the waterlogged trenches, the result being that in some cases units were so reduced in strength that they were unable to do anything beyond holding the front line. To add to the discomfort, the enemy now commenced using gas and lachrymatory shells to a greater extent than hitherto. This necessitated the constant use of gas-helmets, sometimes for hours at a time, not only in the front line but as far back as Albert and the neighbouring villages.

Work of R.E. and Pioneers.

In spite of all difficulties, however, an enormous amount of work was accomplished by the sappers and pioneers, as will be seen from the following résumé of their doings from the com-

Oct.-Nov. 1916. Work of R.E. and Pioneers.

mencement of October to November 3, when the Division left the line.

To begin with, the 73rd Field Company worked in the front line, the 91st on tram-lines, and the 74th, in reserve, on shop work and roads, the 9th Gordons (Pioneers) being employed on the construction of communication trenches. Assisting them were the 1/1st Northumbrian Field Company (50th Division) and three companies of the 1/7th Durham L.I. (50th Division Pioneers), engaged on road and tram-line construction. On October 25 these were relieved by similar units from the 48th Division, and two days later the 74th Field Company took the place of the 73rd in the front line.

At first work was concentrated in assisting the infantry to construct a series of strong-posts in front, and later in connecting these up to form a new front line north of Le Sars. At the same time a large number of German dug-outs were cleaned out, repaired, improved, and the entrances (which all faced the enemy) were protected as far as possible. This alone was a huge job. It is recorded in one battalion diary that out of one dug-out alone 800 sandbags of rubbish were removed, *also half a dead pig*. In another six very dead Germans were removed before the place could be made habitable. Bomb stores were constructed, and trenches labelled and put in order. The pioneers dug two main communication trenches six feet deep—Gilbert Alley on the left, and William Alley on the right.

Directly the front line was continuous, strong-posts were pushed out in front, and a new front line, about 200 yards ahead, formed by joining these (Scotland Trench). This was intended for a jumping-off line. The pioneers also dug a cable trench, 6 feet deep, from Martinpuich to the front line, 4000 yards in length.

Owing to the shell-riven state of the ground, few communication trenches, and weather, it was difficult for reliefs and carrying parties to find their way to and from the front line. Two overland routes were therefore laid out. These were bounded by pickets painted white at the top, fenced with wire, and trench-boards laid down over the worst places.

The tramway (16 lb. Decauville) was put in good working order from Peake Wood to Martinpuich, the rails straightened and packed where necessary, sidings were put in, and a regular service run. The petrol locomotives were then able to run right up to Gunpit Road. This railway track was also chalk ballasted, and gratings laid along it for some distance for the use of troops proceeding to or from the line. In addition to this, the line itself was extended for 3200 yards farther back. All this was properly ballasted, and planks laid along the centre to prevent pockets being formed between the sleepers.

Oct.-Nov. 1916. Work of R.E. and Pioneers.

The Contalmaison-Martinpuich road, which was exceedingly bad when the Division first came into the line, was cleared, drained, repaired, and made fit for use from the Cutting up to a point 500 yards north-west of Contalmaison villa. In the vicinity of Bazentin-le-Petit the road was also in a very bad condition. This was corduroyed, and a lot of work done on it for two weeks, but unfortunately heavy traffic nullified these efforts, and it was found necessary to concentrate on the Bazentin-le-Petit-Martinpuich road alone.

Four sites for battalion camps were prepared at Contalmaison, and about eight Nissen huts erected up to the date the Division left the line.[1]

On November 2 and 3 the Division was relieved by the 48th, and became III. Corps Reserve, being billeted as follows :—

To Corps Reserve.

Divisional Headquarters at Baizieux.
44th Brigade at Bresle.
45th Brigade at Franvillers and Baizieux.
46th Brigade at Henencourt, Millencourt, and Baizieux.
Field Ambulances at Contalmaison, Ebart Farm, and Becourt.
Divisional Train at Frechencourt.
R.E. and Pioneers at Mametz Wood, Fricourt, and Contalmaison.

---

[1] In addition, the following work was carried out :—

(1) Four drying sheds built for the reserve brigade.

(2) Erection of divisional baths commenced.

(3) A bath-house built at Martinpuich.

(4) Three wells repaired at Martinpuich and Le Sars.

(5) The field companies constructed their own, and assisted other units in building, covered horse-standings.

(6) The 9th Gordons (Pioneers) made their own camp, the material for which was all brought up by their own battalion transport.

(7) Two field company camps were built.

(8) Winter hutting commenced at Divisional Headquarters.

It must be admitted that the above was, considering the conditions under which the work was accomplished, a marvellous performance on the part of the sappers and pioneers.

Nov. 1916.

Although there had been no fighting other than the ordinary trench warfare, the casualties during the past tour had been fairly heavy.[1] The first few days therefore were devoted to reorganising and cleaning up, more necessary than ever before owing to the sea of mud in which the Division had lived for the past few weeks. Training then began in earnest, and with fine cold weather a lot of very necessary work was accomplished.

On November 4 the Commander-in-Chief visited all brigades in the Division. Work was not interfered with in any way, but he saw all men not otherwise employed, and complimented them on the good work done by the Division. His remarks on the general appearance of the troops were commendatory, and his visit gave great satisfaction to every one. Two paragraphs from the official despatches may be quoted as showing what he thought of the troops engaged in the Somme battles. On page 53 he says: "Among all the long roll of victories borne on the colours of our regiments, there has never been a higher test of the endurance and resolution of our infantry. They have shown themselves worthy of the highest traditions of our race, and of the proud record of former wars." Again, on page 59, he says: "Our New Armies entered the battle with the determination to win, and with confidence in their power to do so. They have proved to themselves, to the enemy, and to the world that this confidence was not misplaced."

The "rest period" passed uneventfully. No "alarms" or "noise from without" marred its placidity, and, free from the wet and discomfort of the trenches, the health of the Division rapidly improved, and by the end of the month it was fit and ready to take its place once more in the front line.

Into Albert sector.

November 30 and the following day found the Division moving once more up towards the front line. This time it relieved the 50th in the neighbourhood of Albert (44th Brigade), Mametz Wood (45th Brigade), and Becourt (46th Brigade).

[1] Casualties for October:—

	Killed.	Wounded.	Missing.
Officers	10	43	...
Other Ranks	172	1109	19
Total casualties . .		1353.	

Dec. 1916. To Butte de Warlencourt sector.

A fortnight later, on December 14, the Division began to relieve the 48th in the left sector of the Corps front, the operation being completed by 10 A.M. on the 16th, when General McCracken assumed command of the line, with headquarters just behind Shelter Wood. The line ran almost due east and west opposite the famous Butte de Warlencourt from the Tail Trench on the right to the chalk pit on the left. Divided into two sections, the right was first held by the 46th Brigade, the left by the 45th, whilst the 44th were held in Divisional reserve at Scott's Redoubt and Shelter Wood.

Conditions in the line.

Conditions were as bad, if not worse, than formerly. The front line consisted of a series of shell-holes linked up in places by shallow trenches. There were no defences in the shape of wire or other obstacles, and no communication trenches between the front and support lines. Each shell-hole post was garrisoned by six or seven men, and it was impossible to visit these posts during daylight. It can be readily understood that such a precarious line was always liable to enemy raids. On several occasions these took place, but, fortunately, they were carried out in a half-hearted fashion, and were easily repulsed with considerable loss to the enemy.

At this period it was decided to keep no man longer than two days in the front line, and to see that every one had frequent chances of dry boots and clothing. This, of course, entailed more inter-brigade and battalion reliefs than usual, and added greatly to the labour, but the method certainly saved much sickness. One institution in particular must be mentioned—the Divisional soup-kitchen, which was started in November at Contalmaison. Supervised by Captain Home of the K.O.S.B., it became one of the best-known spots in the Divisional area. Battalions or working-parties going up or coming down from the front line could always rely on a good supply of hot soup at any hour of the day or night to warm them on their journey. The remembrance of this cheery half-way house will live long in the memories of all who patronised it.

Towards the close of the year snow and mist greatly hindered patrol activity, but in spite of these drawbacks parties were out in No Man's Land every night, and were successful on many occasions in taking prisoners and doing much damage to the enemy's listening

Dec. 1916.

posts, &c. On one occasion, on December 23, a prisoner volunteered the statement that his regiment would be relieved the following night. As the official diary states, "suitable steps were accordingly taken." These consisted of bringing heavy artillery and machine-gun fire to bear at irregular intervals throughout the night on the German communication trenches and roads leading up from the reserve area, whilst trench-mortars "attended to" the front line.

From the front posts any enemy movement in the vicinity of the Butte de Warlencourt could be clearly seen, and the Divisional snipers took full toll of Germans rash enough to work in the open during daytime. As one diary says: "Our snipers caused all enemy work near the Butte to be done at the double. This morning seven hits are claimed."

The energetic measures taken at this time to prevent trench feet and other sickness were very successful, with the result that on December 31 the percentage of sickness dwindled down to ·33, and there were only nine cases of trench feet in the whole Division.

Jan. 1917. Raid on the Butte.

Christmas and New Year passed without incident, as also did January 1917. On the whole, the weather was fairly good, and a great deal of work was done to better the trench system. Towards the end of the month rumours of a move elsewhere commenced to circulate throughout the Division, but before it took place a raid on the Butte was organised by the 44th Brigade, and carried out most successfully by "B" and "D" Companies of the 8/10th Gordon Highlanders (Lieut.-Colonel Thom).

This raid was so well planned and executed that no excuse is necessary for reproducing the Brigade Orders issued in connection with it.[1] The famous Butte de Warlencourt, against which the operation was directed, requires a few words of description.

The opposing lines at this point ran along each side of a shallow valley. On the British side the ground sloped gently down from the ruins of Le Sars village, the front line being about half-way down the slope. On the opposite side of the valley were the German trenches in a somewhat similar position, and immediately behind their front line rose the Butte, an artificial mound of chalk, the material for which

[1] See end of chapter and Map 6.

Jan. 1917. Raid on the Butte.

had been taken from the Quarry immediately north-west of it. About 100 feet in height and the same in diameter, this mound dominated not only No Man's Land but the British trenches on the opposite slope. It had been tunnelled into by the enemy, and was suspected of containing a number of dug-outs and machine-guns. The Quarry to the north-west was also known to contain dug-outs, shelters, and trench-mortar emplacements; this was also to form part of the raiders' objective.

On account of the numberless shell-holes and the condition of the intervening ground, it was decided that the raiding party should form up in No Man's Land, and, as there was deep snow on the ground at the time, the men wore white smocks over their equipment and had their steel helmets whitewashed.[1] To eliminate further any chance of confusion, black tapes were laid out beforehand, on which the lines formed up prior to the attack. As was the custom on all raids, the enemy wire was previously cut by artillery fire, and in this instance the work was exceedingly well done. There was no preliminary bombardment, the strictest injunctions being given that the enemy were to be left undisturbed until the raid started. At zero hour things were to liven up. The Divisions on the right (the 2nd) and on the left (the 1st Australians) were to simulate attacks, in order to deceive the enemy as to the real point of attack, and the Fifteenth Divisional Artillery, assisted by the III. Corps Heavy Artillery, were to open an intense barrage on the German front line. This barrage was after one minute to lift at the rate of 50 yards a minute until it reached a point well behind the Butte and Quarry. At the conclusion of the raid, twenty-five minutes after zero, the barrage was to return to the German front-line trenches, by which time the raiders were to be back in their own lines.

The 44th Brigade was the one chosen to carry out the operation, and General Marshall selected the 8/10th Gordon Highlanders for the work. From his battalion Lieut.-Colonel Thom detailed "B" and "D" Companies, putting them through a thorough preparation and

[1] Some of these were ladies' night-gowns, bought in Amiens by two Highland officers, who caused much amusement in the shops when they informed the fair assistants what they wanted.

Jan. 29-30, 1917. Raid on the Butte.

rehearsal behind the lines. Every imaginable contingency was provided for, and this care and forethought was largely responsible for the success of the raid.

At 11 P.M. on the night of January 29 the two companies left their shelters just behind the support line. Although they had barely 700 yards to travel, it took them two hours to reach the positions of attack in No Man's Land. The utmost care had to be taken to avoid arousing suspicion in the minds of the enemy, and the raiders crawled out in small parties through gaps cut in the wire, and formed up on the black tapes without trouble and without opposition from the enemy. Due credit should be given to Captain Martin for the way in which the tapes were laid out, barely 100 yards from the foremost line of German sentries.

By 1.15 A.M. on the 30th the attackers were in position. They were formed up in two waves, each wave consisting of two platoons from each company. On the right Captain Mutch was in command of "B" Company, having with him 2nd Lieutenants Kemp, Wallace, and Hofford. On the left Lieutenant Kenyon commanded "D" company, with 2nd Lieutenants Knowles and Forster. "B" Company's objective was the Butte itself, whilst that of "D" was the Quarry. The task of both parties was to take prisoners, do as much damage as possible, and be back in their lines within twenty-five minutes of zero hour, a short enough time for any but well-trained troops.

Sharp to the second, at 1.30 A.M., the barrage fell on the German lines, and one minute afterwards the two companies went forward. Practically no opposition was met with except on the left flank, which was held up for a short time by a machine-gun in the Quarry. On the right, just as the barrage lifted from the front line, two enemy machine-guns opened fire, and the line hesitated. With a shout of "Come on, Gordons!" Captain Mutch dashed forward, followed by his company, and the guns were at once silenced. On crossing the German front line "B" Company discovered a trench-mortar, which they demolished by dropping a Stokes' bomb down the barrel, and then ramming a tuft of earth and grass into the muzzle. Once past the front line, parties went forward north of the Butte to act as a screen

Jan. 30, 1917. Raid on the Butte.

for those detailed to deal with the Butte and its dug-outs. On the left " D " Company had discovered an enemy strong-point garrisoned by six men. These, half dazed by the sudden attack, surrendered without a struggle, and the line swept on to the Quarry, where many dug-outs were bombed and destroyed. On the right " B " Company was investigating the Butte itself. Discovering several entrances on its northern side, the garrison was summoned to surrender. A few wisely obeyed, but at two entrances, as no reply was received, Stokes' shells and Mills' bombs were thrown down, which demolished the passages and bottled up the inmates. Here the " bag " in prisoners amounted to 12, who were sent back at once, and the work of destruction continued. By a stroke of good-fortune a Stokes' shell exploded at the bottom of one entrance, and set alight some tins of petrol, and the fire spread to the recesses of the Butte itself.

By this time the party had done all the damage they could, and it was time to get back to their lines. Twenty minutes after the raid started the covering parties withdrew, and five minutes later, as the two companies reached the safety of their lines, the Divisional artillery barrage fell once more on the German front line. Looking back on the scene of their exploit, what they saw must have given the raiders great satisfaction. Flames were shooting out of the Butte, the German lines were being pounded into fragments by the gunners, many of the enemy had been killed in hand-to-hand fighting, 17 prisoners were on their way to the cage, and not one single rifle-shot or machine-gun stutter was heard from the area they had just left—a truly remarkable performance. A prisoner, who spoke a certain amount of English, told one of his captors that the dug-outs in the Butte contained 150 men. Of these, 12 had surrendered; the remainder were—well, " accounted for," by the fire, which was still burning two days later.[1]

Both during and after the raid the enemy's artillery fire was feeble. Apparently he was taken completely by surprise, and made no attempt whatever to drive back the invaders.

Casualties.

Whilst they had inflicted severe casualties on the enemy, the party got off comparatively lightly. 2nd Lieutenant Knowles was missing,

[1] At 3.15 A.M. the Butte exploded, flames rising thirty feet in the air, the noise of bursting bombs and S.A.A. telling its own tale.

Jan. 30, 1917. Raid on the Butte.

and it is thought that he was killed whilst dealing with the machine-gun near the Quarry. 2nd Lieutenants Forster and Walker were slightly wounded, 4 other ranks were killed and 10 wounded, the number of prisoners thus exceeding the total casualties suffered by the party.

Thus concluded one of the most successful raids undertaken by the Division. Well thought out, well rehearsed, and exceedingly well carried out, it reflects the highest credit on Lieut.-Colonel Thom and every officer, N.C.O., and man who took part in it; also unstinted praise is due to the gunners, whose barrage was so accurate and destructive. The operation called forth well-merited praise from many sources, including the 1st Australian Division.[1]

Relief of Division.

Two days later the 5th Australian Division commenced to relieve the Fifteenth, and by February 4 the latter was stationed as follows, with headquarters at Baizieux:—

44th Brigade and 91st Field Company at Bresle and Contay.
45th Brigade and 73rd Field Company (less two sections) at Franvillers.
46th Brigade and 74th Field Company at Warloy.
45th Field Ambulance at Vandencourt.
9th Gordons (Pioneers) at Warloy.

On February 2 the 72nd Brigade, R.F.A., left the Division, and became an Army brigade, remaining, however, under C.R.A., Fifteenth Division, for tactical purposes. The remainder were relieved on the 5th by the 2nd Australian Divisional Artillery, and proceeded to Molliers au Bois (70th Brigade), Pierregot, and Miriaux (71st Brigade), trench-mortar batteries to camp near Lavieville. They had to leave nine 18-pr. guns, one 4.5 howitzer, and eighteen dial sights in the line to complete the Australian batteries.

Work of the R.A.

This period on the Somme cannot be closed without special mention being made of the work done by the Divisional artillery. It was

[1] The following awards were given for work in connection with this particular raid:—

Captain Mutch received the D.S.O.
Captain J. Martin received the M.C.
Three other ranks received the D.C.M.
Sergeant Donelley received the M.M.

during this time that the British artillery may be said to have begun to "come into its own"; and although their work was increased tenfold, the gunners never failed. A Division staff officer writes: "The work of the Fifteenth Divisional Artillery in the mud of the Somme was perfectly magnificent."

Feb. 1917.

Here reorganisation and training occupied the next ten days. The weather was fine but intensely cold, billets were good, and, after its experience of the past six months, the Division eagerly looked forward to the coming move to a new area.

Farewell to the Fourth Army.

Before leaving, General McCracken received the following letter from General Sir H. Rawlinson, commanding the Fourth Army, which was communicated to all ranks:—

"I cannot allow my old friends in the Fifteenth Division to leave the Fourth Army without expressing to them my gratitude for, and admiration of, their excellent services during the battle of the Somme.

"The capture of Martinpuich with more than 1000 prisoners, accomplished as it was after six weeks of hard and continuous fighting in the line, was a feat of arms deserving the highest praise, and illustrates the endurance and fine fighting spirit for which the Division has always been renowned.

"The work they have done at and about Le Sars has been of the same high standard as that which they accomplished at Loos, and I know no division in which a higher standard of discipline and moral exists, nor one to which I would entrust a difficult undertaking with greater confidence.

"The close co-operation between the artillery and infantry of the Division has been a factor which has contributed greatly to their successes, and shows that the training of the artillery has been no less thorough than that of the infantry.

"In the operations of the coming spring, the Division will, I am sure, maintain the same high reputation that they have won in the IVth Corps and in the Fourth Army, and I trust that at some future date I may again have the honour of finding them under my command.

"I wish all ranks every possible good-fortune.

"(Signed) H. RAWLINSON, *General*,
"*Commanding Fourth Army.*"

Thus ended the tour of the Division in the Somme area. Enough has been said to give the general reader some idea of the conditions under which it lived and fought for six months. More might have been said of the discomforts and hardships endured during this trying

Feb. 1917. Schools of instruction

time, but the tale as it stands needs little embellishment, and the glorious part played by the Division throws into the shade the sufferings endured cheerfully by all ranks.

As methods of warfare were constantly changing and new devices came into use on any part of the front, it was necessary that information regarding them should be available to all ranks. To do this, and also to keep up their training in the various subjects, schools of instruction were again established behind the line wherever the Division was engaged, to which parties of all ranks were sent. These schools are mentioned occasionally in brigade and Division diaries, but it is a pity that there is no record of the most excellent work accomplished by them.[1] Apparently they kept no diaries, and the only proof of their usefulness is the manner in which the Division invariably carried out its work. Whenever the enemy produced some new weapon of warfare or tried some fresh method of attack, it was only a matter of a few days before news of it reached the Division, and steps were taken to deal with each as it became known.

By 1916 it was recognised that the continual strain of trench warfare was telling on officers and men alike, and rest camps were established on the sea coast. The first mention of them is found in the Division diary of September, where it states, "Vacancies given for 4 officers and 100 men in a rest camp near the sea."

FIRST APPENDIX.

ORDERS FOR RAID BY 8/10TH GORDONS, 29/30TH JANUARY 1917.
44TH BRIGADE O.O. No. 137.

Reference— 26-1-17.

LE SARS to LOUPART WOOD Map.
Dated 19-12-16.

1. The 44th Infantry Brigade will carry out a raid on the night of 29/30th January 1917 on the Butte de Warlencourt and Quarry in M.16.b.9½.6.

The object of the raid is to capture prisoners, and to destroy the enemy works in the Butte and Quarry.

---

[1] Colonel H. H. S. Knox, at this time G.S.O. 1, Fifteenth Division, writes:—

"There is not much more to say about these schools. I used to attend each class at least once, and lecture on tactics and leadership. No lecturer ever had an audience to equal the grand platoon commanders of the Fifteenth Division."

2. In order to mislead the enemy as to the point about to be raided—

(*a*) The 1st Australian Division will be asked to assist by simulating an attack in N. 13.

(*b*) The 2nd Division are arranging to barrage the Dyke Road in M.9., and to simulate an attack on their front, possibly about the Quadrilateral M.8.d.

(*c*) The 3rd H.A.G. will at zero hour open an intense bombardment in Little Wood, and on the Gallwitz Line south of it.

The 45th Infantry Brigade will co-operate with the 3rd H.A.G. with rifle, machine-gun, and trench-mortar fire to induce the enemy to expect an attack on Little Wood.

3. The left group Divisional artillery (Brig.-General Macnaghten, D.S.O.) will issue detailed instructions for the artillery, arranging with artillery of flanking divisions.

(i) In preparation for the raid—

Wire is being cut at—

M.17.a.9.5.
M.10.d.1.4.
M.10.c.0.6.
M.9.d.1.5.

And the gaps are being kept under shrapnel and machine-gun fire.

The Heavy Artillery are paying daily attention to the Butte and Quarry and to Little Wood, especially to Little Wood.

(ii) (*a*) At zero hour an intense 18-pr. barrage will be placed on the Butte Trench M.17.a.8.3. and westward to M.18.b.5.3.

(*b*) Commencing at 0, plus 1,[1] the barrage will lift 50 yards a minute until on the line M.11.c.8.1.—M.11.c.0.1.—M.16.b.9.9½., and thence along trench to M.10.d.5.1.

(*bb*) From 0.30-0.32 18-prs. will fire on M.17.8.5.—M.16.b.8.8.

(*c*) 18-prs. will also cover the right flank of the attack, forming a barrage along the track M.17.a.8.4. to M.11.c.8.1., and searching to the east of the track.

(*d*) At zero hour 18-prs. will engage the enemy line and posts about M.10.c.9.5., and during the raid will search the approaches in M.10.d.

(*e*) At zero hour 18-prs. will open on the Butte de Warlencourt and posts west of it, lifting off the objectives with the creeping barrage.

(*f*) 4.5-in. howitzers will engage trenches about M.17.b.5.0., dug-outs about M.11.d.8½.5. road M.10.d.5.0. to M.10.b.5.0. from zero till 0.30.

(*g*) Heavy Artillery will engage the Coupe Gueule, cross roads M.11.a.6.4., eastern exits of Warlencourt, and headquarters in M.5.a.3.3.

4. Two companies 8/10th Gordon Highlanders will deliver the assault on a front from M.17.a.6.0. to M.16.b.9.0.

5. (i) The assaulting troops will be drawn up in two waves at twenty minutes before zero.

(ii) The first wave will be in Maxwell Trench from M.17.a.6.0. to about M.17.a.4.0., thence along a taped line to M.16.b.9.0.

[1] Minutes.

(iii) The second wave will be on a taped line about 50 yards in rear of the first wave.

(iv) Each wave will consist of 4 platoons (2 from each company). The first wave will be organised as bombers and riflemen, except that each platoon will find the garrison of one of the covering posts mentioned below in sub-para. (vi). Each of these garrisons will consist of 1 leader, 1 Lewis-gun (4 men), 4 rifles, 4 rifle bombers.

(v) The platoons of the second wave will consist of riflemen, except that each platoon will provide a special clearing party of 1 leader, 6 bombers, 2 rifles, 4 men carrying 2 Stokes' bombs each prepared as bombs, 4 men carrying 4 " P " bombs each. Also each of the assaulting companies will provide one Lewis-gun team (4 men) for the second wave.

(vi) The covering parties referred to in sub-para. (iv) above will occupy positions approximately as follows :—

(*a*) Right platoon, M.17.a.6.3.
(*b*) Second platoon, M.17.a.4.4½.
(*c*) Third platoon, M.17.a.2.8.
(*d*) Fourth platoon, M.16.b.9½.8½.

Their duties are to protect the raiders from interference, and to cover their withdrawal.

(*c*) and (*d*) parties will withdraw at zero, plus 23 minutes.

(*a*) and (*b*) parties as soon as the remainder of the raiding party have withdrawn behind them, or in any case at zero, plus 26 minutes.

(vii) (*a*) The duty of the first wave is to seize the objectives, make prisoners, and capture machine-guns or trench-mortars.

(*b*) The duty of the second wave is to explore and clear the dug-outs and underground passages in the neighbourhood of the Quarry and Butte.

Lewis-guns should be freely used underground to clear the way for exploring parties; " P " bombs and Stokes' bombs are not to be thrown into the dug-outs until they have been explored, or unless it is found impossible to gain entrance to them.

In any case, at least 2 " P " bombs and 1 Stokes' bomb are to be thrown down each dug-out before the party withdraws to our lines.

(*c*) The assaulting troops will commence to withdraw to our own lines at zero, plus 25 minutes (except as stated in sub-para. (vi) above).

(viii) Dress—skeleton equipment ; 120 rounds S.A.A. ; bombers, 12 Mills' ; rifle bombers, 12 No. 23 ; Lewis-guns, 20 drums.

If snow is on the ground, white shirts will be provided, and helmets will be whitewashed.

(ix) The assaulting troops will reassemble in Maxwell Support.

6. (i) 44th Trench-Mortar Battery will co-operate as follows :—

In addition to the guns at M.17.d.0.7½. and M.17.c.2.7., four more Stokes' guns will be placed in Maxwell Support, and one gun will be placed in the neighbourhood of Warlencourt Alley.

At zero the six guns in Maxwell Support will open an intense bombardment on the line M.17.a.8.3.—0.2¾. for one minute. Thereafter the two right-hand guns will maintain a steady rate of fire on the Butte Trench between M.17.a.9.4. and a.7.3½. until zero, plus 30.

The gun near Warlencourt Alley at zero will open an intense bombardment of enemy post at M.16.b.4½.9. for one minute, and thereafter maintain a steady rate of fire about the same target until zero, plus 30.

O.C. 44th Trench-Mortar Battery will be responsible that emplacements are made, and sufficient ammunition available in them before 6 A.M., January 27.

(ii) The two medium trench-mortars in Hexham Road will fire as follows:—

No. 1 *gun* at zero will fire at the Quarry as many rounds as possible for 3 minutes, thereafter to cease fire until zero, plus 30, when 2 rounds will be fired at the same target.

No. 2 *gun* at zero will fire at M.16.b.9.8½. as many rounds as possible for 4 minutes, thereafter to cease fire until zero, plus 30, when 2 rounds will be fired at the same target.

7. 44th Machine-Gun Company will arrange to keep all approaches to the Butte under fire at intervals from zero to daylight.

45th Machine-Gun Company will co-operate.

8. O.C. 8/10th Gordons is responsible that—

(i) Sufficient gaps are cut in our wire to allow of the uninterrupted advance of the assaulting troops. These gaps are not to be cut before the evening of January 29, and are to be clearly marked.

(ii) The tapes from which the assaulting troops form up are correctly sited. This may be done on night 28/29th January. If snow is on the ground, the tapes should be coloured black or red.

9. Brigade Signal Officer will (*a*) establish direct communication from Company Headquarters, Hexham Road, to Brigade Headquarters; (*b*) arrange for existing communication between these points to be duplicated.

10. Regimental aid-posts in Hexham Road at about M.17.c.2.5., and at Le Sars cross-roads at M.16.c.2.4.

11. Prisoners to Corps cage at Bazentin-le-Petit.

12. Reports to Brigade Headquarters.

13. Zero hour will be notified later.

(Signed) E. CAMPBELL, *Major,*
Brigade-Major, 44th Infantry Brigade.

Note.—Zero hour will be at 1.45 A.M. on night of 29/30th inst.

SECOND APPENDIX.

During the past year (1916) a good many changes had taken place on the Division and brigade staffs. The following are the principal ones :—

January.—Captain J. C. Cook, General List, became Brigade-Major, 46th Brigade, vice Major G. W. Howard, D.S.O., the Essex Regiment, to G.S.O. 3, Second Army.

February.—Major J. C. Thornhill, Seaforth Highlanders, to be G.S.O. 3, vice Major F. G. Spring, Lincoln Regiment, to the Division as G.S.O. 2.

March.—Lieut.-Colonel R. S. Walker from IV. Corps to be C.R.E., vice Lieut.-Colonel G. S. Cartwright, appointed C.R.E., VIII. Corps. Major Smott, 7th K.O.S.B., appointed D.A.A. and Q.M.G.

April.—Major P. W. L. Powell from Brigade-Major, 95th Brigade, to be D.A.A. and Q.M.G., vice Captain H. W. Snow, R. of O., to A.A.G., III. Corps. Brig.-General W. H. Allgood, R. of O., to command 45th Infantry Brigade, vice Brig.-General E. W. B. Green, Royal Sussex Regiment, to England (invalided). Captain M. O'Connor, late R.N.R., Staff Captain, 44th Brigade, to England (invalided). Lieut.-Colonel C. R. Berkeley, D.S.O., to D.A.A. and Q.M.G., vice Major P. W. L. Powell, to D.A.A. and Q.M G., 25th Division. Brig.-General F. J. Marshall to command 44th Brigade, vice Brig.-General M. G. Wilkinson, to England (invalided). Brig.-General E. B. Macnaghten, D.S.O., to command 15th Divisional Artillery, vice Brig.-General E. W. Alexander, V.C., R.A.

May.—Major K. Henderson from Brigade-Major, 21st Division, to be G.S.O. 2, vice Major E. G. Wace to 32nd Division as G.S.O. 1. Captain L. Carr, from Staff Captain, 20th Brigade, to be Brigade-Major, 45th Brigade, vice Major J. Rainsford Hannay, to Chief Instructor, First Army School. Captain A. Rollo to be Staff Captain, 44th Brigade, vice Captain O'Connor, late R.N.V.R. Rev. Meek, Senior Presbyterian Chaplain, to England for East Africa.

June.—Rev. S. C. Fitzgerald to be Senior Chaplain.

July.—Captain C. F. N. Ryan, R.E., to be G.S.O. 3, vice Major J. E. Thornhill, to England (invalided).

August.—Lieut.-Colonel C. R. Berkeley to be A.A. and Q.M.G., vice Lieut.-Colonel E. F. Taylor, R.A.S.C., to England as A.D. of S. and T. Western Command. Captain J. F. Chevenix-Trench from Staff Captain, 52nd Brigade, to be A.A. and Q.M.G., vice Lieut.-Colonel E. F. Taylor.

September.—Captain K. Barge, 17th Lancers (Indian Army), to be Brigade-Major, 44th Brigade, vice Major E. A. Beck, D.S.O., to Fourth Army as G.S.O. 2. Captain W. G. Wright, A. & S. Highlanders, to be Staff Captain, 45th Brigade, vice Captain H. G. Fowler (wounded).

October.—Major H. F. Baillie, D.S.O., Seaforth Highlanders, to be G.S.O. 2, vice Major K. Henderson, D.S.O., to England (invalided).

December.—Captain W. H. Horsley, 21st Lancers, to be D.A.Q.M.G., vice Captain W. H. Annesley, R. of O., to 31st Division as A.A. and Q.M.G.

SERGEANT J. C. RAYNES, V.C.

71st Brigade Royal Field Artillery.

CHAPTER V.

THE BATTLE OF ARRAS.[1]

Feb. 1917.

On all occasions rest and change invariably worked wonders with the Division. No matter what the weather had been, or how hard the fighting, once in rest it was only a matter of a few days before all units had reorganised and were again ready for work. On this occasion ten days elapsed before a move was made elsewhere. The weather was fine but intensely cold, and excellent work was accomplished both as regards drill and "recreational training." Higher authority always recognised that as much good could be obtained by the latter as by the former method of training, but this time more opportunities were afforded for football, boxing, &c., and there is no doubt that the troops benefited in consequence.

Move to Arras area.

On February 13 the Division ceased to be part of the III. Corps, and joined the VI., Lieut.-General J. A. L. Haldane, in the Third Army, General E. H. H. Allenby, and the same day commenced moving northwards to the Arras area. Marching in brigade groups and billeting in Beauval, Rebreuve, Boquemaison, and the neighbouring villages, the Division was concentrated in the vicinity of Duisans by the 18th, with its artillery at St Michel. Although favoured by fine weather throughout, the march was trying to a degree. Life in the mud and shell-holes of the Somme area had caused much sickness, and lessened the men's ability to march long distances. Added to this, the icy wind that blew all the four days made the usual hourly halts anything but a comfort. It was extraordinary, however, how few men fell out. In the diary of one unit it is noted that "Notwithstanding our long, quick, and tiring march, fully 50 per cent of the

[1] Maps 7 and 8.

Feb. 1917.

battalion returned to spend the evening in St Pol (two miles from their billets). Such is the attraction of a decent town to men who have been away from one for so long."

Description of Arras front.

The following three days were spent in preparations for taking over the line east of Arras from the 12th Division, the left sector of the VI. Corps front, and in reconnoitring the position. Here the front line ran from a point a quarter of a mile east of Arras Cemetery, due north-east, by Blangy village to the river Scarpe, the Divisional boundary. Till now no operations on a large scale had been undertaken east of Arras, and in consequence the trenches were in excellent order. Communication trenches led from the city to the front line, making it possible to relieve troops in the line during the day, thereby eliminating the extra fatigue caused by night reliefs. Dug-out accommodation was plentiful and good, No Man's Land was fairly wide, and, on the whole, the sector was reputed to be comparatively peaceful. Although the centre of the city was barely a mile and a quarter from the front line, it was possible to accommodate support and reserve troops with perfect safety in the cellars with which Arras abounds. These require a passing word, as they played no small part in the defence of the city and in the forthcoming operations. Dating back to the eleventh and twelfth centuries, these cellars, or " boves," as they are called, were originally quarries from which the stone required for building the houses over them was taken. On many occasions in the history of the city these cellars had afforded protection to the inhabitants in time of war. Once more they played their part in history, and this time not only did they give shelter to the inhabitants and garrison, but, as will be seen later, they enabled a vast host to gather in Arras, unnoticed by the enemy, which host two days later was to overwhelm him and free the city from the fire of his guns.

Into the line.

On February 23 the Fifteenth Division commenced relieving the 12th in the front line, General McCracken assuming command the following day (with headquarters at Duisans), although the relief was not completed until the night of the 27th. The length of this relief was due to the fact that, as the western approaches of Arras were under direct enemy observation, all movement into the city from that side by daylight was out of the question. Every night about dusk, at a certain point on the St Pol-Arras road, columns of troops and transport congregated, waiting to cross the danger zone. Directly it was dark these moved forward, sometimes infantry, horsed vehicles, and motor transport all abreast. On arrival in Arras the resulting confusion in its narrow streets may well be imagined. A company officer, describing his experience on this occasion, writes as follows :— Feb. 1917.

"That night Arras was a seething mass of men, horses, guns, and transport. You can imagine my predicament when I suddenly found myself pitchforked into this rabble, out of touch with the company in front, never having been there before, and not knowing in which direction my billets lay. In addition, the noise was deafening. Guns seemed to be firing from behind every house, and, to cap all, German shells fell continually in the city, the noise of their explosion being accentuated by the rebounding echoes of the narrow streets. Language on all sides was hot and flowery, and generally the place might have been mistaken for Hades instead of Arras."

To commence with, the 46th Brigade (Brig.-General Matheson) held the whole of the front line, the remainder of the Division moving as follows: 44th Brigade and 9th Gordons (Pioneers) from Buneville to Ambrines; the 45th from Foufflins to Habarcq area. 91st, 73rd (less two sections), and 74th Field Companies, R.E., moved with the 44th, 45th, and 46th Brigades respectively. Before taking over this sector a change had been made in the Fifteenth Divisional Artillery. On February 2 the 72nd Brigade, R.F.A., left the Division and became an Army brigade, but for the time being remained under the orders of C.R.A., Fifteenth Division, for tactical purposes.

A quiet time.

From now to the commencement of the spring offensive the Division enjoyed a comparatively quiet time. Until the end of February the sector was held by one brigade in the front line, one in support, and the third in reserve. The weather was fine, and the enemy surprisingly inactive. Day after day entries such as the following occur in the Divisional diary: "Enemy very quiet," "No change, quiet day," &c., &c.

Although the Germans were so unenterprising, the Division by no means followed their example. Almost daily the enemy lines were subjected to bombardments by artillery and trench-mortars, and raids were made on his trenches, a particularly successful one being carried out on April 5 by two platoons of "C" Company, 13th Royal

Mar.-April 1917. Raids.

Scots, under Captain J. A. Turner, against the enemy lines east of Blangy. Eight prisoners were taken, and, as usual, dug-outs bombed and damage done to the German trenches. At this time, and on this particular portion of the front, the Allied supremacy was unquestioned. This is shown by many incidents, but two will suffice. Both are experiences of the 7/8th K.O.S.B. On one occasion, east of Blangy, an officer and private—Lieutenant Strachan and Private Henderson—entered the German front line. Here they discovered a sentry standing with his back to them. To give him a chance for his life, Strachan threw a brick at him, hitting him on the head. The sentry turned round and put up his hands at once. On second thoughts, however, he turned and ran, whereupon Private Henderson "added him to the bag." In connection with this incident, General Allgood, 45th Brigade, writes: "We knew of this sentry, and kept him tame. You could always see him when you wanted to by climbing into a ruined house near-by. Orders were issued that he was not to be molested, so that we could bag any officer visiting him. This order was handed over by units on relief. Strachan spoilt the game: he couldn't resist it. The sentry looked such a fool that we waited for higher game." On another occasion, March 26, No. 2651, Private T. Flatt, 10th Scottish Rifles, crawled over to the enemy's lines in broad daylight and brought back a German sentry. At 12.30 noon, Flatt was on the top of a building near the "Boiler House" in Blangy, from which he could see down into the enemy's trench, which appeared to be empty. He went over to the trench to investigate, and there found a sentry with his back to him looking through a loophole. On turning round, the German, seeing Flatt had a grenade in his hand, threw up his arms and shouted "Kamerad!" and then tried to run away. Flatt thereupon hit him on the head with the bomb, made him climb over the parapet, and brought him into the Scottish Rifles' lines. He also obtained much useful information regarding enemy dug-outs during his visit.

Preparations for offensive.

Whilst the troops were living this comparatively easy existence, Army Corps, Division, and Brigade staffs were engaged in perfecting their arrangements for the coming operations. Weather alone had stopped the British advance in the autumn of 1916, and the Commander-in-Chief was determined to resume the offensive at the earliest opportunity. Throughout the winter his plans for this had been maturing. Roads and railways were improved and built, stores of shells and munitions of all kinds accumulated, and the numberless details, such as accommodation, water supply, &c., necessary for the successful concentration of the large number of troops engaged, had all been thought out.[1]

Mar.-April 1917.

Plan of offensive.

In the operations now known as the battle of Arras the Commander-in-Chief's intention was to capture the Vimy Ridge, the village of Monchy-le-Preux, and the high ground north of Croisilles and west of Fontaine les Croisilles, thereby compelling the enemy to retreat for some distance or take up positions on the low ground eastwards, over which, as on the Somme, observation would be easy and a farther advance facilitated. To the Third Army was given the task of taking Monchy-le-Preux and Guemappe, its boundaries being the rivers Cojeul and Scarpe, on the south and north respectively.

By this time the Germans had adopted the plan of defence in depth, and had constructed several lines behind their front system, each well wired and provided with strong-points ready for defence in case those in front were captured. Knowing this, and profiting by experience, it was laid down that the attack on the enemy positions was to be carried out in successive stages, each limited to one particular portion or line of the enemy's defences. On the VI. Corps front these lines consisted of four (see Map No. 7), designated respectively the Black, Blue, Brown, and Green Lines.

The vital tactical position on the Corps front was the village of Monchy-le-Preux. From it a good view of nearly the whole ground as far as Arras can be obtained, and although the Vimy Ridge and the high ground south of the Cojeul River might fall into British hands, so long as Monchy remained in possession of the enemy farther advance

[1] "In particular, advantage was taken of the existence of the large system of underground quarries and cellars in Arras and its suburbs to provide safe quarters for a great number of troops. Electric light was installed in these caves and cellars, which were linked together by tunnels, and the whole connected by long subways with our trench system east of the town.

"A problem peculiar to the launching of a great offensive from a town arose from the difficulty of ensuring the punctual debouching of troops, and the avoidance of confusion and congestion in the streets both before the assault and during the progress of the battle. This problem was met by the most careful and complete organisation of routes, reflecting the highest credit on the staffs concerned."—Sir Douglas Haig's Despatches, 85 and 86.

April 1917.

from the north and south would be wellnigh impossible. Between Monchy and Arras were two other important positions—namely, Orange Hill and Observation Ridge, whilst on the right due south of Monchy, and in the Corps area, lay the village of Guemappe in the valley of the Cojeul River.

The Corps Objectives.

Roughly, the Black Line included the enemy first-line and support trenches; the Blue Line, Observation Ridge and Thilloy village; the Brown Line, Himalaya Trench, on the western slopes of Orange Hill; and the Green Line, the final objective, the villages of Monchy-le-Preux and Guemappe.

In the first orders received, on which the initial attack was carried out, the taking of the first three lines—Black, Blue, Brown—was entrusted to the 3rd, 12th, and Fifteenth Divisions, from right to left, the 37th Division being detailed to advance through them when the Brown Line had been captured and take the villages of Monchy and Guemappe.

The dividing line between the 12th and Fifteenth Divisions ran almost due east and west from Arras Cemetery to Hart Work, thence just south of Broken Mill, and then on to the north-western slopes of Orange Hill. On the left the boundary between the Fifteenth and 9th Divisions was the river Scarpe.

Dispositions of Divisions.

The attack was divided into two distinct phases. The first phase consisted of taking the enemy's front and support trenches, the Black and Blue Lines respectively; the second phase was the capture of the Brown Line, the third and last German line west of Monchy-le-Preux. General McCracken decided to take the Black and Blue Lines with two brigades, 44th on the right and 45th on the left, keeping the 46th in reserve for the attack on the Brown Line.

On the right General Marshall attacked with the 8/10th Gordons on the right and 9th Black Watch on the left, keeping the 7th Camerons in support and 8th Seaforths in reserve. On the left General Allgood, 45th Brigade, had the 6/7th Royal Scots Fusiliers on the right, 11th A. & S. Highlanders in the centre, and two companies of the 13th Royal Scots, under Captain J. A. Turner, on the left, keeping the 6th Camerons and 13th Royal Scots, less two companies, in reserve.

April 9, 1917. The attack launched.

Starting at 5.30 A.M. on April 9, under cover of an intense artillery barrage, the attack was at once successful. By 6.15 A.M. the 44th and 45th Brigades had reached the Black Line, the first objective, and quarter of an hour later reports reached General McCracken that the whole of it had been taken, and that both flanks were secure.

On the left the 45th Brigade, which was led into action on this occasion by Brig.-General Allgood, found its task a formidable one. Blangy, the Railway Triangle, and its embankments proved serious obstacles, together with a maze of ruined factories and buildings, through which the attack had to force its way. For this reason the two companies, 13th Royal Scots, were specially detailed to deal with Blangy village as a separate operation, whilst the 11th A. & S. Highlanders were ordered to leave Blangy alone. Writing of this, General Allgood states: "The two companies fought hard, but did not subdue Blangy till half an hour after The Triangle had been taken; in other words, the Germans in the village were cut off and surrounded—which I don't suppose they realised—long before they died or surrendered." [1]

Railway Triangle.

Between the first and second objective, the Black and Blue Lines respectively, lay the Railway Triangle. On its eastern face the railway ran along an embankment some 50 or 60 feet high, which overlooked the ground westward, and was defended by numerous machine-guns. This was another formidable obstacle on the 45th Brigade front, and delayed its advance for some time. Material assistance in reducing The Triangle was rendered by a battery of the 9th (Scottish) Divisional Artillery. In addition, General Allgood, with the consent of General McCracken, brought back his barrage and attacked again, which enabled the 9th to get forward, and by bringing flanking fire to bear on The Triangle from the north, made it untenable by the enemy. A company of the 8/10th Gordons was able to work round Feuchy Switch Trench, and, with the aid of the 12th H.L.I., 46th Brigade, then coming up to attack the third objective (Brown Line), they captured Hart Work, and outflanked The Triangle, which was

[1] If Blangy had not been dealt with in this manner, it is probable that its capture might have delayed the advance of the remainder of the Division and, possibly, have jeopardised the result.

April 9, 1917. Second objective gained.

shortly afterwards captured by the 45th Brigade, with the help of a tank. By 12.40 P.M. the Division had taken its second objective, and commenced to consolidate its gains.

2 P.M.

At 2 P.M. General Fagan, with the 46th Brigade, advanced through the 44th and 45th on the final objective, the Brown Line or Himalaya Trench. On the right the 12th H.L.I., who had suffered somewhat severely during the morning in assisting the 44th Brigade, at once came under fire from the enemy guns in Battery Valley a few hundred yards in front of them. Silencing these with rifle and machine-gun fire, the battalion continued its advance, in the process of which it captured four guns, and had no further difficulty in reaching its objective. In the centre the 10th Scottish Rifles met with practically no opposition. So eager was this battalion to complete the task allotted to it that it dashed through the British barrage, and was obliged to wait for the 7/8th K.O.S.B. on its left to come up before proceeding farther. The Borderers met with no difficulties until they reached Feuchy Redoubt. Here they were held up by fire from the railway bridge near Spider Corner, and it was not until 2nd Lieutenant Strachan and five men very gallantly rushed the position that they were able to push on. This little party captured 17 Germans in the Redoubt, and accounted for the remainder of the garrison. From this point onwards little opposition was encountered. Feuchy village was cleared with ease, several guns in it being captured.

Final objective gained.

The Brown Line was reached at 4 P.M. through gaps in the enemy wire. It had been the third line of the German system east of Arras, and was well prepared for defence. The British guns had not been able to deal with it as effectively as they had with the first and second lines, with the result that parties of the enemy were found still in occupation interfering with the advance of the 12th Division on the right. It was therefore necessary to clear Himalaya Trench southwards to assist that division, and to make the right flank secure. This was done at once by the 6th Camerons from 45th Brigade,[1] and consolidation commenced. The 91st Field Company now arrived on the scene, and put in very useful work in the construction of strong-points. Fortunately here, as at Martinpuich, an enemy dump full of wire,

[1] Lent to 46th Brigade for this purpose.

pickets, &c., was discovered in front of the position, and saved the necessity of carrying material up from Arras.

April 9, 1917.

Just as they had reached their final objective for the day, the Division was cheered at the sight of cavalry, accompanied by R.H.A., coming up. Unfortunately the cavalry were unable to proceed far owing to uncut wire, and after capturing a few prisoners, the force was withdrawn the same evening to positions west of Arras.

6.30 P.M.

At 6.30 P.M. the 37th Division passed through the Fifteenth, with the object of capturing Monchy-le-Preux and the Green Line, or fourth objective. To support them the 45th Brigade was ordered to move up two battalions. In compliance with this the 6th Camerons, who by this time had completed the clearing of Himalaya Trench and had returned to its own brigade, were moved from the west of Feuchy to the east of that village, the 6/7th Royal Scots Fusiliers from the Railway Triangle, and the 13th Royal Scots from Blangy, to a point just south of Feuchy and to the Feuchy Redoubt. Whilst this was going on, the 44th Brigade, which had remained in the Blue Line, continued its work, and, with the 74th Field Company, R.E., thoroughly consolidated that position. Strong-points were erected, communication trenches commenced, dumps made and filled, &c.

Bitter weather.

It is necessary here to say something regarding the atmospheric conditions, which had an adverse effect on the operations that followed. Up to the day of the attack the weather had been fine. Unfortunately, just as operations started, rain commenced to fall, and by dusk it was snowing heavily. This and squalls of wind made life in the half-dug trenches in the captured ground almost unbearable. With no greatcoats or protection of any kind, working in snow and mud to consolidate the ground it had won so well, the position of the Division was far from enviable, but, conscious of what it had accomplished, it is doubtful if at any period of its existence the *moral* of the Division was higher than it was on the night of April 9, 1917. Between dawn and dusk it had advanced 4000 yards, taken all its objectives, and captured over 500 prisoners, over 40 guns, besides numerous machine-guns and material. Its losses had not been excessive, and the blow dealt to the enemy is best shown by the following sentence from General Ludendorff's 'Memoirs': "The battle near Arras on

Achievements of Division.

April 1917.

April 9 formed a bad beginning to the capital fighting of this year."

The following day, April 10, passed without incident, except that the front line on Orange Hill was shelled severely all day. In snow and sleet, wet through, the Division spent the time in completing the work of consolidation. In front the 37th Division was endeavouring to capture Monchy-le-Preux, but without success. By this time the Germans had brought up fresh troops, additional artillery, and many more machine-guns, with the result that Monchy still defied capture.

During the day the Commander-in-Chief visited Divisional Headquarters, situated in a dug-out east of Arras, and congratulated General McCracken on the grand performance of his Division. A staff officer writes: "During the eighteen months' hard fighting during which I was with the Division, the 9th of April was by far the most successful day we had."

At 11 P.M. orders were received from VI. Corps that the Fifteenth Division would continue the advance the following day at 5 A.M. between Monchy and the Scarpe, in conjunction with the 37th, who were to take Monchy village. On this occasion the objective was a line from Boiry-Nôtre-Dame, due north to the Scarpe, about two miles east of Monchy.

General McCracken at once warned brigade commanders of the coming attack, and ordered all construction work to cease, and the men to get as much rest as possible in the hours remaining before the assault. Divisional Orders for the operation reached brigade commanders about 1 A.M., and battalions about two hours later. On receipt of these, as time was so short, in some cases brigadiers issued their orders verbally to commanding officers, and in others by telephone, supplementing them afterwards by written orders.

Dispositions for next attack.

The attack was carried out by the 46th Brigade (right) and the 45th (left), the dividing line between brigades running due east and west through the southern corner of Lone Copse. The 44th Brigade remained in Divisional reserve in the vicinity of Himalaya Trench and west of Orange Hill. On the left the Scarpe formed the dividing line between the Fifteenth and 4th Divisions, whilst on the right the 37th Division were to attack Monchy-le-Preux and the enemy position to the south of it, the dividing line between it and the Fifteenth Division running due east and west, north of Monchy village.

April 11, 1917.

On the right Brig.-General Fagan attacked with the 10/11th H.L.I., supported by the 7/8th K.O.S.B., keeping the 12th H.L.I. and 10th Scottish Rifles in support and reserve. On the left the 45th Brigade had two battalions in front, the 6th Camerons on the right and 6/7th Royal Scots Fusiliers on the left, with the 13th Royal Scots in support and 11th A. & S. Highlanders in reserve.

The first objective—the only one that matters, as the second was not reached—was the Pelves Ridge, running north-east from Monchy to the Scarpe. Looking at the map it will be seen that this position commands a slight valley, over which it is impossible to advance unseen by the enemy holding the ridge. In front of it lies another ridge overlooking Happy Valley, at the bottom of which is Lone Copse. This ridge was also in German hands, and had to be taken before a farther advance could be made on the Pelves position. Farther to the left, and on the north bank of the Scarpe, Mount Pleasant and Roeux village were held by the enemy, and machine-gun fire from both places swept the ground over which the Fifteenth Division had to advance. On the right Monchy village, a veritable nest of machine-guns, commanded the ground west and north-west of it.

The attack launched, 5 A.M.

At 5 A.M., in a heavy snowstorm, the attack was launched. So short had been the notice that one of the leading battalions of the 45th Brigade, 6th Camerons (Lieut.-Colonel J. C. Russell), marched straight up from Feuchy and deployed for the attack without a halt. Too much cannot be said for the manner in which battalions moved to their positions of assault, and the vigour with which the subsequent advance was carried out. Although it was almost impossible to see more than 50 yards in front on account of the blinding snow, units marched correctly on compass bearings, and, on reaching their respective positions, deployed without hesitation or delay.

At first snow and darkness hid these movements from the enemy, and casualties were consequently few, but the leading lines had not gone far before the enemy sent up S.O.S. signals from Monchy, and heavy artillery and machine-gun fire was opened on the advancing troops. Most of the machine-gun fire came from the vicinity of Monchy,

April 11, 1917.

and this was responsible to a great extent for what now occurred. Attracted by the fire of the machine-guns in and around the village, the left of the 45th Brigade somewhat lost direction, and advanced on the south side of Lone Copse, whilst the leading lines of the 46th Brigade swung to the right to meet the fire from Monchy. The result was that a gap occurred between the 6th Camerons of the 45th Brigade and the 6/7th Royal Scots Fusiliers on their left. The Camerons, keeping in touch with the 10/11th H.L.I. of the 46th Brigade and with that brigade, advanced straight on Monchy itself, although the village had been allotted to the 37th Division.[1]

Monchy.

On reaching Monchy ahead of the 111th Brigade of the 37th Division, the leading lines of the 10/11th H.L.I. and 7/8th K.O.S.B. pushed on eastwards south of the village, and endeavoured to continue the advance on Boiry-Nôtre-Dame, but were checked by heavy fire before they had proceeded more than a few hundred yards. Close behind them followed the remaining companies of the 10/11th H.L.I., the 12th Battalion of that regiment, and the 10th Scottish Rifles (the latter had joined in the general advance, and at 6.10 A.M., when Brig.-General Fagan ordered it to support the leading battalions of his brigade, he found it was already committed to the attack). On reaching Monchy the supporting companies of the 10/11th H.L.I. cleared the houses and cellars as they went, assisted by the Scottish Rifles and 12th H.L.I. Shortly afterwards, about 7 A.M., the 111th Brigade arrived, completed the capture of the village, and undertook the work of "mopping up" and consolidation, being assisted by men of the 3rd Dragoon Guards, Essex Yeomanry, and 10th Hussars, 8th Cavalry Brigade, who had been sent up in view of a possible pursuit should the enemy's line be broken. Unfortunately this was not to be, but the cavalrymen gave exceedingly valuable help in holding the position throughout the day by filling the gaps in the attacking line and in the work of clearing Monchy. A tank, too, whose commander's name is not men-

[1] This loss of direction by the 45th Brigade was partly accounted for by the fact that Lone Copse consisted of long grass and shell-torn stumps of trees, and was therefore hardly recognisable, but there can be little doubt that the presence of the enemy in Monchy had a good deal to do with it. It was a case of Hill 70 over again. The fiercer the fire the more attraction it always had for the Fifteenth Division. The fire from the Dynamitiere at Loos, and here again at Monchy, irresistibly drew the Scotsmen to it.

tioned in any diary, was very skilfully and gallantly handled, and was of great assistance in the capture of the village.

April 11, 1917.

The left held up.

On the left the experiences of the 45th Brigade were as follows: As the leading waves were nearing Lone Copse they suffered severely from machine-gun and artillery fire from Mount Pleasant and Roeux. The 11th A. & S. Highlanders, then lining the river bank north-east of The Triangle, did what they could to counteract this fire from the north bank, and thus protect the left flank of the Fusiliers; but they could not do much, especially as the barrage was by now practically non-existent,[1] and the attack was held up all along the line. Realising the situation, 2nd Lieutenants Hyslop and Grindall of the Camerons rushed forward, and by their own personal bravery steadied the line, and led it forward to an enemy trench 60 yards south-east of the Copse, which was then captured. Here 30 prisoners were taken and machine-gun crews dealt with. By now the Camerons had lost all but four officers, and on reaching the northern outskirts of Monchy were obliged to dig in on a line of strong-points from the north of the village in a north-westerly direction. On the extreme left the 6/7th Royal Scots Fusiliers had been unable to advance very far. Some men had accompanied the Camerons in their advance towards Monchy, but the remainder of the battalion were held up on the north-eastern spur of Orange Hill, and had lost touch with the Camerons on their right.

Shortly before 9 A.M. General McCracken, realising that the attack was definitely checked, especially on the left, ordered the 44th Brigade to advance through the 45th and 46th, and occupy the Monchy-Pelves ridge.

Advance of the 44th Brigade.

At 10.30 A.M. General Marshall advanced, with the 7th Camerons on the right and 8/10th Gordons on the left, the 8th Seaforths being in support and 9th Black Watch in reserve. As had been the case earlier in the day, this attack was met by heavy machine-gun and artillery fire from Mount Pleasant and Roeux, and was likewise checked on the north-eastern slopes of Orange Hill. At 3 P.M. another attempt was made under cover of a creeping barrage, but could only make slow progress. The 7th Camerons swung to the right, and were eventually able to establish a line of posts west and south-west of Lone Copse,

[1] Owing to mud the guns were unable to get forward.

April 11, 1917.

whilst the majority of the battalion proceeded south-east towards Monchy, some eventually reaching the village. About 4.20 P.M. the 8/10th Gordons, under cover of a violent snowstorm, successfully pushed forward some 500 yards up to Lone Copse, but as it was found that both flanks were in the air, and that the position would become untenable when the weather cleared, the battalion was withdrawn to its original line. The 7th Camerons at dusk, withdrawing what men it had in Monchy, took up a line running from the enclosures to the north of the village almost due east and west, south of Lone Copse, to the eastern slopes of Orange Hill, where touch was regained with the 8/10th Gordons.

Events on the right.

To return to the right. Throughout the day mixed parties, consisting of men of all units of the 46th Brigade, with some of the 111th, held the line of shell-holes east of Monchy all day, until the former was relieved early on April 12. It is not possible to give any detailed account of the doings of the various battalions engaged in and around Monchy that day. Men from eight or ten units, infantry and cavalry, to say nothing of R.E., were inextricably mixed up. Most of the officers had become casualties, and it remained to junior officers and N.C.O.'s to "carry on." Right well did they do their work. The following extract, taken from an official diary, shows not only the confusion that existed but gives some idea of the spirit of the men, who, with few leaders to inspire them and left to their own initiative, held the somewhat precarious line until relieved :—

"The spirit of the men throughout was excellent. . . . That many should find themselves committed to fight with other units was inevitable. In Monchy, and engaged in clearing cellars, &c., there was a mixed crowd of soldiers of different units, brigades, and divisions. As the day wore on these sorted themselves out in groups of varying size to hold and consolidate shell-holes and strong-points in and around the village. I am convinced that these men did most excellent work. One lance-corporal—I do not know who he was—was discovered by one of my officers holding a shell-hole with a Lewis-gun and the remnant of a team about 100 yards in advance of the nearest infantry post east of Monchy. Here he remained, oblivious to the fact that a relief had taken place behind him, until the morning of April 12, when he and the remainder of his party came down with some men of the 10th Hussars."

At dusk the Divisional line was a curious one. On the right elements of the 46th Brigade held a line of shell-holes east of Monchy to the north of the village, where the line turned almost at right angles and ran due east and west as far as Lancer Lane, where it again turned north, east of Lone Copse, across Happy Valley to the Scarpe.

April 11, 1917. The line at dusk.

Throughout the day the enemy made repeated attempts, accompanied by heavy artillery fire, to retake Monchy, but without success. Each attack, as it showed signs of developing, was met by withering machine-gun and rifle-fire. Owing to the state of the country it had been impossible to advance the Divisional artillery far enough to protect properly the advanced troops, but notwithstanding this, not one of the enemy attacks succeeded in reaching the Division's front-line trenches.

Relief of Division.

By nightfall heavy casualties, the result of three days' almost continuous fighting, and the appalling weather conditions—snow, sleet, wind, and rain—under which its success had been achieved, had exhausted the Division, and at 5.30 P.M. on the 11th orders were received that it would be relieved during the night by the 17th Division. Starting shortly after midnight, this operation took more time than usual to carry out, and it was not until 8 A.M. on the 12th that it was completed, and the Division once more concentrated in the eastern outskirts of Arras, round the Railway Triangle, and in the original British front line.

Work of the R.A.

Seldom did the gunners get much rest, and the manner in which they worked will ever be remembered with gratitude by the infantry they invariably supported so well. On April 9 and the following night, artillery commanders did their utmost to get their guns forward in spite of snow, mud, no roads, and obstacles in the shape of enemy trenches, shell-holes, &c. Although little of this is mentioned in official diaries, the gunners used every ounce of energy to get their guns as far forward as they did. The following extract from Major F. Graham's letters from the front is worth quoting :—

> "The weather has, of course, been against us. Continual storms of snow, hail, and rain do not make it any easier to move guns across country which has undergone a five days' intense bombardment. Albeit, we got 'em up somehow by relays, with twelve to fourteen horses in the guns, and the gunners harnessed to the waggons."

April 9-11, 1917. Work of the R.A.

Another artillery officer writes :—

"On Easter Monday at 2 P.M. all battery commanders went forward to reconnoitre four miles, and found our infantry hung up for want of artillery support. All guns were stuck in the mud miles behind. Graham and I watched the infantry for an hour, and then found a German field-gun which had been made useless, but we gathered up some bits and managed to repair it. Then with the help of some of the infantry we slewed it round and got the range, fired for two hours, drove the Huns out of Himalaya Trench, and allowed the infantry to get through. Range, 800 yards. Very heavy machine-gun fire, but luckily neither of us hit."

Whilst the remainder of the Division was resting, the sappers were hard at work repairing roads to enable the guns to advance, and directly they were fit for use batteries went forward to positions in the neighbourhood of Tilloy and Feuchy Chapel. As the number of these positions was few, and all were obvious to the enemy, who had been in occupation of the ground for so long, they came in for special attention from the enemy, with the result that the personnel of the batteries, especially of the howitzers, suffered heavy casualties, and several of their guns were damaged by direct hits.[1]

On the following day the Division moved back into billets in Arras, with the exception of the 46th Brigade and the Divisional Headquarters, which moved to Duisans. Disposed thus the Division remained for

[1] The work of the field companies, R.E., had been extraordinarily heavy. Before and during the fighting they carried out the following, in addition to assisting the infantry in consolidation of the ground gained :—

During the attack—

- Seven strong-points erected.
- Two tracks prepared, levelled, and trenches bridged up to Battery Valley (south of Feuchy).
- One track from there on to Feuchy-Feuchy Chapel road.
- River Scarpe cleared for pontoons up to Athies Lock.
- 1200 yards of tramway laid, with 500 yards of trench-boards on either side and 700 yards of boards down the centre.
- 260 yards of support trench dug.
- Reconnaissances carried out and reported on.
- Water supply arranged for.
- Broad gauge railway repaired.
- Dumps constructed.

Prior to the attack—

- 2100 yards of assembly trenches dug.
- Tracks marked out.
- R.E. stores carried up.
- 1500 yards of trench-board track laid.
- Prisoners' cages erected.

a week, during which the necessary reorganisation was carried out. Every unit and formation in the Division had not only worked hard for some time prior to the actual attack, but had lost severely during the operations, and all required rest badly.[1] As was usually the case, the Divisional artillery did not leave the line, but remained in, covering the attacks that went on against the enemy positions east of Monchy. In these operations the gunners lost heavily.

April 1917.

Whilst the Division was resting, changes had taken place in the main plan of operations. On April 13, in view of the limited number of reinforcements expected to be forthcoming for some time, it was decided that no great offensive operation should be undertaken by the Third Army, but that every effort should be made to gain ground by deliberate methods. To give effect to these it was decided to consolidate thoroughly the Monchy position by taking Guemappe and the high ground south of the Cojeul River, and if possible the villages of Vis-en-Artois and Boiry-Nôtre-Dame.

Plan for attack, April 23.

On April 17 the Division received a warning order that the advance of the Third and First Armies would continue on the 21st, afterwards postponed till the 23rd. In this operation the Fifteenth Division was to attack south of the Cambrai road, with the object of capturing the village of Guemappe and the enemy positions east of it, up to and including the village of Vis-en-Artois, 4000 yards east of Guemappe. The first objective, the Blue Line, included Guemappe village and the enemy trenches running due north from the Cojeul, through Cavalry Farm and Saddle Lane to Twin Copses east of Monchy. The second, the Red Line, included the German support trenches east of St Rohart Factory and Bois du Vert ; whilst the third, the Green Line, ran east of Vis-en-Artois and Boiry-Nôtre-Dame.

On the right of the Fifteenth Division was the 150th Brigade, 50th Division, and on the left the 88th Brigade of the 29th, dividing lines being the Cojeul River on the south and east and west line from La Bergere on the Arras-Cambrai road through the southern corner of the Bois-du-Vert.

The attack was to be carried out by the 44th and 45th Brigades,

[1] See Appendix I for casualties.

April 1917. on the right and left respectively, the 46th being kept in Divisional reserve. The dividing line between brigades was from the bend in Spear Lane eastwards, just north of Cavalry Farm, which was in the 44th Brigade area.

Objectives of Division, April 23. The object was the capture and consolidation of the Blue and Red Lines, the attack on the latter being timed to commence seven hours after zero. In order to make special provision for the capture of Guemappe village, General McCracken instructed Brig.-General Marshall to detail one battalion to deal with it alone, whilst the remaining three battalions pushed forward to the Blue Line. On the left, as the front of the 29th Division was farther forward than that of the Fifteenth, the right battalion of the 45th Brigade was directed to keep in line with the left battalion of the 44th, whilst the left had to advance in echelon forward, to connect with the right flank battalion of the 88th Brigade.

Dispositions. To comply with these instructions, Brig.-General Marshall disposed the 44th Brigade as follows. The 8th Seaforths were detailed to capture and consolidate Guemappe, sending one company round the north of the village to block its eastern exits. The 7th Camerons, followed by the Black Watch, who were to leave their assembly trenches twenty minutes after zero, were to push past the northern end of Guemappe, and when clear of it extend to the right as far as the Cojeul, advance and capture the Blue Line, from the river to Cavalry Farm inclusive, preparatory to a further advance on the Red Line. The 8/10th Gordons were kept in reserve to provide carrying parties for dumps and R.E. stores. General Marshall also sent one trench-mortar and two machine-guns with each of the attacking battalions, detailing the remaining guns of the 44th Trench-Mortar Battery and 44th Machine-Gun Company to assist in covering the Seaforth attack of Guemappe and the advance of the Camerons and Black Watch on the Blue Line. He also arranged that one section, 74th Field Company, and one platoon 9th Gordons (Pioneers) would construct a strong-point just south of Cavalry Farm when captured, and that one section, 91st Field Company, R.E., would bridge the Cojeul River south of Guemappe as soon as it could get forward.

On the left Brig.-General Allgood had a somewhat easier task.

He arranged to attack with the 11th A. & S. Highlanders on the right, 13th Royal Scots on the left, keeping the 6/7th Royal Scots Fusiliers in support and the 6th Camerons in reserve. He ordered the 13th Royal Scots to advance in echelon forward to connect with the left battalion of the 88th Brigade (8th Battalion Worcester Regiment), whilst the 11th A. & S. Highlanders were to attack in line with the 44th Brigade.[1] He also sent a section of the 73rd Field Company with the leading battalions for the usual consolidation work, the remainder of the R.E. and 9th Gordons (Pioneers) working directly under orders from the C.R.E.

Preparations for attack on April 23, 1917.

The attack was covered by the combined artillery of the 3rd, under Lieut.-Colonel G. T. Mair, D.S.O., and Fifteenth, under Lieut.-Colonel H. Christie, D.S.O., Divisions, under Brig.-General E. B. Macnaghten, D.S.O., the first covering the advance of the 44th Brigade and the second that of the 45th. In addition, barrage fire from the 46th, as well as from those guns of the 44th and 45th Machine-Gun Companies that did not accompany the attack, was arranged for. Lastly, one male and one female tank were attached to the 44th Brigade to assist in the capture of Guemappe.

From the above it will be seen that every detail had been well and carefully thought out. It was a somewhat complicated operation, but one that would have succeeded had not fate and the Germans intervened. Unfortunately, by this time thoroughly alarmed by what had taken place during the last fortnight, the Germans had reinforced their front line very strongly both with men and machine-guns, to say nothing of artillery. The enemy troops holding the line on the Divisional front were the 18th Bavarian Regiment of the 3rd Bavarian Division. In addition to the usual garrison, Guemappe, like Monchy, was full of machine-guns, and formed an exceedingly strong post in the German line. More guns were also on the rising ground at and around Cavalry Farm, whilst others, south of the Cojeul, commanded the ground between the farm and village.

During the night of April 19th/20th the 44th and 45th Brigades relieved the 87th in the front-line trench east of La Bergere and Marliere. The weather was dry, and, though the ground was still soft,

[1] Map 8.

Preparations for attack on April 23, 1917.

this relief was fairly quickly carried out, some difficulty being experienced owing to no moon and lack of landmarks. The line taken over consisted of a single untraversed trench, running roughly due north and south from Marliere to La Bergere, with a support line some distance behind it. On the right, in front of the 44th Brigade, were two strong-points, but otherwise the line had nothing to commend it in the way of security.

The 44th Brigade (right) put the 8/10th Gordons in the line, with the 9th Black Watch in support, keeping the 8th Seaforths and 7th Camerons in Arras for the time being. On the left the 6/7th Royal Scots Fusiliers and 6th Camerons of the 45th Brigade took over the line, the 13th Royal Scots and 11th A. & S. Highlanders remaining in Arras.

For the next two days both brigades were engaged in completing their preparation for the attack. During darkness patrols went out to discover what they could of the enemy's position, and, where possible, to establish advanced posts. The 44th Brigade successfully pushed forward a chain of strong-points in front of Spear Lane and between it and the Cojeul. "Jumping-off" trenches were dug by both brigades; dumps for bombs, S.A.A., &c., were built, and by the morning of the 22nd all was in readiness. The same night the assaulting battalions moved into their positions of assembly in the front line and newly dug trenches, and at 4.45 A.M. on the 23rd the assault was launched.[1]

The attack launched.

The morning was darker than usual, and owing to this the 7th Camerons inclined rather too much to their left, thus leaving a gap between their right flank and the left of the Seaforths. For some reason the 9th Black Watch left their trenches some minutes too soon, with the result that, knowing nothing of the loss of direction of the Camerons, they filled the gap between that battalion and the Seaforths, and before it had proceeded far the centre of the 44th Brigade attack consisted of mixed parties of Black Watch, Seaforths, and Camerons.

[1] An interesting story is related by Major-General Pollock, who writes: "During this period a company kitchen was established in a certain ruined house. One morning, as the cooks were preparing 'gun-fire tea,' an enemy 'plane came over, flying very low. One of the cooks grabbed a rifle, fired one shot, and down came the machine, bursting into flames as it fell."

Almost as soon as the attack started the enemy put down a heavy and accurate artillery and machine-gun barrage along the whole front, and brought enfilade fire to bear on the 44th Brigade from the high ground south of the Cojeul, causing severe casualties, especially to the Seaforths. The advance was checked by this barrage about 300 yards west of Guemappe, and a desperate fight for fire superiority ensued, during which the Seaforths, creeping from shell-hole to shell-hole, were able to advance about 100 yards.

April 23, 1917.

The situation remained thus till about 7.30 A.M., when the enemy holding Guemappe showed signs of giving way. This was due to two reasons. On the south of the Cojeul the 50th Division had worked forward and dealt with the enemy holding the high ground near Wancourt Tower, thus relieving the 44th Brigade from the galling enfilade fire coming from that direction. The other reason was that the 7th Camerons and a party of about seventy men, chiefly 9th Black Watch, had been able to work round the north of Guemappe and threaten to outflank it. The advance of this Black Watch party, under Captain Morrison, was very largely due to the gallantry of No. 240046, Sergeant J. Gibb, who, single-handed, worked his way round the end of a trench and destroyed an enemy machine-gun and its crew who were holding up the advance. By 9.30 A.M. the advance of the 50th Division had cleared the remainder of the enemy from the high ground south of the Cojeul, and shortly afterwards the 8th Seaforths were able to advance right through Guemappe, and the 44th Brigade line then went forward to the east of the village.

Guemappe taken.

Whilst this was going on the 45th Brigade, although meeting with less resistance than had the 44th, had not been able to get very far, first on account of the 44th having been held up, and secondly, because they, too, had suffered severely from the enemy's barrage fire. They, too, like the 44th, had become mixed up almost from the start. The A. & S. Highlanders, with some of the Royal Scots, had succeeded in occupying Bullet Trench, whilst some of the latter battalion had pushed farther forward towards the Red Line in the direction of Pick Trench.

At 7.15 A.M. Brig.-General Allgood, learning how matters stood, sent up one company, " C " Company of the 6/7th Royal Scots Fusiliers,

April 23, 1917.

to support the leading troops of the Royal Scots; another, "D" Company, to support the A. & S. Highlanders; and a third to make a detour to the north, and thus, by attacking String Trench from that direction, take the enemy still in it from behind. Artillery support for this movement was arranged, and at 11.30 A.M. the Argylls reported that they had captured part of String Trench, but that the enemy still held the remainder of it, and Shovel Trench just behind it.

For some time after this no definite news was received from the front line. From the very commencement of the action all units became more or less mixed up, and authoritative reports were difficult to obtain. What further complicated matters was the fact that visual signalling was out of the question, owing to the dust and smoke caused by exploding shells. At 10 A.M., however, the F.O.O. of the 45th Brigade sent in a report, from which it was gathered that the situation was as follows: parties of the Seaforths, Black Watch, and Camerons held the 44th Brigade line running in an irregular line from the Cojeul northwards, just east of Guemappe, thence to and along Dragoon Lane, where it joined the 45th Brigade. Parties of Seaforths and Black Watch were in Guemappe itself, whilst others of the latter battalion and Camerons held Hammer Trench and the Guemappe-Les Fosses Farm Road. On the left similar mixed parties of A. & S. Highlanders, Royal Scots Fusiliers, and Royal Scots were holding Bullet Trench, and part of Dragoon Lane north of the Cambrai road.

At 10.45 A.M., as both the 50th and 29th Divisions had made good progress, General McCracken decided to launch a fresh attack with the 46th Brigade at noon, but before this could take place the situation had altered.

Guemappe lost.

On the right an enemy counter-attack drove back the left of the 50th Division, and enveloped the right flanks of the 44th Brigade, which once more became exposed to enfilade fire from the south. All detachments north of Guemappe held their ground, but as the enemy attack developed and the right flank of the brigade became more and more exposed, the Seaforths and Black Watch east of Guemappe were compelled to withdraw to the west of the village. The posts of the 7th Camerons, on the high ground to the north, held firm, thereby preventing further enemy movement north of the Cojeul. These posts, although both their flanks were in the air, gallantly held out for four hours, until ordered to return to the old German front line. During all this no change had occurred on the front of the 45th Brigade.

April 23, 1917.

Shortly after noon, as a fresh enemy counter-attack appeared imminent, Brig.-General Marshall sent up two companies of the 8/10th Gordons to be in readiness, if such attack developed, and arranged for an artillery barrage on Guemappe, the western and northern faces of the village across Hammer Trench, and up to Dragoon Lane. Unfortunately the artillery did not know that the whole line had not been withdrawn, with the result that Captain Morrison's party suffered somewhat severely until withdrawn according to orders.

Further German counter-attacks.

As the day wore on the enemy made several further counter-attacks on the Divisional front, none of which met with the slightest success. As General McCracken says in his report: "The 44th and 45th Brigades kept on fighting, gradually breaking down the enemy's resistance and causing him severe casualties." From the commencement the fight had been a "soldier's battle," and its ultimate success is very largely due to the stubborn manner in which the mixed parties of men who, with very few officers remaining, and in spite of heavy losses, defied defeat, and against whom the German counter-attacks in the afternoon failed one after another.

At 2.50 P.M. General McCracken sent the following Division telegram, G. 126:—

"Situation from reports up to 2 P.M. There is no one in Guemappe village. Enemy holds Guemappe Cemetery, Tank Trench, and southern portion of Shovel Trench. Our troops hold Dragoon Lane from Northern houses of Guemappe up to Bullet Trench. We also hold Shovel Trench as far south as main road. 44th and 45th Brigades will capture at once the southern portion of Shovel Trench and Guemappe Cemetery. Heavy artillery will continue to engage Guemappe village and isolate it. At 6 P.M. 46th Brigade will pass through the front line of 44th and 45th Brigades, leaving Guemappe on their right. 46th Brigade will capture the Blue Line. Line to be consolidated and communication established with flanking divisions. 50th Division, south of the river, are carrying out a simultaneous attack. 44th and 45th Brigades, under cover of 46th Brigade attack, will consolidate the ground already gained."

As the whole of his Division would now be committed to the action, the 8th Brigade, 3rd Division, was placed at General McCracken's

April 23, 1917.

disposal to be used if required. It did not, however, take part in the fighting, and returned to its own Division the following afternoon.

In compliance with the above orders, Brig.-General Fagan directed the 10th Scottish Rifles (right), and 10/11th H.L.I. (left) to lead the attack of the 46th Brigade on the Blue Line, in conjunction with that of the 44th and 45th on their limited objectives. He put the 12th H.L.I. in support behind the 10th Scottish Rifles, keeping the 7/8th K.O.S.B. in brigade reserve. At the same time he arranged for a machine-gun barrage from all available guns of the 46th Machine-Gun Company, in addition to one by the Divisional artillery that had already been ordered.

Successful attack of 46th Brigade.

The attack was well carried out. On the right Captain Morrison, the Black Watch, who had done so well throughout the day, collected and organised the men round him—Camerons, Seaforths, and Black Watch,—and led them forward to the cemetery. Unfortunately this very gallant officer was killed before he got more than a few yards, but the attack he initiated swept on and reached its objective, thus regaining all ground taken by the 44th Brigade in the morning east of Guemappe.

Shortly before the attack commenced, at 5.30 P.M., General Fagan received a message from General McCracken that, as there was some uncertainty regarding the situation on the flanks of the Division, the artillery barrage would rest for half an hour on a north and south line just west of Cavalry Farm. Orders to this effect were at once sent out, but did not reach the 10/11th H.L.I. in time. This battalion had already left its position of assault, and, knowing nothing of the alteration, passed through the barrage, suffering severely whilst doing so, not only from the British artillery but from the enemy machine-guns from Cavalry Farm, especially the right leading company, "B." This unavoidable occurrence somewhat disorganised the whole of the left attack, but the support company, "C," came up, and, taking the place of "B," the attack swept on.

By 6.30 P.M. the Blue Line was reached by the leading companies of H.L.I., who at once commenced to consolidate on a line running from The Copse in 0.8. to a point about 300 yards north-east of Cavalry Farm. Here they remained for some time, inflicting severe loss on the enemy by rifle and machine-gun fire. On the right the Scottish Rifles had advanced in artillery formations with the remainder of the 44th Brigade, and when clear of Guemappe had increased their frontage so as to protect the right flank of the Division. They found that Cavalry Farm was still strongly held, and, seeing the 10/11th H.L.I. in Knife Trench, decided to dig in on a line level with them. Unfortunately the artillery barrage stopped short of the farm, which otherwise could have been easily taken. The situation remained thus till 8 P.M. Neither the 29th nor 50th Divisions had been able to get forward at all, with the result that the Fifteenth Division found both its flanks exposed.

April 23, 1917.

Shortly after 8 o'clock the enemy, taking advantage of shell-holes and folds in the ground, commenced massing in considerable numbers on both flanks of the H.L.I. Realising their position, and not being able to prevent the enemy from getting behind their right flank, the two companies in the Blue Line withdrew at 8.30 to Shovel Trench, taking all their wounded—a considerable number—with them. Seeing the H.L.I. move back, the Scottish Rifles followed suit, and commenced to dig and consolidate a new trench south and a little east of Shovel Trench, both battalions working under heavy and continuous shell-fire.

Position at nightfall.

At nightfall the position of the Division was as follows: 46th Brigade in the front line, from right to left, one company (D) 12th H.L.I., 10th Scottish Rifles, 6/7th Royal Scots Fusiliers, from the 45th Brigade, and remainder of 10/11th H.L.I. in Shovel Trench; whilst the 12th H.L.I., less one company, were in support, just behind the 10th Scottish Rifles, and the 7/8th K.O.S.B. in reserve between Guemappe and La Bergere. 45th Brigade, less one battalion, in support of the left of the 46th, in the vicinity of Spear Lane and La Bergere. 44th Brigade in support of the right of the line, north and west of Guemappe.

During the night of the 23rd/24th the 44th Brigade was withdrawn, and became Divisional reserve, the 8/10th Gordons remaining in the original front-line trenches west of Guemappe in support of the 46th Brigade.

The night passed quietly, troops in the front line being engaged

April 24, 1917.

in deepening and strengthening their trenches and wire. A party of 80 men from the 7/8th K.O.S.B. succeeded in getting up water and S.A.A. to the two leading battalions. This party did magnificent work, and only returned to its battalion at 5 A.M., just as dawn was breaking.

The morning of the 24th brought no enemy counter-attack, and until the afternoon conditions were more or less "normal." At 2 P.M. Brig.-General Fagan received orders to resume the attack at 4 P.M., and a warning order was at once sent out to battalions. So short was the time that the actual orders for the attack in some instances only reached company commanders five minutes before the attack started.

The advance resumed.

On the right were the 10th Scottish Rifles and one company, 12th H.L.I., "D" Company, with the 8/10th Gordons from the 44th Brigade in close support. This latter battalion had taken the place of the 10/11th H.L.I., who had been withdrawn on account of the heavy casualties it had suffered the day before. On the left the 12th H.L.I., less one company, attacked with the 7/8th K.O.S.B. in support, and 6th Camerons (45th Brigade) in reserve. The Borderers, having been able to move up from their position in reserve by platoons, had suffered little loss in so doing, the dividing line between battalions being an east and west line through the junction of Cyclist Lane and the Cambrai road.

At the very start the Scottish Rifle advance encountered a murderous machine-gun fire from Cavalry Farm, and, unable to advance through the hail of bullets, dug in on a line just west and north of the farm. On the left there was some confusion to begin with. "B" Company, 12th H.L.I., was caught in the German counter-barrage, and had one platoon put out of action. In spite of this, the remaining three platoons and "C" Company continued the advance, and by 4.35 P.M. had reached the Blue Line, but, as on the previous day, owing to fire from Cavalry Farm, they were compelled to dig in on a line running from The Copse south to Saddle Lane, and thence along Knife Trench. During the evening it was found that the battalion was too much to the right. This was at once rectified by Major Dennis, 7/8th K.O.S.B., who, seeing the gap, sent up twelve

Lewis-guns and two platoons of his battalion to form posts in the interval between the 12th H.L.I. and The Copse. In his report on the operations, Lieut.-Colonel St John says: "No doubt the promptitude with which we were supported by the 7/8th K.O.S.B., and the line prolonged, did much to ensure the safety of the left flank."

April 24, 1917.

By five o'clock the whole attack had come to a standstill. The enemy, now in considerable force, and occupying a line of shell-holes, was evidently prepared to move back if pressed, but intense machine-gun fire from Cavalry Farm and from the neighbourhood of the Bois du Vert put farther advance of the 46th Brigade out of the question.

Line at nightfall.

At nightfall the line ran from The Copse south to Saddle Lane, thence along Knife Trench to the Cambrai road, and from these south and south-west, west of Cavalry Farm, to the Cojeul. Although the line was not continuous, it was consolidated during the night, and a communication trench dug by the 9th Gordons (Pioneers) north of the Cambrai road. By this time the opposing lines were very close together, so close indeed that it was found impossible, owing to heavy sniping at close range that night, to bring up either water or rations to the front line.

The following day, the 25th, passed quietly. During the day General McCracken decided to relieve the 46th Brigade, and to entrust the task of completing the capture of the Blue Line to the 44th and 45th Brigades. He therefore relieved the 46th Brigade by the 44th (right) and 45th (left) on the night of the 25th/26th, and issued his orders for the forthcoming attack.

April 26, 1917.

In preparation for the assault on the farm, the trenches held by the Division opposite it were evacuated on the 26th, and the enemy positions subjected to a continuous and heavy bombardment during the whole of the 26th, after which the attack was to be delivered under cover of darkness. For the capture of Cavalry Farm, Brig.-General Marshall disposed his brigade as follows: 9th Black Watch on the right, 7th Camerons on the left, with the 8/10th Gordons in right support and 8th Seaforths left support.

Capture of Cavalry Farm.

Advancing close up to an exceedingly good and accurate barrage, the assault was delivered at 10.30 P.M. On the right the Black Watch reached the Blue Line, and established a series of posts on the crest

April 27, 1917.

line from the river northwards. On the left the Camerons cleared the farm with some slight opposition, and reached an enemy trench on the Cambrai road about 150 yards east of it. Unfortunately they found the enemy in strong force, evidently expecting an attack on a much larger scale, and, coming under heavy enfilade fire from Tool Trench, they were obliged to withdraw, leaving a post 50 yards east of the farm. This post was rushed by the enemy about midnight, and the garrison forced to retire. About 2 A.M. the Camerons sent out two officer patrols to secure the farm and gain touch with the Black Watch. These patrols established three posts to the south and south-east of the farm, but, owing to the approach of dawn, they were not able to get in touch with the Black Watch, but the three posts established effectively denied the enemy access to the farm.

At 8 A.M. the Germans rushed two of the Black Watch posts near the river, but the remainder and the Cameron posts held their ground and inflicted heavy casualties on the enemy throughout the 27th and night of the 27th/28th, when they were relieved by the 8th Seaforths and 8/10th Gordons.

On the left, north of the Cambrai road, the 45th Brigade had taken over from the 46th, and held the line with the 6th Camerons and 11th A. & S. Highlanders, the 13th Royal Scots and 6/7th Royal Scots Fusiliers being kept in reserve. Until Cavalry Farm had been definitely taken no advance on this part of the line was possible; the brigade were therefore employed on the work of consolidation and defence until the night of the 27th/28th, when it was relieved by the 167th Brigade.

By this time, after some of the heaviest fighting it had yet experienced, fighting that had been spread over five days, the Division was not in a state to undertake further offensive action. Every unit had lost heavily, and all required time for reorganisation and refitting.

Relief of Division.

On the night of the 27th/28th the 56th Division commenced taking over the line, relief being completed and command passing at 10 A.M. on the 29th, by which time the Division had withdrawn to rest, refit, and train in the area Dainville, Warlus, Duisans, Berneville, and Siemencourt, with headquarters at Warlus. The following, taken from a Gordon diary, will show the state of battalions when they were relieved: "About midnight on the 28th/29th the London Division arrived to relieve us. They were a very strong Division, so much so, in fact, that the battalion that relieved us only sent up one company to relieve the entire battalion. . . . That company alone was stronger than our whole battalion. . . . During the six days we had advanced altogether about 2250 yards, and taken several hundred prisoners. It was not an enormously successful battle, considering that we lost nearly half the Division; our own battalion came out with only about 98 men and 5 officers."

April 1917.

Casualties.

It is somewhat difficult to speak with accuracy regarding the casualties suffered by the Division on this occasion. The Divisional main dressing-station had been situated at Nouveau Quai, Arras, and a good many of the wounded found their way there, but, owing to the extraordinary nature of the fighting, many reported to the nearest dressing-station, and from there were sent to various casualty clearing stations. In one diary it states: "It is almost impossible to form an accurate estimate of casualties, as small parties continued to come in from other regiments to right and left of us, with which they had been mixed up." Some diaries only mention the number of officers killed, giving no names. On April 9 the strength of the Division going into action was 433 officers and 11,499 other ranks. The total casualties for the month are given in A. and Q. diary as follows:—

Officers—
Killed, 80; wounded, 203; missing, 10—293.

Other Ranks—
Killed, 887; wounded, 4410; missing, 723—6020.

Total—6313.

Of these, the first phase was responsible for about 2700, and the second, the attack on Guemappe, for about 3000, of which 144 were officers.

On May 3 the VI. Corps Commander, General Haldane, visited Warlus, and presented decorations to seventy-six recipients for good work done during the recent fighting.

May 1917.

Now followed the longest "rest" period enjoyed by the Division throughout the war. From April 29 until the middle of June training and recreation was carried out some distance behind the line, in good weather and amongst peaceful surroundings. For the first ten days the Division remained in the Warlus area to support another attack on May 2. Its services were, however, not required, and on the 4th and following days it moved to Le Cauroy, on transfer from the VI. to the XVIII. Corps (Lieut.-General Maxse), Third Army. By the evening of the 8th the move was completed, and brigade groups were billeted as follows, with Divisional Headquarters at Le Cauroy:—

44th Brigade group at Grand Rullecourt.
45th Brigade at Sus St Leger.
46th Brigade group at Barly.
Field companies and 9th Gordons (Pioneers) at Gouy-en-Artois.

The R.A.

The Divisional artillery remained in the line under command of G.O.C. 56th Division until May 25, when it moved to Rebreuve, and once more came under its Divisional Commander's orders.

On May 21 Divisional Headquarters moved to Willeman, and by the evening of the 23rd brigade groups were billeted as follows:—

44th Brigade group at Wail.
45th Brigade group and 45th Field Ambulance at Fontaine L'Etalon.
46th Brigade group and 46th Field Ambulance at Vaulx.
C.R.E. and field companies at Nœux.
9th Gordons (Pioneers) at Oeuf.

In this quiet and comfortable area the Division remained until it moved north. One rest period is much the same as another; all are delightful memories to look back on, but the historian can seldom find incidents of sufficient importance to warrant mention. Whilst training of all kinds was carried out, recreation was not overlooked. Although the middle of summer, football shared the honours with cricket, but alas! the recent fighting had deprived most units of their best men. A Gordon Highlander, writing on this subject, states: "All forms of sport were resuscitated. It was when trying to get a team together that one realised the gaps the late battle had made in our ranks. In my platoon alone eight of my champion eleven were now casualties. Four of these, the best I had in the platoon, had been killed. . . . These four had been out since June 1915, and had come through the fighting at and round Loos and on the Somme without a scratch."

May 1917.

On May 13 a Divisional horse show was held near Bullecourt, which was attended by the Commander-in-Chief, the Army Commander, and others. On this occasion the massed pipes and drums of the Division, 232 men in all, supplied the music. It was an inspiring sight—and sound,—and greatly impressed the Commander-in-Chief.

The Horse Show.

A new formation joined the Division during May—namely, the 216th Divisional Employment Company. It was composed of men who were not fit enough to take their place in the fighting line, but who were able to carry out work behind it, thus releasing others. It was a sound move, as experienced men were scarce, and this company did exceedingly good work whilst with the Division.

The first fortnight in June was devoted to Brigade field firing and tactical exercises, and by the middle of the month the Division was once more fit and ready to resume its position in the front line.

By this time it had become known definitely that the next sphere of operations would be the notorious Ypres salient. No one was therefore surprised when, on the 11th, orders for the move were issued.

There was, however, an unpleasant surprise in store for the Division. In the Divisional G.S. diary, under the date June 15, the following entry occurs: "Verbal information received that G.O.C. Fifteenth Division is to take over command of XIII. Corps." No one could grudge General McCracken his promotion, but all ranks could, and did, regret his loss. Knowing the Divisional Commander as he does, the author can well imagine his feelings when he penned the following farewell message:—

G.O.C. leaves Division.

"SPECIAL ORDER by Major-General F. W. N. McCracken, K.C.B., D.S.O., Commanding Fifteenth (Scottish) Division.

"In bidding farewell to the Fifteenth (Scottish) Division, I wish to express my heartfelt thanks to all ranks for their continued assistance to me throughout the period of over two years since I assumed command.

June 1917.

"The standard of discipline and training which has enabled the Division to achieve the results already obtained will, I am convinced, lead in the future to still greater successes. The maintenance of this standard, added to the high sense of duty of all ranks in the Division, will inevitably enable them to obtain the final victory before returning to the land of their birth, which is already so justly proud of their fine achievements.

"I shall at all times watch their movements with the deepest interest, and I wish them every possible success in the future.

"(Signed) F. W. N. McCracken, *Major-General,*
Commanding Fifteenth (Scottish) Division."

June 16, 1917.

Appointed to the Division in March 1915, General McCracken took over a body of men nearly all with only a few months' experience of soldiering. With infinite patience and consummate knowledge of men and their capabilities and limitations, he produced a Division second to none—one that, within a few weeks of landing in France, fought and won at Loos what was then considered to be the most sanguinary battle in modern history. Later, on the Somme, and again at Arras, his Division had more than maintained its high reputation. It may be truly said that the successes of the Fifteenth Division, and the reputation it gained during his period of command, were very largely due to the personality of its commander.

Major-General H. F. THUILLIER, C.B., C.M.G.

CHAPTER VI.

THE BATTLES OF YPRES, 1917.[1]

June 1917.

GENERAL McCRACKEN was succeeded by Major-General H. F. Thuillier, C.B., C.M.G., R.E. A Major in 1914, General Thuillier had been successively C.R.E., 1st Division, in 1915; Brig.-General commanding 2nd Infantry Brigade, 1915-16; and Director of Gas Services at G.H.Q., 1916-17.

The move to Ypres.

On June 16 the move northwards to join the XIX. Corps (Major-General H. E. Watts) commenced. The 46th Brigade group, consisting of the 46th Infantry Brigade, 73rd Field Company, R.E., 9th Gordons (Pioneers), 46th Field Ambulance, and No. 4 Train, moved by train from Bouquemaison and Bonnieres to Vlamertinge, accompanied by the C.R.E. and 91st Field Company, R.E.; while the artillery, starting the same day and halting at Bergueneuse, St Hilaire, and Steenbecque, proceeded by road to the new area.

46th Brigade in the line.

On the 19th and 20th the 46th Brigade relieved the 166th (55th Division) in the right sector of the XIX. Corps front. The length of the Divisional line was, roughly, 1300 yards, and ran from the Ypres-Roulers railway on the right to Warwick Farm. This was held for the first time by the 7/8th K.O.S.B. on the right and the 10/11th H.L.I. on the left, the 10th Scottish Rifles being in support, and the 12th H.L.I. in reserve in Toronto Camp between Poperinghe and Vlamertinge.

The remainder of the Division started by road on the 21st. Their departure was a source of great regret to the inhabitants of the villages they had occupied for so long. The following entry in a private diary testifies to the somewhat misplaced generosity of their hosts

[1] Map 9.

June 1917.

on this occasion: "June 21. Left . . . with regret . . . Arrived at . . . late at night. We had to leave an officer behind to look after about twenty or thirty of our 'weaker brethren,' who could not march owing to the thoroughness of their farewell to the place. . . . Nearly every man in 'D' Company had his water-bottle filled with beer (instead of the regulation water), in spite of orders to the contrary. . . . When we got on the move the beer became frothy and bubbled over. Major W.—this was his first experience in command—dealt most admirably with this somewhat difficult situation." The march was accomplished in eight days. The weather was good, and, with the exception of an air raid on the 26th, no untoward incident occurred.[1]

The Ypres battle-ground.

It is now necessary to describe the ground over which the Division, concentrated in the XIX. Corps area, with Divisional Headquarters one mile south-west of Vlamertinge, was to operate for the next two and a half months.

Many word-pictures have been painted of the sinister "salient," but no writer will ever be able to describe it as it appeared, and still appears, to those whose fate it was to enter it between 1914 and 1918. Imagine a huge semicircle of ground with a radius of some three miles, and in the centre of the circle the battered shell of an ancient city. From the ruins the ground slopes gently upwards to the east and south-east to a crest-line running, roughly, from St Eloi in the south, through Zwartelen, north-east and east of Hooge, thence north to Frezenberg, and on the north-west gradually sloping downwards to Weltje and Pilckem, where the ridge disappears in the flat plains of Flanders. This crest-line had been held by the enemy for the past

[1] Brigade groups billeted at the following places on the march:—

June 21, 44th	Brigade	Group,	St Croix.
45th	"	"	Blangermont.
June 22, 44th	"	"	Pernes.
45th	"	"	Tangry area.
June 23, 44th	"	"	St Hilaire area.
45th	"	"	Ligny les Aires area.
June 25, 44th	"	"	Thiennes area.
45th	"	"	Boesenghem area.
June 26, 44th	"	"	Caestre area.
45th	"	"	Hazebrouck area.
June 28, 44th	"	"	Toronto and St Lawrence Camps.
45th	"	"	" "

three years, and from it they had been able to make life almost unendurable for the defenders of Ypres. June 1917.

Nearly the whole of this semicircle is not more than 20 feet above sea-level. Much of it was little better than a marsh even in dry weather, water being met with a few feet below the surface. Owing to this, and to the fact that the Germans were able to drain their position on the ridge into that of their opponents on the lower ground, it was necessary to provide some sort of defence other than deep trenches. In the front and support lines the trenches were barely 3 feet deep, further protection being obtained by building up breastworks and parados of sandbags and brushwood. With the exception of the front system and main communication trenches, there were no parados to give protection from shells bursting behind.

The Divisional sector.

The sector occupied by the Division lay to the east-north-east of Ypres, and extended from the Roulers Railway on the right to approximately the line of the Potijze road on the left. The town of Ypres formed the only means of approach by road to the sector; in fact, the sole means of communication for wheeled transport was along the main road, passing the famous Cloth Hall and through the Menin Gate. This road was subject at all times, day and night, to shell-fire, sometimes of great intensity. In consequence of this, its use by troops was forbidden by day, and tracks skirting the city to the north and south were used instead. By night, however, supplies and munitions for the line had necessarily to be conveyed along this road, and, as the enemy had a preference for using gas-shells during the hours of darkness, a procession of transport, the drivers, and often the horses too, either wearing gas-masks or with these in a position for immediate wear, would be seen streaming through the Menin Gate for several hours every night.

From the outskirts of the city to the front trench line, a distance of between two and three miles, the country was overlooked by the high ground occupied by the enemy to the east. Up to the reserve line no communication trenches existed, but unseen approach to this line could always be obtained by exercising due caution, owing to the existence of numerous hedges and trees. Similarly it was not difficult, when the Division first went in, to find positions giving

June-July 1917. The Divisional sector.

concealment for the Divisional artillery; but prior to the attack of July 31, when the artillery was greatly augmented, this was no longer possible, and many of the guns had to be put in the open under rough camouflage cover.

From the reserve line to the front system communication trenches existed, but owing to the water level they were to a large extent built up instead of excavated, and in many places consisted of little more than screening, giving a bare cover from view. There were, when the Division went in, no dug-outs, and the only cover was some cellars in Potijze and in the ruins of l'Ecole; also others in the convent and certain selected buildings in Ypres.

From the front trenches the crest of the Frezenberg Ridge, about 1500 yards away, was visible, but in some parts the view was restricted by a low ridge only some 400 yards distant. From observation-posts in the rear could be plainly seen, not only the brown outline of the Frezenberg Ridge, but also, behind it, other ridges in succession, till on the far sky-line could be distinguished, with the aid of a telescope, a village with a white church spire, Passchendaele. This was known to be the ultimate objective which would give command over the Ghent plain, and consequently was looked at with great interest by the Division during the period of preparation for the battle. The Fifteenth Division, however, was not fated to reach that goal, for it was not till two months after it had left the salient, and after long and bitter struggles in mud and blood, that the Passchendaele Ridge was gained by other formations.

Even at this early stage the ground on the enemy's side of the line was mostly a waste of rolling brown ridges with few distinguishing features. It was just possible to pick out the line of the Ypres-Roulers railway, the remains of North Station Buildings, and a few others, such as Grey Ruin, Bavaria House, and Square Farm just behind the German front line. These latter were known to have been reinforced with concrete, strongly wired, and held by machine-guns, thus constituting formidable strong-points in the enemy system of defence. Other buildings treated in like manner, such as Borry Farm, Beck House, Potsdam, &c., were known to exist farther back, but were not visible from the British trenches. These ruins were very much alike, and it is important to remember this, for later, in the excitement of battle, mistakes were made regarding the situation of some of these fortified fragments in the sea of mud and fortified shell-holes.

June-July 1917.

But, desolate and featureless as this ground looked in June when the Division first saw it, its condition was infinitely worse in August after every yard of it had been churned by the unprecedented bombardment to which it was subjected, and after the torrential rain of the first few days of that month. Of its condition, then, and the effect of that condition on the operations of the battle, more will be said in due course.

Preparations for the Offensive.

The Division had hardly taken over the line before it became apparent that operations on a large scale would soon take place. Army and Corps instructions followed one another in quick succession. From these it was seen that the Commander-in-Chief was about to launch the offensive in Flanders which he had originally planned some months before. It had been put off owing to the wishes of the French, and the Arras offensive had taken its place. When that phase was over, however, Sir Douglas Haig turned his attention northwards. During the spring and early summer he had perfected his plans, and, by minor operations on other parts of the front, had kept the enemy busily engaged and in a state of uncertainty as to where the blow would eventually fall.

Raids.

As usual on these occasions, units in the front line were employed nightly in carrying up stores and material for the coming fighting, whilst behind the line brigades resting practised the attack over taped-out trenches in the training areas of Watou and Roubrouck.

Periodically raids were carried out for the purpose of obtaining prisoners and gaining information as to the state of the enemy positions. Two of these were brilliant successes, and merit description. The first took place on July 24 in daylight by " C " and " D " Companies, 12th H.L.I. (Lieut.-Colonel St John), under Captain T. B. Myles in command, with 2nd Lieutenant Bannatyne and Captain Hannah commanding " C " and " D " companies respectively.

The following is the official account of the operation, which, carried out in broad daylight, deserved every word of the praise it received.

July 1917.

The fact that stubborn opposition was not encountered in no way detracts from the brilliancy of the exploit, but tends to show the mental state to which the enemy had been reduced at this particular time.

REPORT ON RAID BY 12TH H.L.I. ON JULY 24, 1917.

Raid by 12th H.L.I.

1. Strength of raiding party—10 officers and 186 other ranks, under command of Captain T. Myles.

2. Party left their trenches at 1 P.M. as arranged.

3. At 1.5 P.M. the German first-line trenches were taken with no opposition. The enemy wire proved no obstacle. The trenches were badly damaged, poorly revetted, and duck-boards were not visible. There were four concrete dug-outs, two battered by shell-fire and unfit for use; two held, each containing six men, who came out when called upon to do so. Only one attempted to get away; he was shot at, wounded, and recaptured. The estimated number of prisoners taken in this line was 25.

4. Prior to the capture of the front line the "Mound" and "Stables" were dealt with. No wire was found in front of the "Mound," but the whole of the top was covered with it. In rear of it was a concrete dug-out, where 12 prisoners were taken.

5. No opposition was encountered in the support line or in Eitel-Fritz Farm; the buildings contained no dug-outs, and the line was badly knocked about.

6. The final objective, the German reserve line, was reached at 1.10 P.M. Here the wire had been completely smashed by our artillery, and presented no obstacle. Iberia Avenue and Iberia Walk had been almost obliterated, and were only knee-high. In the reserve trenches there were three concrete shelters, capable of holding about 20 men each. Approximately 50 prisoners were taken from these shelters. They came out freely when called upon to do so. The tram-line beyond the reserve trenches was destroyed; there were no works of any kind between the tram-line and the reserve line. There were no machine-gun emplacements discovered. When the final objective was taken, a few men were seen retiring about 300 yards away, and were fired on.

7. Withdrawal. This commenced at 1.25 P.M., and the raiding party were back in their trenches by 1.38 P.M.

8. Our artillery. All barrages were excellent. All officers concerned in the raid speak in the highest terms of the artillery co-operation. There were a few casualties from the creeping barrage during the advance to the first objective, but these were caused by raiders keeping exceptionally close to the barrage (I understand from 35 to 50 yards), and it was not the fault of the artillery.

9. During the raid very little interference seems to have been experienced from artillery fire. A few stray shots were put into his own front

line about 1.15 P.M., and after the withdrawal he shelled it, lifting from there to our front line and Cambridge Road.

July 1917.

10. Our machine-gun barrage was very effective.

11. Generally speaking, the enemy machine-gun fire was very slight.

12. Our Lewis-gun fire was of valuable assistance. There was scarcely any rifle-fire on the part of either the enemy or ourselves.

13. The estimated number of prisoners (all of the 90th Fusilier Regiment) is : 2 officers and 77 other ranks, 12 of whom were wounded.

14. The estimated casualties to the raiding party are : 1 other rank killed, 17 other ranks wounded (mostly slight), 3 missing. These casualties all occurred during the advance from the enemy front line to the final objective. No enemy dead were seen, but doubtless many were buried during our bombardment.

15. General. All reports indicate that our artillery preparation is very severe. The whole country is described as being churned up. The success of the raid reflects great credit on all officers, N.C.O.'s, and men engaged in it. Undoubtedly very little opposition was experienced, but the manner in which all ranks carried out their allotted task and time-table was most satisfactory. The medical arrangements made by Lieutenant Campbell, R.A.M.C., were excellent. No special signalling arrangements were available from battalion headquarters, but, owing to the initiative of 2nd Lieutenant W. F. Burton, communication was established, and reports on the progress of the raid were able to be forwarded.

(Signed) W. E. ST JOHN, *Lieut.-Colonel.*
Commanding 12th H.L.I.

Raids by 7th Camerons.

In conjunction with the above raid, another was carried out by twelve men of "A" Company, 7th Camerons, under 2nd Lieutenant J. Miller. It resulted in one prisoner and a machine-gun being captured. This weapon was in a tunnel under the Ypres-Roulers railway in an advanced post. As from its position it could enfilade No Man's Land, its elimination before the big attack was important. Three raids were made on different dates with the object of capturing the gun. On the first it was taken. On this, the second occasion, its successor was also captured, and on the third occasion on a later date the tunnel was found to be empty, the enemy having given up the idea of keeping a gun there.[1]

[1] This is of interest, as it shows that the Germans could not keep a machine-gun in No Man's Land on the Fifteenth Division front, even in the Ypres Salient.

The following telegrams were received on the 24th :—

From G.O.C. 46TH BRIGADE *to* O.C. 12TH H.L.I.

"The Brigade Commander wishes to send you heartiest congratulations on your splendid success to-day, in which all ranks of the Brigade join."

"Fifteenth Division wire begins—'Please convey to Col. St John and Officers,

July 1917. Raids.

The second raid was made by the 7th Camerons (Lieut.-Colonel McLeod) and two fighting patrols of the 10th Scottish Rifles (Lieut.-Colonel A. Stanley Clarke) at 7 P.M. on July 28. The Cameron party consisted of "D" Company and three platoons of "A," all under Captain J. L. C. Jenkins. Its objective was the enemy front, support, and reserve lines in the immediate north of the railway—the extreme right of the Division front. Closely following a most excellent artillery barrage, the raiders had no difficulty in reaching the German front line. They found this almost obliterated by shell-fire, and a number of the enemy, who had survived the barrage and bombardment, were either killed or taken prisoners. The party then proceeded to the support and reserve lines, where more prisoners were captured. Whilst this was going on a party under 2nd Lieutenant Elliot had worked along the railway looking for the machine-gun which had already been twice captured in previous raids. They did not discover it, but bombed the culvert and dug-out, taking a few prisoners. Both parties were back in their own lines within half an hour, bringing with them, in all, 1 German officer, 39 other ranks, and a machine-gun, and having inflicted many casualties. Their own loss was slight—1 man killed, 2 missing, and 1 officer (2nd Lieutenant Fraser) and 6 other ranks wounded.

Farther to the left, and over almost the same ground visited by the H.L.I. on the 24th, the patrols of the Scottish Rifles raided the "Mound," the "Stables," and the German front line between these points. The parties, under 2nd Lieutenant Killeen (right) and 2nd Lieutenant Hunter (left) each consisted of 1 officer and 21 other ranks, and 2 stretcher-bearers. Like the Camerons, they had no difficulty in reaching their objectives. The right patrol found the "Stables" wrecked and unoccupied. It then pushed on to Ibex Trench, where

N.C.O.'s, and men of 12th H.L.I. my congratulations on their very successful raid, and to the patrol of the 7th Camerons on their successful exploit.'—*From* General Thuillier."

Following copy of a memo., dated July 26, received from 5th Army G.S. is forwarded for communication to all concerned:—

"The Army Commander wishes his congratulations conveyed to the 12th H.L.I., the 7th Camerons, and the Artillery who assisted them, on the success of the daylight raid carried out by them on July 24. The organisation of the raid and the manner in which it was carried out reflects great credit on all the officers and men concerned.

"(Signed) H. F. BAILLIE, *Lt.-Colonel,*

26/7/17. "*General Staff, Fifteenth Division.*"

July 1917. Raids.

a concrete shelter containing 8 Germans was discovered; 2 of these were killed, and the remaining 6 taken prisoners. Moving northwards, the raiders found the trench unoccupied, and returned across No Man's Land to their own lines. The left patrol found the "Mound" also unoccupied, and also proceeded on to Ibex Trench. Here a number of Germans were seen running away. Six were either shot or bayoneted, and 16 others, found in a shelter, surrendered of their own accord. A machine-gun was also discovered, its team being amongst the prisoners. The party then worked south along the trench, and, finding it unoccupied, likewise returned to their own lines. Neither party suffered many casualties, retaliatory fire being practically nil.[1]

These operations had been carried out with the express object of ascertaining whether any change had taken place in the dispositions of the enemy troops, and of getting as much information as possible of his strength and *moral*. It was impressed on the raiding parties that, to ensure information, a considerable number of prisoners was required; each party had therefore been urged to secure at least twenty. On the day after the raid the Divisional Commander, while walking through the trenches occupied by the 10th Scottish Rifles, came across some of the party which had carried out the raid. The General had a conversation with their N.C.O., a big hard-bitten sergeant. He asked him how many prisoners they had brought back.

"Twenty," was the reply.

"Were there many Germans in the part of the trench where you went?"

"Yes, sir, a great many."

[1] The following messages were received the next day by the battalions concerned:—

To O.C. 10TH SCOTTISH RIFLES.

"I wish to very heartily congratulate you and the officers and men of your battalion who took part in the raid yesterday. When you came into the line the night before, you had not been warned that any immediate offensive action would be required of you, yet without any special preparation the operation was carried out with the utmost success.

"I thank you most cordially for your vigorous co-operation.

"(Signed) J. MARSHALL, *Brigadier-General*,
Commanding 44th Infantry Brigade."

29/7/17.

From FIFTEENTH DIVISION.

"Please convey to Col. McLeod and 7th Camerons, and to Col. Stanley Clarke and 10th Scottish Rifles, my congratulations on the very successful raid to-night, which reflects the greatest credit on all.—GENERAL THUILLIER."

July 1917.

" Why didn't you bring back more than twenty ? "

" Your orders, sir, were to get twenty ; so when we had got twenty, we did not try to get any more."

Throughout July it became apparent that the enemy was getting nervous. His aircraft flew low and frequently over the British trenches and back areas, and, like the British, he endeavoured to obtain information by means of raids. None of these succeeded in penetrating the line, but one caused heavy loss to the 11th A. & S. Highlanders. It took place on the night of the 9th/10th July against the line held by the 8th Seaforths. Unfortunately their relief by the Argylls was in progress, and the leading companies of that battalion were caught in the German box barrage, with the result that they lost 85 men from shell-fire. It was extremely bad luck ; many of those killed had only just arrived from Scotland, and had never seen a trench before, much less an armed German.

Mustard gas.

On July 19 the enemy introduced a new form of " frightfulness "—to wit, " mustard gas." Up to this time his efforts in this direction had been rendered innocuous by the use of gas-helmets. On the 13th the following entry occurs in the Fifteenth G.S. diary : " At night, between 10 P.M. and 1 A.M., between 3000 and 4000 gas-shells were fired against battery positions, causing many casualties, which affected the eyes and stomach." When this bombardment started the usual precautions were at once taken, but shortly afterwards men began to go blind, and later on great blisters formed on those so affected. The casualties ran into hundreds, mostly artillerymen, but it was soon found that, although its effects put a man out of action for periods up to fourteen days, the gas was not fatal. It is related that a certain artillery officer put a small portion of one of these new shells in his pocket, with a view to further investigation by the medical authorities. As the fragment had an odour of decaying vegetables, and as, of course, he knew nothing of the effect it would have, he gave it to his orderly to carry. Before they reached headquarters the unfortunate orderly was unable to walk, the chemical having raised a blister the size of a tea-plate on his thigh.

It was about July 29 that Brig.-General Fagan, commanding

the 46th Brigade, had the misfortune to be gassed when on his way to the front line. The result was that he was sent to hospital, and was unable to take part in the battle. His successor, Brig.-General Sladen, only arrived a few days before the attack, and did not take command until after the first phase, during which the brigade was commanded by Lieut.-Colonel K. G. Buchanan.

July 1917.

The enemy was not allowed to continue his employment of "mustard gas" without any form of retaliation. Although "mustard gas" shell were not available on the British side, numerous discharges of "white star" gas were made from Livens' projectors during the second half of July, three such operations being successfully carried out on the Fifteenth Divisional front by "A" Special Company, R.E., under Captain E. V. Slater.

Divisional preparations for the Offensive.

Having received advance instructions regarding the coming operations, General Thuillier decided early in July to make a temporary change in the composition of the two brigades with which he proposed to lead his attack, in order that they should have as much rest and training as possible. To do this he therefore held the line during the last week before the attack with one "mixed" brigade, composed of two battalions from each of the two leading brigades.

The 45th Brigade took over the line from the 44th on July 10, and the following day the latter proceeded by train to the Roubrouck area. Here, and at Watou, the "mixed" brigades were formed. The 44th consisted of the battalions destined to lead the attack—namely, the 9th Black Watch and 8/10th Gordons from the 44th Brigade, and the 7/8th K.O.S.B. and 10/11th H.L.I. from the 46th, with half the 44th Brigade Machine-Gun Company and Trench-Mortar Battery, the 46th Brigade being composed of the remaining four battalions of both brigades.

In these areas both brigades practised the attack over taped-out ground, representing the enemy system they would attack later. The utmost secrecy was observed, owing to the frequent visits of enemy aircraft endeavouring to discover any unusual movement behind the British front. All practice was therefore carried out either at night or in the early hours of the morning, before the sun had dissolved the ground haze. Other arms of the service took part in this training.

July 1917.

As one historian quaintly remarks: "The frequent presence and co-operation of tanks added a *graceful* feature to these exercises."

On the 19th the 46th "Mixed" Brigade took over the front line from the 45th, who then proceeded to Toronto Camp, the 44th continuing its training.

Divisional Orders for the Offensive.

The Divisional Orders for the coming attack were issued on July 21 (o.o. 163), but numerous "instructions" had been already issued from time to time regarding the details of the operations. These were marvellously complete. Every contingency humanly possible to foresee was arranged for. The main points were as follows:—

On zero day the Fifth Army was to attack the enemy positions east and north of Ypres, in conjunction with a French offensive farther north, with the object of driving the enemy from the high ground east and north of Ypres. The II. Corps were to attack on the right, the XIX. in the centre, and the XVIII. on the left.

As regards the XIX. Corps, the Fifteenth Division was on the right, the 55th on the left. On the right of the Fifteenth was the 8th Division (II. Corps).

The frontage allotted to the Division was about 1300 yards in length, and formed part of the Frezenberg Ridge, the ground between that village and north of Zonnebeke, the actual front which had been held by the Fifteenth since their arrival in the salient.

On the right the dividing line between the 8th and Fifteenth Divisions was the Ypres-Roulers railway, inclusive to the Fifteenth; whilst on the left, that between the Fifteenth and 55th ran from Warwick Farm to Iberian Farm, thence north-east of Hill 37 to the Langemarck-Zonnebeke road and on to Gravelstafen.

The attack was to be carried out in three phases, each with a limited objective. The first, or Blue Line, comprised the German front and immediate support lines. The second, the Black Line, included the enemy's second position; and the third, the Green Line, a system of trenches and concrete defensive points some 1500 yards farther back (see Map 9). Should the Green Line be reached, a further advance was to be made to the Red Line, the Gravelstafen-Broodseinde road.

General Thuillier ordered the attack on the first two objectives to be made by the 44th Brigade (right) and the 46th (left), keeping the 45th in reserve for the moment and for the attack on the Green Line later. The dividing line between brigades ran from Oskar Farm (to 44th Brigade) north, east, north of Frezenberg and south of Frost House (to 46th Brigade), and on to the Black Line.

The task of the leading brigades was the capture and consolidation of the Blue and Black Lines.[1] When this had been accomplished, the 45th

[1] See Map 9.

were to pass through them and take the Green Line. Should this be successful, the brigade was then to push forward posts to Hill 40 and Dochy Farm, north of the Winnipeg-Zonnebeke road. As soon as this had been established, the 44th was to take over from the 45th, and send out patrols, supported by one battalion, as far as the Red Line, and there establish a line of outposts, the 45th being then withdrawn into Divisional reserve in the old German front trenches.

July 1917. Divisional Orders.

To each of the leading brigades was allotted half the Divisional Machine-Gun Company, and to all three one section of the R.E. for consolidation purposes—one section, 91st Field Company, to the 44th Brigade; one section, 74th, to the 45th; and one, 73rd, to the 46th.

Barrage fire from the guns of the 47th Machine-Gun Company (16th Division) and half the 44th and 46th Machine-Gun Companies was arranged for. In all, eighty machine-guns were employed. Of these, 32 were detailed for barrage fire alone. These, acting under the direction of the Divisional machine-gun officer, were divided into two groups, each consisting of two batteries of eight guns each. These fired six separate and distinct barrages. Of the remainder, 16 guns were allotted to each brigade—2 to each battalion.

One trench-mortar accompanied each battalion.

Two companies of tanks had been lent to the Division for the operation, Nos. 7 and 9 of "C" Battalion. The latter company was detailed to work with the 44th and 46th Brigades, and the former kept with the 45th to assist in the capture of the Green Line.

Forward dumps of S.A.A., bombs, R.E. material, &c., were formed in the front and support lines prior to the battle, and in addition to these each brigade had a mobile dump, or pack column, consisting of 100 animals. These were under the orders of the respective brigadiers, and it was arranged that they should work forward as far as possible just behind the advancing troops. A Divisional dump, on similar lines but directly under Divisional orders, was also arranged. It consisted of 20 pack animals, 8 G.S. waggons, and 3 water-carts. Designed to supplement the brigade dumps, it carried water and explosives only.

As regards the artillery programme, for twelve days prior to the attack the German trenches were subjected to a heavy and continuous bombardment. The Divisional artillery group then consisted of the Fifteenth, 16th, and 5th Australian Divisional Artilleries, together with part of the XIX. Corps Heavy Artillery, 34 heavy and siege batteries, the latter working under Corps orders.

The Field Artillery was divided into right and left sub-group, covering the fronts of the 44th and 46th Brigades respectively during their advance. The Corps Heavy Artillery was organised into—

(*a*) Two counter-battery groups, each divided into two sub-groups.

(*b*) Three bombardment groups—Northern, Central, and Southern—the latter covering the Fifteenth Division front.

Finally, the most careful arrangements were made by the A.D.M.S. for the collection and evacuation of wounded. (See Appendix H.).

July 1917.

For over a month before the battle the R.E. and pioneers were hard at work preparing for it. In that time the following are some of the tasks they accomplished :—

Many roads repaired.

Battle headquarters constructed (3).

Trench shelters made.

Seven special tracks prepared and marked with pickets.

10,170 yards of deep cable trench dug and filled in.

Two brigade S.A.A. and bomb stores made.

Water supply of Ypres repaired.

8 water points and two wells dug.

6 bivouac camps and 14 Nissen huts erected.

Road diversion round Ypres made.

Of the above works the most remarkable was the construction of battle headquarters and of the road diversion south of Ypres. To make deep-mined dug-outs on the water-infested soil of the salient seemed at first impossible, but geological data supplied by G.H.Q. showed the existence in certain areas of pockets of blue clay impervious to water. In these it was possible to mine without danger of being flooded out, and advantage was taken of them to create dry, roomy, deep, and safe headquarters for each of the brigades by the agency of the Tunnelling Company, R.E.

The conditions previously described regarding communications were such that at any time the enemy chose to put down a barrage on the Menin Gate, all movements of troops, artillery, or supplies to the front would be stopped. It was therefore imperative that alternative lines of communication avoiding this dangerous defile should be established. Two infantry tracks were marked out starting from Kruisstraat, crossing the Ypres-Lille road some 300 yards south of the city, and ultimately joining the Ypres-Menin road east of l'Ecole. These were for the use of the battalions moving into their assembly positions in the line before the attack.

To ensure that when the break-through had been accomplished the forward movements of supplies (and of artillery, whose original positions were to the west of Ypres) should be facilitated, a slab road was constructed from a point outside the Lille Gate, and following the northerly side of the embankment of the Ypres-Roulers railway to a point south-east of l'Ecole, where it turned north and joined the Menin road. This work was entrusted to the Divisional Pioneer Battalion, the 9th Gordons, who stuck to this laborious task night after night for a period of over a fortnight, and completed it in good time, under constant fire from high-explosive and gas-shell, with admirable spirit, in spite of many casualties.

July 1917.

Under ordinary war conditions the above would have been no light task, and it was far more formidable in the salient, where, on account of enemy fire, work was only possible about every other night. Too much cannot be said of the manner in which the work was carried out by the sappers, pioneers, and tunnelling company.

Assembly of Division.

On the evening of July 29 the Division began to close up. The difficulties of this move, and the brilliant manner in which it was conducted, merit more than a passing word.

The attack had been originally staged for the 28th, but on grounds of high policy it had been necessary, almost at the last moment, to postpone it for three days. Brigade reliefs had been so planned that on July 24 there should be two battalions each of the 44th and 46th Brigades in the line, the others remaining in Toronto Camp. On the night of the 25th/26th one battalion of each brigade was to move up from Toronto to bivouac camps nearer the line, and on the following night, the 26th/27th, these two would move up into the line, and the remaining two would move from Toronto to the camps the former had vacated. Then, on the night of the 27th/28th, these last two battalions were to move up, followed by the 45th Brigade.

Postponement.

Such was the plan, but on the 24th news of the postponement reached General Thuillier. The problem that now presented itself to him was one of great difficulty. If the original plan was adhered to, it meant that three battalions from each of the assaulting brigades would be sitting in the line for three days under heavy shell-fire, waiting for the curtain to go up, which might have a bad effect on their *moral* and physical condition. An alternative was to bring back the 45th Brigade, which had only recently gone out of the line, from Watou into the line for three days. If this had been done, the 45th Brigade

July 1917. would have been exhausted instead of the 44th and 46th, and it had to be remembered that the 45th was destined for the capture of the Green Line, the most distant objective.

New plans for assembly.

In this quandary it was decided to discard both these plans, and, relying on the efficiency of the Division, to accept an undoubted risk in order to give the greatest possible amount of rest and freedom from shell-fire to the two leading brigades preparatory to the attack.

It was therefore arranged that the 44th and 46th Brigades should hold the line for the last two days with one battalion each, the remaining six battalions resting behind in Toronto and bivouac camps west of Ypres, and that during the hours of darkness immediately preceding the attack, these six battalions, as well as the whole of the 45th Brigade, should move up from their camps, *viâ* the newly marked infantry roads south of Ypres, and get into their assembly positions in time to start on their respective tasks by their appointed hours.

As soon as this decision was made, all ranks and grades of those to whom it was communicated worked hard to ensure its success. Battalion commanders, their staffs, and company commanders all personally reconnoitred the tracks they were to follow by day and by night. The whole movement was rehearsed with the greatest care, each battalion taking the opportunity of a previous relief to traverse by night the route allotted to it, so that on the battle night the track would not be unfamiliar. Every precaution that the foresight of staff and regimental officers could suggest to prevent any mischance was taken.

As General Thuillier saw it, the risk was not that the enemy might attack a weakly held line whose nearest supports were west of Ypres, but that one or more of the ten battalions moving up on the night of the 30th/31st in darkness, by foot-tracks through a heavily shelled zone, might go astray and not be in position for the attack the following morning. Had this occurred, and the Division in consequence failed to reach its objective, the inevitable verdict would have been that the risk entailed by keeping six out of the eight battalions of the two assaulting brigades west of Ypres until a few hours before zero was too great to be justified. Writing on the subject, General Thuillier says: "It cannot be denied that the above criticism would have been sound"; but he adds: "only from any one who did not know the quality of the Division." July 1917.

The Division did not fail its commander. Everything worked with the precision of clockwork. The six battalions of the attacking brigades left their camps between 9 and 11 P.M., and reached assembly positions in the front system in time to get a couple of hours' rest before zero hour. The 45th Brigade commenced filing up the same tracks at zero hour itself, and was in position by 7.30 A.M. between Cambridge Road and the British front line ready to advance at the appointed hour—namely, 9 A.M. Although in the earlier hours of the night considerable shell-fire was experienced, the movements were carried out in perfect order, and with few casualties. The freshness and fitness of the troops, who had by this daring plan been preserved from fatigue and undue losses, was shown by their achievements in the battle that followed.

In his account of this operation there is one statement made by General Thuillier which cannot but be of interest to all ranks of the Division. It is as follows:—

> "The actual facts reflect so much more credit on the commanders, staffs, and all ranks than does the official account that I should be sorry if they were not included, although they differ from the official narrative. . . . It was such a fine feat that it would be a pity if no mention were made of it in the history of that grand Division."

Such is the story of a risk boldly taken by a commander who knew his men, and of a difficult movement carried out by thorough-trained, tried, and disciplined troops.

In readiness.

During the night the troops moved up, the R.E. and pioneers put the finishing touches on their work. Bridges were made over the trenches, and tracks and extra roads leading forward were laid out, and by midnight all was ready.

Unfortunately the element of surprise was lacking. This was due to the attack having been postponed after the preliminary bombardment had started, which, of course, warned the enemy that something was coming. Another reason was that, owing to the desertion of a non-commissioned officer from another division, the

July 31, 1917.

Germans knew that an attack on a large scale was pending, and prepared for it.

The attack launched.

Punctually at zero, 3.50 A.M. on July 31, the assault was launched. The weather was dull and threatening, and the ground was in a terrible state, due to rain prior to the 31st. In spite of this the troops went forward under cover of a highly satisfactory barrage. Little opposition was met with at first. The German front line had been almost wiped out, but a number of concrete dug-outs were found still intact. These were cleared, and the advance continued to the Blue Line without a check. On reaching this the battalions reorganised. On the right a portion of the 8th Seaforths had been drawn into the fight almost at once, but by so doing had luckily escaped the enemy barrage which was put down on Cambridge Road (their "jumping-off" position) five minutes after zero. On the left, owing to the darkness and state of the ground and to the fact that three of the company commanders had become casualties at the commencement of the attack, the leading lines of the 7/8th K.O.S.B. became somewhat disorganised. On reaching the Blue Line this was put right, and shortly after 5 A.M. both brigades swept on towards the second objective. By this time the whole line had to face heavy enemy machine-gun and artillery fire, and the advance moved forward by section rushes. On the right the 44th Brigade found that the wire round North Station Buildings and Frezenberg had been well cut by the preliminary bombardment, and, in face of heavy fire from these places, the leading companies of the Black Watch and Gordons fought their way through the village and on to the Black Line. One of the tanks, "Challenger," was of the greatest assistance in the capture of Frezenberg. Under command of 2nd Lieutenant C. S. Walker, she entered the village, and dealt with many fortified houses that were holding up the advance. It was an exceedingly fine performance to get a tank over such bad ground, and the assistance it gave was of immense value to the brigade. Unfortunately most of the remaining tanks had been put out of action by this time through either being bogged in shell-holes and marshy ground, or hit by artillery fire before reaching the Blue Line.

Frezenberg captured

On the left serious opposition was encountered by the 46th Brigade in their attack on the Frezenberg Redoubt, on the Ypres-Zonnebeke road. This work lay just behind the crest-line, and directly they reached it the leading waves of the K.O.S.B. were met with machine-gun fire from concrete emplacements on either side of the road, suffering heavy casualties. The advance on this part of the line was momentarily checked, but the Borderers were not to be denied. Finding that it was impossible to get forward in the face of such heavy fire, a party from the left company, under 2nd Lieutenant Causley, worked round to the north of the Redoubt. "Here Causley and another company officer, 2nd Lieutenant Connachie, were killed, and it was under the command of 2nd Lieutenant Houston that the gallant little party finally captured the strong-point."[1]

July 31, 1917.

In the Redoubt itself 160 prisoners were taken, and the centre of the line continued its advance.

Farther to the left the 10/11th H.L.I. had also met with stout resistance from Square Farm and Hill 35, and also from enfilade fire from Frost House. In spite of this, the battalion pushed on, and succeeded in taking Square Farm, and in it 130 Germans. This enabled the 55th Division, who had been held up by fire from the farm, to get forward. Continuing their advance, the H.L.I. then took Low Farm without serious opposition, but were again checked by fire from Pommern Redoubt (Castle) and Hill 35, and it was 10 A.M. before they reached the Black Line.

The second objective gained.

On the right the 44th Brigade had reached the Black Line some time in advance of the 46th, and were engaged in linking up a series of shell-holes on a line of concrete "pill-boxes" some 500 yards east of Frezenberg. Whilst so employed they, with the assistance of a tank, dispersed an enemy counter-attack delivered at 8.30 A.M., and another which developed about 10 A.M. On the left the K.O.S.B. and the H.L.I. dug in slightly in rear of the Black Line—the former from Frost House, through Low Farm to 150 yards east of Beck House; and the latter from there to Iberian Farm.

Whilst the leading battalions had been thus engaged, those in support had been occupied in "mopping up" and clearing out parties of the enemy left in the front system. They had also brought up stores to the Blue Line, and formed dumps and consolidated that position.

[1] From 'A Border Battalion, the 7/8th Battalion K.O.S.B.'

July 31, 1917.

At 10 A.M. General Marshall moved the reserve battalion, 7th Camerons, up to the original German front trenches, in closer support of his leading lines, the Seaforths occupying the Blue Line. As regards the 46th Brigade, two companies of the 10th Scottish Rifles had pushed forward in close support of the attack, and at 10 A.M. were just south of Square Farm, and about 500 yards behind the front line, whilst the other two remained in the vicinity of Grey Ruin. At the same time the brigade commander moved the 12th H.L.I. up to the original Divisional front line in support.

The third phase of the battle was now about to begin—namely, the attack on the Green Line by the 45th Brigade.

In order to provide a barrage to support their advance, three brigades of the Field Artillery—*i.e.*, half the artillery at the disposal of the Division—had already moved up from its original positions to new positions in the neighbourhood of Cambridge Road, just behind the old British front line. The remainder of the Divisional artillery began to move forward as soon as the infantry advanced from the Black Line, and took up more advanced positions in the vicinity of the Blue Line, with a view to bringing fire to bear on the ground in advance of the Green Line.

Attack on the final objective.

At about 9 A.M. the 45th Brigade began its advance from its assembly position between the Cambridge Road and the old British line towards the Black Line. It was disposed so as to cover the whole of the Divisional front, with the 6/7th Royal Scots Fusiliers on the right and the 6th Camerons on the left. In support were the 11th A. & S. Highlanders behind the Fusiliers, and the 13th Royal Scots behind the Camerons.

At 10.18 A.M. they passed through the leading troops of the 44th and 46th Brigades and began the advance to the Green Line under cover of a creeping barrage.

Some time before they reached the Black Line, however, it became apparent that that position had not been completely consolidated. Many Germans were killed by the Camerons between Frezenberg and the Black Line, and the battalion came under heavy fire from Beck House and Iberian Farm. The leading companies pressed on, however, without undue casualties, until they reached a belt of uncut wire about 10 yards thick and 2 feet high just east of Beck House. Through this the leading waves cut a passage, and the advance continued without losing touch with the barrage—a remarkable performance. From this point onwards strong opposition was met with, especially from Hill 37, where 150 prisoners were eventually captured and many Germans accounted for. The Green Line was eventually reached by this battalion about 11.25 A.M., and consolidation was at once commenced. While they were thus engaged so well, a most unfortunate occurrence took place. As their C.O., Lieut.-Colonel J. C. Russell, and his adjutant were moving up behind the battalion, both of them were killed near Grey Ruin. Hearing of this about 1.30 P.M., Colonel Hannay, 13th Royal Scots, ordered Captain Christison of the Camerons to take command. This officer could not be found for some time, and for many hours the Camerons fought on without orders of any kind, hanging on to their position in the Green Line. Patrols were sent out to Otto and Bochy Farms, but their results were never ascertained, as they were all either killed or became casualties during the German counter-attack delivered an hour or two later.

July 31, 1917.

On the right matters had not gone so well. At the very commencement of the advance the left leading company of the Fusiliers had been held up by machine-gun fire from the Black Line, and suffered some casualties. It was at once reinforced by the support company, and the advance continued for a short distance until the line came under enfilade fire from the right. It was then found that the 25th Brigade, 8th Division, had not gone beyond the Black Line, and directly the Fusiliers passed that line they became exposed to enemy fire from their right rear. How far the battalion actually advanced is not certain, but an officer wounded at the wire in front of Bremen Redoubt was assisted back from that point by his servant. Most of the officers had become casualties, and the position of the front line on this flank was somewhat uncertain.

Position at 11.30 A.M.

At 11.30 A.M. the position on the brigade front was as follows: on the right it was not known where the 2nd Rifle Brigade (25th Brigade) was south of the railway, but it was thought that it was engaged in consolidating South Station Buildings and Rabbit Villa. The Scots Fusiliers had one company just east of Potsdam, but it was

July 31, 1917.

not in touch with two others of the battalion, who were just west of Bremen Redoubt, the remaining company being just south of the Ypres-Zonnebeke road, and about 500 yards west of Potsdam. On the left the Camerons were consolidating on the Green Line, and in touch with the 1/4th North Lancashire Regiment on the left, but not with the Scots Fusiliers at Bremen Redoubt. In support, on the right, the A. & S. Highlanders had stopped in consequence of the inability of the Fusiliers to reach their objective, and, realising that there was no attempt being made by the Division on the right to advance south of the railway, they dug in on a line facing north-east, and about 400 yards west of Potsdam, with a company in support on the right ready to form a defensive flank along the railway.

Between noon and 1 P.M. three enemy 'planes flew very low over the Division front, carrying out a thorough reconnaissance of the position without receiving any attention on the part of the R.F.C. The result was soon apparent. An hour later the enemy commenced to attack the 164th Brigade of the 55th Division on the left of the 6th Camerons. The Camerons drove off the first attack, but, owing to the retirement of the 164th Brigade, they found that both their flanks were in the air and that they were running short of ammunition, and in the face of a second and much heavier attack they commenced to withdraw slowly from the Green Line to a position on a ridge some 400 yards west of that line. Here they made a stand for a quarter of an hour. At 3.10 P.M. Colonel Hannay, 13th Royal Scots, received a message from the Camerons that they were being heavily attacked. He at once decided to reinforce the Camerons with every available man at his disposal. This consisted only of two and a half companies. Two platoons had been engaged in "mopping up," and had gone forward with the 6th Camerons in their initial attack. Of these, very few ever returned. The remaining company was employed on carrying work, and was not available. Colonel Hannay moved forward two companies to reinforce the Camerons, who were now retiring after their temporary stand, and sent one platoon of the two in reserve to form a defensive flank facing Hill 35, and to get in touch with the 164th Brigade on the left, with instructions to stop all men withdrawing and utilise them for defence.

Colonel Hannay's stand.

July 31, 1917.

About 4 o'clock the situation was serious. Before the two companies of the Royal Scots had time to act, the Camerons had, in face of heavy fire, withdrawn from their position, and the enemy was pressing on. Seeing this, Colonel Hannay ordered his right company to hold on at all costs, and his left to throw out a defensive flank and gain touch with the platoon of the reserve half-company which he had sent to strengthen that flank. This formed a line running, roughly, from Pommern Redoubt south-south-east along the spur of the ridge north and east of Beck House. He ordered this line to be held at all costs, *no matter what happened on either flank.* With all his available officers and a few of the Camerons, he himself went forward and rallied the retiring line. He then put it under 2nd Lieutenant Sandeman, thus prolonging his line to the right. At the same time he sent a message asking for reinforcements, in answer to which two Vickers-guns were sent up by the 45th Brigade, and the 12th H.L.I. were ordered to be in readiness to support the 45th Brigade if required. In addition, eleven Vickers-guns of the 45th Brigade were hurriedly sent up, got into position, and fired on all targets presenting themselves, especially on Hill 35, with marked success.

At 4.15 P.M. the enemy attack began to die away under the heavy fire from Colonel Hannay's mixed force and the machine-guns of the 45th Brigade. In the meantime Colonel Hannay's Intelligence Officer had succeeded in getting together some 200 more men, reorganised them, and placed them in the Frezenberg (Black) Line. At the same time the 10/11th H.L.I., 46th Brigade, were moved forward to Iberian Farm to strengthen the left flank, with the 10th Scottish Rifles in support and the 12th H.L.I. in reserve. At 5.30 P.M. the enemy fire died away, and, except for slight shelling, all became quiet.

The situation at dusk was as follows :—

Situation at dusk.

It was now possible to reorganise the front line, but, as had been the case throughout the day, great difficulty was experienced in finding out where it was.

On the right the 11th A. & S. Highlanders, owing to the failure of the 8th Division, had sent two platoons with Lewis-guns to the south side of the railway, forming a defensive flank between the Fifteenth and 8th Divisions, the front line of the latter being some

July 31, 1917. 200 yards behind that of the former. They were reinforced later, as the retirement of the 25th Brigade made that flank insecure. On the left of the Argylls a few of the 6/7th Royal Scots Fusiliers linked up with the shattered remnants of the 6th Camerons under 2nd Lieutenant Sandeman, and two companies of the 13th Royal Scots. The remainder of the Fusiliers, who had been forced back from Potsdam, were about 100 yards behind the Argylls, and the reserve company, under Captain Jape, which had been isolated in an advanced position for some time, now withdrew to the general line held by the Argylls, thus strengthening the line to the left. On their left the line to Iberian Farm was held by the 10/11th H.L.I. (46th Brigade). At 8.30 P.M. the 44th and 46th Brigades were ordered to relieve the 45th during the night. Heavy rain, mud, and the churned-up state of the ground rendered this a difficult task. On the right the 44th Brigade were able to carry out their orders, and held the right half of the Divisional line, with the 8/10th Gordons on the right and the 8th Seaforths on the left, as far as the Ypres-Zonnebeke road, 100 yards east of Frost House. In addition, General Marshall moved the 7th Camerons up in support, and withdrew the 9th Black Watch from the Black Line to the old German front line. On the left the 46th Brigade only received its orders about midnight, and although every effort was made to relieve the sorely tried troops in the front line, it was 3.15 A.M. before the first relieving troops arrived. As there was not then sufficient time to carry out the relief before daylight, Colonel Hannay sent them back, and continued to hold the line with the troops he had there.

Aug. 1, 1917. When dawn broke on August 1 it was found that the line held by the Seaforths ran along the road from Frost House southward, just east of the Black Line, and about 500 yards behind the position

A gap in the line.

held by the 13th Royal Scots, thus leaving a gap between the two battalions.[1] Efforts were at once made to get the Seaforths line forward level with the Royal Scots at Borry Farm. This was not done during the morning, and while the gap existed enemy aircraft again flew over the Divisional front investigating the situation. The result of

[1] In 46th Brigade report it is stated that the 8/10th Gordons held this part of the line. This is incorrect.

Aug. 1, 1917. German counter-attacks.

this was that about mid-day small parties of the enemy were seen advancing from the Zevencote-Bremen Redoubt line to another just east of Vampire Farm. At first no significance was attached to these parties, but about 2.20 P.M. the Royal Scots at Beck House reported that the enemy was penetrating the gap. Captain Christie of that battalion at once collected every spare rifle he could find, and formed a defensive flank facing south from Beck House. An hour later the enemy was advancing in considerable strength. Captain Christie's party held out until he was wounded, and then, as the other company commander, Captain Logan, had been killed, and they were being overwhelmed and exposed to very heavy machine-gun fire, they were forced to give way, and the enemy occupied both Beck House and Borry Farm.

Realising the serious situation, Colonel Hannay, whose headquarters were then at Square Farm, at once organised his headquarters staff, and, together with eleven guns from the 46th Machine-Gun Company, prepared to counter-attack.

Whilst this occurred on the left, what took place on the right was as follows: Between 3 and 3.30 P.M. the enemy launched an attack astride the Ypres-Roulers railway line against the right of the Fifteenth Division and the left of the 8th Division. This having been anticipated, the Fifteenth Divisional Artillery at once opened a heavy barrage fire, which caused the leading waves of the attack on the north side of the railway to melt away. Against the Division on the right the attack got home, and forced a withdrawal of their line.

This exposed the right flank of the 8/10th Gordons, and although their line was thrown back to meet the assault, they were unable to hold their ground against the attack of succeeding waves, and were obliged to move back to the rear crest of the Frezenberg Ridge, uncovering as they did so their battalion headquarters.

Here the adjutant, Lieutenant Geddes, had already turned out every available man, and, taking command of all men near him, established a line of defence about North Station Buildings. In the meantime the left of the Gordons and the right of the Seaforths stood firm, and, with the help of two Vickers-guns of the 44th Machine-Gun Com-

Aug. 1, 1917. pany, poured a devastating fire into the rear lines of the attacking Germans. Their casualties from this fire must have been exceptionally heavy, but alas! so were those of the Gordons. Of Lieutenant Geddes's party round the station only thirty men remained.

Notwithstanding this resistance, the Germans pushed forward to within 200 yards of the crest of the ridge, and the situation became critical. Had they reached the crest they would have overlooked at short range the positions of the advanced brigades of artillery, by this time a little to the east of the Blue Line.

At this juncture the leading company of the 7th Camerons, under Captain Symon, which had been sent up to Geddes in support, reached the crest of the spur south-east of Frezenberg. Seeing them coming and realising his chance, Lieutenant Geddes got his men together, and with the Camerons charged the right flank of the attacking Germans. At this moment the reserve company of the Seaforths, under 2nd Lieutenant Brodie, arrived on the scene, and joined in the charge from a north-westerly direction. Firing with good effect as they advanced, this resolute charge took the Germans entirely by surprise. They were only able to stand it for two minutes, and, when the advancing Highlanders were within 50 yards of them, their *moral* broke, and they fled before the rush. By 4.15 P.M. the 44th Brigade had re-established its line as it had been before the attack. In this most gallant charge 1 officer and 70 other ranks of the German 221st Division were taken prisoners.

Germans finally repulsed on right.

Throughout this fight the work of the artillery was of great value. The protective barrage was gradually drawn close in, with the result that exceedingly heavy casualties were inflicted on the enemy, a number of whom, seeing themselves cut off by the barrage from their own lines, endeavoured to surrender, but only a few succeeded in reaching the Scotsmen's lines in safety. While the conflict was at its height the leading batteries saw numbers of their own troops retiring over the ridge, which was only a few hundred yards in front of them, and were in constant expectation of seeing the Germans appear over it also. They coolly continued to maintain their fire, and their firm bearing had a heartening effect on the defenders of the ridge.

Events on the left.

To return to the left. The situation was first clearly reported to General Allgood about 4.45 P.M. He at once ordered the Scots Fusiliers and Argylls to stand to. At 5 P.M. the former battalion, whose total strength was then only about 130 all ranks, was ordered to send one company forward to Square Farm, whilst the remainder of the battalion was to move forward to the Blue Line and be prepared to counter-attack if necessary. In the meantime the 46th Brigade, most of whose troops were already mixed up with those of the 45th in the vicinity of the Black Line, sent word to General Allgood that the only men it had available for counter-attack was one weak company of the 10th Scottish Rifles. This turned out to consist of only twenty rifles, with no officers, but as there was some doubt as to whether the enemy had reached the Black Line, it was sent forward as a strong (?) patrol to investigate the situation near Beck House. What happened to this patrol is not certain. No report was received from it. In order to clear up the situation, the 6/7th Royal Scots Fusiliers (left) and the 11th A. & S. Highlanders (right) were ordered to counter-attack against the Black Line, and, having captured it, hold and consolidate it, and relieve all other units of the 45th and 46th Brigades in that part of the front line.

Aug. 1, 1917.

Before this attack started the company of the Fusiliers under Captain Jape had reached Square Farm at 8.40 P.M., and was ordered by Colonel Hannay, who was still there, to dig in on a line running north and south from Low Farm to the northern Division boundary, which they did.

Advance of the Argylls.

On the right the Argylls moved off from the original British front-line trenches in artillery formation about 8.45 P.M., and advanced in this manner without a single casualty right up to the Black Line. The following is taken from the 45th Brigade diary referring to this advance :—

" The circumstances of this advance are worth recording. It was at the end of the second day of very heavy fighting, and for the whole of that day the men had been ' resting ' in torrents of rain in waterlogged trenches. Officers and N.C.O.'s had not been able to make any previous reconnaissance of the ground, and darkness set in almost immediately after the start. The ground in the vicinity of the objective was similar to that of the Somme area in the wettest time of the winter. In spite of this, however, the objective was reached, well consolidated, and patrols

Aug. 1-2, 1917.

sent out, and the commanding officer reports that on going round his line the next morning he found his men, heavily laden and exhausted as they were, alert and cheerful in spite of a night of incessant rain. . . "

What happened to the Fusiliers is not clear. In the morning (August 2) they were found to be in trenches near Square Farm, and as it was not possible for them to move up during the daylight, the Argylls held the whole front during that day. On relief by the Argylls, what was left of the 13th Royal Scots and the Camerons withdrew to the old British front line and Cambridge Trench, and were not called upon to take part in any further operations during this phase of the battle.[1]

On the right, after the enemy attack during the afternoon, and when touch had been gained with the Argylls on the left, the 44th Brigade sent out patrols and occupied a line of concrete shelters 200 yards in front of the line held by the Seaforths. Nothing more of note took place on the Division front that day, and the night of the 1st/2nd passed without incident.

August 2 passed fairly quietly. As information had been received from a prisoner that the enemy contemplated another attack, the two battalions lent from the 16th Division were moved up to the Blue Line. On the left, about 1.30 P.M., after a very heavy bombardment of the Frezenberg Ridge, the enemy developed an attack against Pommern Redoubt. This was driven off with ease. Another was attempted on the same flank at 5 P.M., and this time it was caught and crushed by an intense artillery barrage before it had a chance of developing.

Nothing further occurred throughout the day, and during the afternoon the 46th Brigade was withdrawn and proceeded by

[1] It should be mentioned that, during the afternoon of July 31, General Thuillier had asked for reinforcements, as the Division had suffered very heavy casualties. In answer to his request the 7th Royal Irish Rifles and 9th Dublin Fusiliers of the 48th Brigade, 16th Division, were placed at his disposal. He sent the former to the 44th Brigade, and the latter to the 45th, to be used in case of emergency. Both these battalions were moved up to the original British front line during the night of July 31/August 1, but took no part in the fighting. In the afternoon of August 1 they were relieved by two battalions of the 47th Brigade (16th Division), and in view of the critical nature of the situation which had developed, General Thuillier retained the two original battalions as an additional reserve east of Ypres till the following morning, when they rejoined their own division.

'bus to the Winnezeele area, less the 12th H.L.I., who rejoined the following day, and the 46th Machine-Gun Company a day later. That night the 47th Brigade, 16th Division, relieved the 45th, which was withdrawn to bivouacs west of Ypres, the 44th remaining in the line.

Aug. 2-3, 1917.

Apart from intermittent shelling the 3rd also passed quietly. Considerable movement of the enemy was observed from time to time, but no attack took place. The weather remained bad; heavy rain fell throughout the day, rendering movement and work on the trenches extremely difficult. That night the 44th Brigade was relieved by a battalion of the 47th, and withdrew to camps west of Ypres. Command of the line passed to G.O.C. 16th Division. At 10 A.M. on the 4th, Divisional Headquarters moved to Winnezeele, the 44th Brigade proceeding there the same day by 'bus.

Relief of Division.

The fight was over. It was now possible to balance gains and losses. The third objective had certainly not been held though it had been reached, and on the left over-reached by the 45th Brigade. The most forward positions had been retained as long as humanly possible, and not a unit of the Division had retired until outflanked, overcome by immensely superior numbers and harassed for hours by galling artillery fire.

Retrospect.

When the Division was relieved its front line had been advanced over 2000 yards, the Frezenberg Ridge securely consolidated, and very heavy casualties had been inflicted on the enemy. The cost, although high, was not out of proportion to the result, the total casualties being 3576 out of a fighting strength of 513 officers and 12,078 other ranks.

In achieving the above results the Division had to contend with other enemies hardly less formidable than the Germans—namely, weather and ground. On the opening day, though rain held off, the going was heavy from the rain of the previous week. On August 1 at mid-day rain again came down in torrents, and continued with little intermission till after the Division had left the line. The state of the ground on the 2nd and 3rd can hardly be imagined by those who did not see it. In the first place, the whole of the area in which the fighting took place had undergone a bombardment of unexampled

July 31–
Aug. 3, 1917.

severity for fifteen days. It consisted, therefore, of one mass of intersected shell-holes of great size, without a yard of original surface between them anywhere. Progress could only be made by walking on the soft greasy rims of the shell-holes, and with difficulty it was possible to avoid falling into the water and mud with which the shell-holes were filled, and in which there was considerable risk of drowning. Those who tried walking over the ground carrying only the light load of a staff officer wondered at the strength and endurance which must have been required to do so by men laden with rifle, ammunition, pack, rations, &c. Justice compels the admission that the enemy, when making his counter-attacks, must have suffered equally from this appalling hindrance to movement.

The co-operation between all arms was marvellous throughout the battle. Success was due to this as much as to anything else. Tanks were of not much assistance except in the initial stages of the attack. Well handled, it was not their fault, but was almost entirely due to the appalling condition of the ground. Their moral effect during the assault was very great, but those abandoned were later fortified by the enemy, and served as strong-points, which had to be taken in the subsequent phases of the battle.

The machine-guns.

Too much cannot be said of the action of the machine-gun companies. One instance alone will suffice to show how gallantly they fought. Of the Vickers-guns that went forward two got into Beck House, and did great execution during the counter-attack on the 2nd. When the Royal Scots were forced to retire from this position these two remained behind covering their retreat. Only one man of the teams got back to tell the tale. The last he saw of the officer commanding the guns was when the Germans were within ten yards of him. HE WAS STANDING UP FIRING HIS REVOLVER AT THEM.

R.A. and Infantry.

Between the artillery and the infantry of the Fifteenth Division the sense of comradeship was very high. To the gunners working at their guns it was enough to know that the "Jocks" were advancing against the enemy, or that they were being counter-attacked, to ensure that their utmost effort and most careful laying would be forthcoming. Neither enemy shell-fire, gas, or exhaustion could stop or check their hurricane of shrapnel and high-explosive as long as a covering barrage was necessary, and sometimes these were of extremely long duration. The same spirit actuated the personnel of the Irish and Australian divisional artilleries attached to the Division during these operations.

July 31–Aug. 3, 1917.

Although communication was constantly broken, fire was always brought to bear when asked for. There is no doubt whatever that, had it not been for the heavy and accurate artillery fire during the counter-attack on the 2nd, the situation might have been very different. A brigade commander writes :—

> "The liaison officers, R.A., attached to the brigade carried out their duties in a most satisfactory manner, and, by their prompt adjustments of the barrage and by the co-operation and support of their guns, very greatly contributed to the success of the operations."

The infantry reciprocated this comradeship by a thorough confidence in their gunners, particularly, of course, in those of the Fifteenth Division, behind whose barrage they had advanced on many other fields of battle.[1]

The trench-mortar batteries were not of great use. In the appalling state of the ground the question of ammunition supply was a serious one, and all reports agree that, except in the initial stages of the attack, they played no great part in the fighting.

R.A.M.C.

No account would be complete without reference to the carrying parties from infantry units attached to the R.A.M.C. to assist in the collection of wounded. It has been the fortune of the author to obtain access to a diary kept by an officer in charge of one of these parties (Lieutenant R. L. Mackay, 11th A. & S. Highlanders). His party of 50 moved into l'Ecole, east of Ypres, early in the morning of the 31st. He says :—

> "We are in a cellar indescribably filthy, with an appalling smell and three inches deep in water. Here we have to rest, sleep, and eat if we can.

[1] It was during the weeks of preparation for the Ypres battle that the Divisional Artillery Commander, Brig.-General E. B. Macnaghten, came to the General Officer commanding the Division and conveyed to him a request from the men of the Fifteenth Divisional Artillery to be allowed to show their pride in the Scottish Division by wearing a distinctive mark to show they belonged to it. The request was granted, and thereafter all ranks of the Divisional Artillery wore on the sleeve, below the shoulder, a small disc of Royal Stuart tartan.

July 31–Aug. 3, 1917. The stretcher-bearers.

. . . Began work at 3.50 A.M. Searched ground up to Blue Line in terrific rain and under heavy bombardment. We could scarcely move one foot after another. . . . Tuesday (August 1). Nobody rested. In response to an urgent message, we were off at 11 A.M. Had to pass through three very bad barrages on the way up. . . . Never before have I seen artillery fire like it. The Somme was a picnic and Arras a joke. Got to blockhouse on Frezenberg Ridge, barrage closed down all round us. Took down wounded, and sent off men in parties until I had only three left. Found at last, when no other men could be seen, a demented Boche, wounded. Got him on a stretcher and took an end myself. Then the enemy turned a machine-gun on us as our little party stumbled down the Roulers railway. . . . Dumped the Boche at the 8th Division dressing-station, and got a Britisher in exchange. . . . Cruel work for men with stretchers owing to mud, shell-holes, and wire. Finally, got back to l'Ecole at 5 P.M."

This officer and his party worked the whole of the following two days, and did not rejoin his battalion till the 4th, after it had been withdrawn to Winnezeele. He took back 16 of his original party of 50!

Owing to officers and men of this stamp, it is very worthy of note that, when the Division left the front line, only four cases remained which could not be got away until darkness. During the fighting the total number of wounded (of the Fifteenth Division) who passed through the Corps dressing-station was 86 officers and 2186 other ranks, walking wounded only.

Piper D. LAIDLAW, V.C.

7th Battalion King's Own Scottish Borderers.

STATEMENT OF CASUALTIES, 29/7/17 TO 4/8/17.

Unit.	Killed.		Wounded.		Missing.		Totals.
	O.	O. R.	O.	O. R.	O.	O. R.	All Ranks.
44th Infantry Brigade.							
9th Black Watch	1	26	11	207	..	22	267
8th Seaforth Highlanders	3	26	8	153	..	13	203
8/10th Gordon Highlanders	2	38	14	245	..	51	350
7th Cameron Highlanders	..	16	8	251	..	47	322
44th Machine-Gun Company	2	8	..	26	..	..	36
44th Trench-Mortar Company	..	..	..	..	..	..	..
45th Infantry Brigade.							
13th Royal Scots	2	13	6	148	6	191	366
6/7th Royal Scots Fusiliers	2	43	10	205	..	28	288
6th Cameron Highlanders	7	19	6	145	5	108	290
11th A. & S. Highlanders	4	15	5	110	..	21	155
45th Machine-Gun Company	1	6	1	32	1	8	49
45th Trench-Mortar Battery	..	1	..	6	..	3	10
46th Infantry Brigade.							
7/8th K.O.S.B.	4	38	10	240	..	19	311
10th Scottish Rifles	6	20	6	118	2	64	216
10/11th H.L.I.	6	23	5	188	5	80	307
12th H.L.I.	2	15	6	88	..	19	130
46th Machine-Gun Company	..	11	2	23	..	11	47
46th Trench-Mortar Battery	..	..	..	9	..	1	10
225th Machine-Gun Company	1	5	1	12	..	4	23
9th Gordon Highlanders (Pioneers)	..	2	6	52	..	2	62
70th Brigade, R.F.A.	1	9	..	16	1	..	27
71st Brigade, R.F.A.	1	9	..	26	..	2	38
Heavy Trench-Mortar Battery	..	1	..	3	..	..	4
Medium Trench-Mortar Batteries	..	..	..	3	..	..	3
Fifteenth Div. Ammunition Column	..	..	..	1	..	..	1
73rd, 74th, 91st Field Co.'s, R.E.	..	2	..	8	..	..	10
Fifteenth Div. Signal Coy., R.E.	..	..	..	8	..	..	8
Fifteenth Divisional Train	..	..	..	..	..	..	..
45th, 46th, 47th Field Amb., R.A.M.C.	..	3	1	40	..	..	44
R.A.M.C., attached infantry	..	..	1	..	1	..	2
Presbyterian Chaplain	1	..	..	..	..	..	1
Total	46	349	107	2363	21	694	3580

CHAPTER VII.

THE THIRD BATTLE OF YPRES (*continued*),[1] AND UP TO THE END OF 1917.

Aug. 1917.

THE Division was relieved by the 16th (Irish) Division on the nights of August 3 and 4, and by the evening of the latter date it was concentrated round Winnezeele and Oudezeele, about sixteen miles west of Ypres, with headquarters at Winnezeele. The artillery remained in the line under C.R.A., 16th Division. The camps allotted to the Division were in a terrible state, especially those at Oudezeele. Not only were the men crowded, but many of the tents were not waterproof, and the whole area was a sea of mud. Under these adverse conditions reorganisation took place. The recent fighting had reduced battalions to skeleton strength, and to replace casualties drafts amounting to 51 officers and 3696 other ranks arrived. Unfortunately they were only partially trained, and there was neither time nor facilities for doing much in that way. The most that could be done was to send parties of 250 from each brigade in turn to the Fifth Army Musketry School, but beyond this nothing was possible. This lack of training was very noticeable, especially during a practice attack carried out on the 19th, and it was a very different Division that went into the line the next time.

Reinforcements.

It was not that the quality of the reinforcements was in any way inferior. The officers and men of the new drafts were of a good stamp, and, could the Division have had a month out of the line, there is no reason to suppose that it would not have been as fine a fighting force as it was when it left the Willeman area for the salient in June. But the necessity for an early return to the battle did not give time

[1] Map 9A.

for platoon commanders even to get to know their men, much less to have sufficient practice in handling them in attack.

Aug. 1917.

Whilst resting, all battalions were inspected by the Divisional Commander, who warmly complimented them on their achievements at Frezenberg. A still better testimonial was furnished later by the Germans themselves. In a list captured shortly afterwards, giving the British divisions they feared most, the enemy placed the Fifteenth second on the list.

Weather causes delay.

In the meantime the appalling weather conditions had made it impossible to continue operations. To quote from Sir Douglas Haig's despatches :—

> " The low-lying clayey soil, torn by shells and sodden with rain, turned to a succession of vast muddy pools. The valleys of the choked and overflowing streams were speedily transformed into long stretches of bog, impassable except by a few well-defined tracks, which became marks for the enemy's artillery. To leave these tracks was to risk death by drowning, and in the course of the subsequent fighting on several occasions both men and pack-animals were lost in this way."

This delay was of great assistance to the enemy. It gave him time to recover from his defeat, to reorganise his defences, and to complete a number of concrete strong-points behind his front line.[1]

The weather improved about the middle of August, and the attack was resumed on the 15th. Unfortunately it did not go particularly well on the right of the Fifth Army front. The 16th Division was unable to advance very far, held up as it was by fire from strong-points such as Beck House, Iberian Farm, and Borry Farm.

46th Brigade in the line.

On the 17th the move to the front line began, and that night the 46th Brigade took over the whole of the right sector of the V. Corps front from the 16th Division, the ground it had occupied a fortnight earlier. The position of the front line had not changed greatly (see Map 9). The fortified farm buildings still defied capture, and it had become evident that in addition to these the enemy had studded the whole of his defensive zone with concrete defensive posts of the type which came to be known as " pill-boxes." Since these could

[1] Operations were also greatly hampered owing to weather conditions being so bad that it had been impossible to get any air photos for some time prior to the assault.

Aug. 1917.

not be knocked out by heavy artillery fire owing to their small size and concealment, it became the task of the Division to take them. Operation orders had been received, and the attack practised by the 44th and 45th Brigades on the 19th. That same day both brigades moved up nearer the line to Toronto Camp and others just west of Ypres, and during the night 20th/21st they relieved the 46th Brigade and part of the 183rd (61st Division) in the front line, preparatory to the attack the next day.

A fresh attack.

The XIX. Corps were about to resume the offensive in conjunction with the right of the XVIII. Corps. The Fifteenth Division was to attack on the right of the XIX. Corps front, with the 61st on the left. In order to protect the right flank of the Fifteenth Division, the II. Corps arranged to cover that flank with artillery and machine-gun fire and also with smoke. Its commander also arranged to send forward troops from the 141st Brigade (47th Division) to establish posts on the railway midway between Railway Dump and Potsdam. On the left of the Division the 61st was to attack with the 184th Brigade, the 182nd and 183rd being in reserve.[1]

The reserve brigade, then in camps just west of Ypres, was directed to move up at zero hour to a position of assembly in the old British lines east of Ypres, and be ready to advance when ordered.

R.A. arrangements.

Covering the attack, and acting under the orders of the Divisional Commander, the artillery consisted of the whole of the Fifteenth, 16th, and 5th Australian groups, together with the 150th Brigade, R.F.A., and were organised as follows :—

Right Sub-Group (Commander, Lieut.-Colonel C. M. Ingham, D.S.O.)—
- Fifteenth Divisional Artillery.
- 13th Brigade, Australian Field Artillery.

Centre Sub-Group (Commander, Lieut.-Colonel H. M. Thomas, C.M.G.)—
- 16th Divisional Artillery.
- 14th Brigade, Australian Field Artillery.

Left Sub-Group (Commander, Lieut.-Colonel F. A. Dixon, D.S.O.)—
- 150th Brigade, R.F.A.

In addition, Corps Heavy Artillery was divided into two counter-battery groups and two bombardment groups, of which the southern

[1] Map 9A gives the objective, dividing lines, and disposition of the two assaulting brigades. It will be seen that the divisional front had been extended somewhat to the left, in order that the whole of the ridge which runs east from Hill 35 should be included in it.

and part of the northern covered the Division front. Barrage fire from the 225th and 46th Machine-Gun Companies was arranged by the Divisional machine-gun officer.

Aug. 1917.

Just in front of the left battalion of the 44th Brigade lay Hill 35, a low mound that had given a good deal of trouble in the previous battle. In order that this should be dealt with effectively, General Thuillier ordered that the 9th Gordons (Pioneers) should detail six platoons for the sole purpose of consolidating and holding the hill when taken, the remainder of the battalion acting directly under the orders of the C.R.E.

For the five days prior to the attack, harassing fire was kept up every night by both artillery and machine-guns, and all known strong-points were freely bombarded by Heavy and Field Artillery. Throughout the same period infantry patrols were active along the whole front, and every endeavour was made to discover the positions occupied by the enemy. On the 21st a patrol of the 11th A. & S. Highlanders got as far as Beck House, and threw bombs into it. As the house was reported unoccupied, half a platoon went forward to take possession, but were met by a strong party of Germans, and withdrew to a trench some 50 yards to the west of the house.

The attack of the 22nd.

At 4.45 A.M. on the 22nd the attack was launched under cover of a creeping barrage and fire from thirty-two machine-guns. Within thirty seconds down came the enemy barrage on the line Frezenberg-Square Farm, and within a minute very heavy machine-gun fire met the assaulting battalions, support and reserve companies of the 44th Brigade in particular suffering from this fire before they had left their trenches.

Failure on the right.

On the right the fate of the leading companies of both the 13th Royal Scots and 11th A. & S. Highlanders will never be known. So heavy was the machine-gun fire that no information could be sent back or supports sent up. Two hours after the attack started the company commander of the left front company of the Royal Scots had only nine men and one Lewis-gun team remaining. Of the Argylls only three officers came back (McClure, Chesney, and Muirhead), all three being badly wounded. It was made out, however, that, advancing steadily, the lines reached Potsdam, Vampir, and Borry Farms, as flares were shown at these places later, but beyond this nothing definite can be said. The few men of the Royal Scots and Argylls who returned

Aug. 22, 1917. were rallied on a line north-west from the Railway Dump along the road running to Beck House.

Progress on the left.

On the left the 44th Brigade met with much the same experience. The right assaulting company of the Seaforths mistook the Steenbeke stream for the Zonnebeke brook, and thus lost direction. No confirmation of this is possible, as no survivor of this company came back, all being either killed or seriously wounded. It appears, however, that the company reached a point well east of Beck House before they were annihilated by fire from machine-guns in the house behind them. The left company of the Seaforths advanced steadily towards Iberian Farm, and reached a point about 30 or 40 yards west of the farm, also losing heavily in doing so. To help them, the support company was pushed forward. This advance was carried out in the most admirable manner. Although under exceedingly heavy machine-gun fire, the company went forward by rushes from shell-hole to shell-hole, and, in spite of heavy losses, managed to reach the forward troops, and, with one platoon on the left, prolonged the line, and linked up with the 7th Camerons. The two leading companies of the Camerons advanced up the slopes of Hill 35, but were held up on reaching the crest by machine-gun fire from Gallipoli, and dug in where they were.

In front of the Seaforth area Iberian Farm still held out, making the position of the Camerons on the hill extremely precarious. The reserve company was pushed forward, and repeated efforts were made to outflank the farm, but without success. The enemy fought with grim determination, and his new system of defence by lines of "pill-boxes" defied the efforts of the Division.

On the left of the Camerons the platoons of the 9th Gordons, who, under Captain R. Lumsden, had come up to consolidate Hill 35, had reached Pommern Redoubt, and proceeded towards Hill 35. Finding the position somewhat obscure, it was decided to dig in and form a defensive flank from the hill to Pommern and onwards in the direction of Somme. To do this, Lieut.-Colonel T. G. Taylor, 9th Gordons, who had accompanied the six platoons, ordered two of them to consolidate a line running, roughly, along the road leading north from Pommern and about 120 yards behind the leading infantry, two more to prolong the line from Pommern towards Somme, one section, two Lewis-guns, and one Vickers-gun to occupy Somme itself, and one platoon to dig trenches in rear, facing east, about 300 yards south-east of Somme, to protect his left flank. He ordered his remaining platoon to dig posts, 30 yards apart, behind his leading platoons.[1] In carrying out this work the pioneers suffered rather heavily. In quick succession Lieutenant Milne was killed, and Lieutenants Cantlay, Crowe, and M'Laren wounded, together with a number of N.C.O.'s and men; but in spite of this the work went on, and as the trenches deepened casualties grew less.

Aug. 22, 1917.

Situation at 7 A.M.

By 7 A.M. it was clear that little or no progress had been made. On the right the line had only been able to advance a few yards, whilst in the centre, what was left of the assaulting troops had been compelled to withdraw to their original line. Farther north, at 8 A.M., the right flank of the 61st Division commenced to retire. It was rallied by Captain Lumsden of the Pioneers, and dug in on a line selected by him, and a gap between the two Divisions, just north of Somme, was filled by a mixed body of troops from the 61st Division, 7th Camerons and 9th Gordons.

The action of the 7th Camerons and six platoons 9th Gordons attached to that Battalion was of the greatest value. They secured and maintained a footing on the ridge, which was a valuable buttress to the left of the Division and to the right of the 61st Division. But for this it is probable that before night both would have been back in the line from which they started. This was the first time that the 9th Gordons had been used to take part in an attack since Loos, and their enthusiasm, energy, and endurance under a severe fire, which caused them 25 per cent of casualties in a short time, were worthy of all praise.

No advance possible.

For the rest of the day the situation remained unchanged. On the right the 13th Royal Scots made repeated attempts to get forward by jumping from shell-hole to shell-hole, but without success. No forward movement was possible in face of the heavy fire from various

[1] Regarding this phase of the battle General Thuillier writes:—

"There is great uncertainty as to the exact location of these trenches, and I doubt if this description is correct. Broadly speaking, they were on the ridge between Pommern and Hill 35, and they faced *north*."

Aug. 22, 1917. farms and strong-points. Between one o'clock and three the enemy made two faint efforts to counter-attack. These were dealt with by rifle and artillery fire, and failed to materialise. From one o'clock onwards enemy fire gradually decreased in face of the heavy and accurate rifle and Lewis-gun fire from the Division.

Night attacks fail.

Late in the evening, as it was reported that men of the Division were still in the vicinity of Beck House, Borry and Iberian Farms, and Gallipoli, General Thuillier issued orders that these points would be rushed at night. On the right General Allgood entrusted the attack on Beck House and Borry Farm to the 6th Camerons. On the left the 44th Brigade attack on Gallipoli was carried out by the 9th Black Watch, the 8/10th Gordons and 8th Seaforths being instructed to converge on and capture Iberian Farm.

None of these attacks succeeded. The enemy was found to be on the alert. The Black Watch, although attacking under adverse conditions and having had little time to reconnoitre the ground, managed to advance their line some 80 yards nearer to Gallipoli, but could not get farther on account of heavy enfilade fire from both flanks. They consolidated the ground gained, and dug a communication trench to link up with the platoons of the 9th Gordons on their left. Elsewhere the line remained unchanged, and the rest of the night was quiet.

Reorganisation.

August 23 passed in a curious peace. The enemy rifle and artillery fire was surprisingly light, and energetic sniping on the part of units in the front line kept down that of the enemy. By this time battalions in the front line had become considerably mixed up, so much so, in fact, that during the day General Allgood decided to withdraw the 11th A. & S. Highlanders and 13th Royal Scots and to allow them to reorganise and re-equip in the Toronto Camp area, their places in the line being taken by the 6/7th Royal Scots Fusiliers and the 6th Camerons. Every available fighting detail that these battalions had left behind them was sent up, and in addition the 12th H.L.I. from the 46th Brigade was placed at General Allgood's disposal as a reserve.

This reorganisation of the two battalions was all the more necessary, as General Thuillier designed to use them for another attack on Borry Farm and Beck House on the 28th. A somewhat similar reorganisation took place on the left. The 10th Scottish Rifles, lent from the 46th Brigade, relieved the 8th Seaforths on the right of the 44th Brigade front, the left being held by the Black Watch, the 8/10th Gordons relieving the 7th Camerons in support. On relief, the Seaforths moved to St Lawrence Camp, and the Camerons to one just west of Ypres to refit and reorganise.

Aug. 23-27, 1917.

The night of the 23rd/24th and the two following days passed quietly, the enemy making no attempt to attack, nor did he harass the front line with artillery fire.

During this lull, General Thuillier completed his plans for his next attack. On the right a party of the 9th Gordons under Captain Burnett dug jumping-off trenches for the Argylls and Royal Scots. This work was exceptionally difficult on account of heavy rain and the appalling state of the ground, but in spite of this the task was performed in time. On the left the 9th Black Watch and the 9th Gordons dug similar trenches just north-east of Pommern, thus securing the western slopes of Hill 35.

On the 25th another attempt to capture Gallipoli was made by two companies of the Black Watch under Captain J. Donaldson. The advance was made in two parties at 11 P.M. under a creeping artillery barrage, assisted by fire from four Stokes mortars. Although the farm buildings were reached, the companies suffered severely in the advance. The right company overran a concealed machine-gun position, and was taken in reverse by intense machine-gun fire. Faced with fierce fire from the farm buildings and from a derelict tank close by, both were then compelled to fall back to a line about 170 yards in advance of their original position. Here, with the assistance of some men of the 9th Gordons, they consolidated the position, and linked it up with the original front line. Whilst this took place a patrol of the 10th Scottish Rifles attempted to reach Iberian Farm, but without success.

Minor attacks fail.

On the 26th the 10/11th H.L.I. relieved the 9th Black Watch and 8/10th Gordons in the front line, the two latter moving to camps west of Ypres, whilst the 7/8th K.O.S.B. were sent up to occupy the old British trenches east of Ypres.

On the 27th the general offensive was resumed. As far as the Fifteenth Division was concerned, the only part played by it on this

Aug. 27-31, 1917.

occasion was another attempt to take Gallipoli Farm. This time the attack was made by 120 men of the 10/11th H.L.I. As in the previous assaults, heavy machine-gun fire was encountered, and the party was compelled to fall back after it had succeeded in reaching the farm buildings.

Once more the weather greatly assisted the enemy. Rain fell heavily, trenches and tracks became almost too bad for use, and it was apparent that further operations on any large scale could meet with little success. It was not surprising, therefore, that, on the morning of the 28th, orders were received cancelling the arranged attack, and that General Thuillier issued instructions for the front line to be thinned out. The relief of the 44th and 45th Brigades by the 46th took place during the night of the 29th/30th, and the two former brigades proceeded to camps west of Ypres. The following night the 46th Brigade were relieved by the 125th, 42nd Division, and General Thuillier gave over command of the line on the completion of the relief at 10 A.M. on the 31st. The same day the 44th Brigade marched to Watou area, the 45th and 46th moving by road and 'bus to Wormhoudt.

Relief of Division.

On the morning of the 31st General Gough personally visited the Division Headquarters near Brandhoek, and expressed to the Divisional Commander in warm terms his appreciation of the determination and endurance displayed by all arms and all ranks of the Division during its stay in the Ypres salient. At the time of his visit it had been the intention of General Thuillier to go to meet the 45th Brigade on the road on their march to Wormhoudt. He invited General Gough to accompany him and have a last look at a portion of the Scottish Division. At the same time, he warned General Gough that only twenty-four hours had elapsed since the brigade had left the trenches, and that they would be showing signs of hardship and fatigue. General Gough went with him to a point west of Poperinghe, where all four battalions of the 44th Brigade defiled before the two commanders. General Gough was astonished at what he saw. During the one day's halt in the bivouac camps all traces of mud and dirt from the trenches had been removed. Uniforms and equipments were clean. The men were alert and vigorous, and stepped out well. It was difficult to believe that they had been through such bitter fighting under the worst conditions for a fortnight without a rest. The Army Commander was outspoken in his admiration of their bearing. "What splendid men!" he said. "Look at their hard, stern, Scottish faces, their upright carriage! They look as if they would be ready for another fight now if need be!" General Thuillier adds: "I am certain they *would* have been ready if called on, although they had been through more than most men could stand!"

Aug.-Sept. 1917.

General Gough's compliment.

On September 1 the Division, less artillery, which remained four days longer in the line, commenced moving south to the Arras sector of the front. Proceeding by train, it arrived the following day in XVII. Corps area, Third Army, commanded respectively by Lieut.-General Sir C. Fergusson and General Sir J. H. Byng.

Move to Arras sector.

By the evening of Sept. 2 the Division was billeted as follows:—

44th Brigade Group in Agnes les Duisans, Montenescourt, and Gouves area;
45th Brigade Group in "Y" Camp, Etrun;
46th Brigade Group in Duisans area;

with Divisional Headquarters at the Chateau, Hermaville. The artillery arrived on the 4th, and occupied Habarcq and Noyellette areas. Here two days were spent in reorganising and refitting, and on the 5th the relief of the 4th Division, in the centre of the XVII. Corps, commenced.

Whilst thus engaged the following message was received:—

"The commander of the Fifth Army bids good-bye to the Fifteenth Division with great regret. Its reputation has been earned on many battlefields, and has never stood higher than now. He wishes it all good fortune and many further successes in the future. 'Will ye no' come back again'?"

Farewell to the Fifth Army.

Whilst this message was appreciated by its recipients, the reply was obvious. One battalion records that the unanimous answer was contained in three words, "No b——y fear!" The diarist concludes, "The Army commander was simply 'asking for it.'"

The move occupied three days, and at 10 A.M. on the 8th General Thuillier assumed command of the section, the 12th Division being on the right and the 17th on the left. On this occasion the 46th Brigade

Arras trenches again.

Sept.-Dec. 1917.

relieved the 11th in the right sub-section and the 45th relieved the 10th in the left, the 44th remaining in reserve in camps in the vicinity of Blangy, two battalions on each side of the Scarpe.

The Scarpe sector.

The front held was over two miles in length. It ran almost due north and south from Twin Copses, east of Monchy, to a point midway between Roeux and the Chemical Works, north of the Scarpe, which river was the dividing line between the two brigades. The line consisted of a continuous front and support system, except for about 600 yards south of the river, on the left of the right sub-section. Here, owing to the marshy nature of the ground, strongly wired posts took the place of trenches. At this point a curious situation existed. The operations following the capture of Monchy had resulted in the taking of Roeux, east of which ran the British front line. South of the river the line had not advanced so far. Pelves was still in German hands, and their front line ran some 500 yards west of that village. Thus the opposing lines north of the river were about 600 yards east of those on the southern side of the river. In consequence of this the ground between Roeux, the Scarpe, and Pelves constituted No Man's Land on this part of the line.

The section was a particularly quiet one; in fact the last quarter of 1917 was the most peaceful period of trench warfare ever experienced by the Division. The following, taken from 'A Border Battalion,' will give some idea of how this peaceful sector struck those fresh from the mud of Flanders:—

"All was comparatively quiet. Arras was reviving; flowers could still be seen in some of the gardens, and even the trees in Blangy were green. . . . At that time there was a regular time-table of sailings on the Scarpe, not to speak of the light railway system in the valley, with branches running to every useful corner hidden from direct enemy observation. It all seemed magical. The 12th Division ran 'The Spades' in the Arras Theatre; the New Zealanders had a tennis-court; and an officer's 'Rest House' was being built in the Public Gardens."

From September to the end of December, when the Division was relieved, the entry "Quiet day" occurs in the diaries with monotonous regularity. This want of enemy enterprise was of the utmost value to the Division. After its heavy losses in the salient the ranks of all units had been filled by half-trained troops, who, no matter how willing, were quite unable to cope with the intensive warfare now prevailing. The losses in officers had been particularly heavy, and in consequence the Division suffered from a shortage of trained company, platoon, and section commanders. During these quiet winter months training of all kinds continued, and in that period the Division laid the foundation on which was built the brilliant record of 1918.

Sept.-Dec. 1917.

Although attention has been called to the somewhat remarkable lull in operations, it must not be thought that the Division lacked enterprise. Raids and artillery bombardments were of constant occurrence, the enemy being harassed from morning to night. The following is taken from the diary of an officer in a trench-mortar battery :—

> "September 7 to 23. Sixteen days' tour in the line. Trenches quiet when we entered them, but our aggressive spirit stirred them up. . . . As was usual with the Fifteenth Division, trench raids continually annoyed the enemy. Stokes mortars were in great request for retaliatory fire. During this tour my battery fired 2530. . . . At dusk and dawn exciting trench-mortar duels usually ended in our favour. Our policy was instant retaliation and free firing."

Later, during another tour, this battery fired 2850 rounds, with the loss of only one man wounded by retaliatory fire.

"A" and "Q" activities.

Great credit must be given to "A" and "Q" branch for the manner in which they worked and devised means for bettering conditions both in the front line and elsewhere. Although the trenches and dug-outs were in good order when taken over, the Division set to work to improve them. Large parties of R.E., pioneers, and infantry were engaged on this throughout the winter, and when the area was handed over to the Guards in January, "A and Q" diary records :—

> "The area to be handed over is in a much better condition than when handed over to the Division in September."

To start with, a scheme for winter accommodation was arranged—horse lines built, baths improved, camp sites chosen, cook-houses erected as close to the front line as possible, and much done to improve billets in Arras and other places. To quote again from "A and Q" diary :—

> "September 7. This is the first time this year that there have been facilities, whilst in the line, for promoting the comfort of the troops."

Oct. 1917.

On October 10 Major-General Thuillier left the Division on appointment to the Ministry of Munitions, and the following day Major-General Reed, V.C., assumed command. Major-General H. L. Reed had been G.S.O., 27th Division (Western Front), November 1914 to June 1915; Brig.-General, General Staff, IX. Corps, Gallipoli and Egypt, June 1915 to February 1916; Brig.-General, R.A., 40th Division (Western Front), May 1916 to December 1916; and G.O.C., R.A., X. Corps (Western Front), January 1917 to date of appointment to command the Fifteenth Division.

Raids.

In describing a quiet tour such as this proved to be, it is difficult to pick on any incidents worthy of record. Diaries are full of references to patrol activities throughout the period from September to December, and in October and November, when the Division had settled down, the number of raids carried out show that it had not lost the aggressive spirit for which it had always been renowned. On most occasions the enemy was found to be alert and his trenches strongly held, thus little information was gained by the raiders; but the fact that during the four months the enemy only attempted to raid the sector on four occasions, all of which were repulsed, proves that the Division dominated the situation.

One raid may be mentioned as an example of others that took place. On the night of 7th/8th October a party of about 50 all ranks of the 11th A. & S. Highlanders proceeded to raid the German lines. Unfortunately the wire had not been sufficiently well cut; the enemy were on the alert, and only two of the party, Lieutenant Muirhead and Private Blackwood, succeeded in reaching the German wire. Getting through a gap and into the trench, they found four Germans. Blackwood dispatched two with his bayonet, and Muirhead shot a third as he was about to club Blackwood with his rifle. They then hustled the fourth out of the trench and started back. By this time all three had been wounded by shell-fire. Unfortunately Blackwood and the prisoner were killed when half-way across No Man's Land, and Muirhead again wounded. Notwithstanding this, he managed to cut the shoulder-strap from the dead German as identification before returning to his lines—a very fine piece of work.

Throughout September the weather was fine, but as the year drew on it changed, the remaining three months being cold and wet. Thanks, however, to the care and forethought of the R.A.M.C. and "A and Q," cases of sickness were few. By October 31 all winter accommodation had been completed; in addition, drying-sheds had been erected, and conditions were vastly different from those on the Somme the year before. It is worthy of record that there were only eight cases of "trench feet" in the Fifteenth Division throughout the whole tour.

Oct.-Dec. 1917.

On November 27 orders were received that the XVII. Corps front would be reduced, and the 61st Division, on the left of the Fifteenth, would be withdrawn. This necessitated "side-stepping." On the right the Fifteenth handed over the line from Twin Copses to Scabbard Alley to the 4th Division, whilst on the left it took over from the 61st that part of the line as far as the Arras-Douai railway (see map). The relief was somewhat complicated, but, in spite of heavy enemy shelling during the afternoon of the 28th, was completed by the evening of the following day.

A "side-step."

On December 4 the gas area, in which respirators had to be worn in the "alert" position, was deepened, as the enemy were now using gas-shells to a far greater extent than formerly. On this particular day he sent over a thousand of these gas-shells on one small area alone; other positions suffered similarly.

Throughout December every available man was engaged on strengthening the line. Many new trench systems were constructed behind those already in existence, in view of a suspected move by the enemy on a large scale. Speaking of this work in his despatches, the Commander-in-Chief states:—

Work on defences.

> "Though time and labour available were in no way adequate if, as we suspected, the enemy intended to commence his offensive operations in the early spring, a large portion of this work was in fact completed before the enemy launched his great attack. That so much was accomplished is due to the untiring energy of all ranks of the fighting units, the Transportation Service, and the Labour Corps."

At the close of the year, with the exception of the first week in September, the Division had been for six and a half months in the line, of which two and a half had been spent fighting in the Ypres salient.

Dec. 1917–Jan. 1918. Relief of Division.

It was therefore with unmixed feelings that orders for its relief by the Guards Division were received towards the end of December. The move took place during the first three days of the New Year, General Reed handing over command of the sector on January 3. As usual, the artillery were the last to leave the line, but by the evening of the 5th the Division was billeted as under, headquarters moving from Arras to Noyelle-Vion on the 8th :—

44th Brigade, Arras.
45th Brigade, Warlus.
46th Brigade, Berneville.
Divisional Artillery (less 74th Brigade, R.F.A.), Habarcq.
74th Brigade, R.F.A., in position of readiness just north of Tilloy les Mafflaines.
73rd Field Company, R.E., Limencourt.
74th Field Company, R.E., Arras.
91st Field Company, R.E., Arras.

Work of the R.A. in 1917.

When reviewing the narrative of 1917 it may seem that sufficient had not been said regarding the Divisional artillery. Never once did the gunners fail the infantry. The worst period for all arms was, undoubtedly, that spent in the salient. The following are extracts from the letters of the late Major Francis Graham, D.S.O., M.C., R.F.A., commanding C/71 Battery, relating to the operations east of Ypres :—

"August 2, 1917. The weather has again intervened on the side of the enemy. The water-level is never very far removed from the surface in these latitudes, and if we have another couple of days' rain we shall be able to hand over to the Navy, put on our bathing drawers, and swim home. . . . The ground is like one large sponge—the poor old tubes sink farther and farther in. Soon there will be nothing left above-ground but the cowls of our dial-sights, and we shall be loading through a periscope. The Hun is putting up a very fine fight. The way he counter-attacked yesterday against the mud, rain, and the Jocks was a remarkable performance, even if unsuccessful. The Jocks were, as usual, magnificent! They carried all before them, and their advance was only limited by the progress of the people on their right and left."

On August 31 he writes :—

"We are now busy 'resting' at a place called, inaccurately, by the Army 'What Ho!' (Watou—Ed.) I have spent the last few days pulling on a rope trying to heave my guns out of a bog and the relieving guns into their place. The relieving crowd had only had experience of peaceful sectors, where all was nice and clean, cartridge cases burnished, &c., and I am afraid they will hardly appreciate our little mud holes. They were much distressed because we had no 'ablution benches' to hand over to them. (I told them we had been too busy fighting the Boche to think of washing.) We left them full of the offensive spirit, but a trifle apprehensive."

1917.

Retrospect.

During the past year the Division had served in five different corps, and had taken part in two great and successful offensives. On both occasions it had suffered severe casualties, but, with care and attention, was being nursed back to strength and efficiency, and the close of the year found it as good in discipline, *moral*, and fighting spirit as it had ever been in its younger days.

It cannot, however, be denied that an opportunity for training was sadly needed. A period of fighting, with very heavy casualties, followed by an exceptionally long spell of duty in the front line, gave no facilities for the instruction of the young N.C.O.'s and soldiers who had taken the place of those killed and wounded. It is only whilst at rest, clear of the immediate possibility of fighting, that battalion, battery, and company commanders can get hold of units as a whole, supervise their training, and, by instruction and observation, gain a thorough knowledge of the capabilities of their officers, N.C.O.'s, and men.[1]

APPENDIX TO CHAPTER VII.

Many changes had taken place in commands and on the staff, the chief of these being, of course, the departure of Major-Generals McCracken and Thuillier and the arrival of Major-General Reed. Amongst others, the following were the chief alterations :—

January.—Brevet-Major Hon. E. O. Campbell, Seaforth Highlanders, to Brigade-Major, 44th Infantry Brigade, vice Captain K. Barge.

[1] In December the Division suffered a severe loss in the death of Lieut.-Colonel D. McLeod, D.S.O., 8/10th Gordons, on December 19. He was a splendid soldier, and had risen from the ranks of his regiment (the Cameron Highlanders), and had seen much active service in various parts of the world. His death was due to pneumonia, possibly attributable to gas poisoning, accelerated by his refusal to leave his battalion when ill until ordered to do so.

February.—Captain Sir E. P. Duncombe to G.S.O. 3, vice Captain C. M. F. N. Ryan, M.C., appointed Brigade-Major, 45th Infantry Brigade, vice Major L. Carr, D.S.O., to G.S.O. 2, 51st Division. Major J S. Drew, M.C., Cameron Highlanders, to G.S.O. 2, vice Major H. F. Baillie, D.S.O., to G.S.O. 2, III. Corps.

April.—Lieut.-Colonel, Temp. Brig.-General, A. E. Fagan, 36th Horse, I.A., to command 46th Infantry Brigade, vice Brig.-General T. G. Matheson, to command 20th Division.

May.—Major H. F. Baillie, D.S.O., Seaforth Highlanders, from G.S.O. 2, III. Corps, to G.S.O. 1, vice Lieut.-Colonel H. H. S. Knox, D.S.O., to B.G.G.S., XV. Corps. Captain P. T. Blair, Royal Scots, T.F., to Brigade-Major, 44th Infantry Brigade, vice Major Hon. E. O. Campbell.

July.—Lieut.-Colonel, Temp. Brig.-General, D. R. Sladen, K.O.S.B., to command 46th Infantry Brigade, vice Brig.-General A. E. Fagan, to England, gassed. Captain W. P. Haviland, A. & S. Highlanders, to G.S.O. 3, vice Captain Sir E. P. Duncombe. Major J. F. Rankin, A.V.C., T.F., to A.D.V.S., vice Captain T. S. G. Pallin, A.V.C. Captain R. C. Money, Scottish Rifles, to Brigade-Major, 44th Infantry Brigade, vice Captain P. T. Blair.

October.—Captain A. Y. G. Thomson, Cameron Highlanders, to G.S.O. 2, vice Major J. M. S. Drew, M.C., to G.S.O. 2, XVIII. Corps. Lieut.-Colonel J. M. Arthur, D.S.O., R.E., T.F., to be C.R.E., vice Lieut.-Colonel R. S. Walker, D.S.O., C.R.E., to Home Establishment.

November.—Brig.-General E. Hilliam, Nova Scotia Regiment, from 10th Canadian Infantry Brigade, to command 44th Infantry Brigade, vice Brig.-General F. J. Marshall, to Commandant Senior Officers' School, Aldershot.

December.—Major A. P. D. Telfer Smollett, H.L.I., to G.S.O. 2, vice Captain A. Y. G. Thomson, killed. Captain T. K. Newbigging to Brigade-Major, 46th Infantry Brigade, vice Major R. V. G. Horne, to G.S.O. 2, 20th Division.

[STATEMENT OF CASUALTIES

UNIT.	Killed.		Wounded.		Missing.		TOTALS.
	O.	O. R.	O.	O. R.	O.	O. R.	All Ranks.
44TH INFANTRY BRIGADE.							
Headquarters . . .	..	..	1	..	..	..	1
9th Black Watch . .	3	44	6	101	..	23	179
8th Seaforth Highlanders .	2	37	6	223	3	122	393
8/10th Gordon Highlanders	2	24	4	161	..	13	204
7th Cameron Highlanders .	4	8	6	134	..	59	211
44th Machine-Gun Company	..	3	1	22	..	4	30
44th Trench-Mortar Battery	..	..	..	..	..	..	..
45TH INFANTRY BRIGADE.							
13th Royal Scots . .	5	16	3	144	3	112	283
6/7th R.S. Fusiliers . .	..	26	7	157	..	22	212
6th Cameron Highlanders .	1	11	3	99	..	..	114
11th A. & S. Highlanders .	2	26	8	168	5	114	323
45th Machine-Gun Company	..	10	2	32	..	5	49
45th Trench-Mortar Battery	..	8	..	10	..	1	19
46TH INFANTRY BRIGADE.							
7/8th K.O.S.B. . .	1	17	7	77	..	3	105
10th Scottish Rifles . .	..	22	2	157	..	5	186
10/11th H.L.I. . . .	..	16	1	86	..	13	116
12th H.L.I.	..	10	1	57	..	2	70
46th Machine-Gun Company	..	5	..	12	..	5	22
46th Trench-Mortar Battery	..	2	..	2	..	..	4
9th Gordon Hrs. (Pioneers)	3	23	7	102	..	5	140
225th Machine-Gun Company	..	..	1	14	..	..	15
70th Brigade, R.F.A. .	1	9	2	50	..	1	63
71st Brigade, R.F.A. .	..	6	2	45	..	..	53
Fifteenth Div. Ammn. Col.	..	1	..	4	..	..	5
Hvy. & Med. T.-M. Battys.	..	..	..	18	..	..	18
73, 74, 91 Field Coys., R.E.	..	1	3	23	..	..	27
Fifteenth Div. Sig. Coy., R.E.	..	..	..	2	..	..	2
Fifteenth Div. Train, A.S.C.	..	..	..	1	..	..	1
45th, 46th, and 47th Field Ambulances, R.A.M.C. .	..	5	3	34	..	..	42
R.A.M.C., attached infantry and Divisional Artillery .	1	..	1	..	..	..	2
C.F. (Pres.) attached infantry	1	..	..	..	..	..	1
Total . .	26	330	77	1935	11	509	2888

CHAPTER VIII.

THE GERMAN OFFENSIVE, MARCH 1918.[1]

Jan. 1918.

THE weather for the first half of January 1918 was of the vilest. First, heavy snow, then rain, made the slush knee-deep round most of the billets. Even the lasting good-humour and "make-the-best-of-it" custom of the Scots was now sorely tried. They had come out for "rest" and to refit after months in the line, but the conditions were not one whit better than the trenches. Some of the hut encampments were in a disgraceful condition. Trench-boards had disappeared, and even the flooring had, in some instances, been torn up, possibly used as firewood by some former occupants. Yet in these districts Town Majors were to be found whose duty it was to see to the upkeep of the encampments. Thus the "fighting-line" soldiers "rested" in discomfort, whilst troops whose duties kept them behind the line, and who had, of course, taken up nearly all the best billets, lived in comfort. In January, Colonel C. E. Pollock, A.D.M.S. of the Division, was promoted to be D.D.M.S. of a Corps, and left the Fifteenth Scottish Division, to the regret of all.

Much training was, however, carried out, culminating in the brigade exercises on the 25th, 26th, and 29th in the area round Wailly. By this time it was well known that the enemy contemplated an attack in the near future, and every nerve was strained to complete the arrangements necessary to meet it. To do this the three Field Companies, R.E., and the 9th Gordons were only given a few days in which to carry out training in musketry before returning to work on the third line (the Army Line, and others connected with it) immediately east of Arras.

[1] Maps 10 and 11.

Jan.-Feb. 1918. Reduction of Brigades.

Early in January orders were received entailing a change in the composition of infantry brigades, each being reduced by one battalion. It is unnecessary to enter into the reasons for the change, beyond stating that decrease in man-power and increase in the front held by the British forces made it inevitable. It was with great regret that certain battalions learnt that they would leave the Division. Early in February the change commenced. On the 1st the 10/11th H.L.I. left the 46th Brigade to join the 40th Division. Two days later the 12th H.L.I.[1] left the same brigade for the 35th Division, Fourth Army. To replace these, on the 8th, whilst in the front line, the 9th Black Watch was transferred from the 44th to the 46th Brigade. On the 21st the 45th Brigade lost the 6/7th Royal Scots Fusiliers, on transfer to the 59th Division, the three brigades being then composed as follows :—

44th Brigade (Brig.-General E. Hilliam)—

- 8th Seaforth Highlanders.
- 8/10th Gordon Highlanders.
- 7th Cameron Highlanders.

45th Brigade (Brig.-General W. H. L. Allgood)—

- 13th Royal Scots.
- 6th Cameron Highlanders.
- 11th A. & S. Highlanders.

46th Brigade (Brig.-General A. F. Lumsden [2])—

- 7/8th K.O.S.B.
- 10th Scottish Rifles.
- 9th Black Watch.

Back to the Arras front.

On February 3 orders were issued for the relief of the 4th Division by the Fifteenth in the right sector of the XVII. Corps front. Two days later the move commenced, when Divisional Headquarters moved

[1] Shortly after the battalion left the Fifteenth Division, its C.O., Lieut.-Colonel W. H. Anderson, was killed in action at Maricourt on March 25. For his very gallant conduct there he received a posthumous reward of the Victoria Cross. Twice that day Colonel Anderson personally organised and led two counter-attacks, and, to quote from the 'London Gazette' of May 3, 1918, "this very gallant officer died fighting within the enemy's lines, setting a magnificent example to all who were privileged to serve under him."

[2] Brig.-General Lumsden succeeded Brig.-General D. R. Sladen on February 9, 1918, on the latter's return to England.

Feb. 1918.

from Noyelle-Vion to Arras. That day the 44th Brigade took over the right section, and the following day the 45th took over the left from the 12th and 10th Brigades respectively, the 46th moving up to Arras in reserve. General Reed assumed command of the sector at 9 A.M. on the 7th.

Organisation of front.

On the 8th the northern boundary of the sector was extended as far as the Lagoon, immediately south of the Scarpe (see Map 10). General Reed then decided to reorganise the front line, and to hold it with his three brigades, each furnishing their own supports and reserves. This move was completed by the morning of the 9th, when the Division was disposed as follows :—

44th Brigade—Right (Cambrai road) Section.
45th Brigade—Centre (Monchy) Section.
46th Brigade—Left (Pelves) Section.

Each brigade held the front line with one battalion, a second in support, with two companies in Nova Scotia, Halifax, MacKenzie, and California Trenches, and the third battalion farther back in reserve.

The Divisional front was held in this manner up to March 23, when the forward defences were evacuated in accordance with orders. The reason for this was that the French had found that the enemy invariably obliterated the front trenches prior to their attack, and they therefore held their front line lightly, keeping most of their men farther back. Hence the scheme was to hold the forward line east of Monchy lightly, whilst the main line of resistance, running on a line, roughly, north and south through Monchy, was strongly held.

As February wore on the enemy activity, both artillery and patrols, increased. In consequence the Divisional artillery and machine-gun companies harried their back areas by day and night, whilst all brigades carried out more or less successful raids on their front line.[1] These

[1] The following minor operations took place during this period :—

February 22.—7th Camerons, 44th Brigade, raided the enemy trenches west of the Bois du Vert. Three prisoners of the 65th Regiment (185th Division) were taken, and the party returned after having suffered no casualties.

March 6.—10th Scottish Rifles, 46th Brigade, raided the German front line in the Pelves sector. The trench was found to be empty, and the raiders returned, having had two men wounded.

March 9.—8th Seaforths, 44th Brigade, raided Strap Trench in the Cambrai Road sector. No identification was obtained, and unfortunately the party suffered somewhat

raids kept the German activities well in hand, and the enemy showed marked disinclination to trouble the Fifteenth Division at that time.

Feb.-Mar. 1918.

Throughout the month of February elaborate instructions in the shape of defence schemes, with alterations, amendments, and additions, were issued from Division and Corps. Unfortunately no copies of these are preserved in the Divisional diaries, but their completeness is shown by the voluminous nature of those issued by the three infantry brigades, artillery, and R.E. These documents are far too lengthy to quote, but in them directions are contained which left little to the imagination should the enemy attack in strength.

Early in March it was established without a doubt that the German attack would soon be delivered, and the Division proceeded to prepare for it. On the night of the 11th/12th, in accordance with the directions contained in the defence scheme, Brig.-General Allgood, acting G.O.C., thinned out the advance line east of Monchy, and moved up the battalions in brigade reserve to prepared positions nearer to the front line.[1] Beyond an increase in artillery activity on both sides, nothing of importance occurred for the next ten days, but on March 21 the storm broke.

That day the Fifteenth Division was disposed as follows :—

Dispositions on Mar. 21.

44th Brigade. *Right:* 8/10th Gordons in the front system. Two companies of the 7th Camerons in support, and two in trenches and caves near Les Fosses Farm. The 8th Seaforths in reserve in Bois des Bœufs Camp.

45th Brigade. *Centre:* 6th Camerons in the front line east of Monchy, with two companies of the 11th A. & S. Highlanders in Orchard Trench, just north of the village, the remaining two companies of that battalion being in support in Congo Trench, with the 13th Royal Scots in reserve in Wilderness Camp.

46th Brigade. *Left:* 10th Scottish Rifles in the front system, the 9th Black Watch in support, and the 7/8th K.O.S.B. in reserve in Tilloy Camp.

severely, one officer being killed and another wounded ; two men killed, 24 wounded, and 6 returned as missing.

March 11.—6th Camerons, 45th Brigade, attempted to enter Long Trench, Monchy sector. Owing to uncut wire the party did not enter the enemy's trench, but, lying down outside the wire, they inflicted casualties on them by means of bombs and rifle fire. Casualties : one officer killed and three men wounded.

[1] Major-General Reed was away ill for four weeks, and did not resume command of the Division until March 23.

Mar. 21-22, 1918.

The 9th Gordons (Pioneers) were in the eastern outskirts of Arras, with the three Field Companies, R.E.

The German bombardment.

At 5 A.M. on the 21st the enemy heavily bombarded the Divisional front, especially the right and centre sub-sectors, at the same time discharging gas and using gas-shells. Fortunately the attack had been anticipated, and very few casualties occurred, although the trenches were considerably damaged. The bombardment lasted for four hours, but was not followed by any infantry assault. Farther south the roar of the guns, and reports which came through from the Corps, confirmed the fact that the long-looked-for attack had commenced.

The 22nd passed without incident, but news from the south made it apparent that the enemy was making progress, and that as the attack spread northwards the Divisional front would soon become involved.

In the course of the afternoon it became clear that the enemy had broken through the Allied line on a wide front south of Bullecourt, and, although the 3rd Division on the right had so far beaten off all attacks, its right flank was dangerously exposed by the enforced retirement farther south, and it was obvious that our line here must be readjusted in conformity. It was decided, therefore, to draw back the Fifteenth and 3rd Divisions during the night of 22nd/23rd to positions prepared farther back, and thus ensure a continuous front from the left of the Fifteenth Division to the division on right of 3rd Division.

Withdrawal.

The likelihood of this move had been anticipated. Instructions regarding it had been issued some time before, with the result that all ranks knew exactly what to do. The actual orders for the retirement did not reach the Division Commander until 9 P.M. on the 22nd, but, in spite of such short notice, the operation was successfully carried out, without opposition or interference on the part of the enemy, and the Division was in its new position by 3 A.M. on the 23rd, with rear-guards from all three brigades still occupying the evacuated outpost line to the east of Monchy.

This retirement was carried out in a masterly manner. First, the front-line troops withdrew, leaving patrols and the companies detailed as rear-guards. They were followed by those in the support line, and lastly, those in the front line of the second system—Congo

MAJOR-GENERAL H. L. REED, V.C., C.B., C.M.G.

and Morocco Trenches—withdrew to the third system—Corsica and Jerusalem Trenches—on a north and south line, just east of Orange Hill.

Mar. 22-23, 1918.

It was impossible to remove all stores. A good deal were saved, and the remainder were either destroyed or thrown into shell-holes full of water. All telephone wires and test-boxes were destroyed, and as much damage as possible was done to the dug-outs, which could not be destroyed or blown up on account of the noise warning the enemy of what was taking place. In connection with the salving of material, it is worth recording that the 11th A. & S. Highlanders, taking advantage of the early morning mist on the 23rd after they had taken up their new positions, sent out parties, who collected a further amount of S.A.A., bombs, &c., and formed dumps with them in the new line, which materially assisted them in repelling the German attack later on.

Throughout the night of the 22nd/23rd active patrolling was carried out. Véry lights were fired as usual all along the line, and the fact that a hostile patrol approaching one of the posts held by the 45th Brigade retired hastily when fired on, shows that the enemy had no idea that a withdrawal was taking place.

Dispositions at dawn, Mar. 23.

At dawn on the 23rd the Division was disposed as follows: Rear-guards from all three brigades occupied the old front line south and east of Monchy. On the right one company of the 8/10th Gordons, one company of the 7th Camerons, and two Vickers-guns held the original line of the 44th Brigade. On their left the 45th Brigade left a company of the 6th Camerons and two machine-guns east of Monchy; whilst farther north a company of the 10th Scottish Rifles and two guns of "C" Company, Fifteenth Divisional Machine-Gun Battalion, covered the retirement of the 46th Brigade. In the third system the 44th Brigade had the 8th Seaforths in the front, support, and reserve lines; whilst three companies of the 7th Camerons occupied the front and support lines of the Army Line farther back; the 8/10th Gordons, less one company, being in reserve in Artillery Camp.

In the centre the 11th A. & S. Highlanders held the front and support lines of the third system for the 45th Brigade. Two companies of the 13th Royal Scots occupied the Army Line, under tactical

Mar. 23, 1918. Dispositions at dawn.

command of the O.C. A. & S. Highlanders, the remaining two being in Wilderness Camp, together with two companies of the 6th Camerons, whilst the fourth company of the latter occupied the old British trenches east of St Saveur and north of the Cambrai road.

On the left the 46th Brigade had formations from all three battalions in the new front line. On the right a company of the 10th Scottish Rifles occupied the new line—Jerusalem Trench,—with another in support, and a third in Invergordon Trench. Next them the 7/8th K.O.S.B. had six platoons in Jerusalem Trench, two in Jericho Trench north of them, one company in support, and the fourth in Invergordon Trench. On the left the 9th Black Watch had a company in Jericho Trench and Lancer Avenue, another in a line of consolidated shell-holes between Lancer Avenue and the Lagoon, and the remaining two in support about 400 yards behind them.

The line now ran from the point marked "W"[1] on the map, almost due north, to point "Y," just east of Orange Hill, in Jerusalem Trench, bending north-east from there to point "Z" and the Lagoon. Of this, the 44th Brigade held from the right of the Divisional boundary to the Cambrai road, the 45th from there to point "X" on Map 10, whilst the 46th held from the latter point to "Z," and thence to the Lagoon.

During the withdrawal of the infantry, Brig.-General Macnaghten, C.R.A., Fifteenth Division, arranged the retirement of the artillery to prepared positions farther back, batteries destroying their dug-outs before leaving them. The sappers and pioneers were also moved from their positions east of Arras into the city itself, and all transport lines went back to the west of Arras.

This retirement was a difficult operation, and the manner in which it was carried out, unknown to the enemy, was beyond doubt a great achievement. Unpleasant as it was to have to give up ground won so gallantly by them the year before, Monchy village included, all recognised its necessity if Arras was to be held. Had the city fallen, Vimy Ridge and all positions north of the Scarpe would have been outflanked, and the whole line northwards would have gone. Arras was the chief bastion of the whole line, and its safety was now entrusted chiefly to the Fifteenth (Scottish) Division. Three days later,

[1] Map 10.

on the eve of the main attack on Arras, the XVII. Corps Commander, Sir Charles Fergusson, in a message to General Reed, says :—

Mar. 23, 1918.

"The Division is now in a post of honour. The ground it holds is of the utmost importance, and it is to be held at all costs. I am glad it is in the hands of a Scottish division, who, I know, will never let the enemy pass."

Thus disposed, the Division awaited the German attack with confidence.

Rear-guards drawn in.

At 5 A.M. on the 23rd the attack opened with a heavy bombardment of the original advanced line east of Monchy, which continued for an hour and a half. At 7 A.M. it recommenced, and lasted until 8 A.M. Two hours later, at 10 A.M., the enemy were seen advancing in force from the direction of Guemappe, and the rear-guard of the 44th Brigade commenced to retire. This withdrawal was somewhat earlier than had been expected, and was due to the fact that the left brigade of the 3rd Division had been unable to leave out patrols, with the result that the right flank of the 44th Brigade became exposed. The 8th Seaforths withdrew fighting, according to orders, inflicting severe losses on the enemy during the process, and suffering only very slightly themselves.

At 9.30 A.M. three companies of the enemy infantry were seen by the rear-guard of the 6th Camerons, centre brigade, advancing from the Bois du Verts towards Cavalry Farm. Rifle and machine-gun fire was at once opened on them from East Trench, north of Vine Avenue, with good results. As no firing could be heard on the right, where the rear-guard of the 44th Brigade should have been, efforts were made to get into touch with it, but it was found to have withdrawn, as stated above, and in consequence the Camerons were obliged to follow suit. On the left the rear-guard of the 46th Brigade, 10th Scottish Rifles, did not retire until actually ordered to do so by General Lumsden, but, shortly after 11 o'clock, all had withdrawn through the troops holding the new line.

The enemy advanced cautiously in groups, which proved superb targets for rifle, Lewis-gun, and artillery fire, of which full advantage was taken. The Germans appeared to be somewhat at a loss on finding the advanced position unoccupied, and did not seem to know what

Mar. 23-24, 1918.

to do. By noon they had reached a line running, roughly, north and south through Les Fosses Farm, and here they proceeded to dig in.

Describing the enemy advance, the 46th Brigade diary states :—

"Their consolidation was in full view of the 11th A. & S. Highlanders, who forwarded valuable reports from time to time. Throughout the day they were continually harassed by rifle and Lewis-gun fire from the two front companies of the Argylls, who, between 11 A.M. and 6 P.M., expended 15,000 rounds of S.A.A., all at excellent targets. There is no doubt that this day's shooting was very valuable to the battalion, and really demonstrated to the men the value of the rifle and its effect when firing on large parties of men who had been scattered by artillery fire."

About noon, in order to guard the southern flank of the Division, Brig.-General Hilliam, 44th Brigade, moved up the 7th Camerons from the Army Line, east of Tilloy, nearer to the front line, their place being taken by the 8/10th Gordons from Artillery Camp. At the same time, the 45th Brigade moved up the 13th Royal Scots, less two companies, from the Army Line to the ridge south of Chapel Road, in N.8.d., where they commenced digging a trench, known later as part of the Neuville-Vitasse Switch Line. Later in the day they were moved farther north-east, and continued the trench along Chapel Road, assisted by the 74th Field Company, R.E., their place being taken by the 7th Camerons from the 44th Brigade.

Except for intermittent shelling, the rest of the day, the 23rd, and the following three days passed off without incident on the Fifteenth Divisional front. Patrols were constantly out at night, and were successful in capturing a few prisoners. From these and from what they saw, it was evident that the enemy were consolidating their positions with a view to a further attack in the near future.

Germans repulsed farther south.

On March 24 the Germans attacked the 3rd Division during the morning, but were repulsed. In this attack the 44th Trench-Mortar Battery took part, and, having expended all their shells, the teams of the four guns engaged, led by Lieutenant McEwan, 8/10th Gordons, went forward to the front line, and assisted in repelling the attack with rifle-fire. The right of the 44th Brigade, Seaforth Highlanders, was also involved in this attack, and their conduct drew forth an expression of admiration from the G.O.C. 3rd Division, and also a message from the XVII. Corps Commander as follows :—

Mar. 24-27, 1918.

"Please convey my congratulations to the 44th Infantry Brigade and 8th Seaforth Highlanders, who, with the assistance of the artillery, repulsed the German attack on March 24."

The late Lieut.-Colonel Hon. E. Campbell commanded the Seaforths on this occasion. He had a complete view of the German advance, and told General Reed later that no praise could be great enough for the daring of the German method of getting through the wire. He saw a party of 50 men, under an officer, who carried a stick, get outside into the open, barely 400 yards from the Divisional front line, and proceed to cut a gap in the wire. Although many were shot down whilst doing so, including the officer and his relief, others took their places and carried on the work.

Whilst the situation thus remained unchanged on the Divisional front, exceedingly heavy fighting had taken place farther south. The enemy had attacked on a front of fifty-four miles with sixty-four divisions, and had forced the Allies back in many places.[1]

A critical situation.

On the 24th the situation was so serious that the Commander-in-Chief issued the following Special Order of the day :—

"*To all ranks of the British Army*
in France and Flanders.

"We are again at a crisis in the war. The enemy has collected on this front every available division, and is aiming at the destruction of the British Army. We have already inflicted heavy losses on the enemy in the course of the last two days, and the French are sending troops as quickly as possible to our support. I feel that every one in the Army fully realises how much depends on the exertions and steadfastness of each one of us, and will do his utmost to prevent the enemy from attaining his ends."

Two days later the Governments of the Allies placed General Foch in supreme command of all operations on the Western Front.

Strengthening the defence.

During these four days much construction work was done behind the line held by the Division. The Army Line, running due north and south through Neuville Vitasse and east of Tilloy and Blangy, was

[1] Against this onslaught the British had twenty-nine infantry and three cavalry divisions, of which nineteen infantry divisions were in the line. As the line was forced back, the flanks of Corps and Divisions to the north were obliged to conform to the movement. Thus the battle widened until, by the 25th, it was apparent that the right flank of the Fifteenth Division might soon have to withdraw also.

Mar. 25-28, 1918.

completed and heavily wired, and various switch lines were constructed connecting it with the trench systems farther east. Of these, the Neuville Vitasse line is the one with which the Division was mainly concerned. It ran approximately from Neuville Vitasse along Chapel Road to the Cambria road east of Feuchy Chapel, where it joined Nova Scotia and Halifax Trenches in the support line of the front system. At least half this line was dug in the last four days before the attack by men of the 44th and 45th Brigades, assisted by the Pioneers (9th Gordons) and Field Companies, R.E. It proved of enormous importance later on, when the right of the Division had to be slightly thrown back.

On March 25 Divisional Headquarters were informed that information had been received from the Fifth Army that the enemy intended to attack the line north of the Scarpe the following day. This attack was to be carried out by the 219th, 23rd Reserve, and 50th Bavarian Divisions. This information proved correct, except the date, which was the 28th.

Dispositions, midnight, 27-28.

At midnight on the 27th/28th the Division was disposed as follows :—

44th Brigade. *Right:* Two companies 7th Camerons in the front line, Minorca Trench, with the right company in touch with the 2nd Battalion Suffolk Regiment, 76th Brigade, 3rd Division, and the other two companies in Nova Scotia Trench.

8/10th Gordons in strong-points and old communication trenches about 500 yards behind, in support.

8th Seaforths in reserve in the Army Line and dug-outs on the eastern slopes of Telegraph Hill.

45th Brigade. *Centre:* 13th Royal Scots in the front-line system, Corsica and Cromarty Trenches, with two companies of the 6th Camerons in support in Plaid and Dagger Trenches, under tactical command of the O.C. Royal Scots, the remaining two companies being in the Neuville Vitasse line east of Chapel Road.

11th A. & S. Highlanders in the Army Line south of Tilloy.

46th Brigade. *Left:* 9th Black Watch on the right, and 7/8th K.O.S.B. on the left, held Jerusalem and Jericho Trenches, furnishing their own supports.

10th Scottish Rifles in the Army Line in reserve.

The general attack.

On the morning of the 28th the long-expected attack took place. The historian of the 7/8th K.O.S.B. aptly describes the commencement of the enemy operation: "If ever the lid was taken off hell, it must have been on March 28, 1918."

Mar. 28, 1918.

At 3 A.M. on the 28th the enemy opened an extremely heavy bombardment with gas and high-explosive along the whole of the Divisional front, especially on the part held by the 44th and 45th Brigades. With an interval of half an hour, between 4 and 4.30 A.M., this hail of shells continued, gradually increasing in volume until 5.30 A.M., when his infantry, using liquid-fire projectors, advanced to the assault. On the right the front line held by the 7th Camerons and the right of the 3rd Division had been obliterated by the bombardment. Few of the Camerons occupying it remained alive, but those who survived opened a heavy fire on the dense masses of Germans, who, under cover of the smoke and dust, could be seen about 100 yards away advancing from Minorca Trench. The S.O.S. signal was at once sent up on the 44th Brigade front, and, although it was not seen on account of the smoke, the gunners were fully alive to the situation, and opened fire on their S.O.S. lines. On the right, as the left of the 3rd Division did not exist, the enemy had no difficulty in getting round the right flank of the surviving Camerons. It is difficult to describe what actually took place during the first few minutes, as very few men of the leading companies were left to tell what occurred. The flanks of both were annihilated. Not an officer or man of the three platoons on the left or the one on the right returned, and only one from the next two came back. Smoke and dust hid all movement, but it can be safely conjectured that every man fought to the last before being overwhelmed. An attempt was made to form a defensive flank facing south, but it was too late, and the few remaining men of the 7th Camerons withdrew, under cover of rifle and Lewis-gun fire, to the Switch Line, where they got in touch with the 6th Battalion on their left.[1]

The right flank turned.

Whilst this was taking place on the right, no attack had as yet been made farther north, although the trenches were being heavily bombarded. At 6 A.M. the O.C. 6th Camerons in Plaid Trench, seeing the plight of the 7th Battalion, moved up two of his platoons in support of them, and informed the O.C. 13th Royal Scots of what he had done. Twenty minutes later the enemy artillery fire on the 45th

[1] Map 11.

Mar. 28, 1918. Brigade front increased in violence, and at 7.10 A.M. Germans were seen advancing in mass formation from Les Fosses Farm. The left of the brigade line held on for some time, but the right and support companies, who had suffered more severely from the bombardment, found, as had those of the 44th Brigade, their flank turned, and, with the enemy behind them, they too were overwhelmed after a short but stubborn resistance. The left company, now reduced to forty men, on the initiative of the sole surviving officer, Lieutenant Farquharson, manned the firing line and poured a hot fire into the advancing Germans and those who had by this time worked round his right flank. The latter were, however, too strong, and this gallant band was forced to withdraw to the position held by the left support company of the battalion in Cromarty Trench, where a further stand was made. Half an hour later, what remained of these companies was obliged to withdraw farther back still to the small trench between Vine Avenue and Chapel Alley. Here they found a Vickers-gun and two trench-mortars. Determined not to give way, they made another stand in this position. Again they were outflanked on their right and, unfortunately, on their left also, so, after doing their utmost to stem the enemy's advance, they withdrew to Plaid and Dagger Trenches.

As regards the 46th (left) Brigade, at 8.30 A.M. the enemy had not penetrated its line. A quarter of an hour later the 9th Black Watch were forced to withdraw, fighting a rear-guard action ; but the 7/8th K.O.S.B. on their left continued to hold on, and formed a defensive flank facing south, connecting with the Black Watch. Lieut.-Colonel Innes, O.C. Black Watch, had to give up command through illness on the 22nd. Major W. B. Binnie, who succeeded him, was severely wounded on the early morning of the 28th, and the command devolved on Captain Hamilton, adjutant, who had a difficult situation suddenly thrust on him.

Situation, 9 A.M.

Such was the general situation about 9 A.M. on the Division front. It was certainly serious. It appears that the enemy adopted somewhat novel tactics on this occasion. He did not attack on the whole front simultaneously, but, starting from his left, launched one attack after another in succession from the left, waiting until each formation opposing him in turn was in danger in being outflanked and was fully engaged on its own front before attacking farther to the right.

To return to the Division's right. At 9 A.M. reports reached the 44th Brigade Headquarters that the Neuville Vitasse Switch Line was held by the 8/10th Gordons and the 7th Camerons, then only 6 officers and 150 other ranks strong, on the right and left respectively, in touch with the 6th Camerons of the 45th Brigade. The brigade trench-mortar battery had by this time lost all its guns, and the personnel, now mustering 1 officer and 8 men, joined the 7th Camerons with their rifles. Communication either by telephone or runner from the front line was out of the question ; short wires were cut, and the shelling was so intense that it was useless to attempt to repair the lines. All communications had to be sent through the 45th Brigade Headquarters, and thence by runner to the 44th Brigade.

March 28, 1918.

At 9.30 A.M. Lieut.-Colonel Norman MacLeod, 7th Camerons, and Captain J. B. Wood, 8/10th Gordons, the latter being in command of the two forward companies of his battalion, decided to counter-attack from the Switch Line. Messages were sent off asking for supporting artillery fire, but, as this was not forthcoming an hour later, owing to the messages not having reached their destination, the attack was held up, and Colonel MacLeod then proceeded along the line to ascertain the situation on the 6th Battalion front. Finding their line was strongly held, he arranged with them to form a defensive flank, and gave up all idea of a counter-attack. Whilst thus engaged, the enemy was seen advancing along the Cambrai road in considerable force, having reached the Feuchy Chapel cross-roads. Here he was checked for the time being by the fire of the 13th Royal Scots Battalion Headquarters, just west of the Chapel.

Farther north the other battalions of the 45th Brigade had been fighting hard. No reports of this reached brigade headquarters for some time, and when they did, only confirmed what was known from other sources. At 9.40 A.M. the 9th Gordons (Pioneers) were moved from Arras to the old British trenches north-east of Tilloy, just south of the Cambrai road, with orders to send out patrols to Telegraph Hill. At the same time, General Reed ordered half the 7th Machine-Gun Squadron, Household Cavalry, which had been lent by Corps, to take up positions in the vicinity of the hill itself, as it appeared by this time that the enemy were seriously threatening the right flank

March 28, 1918. The Army Line to be held.

of the Division in the Army Line east of Tilloy. He also sent out an order to all brigades and battalions that the Army Line was to be held at all costs, and that if possible the forward system (Brown Line) was to be reoccupied.[1]

The 46th Brigade had also been heavily engaged. About 9 A.M., when the Black Watch had been driven back, Colonel Dennis, K.O.S.B., at once formed a defensive flank with the support companies of the K.O.S.B., and linked up with the Black Watch in their new position. This was accomplished with the help of a company of the 10th Scottish Rifles, which had been ordered up to fill the gap reported to exist between the Black Watch and the Borderers. It had been intended to send up two companies, but, owing to the dangerous situation farther south, and the fact that little was then known of the situation of the Borderers, who were, as it turned out, gallantly holding their own, only a small force could be spared. The advance was brilliantly carried out. Personally directed by the commanding officer, Lieut.-Colonel A. Stanley Clark, the company advanced under heavy fire, and succeeded in driving back strong parties of the enemy, who had penetrated to the west of the Feuchy road, thus somewhat restoring the situation.

At 9.30 A.M. the G.O.C. XVII. Corps (Sir C. Fergusson) got into communication with General Reed, and the vital importance of holding Arras was discussed. It was decided that the Army Line must be made the main line of resistance if necessary, and held to a finish. Orders were therefore issued that the enemy were to be held in check as far forward as possible, but *under no conditions* was he to be allowed to pass the Army Line.

He did *not* pass it.

Withdrawal towards Army Line.

At 1.30 P.M., owing to a further withdrawal of the 3rd Division on the right, the 44th and 45th Brigades fell back, fighting desperately, towards the Army Line, and a little later the 46th Brigade conformed to their movement. By 3 P.M. all three brigades were almost back in this line. This position had been heavily shelled all day, and the reserve battalion of the 45th Brigade, 11th A. & S. Highlanders, had lost many men, their commanding officer, Lieut.-Colonel Mitchell, and

[1] Map 11.

the acting 2nd in command, Captain Wilson, being wounded early in the day.

March 28, 1918.

Although the Division had been driven from its original position, it must not be imagined that this had been done without severe cost to the enemy. Throughout the morning, and especially in the early afternoon, as they retired, the rifles, machine-guns, and Lewis-guns of the Division, to say nothing of its artillery fire, had inflicted unusually heavy losses on the Germans. These now had a great effect on the enemy's advance, and between 2 and 3 P.M. it began to slacken. At certain points his advance continued, and a party of about twenty actually occupied the Bois des Bœufs. Fortunately the 6th Camerons had been able to reorganise just before this occurred, and Lieut.-Colonel Anderson, 6th Camerons, counter-attacking them, not only drove the enemy out of the wood, but established the foundation of an outpost line east of the wood, in conjunction with the 13th Royal Scots on his left.

A successful counter-attack.

By 5 P.M. the German attack had been definitely stopped on the Division front, and the situation became "quiet." An hour later the 45th and 46th Brigades, advancing from the Army Line, established themselves on another about 500 yards farther east, as far north as the Cambrai road, the 4th Division continuing the line northwards from that point. On the right the 44th Brigade also advanced its line, but did not occupy quite so advanced a position, being obliged to conform with the 3rd Division farther south.

5 P.M.

Whilst this advance was being made a number of Germans were seen, not "encountered," in shell-holes. These men, apparently thinking that a counter-attack was being launched, fled on the approach of the Scotsmen—good evidence of the regard in which the enemy held troops of the Fifteenth Division, who, after twelve hours' continual fighting, and after being driven back by immensely superior numbers, could turn on their adversaries and retake a portion of the ground they had lost. The new line, consisting of shell-holes and a few old communication trenches, was occupied without opposition, and more or less consolidated during the night.

Before closing the account of this fighting, mention must be made of the reserves General Reed had at his disposal, of what they con-

Disposal of the Reserves.

March 28, 1918. Disposal of the Reserves.

sisted, and how they were used. Although the importance of defending Arras successfully was recognised by higher authority, there were no troops, other than those directly under the Fifteenth Division command, immediately available to reinforce this part of the front, and any support considered necessary had to be found by the Division itself. General Reed's reserves consisted of the personnel of the three Field Companies, R.E., 9th Gordons (Pioneers), and the various details and reinforcements left behind by infantry battalions when going into action. In addition, there were certain small units from Corps Headquarters that might be available if called for, including the 7th Machine-Gun Squadron, Household Cavalry, which was employed and fully maintained the magnificent reputation of its regiment.

As will be seen from the foregoing narrative, the situation had become very serious during the day, and at noon it was apparent that every available man would be required if Arras was to be saved. During the afternoon General Reed ordered up the three Field Companies, R.E., to man the old British trenches immediately east of Arras, astride the Cambrai road. At the same time, he directed that a battalion should be formed from the details left behind by the infantry battalions. The command of this battalion, the "S.O.S. Battalion," was given to Major Kennedy, 6th Camerons, and included details such as cooks, tailors, shoemakers, &c. Within two hours this force was ready and marching up. By the time it arrived in the support line the situation had become easier, and, beyond doing some excellent work in the construction of trenches, the battalion was not required, and was withdrawn the following day on the arrival of the 1st Canadian Battalion. The only other reserve available was the XVII. Corps Cyclist Battalion and the 7th Machine-Gun Squadron, Household Cavalry. The former was placed under the orders of Brig.-General Allgood, 45th Brigade, but unfortunately it lost its way, and only 1 officer and 60 other ranks reported on the night of the 28th, another 60 arriving the following day.

"S.O.S. Battalion."

So ended the fight. The Division had certainly given ground, but Arras had been saved. The Division had lost heavily (see Appendix I), but all ranks knew that they had played no small part in the battle. The troops were full of confidence, perhaps more so at the close of the day than they had been that morning.

March 28, 1918.

On the 29th the following message was received and communicated to all troops :—

> " It is with great pleasure I pass on the following message from the Corps Commander, which should be communicated to all ranks as far as possible. It is impossible for me adequately to express my thanks and admiration for hard work done and gallantry displayed by the Division.
>
> " (Signed) H. L. REED, *Major-General,*
> " *Commanding Fifteenth Scottish Division.*"

Sir Charles Fergusson's message ran as follows :—

> " I knew you could be relied on to stick it out to the end. Well done! There are fresh troops in support of you now, but I want the honour of holding Arras to be yours alone."

Work of the R.A.

Throughout the day the action of the artillery was magnificent. Obliged to withdraw their guns and yet cover the retirement of the infantry, the gunners did both with the greatest skill. At 10.15 A.M. the forward gun positions became too close to the battle line, and artillery brigades commenced to retire, one battery at a time, keeping up fire with the guns that remained until the others had reached their new positions. Their fire inflicted heavy losses on the enemy each time that he attacked, the liaison between artillery and infantry leaving nothing to be desired.

As has been already explained, nearly all the trench-mortars were knocked out early in the day. The same applies to the machine-guns. Of the twelve in the front line, only one, the extreme left gun, returned, and its team, under Lieutenant J. H. S. Peterkin, although at one time surrounded by Germans, fought their way back.

Casualties.

To the casualties suffered on the 28th must be added those incurred during the fighting between March 21 and 28—namely, 110 officers and 2664 other ranks, bringing the total up to 204 officers and 4887 other ranks, 5091 in all, in eight days' fighting.

Summing up the events of the 28th, it would appear that the reason

March 28 to April 1, 1918.

the outpost line had to be given up was on account of the severity of the enemy's preliminary bombardment, which not only annihilated most of the garrison, but enabled the attackers to outflank those remaining. The ground farther back had to be given up on account of the breach between the right flank of the Division and the left of the 76th Brigade.

The 45th Brigade account of the fighting ends with the following significant sentence :—

> "The power of the rifle was once more demonstrated. All ranks have gained confidence in this weapon when they have been allowed to use it freely. As they were forced back to our present outpost line, they used their rifles with very great effect, and the experience to the man was as good, or better, than any offensive victory, in which the rifle would probably not have been used at all."

Relief and Readjustments.

Various battalion reliefs were carried out during the night of March 28th/29th, and at 5 A.M. the 2nd Canadian Battalion, 1st Canadian Brigade, relieved the 44th in the right sub-section, on completion of which the latter proceeded to Arras, in Divisional reserve, to refit. Owing to the general situation, not much time could be given for this. Every available man was required, as further attacks were expected, and the 44th could only be given a few hours in which to reorganise.

On April 1 certain readjustments of the line were made, a portion of the right sub-section being handed over to the Canadians, who had relieved the 3rd Division on the right. At the same time the front of the Fifteenth Division was divided into two, instead of three, sub-sections. That day the 44th Brigade relieved the 45th in the right sub-section, the latter going into Divisional reserve in Arras; whilst the 46th Brigade, which had not suffered so severely during the recent fighting as had the other two, still held the left of the Divisional line.

In his despatch, dated December 21, 1918, the Commander-in-Chief lays stress on the critical situation of the Allies at this period. Many of the British divisions were greatly under strength, and nearly all required rest and training. Fortunately the enemy were in much the same predicament, and in addition he required time in which to reorganise his communications through the devastated area behind his new front line. The Commander-in-Chief goes on to say that the reasoned opinion of the Allied commanders was that "if the Allies could preserve their front unbroken until August at the latest, there was every hope that, during the later portion of the year, they would be able to regain the initiative, and pass to the offensive in their turn."

April-May 1918.

It was known that the enemy contemplated renewing his attack at the earliest possible moment, but it was also known that the discipline of the German Army was on the wane, and that the enemy was coming to an end of his resources. A striking series of corroborations of the state of affairs behind the German lines occur in various entries in the Fifteenth Division H.Q. diary of this period. It is mentioned that on May 4 three men of the 7th Camerons—Privates A. Wood, E. Tulloch, and M. McPherson,—who had been captured on March 28, escaped and reached the lines of the 1st Canadian Division. Four days later three more, belonging to the 13th Royal Scots, 8th Seaforths, and 7th Camerons, and on the 20th another four, none of whose names are recorded, also escaped. All confirmed the statements regarding the shortage of food, leather, soap, rubber, and transport generally, also the lack of discipline in the front-line troops. They had heard nothing of the coming attack on the Arras front, and stated that the chief topic of conversation amongst the German troops was an impending Franco-American offensive.

Although as much in need of rest as many others, it was not found possible to withdraw the Fifteenth Division for this purpose for some weeks, during which the enemy made no attempt to attack, but daily subjected the area to bombardment, principally with gas-shells, of which numerous entries occur in the diaries of April.

In spite of their experiences in March, the men had lost nothing of that offensive spirit for which the Division had always been famed. Along the whole front held by the Division, snipers and patrols were active, whilst, "owing to the harassing fire of our artillery, enemy movements over the open in forward zones were observed to be carried out at the double." Early in the morning of April 20 a most successful operation was carried out by the 11th A. & S. Highlanders. As this was exceedingly well executed and a number of prisoners taken, it seems

Minor operation by 11th Argylls.

April-May 1918.

desirable to include both the report of and orders connected with it. It is regretted that the air photos alluded to are not available.

Secret.

45TH INFANTRY BRIGADE OPERATION ORDER, NO. 87.

HEADQUARTERS, 45TH INFANTRY BRIGADE,
19*th April*, 1918.

Reference:—
1/10,000 CAMBRAI ROAD
TRENCH MAP.
Air Photos attached,
15 AB 138, & 143.

1. (*a*) The 11th A. & S. Highlanders will capture and consolidate the old gun-pits about H27.c.80.50 (marked X on attached photos), now thought to be held by the enemy, on the morning of the 20th inst.

(*b*) Zero hour will be 6.30 A.M.

2. (*a*) The attackers will be divided into 4 groups—" Q," " M," " R," and " S "—of 4, 3, 1, and 1 sections respectively.

(*b*) Lewis-gun sections will be included with Groups " M " and " S."

3. (*a*) Before zero, groups will be in position as follows:—

" Q " at gun-pits marked " Q," H.27.d.1.9.
" M " in large shell-holes marked " M," H.27.c.9.8.
" R " in gun-pits marked " R," H.27.c.45.85.
" S " in shelters in the bank marked " S," H.27.c.65.45.

(*b*) All the above places have been visited by our patrols every night since the 14th, and have been found to be unoccupied.

4. (*a*) At zero, groups " R " and " S " will demonstrate by opening rifle, Lewis-gun, and rifle-grenade fire on the objective.

(*b*) At zero plus ½ minute, groups " Q " and " M " will move as quickly as possible on the objective from the N. and N.E., taking the enemy from the flank and rear.

5. (*a*) As soon as the gun-pits have been captured, O.C. raiding party will reorganise and consolidate a line of shell-holes E. of objective, and will fire a red Véry Light.

(*b*) Subsequently, according to circumstances, O.C. raiding party will decide whether he will attack gun-pits about 100 yards to the E., H.27.d.05.25 (marked " Y "), thought to be unoccupied, and shelters in gun-pits about 100 yards to the S. in the area H.27.1.c.85.15 (marked " Z "), thought to be occupied by the enemy.

6. Throughout the operation the left flank of the attacking party will be protected by a Lewis-gun section, which will remain in gun-pits " Q," and will take on any hostile movement seen.

7. The artillery programme for 18-prs. and 4.5 howitzers is as follows :—

(i) From zero to zero minus 10 minutes desultory harassing fire on all old gun-pits in the vicinity of the objective as for this morning.

(ii) From zero to zero minus 10 minutes no fire in the vicinity of the above area, but 2 rounds per minute into the vicinity of the Stone Dump, H.33.c.1.1.

(iii) At zero :—

3 guns on the objective H.27.c.80.45.
3 guns on area H.27.c.75.15.
3 guns on area H.27.c.90.15.
3 guns on gun-pits H.27.d.05.25.
3 guns on gun-pits H.27.d.30.65.
3 guns on gun-pits H.27.d.50.90.
3 guns on gun-pits H.27.d.58.60.
2 guns on gun-pits H.33.b.9.6.
2 guns searching area H.36.a. and b.
2 guns on Stone Dump, H.33.c.1.1.
1 howitzer on Feuchy Cave, H.28.c.3.3.
5 howitzers searching area H.34.a.0.5.-H.34.d.0.5.-4.b.0.5.-H.34.a.0.5.
1 howitzer on gun-pits H.34.a.50.20.
1 howitzer on gun-pits H.34.c.50.90.
2 howitzers on gun-pits H.33.d.8.0.

(iv) At zero plus 1½ minutes the three guns on H.27.c.80.45 will lift, and search Pelves Lane eastwards from H.33.a.90.85. Other guns no change.

(v) At zero plus 2 minutes the three guns on H.27.d.05.25 will lift to other gun-pits at H.27.d.30.65. Other guns no change.

(vi) At zero plus 10 minutes, *or earlier if a red Véry light is seen*, the three guns on H.27.c.75.15 and the three guns on H.27.c.90.15 are ceasing fire, and standing by to take on any target that may present itself.

Other guns no change.

(vii) (*a*) At zero plus 20 minutes all fire is ceasing.

(*b*) At zero fire is being opened with a salvo, from zero to zero plus 2½ minutes fire will be intense, and from zero plus 2½ minutes to zero plus 15 minutes rapid; from zero plus 15 minutes it will gradually die away to zero plus 20 minutes, when it will cease.

8. (*a*) In the event of the enemy counter-attacking the captured gun-pits, a green (S.O.S.) Véry light will be fired, preceded by a red Véry light.

This will indicate that the attack is on the gun-pits H.27.c.80.45 to H.27.c.90.15, and artillery fire can be concentrated on this area.

(*b*) If the enemy attacks elsewhere the ordinary S.O.S. signal will be given—*i.e.*, a green Véry light,—and the ordinary barrage should be put down along the S.O.S. lines, which will be as follows :—

300 yards E. of the track from Broken Mill to H.27.c.80.35, to Pelves Lane at H.33.a.90.85, and thence southwards along present S.O.S. line.

9. All prisoners will be collected as soon as possible in Battery Valley and searched, but O.C. raiding party must use his own discretion as to whether he will evacuate them by day or wait till the evening.

They will subsequently be sent to the prison, Arras, unless orders to the contrary are received at Brigade Headquarters.

10. (*a*) All ranks taking part in the attack will be warned to only give their rank and name if captured, *and no further information at all.*

(*b*) The staff captain is supplying the necessary identity discs.

11. If the operation is successful, it will be notified by the code-word "Bon."

12. The Brigade Signal Officer will arrange that all the available means of communication are used by the 11th A. & S. Highlanders in order to pass information back *quickly*.

13. Watches will be synchronised by an officer of Brigade Headquarters as follows :—

9.30 P.M. 19th inst. and 3.30 P.M. 20th inst. at Brigade Headquarters with 70th and 71st Brigades, R.F.A.

10.30 P.M. at headquarters, 11th A. & S. Highlanders, with 11th A. & S. Highlanders.

Acknowledge by wire.

(Sgd.) C. R. RYAN, *Captain,*
Brigade-Major, 45th Infantry Brigade.

REPORT ON OPERATIONS

BY 11TH BATTALION A. & S. HIGHLANDERS

ON 20/21ST APRIL 1918.

To be read in conjunction with 45th Infantry Brigade Operation Order, 87. 19/4/18.

PHASE "A." Operations as ordered in 45th Brigade Operation Order, 87.

PHASE "B." Events following taking of objectives as in Phase "A."

PHASE "C." Enemy counter-stroke and events following it.

20/4/18, 6.30 *a.m. zero.*—Attack opened up to time. Artillery action as arranged.

6.38 *a.m., zero plus* 8.—Gun-pits taken. Red signal put up zero plus 9, but, owing to glare of sun, observers were unable to spot it.

Zero to zero plus 15.—Enemy machine-gun fire neutralised.

6.45 *a.m., zero plus* 15.—Enemy machine-guns began to be active while posts were being pushed out eastwards from these works. Machine-guns from H.33 central hampered the movement of the southernmost of these posts.

6.50 *a.m., zero plus* 20.—Enemy machine-guns very active. Outposts were, however, in all cases, pushed 60 yards (approx.) east of the gun-pits.

6.55 *a.m., zero plus* 25.—All positions being consolidated. Artillery active, called for at 6.50 A.M. on machine-guns mentioned above (H.33 central); opened accurately and quickly, and again neutralised the fire by zero plus 30.

NOTES ON PHASE "A."

Artillery (*Ours*).—Exactly as arranged. Most accurate. One gun out of first three rounds on one of the gun-pits was observed to get two direct hits, smashing one of the enemy machine-guns, which was found there later.

Theirs.—Did not open until zero plus 10, and then fell between outposts and Feuchy Switch. Retaliation of Army Line did not do much damage.

Machine-guns (*Ours*).—Did good work.

Theirs.—Accurate when able to fire, but greatly hampered by our artillery.

Communications.—Between battalion headquarters and new outpost line was established by wire and visual by zero plus 30.

Surprise.—Of the prisoners taken, 8 were not discovered until the gun-pits had been occupied half an hour. They were then found *still asleep* in an unexplored part of the dug-out.

Prisoners.—1 officer and 30 other ranks (of whom one was killed on the way down.) These were all taken in the vicinity of the gun-pits, with the exception of a machine-gun party of 7, who were in a small chalk-pit about 60 yards south of the gun-pits. This party was bombed by us before capture, causing two deaths.

Casualties (*Ours*).—1 officer (2nd Lieutenant V. A. Smith) wounded, 5 other ranks wounded, all by machine-gun fire.

Theirs.—Estimated 12 enemy killed by rifle-fire, Lewis-guns, and bombs. They must also have lost from our artillery fire.

PHASE "B."

Throughout the day posts were pushed farther out till, finally, they were some 150 yards in front of the gun-pits.

7 *a.m., zero plus* 1 *hour.*—Two posts were pushed forward by "A" Company to form a defensive flank to fill the gap between our new line and old outpost line at H.33.a.30.95 (1 L.G. team and 2 R.G.'s), H.33.a.70.90 (8 riflemen). Movement to these positions was made difficult by the enemy machine-gun fire, but was accomplished with 1 casualty (2nd Lieutenant H. W. Robertson).

Captain Irvine, M.C., worked a post of 2 N.C.O.'s and 10 men up in line with the left of the outpost line in front of the gun-pits and "Q" garrison.

All Day.—Movement was impossible. Sniping, Lewis-gun fire, and rifle-fire was active on both sides. During the afternoon continual enemy movement was observed, small parties doubling over the ridge in H.34.d. into H.28.d.

Operation orders were sent to companies, received by them at 5.30 P.M., to the effect that the outpost line was to move forward (" A " and " C " Companies), and conform with the positions taken in the morning's attack. " D " Company to withdraw when outpost line was in new position and in touch. Above not to commence until after 9 P.M.

Artillery (*Ours*).—Quiet, except when called for on the parties mentioned in movement above.

Theirs.—Quiet till about 8 P.M., when some salvoes were fired into Battery Valley.

Casualties (*Ours*).—1 officer wounded (2nd Lieutenant H. W. Robertson, since died of wounds), 1 other rank killed.

Theirs.—4 killed by our snipers, probably others by Lewis-gun and rifle-fire.

PHASE "C."

At 9 *p.m.*—All was quiet on the battalion front. According to Operation Orders referred to in Phase " B," the relief of " D " Company by " A " and " C " Companies started at this hour.

At 9.30 *p.m.*—An enemy bombardment started on the whole front. Barrage between the line of outposts and Feuchy Switch and on the Switch itself, and heavy shells on to Battery Valley. Barrage was reported to be very heavy.

On the right " A " Company had two platoons forward taking over the line.

On the left " C " had taken over from " D " up to the inter-company boundary, and were at the stage of shifting forward the old outpost line to conform with the new one.

At 9.40 *p.m.*—No infantry action was reported by the forward companies. Connection to them was broken shortly after this.

At 10.6 *p.m.*—The S.O.S. signal was put up, and was reported to battalion headquarters. This was afterwards found to have been put up by the left outpost company holding " Q " gun-pit.

At 10.10 *p.m.*—Our artillery barrage came down in full force. It was a very good one, a few shells falling short in the direction of Broken Mill. The enemy had worked his way down Pelves Lane into some old trenches and works about H.27.a.0.0, and was advancing on the gun-pits captured in the morning.

The outpost line east of the gun-pits was still intact at this time. O.C. " D " Company (Captain Irvine), whose headquarters were in the southern gun-pit, turned out his company headquarters, and kept off this attack with rifle-fire.

Meanwhile the O.C. " A " Company, who was in " D " Company's headquarters arranging the relief, got hold of one platoon of his company and brought it up to counter-attack.

The enemy in the old works referred to above saw this coming, and did not wait for it.

At 11 *p.m.*—The Canadian S.O.S. was put up, and at the same time a message, timed 11 P.M., was received from O.C. left company, which stated that all was clear on his front.

At 11.10 *p.m.*—Again visited his line, and met Lieutenant Stewart, whose platoon was responsible for "Q" gun-pit. This officer reported that "Q" gun-pit was lost. The enemy had worked round the flanks and had bombed the post, killing the N.C.O. in charge. The remainder of the garrison withdrew.

At 11.20 *p.m.*—Captain Hood, the left company commander, ordered a counter-attack on "Q" gun-pit. Lieutenant Stewart took No. 10 Platoon, and carried out the orders given him. Owing to the quantity of wire, however, put up in front of Feuchy Switch, there was only one gap through which the counter-attack could go. The enemy were shelling this gap heavily, and Lieutenant Stewart was killed. The platoon was taken forward by the company sergeant-major, but movement was impossible at the gap.

At 11.30 *p.m.*—The O.C. left company warned the O.C. right outpost company, Captain Irvine, of the fate of "Q" gun-pit, and Captain Irvine withdrew the posts, which had been pushed 150 yards east of the captured gun-pits, to about 20 yards east of them. He also pushed out a fresh post to guard his left flank.

Touch was gained on the right at Pelves Lane with the 8/10th Gordons, who had relieved the Royal Scots.

At Midnight.—The left outpost company brought up posts from the old outpost line to conform with the right outpost company, and the line then ran from Broken Mill to point marked on the accompanying photo. All infantry action seemed to be over by this time, and the relief by the 8th Seaforths was pushed on.

At 4.14 *a.m., April* 21.—The relief was reported complete. It had to be carried out in small parties, and rifle and machine-gun fire hampered movement greatly.

NOTES.

The artillery barrage put down in reply to the S.O.S. was very fine, and must have caused considerable damage to the attacking party.

The machine-guns forming the barrage were heard to open directly the S.O.S. was put up.

The counter-attack on "Q" gun-pit would have succeeded but for the heavy wire, and the fact that only one gap existed in it at such a clearly marked place.

The relief being in progress at the opening of the attack caused a great deal of movement to and fro, and the advanced outpost line and the enemy party who worked up from Pelves Lane must have been confused for part of the relief.

I am of opinion that, but for the relief, any enemy movement would have been observed, and warning given to the whole line.

(Signed) G. L. WILSON,
Commanding 11*th A. & S. Highlanders.*

After this highly successful operation the following congratulatory messages were received :—

From XVII. Corps Commander :

Please congratulate 11th A. & S. Highlanders upon the success of their operations carried out this morning.

From G.O.C. Fifteenth Division :

Congratulations to Colonel Wilson and 11th A. & S. Highlanders on most successful enterprise.

From B.G.C., 44th Infantry Brigade :

Heartiest congratulations to all ranks of the 11th A. & S. Highlanders on successful enterprise.

For services in connection with the operation, Lieut.-Colonel Wilson received the Croix de Guerre, Captain Irvine a bar to his Military Cross, 2nd Lieutenant Christie the Military Cross, Corporal Porteous the Medaille Militaire, and eleven other ranks were awarded the Military Medal.

CHAPTER IX.

THE EARLY SUMMER OF 1918.

April-May 1918. Relief of Division.

On April 20 orders were received that the line would be taken over by the 56th Division a few days later, and that the Fifteenth would be transferred from the XVII. Corps to the XIII., then in Army reserve in the neighbourhood of Auchel. Commencing on the 23rd, infantry units moving by motor-lorries and the remainder by road, the move was completed by 10 A.M. the following day, when General Reed handed over command of the sector. The next day the Division, less its artillery, who as usual remained in the line, was concentrated occupying billets as under, with Divisional Headquarters at Auchel :—

44th Brigade and 91st Field Company, R.E., at Auchel.
45th Brigade and 73rd Field Company, R.E., at Marles les Mines.
46th Brigade and 74th Field Company, R.E., at Raimbert (together with 46th Field Ambulance).

The 9th Gordon Highlanders (Pioneers) were billeted at Raimbert until the 27th, when they proceeded to camp in the Bois du Reveillon, where they were employed on a new line of trenches between Choques and Gonnehem. On the 30th the Divisional artillery left the line, and went into billets in Acq, the Divisional Trench-Mortar Battery remaining in Arras.

On this occasion the rest period was of short duration, for on May 3 the Division moved back to Arras. Originally ordered for April 28, the move was cancelled at the last moment after several battalions had entrained. The short period out of the line was uneventful, and taken up in training and the usual inspections. A reconnaissance was also made of the XIII. Corps front, with a view to action as reserve Division in the event of a German attack. This

May 1918. Into line again.

time the Division took over a new, to them, sector of the line from the 1st Canadian Division. Moving by train on the 3rd, the 45th and 46th Brigades were the first to leave, followed the next day by the remainder of the Division. On May 4 the 46th relieved the 2nd Canadian Infantry Brigade in the right section of the Divisional line, and on the 5th the 45th relieved the 1st Canadian in the left, the 44th Brigade being in reserve in Victory Camp. Divisional Headquarters opened at Etrun on the 5th, when General Reed assumed command of the centre sector of the Corps front, with the 51st (Highland) Division and 56th (London) Division on the left and right respectively.

The Feuchy front.

The front line ran from the southern outskirts of Feuchy village, along the river Scarpe, south and east of Fampoux, thence due north to Bailleul Alley, south-east of the village of that name. Over 6000 yards in length, the line was a difficult one to hold, especially that part to the south where it crossed the Scarpe. So long was it that, on May 6, about 1500 yards, from Town Alley to Bailleul Alley inclusive, was handed over to the 152nd Brigade, 51st Division. The dividing line between brigades ran, roughly, north of Fampoux, due east, north of St Laurent Blangy. The right section of the line, from Feuchy to Fampoux, was rather extraordinary. South of the river the opposing lines were just east of Feuchy village. To the north lay marshes and the Scarpe, covering ground where it was impossible to dig trenches. On the north bank of the river the British front line was more advanced than on the south, with the result that the enemy front line south of the river was some 600 to 700 yards west of his front line on the north bank.

Thus, between Feuchy and Fampoux, the lines faced each other in a north-easterly and south-westerly direction, and between them lay the marshes and the Scarpe, overlooked from the high ground both south and north of the river. This section of the front was held by a series of posts about 150 yards apart, with others, manned only at night, between them. The left section, from Fampoux northwards, offered no such difficulties. It was in excellent order, and, although somewhat long, was of the ordinary type.

On the whole, this tour in the trenches was quiet, and, with the exception of various raids, devoid of incident. The Germans showed no disposition to attack, and scarcely even troubled to retaliate when harassed by artillery fire. More mention than heretofore is, however, made of enemy aircraft activity. Scarcely a day passed without allusion being made in the diaries to low-flying 'planes, which seem to have caused some damage, but otherwise there is very little of importance to chronicle. The usual tour consisted of sixteen days in the front line and eight out.

May 1918.

One entry in "A and Q" diary, May 12, will show how uneventful, from the staff point of view, was the commencement of the tour. It runs: "*Moral* of the Division very high. Casualties very light, and sick rate very low." This state of affairs was not destined to last long. Influenza broke out, and that, combined with the shortage of men available to fill the gaps caused by it and battle casualties, made a change in the composition of brigades imperative. On this account it had already been found necessary to reduce the number of divisions then in France. Eight had disappeared, their brigades and battalions being formed into training cadres or sent to reinforce other divisions, amongst them the Fifteenth, who were far below war strength.

Reorganisation of Brigades.

It was unfortunate that the changes meant that certain units practically disappeared, whilst others took their places. This, of course, caused a very great regret in those battalions which were now to lose their identity after nearly three years of hard fighting; but the reason and wisdom of the change was obvious, and all ranks loyally accepted the unpleasant situation. Although warning of the impending changes reached the Division in May, it was not until early in June that they actually took place, and they are officially recorded as having taken place on the 9th as follows:—

44TH BRIGADE.

The 4/5th Black Watch, which had joined the 46th Brigade from the 51st (Highland) Division on May 16, absorbed the 9th Battalion, and was transferred from the 46th to the 44th Brigade.

The 8th Seaforths remained intact.

The 1/5th Gordon Highlanders, from the 61st Division, absorbed the 8/10th Battalion.

The 7th Camerons were absorbed by the 6th Battalion, 45th Brigade.

May 1918. Reorganisation of Brigades.

45th Brigade.

The 13th Royal Scots remained intact.

The 6th Camerons absorbed the 7th Battalion from the 44th Brigade.

The 1/8th A. & S. Highlanders, which had joined the brigade from the 61st Division on June 1, absorbed the 11th Battalion.

46th Brigade

The 4/5th Black Watch, which had practically absorbed the 9th Battalion, was transferred to the 44th Brigade.

The 9th Royal Scots joined the Brigade from the 61st Division on June 1.

The 7/8th K.O.S.B. remained intact.

The 10th Cameronians (Scottish Rifles) remained intact.

After the above changes had taken place, selected training staffs, consisting, roughly, of about 10 officers and 60 to 70 other ranks of the absorbed battalions, were sent to the 39th Division to assist in training American troops, by this time arriving in France in large numbers. The remainder of the officers and other ranks surplus to establishment were despatched to the base, comforted by assurance from higher authority that they would only be used as reinforcements for their own units. Alas ! owing to the exigencies of the service, these pledges could not be kept in every case, and many officers, N.C.O.'s, and men found themselves transferred to other battalions. In all, 36 officers and 1310 other ranks were thus disposed of, and on June 15 the strength of the Division was 10,035.

About this time a mysterious ailment, known as " P.U.O.,"[1] made its appearance throughout the army, and spread so rapidly that soon every hospital and field ambulance was full to overflowing. Arrangements had to be made for extra accommodation, and every precaution was taken to stop the spread of the disease. Fortunately, the malady only lasted for from three to four days, after which the patient soon recovered sufficiently to rejoin his unit. When it was at its height, however, at the end of June, there were as many as 1700 cases from the Fifteenth Division alone. With the exception of this epidemic, the health of the Division was wonderfully good. Casualties, too, were not great, but two amongst them cannot be passed over without

[1] Pyrexia, of unknown origin.

notice. On the morning of May 19, as he was returning from a tour of the trenches, Lieut.-Colonel M. F. B. Dennis, D.S.O., 7/8th K.O.S.B., was struck by a trench-mortar shell and killed. A most gallant officer, his death was felt, not only by the battalion he had commanded so well, but by the whole Division. A month later, on June 24, Brig.-General A. F. Lumsden, commanding the 46th Brigade, was killed by shell-fire in Battery Valley whilst accompanying General Reed on a tour round the trenches. A splendid leader, beloved by all, his death was a great loss to the Division.

May-June 1918.

Amongst the numerous raids carried out in May, June, and the commencement of July, the following were the chief :—

Raids.

May 16.—Three platoons of "A" Company, 13th Royal Scots, under 2nd Lieutenant T. Smith, raided Newton Trench. The party captured 7 prisoners, 4 of which were killed on their way back by German artillery fire. In addition, it was estimated that at least 40 of the enemy had been killed. The raiders lost their commander, missing, and 9 other ranks killed, 16 wounded, and 1 missing.

June 17.—31 other ranks of "C" Company, 4/5th Black Watch, under 2nd Lieutenant J. E. C. Harvey, entered the German trenches, and brought back 3 prisoners of the 91st Regiment, with a loss of only 3 men wounded and 1 missing—a very successful little raid.

June 21.—18 officers and 351 other ranks of the 13th Royal Scots, with Lieutenant Scott, R.E., and 18 other ranks from the 74th Field Company, R.E., the whole under command of Lieut.-Colonel J. A. Turner, 13th Royal Scots, raided the enemy trenches north of Fampoux. It was a brilliantly carried out raid. Much damage was done to the enemy positions : fifteen dug-outs were set on fire, destroyed by the sappers ; severe casualties, estimated about 130, were inflicted on the enemy ; and 10 prisoners of the 188th Regiment, with 4 machine-guns, were brought back. The force lost 1 officer (Captain West) killed and 2 wounded, 40 other ranks killed, 15 wounded, and 4 missing. For this fine performance congratulatory messages were received by the battalion from the Corps Commander and other high commanders.

June 24.—2 officers and 60 other ranks of the 7/8th K.O.S.B., under 2nd Lieutenant Dryburgh, entered the enemy trenches near Feuchy, on the south side of the railway. 5 prisoners and a machine-gun were

July 1918. Raids.

brought back, 9 dead Germans were counted, and one dug-out was bombed. Unfortunately 2nd Lieutenant Dryburgh was mortally wounded on the way back, and died in hospital a few hours later.

July 7.—Lieutenant R. Philips and 3 men of "A" Company, 10th Scottish Rifles, went over to the German front line and brought back 3 men of the 223rd Regiment.

The Division had now been in the line since early February, except for a few days in April, which were spent almost entirely (artillery excepted) moving to and from XIII. Corps. It had during this period suffered the intense strain of awaiting the great German offensive, had met it in front of Arras, and had repulsed it on that front. From April 1, 1917, to April 1, 1918, the casualties—killed, wounded, and missing—in the Division had been approximately 20,000. Later there had been the influenza epidemic. Higher authority, from G.H.Q. downward, fully realised that time for rest, refit, and some training was long overdue.

Rumours were constantly rife, and on the 10th a warning order was received to the effect that the 1st and part of the 4th Canadian Divisions would relieve the Fifteenth on July 11 and the three following days. The first day a battalion of the 11th Canadian Infantry Brigade relieved the 10th Scottish Rifles in the left sector. On the 12th the 1st Canadian Brigade took over from the 45th, then in Divisional reserve, and also relieved the remainder of the 46th Brigade, which then proceeded to Arras for the night. The following day the 44th Brigade was relieved by part of the 1st and 2nd Canadian Infantry Brigades, and on the 14th General Reed handed over the command of the section to the G.O.C. 1st Canadian Division.

Relief of Division.

The relief of the field companies and artillery was as follows: the 73rd Field Company, R.E., and the 9th Gordons (Pioneers) were relieved by the 1st Canadian Battalion, R.E., on the 13th. The following day the 91st and the 74th were relieved by the 2nd Canadian Battalion to Villers Chatel. The 1st Canadian Artillery took over from the Fifteenth Divisional Artillery on the nights of July 13th/14th and 15th/16th, the latter moving to Acq on relief.

As formations were relieved, they proceeded by road and light railway to the Villers Chatel area, ten miles north-west of Arras. Concentrated in this area, the Division was now in G.H.Q. reserve, and all ranks looked forward to a long and well-deserved rest ; but well as it had earned a period of quiet, its services were required elsewhere, and three days later orders were issued for a move by train to an unknown destination. On the night of July 15 and the early morning of the 16th, in pouring rain and wet to the skin, the Division left the XVII. Corps area.

July 1918.

CHAPTER X.

THE MOVE TO THE MARNE.[1]

May-July 1918.

WHILST the Fifteenth Division had been having a more or less quiet period east of Arras, heavy fighting had taken place farther south. On May 27 the enemy launched a heavy attack with twenty-eight divisions on a front of thirty-five miles against the French Sixth Army and the British IX. Corps north-west of Rheims. Another enemy attack on the Marne front was launched early in June, and by the commencement of July continuous fighting, in which French, American, and British troops were involved, was proceeding in the Aisne and Marne areas.

Early in July, Marshal Foch, thinking that the German attack might spread farther east, made certain readjustments of the French forces, and asked Sir Douglas Haig to move four British divisions south to replace four French divisions which he had been compelled to move farther east to protect the threatened sector. Sir Douglas Haig accordingly ordered the Fifteenth, 34th, 51st, and 62nd Divisions, forming the XXII. Corps under Lieut.-General Sir A. Godley, to move south towards the Marne front.

The move south.

On July 13 Marshal Foch asked that these divisions might be placed unreservedly under his orders, and that four more might be sent to take their place. To this Sir D. Haig agreed, but, as some of the troops of the XXII. Corps were already on their way, the change necessitated counter orders, which affected, although not seriously, the Fifteenth Division.

On the 17th General Reed received a telephone message at Beauvais whilst on his way south, informing him of the change of plan, and ordering the Division to detrain at Clermont, Liancourt, Laigne-

[1] Maps 12, 13, and 14.

ville, and Pont St Maxence. These instructions were carried out by the 18th, when, with G.H.Q. at Liancourt, the Division came under the orders of the G.O.C. Third French Army. In this area the inhabitants had never before seen Scottish troops, and the kilted battalions aroused great interest.

July 1918.

The French attack.

The day the Division arrived in the area, July 18, Marshal Foch launched the attack he had been long preparing. Late that night General Reed received a warning order to be ready to move at any hour after 3 A.M. the following morning to join the Tenth French Army (General Mangin), XX. (French) Corps (General Berdoulat), then hotly engaged, together with American troops, south of Soissons. Staff officers of brigades and representatives of units were hastily summoned to Divisional Headquarters, where they received verbal instructions for the move, which commenced at dawn the following morning.

That day infantry and dismounted units moved by march and motor-omnibus to the Montigny, Haute Fontaine, and Breuil areas, with headquarters at Cuise Lamotte, artillery and transport proceeding by road, and halting half-way on the night of the 19th/20th. Those who took part in this long journey by 'bus are not likely to forget it. The day was hot, the roads bad and dusty, and for twelve weary hours the long procession of motor-lorries wound its way through village after village towards the front line. Every town and hamlet was packed with French and American troops, and news of the successful Franco-American attack south of Soissons made every man in the Division eager to reach the front.

By the evening of the 20th the Division was concentrated, and late that night orders arrived that it would march the following day to join the XX. (French) Corps in the Montgobert area. This move was postponed shortly afterwards, and, with the exception of the 44th Brigade Group, which moved from Breuil to Chelles in order that the Division should be concentrated farther east, units remained stationary until 9 P.M. on the 21st, when the Division set out for St Pierre Aigle Le Jardin.

This night march was trying in more ways than one. The weather was fine, and a full moon lit the dust of the long columns of moving troops. The 1/8th A. & S. Highlanders met with bad luck that night.

July 1918.

Just as the head of their battalion cleared Coeuvres village, an enemy bombing-machine flew low over the road. The observer must have caught sight of the columns of dust, for the machine turned back and dropped its load of eight bombs. One officer was wounded, 4 other ranks killed, and some 20 wounded. The 8th Seaforths had a similar experience, Captain S. Murray's company losing 1 officer and 6 other ranks killed, and about 25 wounded. Throughout the night the German airmen were particularly busy, and during the march several flew low over the columns; but little other damage was done, and by 6 A.M. on the 22nd the whole Division was concentrated in the villages round Coeuvres.

Isolated from the British Army, the Division was now in close support of the French and American troops, then engaged in attacking the heights between Tigny and Belleu. So far the combined attack had been a complete success, but losses had been heavy, and fresh battalions were required to exploit the advantage already gained.

General Reed received short notice that the Division would be required. At 9.20 P.M. on the 22nd, Corps orders arrived to the effect that the 10th French Army would resume the offensive on the morning of the 23rd, and that the Fifteenth, taking over from the 1st (American) Division (General Summerall), would attack the enemy positions between Berzy-le-Sec and the north-west corner of Buzancy, adding that zero hour would be 5 A.M.[1]

Orders to attack.

Under such conditions it was impossible to make anything like a proper reconnaissance of either the line to be taken over or of the position to be attacked. This proved unfortunate, as will be seen later. Never did the Division carry out such a relief, for little or no information could be obtained from the relieved troops. The following

[1] After relieving the Americans on the battlefield, it was found that they had not had time to bury their dead. A large number still lay where they had fallen, and it was the privilege and sacred duty of the Fifteenth Division to render the last rites to their most gallant American allies, as the fighting in front progressed. All identity certificates were carefully collected and forwarded to General Summerall, the American commander, who wrote a letter to General Reed, full of gratitude for what his Division had done, adding: "It was a peculiar privilege to be associated with you and your splendid Division, who, to my mind, represent the highest state of efficiency and *moral*. It was an inspiration to us to see the able way in which your Division took hold of the situation and relieved us of our arduous burden." High praise indeed from one of America's most distinguished soldiers.

July 1918. A difficult relief.

is an instance of what took place that night. An officer of the 1/8th Argylls took over a portion of the line south of Berzy village. He met the officer commanding the French company he was to relieve, who, standing in the darkness, pointed in various directions, and said, " Mitrailleuse la, et la, Boche la. Moi, je vais." And he went, without another word! Not one of that officer's company saw a single French soldier, with the result that one platoon walked right on top of a German post, and the enemy, thus made aware that a relief was in progress, at once opened a heavy bombardment with artillery and machine-guns on the whole Divisional front.

Notwithstanding the conditions under which the relief took place, it was completed by 3 A.M. on the 23rd, just two hours before zero hour. How it was done is not told in any diary, but in nearly all, mention is made of the short time available to commanders in which to make preparations for the attack. What added to the difficulty was that the front line as taken over from the French and American troops by no means coincided with that shown on the map, and even its approximate position was extremely difficult to find in the dark. The result was that when the barrage fell on the supposed German front line it overshot a number of enemy machine-gun nests, the fire from which caused heavy casualties. The line was quite different to any the Division had as yet occupied. There were no trenches, and very little shelter was available, even for the support and reserve troops. In fact this fighting may be described as " open warfare " —the first in which the Division had taken part.

Description of front taken over.

The front taken over by the Division from the American Corps extended from the western outskirts of Buzancy to the western edge of Noyant.[1] About two miles behind the front line a cultivated plateau, open, devoid of hedges, and intersected by sunken roads, sloped gently downwards from the Villers-Cotterets road on the north-west to more undulating country some five miles to the south-east. Its forward or north-eastern slope was more precipitous, and, being split by two valleys, had its slope broken up into several steep and commanding spurs running out to the north-east. Facing the ridge along the whole front was the very similar plateau of Buzancy, which

[1] Map 12.

July 1918.

at its northern end falls back sharply to the east, and looks down on the valley in which lie Noyant and Septmonts, Buzancy itself lying in a small side glen.

The Divisional front was divided into two brigade sectors, which, however, were marked by no natural boundary. In the right sector the line followed the crest of Buzancy Ridge, and looked out over the plateau, whilst the reserves behind the line were sheltered in the re-entrant below. The ground in the left brigade sector sloped gently downwards from right to left—*i.e.*, from Buzancy to Noyant,—and included as its only striking feature a railway cutting, which formed the northern extremity of the Divisional front. On both flanks French troops held the line, and were in touch with the Divisional flank posts.

On the right the dividing line between the 87th (French) Division and the Fifteenth ran almost due east and west from Visigneux to about 200 yards north of Buzancy. On the left that between the Fifteenth and 69th French Division followed the course of the Crise River from the northern outskirts of Berzy-le-Sec to the south of Septmonts. As he had received instructions to attack on a front of two brigades, General Reed fixed the dividing line between brigades as from Anconin Farm, due east to the Crise, south of Noyant.

Objectives and dispositions.

The objective of the right brigade, the 46th, was the village of Rozières and the high ground between that village and Buzancy. The task of the left brigade, the 45th, was the capture of Le Sucrerie, south-west of Noyant, and the crossings of the river Crise east and north of it. In reserve was the 44th Brigade, just east of Cravancon.

On the right Brig.-General Fortune attacked with the 7/8th K.O.S.B. on the right and 10th Scottish Rifles on the left, keeping the 9th Royal Scots in reserve. The 45th (Brig.-General N. A. Orr Ewing) attacked with the 6th Camerons on the right and 8th A. & S. Highlanders on the left, the 13th Royal Scots remaining in reserve south of Ploisy. Owing to the short notice and the impossibility of relieving all the American artillery covering the Divisional front, it was arranged that their gunners should remain in the line and cover the Fifteenth Division attack.[1]

[1] In a memorandum issued on this occasion Colonel L. R. Holbrook, commanding the First American F.A. Brigade, says: "It is noted that for the first time in history, French, British, and American artillery are working together under the same command."

July 23, 1918. The assault launched.

At 5 A.M. on the 23rd the assault began, and was at once held up by heavy machine-gun fire from nests of guns overlooked by the barrage. In addition, the barrage itself was poor, and in fact the left of the 10th Scottish Rifles was not covered by it at all. This was due to the fact that the Franco-American front line was supposed to be some 600 yards in advance of what it actually proved to be, with the result that the barrage fell far behind the actual German front line.

On the right the K.O.S.B. and Scottish Rifles managed to work forward a few hundred yards, but at 8.15 A.M. Brig.-General Fortune reported that his brigade was unable to advance farther owing to heavy losses and lack of artillery support. On the left the 45th Brigade had also suffered severely. The Camerons had captured the Sucrerie, and then, finding their left flank exposed, gradually extended their line northwards until they held the whole of the 45th Brigade front as far as the railway crossing over the Crise, Lieutenant Fraser being in command of the left post of the Camerons at this point.

Farther north the Argylls had met with bad luck. Owing to heavy enemy shelling during the relief, the short notice given them, and the extraordinary manner in which this part of the line had been handed over, very little was known of the two companies in the front line. Many of the runners had been killed, and in some instances orders for the attack never reached the front line before zero hour. Eventually it was found that "A" Company on the right had been able to advance a short way down the forward slope east of Berzy, but it had ultimately to come back and take up a position about 100 yards in advance of its original line. Even here it suffered heavy losses owing to lack of cover. On the extreme left, what remained of "B" and "D" Companies had concentrated in the western outskirts of Berzy during the morning, and were in touch with the French troops on their left. On this flank the situation was obscure for most of the day, and it was largely due to the intrepidity of Lieutenant R. L. MacKay, 8th A. & S. Highlanders, that accurate information regarding the situation was ultimately received. This officer, together with his runner, Private Langridge, went forward and searched the whole of his battalion front, being most of the way in full view of the enemy, and returned with a full report of the situation.

July 23, 1918.

When he heard that the advance was thus held up, General Reed arranged for a further artillery barrage to be put down, but later, as the French were unable to co-operate, it was decided to suspend for the moment any further attack.

Both flanks in the air, 10 A.M.

About 10 A.M. it was discovered that neither of the French Divisions on the flanks had been able to advance, and both flanks of the Fifteenth were consequently in the air. To remedy this a company of the 10th Scottish Rifles, who had not lost as heavily as had other battalions, was placed at the disposal of the O.C. 7/8th K.O.S.B. to form a defensive flank on the right, whilst on the left the Argylls held the left flank of the Division.[1] Later in the day General Reed further reinforced the Borderers with the personnel of the 46th Trench-Mortar Battery, formed into a company of infantry for the moment. In the centre the Scottish Rifles and Camerons were able to hold on to the ground they had gained throughout the day, but in the evening, owing to the fact that the Sucrerie was well in advance of the rest of the line, it was decided that the Camerons should withdraw to the railway embankment and straighten out the position.

A German counter-attack, 6 P.M.

About 6 P.M. the enemy launched a strong counter-attack from Chivry Farm under a fairly heavy artillery barrage. This was repulsed without difficulty by artillery and machine-gun fire, and he made no further effort to interfere with the work of consolidation, which was at once commenced. During the evening all the American guns left in the line were withdrawn, and command of artillery passed to Lieut.-Colonel Ingham, acting C.R.A., Fifteenth Division, who, in addition to his own, had the guns of the 253rd French Artillery Regiment, consisting of three brigades, each made up of three four-gun batteries of .75's.

By this time things were quieter, and battalions in the front line were able to reorganise. In order to make his left flank secure, the O.C. 9th Gordons (Pioneers) was instructed to send up one company to reinforce the 45th Brigade in the event of any enemy counter-attack that night. When night fell the Divisional front line ran as shown

[1] On this occasion the 7/8th K.O.S.B. lost 4 officers killed, 10 wounded; 32 other ranks killed, 214 wounded, and 63 wounded and missing, whilst the Argylls lost almost as heavily.

on Map 12. Under cover of darkness both the 45th and 46th Brigades relieved their front-line battalions. On the right the 9th Royal Scots took over the whole of the 46th Brigade line, whilst the 13th Royal Scots did the same on the 45th front, both reliefs being completed before dawn.

July 23-25, 1918.

Thus ended the first day's fighting. It was not the fault of the Fifteenth Division that its gains were small. Thrown into the line without proper reconnaissance, it seems extraordinary that even a yard was gained. Still, as it did on every occasion, it not only advanced a certain distance, but inflicted severe losses on the enemy. It was indeed a creditable performance. To take over an ill-defined line at night, in unknown country, with orders to attack a position that has not been seen by or even explained to 90 per cent of the attacking forces, is a task which is rarely demanded of troops. Yet the Fifteenth Division accomplished it, and not only that, but, as will be seen later, "came again" in two days' time, and definitely smashed the German resistance between Villemontoire and Buzancy.

The 1st American Division.

Before closing the record of the first day's fighting, tribute must be paid to the assistance rendered by all ranks of the 1st American Division during the difficult operation of handing over their line. All ranks gave every assistance in their power, in spite of the fact that they had lost heavily, and must have been feeling the strain. Alluding to the American artillery and ambulance service, General Reed, in a letter to General C. P. Summerall, commanding the 1st U.S.A. Division, says:—

"To your artillery commander (Colonel Holbrook) and his staff, and to the units under his command, our special thanks are due. Without hesitation (when you and he saw our awkward predicament as regards artillery support) the guns of your division denied themselves relief in order to assist us in an attack. This attack was only partly successful, but the artillery support was entirely so. Without the help of Colonel Habee and his establishment of ambulance-cars, I have no hesitation in saying that at least 400 of our wounded would still be on our hands in this area."

No infantry action took place on either the 24th or 25th, but throughout these two days the Divisional area was subjected to constant and heavy enemy shelling. On the night of the 25th/26th the 44th Brigade

July 26-27, 1918.

relieved the 46th in the front line, the latter becoming Divisional reserve.

Extension of line southwards.

On July 26 orders were received from the XX. French Corps to the effect that the Division would extend its line southwards the following night, taking over part of the line then held by the 91st Regiment, 87th French Division, immediately west of Buzancy. This was carried out without any of the difficulty experienced on the 22nd. Everything possible was done by the French to make the relief easy, and General Reed subsequently sent a warm letter of appreciation to General Dehers, the 87th Division commander, thanking him for the assistance given by his division.

Just before this relief took place the Division lost a most brilliant young soldier (he was only twenty-seven) in Lieut.-Colonel J. A. Turner, O.C. 13th Royal Scots, who, together with his assistant adjutant, Lieut. Henderson, was killed at battalion headquarters by shell-fire. A born leader and a splendid athlete, his loss was felt by the whole Division.[1]

When the relief was complete the southern boundary of the Divisional area ran due east and west from a point immediately south of La Foulerie to just north of the Bois l'Eveque, and that between brigades, roughly, from Anconin Farm, in the left sector, eastwards to Ecuiry. Opposite the position now held by the right (44th) Brigade was the village of Buzancy, with woods between it and the front line.

Orders for attack on Buzancy.

Nothing of interest occurred on the 27th until 7 P.M., when General Reed, in accordance with Corps instructions, issued his orders for an attack on Buzancy by the 44th Brigade the following day. The 87th French Division had captured Villemontoire that morning, and it was of importance that Buzancy and the high ground east of it should be taken, in order to facilitate a further advance.

In this attack five companies of the 91st French Regiment were detailed to co-operate on the right. Two of these were to advance from Villemontoire and capture the ground south of Buzancy as far

[1] Perhaps an extract from one of the last letters Colonel Turner wrote, to his mother, is the most fitting tribute to his memory: "Pray that I may have more strength to carry on; more courage to face the very worst that comes; victory without giving my men unnecessary pain; that I may be spared to return to you. If that may not be, I have not lost my faith; my conscience is clear, and I am not afraid to 'go over the top' to meet my Maker 'for everlasting peace.'"

north as the road leading from the village to the Bois l'Eveque. Another, attacking in a northerly direction, was to clear the wood south-south-west of the village. A fourth, on the immediate right of the 44th Brigade, had to capture the "Grenade Work" on the high ground south-west of Buzancy, and clear the wood between it and the village, whilst the fifth remained in reserve in Villemontoire. The above is of importance, as it shows the careful arrangements made between General Reed and the French commander to secure the right flank of the Division. Had these been carried out in entirety, the result of the subsequent fighting would have been far different.

July 27, 1918.

Brig.-General Thomson was directed to carry out the main attack with the 44th Brigade, and issued his orders on the following lines: Two companies were to attack Buzancy, moving by the north of the Chateau. They were then to clear the village, working in a south-easterly direction, and link up with the French troops of the 91st Regiment. Another was to attack the Chateau, and clear it and its grounds. Three companies were to attack the position from the road running from Buzancy to the Bois l'Eveque to the southern edge of the wood south of Chivry Farm. To assist him Brig.-General Thomson also had the 10th Scottish Rifles from the 46th Brigade, one section of the 91st Field Company, R.E., the 45th Light Trench-Mortar Battery, and half a section of French flammenwerfer. On the left of the 44th Brigade the 45th was ordered to co-operate by establishing posts on the northern edge of the wood south of Chivry Farm.

Dispositions of 44th Brigade.

Of the tasks allotted by him Brig.-General Thomson gave the first two to the Seaforths, sending with them the section of R.E., two teams of the 45th Light Trench-Mortar Battery, the half section of flammenwerfer, and one company of the Black Watch. He also instructed the Seaforths to furnish a platoon to keep touch with the French on the right. The third he gave to the 5th Gordons. As regards the left, Brig.-General Orr Ewing detailed the 8th Argylls, right, and 13th Royal Scots, left, to carry out the attack, keeping the 6th Camerons in reserve.

For fire supports, in addition to his own artillery and that of the 15th Machine-Gun Battalion, General Reed had the guns of the 87th French Division, the 253rd French Artillery Regiment, and the 5th

July 28, 1918. Group 130th Regiment, 69th Division. With these barrages were arranged, and certain areas allotted to groups of guns for special bombardment both before and during the attack (see Map 13).[1]

The Seaforth battle order was as follows: "A" Company was to lead the attack, together with the teams of Stokes' mortars. Immediately behind them came "C," with the section of the 91st Field Company, R.E., the half section of flammenwerfer, and "B" Company, Black Watch. Next followed "D," "B," less one platoon remaining in reserve, that platoon being the one detailed to keep touch with the French. "A" Company's task was to take the Chateau and grounds, and consolidate on the eastern side of it. That of "C," assisted by the Black Watch and R.E., was to capture Buzancy, and, if required, assist "A." "D" Company was to move forward on the right of the Gordons, and take the final objective on the high ground east of the village.

On the left the Argylls attacked with "B" and "C" Companies, "D" being in close support and "A" in reserve.

Zero hour was fixed for 12.30 P.M. This somewhat unusual hour had been decided upon after consultation with General Berdoulat, the French Corps Commander, the main reasons being "surprise" and to ensure good aeroplane observation. For some time previously, and during the morning of the actual day itself, artillery barrages had been put down at irregular intervals in order to make the Germans expect an attack. Of course nothing followed these demonstrations, and it was hoped by this means to train the enemy to take no notice of them. Besides, this 12.30 P.M. was the enemy's dinner hour, and the barrage put down at that hour on the 28th was of exceptional fury.

At 9.30 A.M. Divisional Headquarters moved forward to Battle Headquarters, just north of Glaux Farm. Earlier in the morning General Orr Ewing reported that his brigade, which had only a short distance to go, had almost reached its objective during the night, and were then ready to conform with any movement of the 44th.

The attack launched, 12.30 P.M.

Two minutes before zero the barrage fell on the German positions, and punctually at 12.30 the attack was launched.

Half an hour later the Gordons reported that their advance was proceeding well, and that prisoners were coming in. This was confirmed

[1] Barrage areas are shaded.

PRIVATE R. DUNSIRE, V.C.

13th Battalion The Royal Scots.

July 28, 1918. The fight for Buzancy.

shortly afterwards by the 45th Brigade, who said that troops could be seen on the plateau south-east of Buzancy. For some time no definite news came from the Seaforths, and nothing at all regarding the French companies on the right, but at 1.30 the 60th French Division on the left reported that columns of the enemy could be seen moving through the village of Septmonts. Of this news full advantage was at once taken by the artillery, with dire results to the Germans.

The first information received by the G.O.C. that there was a check was a message dropped by a French contact 'plane, to the effect that Germans could be seen in Buzancy.[1] Half an hour later French artillery observers on the right flank reported that the enemy could be seen counter-attacking from the east. What had occurred was as follows :—

At zero the Seaforths moved forward close to the barrage. Twelve minutes later "A" Company had taken the Chateau and grounds, and established posts east of it. "C" and "B" of the Black Watch, the second line, experienced considerable resistance from isolated strong-points, chiefly from a house in the north-east corner of the village. This house, however, was dealt with in a very effective manner by the Flammenwerfer squad, who set the buildings on fire, and thus enabled the Seaforths to rush it and capture the garrison.[2]

[1] The story of this message and the conditions under which it was received are rather amusing and clearly show the gallantry, resource, and, be it whispered, the superstition of our brave Allies. General Reed tells the story as follows: "I was occupying a small dug-out lit by three candles when a French officer brought in the message. He at once blew out *all* the candles and was understood to say that no operation could possibly succeed if directed from a headquarters lit by three candles. This plunge into darkness complicated matters somewhat, but eventually I was allowed to relight *two*, by the light of which the message was examined. It proved to have been written on the back of a photograph of a very charming lady, and at the end of the message the writer stated that he had lost his notebook, and requested that the photo might be returned to a given address. Shortly afterwards another message came in from the same observer. It also was written on the back of a photograph, but of *another* and, if possible, still *more* charming lady! I returned both photographs the next day, and have often speculated on the romance that lay hidden in the lives of this most gallant airman and his *two* most charming friends. Nothing could exceed the intrepidity and determination of these French flying officers in their endeavours to help their Scottish comrades to the utmost of their ability."

[2] Alluding to the French flammenwerfer men, Brig.-General Thomson says: "They were in 'high spirits' the evening before the battle, and were determined to show the enemy how his own invention *should* be used. The very appearance of these 'Firebrands' increased, if it were possible, the *moral* of my Brigade. The work they

July 28, 1918. Another post held out until the sappers exploded a heavy charge inside the building. About this time, as both companies were under heavy machine-gun fire, Lieutenant Badenoch, Black Watch, collected a few men, and successfully cleared the house from which the fire came. Fierce fighting was now taking place throughout the village, and the enemy were being driven steadily back. At one point over 100 Germans were located in a cellar. This was rushed by the Seaforths and Black Watch, and all were taken prisoner.

Buzancy taken, 1 P.M. Shortly after one o'clock Captain Murray, commanding "D" Company, Seaforths, reported that he was consolidating on the high ground east of Buzancy, and had captured a strong-point held by about 50 Germans, who had apparently fled during the "mopping up." He also reported that the French troops on the right had not advanced, and that in consequence he had ordered "B" Company, Black Watch, to establish posts on his right flank, and to conform to the position as much as possible. Another post was also established in the centre of Buzancy, and one between it and the front line to defend the village.

3 P.M. At three o'clock the position of the Seaforths was far from enviable. Buzancy, being in full view of the enemy from the east and south, was subjected to heavy rifle and machine-gun fire, and the enemy now commenced to push up small bodies of troops with the obvious intention of counter-attacking from the south. It was quite clear now that the French had been unable to advance according to plan, and that the village and ground so gallantly won by the Seaforths, sappers, and Black Watch was in danger of being lost.

As for the attack by the 5th Gordons, for the first 300 yards it met with no opposition. Here, however, a strong-point at the edge of a cornfield was encountered. This gave some trouble, but, after a rather lively bombing fight, its resistance was overcome, and the advance continued. On reaching the wall of the Chateau grounds the attack was again held up by fire from a post in the wall. Another platoon, under Lieutenant Lovie, worked round this obstruction and

did in Buzancy filled every one with admiration, tinged with compassion, for a foe whose own barbarous weapon was now turned against him in such a competent, ruthless, and deadly manner."

rushed it, capturing the gun and its team, but unfortunately lost heavily in doing so. No further opposition was encountered, and by 1.30 P.M. the battalion had reached its objective north-east of Buzancy, and were in touch with the Seaforths on the right and the Argylls on the left. Covering points were at once thrown out, and consolidation commenced, despite heavy machine-gun fire from both Buzancy and Noyant.

July 28, 1918.

About three o'clock the situation on the Divisional front was as follows: One company of the Seaforths held the south-east corner of Buzancy. Two others were in the village itself, having been driven from the positions they had gained in the morning on the high ground east of it. They and the Black Watch company now held the village, and, together with two companies of the latter battalion which had been sent up for the purpose, formed a defensive flank facing south, guarding the right of the Division. On their left the Gordons occupied the high ground north of the village, in touch with the 8th Argylls south of Chivry Farm.

Situation at 3 P.M.

The weak point was the right flank. At 3.35 P.M. the Seaforths reported that they could no longer continue the advance in view of heavy counter-attacks, also that the French were back in their original line, adding that the right flank of the Division seemed dangerously exposed.

This situation was explained to Corps, and arrangements made through Brig.-General Thomson to get in touch with the 91st (French) Regiment, and also to subject the "Grenade Work," still holding out, to an intense artillery bombardment. Before this could be done, however, an S.O.S. signal went up from the south-east corner of Buzancy.

This came from the Seaforths. With their right exposed and subjected to heavy German counter-attacks from the sunken road leading south from the village, outnumbered and outflanked, the heroic remnant of the battalion, and what remained of the Black Watch, withdrew, fighting, through Buzancy to their original line.

On the left about half-past 4 the Gordons had also been compelled to withdraw, leaving both flanks of the Seaforths in the air. It was therefore impossible to hold on any longer to the forward position. The post east of Buzancy was withdrawn to the western edge, the

4.30 P.M.

July 28, 1918. garrison of the Chateau still holding out, although almost surrounded, and it was soon seen that they too would have to come back. To help this retirement a small party of twelve Seaforths under a C.S.M. went to their assistance. It was found that the enemy had managed to bring up a machine-gun to within 15 yards of the exit through which the withdrawal had to take place. The man in charge of this gun was shot, and his team scattered by German bombs thrown by the Seaforths from within the walls, thus enabling the garrison to get away, although they suffered many casualties in doing so from other enemy machine-guns that had crept up in the meantime. In their diary, the Gordons, doubtless writing of this, say that the enemy used his light machine-guns very skilfully, and, "pressing on, forced our men back to their original line." [1]

5.45 P.M.

At 5.45 P.M. orders reached General Reed from Corps to the effect that a fresh artillery barrage was to be put down on the "Grenade Work" and the woods south of Buzancy, under cover of which the 91st French Regiment would attack again with the object of linking up with the Fifteenth Division. It was too late. Both the 44th and 45th Brigades had been compelled to withdraw; and at 6 P.M. the officer commanding the 91st Regiment was ordered not to develop his attack, and directions were given that the original front line was to be strongly held.

Situation at nightfall.

Such was the situation when night fell. Comment on the result is superfluous. What occurred may be summed up in a few words. The Highland Brigade took Buzancy and the plateau east of it. The 45th Brigade also carried out its task. Both brigades, although losing heavily themselves, inflicted severe losses on the enemy, whose losses, in addition to killed and wounded, amounted to 6 officers and over 200 other ranks taken prisoner.

The forced retirement of both brigades was due to the failure of the French troops on the right to carry out the task allotted to them. In justice, however, it must be stated that their Division had been fighting hard for a considerable period; the men were strained to

[1] In the hour of victory the Gordons lost their Commanding Officer, Lieut.-Colonel G. A. Smith, D.S.O., "a most capable and gallant officer." He had been a lifelong volunteer, and the 5th Battalion suffered a very great loss when he was killed that day.

almost breaking point, and, above all, they had a most difficult task to perform through wooded and well-fortified country.

July 28, 1918.

Although unsuccessful in retaining the ground won, the Fifteenth Division that day inflicted a blow on the enemy, the result of which was speedily apparent.

The account of this day's fighting cannot be closed without allusion to the work of the sappers, 45th Light Trench-Mortar Battery, and 15th Machine-Gun Battalion (Lieut.-Colonel R. Nasmith, H.L.I.). The section of "A" Company, 15th Machine-Gun Battalion, with the Seaforths, took their guns actually into Buzancy, remained there all day, and did great execution before being forced to withdraw. As regards the two trench-mortar teams, on reaching the village the officer in charge of them reported that, owing to casualties, he was unable to get his guns into position. He volunteered to go forward with the R.E. section and the few men he had left, and with them he succeeded in "mopping up" the most obstinate strong-points in his neighbourhood.

Work of the R.E.

The section of the 91st Field Company, R.E., had been allotted to the Seaforths to be used for demolition purposes. As at Loos, and on subsequent occasions, here again the sappers covered themselves with glory. At zero hour their commander, 2nd Lieutenant Arbuthnott, was hit, and, after seeing him carried to a place of safety, Sergeant Coleman, R.E., took command of the section. What this party did is best described in the short report written by Lieutenant Lamb, commanding the company. He says:—

"The first wave (of the Seaforths) captured the Chateau, and the second passed through the Chateau grounds. . . . The sappers got mixed up with the infantry. . . . Sergeant Coleman then told the party to stop in the grounds until he got in touch with the O.C. company clearing the village. At this point the section came under machine-gun fire from the vicinity of the Chateau, which had not been properly 'mopped up,' and got split up. Each party separately engaged the enemy, and Lance-Corporal Brazier, with four sappers, got in touch with O.C. "A" Company, 8th Seaforths—I think, Captain McElderney,—who told him to report to Lieutenant Thomson. Lance-Corporal Brazier then blew up a cellar close to the church, which contained enemy machine-guns, silenced them, and killed several of the enemy. He and his men then returned to the Chateau, and, with Lieutenant Thomson and one platoon of the Seaforths, rushed a cellar, and captured between 100 and 120 Germans.

July 28, 1918.

"At this point the enemy counter-attacked on our exposed right flank, and practically the whole of the sappers fought their way back to our old front line, as they were nearly surrounded. . . . O.C. 8th Seaforths has nothing but praise for the conduct of the sappers."

A modest report, indeed, considering what this little party accomplished. Their casualties were not excessive—namely, 1 officer wounded, 2 other ranks killed, 2 wounded and missing, and 4 missing.

During the night of the 28th General Reed sent the following message to Brig.-General Thomson :—

"Please let me congratulate you and your brigade on the work of to-day. There is no question about the complete initial success, thanks to the plans well made by you in a short time, and carried into effect by the Highland brigade with great gallantry. The fault that the ground gained had to be given up was due, as far as I can judge, to no fault of the Scottish Division."

At eleven o'clock that night orders were issued for the Fifteenth to relieve parts of the 87th and 12th (French) Divisions, half the relief to be carried out that night and the remainder by 3 A.M. on the 30th. This was a heavy demand, but doubtless the French Corps Commander found it unavoidable. To carry out *any* relief at twenty-four hours' notice is a difficult matter, and requires more than ordinary foresight, but to do so without notice and immediately at the close of a battle, when most of the units were more or less in confusion, and when parts of two different Divisions had to be relieved, was a Herculean task, the language question not making matters any easier.

Relief of French.

On that night, 28th, the 7/8th K.O.S.B. and 9th Royal Scots relieved one battalion of the 72nd Regiment, 87th Division, one of the 67th Regiment, and a company of the 54th, both of the 12th Division. The next night the 9th Gordons (Pioneers), lent to the 45th Brigade, and the 13th Royal Scots, took over from the 136th and 91st Regiments, 87th Division, the 10th Scottish Rifles relieving one battalion, 72nd Regiment, then in support. The 44th Brigade was relieved in the line by troops of the 87th Division, and then became Divisional reserve, west of Lechelle and Chazelle. It speaks well for the Division that the relief was carried out successfully under rather difficult conditions, for, owing to the enemy using gas-shells freely on both nights, respirators had to be worn practically the whole time.

July 29, 1918.

The new line of the Division.

The new line (see Map 14) ran from Bois de Tigny north to a point just south of Ru Gailet Farm, and was held, from right to left, by the 9th Royal Scots, 7/8th K.O.S.B., 9th Gordons, and 13th Royal Scots. On all parts of this new front the Divisional front was overlooked by the enemy. On the extreme right the line was faced by a ridge 1000 yards long, above which rose three hillocks, known as "Les Trois Mamelons" or "The Three Breasts." These were in the hands of the enemy, and formed three very formidable strong-points in their front system. From the northern edge of these hillocks the Division line followed the main road, passing east of Villemontoire, and confronting an open and regular upward slope—the southern limb of the Buzancy Ridge,—which also afforded no kind of cover to an attacking force. On the other hand, two deep and narrow re-entrants, cutting into the eastern edge of the slope, gave the Germans a covered approach to their front line and shelter for support and reserve troops. No change was made in the position of the artillery. That of the Fifteenth Division remained where it was, covering the 87th (French) Division front, whilst the latter's guns covered that of the Fifteenth.

During the morning of the 29th orders reached Division Headquarters from G.O.C., XX. (French) Corps, that the Fifteenth would, in conjunction with the 12th on their right, attack the enemy positions the next day.

The operation was to consist of an enveloping movement round the Bois d'Hartennes, the 12th Division working round it by the south and the Fifteenth by the north. The scheme was dependent on the success of another attack farther south, which was to take place on the 30th. If that was successful, the attack on the Bois d'Hartennes would be made the following day, and the Fifteenth Division was to be ready to move forward and take a series of wooded hills lying between Tigny and Villemontoire, having as their objective the main Soissons road. It was originally intended that this attack would be carried out whether the other farther south was successful or not, but on the evening of the 29th it was settled that it should

July 29-31, 1918.

form part of the whole operation, and would take place in conjunction with the southern attack, which was now fixed for August 1.

Although not actually in the line, brigades behind lost several officers and men from the persistent enemy shelling prior to the day of attack. Amongst these was Lieut.-Colonel H. H. Kennedy, commanding the 8th Seaforths. A regular officer of that regiment, he had served for a considerable period with the Fifteenth Division, in which his sterling worth and intense devotion to duty were fully appreciated by all who came in contact with him.

During the night of July 30th/31st, much to their disgust, the 9th Gordons were relieved by the 13th Royal Scots. In their diary it is stated :—

> "The battalion were expecting to attack in the morning, and were in fine spirits. All ranks were really disappointed to hear that the attack had been postponed, and that they would be relieved that night without a fight."

Plan for next attack.

A conference of brigade commanders was held at Division Headquarters on the 31st, when General Reed explained his plan of attack. On the right the 46th Brigade was to attack the two wooded hills west of the Soissons road and go forward as far as Taux, forming as they went a defensive left flank along the German trenches running in a south-easterly direction from the road. On the left the 45th Brigade were to conform with the right attack, having as their objective the Soissons road from Villemontoire as far south as the German trench where it crossed the road. When Taux had been captured by the 46th Brigade, the 44th, who were to be in close support, was to move up and go through the 46th to the final objective—namely, the northern end of the Bois d'Hartennes,—where they would link up with the French advancing from the south. They were also directed to continue the defensive flank formed by the 46th along the German trenches.

The difficult part of the operation was the move forward of the 44th Brigade to their assembly positions, as the ground was in full view of the enemy occupying the woods between Buzancy and the Bois d'Hartennes. On this account it was settled that the brigade and the 10th Scottish Rifles (supporting battalion of the 46th Brigade) should get into position during the night, using the fields of standing corn to conceal them as far as possible from the view of the enemy.

Aug. 1, 1918.

The XX. (French) Corps had arranged that a signal would be dropped from a contact 'plane as soon as it had been ascertained that the French attack farther south had been successful. This signal, and certain salvoes from heavy guns, would notify troops that zero hour would be the moment when the first completed half hour had elapsed from the giving of the signal. Artillery barrages and bombardments were arranged, special attention being paid to the northern edge of the Bois d'Hartennes, the western edges of the Bois de Concrois, and other points. Two sections of "C" Company, 15th Machine-Gun Battalion, were allotted to the 44th Brigade and one of "B" to the 46th, the remaining guns reinforcing the artillery barrage.

Dispositions of Brigades.

For the attack, brigades were disposed thus: On the right the 9th Royal Scots and 7/8th K.O.S.B. were to lead the attack of the 46th Brigade, with the 10th Scottish Rifles in close support. Behind the 46th was the 44th, with the 5th Gordons on the right, 4/5th Black Watch on the left, and 8th Seaforths in reserve. On the left the 6th Camerons, right, and 13th Royal Scots, left, occupied the front line, the 8th Argylls being in reserve.

Before dawn on August 1 all troops were in position, those behind having been able to move up unseen by the enemy, and lay hidden in fields of standing corn ready to advance when the signal was given. They could only have been seen from aeroplanes, and fortunately on this occasion the German machines had been forced down by those of the French.

The attack by the French was launched at 5 A.M., and was so quickly successful that at 8.25 A.M. the prearranged signals were seen, denoting that the Division would advance at 9 A.M. At that hour, accordingly, the troops left their positions.

The attack launched.

From the very start they came under heavy artillery and machine-gun fire. By far the worst came from machine-guns in several derelict tanks in front of the 46th Brigade. The fire from these was so intense that progress forward was impossible. Artillery fire was brought to bear on them, but without success, the result being that the right attack was completely checked. "C" and "D" Companies of the

Aug. 1, 1918. 9th Royal Scots, leading the attack, suffered heavily after advancing with the greatest gallantry barely 250 yards. The K.O.S.B., too, were almost decimated in their repeated and resolute attempts to get forward a few yards. Behind these battalions the 10th Scottish Rifles did not leave their positions, having been ordered not to do so until the first objective had been taken.

Meanwhile the 44th Brigade had come up behind the 46th, and about eleven o'clock were about 700 yards behind in artillery formations ready to advance if required. On the left the Camerons reached the Soissons road about eleven o'clock, but reported that they were not in touch with the K.O.S.B. They at once formed a defensive flank along the lane leading from the cemetery to the main road, and consolidated their gains. Farther north the 13th Royal Scots got as far as the hedge east of the main road about the same time as the Camerons, where they too consolidated.

Realising from these reports that his right attack was definitely held up, General Reed at once arranged for a further artillery and Stokes' mortar bombardment, the targets being the tanks and wooded knolls north of Tigny, and directed that another assault was to take place under cover of it.

Whilst the above events were taking place on the Divisional front, reports reached Divisional Headquarters that the French attack was progressing satisfactorily, and that Tigny had been taken; but at 2.45 P.M. an S.O.S. signal went up from the village, and French troops were seen moving back, having apparently been driven out by fire from the wooded knolls alluded to above. Artillery fire was again opened on these knolls by every available gun, but without effect, and the Germans, counter-attacking the French in force, drove them back, and by 4.50 P.M. the whole line south of the ground held by the Camerons was the same as that held in the morning.

Little success.

Of the many acts of gallantry performed that day one may be mentioned. When the attack of the 9th Royal Scots and 10th Scottish Rifles was brought to a standstill by terrific machine-gun fire, a number of men of both battalions lay wounded in full view of the enemy. Seeing this, Private R. Owenson, Scottish Rifles, went out to help them, and, in defiance of the intense fire his action drew on him, crawled

Aug. 1, 1918.

from one to another, bandaging their wounds until his supply of dressings was finished. Returning to his company, he got a further supply, and went back through the barrage to the wounded men. Later in the day, when another attempt to get forward was made, Owenson continued to assist the wounded men, utterly indifferent to the hail of machine-gun bullets and shrapnel which swept the ground over which he had to work. No decoration could be adequate for the work this soldier performed, but it is gratifying to know that for this Owenson received the D.C.M., Medaille Militaire, and Croix de Guerre (avec Palmes).

It was now decided by the French Corps Commander that the Fifteenth Division would not resume the attack, but would keep in touch with flanking divisions. By this time few, if any, battalions in either the 44th or 46th Brigades could muster more than 250 all ranks, and arrangements were then made to send up 2 officers and 50 other ranks to each battalion that night from a last reserve which had been carefully nursed for each battalion.

That night the 44th relieved the 46th in the right sector, the 4/5th Black Watch on the right, and 5th Gordons on the left, with the Seaforths in support, whilst the 9th Gordons (Pioneers) relieved the 6th Camerons of the 45th Brigade, and, with the help of one company from the 8th A. & S. Highlanders, consolidated the ground won that morning.

It was now being realised by the High Command that units of the Fifteenth Division were feeling the strain after eight days of heavy and almost continuous fighting, and General Reed was informed by a liaison officer from the Tenth (French) Army that the Division would be relieved during the nights of the 2nd and 3rd.

Effect of the day's fighting.

Although there was not much to show as the result of the day's fighting, the moral effect of it was soon apparent. The Division had assisted in keeping a considerable force of the enemy fully occupied whilst the French successfully drove them back farther south. This compelled the Germans to straighten out their line, which they promptly proceeded to do by retiring from the positions they occupied in front of the Division, and those farther south and north, during the night of the 1st/2nd. About half-past 8 on the morning of the 2nd, news

Aug. 2, 1918. Retreat of the Germans.

reached General Reed that the 12th French Division, with cavalry in front, were pushing eastwards, and that the enemy were retiring before them. Orders were at once issued that strong patrols should be pushed out by front-line battalions, and every endeavour made to get in touch with the enemy.

Unfortunately there is little material in the diaries giving any idea of what must have been a dramatic day. The only one is that of the Gordons (Pioneers) :—

11 A.M.

"At 11 A.M. the commanding officer, Major Gourlay, received orders to push forward officers' patrols. . . . He at once proceeded to the front line. On arrival at Villemontoire it became evident that a withdrawal had been effected, as the troops on our right were walking about on the top. . . . The C.O. immediately ordered 'F' Company to move forward as an advance-guard, with a strong protective screen in front. About noon 'H' Company was ordered to follow in support, and 'G' Company in reserve.

"The advance-guard moved very rapidly, and by 4 P.M. had covered all the ground as far as Amberif. Here Captain Lumsden had to halt, as it was becoming impossible to maintain liaison with the units on his flank."

A general advance.

The Tenth (French) Army Orders for a general advance reached the Division at 11.30 A.M. The 44th Brigade was accordingly directed to advance due east through Taux, and effect a junction with the French east of it. When that had been accomplished it was then to turn slightly left, and, keeping in touch with the French on its right and the 45th Brigade on its left, the advance would be continued in a north-easterly direction, with the river Crise as its first objective, the 46th Brigade being ordered to stand by at short notice.

3.30 P.M.

At half-past three in the afternoon reports reached Divisional Headquarters to the effect that the 45th Brigade had gained the edge of the Bois de Concrois, and were pushing forward in touch with the 5th Gordons of the 44th Brigade on the right. General Reed at once moved his headquarters to Vierzy, and ordered the 46th Brigade up to the neighbourhood of Villemontoire.

When night fell the leading troops of the Division had crossed the river Crise north of Chacrise, two and a half to three miles east of the line they had occupied that morning. Very little opposition was met with, and French cavalry, who had been asked for earlier in the day, were out in front of the outpost line, which ran and was held as follows :—

Aug. 2, 1918.

Situation at nightfall.

On the right the Seaforths and 5th Gordons held the line from Chacrise to Amberif, in touch with the French on their right. On the left the 9th Gordons (Pioneers) continued the line from Amberif to Ecuiry, where the 13th Royal Scots took it up, and continued as far as the junction, with the 87th Division on the left, north-east of Buzancy.

The result of the day's operations had been better than the most sanguine could have expected. Brig.-General Thomson writes :—

"The whole day was full of incident. It was certainly a dramatic moment when orders for the advance reached my brigade. In the front line the men formed up in groups on the parapet of their trenches seemingly dazed at these, to them, new conditions of warfare. Fortunately, a few older hands remembered their early training at Aldershot and Salisbury Plain, and I think it is due to this that the dash forward so quickly became general in all. Never on any field day or in action have I seen men press forward in such eagerness when once the game was realised, and when the first mounted officer's horse was brought up—that of Smith, the Brigade Signalling Officer—the pace was hot indeed. We were out of touch with the French on our right, and did not know what the Bois de Concrois and Bois de Phenix might contain. There was, however, no time for delay. One platoon only was told off to deal with the right flank, and the remainder of the brigade pushed boldly across the Crise to the line Amberif-Chacrise, where touch was regained with the French, and the Seaforths and Gordons dug in, in full view of the enemy, in open fields on the high ground east of the road between those two villages. Torrents of rain fell during the evening, but neither this nor the intermittent shelling by the enemy, both during the advance and the occupation of the new position, could damp the ardour of all ranks."

In recording the day's fighting, most diaries mention the fact that whilst retiring the Germans drenched the woods and corn-fields, as well as the dug-outs and caves, for which they now had no further use, with gas, from the effects of which many suffered before its presence was discovered. The officers commanding both the 44th and 45th Brigades, and most of the staff of the latter, as well as the commanding officers of several battalions and many other ranks, suffered from this, but managed to carry on until the Division was relieved that night. Fortunately the effects did not last long, and although a number

Aug. 2-3, 1918.

of cases were admitted to hospital, most of them were back with the Division within a fortnight.

Late that night orders for a further advance reached the Division, but, in view of the state of affairs, it was subsequently decided that the relief, originally planned to take place on two nights, should be completed in one. It was therefore arranged that guides from the 44th and 45th Brigades should meet representatives of the incoming regiments of the 17th (French) Division at the cross-roads south of Villemontoire, due east of Raperie. The first relieving regiment passed Vierzy at 11.30 P.M. on the 2nd, and was led to the 44th Brigade Headquarters on the northern edge of the Bois de Concrois, whilst the second passed at 1 A.M. on the 3rd. These two regiments then formed up on the south bank of the Crise, and at dawn went through the Divisional outpost line, the reserve brigade being relieved at that hour by the 3rd Regiment, 17th Division, who took up a position on the western edge of the Bois de Concrois. The two forward companies of the 15th Machine-Gun Battalion remained in the line to assist the French troops until the afternoon of the 3rd, when they, too, withdrew, and the battalion concentrated at Vierzy.

Relief of Division.

More than passing reference must be made to the 17th (French) Division. Recruited from the country round Nancy, from whence comes probably the finest type of French soldier, the appearance of the leading battalions astonished the Scotsmen. Big stalwart men of the type of the British Guards, spick and span, turned out to the last button as if for a ceremonial parade, in spite of having been hurried up from Verdun and having done a long march before the relief, they were an inspiring spectacle as they arrived to relieve the Division. Perhaps the most striking of all was their commander, General Gassoins, whose letter to General Reed is referred to later. Tall and slim, with a handsome clean-cut face, he looked, and was, the very type an artist would select as a perfect soldier.

Arrangements had been made for motor-lorries and 'buses to convey brigades, &c., to the Vierzy area, but, probably owing to the extraordinary success of the recent fighting, and the fact that their services were required elsewhere, the vehicles did not turn up, and the move was carried out by march route, the 45th and 46th Brigades arriving during the night of the 3rd/4th, whilst the 44th bivouacked at Dommieres, and arrived on the morning of the 4th, after a march of thirteen miles. The Machine-Gun Battalion were more fortunate. Their 'buses met them at Vierzy in the early morning of the 4th, and they proceeded direct to the Liancourt area. On the 4th the Division embused, and by the evening was, with the artillery and transport, which had moved by road after the former had been relieved by the 87th Divisional Artillery, concentrated round Liancourt, south of Clermont.

Aug. 4-6, 1918.

Return to the British area.

The same night orders were issued for the entrainment of the Division, on transfer from the Third (French) to the First British Army on the Arras front, and the move, after having been postponed for twelve hours to allow the artillery and transport to come up, was commenced on the night of the 5th/6th, and by the morning of the 8th the Division was once more concentrated in the Le Cauroy area, again under the orders of the XXII. Corps.

Farewell to the French.

The Division left their French chiefs and comrades with regret. It had been an honour to have served under Generals of such distinction as General Mangin, Commanding the Tenth French Army, a soldier of world-wide renown ; and General Berdoulat, XX. French Corps (The " Corps de Fer "). From first to last these officers showed the greatest consideration and kindness to the Division. It was placed in a post of honour ; much was expected of it, and the French chiefs were more than satisfied with what it accomplished.

At the conclusion of the operations, General Mangin, in consultation with General Berdoulat, allotted the Division eleven Legions of Honour, twenty Medaille Militaire, sixty Croix de Guerre (avec Palmes), and one hundred and twenty Croix de Guerre (avec etoile), with special instructions that they were all to be considered as rewards for good work " on the field of battle."

General Mangin did not forget the Fifteenth Division, for in 1921, on his return from the French official Mission to South America, he had occasion to write to the British Ambassador in Paris. In the letter he said :—

" My reference to the services of the British forces on land and sea during the war were dictated by a regard for truth and a spirit of comradeship which

Aug. 1918.

I felt very strongly, having fought side by side with His Majesty's troops in the summer of 1916, and having had the honour of commanding the Fifteenth (Scottish) and 34th (British) Divisions during the decisive battles fought in July 1918. THESE DIVISIONS CONTRIBUTED LARGELY TO THE ALLIES' VICTORY."

General Berdoulat has since become Governor of Paris. The Division owes much to him. General Gassoins has retired, but has not forgotten the Scottish Division. Only recently (1922) some senior officers of the Fifteenth Division have been made " Membres d'Honneur " of the 17th (French) Division Old Comrades' Association.

Such is the story of Buzancy. During the fighting the Division was entirely under French control. This naturally made administration difficult, especially as regards supplies, ammunition, &c. Realising this, the French did all in their power to assist, and on leaving the area every man, from General Reed downwards, was loud in praise of the manner in which they had been treated by their French comrades. The British Field Force Canteen successfully pushed up stores to the Division in a manner which opened the eyes of the Frenchmen, and by means of it exchange in commodities took place between the Scots and Frenchmen, jam being bartered for *vin ordinaire*, &c.

Before the Division left the French area, General Reed received and promulgated the following messages, fitting tributes to the deeds of the Scottish Division and others of the XXII. Corps :—

1.

2/8/18.

From GENERAL MANGIN, Commanding Tenth French Army.

Forward! The victory of August 1 puts the finishing touch to that of July 18, and is ending in a rout. The roads are bad, but the rain is hurting the Boche too. Follow them up! Trample them down!! Overrun their feeble centres of resistance where they are vainly endeavouring to stop our victorious advance. This evening the Tenth French Army must be on the line of the river Vesle.

2.

To ALL UNITS.

General Mangin, Commanding Tenth French Army, sends the following, dated 2/8/18, to the Fifteenth Division. To-day's success has been made possible by the conduct of all concerned, and particularly by the sacrifices of the Scottish. Aug. 1918.

3.

The French commander also issued the following General Order :—

(*Translation.*)

ARMY H.Q. 5/8/18.

GENERAL ORDER, NO. 343.

Officers, non-commissioned officers, and men of the Fifteenth and 34th British Divisions,

You entered the battle at its fiercest moment. The enemy, already once vanquished, again brought up against us his best divisions, considerably outnumbering our own.

You continued to advance step by step in spite of his desperate resistance, and you held the ground won in spite of his violent counter-attacks.

Then, during the whole day of August 1, side by side with your French comrades, you stormed the ridge dominating the whole country between the Aisne and the Ourcq, which the defenders had received orders to hold at all cost.

Having failed to retake the ridge with his last reserves, the enemy had to beat a retreat, pursued and harassed, for twelve kilometres.

All of you, English and Scottish, young soldiers and veterans of Flanders and Palestine, have shown the magnificent qualities of your race : courage and imperturbable tenacity.

You have won the admiration of your comrades in arms. Your country will be proud of you, for to your chiefs and to you is due a large share of the victory that we have gained over the barbarous enemies of the free.

I am happy to have fought at your head, and I thank you.

MANGIN.

4.

The General Officer Commanding the First Army issued the following Special Order :—

SPECIAL ORDER

BY GENERAL SIR H. S. HORNE, K.C.B., K.C.M.G.,

Commanding First Army.

The following letter from the General Officer Commanding the 17th (French) Division to the General Officer Commanding the Fifteenth Division is published for the information of all ranks :—

Aug.-Sept. 1918.

27th August '18.

MON GENERAL,—After relieving your Division in the pursuit on the Vesle, I established my headquarters at Buzancy. I found there the traces still fresh of the exploits of your Scottish soldiers, and the officers of my staff were able to see clearly what hard fighting you had to gain possession of the village, and, above all, the park.

Wishing to leave on the spot some lasting tribute to the bravery of your soldiers, I entrusted to one of my officers, Lieutenant Réné Puaux, the task of erecting there, with the material at hand, a small monument, emblematic of the homage and admiration of my Division for yours.

This monument has on it a medallion, on which are inscribed thistles and roses, and beneath the words :—

HERE THE NOBLE THISTLE OF SCOTLAND WILL FLOURISH
FOR EVER AMONG THE ROSES OF FRANCE.

and beneath :—

17TH FRENCH DIVISION
TO
15TH (SCOTTISH) DIVISION.

This monument was erected on the highest point of the plateau, where we found the body of the Scottish soldier who had advanced the farthest (on July 28, 1918—Buzancy).

The photograph of this monument has appeared in the last number of the journal 'L'Illustration.' I thought you would be glad to have a few copies of the photograph, which I send you herewith. They convey to you, together with the memories which I have kept of our short meeting at Vierzy, the expression of my esteem and my admiration for your valiant Division.

Will you please accept, dear General, the expression of my sincere regards ?

(Signed) C. GASSOINS,[1]
(*General de Division,*
Commanding 17th (French) Division.)

---

[1] General Gassoins died in Paris on January 11, 1924, after a very short illness. In May 1923 he had written to Major-General Reed informing him that he had succeeded in having the Memorial at Buzancy officially recognised as a "Monument historique," with the result that its care and upkeep was ensured—in his own words, "In order that the mark of confraternity in arms may remain inscribed on the battlefield." General Gassoins had seen much active service. He was perhaps in his element as an organiser, and for a considerable time during the late war (two and a half years) he had supreme military control of all French railways ; but his heart was with the troops in the field, and he resigned his high post to take up command of 17th Division. After the war he retired in order to assume position of General Manager of the Standard Oil Company in France. Arrangements were made immediately on news of his death that the sympathy and condolence of all ranks Fifteenth (Scottish) Division should be conveyed to Madame Gassoins by Colonel Lord Malise Graham, Military Attaché in Paris at the time.

I am confident that this testimony of the true feeling of comradeship which exists between our ally and ourselves will be highly appreciated by all ranks of the First Army.

Aug. 1918.

(Signed) H. S. Horne, *General*
Commanding First Army.

First Army Headquarters,
15th September 1918.

It is worthy of mention that this monument is believed to be the only one erected by the French Army on any battlefield in memory of a British formation.

In order to assist the French relieving troops, each battalion left five officers and four N.C.O.'s in the line for twenty-four hours, when they rejoined their battalions.

With the exception of the move on the 3rd, when owing to congested roads it marched, the Division, less artillery and transport, which proceeded by road, was conveyed by 'buses to Liancourt area, where it entrained for Arras. The arrangements were excellent, and, commenting on them in his report, General Reed says :—

" The bussing arrangements made by the French authorities are worthy of mention. On arrival in the French zone, the whole Division, less artillery, was bussed to the forward area, a distance of twenty-five miles. On leaving the battle zone, the Division, less artillery, together with the 34th Division, were bussed to the entraining areas simultaneously. At the same time, a French division was bussed from the detraining area to the battle zone, passing through the British divisions ; thus *three divisions* were in movement in 'buses in the same area on the same day, and the operation was completed without a hitch."

By the morning of the 4th the Division was concentrated round Viviers, the 44th Brigade having bivouacked at Dommieres on the night of the 3rd.

This transfer to the First Army occupied three days, and on the morning of the 8th Divisional Headquarters opened at Le Cauroy, troops being billeted as under :—

44th Brigade Group in Izel area.
45th Brigade Group in Lignereuil area.
46th Brigade Group in Maizieres area.
9th Gordons (Pioneers) at Beaufort.
15th Machine-Gun Battalion at Ambrines.

Aug. 1918.

73rd Field Company, R.E., at Manien.
74th Field Company, R.E., at Denier.
91st Field Company, R.E., at Villers sur Simon.
Divisional Artillery at and around Estree Wamin and Berlincourt.
Divisional Headquarters at Houvin Houvigneul.

Rest and refitment.

The next ten days were spent resting and reorganising. Large reinforcements (129 officers and 2939 other ranks) reached the Division in August, most of them during the first fortnight, and by the time they went into the line again units were up to strength. Whilst at rest on August 10, 12, and 13, General Reed presented a number of decorations, many of them French, to officers, N.C.O.'s, and men for good services at Buzancy.

Into line south of the Scarpe.

Between August 15 and 18 the Division relieved the 56th (London) Division in the right sector of the XVII. Corps front south of the Scarpe. This time the 44th Brigade relieved the 167th during the night of the 15th/16th in the right section. The following night the 45th relieved the 169th in the centre section, and the next night the 46th relieved the 168th in the left section, the 9th Gordons (Pioneers) relieving the 1/5th Cheshire Pioneers during the second night; whilst the 91st, 73rd, and 74th Field Companies, R.E., took over from the 416th, 512th, and 513th respectively, Divisional artillery and machine-gun battalion relieving those of the 56th Division at the same time. By 10 A.M. on the 18th the relief was completed, and General Reed assumed command of the sector, with headquarters again at Warlus. The line ran from Neuville Vitasse, due north, to the junction of the Cambrai road and Pelves Lane, and was held by all three brigades, each finding its own supports and reserves.

After its recent experiences in the south, this tour, with one exception, proved an exceedingly quiet one for the Division. By this time there were unmistakable signs that the German *moral* was breaking. Evidence of this was obtained from various prisoners taken. On the 18th one of these stated that his comrades had actually retired to a line approximately Monchy, Pelves, Biache (some 5000 yards). On receipt of this news brigades were at once ordered to send out strong fighting patrols, and the Divisional artillery directed to be ready to move forward if required. At midnight these patrols went out, but found the line still occupied by the enemy in force, with the result that they suffered somewhat severe casualties. Five prisoners were taken by the 45th Brigade, but no forward progress was made, and at daybreak the next morning the patrols withdrew.

Aug. 1918.

Although this pressure on the enemy had no immediate effect, constant and vigorous patrolling by all battalions in the front line went on, and advanced posts were established well in front of the line. These were withdrawn on the 21st, as, according to Fifteenth Divisional G.S. Diary, "The recent offensive patrol policy had gained the required information regarding the dispositions of the enemy. Energetic patrolling, however, still went on."

The same night warning orders were issued to the effect that the 2nd Canadian Division would relieve the Fifteenth, commencing the following night, Divisional artillery to remain in the line covering the Canadians. The 44th and 45th Brigades were relieved by the 6th Canadian Brigade early in the morning of the 23rd, twelve hours earlier than had been arranged, and at 9.30 P.M. that night the G.O.C. 2nd Canadian Division assumed command of the sector, Fifteenth Divisional Headquarters opening at Villers Chatel at that hour. The following night the remainder of the Division left the line, and, moving by train (transport by road), found itself once more in the familiar Loos area.

Move to Loos area.

CHAPTER XI.

THE ADVANCE TO VICTORY.[1]

Aug. 1918.

WAS it by accident or design that the last phase of its fighting career should begin round Loos and the Hohenzollern Redoubt, where over three years before the Division had received its baptism of fire? There were then few left in the Division who could remember those early days, but to the few the memories must have been many. As an old officer who had the privilege of serving for all too short a time with the Division, the writer can well imagine (and envy) the feelings of those gallant few in finding themselves back once more in the Loos area.

In the Loos salient.

With headquarters at Bracquemont, General Reed now took over the left sector of the I. Corps (First Army) front from the 11th Division, command passing on the morning of August 26. As the Fifteenth Division guns had been left at Arras covering the Canadian Division, those of the 11th remained in the line.

Dispositions.

At the start the 44th Brigade took over the right sub-sector and the 45th the left from the 34th and 33rd Brigades respectively, the 46th remaining in reserve. On the 27th the Division was ordered to prolong its line to the right, and take over the front held by the 73rd Brigade (24th Division). The 46th Brigade was directed to take over the additional front, and the line was then held by all three brigades, each finding its own supports and reserves as follows:—

Right (Loos) Section—46th Brigade, from Bois Rase almost to Posen Alley.

Centre (Hulluch) Section—44th Brigade, as far as the Vermelles-Hulluch road.

Left (St Elie) Section—45th Brigade, as far north as the boundary between the Fifteenth and 16th Divisions.

[1] Maps 15 and 16.

Although the line, with the exception of that part immediately east of Loos, where it had been advanced about 1500 yards, ran almost as it had in 1916, many changes had taken place. Behind the line things were much the same. It seemed to have been a point of honour to the inhabitants of the various villages to repair any damage done by shell-fire as soon as possible, but the front areas were very different. The old fire trenches were battered out of all recognition, and in consequence the system of defence had been considerably altered. Instead of holding a continuous line of trenches as heretofore, an "outpost zone," consisting of observation posts in No Man's Land, had been substituted. Behind this was the "battle zone," a series of "defended localities," running back to a depth of some 3000 yards. In this area were posts so arranged that the fire from each flanked those on either side, the normal garrison of each post being one platoon. Behind these posts what remained of the old trenches, especially those in the original front line, had been filled in with barbed wire, and formed serious obstacles to any attack.

Aug. 1918.

Another marked change was the existence of a system of tunnels leading from the reserve line to the front posts. These were used not only to allow troops to get up under cover but gave accommodation to the garrisons of "defended localities." The following is a short description of one running from the Hulluch-Vermelles road to Devon and Hay localities:—

The Tunnels.

"The passage was about 4 feet wide, varying in height from 5½ to 7 feet, and, cut out of the solid rock, needed few supports. Down the centre ran an 18-inch tramway for the purpose of conveying rations, water, ammunition, &c., to the front system. At various points other passages branched off, each leading to a post or strong-point, or to large dug-outs, from which could be heard voices of men talking, officers calling orderlies, &c., the garrison of that locality. Farther up one passed an officers' mess, signal and dressing stations, a cook-house, and the headquarters of the battalion. The whole of this glorified rabbit-warren was lit by electricity, and was a marvel of construction. Undoubtedly these tunnels saved many lives, and moreover greatly lessened the fatigue caused by long journeys up miles of traversed communication trenches, often knee-deep in mud or water.

"Close to the exit nearest the enemy was a large block of cement on wheels, so arranged that it could be rolled out to close the passage if required. Just past this the tunnel branched off in five directions, each leading to posts in the 'battle zone.'"

Sept. 1918.

This last tour in the trenches started unfortunately. On August 26 ten rounds from a German high-velocity, large-calibre gun fell in the Fifteenth Divisional Reception Camp, causing many casualties, about 53 killed and wounded, mostly among men about to go on leave, the Royal Scots suffering more than any other battalion.

Throughout September the entries "A quiet day," "Quiet in front," occur in all diaries. It seems that the enemy had now reached his limit of endurance, and contented himself with holding on to his position. He certainly had lost the initiative, and all ranks of the Division saw to it that he was harried in every possible way both by day and by night. Strong fighting patrols went out nightly, but, with few exceptions, met with no opposition, and it was only when they attempted raids deeply into the German defences that they met with strong resistance.

Raids.

During the night of September 4 the 9th Royal Scots raided the German lines north of the Bois Hugo. Strong opposition was met with, and no prisoners were taken. The following day the same battalion carried out a similar raid with a like result, thus demonstrating that the enemy was still alert and holding his second line in force. Nineteen men of the 4/5th Black Watch, under 2nd Lieutenant McGladdery, entered the enemy front trenches on the night of the 6th/7th. The party searched the position for about 200 yards without meeting a single German, and, after staying out from 10.30 P.M. until 2 A.M., returned after having suffered no casualties of any kind.

On the 8th the Fifteenth Divisional Artillery took over from that of the 11th. Left behind at Arras, it had covered the great Canadian attack from August 26 to September 5, and on the 6th had been relieved by the 50th Divisional Artillery, when it proceeded by road to Hersin. In addition to his own guns, Brig.-General Macnaghten, B.G.R.A.,[1] now had those of one regiment of Portuguese artillery and a battery of their 4.5 howitzers with which to cover the Divisional front.

The most successful raid of this period must be credited to the 7/8th K.O.S.B. On the 14th "A" and "B" Companies of that

[1] At the end of September Brig.-General Macnaghten, so long C.R.A. of the Division, left it to take command of an Infantry Brigade in another Division, Lieut.-Colonel C. M. Ingham, commanding 71st Brigade R.F.A., succeeding him as C.R.A.

battalion got into the enemy front and reserve trenches south of Hulluch in spite of heavy machine-gun fire, from the effects of which "A" Company on the right suffered somewhat severely. On the left "B" Company successfully reached the German support line, the enemy flying down their communication trenches before the attackers. Here a good deal of desperate hand-to-hand fighting took place, but the Borderers gradually drove the enemy back to their reserve line, where the resistance stiffened, and the party, having discovered that the German reserve line was their main line of resistance, withdrew. This gallant party lost heavily in officers—3, including Captain Deans, who led the raid, were killed, and 3 more wounded out of a total of 10. 12 other ranks were killed, 30 wounded, and 5 reported missing.[1]

Sept. 1918.

Fighting at the Quarries.

Very desperate fighting took place in and around "The Quarries" from the 12th to the end of September. To start with, the 6th Camerons pushed forward to the north-east side, and established posts on the far side. On the 15th the enemy endeavoured to regain their lost trenches, but were driven back with heavy loss after severe fighting, of which the 13th Royal Scots bore the brunt. The following day the front companies of both battalions pushed forward their line still farther east of "The Quarries," taking some prisoners and two machine-guns. The next night the 1/8th Argylls also went forward. Against these aggressive tactics the enemy did little; a few weak counter-attacks were launched, but each in turn was repulsed without difficulty.

Several readjustments of the front system took place during the month. Both the Division and inter-brigade boundaries were changed more than once on account of operations on either flank. On the 21st the I. (British) Corps, of which the Division formed a part, was transferred from the First to the Fifth Army. The only other move worth mentioning took place on the nights of the 19th and 20th, when

[1] For their services in this raid the Borderers received the following honours: 1 bar to M.C., 2 M.C's., 2 D.C.M's., and 8 M.M's., every one of them thoroughly well deserved. In connection with this raid it is worth mentioning that two Privates, Reid and Morrison, of the Lewis-gun teams of "B" Company, did exceptionally good work. "Their guns took on several German machine-guns which were thinning our ranks and succeeded in silencing them, although Morrison's gun had the whole of the radiator-casing shot off."

Oct. 1918.

the 46th Brigade in the Loos section changed places with the 45th in the St Elie (or left) section.

As September drew to a close it became more and more evident that the continuous pressure exerted on the enemy would compel him to withdraw at no distant date, and in view of such an event, voluminous orders and instructions dealing with every possible contingency were issued. The quantity of these documents and the care with which they were made out show the forethought and attention to detail given by those responsible for their issue. They are far too voluminous to quote, but the keynote of all was that the enemy was to be kept on the move once he showed any signs of withdrawing.

On October 1 nearly all diaries mention that enemy artillery fire was unusually heavy, indiscriminate fire with every kind of shell being opened on points hitherto left undisturbed. High-velocity guns pumped hundreds of gas-shells each night into back areas, and the civil population suffered a good deal. This was no doubt merely emptying of ammunition dumps prior to withdrawal of the guns. This bombardment was kept up all day, but died down completely at night, when a curious quiet was noticed all along the line. It was the beginning of the end.

The German withdrawal.

The first intimation the Division had of a German withdrawal occurred at 4 A.M. on the 2nd, when a deserter informed a patrol of the 8th Seaforths that his regiment had retired during the night. At dawn that morning men rubbed their eyes when they looked for the famous Wingles Towers, the great landmarks of this part of the country. They had disappeared, having been blown up in the night! Orders were at once issued, and strong fighting patrols from all three brigades pushed forward into the German lines.[1]

Advance of the Division.

The right brigade, 45th, got as far as Hercules and Halcyon trenches, from which the leading battalions, 13th Royal Scots (right) and 6th Camerons (left), sent on patrols as far as the Vendin-Douvrin-La Bassee line, the only opposition met with coming from the Bois de Quatorze. In the centre the 4/5th Black Watch and 8th Seaforths got forward

[1] Map 15. So rapidly was the advance pushed forward that in some instances the Scotsmen were on top of the Germans before they could get away. Some of them were just finishing breakfast, and in some instances the shells prepared to destroy their dug-outs were left without nose-caps.

Oct. 1918.

some distance without opposition, whilst on the left the 7/8th K.O.S.B. and 10th Scottish Rifles experienced no difficulty in advancing through the Cite St Elie and eastward of the village. That night the Divisional outpost line ran, approximately, from the Bois de Dix Huit, east of the Bois des Dames, east of Hulluch, and west of the Cite St Leonard, in touch with the divisions on either flank, who had also been able to get on. All through the night explosions were heard and large fires seen behind the enemy's lines—sure signs that a retirement was in progress. These and the satisfactory result of the day's fighting, accomplished with astonishingly light casualties, made every one eager for the next day, when a further advance through the Vendin-Douvrin-La Bassee line and the capture of Wingles and the Metallurgique were to be attempted.

Situation on night of the 3rd.

Shortly after dawn on October 3 news reached General Reed that good progress had already been made, and by ten o'clock all three brigades reported that their advanced troops had occupied the strongly fortified Douvrin line. When night fell the position was as follows: On the right the 45th Brigade advanced posts had reached the railway junction north-east of Annay, the outskirts of Vendin-le-Vieil, but not the village, and from there to a point due north, midway between Vendin and the Metallurgique. The 44th Brigade line skirted the western edge of the Metallurgique, thence along the eastern edge of Wingles, and from there north-west as far as the Flot de Wingles, where the 46th took up the line along the Flot, and then due north to Puits No. 5.[1] Again casualties had been slight, mostly from German machine-guns. From a deserter taken during the day it was ascertained that the enemy had withdrawn to the eastern edge of the Haute Deule Canal after destroying the bridges.

The night was as usual quiet, and patrols were able to get forward some little distance, but at dawn on the 4th fairly heavy machine-gun fire along the whole front gave indication that the enemy had for the present determined to remain where he was. On the right the progress of the 46th Brigade was somewhat hampered by the fact that the left brigade of the 58th Division had so far failed to capture

[1] Lieut.-Colonel N. Macleod, 7th Camerons, commanded the 46th Brigade during these operations, Brigadier-General Orr Ewing being on leave.

Oct. 1918.

Annay. It was able, however, to push on as far as the Coke Ovens, south-east of Vendin, but could not advance beyond that point. Prisoners taken by the brigade confirmed the fact that the enemy meant to hold on as long as possible. The 44th Brigade, owing to the difficulty in clearing the Metallurgique buildings, were not able to advance at all, but on the left the 45th pushed eastwards as far as Puits No. 9 de Meurchin, the 10th Scottish Rifles, who were then north of the Divisional boundary, being relieved that night by the 48th Brigade, 16th Division.

Between October 5 and 10 nothing beyond patrol encounters took place. The enemy were strongly posted on the east bank of the Haute Deule Canal, and all parties approaching its western bank came under heavy machine-gun fire, and under such conditions it was useless to attempt to force a passage whilst operations on either flank might force the enemy to retire voluntarily.

During the night of the 5th/6th the 46th Brigade was withdrawn from the line, leaving the 44th and 45th holding the whole Divisional front.

Preparations for pursuit.

There was now a check in the forward move whilst all preparations were made for a "pursuit." Brigade groups were formed, each with artillery and Field Companies, R.E., attached. In addition, a section from the 3rd Australian Tunnelling Company joined each brigade for the purpose of investigating enemy dug-outs and dealing with "booby-traps." The enemy had, with his usual ingenuity, taken great pains to render his late habitations unfit for use: in some cases poison gas was used, in others delay-action mines were employed. Roads, too, had to be exceedingly carefully examined before either vehicles or guns traversed them. In fact, troops of all arms advanced with great caution, in order to avoid the many traps laid for them, whilst the gallant Australian tunnellers cleared buildings of hidden mines and "booby-traps." To the 9th Gordons (Pioneers) was allotted the task of clearing all roads along which the Division advanced. From the start the enemy had thoroughly blocked these as he retired: telegraph-posts and trees were felled, mines exploded at important points, and, of course, all railways had been put out of order. It is a point worthy of mention that, owing to the untiring efforts of the Australians and Gordons (Pioneers), the passage of the Divisional troops was never once held up throughout the whole advance. "Realising what delay meant in such a contingency, the men excelled themselves."

Oct. 1918.

The 46th Brigade relieved the 45th in the right section on the 11th, the last relief which took place before the pursuit commenced.

Two or three days before this, orders had been issued for the capture of Annay and Vendin on the 12th. The taking of the former was entrusted to the 58th Division, and the latter to the 46th Brigade. It was anything but an easy task; for years the Germans had held Vendin as a bridge-head to the crossing of the canal. It was a most complicated mining village, full of large iron buildings, coke ovens, railway sidings, &c., and had been well fortified with many nests of machine-guns. To the south of it lay the remains of Annay, from which flanking fire could be brought to bear on any direct attack. It was obvious that to attempt to take Vendin before Annay had been captured would lead to useless sacrifice of life, and it was therefore directed that the 58th Division should complete its task before the 46th Brigade moved.

During the afternoon of the 12th news reached Divisional Headquarters that Annay had been captured, and General Reed at once ordered the 46th Brigade to rush Vendin, under cover of a prearranged artillery barrage. In this attack, which was quickly successful, the 9th Royal Scots greatly distinguished themselves. Rushing forward across the open, exposed to the fire from many machine-guns, they entered the village, driving the enemy before them. Here desperate hand-to-hand fighting took place amidst a network of railway sidings, coke ovens, and mine buildings before the enemy were compelled to give ground; but eventually Vendin was cleared, and posts established along the banks of the canal east of the village, the brigade prolonging its line southwards, taking over the front line from the 175th Brigade as far as the Lens-Garvin road. On the left the success of the 46th Brigade had enabled the 44th Brigade to push on, and by nightfall they had established posts along the canal bank in line with those of the 46th Brigade.

Vendin occupied.

The 13th and 14th were occupied in consolidating the position and in reconnoitring the ground for the next move, the crossing of

Oct. 1918.

the Canal itself. The enemy still held on to their positions on the far side, and it seemed as if hard fighting would be required before he was compelled to withdraw. Such, however, was not the case.

Haute Deule Canal crossed.

Early in the morning of the 15th loud explosions in Pont a Vendin and Meurchin gave colour to reports of a further enemy retirement. Soon after daybreak scouts of the 7/8th K.O.S.B., under Corporal Kempshall, D.C.M., successfully crossed the canal, penetrating as far as Epinoy without opposition. On learning this the Borderers at once sent patrols across on hastily constructed bridges made by the R.E. On the left patrols of the 8th Seaforths met with machine-gun fire whilst trying to reach the canal, but the check was only temporary, and by 6 A.M. they and the 5th Gordons had also crossed. Here, as on many former occasions, the energy and skill of the R.E., under Lieut.-Colonel J. M. Arthur, C.R.E., was the admiration of the Division, for an hour later bridge-heads had been established, and work on the bridges themselves was in full swing.

Situation on night of the 15th.

That night the outpost line ran almost due north and south through Fosse 6, with patrols pushing forward unopposed towards Epinoy and Carvin. Eight field-guns were in position east of the canal, and two pontoon bridges had been thrown across it. It was a most satisfactory day ; few casualties marred its success, and it was now clear that the German main line of resistance was definitely broken.

The advance continued at dawn on the 16th, and by the evening the leading troops had reached their objectives. On the right the 9th Royal Scots held the 46th Brigade outpost line from the Oignies road to a point 300 yards north-west of Oignies, whilst the Seaforths and the Gordons held that of the 44th Brigade from east of Epinoy due north through the distillery on the Carvin-Camphin road to the Division boundary. Patrols were out in front working through and north of the Bois d'Epinoy, but found no trace of the enemy.

General Reed now made a change in the composition of his advance-guard, using only one brigade instead of two. At dawn on the 17th the 45th Brigade passed through the outposts of the 46th and 44th, and took up the pursuit, the 8th Argylls relieving the former and the 13th Royal Scots the latter. On relief the 46th Brigade group reformed at Epinoy, and the 44th at Carvin.

Now the aspect of the country changed. Battered villages and shell-torn ground had been left behind, and civilians were met with, all wildly excited at their liberation. The village streets were decked with flags, and the country folk did their utmost to show their gratitude to the Division. Prior to their departure the Germans had removed all live-stock, and either burnt or destroyed most of the food-supplies which they could not take away. A certain amount had, however, been concealed by the inhabitants, and from this scanty store they gave freely to the Scotsmen. As it was ascertained from the inhabitants that the enemy had retired some twenty-five to thirty kilometres, orders were issued for the advance to push on, the next day's objective being the villages of Thouars and Capelle, more than seven miles farther west.

Oct. 1918.

At dawn on October 18 the Division advance-guard, consisting of the 6th Camerons, passed through the outpost line. Moving rapidly and encountering no opposition, they reached La Poissonnerie about 4.30 P.M. Here the leading troops encountered some resistance from machine-gun fire, but were eventually able to establish their outpost line east of the village before nightfall, with Divisional Headquarters at Carvin.

This day, for the first time in the G.H.Q. diary, a list is given of the composition of the three brigade groups :—

The Brigade groups.

The 44th consisted of 44th Infantry Brigade.
73rd Field Company, R.E.
46th Field Ambulance.
" B " Company, 15th Machine-Gun Battalion.

The 45th consisted of 45th Infantry Brigade.
91st Field Company, R.E.
47th Field Ambulance.
" C " Company, 15th Machine-Gun Battalion.

The 46th consisted of 46th Infantry Brigade.
74th Field Company, R.E.
45th Field Ambulance.
" D " Company, 15th Machine-Gun Battalion.

As regards artillery, brigades and batteries were placed under brigade commanders as circumstances might demand.

Oct. 1918. Line at dusk on the 19th.

The pursuit was resumed at 8 A.M. on the 19th, when the 1/8th Argylls passed through the outpost line. They met with some resistance during the morning at La Coquerie and Huquin Farm, but after that pushed forward rapidly, and before dusk had reached their objectives—a line running west of the Bois de Bercu and east of Fournes and La Croix, with patrols out 1000 yards farther east examining the woods. Throughout the day no artillery fire was met with. This was accounted for by an Alsatian deserter from the 12th German Reserve Division, who stated that all enemy guns had been withdrawn on the 18th. That afternoon Divisional Headquarters moved to Thumieres.

On the 20th the 46th Brigade took over the duties of advance-guard, the 10th Scottish Rifles leading. Again little opposition was encountered, but one platoon lost several men whilst outflanking an enemy machine-gun at Toupet, east of which the outpost line was established by 10 P.M., with Divisional Headquarters at Capelle.[1]

The Scheldt reached.

Early on the 21st the Scottish Rifles continued their advance, and by the evening, when Divisional Headquarters opened at Geneche, their patrols were approaching the western banks of the Scheldt. Throughout the day, although no enemy infantry or machine-gun resistance was met with, German artillery fire increased, and it became evident that the enemy meant to make a stand east of the Scheldt and Escaut rivers. This was confirmed the following day, when all patrols approaching the canal were fired on by machine-guns from the opposite bank.

The German position.

The position requires some description.[2] On the west bank of the canal, which was some 40 yards broad, over 20 feet deep, and across which all bridges had been destroyed, the ground slopes down, in some places rather abruptly, to a strip of marshy ground intersected by wide ditches. On the eastern bank, south of Hollain, lay marshes covered by a maze of irrigation ditches and small canals running back for well over 1000 yards. East of this the ground rose gradually, to the north-east and east, to large forests, which effectually screened enemy artillery and infantry from view. From these wooded

[1] During the day a British prisoner was recovered by the 10th S.R.

[2] Map 16.

slopes and positions behind them the Germans were able to keep the whole Divisional front under constant observation and artillery fire. A crossing on this part of the front was therefore rather risky, and before anything of the sort could be attempted it was necessary that flanking divisions should get up in line with the Fifteenth. On the left the 16th Division and on the right the 58th had not as yet reached the vicinity of the canal bank. This occupied some days, and during the pause the enemy flooded the low-lying ground east of Hollain, thereby making it impossible to advance with any success on at least half the Fifteenth Divisional front.

Oct.-Nov. 1918.

Realising the impossibility of attempting to force a passage south of Hollain under such conditions, I. Corps directed General Reed not to attempt it till the 16th Division had made good a crossing. When this was accomplished the Fifteenth were to side-step to the north, and its leading troops, crossing between Hollain and Antoing, were then to move east and south-east, thus outflanking the woods east of the former village.

Nothing of note occurred during the last week of October and the first week of November. The Division established posts along the banks of the Scheldt and fringe of marshy ground, but, with one exception, no patrol was successful in getting across. On October 25 a party of the 7/8th K.O.S.B., led by their C.O., Lieut.-Colonel Sutherland, crossed on a raft and explored the marshes east of the river, but, finding the ground impassable, the party returned unmolested. On October 28 the 44th Brigade relieved the 46th in the outpost line, the Black Watch taking over from the Royal Scots, while the Seaforths and Gordons relieved the Scottish Rifles and K.O.S.B. in support and reserve respectively. With the exception of the actual forward posts, this relief was carried out in broad daylight without interference from enemy artillery.

The curé.

That day the Divisional Headquarters moved up to La Glanerie, where General Reed occupied the curé's house. The old man proved to be a " character." He was over seventy years of age, and had remained with his flock openly throughout the whole war. Never once did he swerve from his opinion, openly expressed, that relief would come in time. Moreover, he vowed he would kiss the first

Nov. 1918. Allied soldier, be he Frenchman, Briton, or Belgian, who entered his village. He had hardly even heard of the Highlanders, and his feelings may be imagined when he espied the leading troops of the Fifteenth Division. Were they *vivandières?* No! They were playing a discordant tune on instruments he had never seen before. They were "great burly men in petticoats," as he explained later to General Reed. (They were actually pipers of the 10th Scottish Rifles.) Notwithstanding this, true to his vow, the curé went forward, and solemnly kissed the manly brow of the leading piper, much to the amazement of the man and the amusement of his comrades.

On November 7, as the 16th Division had now reached the western banks of the Scheldt, Corps orders were received to force the crossing of the river the following day. The 44th Brigade had already been detailed to lead the Division, and Brig.-General Thomson directed the Seaforths to cross west of Crevecourt and secure the line Vezonchaux-Bourgeon, whilst the Black Watch, crossing at Antoing, were to prolong the line northwards through Fontenoy to Gueronde, throwing back a defensive left flank if the 16th Division had not been able to come up. To assist these two battalions the 73rd and 74th Field Companies, R.E., were detailed to throw two barrel bridges across the river, selected places, whilst an elaborate artillery programme was arranged to cover the crossing.

November 7 and the night of the 7th/8th was the last occasion on which the Division came under German artillery fire. As was usual before a further retirement, the enemy subjected the whole front and back areas to heavy and indiscriminate fire, the Black Watch in and around Jollain-Merlin suffering somewhat severely from "Blue Cross" gas-shells.

Early in the morning of the 8th news reached headquarters that the 58th Division were across the river and were in possession of Belloy and Laplaige, but the 44th Brigade reported the enemy still in position on their front. On the left the 16th Division had also advanced, but were soon held up by machine-gun fire from slag-heaps south of Crevecourt.

Crossing of the Scheldt.

The 44th Brigade was now directed to cross according to plan. At noon a patrol of the Seaforths got over, and reported the enemy still in possession of Le Large and the slag-heaps north of it. These points were at once subjected to heavy artillery fire, under which the Seaforths and Black Watch pushed on. By seven in the evening both these battalions had advanced east of Le Large and the canal basin, and that night their outpost line ran between Le Large and Rosoir.

Nov. 1918.

At daybreak on the 9th patrols pushed forward without opposition, and by 8 A.M. the Seaforths had occupied Vezonchaux, and the Black Watch were advancing towards Fontenoy and Bourgeon. Practically no opposition of any kind was encountered throughout the day, and by 5 P.M. the Division had reached its objectives, the outpost line running from Brasmenil, east of Wasmes, to Weyaux.

It was now decided to continue the advance on a front of two brigades, and with that object the 7/8th K.O.S.B. took over the left of the line from the Black Watch, whilst the remainder of the 46th Brigade group moved up to Merlin and Bruyelle, and the 45th, in reserve, proceeded to Deroderie and Petit Rumes.

For the last days of the war the three brigade groups were constituted as follows :—

44th Infantry Brigade (Brig.-General Thomson)—
158th Army Brigade, R.F.A.
73rd Field Company, R.E.
46th Field Ambulance.

45th Infantry Brigade (Brig.-General Orr-Ewing)—
71st Brigade, R.F.A.
74th Field Company, R.E.
47th Field Ambulance.

46th Infantry Brigade (Brig.-General Fortune)—
70th Brigade, R.F.A.
91st Field Company, R.E.
45th Field Ambulance.

For some days previous to the crossing of the Scheldt it was common knowledge that the enemy was suing for peace, and by the 9th all ranks knew that it would not be long before the end came. Few

Nov. 10, 1918.

Germans were even seen from now onwards, and no opposition was encountered.

Line on the afternoon of the 10th.

Starting at 7 A.M. on the 10th, the advance continued, the Division reaching its objectives in the afternoon, when the outpost line ran between Beloeil and Blicquy, with patrols forward towards Ladeuze and Tongres, both of which were reported to be clear of the enemy that evening. What proved to be the last Divisional Operation Order was issued at Vezin on this day. It runs as follows :—

Issued at 18.50. *10th November* 1918.

Cavalry Corps is advancing to-morrow on Soignies and Nivelles. 46th Brigade Group on left will advance to-morrow, construct bridges, and form bridgeheads, covering Blaton Canal on line Hoyes-Attre. 58th Division will extend the line to Neuf-Maison, and 55th will extend it northwards. Right Divisional boundary Beloeil-Bauffe, both exclusive. Left Divisional boundary Blicquy-Moulbaix-Arbre, all inclusive. Inter-brigade boundary Aubechies-Tongres Notre Dame (both inclusive to 46th Brigade)—Chievres (inclusive to 44th Brigade)—Brugelette (inclusive to 46th Brigade). Advance-guard to pass outpost line at 8.30 A.M., when one battalion, 46th Brigade, will revert to command of 46th Brigade. Company Corps Cyclists and K.E.H. will operate on front under O.C. " B " Squadron, King Edward's Horse, and report to 44th Brigade. 44th and 46th Brigade Groups will billet to-morrow east of north and south line through west edge of Moulbaix. 45th Brigade will move to-morrow and billet east of north and south line, through west of Willapuis, but not in Tourpes. 45th Brigade march at 8.30 A.M. Division Headquarters will close at Vezon at 11 A.M. to-morrow, and open at Tourpes at the same hour.

(Signed) W H. DIGGLE, *Lieut.-Colonel, G.S.*

In pursuance of this order the advance was resumed the following morning, November 11. On the right the 5th Gordons covered the 44th Brigade front, whilst the 7/8th K.O.S.B. covered that of the 46th. With the Gordons were one battery, 158th Brigade, R.F.A. ; two sections, " D " Company, 15th Machine-Gun Battalion ; one section, 73rd Field Company, R.E. ; and a section of trench-mortars. The K.O.S.B. also had with them the following troops : " B " Battery, 70th Brigade, R.F.A. ; two sections, " C " Company, 15th Machine-Gun Battalion ; one section, 91st Field Company, R.E. ; whilst both had the usual parties from No. 3 Australian Tunnelling Company.

Throughout the morning the advance continued, and at half-past ten the leading troops of both brigades had just crossed the Dendre Canal, over which the bridges had been destroyed, and half an hour later vehicles were crossing by means of temporary bridges constructed by the Divisional Field Companies, R.E. Here a verbal message reached them that hostilities would cease at eleven o'clock that day. The Division order announcing this runs as follows :—

Nov. 1918.

Issued at 9.10. *a.m.* *11th November* 1918.

The Armistice.

Hostilities will cease at 11 A.M. to-day. All troops will be halted on the line reached, and outposts will be formed and all military precautions will be taken. There will be no communication with the enemy.

(Signed) H. MACKENZIE, *Captain,*
for Lieut.-Colonel.

Thus did the great news reach the Division.[1] The dry official diaries give no sign of how it was received by the men. There were few, alas! remaining of the original Division that left England in July 1915, but to those few the news must have brought back the memory of many a gallant comrade who had given his life for the honour of his country. In several private diaries traces can be found that some were actually disappointed. The enemy had been beaten after a struggle lasting over four years, and there were many who wished to drive the Germans back to their own country, and there give them a taste of the destruction and desolation they had meted out to France and Belgium.

The great climax was taken composedly. The following is taken from ' A Border Battalion ' :—

" The news of the Armistice was received by the men very quietly. They were spread in small parties over a wide area, and had no chance of giving full vent to their feelings, but every face was wreathed in smiles.

" ' I'd like fine to be in Blighty the nicht. It'll be a great nicht this at hame ; something daein', I'll bet.' ' Ay,' said another, ' an' there'll be a guid few tears, too.'

---

[1] As a matter of fact this momentous news reached Division Headquarters (unofficially) at 6 A.M. The Fifteenth Division Signal Company, with their usual alertness, intercepted the wireless message from General Foch to Higher Command announcing the fact. At that moment the —— Cavalry Division was moving up through the Fifteenth, only to retrace its steps a few hours later when, to its chagrin, the "Great War" ceased.

Nov. 1918.

"One man was fastidiously adjusting his steel helmet, when another gave him a resounding slap on the back, shouting, 'There's nae use o' your tin hat noo, ma lad.' It was almost impossible to realise it.

"In eager laughing groups the men stood about, chaffing over the news, with odd little silences that betrayed an undercurrent of deeper feeling. Then the word of command rang out, and we fell in to finish the day's march."

Locations on the 11th.

The day's objectives were reached during the afternoon, when, with headquarters at Tourpes, the Division was billeted as follows :—

44th Brigade—Headquarters at Huissignies.
4/5th Black Watch at
8th Seaforths at
5th Gordons at

45th Brigade—Headquarters at Blicquy (in reserve).
13th Royal Scots at
6th Camerons at
8th A. & S. Highlanders at

46th Brigade—Headquarters at Ormeignies.
9th Royal Scots at
7/8th K.O.S.B. at
10th Scottish Rifles at

Artillery at Tourpes (and neighbourhood).

CHAPTER XII.

CONCLUSION.

Nov.-Dec. 1918.

SUCH is the war history of the Fifteenth Division. Little remains to be told.[1] A few days after the Armistice news reached headquarters that the Division were transferred to the III. Corps, with a view to marching to the Rhine. Every one was delighted, but, unfortunately, the High Command changed its mind, and III. Corps was switched to the Brussels area.

On November 18 the 3rd Australian Tunnelling Company, who had done such fine and most dangerous work during the advance, left the Division. The same day Divisional Headquarters moved from Tourpes to Ormeignies, the 44th Brigade moved to Chievres, and the 46th to Arre, the 45th and Divisional artillery remaining where they were.

Visit of H.M. The King.

On December 7 the G.S. diary records: "His Majesty the King passed through the Fifteenth Divisional area, and saw detachments of every unit." This entry requires amplification. The King was accompanied by T.R.H. The Prince of Wales and Prince Albert, and by General Sir W. Birdwood, G.O.C. Fifth Army. By His Majesty's special desire the Division was formed up by units on either side of a broad road, the men being about twenty deep, and leaving only a narrow passage in the middle of the road for His Majesty. His reception baffles description. As the party walked slowly through the closely packed ranks a veritable roar of cheering greeted them, the men pressing forward to such an extent that the Divisional Commander himself had to force a passage through the dense and cheering

[1] The principal changes on the Staff from the commencement of 1918 to the end will be found in Appendix C.

Dec. 1918–Jan. 1919.

ranks. His Majesty spoke to many officers, and, on leaving after complimenting General Reed on the appearance and turn-out of the men, remarked: "You have indeed a splendid Division." Wherever he goes His Majesty invariably invokes a remarkable enthusiasm, but nowhere during this tour of his victorious troops was he received with greater enthusiasm than by his Fifteenth Division.

Demobilisation begins.

On December 10 the first party of miners left the Division on demobilisation. It is not out of place to mention that, owing to lack of shipping and other reasons, it was found impossible to carry out the elaborately devised schemes for this as quickly as had been arranged. Later, other reasons further delayed the return of the men to civilian life.

Between December 16 and 19 the Division moved eastwards, and by the night of the 19th, with headquarters at Braine-le-Chateau, the move had been completed—the 44th Brigade at Bonquieres, the 45th at Braine-le-Conte, the 46th in Braine-l'Alleud, artillery at Rebec Rognon, R.E. and 9th Gordons (Pioneers) at Tubise, and machine-gun battalion at Lillois Witterzee. Owing to poor accommodation, the 44th Brigade moved three days later to Nivelle.

From this date onwards the expression "Nothing of importance took place" occurs almost daily in the diaries. It is not until late in January 1919 that there is any outstanding event to record. On the 21st of the month colours were presented to the 13th Royal Scots and 6th Camerons by Lieut.-General Sir R. Butler, Commanding III. Corps, after having been duly consecrated.

Reviewed by King Albert.

On January 26 the 45th Brigade and massed bands marched past the King of the Belgians at the Palais du Roi, Brussels, together with representative troops of III. Corps. Besides the 45th Brigade, the Division furnished 73rd Field Company, R.E., "A" Company, Machine-Gun Battalion, the 47th Field Ambulance, with detachments of R.A. and guns. On this occasion the troops were commanded by Brig.-General N. A. Orr-Ewing. General Reed had a somewhat difficult task to perform in choosing which of his three brigades should represent the Division. The 44th was purely Highland, the 46th Lowland, whereas the 45th was composed of two Highland battalions and one Lowland, and he therefore selected it.

Jan.-Feb. 1919.

On the previous day the above troops moved to billets in Brussels, where they were royally entertained by the Belgians. The following day, Sunday, the review took place. Unfortunately the weather was bad; in fact, the parade took place in a blizzard, but nothing could damp the enthusiasm of the crowd. In spite of the snow and wind, all Brussels turned out in thousands to welcome the victorious troops. As the massed pipers of the Scottish Division approached the saluting base, a roar of cheering broke from the half-frozen onlookers. In a place of honour, opposite His Majesty the King of the Belgians, stood a small group of French officers, and as the pipers approached, one heard cries of "Les Ecossais"; and a few seconds later, clear above the cheers of the crowd, came a shout from the French officers, "The Highlanders, la Division de Buzancy!" It was a proud moment for every man of the Scottish Division, whether he was present or not. A fitting reward indeed for what they had done for Belgium, and a most graceful and fully appreciated compliment for their work with the armies of the French Republic.

On January 27, colours, after consecration service, were presented to the 7/8th K.O.S.B. on the field of Waterloo by the III. Corps Commander, Lieut.-General Sir R. Butler. On this occasion the whole country lay under heavy snow, but, in spite of weather conditions, the battalion carried out the ceremony of "trooping the colours" in most praiseworthy style. Curiously, no battalion of the K.O.S.B. had taken part in the battle of Waterloo.

On February 20 the 5th Gordons left the Division, on transfer to the 62nd. On the 24th the 44th Brigade moved to Braine-le-Chateau. During this month, on the 16th, the Division lost a most brilliant soldier, Lieut.-Colonel G. L. Wilson, D.S.O., M.C., who died of pneumonia. He was only nineteen at the outbreak of war, but enlisted in August 1914, and the following month was gazetted 2nd Lieutenant, 11th A. & S. Highlanders. He did brilliantly throughout the war, especially perhaps as machine-gun officer to his battalion at Loos. Although there are many outstanding examples of patriotism, heroism, and devotion to duty to be found in the records of the Division, there are none that can exceed, if equal, that of Gavin Laurie Wilson. He was only twenty-four when he died, but, be he general or private

March 1919. soldier, none who served with Laurie Wilson can forget him, and they will ever mourn the loss of a most gallant comrade, gentleman, and soldier.

On March 5 the 46th Brigade moved to Tubise, with headquarters at Clabecq. On the 22nd all moves of leave men were cancelled owing to strikes at home. One can well imagine the feelings of the men on receipt of this order. On the 25th Major-General H. L. Reed left the Division to join X. Corps as G.O.C. R.A.

The last entry in the Divisional General Staff diary occurs on March 26, when it is recorded that "G.S.O. 1, having been ordered to join the 59th Division, and all other 'G' officers having left or being employed on 'Q' works, this 'G' Office was closed down on this date."

The "A and Q" Diary continues somewhat further. During March, May, and June the cadres of all units of the Division left for Scotland, the last being on June 17, when those of the 6th Camerons, Fifteenth Divisional Signal Company, 73rd Field Company, R.E., and 71st Brigade, R.F.A., departed; and Lieut.-Colonel N. MacLeod, 6th Camerons, who had commanded the Division since the departure of Major-General Reed, left with his battalion.

During the following ten days the various equipment guards that had been furnished by the Division were relieved, and on June 27 the Fifteenth (Scottish) Division ceased to exist.

APPENDICES

APPENDIX A.

TABLE SHOWING ORDER OF BATTLE OF THE FIFTEENTH (SCOTTISH) DIVISION.

CAVALRY.

" B " Squadron, Westmorland and Cumberland Yeomanry. Transferred to XIth Corps, May 1916.

CYCLISTS.

Fifteenth Division Company. Transferred to XIVth Corps, May 1916.

ROYAL ARTILLERY.

11th Motor Machine-Gun Battery.

R.F.A. Brigades.

70th Brigade.
- B/73 joined, and became D/70 (How.)
- C/73 joined, and became C/70 (3/12/16).
- D/70 to 73rd, and became B/73 (22/5/16).

71st Brigade.
- C/73 joined, and became D/71 (How.)
- B/73 joined, and became C/71 (3/12/16).
- D/71 to 73rd, and became C/73 (22/5/16).

72nd Brigade.
- D/73 joined, and became D/72 (How.)
- D/72 to 73rd, and became D/73 (22/5/16).
- Became Army Brigade, and left Fifteenth Division, 1/12/17.

73rd Brigade.

B/73 to 70th Brigade.
C/73 to 71st Brigade.
D/73 to 72nd Brigade.
D/70 joined, and became B/73 (22/5/16).
D/71 joined, and became C/73 (22/5/16).
D/72 joined, and became D/73 (22/5/16).
Half of "A" to "B" and half of "A" to "C" on 1/12/16.
Brigade broken up, 3/12/16.
"B" to 71st Brigade.
"C" to 70th Brigade.

R.A. reorganised 22/5/16, and completed June 7-8 to three 4-gun 18 pr., one 4-gun 4.5 (howitzer) battery per brigade. Again reorganised on 1/12/16 to three 6-gun 18 pr. and one 4.5 (howitzer) battery per brigade.

Royal Engineers.

73rd, 74th, and 91st Field Companies, 15th Signal Company.

Pioneers.

9th Battalion Gordon Highlanders.

Infantry.

44th (Highland) Brigade.

9th Battalion The Black Watch. Transferred to 46th Brigade, 8/2/18.
8th Battalion Seaforth Highlanders.
10th Battalion Gordon Highlanders. Amalgamated with 8th Battalion from 9th Division, and became 8/10th Battalion, 13/5/16. Reduced to T.C., and transferred to 39th Division, 8/6/18.
7th Battalion Cameron Highlanders. Reduced to T.C., and transferred to 39th Division, 10/6/18.
(The above four battalions left England with the Division in 1915.)
4th Battalion The Black Watch. From Meerut Division, 5/11/15. Transferred to 51st Division, 7/1/16.
4/5th Battalion The Black Watch. From 46th Brigade, 5/6/18. (Took the place of 8/10th Gordon Highlanders.)
5th Battalion Gordon Highlanders. From 61st Division, 1/6/18. (Took the place of 7th Cameron Highlanders.) Officers and men of the 8/10th Battalion not required for T.C. joined the 5th Battalion on 8/6/18.

45th Brigade.

13th Battalion The Royal Scots.
7th Battalion Royal Scots Fusiliers. Amalgamated with 6th Battalion from 9th Division, 11/5/16. Transferred to 59th Division as Pioneers, 1/3/18.
6th Battalion Cameron Highlanders. Officers and men of the 7th Battalion, 44th Brigade, not required for T.C. joined the 6th Battalion on 10/6/18.
11th Battalion A. & S. Highlanders. Reduced to T.C., and transferred to 39th Division, 9/6/18.
(The above four battalions left England with the Division in 1915.)
8th Battalion A. & S. Highlanders. From 61st Division, 1/6/18. (Took the place of the 11th Battalion, and absorbed its officers and men not required for T.C.)

46th Brigade.

7th Battalion K.O.S.B. }
8th Battalion K.O.S.B. } Amalgamated as 7/8th Battalion, 28/5/16.
10th Battalion The Cameronians (Scottish Rifles).
12th Highland Light Infantry. Transferred to 35th Division, 3/2/18.
(The above four battalions left England with the Division in 1915.)
4th Battalion Suffolk Regiment. From Lahore Division, 15/11/15. Transferred to 33rd Division, 28/2/16.
10/11th Highland Light Infantry. From 9th Division, 16/5/16. (Took the place of 8th Battalion K.O.S.B., amalgamated with 7th Battalion.) Transferred to 40th Division, 1/2/18.
9th Battalion The Black Watch. From 44th Brigade, 8/2/18. (Took the place of 10/11th Battalion Highland Light Infantry.) Reduced to T.C., and transferred to 39th Division, 19/6/18. Officers and men not required for T.C. absorbed in 4/5th Battalion.
4/5th Battalion The Black Watch. From 51st Division, 16/5/18. (Took the place of 9th Battalion.) Transferred to 44th Brigade, 5/6/18.
9th Battalion The Royal Scots. From 61st Division, 1/6/18. (Took the place of 4/5th Battalion The Black Watch.)

COMPOSITION OF THE BRIGADES IN JULY 1918.

44th Brigade.	*45th Brigade.*	*46th Brigade.*
4/5th Black Watch.	13th Royal Scots.	9th Royal Scots.
8th Seaforth Highrs.	6th Cameron Highrs.	7/8th K.O.S.B.
5th Gordon Highrs.	8th A. & S. Highrs.	10th Scottish Rifles

Note.—On amalgamation of the 8th and 10th Gordons, the 6th and 7th Royal Scots Fusiliers, and the 7th and 8th K.O.S.B., the surplus officers, N.C.O.'s, and men of these battalions were formed into the 11th Entrenching Battalion.

Machine-Gun Corps.

44th, 45th, and 46th Machine-Gun Companies, 225th Machine-Gun Company (joined 20/7/17), amalgamated as 15th Battalion Machine-Gun Corps, 17/3/18.

Royal Army Service Corps.

138*th Company*	139*th Company*	140*th Company*	141*st Company*
H.Q., Artillery Div. Troops, R.E., and Div. Group.	44th Brigade.	45th Brigade.	46th Brigade.

Royal Army Medical Corps.

45th Field Ambulance, 46th Field Ambulance, 47th Field Ambulance, 27th Mobile Veterinary Section.

APPENDIX B.

ORDER OF BATTLE (PERSONNEL), FIFTEENTH (SCOTTISH) DIVISION.

FROM IIIRD CORPS DIARY, DATED OCTOBER 2, 1916.

Corps Commander . .	Lieut.-General Sir W. P. Pulteney, K.C.B., D.S.O.
Divisional Commander .	Major-General F. W. N. McCracken, C.B., D.S.O.
A.D.C.'s	Lieutenant Sir J. H. B. D. Tichborne, Bart., 10th Reserve Regiment of Cavalry.
	Captain Sir E. P. D. Duncombe, Bart., Bucks Yeomanry.
G.S.O. 1	Brevet Lieut.-Colonel H. H. S. Knox, Northants Regiment.
G.S.O. 2	Major K. Henderson, D.S.O., 39th Garhwal Rifles.
G.S.O. 3	Major G. F. H. N. Ryan, Royal Engineers.
A.A. & Q.M.G. . . .	Brevet Lieut.-Colonel C. R. Berkeley, D.S.O., The Welsh Regiment.
D.A.A. & Q.M.G. . .	Captain J. F. Chevenix-Trench, Northumberland Fusiliers.
D.A.Q.M.G. . . .	Captain W. H. Annesley, Royal West Kent Regiment (R. of O.)
A.D.M.S.	T/Colonel C. E. Pollock, Royal Army Medical Corps.
D.A.D.M.S. . . .	Captain G. D. Hindley, Royal Army Medical Corps.
A.D.V.S.	Major S. F. G. Pallin, Army Veterinary Corps.
D.A.D.O.S. . . .	Captain J. G. Hibbert, Army Ordnance Department.
A.P.M.	Captain G. B. Gunston, Coldstream Guards (S.R.)
Divisional Claims Officer .	Captain F. D. Livingstone, Army Service Corps.
Divisional T.-M. Officer .	Captain A. C. Elliot, A. & S. Highlanders.
Divisional Bombing Officer	Captain S. C. McKinnon, Cameron Highlanders.

Divisional Artillery.

Commander . . .	. Brig.-General E. B. Macnaghten, D.S.O.
Brigade Major . .	. Major C. E. Boyce, R.A.
Staff Captain . .	. Captain H. Booth, 3rd Hussars.
A.D.C. . . .	. 2nd Lieutenant J. F. Tallack, R.F.A. (S.R.)
70th Brigade, R.F.A.	. Lieut.-Colonel H. W. A. Christie.
71st Brigade, R.F.A.	. Lieut.-Colonel F. W. Heath, C.M.G.
72nd Brigade, R.F.A.	. Brevet Colonel J. W. Stirling.
73rd Brigade, R.F.A.	. Lieut.-Colonel C. St M. Ingham.
15th D.A.C. . .	. Lieut.-Colonel J. F. Duncan.

Trench-Mortar Batteries.

Medium.

X/15 T.-M. Battery .	. Lieutenant H. J. Daniels.
Y/15 T.-M. Battery .	. Lieutenant H. B. Garrett.
Z/15 T.-M. Battery .	. 2nd Lieutenant R. A. Connor.

Light.

44th T.-M. Battery .	. Captain G. R. W. Stewart.
45th T.-M. Battery .	. Captain A. Gardner.
46th T.-M. Battery .	. Captain G. Craik.

Divisional Engineers.

Commander . . .	. Lieut.-Colonel R. S. Walker, D.S.O.
Adjutant	. 2nd Lieutenant C. de W. Gaussen.
73rd Field Company .	. Captain H. W. T. Palmer.
74th Field Company .	. Captain J. A. Graeme.
91st Field Company .	. Captain A. H. Davenport.
15th Signal Company	. Captain A. Holmes Scott.

Pioneer Battalion.

9th Gordon Highlanders	. Lieut.-Colonel E. H. H. Gordon, D.S.O.

Army Service Corps.

Divisional Train .	. Lieut.-Colonel T. P. Johnson.
Adjutant	. Captain O. F. Baerlein.
S.S. Officer . . .	. Major J. E. Arnold.
Divisional S. Column	. Major J. H. Tweedie.

Medical Units.

45th Field Ambulance .	Major F. Worthington, D.S.O.
46th Field Ambulance .	Lieut.-Colonel A. E. B. Wood.
47th Field Ambulance .	Lieut.-Colonel T. F. Ritchie.
27th Mobile Vet. Section .	Captain U. W. F. Walker.
32nd Sanitary Section .	Captain S. H. Daukes.

44th Infantry Brigade.

Commander . . .	Brig.-General F. J. Marshall.
Brigade Major . . .	Captain K. Barge, 17th Lancers (I.A.)
Staff Captain . . .	Captain A. Rollo, General List.
O.C. M.-G. Company .	Captain C. King.
Brigade Bombing Officer .	Lieutenant A. Inglis, 8/10th Gordon Highlanders.
9th Black Watch . .	Lieut.-Colonel S. A. Innes.
8th Seaforths . . .	Lieut.-Colonel N. A. Thomson, D.S.O.
8/10th Gordons . . .	Lieut.-Colonel D. MacLeod, D.S.O.
7th Camerons . . .	Lieut.-Colonel C. H. Marsh, D.S.O.

45th Infantry Brigade.

Commander . . .	Brig.-General W. H. Allgood, R. of O.
Brigade Major . . .	Major L. Carr, Gordon Highlanders.
Staff Captain . . .	Captain W. G. Wright, A. & S. Highlanders.
O.C. M.-G. Company .	Captain H. V. Wilkinson.
Brigade Bombing Officer .	2nd Lieutenant A. Maclean, 11th A. & S. Highlanders.
13th Royal Scots . .	Lieut.-Colonel G. N. Hannay.
6/7th R.S. Fusiliers . .	Lieut.-Colonel E. I. D. Gordon.
6th Camerons . . .	Lieut.-Colonel G. J. Russell.
11th A. & S. Highlanders .	Lieut.-Colonel N. M'Neill, C.M.G., D.S.O.

46th Infantry Brigade.

Commander . . .	Brig.-General T. G. Matheson.
Brigade Major . . .	Captain J. C. Cooke, General List.
Staff Captain . . .	Captain H. S. Fox, Highland Light Infantry.
O.C. M.-G. Company .	Captain W. F. Morrogh.
Brigade Bombing Officer .	2nd Lieutenant A. McIntosh, 7/8th K.O.S.B.
7/8th K.O.S.B. . . .	Lieut.-Colonel T. B. Sellar, C.M.G.
10th Scottish Rifles . .	Lieut.-Colonel A. V. Ussher.
10/11th H.L.I. . . .	Lieut.-Colonel R. F. Forbes.
12th H.L.I. . . .	Lieut.-Colonel A. A. I. Heyman.

ORDER OF BATTLE, FIFTEENTH (SCOTTISH) DIVISION.

BUZANCY.

Headquarters, Fifteenth Division, Major-General H. L. Reed commanding.

G.S.O.	Lieut.-Colonel W. H. Diggle.
A.A. & Q.M.G. . . .	Lieut.-Colonel C. R. Berkeley.

44th Infantry Brigade (Brig.-General N. A. Thomson).

4/5th Black Watch . .	Lieut.-Colonel R. M. Bulloch.
1/5th Gordon Highlanders .	Lieut.-Colonel G. A. Smith.
8th Seaforth Highlanders .	Lieut.-Colonel H. H. Kennedy.
44th Trench-Mortar Battery .	Captain A. B. Blagden.

45th Infantry Brigade (Brig.-General N. A. Orr-Ewing).

13th Royal Scots . .	Lieut.-Colonel J. A. Turner.
6th Cameron Highlanders .	Lieut.-Colonel N. MacLeod.
1/8th A. & S. Highlanders .	Lieut.-Colonel G. L. Wilson.
45th Trench-Mortar Battery .	Captain J. T. Allardice.

46th Infantry Brigade (Brig.-General V. M. Fortune).

9th Royal Scots . . .	Lieut.-Colonel J. B. Muir.
7/8th K.O.S.B. . . .	Lieut.-Colonel H. P. Hart.
10th Scottish Rifles . .	Lieut.-Colonel A. C. Stanley Clarke.
46th Trench-Mortar Battery .	Captain G. Craik.

H.Q., Fifteenth Divisional Artillery (Lieut.-Colonel C. St M. Ingham (Brig.-General Macnaghten absent on leave).)

70th Brigade, R.F.A. . .	Lieut.-Colonel G. B. Daubeny.
71st Brigade, R.F.A. . .	Lieut.-Colonel C. St M. Ingham.
X/15 T.-M. Battery . .	Captain A. F. Hutchison.
Y/15 T.-M. Battery . .	Captain H. B. Garrett.

9th Gordon Highlanders (Pioneers)	Major G. B. Gourlay (Lieut.-Colonel Taylor on sick leave).
15th Battalion M.-G. Corps .	Lieut.-Colonel R. Nasmith.

H.Q., Fifteenth Divisional R.E. (Lieut.-Colonel J. M. Arthur).

73rd Field Company R.E. .	Major E. W. Nesham.
74th Field Company R.E. .	Major J. F. Readman.
91st Field Company R.E. .	Major A. H. Davenport.
Fifteenth Div. Signal Coy. .	Major T. F. Ormsby.

H.Q., A.D.M.S. (Colonel F. G. Fitzgerald).

45th Field Ambulance . .	Lieut.-Colonel F. Worthington.
46th Field Ambulance . .	Lieut.-Colonel E. Percival.
47th Field Ambulance . .	Lieut.-Colonel H. Monteith.
Fifteenth Divisional Train . .	Lieut.-Colonel R. E. Sanders.
Fifteenth Divisional M.T. Coy. .	Major W. B. Flook.
27th Mobile Veterinary Section .	Lieutenant J. Cane.

APPENDIX C.

COMMANDING OFFICERS AND STAFF, 1914-1918.

	From	To
General Officer Commanding.		
Major-Gen. A. Wallace, C.B.	Sept. 18, 1914	Dec. 1914
Major-Gen. Colin J. Mackenzie, C.B.	Dec. 1914	March 22, 1915
Major-Gen. F. W. N. McCracken, C.B., D.S.O.	March 22, 1915	June 17, 1917
Major-Gen. H. F. Thuillier, C.B., C.M.G.	June 17, 1917	Oct. 10, 1917
Major-Gen. H. L. Reed, V.C., C.B., C.M.G.	Oct. 10, 1917	March 25, 1919
Aides-de-Camp.		
Lt. Sir J. H. B. D. Tichborne, Bart., 10th Reserve Regiment Cavalry		June 1917
2nd Lt. L. E. C. D. Lace, 12th Reserve Regiment Cavalry		
Capt. Sir E. P. D. Pauncefort-Duncombe, Bucks Yeomanry		Jan. 1917
2nd Lt. (Temp. Lt.) J. C. Ferguson, Northumberland Hussars	July 1917	Sept. 1917
Capt. G. H. C. Davy, D. of Lancs. Yeomanry	July 1917	March 1919
Major W. E. Royds, D. of Lancs. Yeomanry	Sept. 1917	March 1919
G.S.O. 1.		
Lt.-Col. J. Burnett-Stuart, Rifle Brigade		Nov. 1915
Lt.-Col. H. H. S. Knox, Northamptonshire Regiment	Nov. 1915	May 1917
Major (Temp. Lt.-Col.) H. F. Baillie, Seaforth Highlanders	May 1917	July 1918
Capt. (Temp. Lt.-Col.) W. H. Diggle, Grenadier Guards	July 1918	

	From	To
G.S.O. 2.		
Major E. G. Henderson, R.E.		Sept. 1915
Major E. G. Wace, R.E.	Sept. 1915	May 1916
Major K. Henderson, 39th Garhwal Rifles .	May 1916	Oct. 1916
Major H. F. Baillie, Seaforth Highlanders .	Oct. 1916	Jan. 1917
Bt. Major J. S. Drew, M.C., Cameron Highlanders	Jan. 1917	Oct. 1917
Capt. A. Y. G. Thomson, Cameron Highlanders	Oct. 1917	Dec. 1917
Bt. Major A. P. D. Telfer-Smollett, H.L.I. .	Dec. 1917	Sept. 1918
Bt. Major R. C. W. G. Firebrace, R.G.A. .	Sept. 1918	Oct. 1918
Capt. (Temp. Major) P. de Fonblanque, R.E.	Oct. 1918 (to	First Army)
Lt. (Temp. Major) J. E. Snell, Royal Highlanders	Oct. 1918	
G.S.O. 3.		
Capt. H. F. Baillie, Seaforth Highlanders .		Oct. 1915
Major H. F. Spring, Lincolnshire Regiment	Oct. 1915	Feb. 1916
Major J. E. Thornhill, Seaforth Highlanders	Feb. 1916	July 1916
Lt. (Temp. Capt.) C. F. M. N. Ryan, R.E. .	July 1916	Jan. 1917
Capt. Sir E. P. D. Pauncefort-Duncombe, Bt., Bucks Yeomanry	Jan. 1917	Aug. 1917
Lt. (Temp. Capt.) W. P. Haviland, A. & S. Highlanders (T.F.)	Aug. 1917	April 1918
Lt. (Temp. Capt.) H. D. Mackenzie, Lovat Scouts	April 1918	
A.A. & Q.M.G.		
Lt.-Col. E. F. Taylor, A.S.C.		1916
Bt. Lt.-Col. C. R. Berkeley, Welsh Regt. .	Aug. 1916	Oct. 1918
Capt. (Temp. Lt.-Col.) C. D. Horsley, 21st Lancers	1918	
D.A.A.G.		
Bt. Major J. F. Chevenix-Trench, Northumberland Fusiliers	July 1918	
Capt. (Temp. Major) C. R. Viscount Erleigh, Inns of Court O.T.C. (Acting) . . .	Aug. 1918	Oct. 1918

	From	To
D.A.A. & Q.M.G.		
Capt. H. W. Snow, R. of O.		April 1916
Major P. W. L. Powell	April 1916	April 1916
Lt.-Col. C. R. Berkeley, Welsh Regiment .	April 1916	Aug. 1916
Capt. J. F. Chevenix-Trench, Northumberland Fusiliers	Aug. 1916	July 1918
Capt. (Temp. Major) J. G. Halstead, N. Lancs. Regiment (Acting)	July 1918	Aug. 1918
D.A.Q.M.G.		
Capt. W. H. Annesley, R. of O.		Dec. 1916
Capt. C. D. Horsley, 21st Lancers . . .	Dec. 1916	Oct. 1918
Capt. (Temp. Major) M. F. Hammond Smith, Royal Inniskilling Fusiliers	Oct. 1918	
A.D.M.S.		
Col. S. G. Allen, R.A.M.C.		Aug. 1915
Col. G. T. Rawnsley, R.A.M.C.	Aug. 1915	Dec. 1915
Col. C. E. Pollock, R.A.M.C.	Dec. 1915	Feb. 1918
Lt.-Col. (Temp. Col.) E. B. Knox, R.A.M.C.	Feb. 1918	June 1918
Lt.-Col. F. G. Fitzgerald, R.A.M.C. . . .	June 1918	
D.A.D.M.S.		
Capt. W. P. MacArthur, R.A.M.C. . . .		1916
Temp. Capt. G. D. Hindley, R.A.M.C. .	1916	May 1918
Major A. S. K. Anderson	May 1918	
A.D.V.S.		
Capt. T. S. G. Pallin, A.V.C.		Aug. 1917
Capt. (Temp. Major) J. F. Rankin, A.V.C. (T.F.)	Aug. 1917	
D.A.D.O.S.		
Hon. Capt. F. S. Smith, D.C. of O. . . .		Dec. 1915
Temp. Lt. J. G. Hibbert, A.O.D. . . .	Dec. 1915	
A.P.M.		
Capt. P. B. Steinman, 3rd East Kent Regt. .		1916
Capt. C. B. Gunston, Coldstream Guards .	1916	Oct. 1917
Capt. Hon. S. L. Holland, Innis. Dragoons .	Oct. 1917	

	From	To
C.R.A.		
Col. (Temp. Brig.-Gen.) E. Lambart, R.A. (Retired List)		1915
Brig.-Gen. E. W. Alexander, V.C., R.A. .	1915	April 1916
Lt.-Col. (Temp. Brig.-Gen.) E. B. Macnaghten, R.A.	April 1916	Oct. 1918
Lt.-Col. (Temp. Brig.-Gen.) C. St M. Ingham, R.A.	Oct. 1918	
AIDE-DE-CAMP TO C.R.A.		
2nd Lt. J. H. L. Lambert, R.F.A. . .	Aug. 1915	1916
2nd Lt. J. F. Tallack, R.F.A. (S.R.) . .		Dec. 1916
R.A. STAFF OFFICER FOR RECONNAISSANCE.		
2nd Lt. (Temp. Lt.) R. Nicholson, R.F.A. .	Jan. 1917	Aug. 1917
Lt. R. M. Mansel-Pleydell, R.F.A. . .	Aug. 1917	June 1918
Lt. C. E. Hughes-Davies, R.F.A. (S.R.) .	June 1918	
BRIGADE MAJOR, R.A.		
Major N. H. C. Sherbrooke, R.F.A. . .		Oct. 1915
Capt. C. E. Boyce, R.A.	Oct. 1915	Nov. 1917
Major R. H. Walsh, R.F.A.	Nov. 1917	
STAFF CAPTAIN, R.A.		
Capt. E. St C. Gray, 34th Poona Horse .	Aug. 1915	April 1916
Lt. (Temp. Capt.) J. J. Pawson, 2nd Dragoons (R. of O.)	April 1916	Aug. 1916
Capt. G. G. Traherne, R.A. (R. of O.) . .	Aug. 1916	Aug. 1916
2nd Lt. (Temp. Capt.) H. Booth, 3rd Hussars (R. of O.)	Aug. 1916	March 1918
Lt. (Temp. Capt.) J. R. C. Jorgensen, R.F.A. (T.F.)	March 1918	
C.R.E.		
Lt.-Col. G. S. Cartwright, R.E.		March 1916
Major (Temp. Lt.-Col.) R. S. Walker, R.E. .	March 1916	Oct. 1917
Lt.-Col. J. M. Arthur, R.E. (T.F.) . .	Oct. 1917	

	From	To
ADJUTANT, R.E.		
Capt. P. J. Mackesy, R.E.		1916
Lt. A. H. Davenport, R.E.	1916	Aug. 1916
2nd Lt. (Temp. Lt.) C. de L. Gaussen, R.E.	Aug. 1916	May 1918
Temp. Lt. (Acting Capt.) L. R. Guthrie, R.E.	May 1918	

44TH INFANTRY BRIGADE.

BRIGADE COMMANDERS.		
Col. (Temp. Brig.-Gen.) M. G. Wilkinson, M.V.O.	Formation	April 1916
Major (Temp. Brig.-Gen.) F. J. Marshall, Seaforth Highlanders	April 1916	Dec. 1917
Lt.-Col. (Temp. Brig.-Gen.) E. Hilliam, Nova Scotia Regiment	Dec. 1917	May 1918
Lt.-Col. (Temp. Brig.-Gen.) N. A. Thomson, Seaforth Highlanders	May 1918	
BRIGADE MAJOR.		
Capt. H. H. M. Harris (R. of O.), Royal West Surrey Regiment (T.F.)		Aug. 1915
Major J. Rainsford Hannay, Royal West Surrey Regiment	Aug. 1915	Jan. 1916
Major E. A. Beck, Royal Scots Fusiliers	Jan. 1916	Sept. 1916
Capt. K. Barge, 17th Cavalry (I.A.)	Sept. 1916	Jan. 1917
Bt. Major Hon. E. O. Campbell, Seaforth Highlanders	Jan. 1917	May 1917
Lt. (Temp. Capt.) P. J. Blair, R. Scots (T.F.)	May 1917	Aug. 1917
Capt. R. C. Money, Scottish Rifles	Aug. 1917	July 1918
Capt. G. J. S. Lumsden (Acting), Cameron Highlanders	July 1918	Oct. 1918
Bt. Major E. F. Tickell, R.E.	Oct. 1918	
STAFF CAPTAIN.		
Temp. Capt. M. O'Connor, late R.N.R.		April 1916
Temp. Capt. A. Rollo, General List	May 1916	March 1918
Lt. (Temp. Capt.) R. N. MacTavish, South Staffordshire Regiment	March 1918	June 1918
Temp. Capt. C. J. Mackenzie Grieve, General List	June 1918	

45TH INFANTRY BRIGADE.

	From	To
Brigade Commanders.		
Col. (Temp. Brig.-Gen.) F. E. Wallerston .	Formation	Oct. 1915
Lt.-Col. (Temp. Brig.-Gen.) E. W. B. Green, Royal Sussex Regiment	Oct. 1915	April 1916
Major (Temp. Brig.-Gen.) W. H. L. Allgood, Reserve of Officers	April 1916	May 1918
Major (Temp. Brig.-Gen.) N. A. Orr-Ewing, Scots Guards	May 1918	
Brigade Major.		
Capt. E. A. Beck, Royal Scots Fusiliers .	Sept. 1914	Jan. 1916
Major J. Rainsford Hannay, Royal West Surrey Regiment	Jan. 1916	May 1916
Capt. L. Carr, Gordon Highlanders . .	May 1916	Jan. 1917
Lt. (Temp. Capt.) C. F. M. N. Ryan, R.E. .	Jan. 1917	July 1918
Capt. M. C. Bell, Royal Fusiliers . .	July 1918	
Staff Captain.		
Temp. Capt. H. G. Fowler	Dec. 1914	Sept. 1916
Lt. (Temp. Capt.) W. G. Wright, A. & S. Highlanders (T.F.)	Sept. 1916	Nov. 1917
Lt. (Temp. Capt.) C. A. Maclean, A. & S. Highlanders	Nov. 1917	Dec. 1917
Lt. (Temp. Capt.) W. G. Wright, A. & S. Highlanders (T.F.)	Dec. 1917	March 1918
2nd Lt. (Temp. Capt.) W. A. Henderson, Royal Scots (S.R.)	March 1918	July 1918
Lt. (Temp. Capt.) R. M. MacTavish, South Staffordshire Regiment	July 1918	

46TH INFANTRY BRIGADE.

	From	To
Brigade Commanders.		
Lt.-Col. (Temp. Brig.-Gen.) Cooper . .		Sept. 1914
Lt.-Col. (Temp. Brig.-Gen.) A. G. Duff, Retired Pay, The Black Watch . . .	Sept. 1914	Aug. 1915

	From	To
BRIGADE COMMANDERS—*continued*		
Lt.-Col. (Temp. Brig.-Gen.) T. G. Matheson, Coldstream Guards	Aug. 1915	April 1917
Bt. Lt.-Col. (Temp. Brig.-Gen.) A. E. Fagan, 36th Horse (I.A.)	April 1917	July 1917
Lt.-Col. (Temp. Brig.-Gen.) D. R. Sladen, K.O.S.B.	July 1917	Feb. 1918
Major (Temp. Brig.-Gen.) A. F. Lumsden, Royal Scots	Feb. 1918	June 1918
Bt. Major (Temp. Brig.-Gen.) V. M. Fortune, The Black Watch	June 1918	
BRIGADE MAJOR.		
Capt. H. H. C. Baird, D.S.O.	Sept. 1914	Feb. 1915
Major Sandilands, D.S.O.	Feb. 1915	May 1915
Capt. G. W. Howard, Essex Regiment .	May 1915	Feb. 1916
Temp. Capt. J. C. Cooke, General List .	Feb. 1916	Oct. 1916
Capt. and Bt. Major R. V. G. Horn, Royal Scots Fusiliers	Oct. 1916	Dec. 1917
Capt. T. K. Newbigging (Acting) . .	Dec. 1917	Jan. 1918
Capt. R. G. Orred, Royal Fusiliers . .	Jan. 1918	Jan. 1918
STAFF CAPTAIN.		
Lt. M. S. Fox, H.L.I.	Sept. 1914	May 1917
Capt. S. W. Neighbour, London Regt. (T.F.)	May 1917	May 1917
Temp. Capt. A. R. Chapman, General List .	May 1917	Aug. 1917
Temp. Capt. H. W. Smith, General List .	Aug. 1917	

APPENDIX D.

RECORD OF THE FIFTEENTH (SCOTTISH) DIVISION.

1914.

Sept. 18. Formed at Aldershot under Major-General A. Wallace, C.B.; artillery and 46th Infantry Brigade at Bordon.

Sept. 26. Inspection of the Division by their Majesties the King and Queen, accompanied by Lord Kitchener.

Oct. 16. Major-General C. J. Mackenzie, C.B., appointed to command the Division vice Major-General Wallace, C.B., who proceeded to Egypt.

Nov. 16. 44th Brigade moved to Liphook, 45th to Bramshott, 46th to Bordon.

Nov. 22. Divisional Headquarters moved to Bordon.

1915.

Jan. . 9th Gordon Highlanders made Pioneer Battalion; 7th Cameron Highlanders joined 44th Brigade in their place.

Jan. 22. Inspection at Frensham Pond by M. Millerand and Lord Kitchener.

Feb. 20. Division moved to Salisbury Plain; Division Headquarters at Cholderton; artillery at Bulford Camp; 44th Brigade Headquarters and two battalions at Draycott Camp; two battalions at Cirencester; 45th Brigade, Basingstoke; Headquarters (46th Brigade) and three battalions at Winchester; 12th H.L.I., Romsey.

March 22. Major-General F. W. N. McCracken appointed to command the Division vice Major-General Mackenzie, to War Office.

April 21. Divisional Headquarters moved to Marlborough; 44th and 45th Brigades to huts at Chisledon Camp, near Swindon; 46th Brigade to Parkhouse Camp, near Bulford.

June 21. Division inspected by H.M. King George between Perham Down and Tidworth.

July 8. First units of Division embarked for France.
Billeted in the neighbourhood of St Omer.
Marched and joined IVth Corps (Lieut.-General Sir H. Rawlinson), with Divisional Headquarters at Gosnay.

Aug. 3. Took over section of the trenches opposite Loos from 47th (London) Division, with French troops on the right and 1st Division on the left; Divisional Headquarters, Douvrin.

1915.

Sept. . 47th Division took over the next sector on the right between the Fifteenth Division and the French.

Sept. 24. Advanced Divisional Headquarters at Mazingarbe.

Sept. 25. Fifteenth Division attacked and took the village of Loos and Hill 70; casualties about 6000.

Sept. 27. Division relieved and billeted in neighbourhood of Lillers; Divisional Headquarters at Labuissiere.

Oct. 21. Having received large reinforcements, the Division relieved the 12th Division in the line opposite the Hohenzollern Redoubt.

Dec. 15. Division relieved by the 47th (London) Division, and proceeded to billets in Lillers area for a rest; Divisional Headquarters at Chateau Philomel, Lillers.

1916.

Jan. 15. Division took over the centre sector in the Loos Salient, relieving the 1st Division, with Headquarters at Mazingarbe.

Feb. . Lieut.-General Sir H. Wilson appointed to command IVth Corps vice Sir H. Rawlinson, to command Fourth Army.

March 2 Division posted to Ist Corps (Lieut.-General Sir H. Gough).

March 25. Division relieved in Loos Salient by 16th Division, and moved by train to Lillers area; Divisional Headquarters at Chateau Philomel.

Lieut.-General Kavanagh appointed to command Ist Corps vice Lieut.-General Sir H. Gough.

April 10. Part of Division inspected by General Joffre near Estrée Blanche.

April 27. Division relieved 12th Division in the Hohenzollern Sector; Divisional Headquarters at Sailly Labourse.

May 11. German attack on "The Kink."

10/11th H.L.I. joined the Division from 9th Division.

July 22 and July 23. Division relieved by 8th Division on the right and 16th Division on the left, and marched to billets at Heuchin, Tangry, Marles les Mines, Lapougnoy; Divisional Headquarters at Chateau Bryas.

Allied Offensive, 1916.

July 24. Division marched *viâ* Frevent-Bernaville-Vignacourt-St Gratien-Baizieux, joining IIIrd Corps (Lieut.-General Pulteney) of Fourth Army (Sir H. Rawlinson).

Aug. 8. Division took over the front line opposite Martinpuich, relieving the 23rd Division.

Aug. 12 to Aug. 17. Operations resulting in capture of the Switch Line.

1916.

Aug. 30. Capture of Intermediate Line and 4 officers and 123 other ranks.

Sept. 15. The Division captured Martinpuich and three lines of trenches, taking 600-700 prisoners, 13 machine-guns, 3 heavy howitzers, 3 77 mm. guns, and 1 trench-mortar, also a quantity of R.E. material; casualties about 1800.

Sept. 19. Division relieved by 23rd Division, and went to billets, with Headquarters at Montigny.

Oct. 9. Division relieved the 23rd Division in the front line (Le Sars).

Nov. 3. Division relieved by 48th Division, and proceeded to billets; Headquarters at Baizieux Chateau.

Dec. 1. Division relieved 50th Division in IIIrd Corps Reserve area; Headquarters, Albert.

Dec. 16. Division relieved 48th Division in the front line, Le Sars Sector, IIIrd Corps front.

1917.

Feb. 3. Relieved by 2nd Australian Division, and proceeded to billets in Fricourt area; Divisional Headquarters at Baizieux.

Feb. 13. Division now in VIth Corps (Lieut.-General J. A. H. Haldane) and Third Army (General Sir E. H. H. Allenby).

Feb. 18. Concentrated Duisans area; artillery in St Michel; Headquarters at Duisans.

Allied Offensive, 1917.

Feb. 24. Took over front line of VIth Corps Sector (east of Arras) from 12th Division.

April 9 to April 11. Took part in attack on Monchy le Preux on the 11th; the Commander-in-Chief visited the Division and congratulated it on its performances.

April 12. Relieved by the 17th Division, and billeted in Arras and Duisans.

April 18. Divisional Headquarters moved to Wagonlieu.

April 23. Took part in attack east of Arras and capture of Blue Line.

April 29. Relieved in line by 56th Division, and proceeded to Arras, thence to Duisans, Simencourt, and Berneville; Divisional Headquarters at Warlus in VIth Corps Reserve.

May 6. Transferred to XVIIIth Corps; Divisional artillery remained in the line under 56th Division.

May 8. Headquarters at Le Cauroy; units of Division at Grand Rullecourt, Sus St Leger, Barly, Wanquetin, Gouy-en-Artois.

May 17. Transferred to XIXth Corps, Fifth Army.

May 21. Headquarters at Willeman; units at Reboeuvre, Bouquemaison, Bonnieres, Sus St Leger, Fontaine L'Etalon, Noeux, and Oeuf.

June 17. Major-General F. W. N. McCracken, K.C.B., D.S.O., left the Division (after commanding it for over two years) to command XIIIth Corps; succeeded by Colonel (Temp. Major-General) H. F. Thuillier, C.B., C.M.G.

ALLIED OFFENSIVE, 1917.

June 29. Relieved 55th Division in the right sector of XIXth Corps front (Ypres-Roulers road); Headquarters at Vlamertinghe.

July 31. Took part in the attack on Frezenberg; casualties, 3581.

Aug. 5 to Aug. 29. Took part in the attacks by XIXth Corps in Ypres Salient; casualties, 2888.

Aug. 31. Relieved by 42nd Division, and proceeded to Wormhoudt area; Headquarters at Watou.

Sept. 2. Transferred from XIXth Corps, Fifth Army, to XVIIth Corps (Lieut.-General Sir C. Fergusson), Third Army.

Sept. 8. Relieved 4th Division in front line east of Arras; Headquarters, Arras.

Oct. 10. Colonel (Temp. Major-General) H. F. Thuillier relinquished command of the Division on appointment to Ministry of Munitions; succeeded by Colonel (Temp. Major-General) H. L. Reed, V.C., C.M.G.

1918.

Jan. 3. Relieved by Guards Division, and moved to billets in Dainville, Simencourt, Bernaville, Habarcq.

Jan. 7 to Feb. 4. Refitting and training; Headquarters at Noyelle Vion.

GERMAN OFFENSIVES, 1918.

Feb. 7. Took over right sector, XVIIth Corps front, east of Arras, from 4th Division; Headquarters at Arras.

March 28. German attack on XVIIth Corps front; casualties, 2317.

March 29. Message received from Corps commander, Sir C. Fergusson.

April 24. Relieved by 56th Division, and proceeded by 'bus and road to XIIIth Corps area (Lieut.-General Sir T. Morland) in First Army Reserve; Headquarters at Auchel.

May 3. Transferred from XIIIth Corps to XVIIIth Corps.

May 6. Relieved 1st Canadian Division in front line east of Arras; Headquarters at Etrun

July 14. Relieved by 1st Canadian Division, and billeted in Villers Chatel area prior to joining Third French Army.

July 18. Division transferred to Third French Army, and from that to Tenth French Army.

July 22. Concentrated in St Pierre Aigle area; Headquarters at Coeuvres.

July 23 to Aug. 3. Relieved 1st U.S.A. Division in the line west of Buzancy (left sector, XXth French Corps), and took part in the attack on and capture of Buzancy and neighbouring villages; casualties, 3516.

Aug. 3. Relieved by 17th Division, and concentrated, with Divisional Headquarters at Vierzy.
Aug. 7. Special Ordre General issued by General Mangin.
Aug. 8. Division came under orders of XXIInd Corps, and concentrated in area Ambrines-Beaufort-Mazieres ; Headquarters at Le Cauroy.
Aug. 15. Transferred from XXIInd Corps to XVIIth Corps.
Aug 18. Relieved 56th Division in front line east of Arras ; Headquarters at Warlus.
Aug. 23. Relieved by 2nd and 3rd Canadian Divisions, and proceeded to join Ist Corps, First Army.
Aug. 26. Headquarters at Braquemont ; Division relieved 11th Division in the front line in the Loos Salient.
Sept. 11 to Sept 20. Hard fighting round The Quarries, which were captured by the 45th Brigade on Sept. 11.
Sept. 21. Ist Corps transferred from First Army to Fifth Army.
Oct. 2. Division advanced to west of Vendin-Douvrin line.
Oct. 16. Advance continued.
Oct. 21. Headquarters at Genech Chateau ; advance held up by enemy rear-guards east of canal.
Oct. 25. Headquarters at La Glanerie.
Nov. 8. Canal crossed by 44th Brigade.
Nov. 9. Advance continued.
Nov. 11. Hostilities ceased at 11 A.M., and Division halted on line east of Peruwelz-Leuze, with Divisional Headquarters at Tourpes.

APPENDIX E.

INSTRUCTIONS FOR THE BATTLE OF LOOS.

G. 600.

Secret.

9 o'c., 44TH I. BDE.

The attached draft instructions are for your own and your Bde. Major's information *only*.

The Divisional Commander will hold a conference at Div. Hd. Qrs. at 11 A.M. to-morrow, the 31st, to discuss these draft instructions.

Please attend without your Bde. Major.

A Divl. car will be sent to fetch the G.O.C.'s 44th and 45th Bdes.

Please acknowledge receipt.

J. BURNETT-STUART, Lt.-Col., G.S.

15th Div.,
30/8/15.

Secret.

DRAFT INSTRUCTIONS FOR ATTACK.

1. The Div. is to take a principal part in an attack on the German positions, probably within the next fortnight.

Objectives of 15th Div.

2. The objectives allotted to the Div. are :—
   (*a*) The front line trenches from G.34.a.6.5 to the German sap at G.22.d.6.3.
   (*b*) The second line trenches from the cemetery in G.35.a (exclusive) to G.29.6.3.9.
   (*c*) Loos village.
   (*d*) Hill 70.

These objectives are shaded in blue on the map.

Objectives of 47th Div. and 1st Corps.

3. In order to form a defensive flank southwards to cover our advance, the 47th Div. will attack with the following objectives :—
   (*a*) The Double Crassier as far as point M.4.d.8.8.

(*b*) The German front system of trenches from M.4.c.3.9 to G.34.a.6.5.
(*c*) The second line trenches from M.4.d.8.8 to the cemetery in G.35.a (inclusive).
(*d*) Enclosure in G.35.d.
(*e*) Fosse in G.36.

These objectives are shaded in green on the map.

On our left, the Ist Corps will attack the villages of Benifontaine, Hulluch, and St Elie.

Bombardment.

4. The attack will commence by a steady bombardment by all available guns day and night for 4 days up to the moment of the infantry assault on the 5th day. This bombardment will be distributed over the whole front of the Ist and IVth Corps.

Gas.

5. On the morning of the 5th day gas, interspersed and flanked by smoke from smoke candles, will be discharged for 40 minutes along the front; this discharge will be followed immediately by the infantry assault.

6. The attack will be pushed home to the full extent of the IVth Corps power.

Preliminary action by 15th Div.

7. (*a*) Up to the night immediately preceding the opening of the action by the artillery, the front of X1, X2, and Y1 will continue to be held by the 45th Bde. with one * Battn. attached from the 1st Div. On this night the 45th Bde. will be relieved by the 44th and 46th Bdes., and will go into Divl. reserve at Noeux-les-Mines and in the trenches of the Sailly line w. of that place.

* *N.B.*—An additional 1½ Battns. and 2 Fd. Coys. R.E. from 1st Div. will also be attached. All these are for work on the front from 14a northwards, which becomes eventually the 1st Div. battle front. The work will be controlled by the 1st Div.

(*b*) For the purposes of this relief the front will be divided up into 2 Sectors—Right and Left.

The Right Sector will extend from the present southern boundary of X1 to the line trench 12, junction of 14a with 14, junction of new comg. trench with 16 (all inclusive), house G.20.a central, level crossing G.20.a, Mazingarbe Church (all inclusive), and will be taken over by the 44th Bde.

The Left Sector will extend from the above line to the northern boundary of the divisional area, and will be taken over by the 46th Bde., plus * the Battn. of the 1st Div., which will remain in position.

(* The other 1½ Battns. 1st Div., and the R.E. Coys. will be withdrawn under 1st Div. arrangements during the bombardment.)

(*c*) During the following 4 days of bombardment the distribution of the troops in the right and left sectors will be :—

	44th Bde.	*46th Bde.*
In front system	1 Battn.	1½ Battns
In Philosophe, Corons de Rutoire, and trenches of Grenay branch of Vermelles line .	1 Battn.	1½ Battns.
In Mazingarbe and in trenches of main Vermelles line .	2 Battns. 1 Coy. R.E. 1 Coy. 9th Gordons.	2 Battns. 1 Coy. R.E. 1 Coy. 9th Gordons.

The keeps will not be occupied during this period. Hd. Qrs. of these two Bdes. will be in the two houses in the new avenue at Mazingarbe, which have been prepared as Divl. and Divl. Art. advanced Hd. Qrs. respectively (see para 20).

Action on night immediately preceding the assault.

8. (*a*) During the night immediately preceding the day fixed for the assault, all troops will move up into their positions of readiness as shown on the attached map. The detailed arrangements for this move will be made by G.O.C.'s Bdes., who will see that companies are told off to their places, guides provided, and sentries with written instructions posted beforehand at junctions of communicating trenches where necessary.

(*b*) The front from trench 14a to the left of Y1 will be taken over on this night by the 1st Div., who will resume command of their detached Battn., and assume all responsibility for this front.

(*c*) Divl., Bde., and Art. Hd. Qrs. will also move to their advanced stations on this night; and Divl. troops not allotted to Bdes. will move to their assigned positions under divisional orders.

Preparation of wire and exits from trenches.

9. The Bde. holding the Right Sector will be responsible that our own wire is cut opposite the points selected for assault on the last night but one before the day of assault. The wire will be cut close to the posts and diagonally, not straight from front to rear.

This Bde. will also be responsible that steps are cut in the front walls of trenches at the forming-up places.

Equipment.

10. (*a*) Packs and greatcoats will not be taken to the forming-up positions, but will be labelled and left under guard in selected houses or dugouts before moving off.

Every infantryman will take with him—

Rifle and equipment (less pack).
2 bandoliers of S.A.A. in addition to equipment ammunition.
1 ration and unexpired portion of day's ration.
2 sandbags (in belt).
Smoke helmet.
Water-bottle.
(Haversack will be carried on back.)

(*b*) 10 selected men per platoon in 44th and 46th Bdes. will carry wire-cutters (attached to a lanyard). Extra wire-cutters to complete to this amount will be provided.

(*c*) 8 selected men per platoon in the two leading coys. of each assaulting column will carry bill-hooks for destroying wire. These men and men with wire-cutters will be provided with hedging gloves.

(*d*) 1 man per platoon throughout the Div. will carry a yellow flag 2′ × 2′ on a 3′ stick to mark the progress of his platoon in the attack; and 1 man per bombing squad will carry a yellow flag 1′ × 1′ on a 5′ stick to mark the progress of his squad. These flags will be *carried*, not *stuck* in the ground. They will be supplied by the C.R.E.

Preparatory arrangements by Div.

11. The following arrangements will be made before the attack commences :—

(*a*) Preparation of advanced dressing-station at Fosse 7.

(*b*) Establishment of depot of sandbags (20,000) at each place, and R.E. stores at Quality St.*

(* Le Rutoire will be dealt with entirely by 1st Div.)

(*c*) Placing of stores of grenades and S.A.A. at the forward ends of our communication trenches. Suitable places are being selected. These will be replenished during the action from Bde. Amtn. Col. wagons in rear.

(*d*) Placing of gas cylinders and smoke candles in trenches. In addition to the gas specialist personnel, one selected man will be told off by O.C. 9th Gordons to discharge the smoke candles in the proportion of one such man to each 15 cylinders.

(*e*) Making of new trenches, forming-up places, deviations round keeps, bomb proofs at various Hd. Qrs., and saps towards enemy's line.

(*f*) Visual signal station on Fosse 3.

(*g*) Burying, duplication, and laddering of wires.

(*h*) Careful labelling of all trenches and communicating ways with labels low down so that they can be read by electric torch at night.

Organisation of assaulting columns.

12. There will be 4 assaulting columns (two from each leading Bde.) consisting of 1 Battn., 1 sect. R.E., and 1 platoon 9th Gordons in each column. These will be formed up in depth on a front of 2 platoons.

No. 4 column will include also a party of 50 picked grenadiers from the 45th Bde.

The Battn. machine-guns of the assaulting Battns. will go forward with them.

Tasks of columns.

13. (*a*) The task of the assaulting columns will be to go straight forward as fast as possible to their final objectives.

Parties for cutting wire, blocking side trenches, and bombing down communicating trenches will be told off from the two leading companies.

(*b*) Assaulting columns will *not* be entrusted with the tasks of occupying and consolidating positions won, or of digging communications back to our own trenches, unless the whole column is hung up. These tasks will be allotted to parties told off from Bde. Reserves.

(*c*) The 4th Coy. in each column will carry a proportion of picks and shovels.

The R.E. section will carry explosives for hasty demolitions.

The platoon of Pioneers will carry 6 sandbags per man, and tools.

(*d*) In the two leading Coys. of each column men will wear their smoke helmets rolled up under their bonnets ready to be let down at once should the men outrun the gas.

(*e*) Each company will move up at once into the place of the one in front of it directly this latter moves on.

Objectives of Bdes. and plan of attack.

14. (*a*) The objectives assigned to Bdes. are as follows :—

44th Bde.

1st. Front trench EF and support trench behind.
2nd. Second line trench GH.
3rd. Loos village.
4th. Puits No. 15.
5th. German work on Hill 70.

46th Bde.

1st. Trench JK and rectangle of communicating trench behind it.
2nd. Second line trench LH.
3rd. Trench MN.
4th. Road from G.36.b.1.6 to Puits No. 14 bis (inclusive).
5th. Work on Hill 70.

(*b*) The assaulting columns of the 46th Bde. must endeavour not to be drawn into a converging attack on Loos, but to push straight on to their 4th objective ; they will thus best assist the 44th Bde., whose attack will be supported from behind.

(*c*) The machine-guns of the 9th Gordons will be placed at the disposal of G.O.C. 44th Bde., and will be used in the first instance, together with No. 3 Trench-Mortar Battery and 2 Coys. from the Bde. Reserve, to hold the front from Sap 18 to the Lens road. Sap 18 will be used as a communication trench by the 47th Div., but emplacements off the sap will be made for machine-guns to fire on the southern face of the salient.

(*d*) The six Vickers guns of the M.M.G. Battery will be placed at the disposal of G.O.C. 46th Bde., and will be used in the first instance, together with ½ Coy. from the Bde. Reserve, to hold the front from the left of No. 4 column to trench 14a. The fire of these guns will be directed on the northern face of the northern salient, and on the German sap G.22.d.6.3.

(*e*) The German trench running from G.35.a.6.3 to G.34.b central is allotted to 47th Div., who will deal with it. This trench (exclusive) will be the right boundary of the 44th Bde. attack.

(*f*) The party of picked grenadiers referred to in para. 12 will go forward with the leading company of No. 4 column, and will bomb northwards towards the Hulluch road along the German front and support trenches, detaching parties to work down the communicating trenches running eastwards from his line. One ½ Coy. infantry will be told off by 46th Bde. as escort to these grenadiers.

The troops holding the line on the left of No. 4 column will move forward (with the machine-guns) and occupy the German front trenches as soon as the grenadiers have cleared them. The troops of the 1st Div. on our left will have orders to conform to this advance.

(*g*) As soon as the assaulting columns have cleared the German front trench, this trench will be occupied by the Brigade reserves, and parties told off to open up (from both ends) communication trenches to join up with our own trenches. These parties will be left behind when the Bde. reserve moves forward, until relieved by other troops.

The Bde. in Divl. Reserve (45th) will move up into our own front trenches as soon as these have been cleared by the two leading Bdes., but will not leave these trenches without orders from Div. H.Q.

Signal for assault.

15. A fixed time will be fixed for the assault, at which moment the leading companies will advance, simultaneously with those of the 47th Div.

Communication.

16. (*a*) A visual signal station will be established on Fosse 3 by the Divl. Signal Coy. Particulars as to this will be given to Bde. and Battn. Sig. officers by O.C. 15th Signals.

(*b*) At least 2 light wires will be taken forward by each Battn. for communication back to Bde. Hd. Qrs. These wires will be in addition to those taken forward by artillery observing officers.

(*c*) To supplement the above (both of which may fail), Battn. commanders will arrange a system of runners to keep up communication with Bde. H.Q. and with their companies—4 selected men per company and 6 per Battn. Hd. Qrs. have been found satisfactory numbers to tell off for this purpose.

(*d*) In the forming-up positions each company or party will keep in touch with the company in front by means of connecting files along the communicating trenches.

Artillery support.

17. The artillery programme will be issued separately to all concerned. During the gas discharge the artillery bombardment will not be interrupted. After the discharge, the artillery will continue to fire on any hostile troops beyond or retiring before the gas, and will prevent the enemy from forming-up for a counter-attack.

When the assault takes place, the artillery fire will be lifted to cover the infantry advance.

It is essential that the advancing infantry, by means of messages and of the flags provided for the purpose, should endeavour to keep the artillery informed of their progress.

The objects of the 4 days' preliminary bombardment will be :—

(i) Removing all obstacles in the hostile front system of trenches opposite the points of assault, and cutting the wire entanglements along the whole line.

(ii) Destroying artillery observation stations.

(iii) Bombarding the defences and communications on the general line Double Crassier-Loos-Hulluch.

(iv) Damaging defended buildings in rear of the hostile trenches to make them more susceptible to gas attack.

(v) Lowering the *morale* of the enemy's supports and reserves by a continuous bombardment.

During and after the launching of the attack, the task of the artillery is to establish curtains of fire in front of our infantry, and barrages on the exposed flanks of attacks; while the counter-batteries continue to engage the German guns.

The R.E. will hold a party in readiness in each sector to go forward and prepare passage for guns over the trenches.

Disposal of prisoners.

18. Any prisoners captured will be collected and sent back under escort to Quality St., when they will be taken over by the A.P.M. and the escorts relieved.

Special warnings to troops.

19. Troops will be warned :—

(*a*) Against relaxing their attack against an enemy who displays the white flag, unless it is quite certain that he has discarded his arms, and is out of reach of support.

(*b*) That all papers and orders are to be destroyed. No papers will be carried by officers or men taking part in the attack except the Auchy-Lens map showing the German trenches. *All messages and reports will refer to this map.*

(*c*) That men in the ranks will not fall out to bring back wounded.

(*d*) That any guns captured which are in danger of being lost again will be rendered unserviceable by destroying the sights and breech mechanism.

(*e*) That hand grenades are difficult to replenish, and must not be wasted. There must be a supply of grenades in hand to meet counter-attacks.

Divl. Hd. Qrs.

20. Divl. Battle Hd. Qrs. will be established in the 3rd house from the northern end of the new avenue in Mazingarbe. All reports will be sent there.

Divl. Art. Hd. Qrs. will be in the next house to this.

Advanced Divl. Administrative Hd. Qrs. will be at the White House in Noeux les Mines.

J. BURNETT-STUART, Lt.-Col., G.S.

15th Div.
30/8/15.

APPENDIX F.

THE BATTLE OF LOOS.

By R. A. Giesecke.

(*Translation.*)

At the same time as the embittered encounters were fought round the Loretto Hill, in which, as just described, the 1st and 2nd Battalions were principally engaged, other encounters blazed up around the village of Loos, in which it was again a hill—namely, the frequently mentioned Hill 70, half-way between Loos and Lens, which formed the centre. In fact the hills, and even lower eminences along the " Wall of Steel," as usual constituted the focuses of the action. But on this occasion they were not only focuses of the engagement, but of decisive encounters in which again our 178th Regiment played an important part, for it was at this point that they had to make the principal counter-thrust. That these were indeed decisive encounters appears from the evidence of Captain von Sanden (see page 82 of his book published by the Supreme Command of the Army, under the title of 'The Autumn Battle of Champagne'): " Already on the evening of 27th September the intended point of irruption by the enemy could be clearly and precisely recognised. Loretto, Arras, and the blood-soaked soil of Champagne, between Aisne and Suippes, were the points at which again the French and the English simultaneously sought to obtain the great final decision." Thus it was this time, not as previously, that the 178th was forced by our hereditary enemy, namely the French; but for the first time the 3rd Battalion was to try conclusions with the principal enemy, the English. Having scarcely returned from Loretto in the night between the 22nd and 23rd, the 3rd Battalion hastened to the assistance of that position in the neighbouring section, respecting which the report of the Supreme Command makes the following statement, on the 25th September 1915: " To the south-west of Lille the enemy succeeded, at Loos, in pressing back a German division from the first into the second line of defence, suffering considerable losses, including damage to buildings and other material of all kinds, between the positions."

To what extent Lens was threatened by this success of the enemy, we shall quickly understand if we reflect that Loos is situated scarcely 5 kilometres from Lens, and if we carefully examine the report of Field-Marshal French, dated 26th September, in the following words : " Yesterday morning we attacked the enemy to the south of the Canal de La Bassée, east of Grenay and Vermelles, captured the first few trenches on a front of five miles. We broke through the lines at some points to a distance of 4000 yards, captured the western outskirts of the village of Loos, the mines in the vicinity, and Hill 70." In what follows, we shall see how this great danger of losing the basin of Lens was mainly avoided by the brilliant exploits of the 178th Regiment, which is graphically represented on our frontispiece : " A hand-grenade thrower, personifying the regiment, covers with his body the village of Lens behind him, with its valuable surroundings, whilst in front of him in the west are situated Loretto, Souchez, Givenchy ; to the north-west, Hill 70 and Loos. In the background—that is to say, in the direction of the enemy's position—the sky seems aflame, presenting a spectacle which in those September nights was particularly striking, and has indelibly impressed itself on our minds. At St Pierre, a working-class suburb of Lens, a large coal-mine was in conflagration. The greedy flames, like ghosts, played around the tall winding-tower, and in the midst of the flames loomed the church tower of St Pierre. Verily a weirdly beautiful spectacle !

Under the impression of this scene and the uninterrupted cannonade which made the ground tremble, we of the 3rd Battalion, in the night of the 24th September, asked ourselves, When is the enemy going to attack, and when shall we be drawn into the struggle ?

The darkness of the horizon was constantly broken by the flashes of a thousand belching cannon-mouths. These were the batteries of Carency, Neuville, and St Ablain, and these in the ravines of Loretto, which had never been silent since the days of the first Loretto offensive. Great sheaves of fire shot into the sky from the impact of heavy projectiles. What senseless frenzy must have possessed our enemies !

About ten o'clock Lieutenant Geiler of the Reserve, Captain of the 11/178, entered the officers' casino, where a number of officers of the 3rd Battalion had assembled, and brought important news : " At 4.30 to-morrow morning the Battalion must be at the western approach to Liévin. At Souchez a French attack is expected." From billet to billet orderlies hastened to warn our comrades, who were lodged with workmen's families.

One of those restless nights was passed. The companies stood at the appointed time with an assault kit, in the darkness, amid cool and rainy weather, partly on the road leading to Liévin and Angres, partly in the suburb streets. Calmly and composed, we waited from hour to hour for further orders. The flashes and thundering of artillery have almost ceased. Only the Véry lights constantly rising — the nocturnal feelers of the infantry—indicate the position of the vigilant sentries. Gradually daylight begins to dawn. Suddenly the news passes along the line : " Back to quarters. Keep in readiness for an alarm." In groups, or even singly, we wander to our quarters, when our attention is attracted by the unexpected rattle of German machine-guns, the noise of grenades, and the appearance of exploding shrapnel in the direction of St Pierre and St Laurent. Now the German barrage-firing begins. From our elevated quarters we can see how the lazy west wind drives towards the trenches of our neighbouring division greenish-yellow and black clouds of smoke from the English position. Out of hundreds of gas-containers at intervals of about 1 metre poisonous little clouds, after rolling forwards for about 50 metres, unite into a single enormous gas cloud. A gush of wind from time to time whirls it about, whilst, kept together by the moist and heavy atmosphere, it advances threateningly into the ranks of our comrades, with baleful effects.[1]

But now we also move! The German artillery begins a furious fire into the cloud; hand-grenades, projectiles of all sizes, endeavour to divert or stop the uncanny approach of the danger. The gas surges to and fro where the projectiles have fallen, but in spite of everything the gas has reached our trenches.

Those gas-masks, however, which have become historical, did their duty; according to the amount of gas inhaled and even according to differences of level, the effect varied from a slight sickly feeling to complete stupor.

The distinctly audible, continuous rattle of the English machine-guns tells us that the gas attack is being at once followed up by the infantry attack. Indians are driven forward in advance, but their attack is beaten off!

The ground is covered with dead and wounded. Again, and a third time, fresh clouds are sent over the Indians. Then our artillery begins to slacken somewhat. Scotch and English troops assault us. The first line of the division next ours is bowled over. Will the reserves now do their duty?

Meanwhile the enemy's artillery is sending their projectiles and shells more and more to the east, beyond Hill 70, towards Lens—a barrage-fire!

Now orderlies rush here and there. The Brigade alarms the battalion at 10.30: "The companies shall hasten by the shortest road to the north of St Laurent." Again messengers carry the order: "Companies shall be ready to march in five minutes, and in a quarter of an hour the four companies must be at the end of the road to St Laurent." The assault kit was shouldered in a moment, and rifles likewise; already the groups begin to move. By a forced march—partly in single file, partly in ranks, on account of the constant circling of hostile aircraft—we hurry through the streets, following Major Gause, our battalion chief, who rides full tilt ahead to reconnoitre the situation. Already the English missiles pop at the walls of the St Laurent houses, and already the English themselves had reached the nearest houses, when our 3rd Battalion rushed up like the wind to save Lens and save our comrades at the Lorette from being cut off. Across the open field which reaches to the suburb of St Laurent we had to run in groups, because, from Fosse 14 and Hill 70, as well as from other directions, the road was fully commanded, and in fact the road right into Lens. Whilst the first shells

[1] According to No. 32 of the 'Beobachter,' of November 16, this is the strongest gas attack so far made by the English. (Supplement of the 'Zeitung der 10 Armee.')

began the work of destruction at the south exit from St Laurent, some trains turned off at the first houses into the gardens, and thus reached Fosse 14 on the north edge of the village, unobserved and under cover. There, Major Gause, Adjutant-Lieutenant Ryssell, and the rest of the staff had made a stand. Major Gause placed the 9th and 12th Companies on the right side of the road, and the 10th and two trains of the 11th on the left of the road, with orders to carry out an enveloping attack.

After pithy addresses by the company leaders the troops advance. About 12 o'clock, the 10th, and afterwards two trains of the 11th Company, taking advantage of the cover afforded by the escarpment of the road to right and left, advanced, creeping and leaping, until they reached the reserve trench running along the north side of St Laurent. The trains of the 11th, moving more to the left, were able without loss to hold on close to a high railway embankment, which, gradually diminishing, led to a trench west of the road between Lens and La Bassée. At an elevation of 4 to 5 metres the embankment afforded good shelter, and by the time the 11th had got so far they noticed that the Scotch had already, in considerable numbers, obtained a footing on the other side of the embankment, so that we were only separated from the enemy by the width of the embankment (about 20 metres), on which ran about 6 trucks. Portions of the 10th, to the left of the road, were at a distance of about 100 to 200 metres from the enemy, whilst other portions on the right side of the road, also the 9th and 12th Companies, which had sustained some losses, had passed through the trench and crossed the railway line, thereafter leaping into the reserve trench 50 metres behind it, and reinforcing the remnants and small reserves of that regiment to such an extent that at length the trench might be considered as sufficiently occupied. In the meantime the Scotch had worked forward on that side up to within 50 metres distance, when, hindered by the strong wire entanglements and the assumed adequate manning of the reserve trench, they began to disappear underground like moles. Whilst this first and feeble company of rifles now paused in their victorious assault, the main strength of the enemy was still on Hill 70, which, distant about 1 kilometre from St Laurent, extended chiefly eastwards to the right of the road. It was, however, a good while before, owing to the intense fire of the enemy, we were able to obtain sufficient information respecting the position and strength of the latter, whom we of course kept under our carefully directed rifle-fire, at the same time beginning to cut several lanes of attack through the wire entanglements. All suffering and privation of the Lorette were forgotten, and after our long passive inactivity, and now reckless of the wild firing of hostile artillery, we were burning to get to close quarters with the English. The machine-guns on the left wing operated with good effect against the Scotch, who were almost taken in flank, and after Captain Starke had continuously moved reinforcements from the right to the left wing, the enemy's lines began gradually to thin out shortly before half-past one, as some of our opponents detached themselves, and, first creeping, tried to gain the eminence behind. We were so keen on the assault that there could be no holding back. Continuing from left to right, we crossed the embankment and pursued the Scotch towards the height, when we for the first time discovered that the Scotch, who had faced us, were twice as numerous as ourselves. Without waiting for orders, we went on leaping and storming forward against that portion of the battalion on the right of the road, when they heard the loud and victorious hurrahs from the left and saw our brilliant advance. Away we went, crossing the trench begun by the Scotch, passing dead and wounded and everything on our way, and already taking our first prisoners.

All those who took part in this action will never forget it. Those who looked on from a distance witnessed a first-class war drama, such as they might never see again, when our 178th Regiment, with the remnants of the reserves, in one wide semi-circle furiously stormed the height, halting now and then to fire while standing, some stopping to relieve the wounded of their arms, whilst the Scotch and English, partly divested of their straps and belts, approached the heights, much outnumbering us. Owing to the clear weather they, for a short time, stood out distinctly silhouetted on the ridge, then disappeared behind us. About 2 P.M. this important engagement was over, and the heights commanding Lens were again in our possession. Now the great thing was to hold the captured position at all costs against the larger numbers of English troops which were still on the right flank at the point of irruption in Bois Hugo, which our comrades had christened "Schottenwald," because it swarmed with Scotch troops. Already the sudden advance of superior forces was announced. Whilst on our side the reserve train, under Lieutenant Krempe, was able to take part in the storming of the hill, now it was replaced by the last reserve, a train of the 11th under Lieutenant Starke, bringing fresh forces, fresh courage, and especially fresh ammunition, at the double-quick, to support the brave assailants.

In order to secure the hill a machine-gun was at once placed in the house close to the road, and it kept up a continuous and effective fire directed against the enemy on the opposite slope of the hill. After being closely inspected by the enemy aircraft, this house received a direct hit in the evening. A short time before that, it had afforded protection for a first-aid station.

The enemy also directed the fire of their heavy ordnance against the battalions stationed at St Laurent and its immediate proximity. Those guns, as vice Colour-Sergeant Birke reported, sent their dangerous greeting with rumbling and crashing to that quarter, and the gable-end of the house received a direct hit; pieces of tiles, flying with considerable force, hit Birke in the nape of the neck. He was just about to disappear into the cellar when suddenly a heavy load fell on his back. Could it be a comrade cut to pieces by a shell? Oh, no! It was only one of our men of the 10th who had lost his balance through fright, and consequently fell nice and softly on to a broad back. Owing to the superior forces facing us and the passage of irruption being still open, besides a shortage of reserve, we were obliged to content ourselves, in the meantime, with the success already obtained, and we employed the evening and the night with entrenching ourselves. The attempted nocturnal attacks by two neighbouring regiments proved futile. Furious artillery fire of the enemy, which we had to endure patiently, was followed by repeated desperate attacks on our position by the English, attacks which several times developed into hand-to-hand encounters. Thus an exciting forenoon followed the first day of the battle of Loos. As the weather cleared and the afternoon was sunny, we were able from the top of Hill 70 to obtain good observation of the little wood at our feet—on the right of the street leading to La Bassée. To the east and north of the wood stood portions of the neighbouring division in a semi-circle. We had not yet succeeded in quite closing the passage of irruption. A second attack was undertaken at this point by the Scotch about half-past two o'clock, after energetic artillery preparations with shells and shrapnel. After this second attack had broken down, thanks to our hot resistance and well-aimed fire, we observed that to our right the infantry regiment . . . . . . was following up the retreating enemy. That was our signal for storming into that section of the wood, led by Lieut.-Colonel Franke, and we reached the wood before the . . . . . . Our ranks were led by the non-commissioned officer L. Deise, a stoutly-built, broad-chested Saxon. He had already reached the middle of the wood and was standing in a dense coppice when he suddenly started. At a distance of less than 10 feet there stood in front of him, in a small clearing, six very tall Scotchmen in a group, anxiously scanning the neighbourhood. When they got sight of him they lifted their rifles hurriedly, but before they were able to fire, Deise had seized his short axe, which flew at the Scotchmen. Each of them tried to shield himself. By this they lost time, which Deise used to make a spring at them and attack them with his bayonet, after having shot a second, for his axe had hit the first Scotchman on the left temple and finished him, whilst the man who had stood beside him was wounded severely in the eye by the handle of the axe. Deise managed to wound the fourth, though a good fighter, in the abdomen. The fifth, although startled by the loud hurrahs of the Germans, succeeded in giving Deise a blow with the butt-end of his rifle, under which he collapsed. Godicke, a volunteer, rushed forward, knelt down beside Deise, and fired wildly at the Scotchmen who were again coming on. Nevertheless, four of them got near and engaged in a hand-to-hand fight. One of the Scotchmen then stumbled and fell on the top of Deise, whom this hard blow roused from his stupor, for fortunately Deise, on account of the hot shrapnel fire, had put on the strong old helmet of one of our men which he had found, and that had weakened the force of the blow. In a moment there was a rush to help Godicke. Loud shouts of "Here" and sharp whistling, which sounded above the roar and rattle of the wood, brought about forty men round Deise, whereupon he led them against the superior force of the Scotch. Non-commissioned officer Reuter was among those who distinguished themselves in this hand-to-hand fight, which once more gave free vent to the Germanic-German joy in fighting and wrestling. In conjunction with the neighbouring division, we now slowly pushed the enemy to the road, threw him across it, and again got possession of trench 14 bis.

This made a satisfactory conclusion to the successes of the day before; the English had been thrown back in a westerly direction towards Loos, and we had obtained a position which we could content ourselves with defending. Five times in the course of the afternoon they rushed out of Loos and from the heights to the north, against us. We had eight, ten, or more skirmishes! Again and again new lines of riflemen appeared, but it was in vain that they threw themselves upon our positions. Annihilated and broken up was one battalion after another by our effective artillery, machine-gun, and rifle fire, as the English newspapers themselves relate. The onrush died away several hundred metres in front of our position, and those who escaped were driven back in absolute confusion. What had appeared impossible was accomplished.

The stormy days have not yet passed, but as adequate reserves have reached us, we are prepared and armed to meet the worst.

It was necessary to detach a number of our regiment who were almost overcome by hunger, thirst, and fatigue. But only a portion of them were able to take a rest in the cellars of St Laurent, near trench 14.

In the evening, under the guidance and leadership of Lieutenant Looff, an entrenching operation was commanded, about which Comrade Sturm relates the following:—

"The object was to dig a fresh flanking trench from which operations might be easily and successfully carried out against any attack of the enemy. On the previous afternoon the English had repeatedly attempted to advance from that flank, but in consequence of German vigilance and preparedness, they had not succeeded. Nor had they got away without sustaining losses. But we wanted to obtain certainty on this point. Here the opportunity presented itself to adorn the laurels of the previous day with the trophies of warlike triumph! 'Volunteer patrol advance.' Non-commissioned officer Lehmann and his substitute, Lance-Corporal Mucke, offered themselves. It was quite possible that on wounded or dead English, left on the field, important material giving information might be found, as, for instance, charts, optical instruments, &c. . . . Lehmann and Mucke crept forward unmolested. They had already advanced a good while from our position when, from a distance, the sounds of moaning and whining were heard. Lehmann listened—heard something, and listened again. He felt impelled to follow these sounds. Without hesitating, and braving the danger, he went forward to investigate, approaching nearer and nearer to the point whence the sounds had proceeded. Once Lehmann turned round to whisper something to his companion, Mucke. Mucke had disappeared! . . . There was no time to think about the matter. Lehmann held on, for had he not almost reached his goal? A noise! Again a rustling was heard, and then silence. He held his rifle ready to fire! He continued listening and looking round keenly! Anxious moments . . . but nothing suspicious was to be discovered, no menacing symptom. He groped about and painfully moved on, following the direction of the muttering and groaning, which became more and more distinct. Only a few metres in front, an English uniform was visible above the flax-grass which here covered the clay soil. He had kept on the right track! This expedition is getting interesting and exciting! Creeping and crawling, and carefully looking around, Lehmann reached his goal. By the uniform he now recognised an English officer. The man was lying with closed eyes, motionless and helpless, seriously wounded and much exhausted. He had lost much blood from a shot in his leg. Lehmann was on the point of taking possession of his gun, when he noticed an English corporal on his left, who was trying to get up. Lehmann tried with gestures to inquire whether he was wounded. The Englishman, however, did not seem to understand, and was about to come forward. But he immediately followed Lehmann's direction to remain lying. Without losing sight of his two foundlings, Lehmann in the first place collected a great number of English arms which were scattered in the neighbourhood, thus removing them from the grasp of the 'sons of Albion.' He could not yet tell but what a third or fourth mortal enemy, concealed by the risings of the ground, might be in the neighbourhood. Here was another rifle to take in charge. It was lying among some thistles. Lehmann was quick, and already held safely in his hand this weapon. But hold! What was that? That slight elevation among the high grass was moving and had human limbs; gradually this puzzle was solved. Actually a third Englishman! Apparently he had just woke up from a deep sleep, was breathing heavily and slightly coughing. As Lehmann observed, this third man was not wounded; possibly he had laid down exhausted and had fallen into a coma-like sleep. Treacherously, the corporal's braiding of the Englishman shone out of the thistles. The Englishman stretched himself and coughed repeatedly. Then he jumped up. In a loud voice Lehmann called to him, so that he evidently was startled and let fall the rifle which he had just taken up. Lehmann presented his revolver, and the Englishman at once resigned himself to his fate without making any opposition. Lehmann's position, however, was becoming more critical. He was alone and could not expect any help, unless luck were to favour him. He was a man, and prepared for anything. He did not lose his usual composure, and it proved that luck did favour him! Comrade Mucke suddenly appeared as if by enchantment! A silent but eloquent 'welcome' from Lehmann's eyes greeted Mucke, who immediately found a way to make himself useful. As yet the question of transporting the three 'gentlemen' was unsolved. It was not possible to discuss the matter with them, for neither in German nor in English could we manage to make each other understand. The officer, whose wounded leg had been roughly put in splint by means of a spade handle, was evidently seriously wounded and showed symptoms of great exhaustion, and was consequently not capable of standing up. He would have to be carried. But there were no carriers or other means of transport at hand. It was necessary to procure men, and it was also necessary to report the whole story to the lieutenant. Now, Mucke, having come up, was the man to take the message. He departed quickly, whilst Lehmann kept close watch over the wounded men. The short time of waiting seemed unending. . . . At last Mucke came back. Shortly afterwards the lieutenant himself arrived, accompanied by three men carrying short swords. Under Lehmann's guidance, the transport was effected smoothly, with the exception of a short and agreeable interruption; for they discovered a machine-gun which had been abandoned by the English and was in perfect condition, and this of course had to be conveyed to the German trench and delivered. As Lehmann discovered on the following morning, the Englishmen had been found at a distance of scarcely 100 metres from the enemy's division."

All the successes described had cost much precious blood, for after the last of the scattered men had been collected on the 28th September, our 3rd Battalion showed very much thinned ranks. Probably nearly one-half had been sacrificed, and of these many a one, after a sad post-mortem examination, found his last resting-place in the cemetery of Lens. Among them was Lieutenant Ryssell, who fell exclaiming: "I have it. Hurrah!" There was also Lieutenant Strauss and Lieutenant Gräber, and many a popular non-commissioned officer, such as Vogel, Hartnick, and Godicke.

Thus we were able to show how, thanks to the part played by the 3rd Battalion, the "victory" of Loos, which, besides Tahure, was won by the Entente over "Dying Germany" in 1915, and which was to bring about her "destruction," was to be traced to an unimportant success: for the final reckoning shows that only Loos still remained in their hands, that a portion of the captured material was again recaptured; but on the other hand, losses of their own material had to be booked. And what efforts the enemy had to make, what an enormous expenditure of ammunition, and, "last not least," to use a favourite English expression, the great hopes which they had to bury! For the decisive irruption which was to cast us out of the north of France and Belgium was described by the chief of the English Guards on the eve of "the greatest battle of all times," with the words that from this battle "depended the fate of future English generations."

APPENDIX G.

CASUALTIES AT LOOS, 25/9/15.

	Officers.					Other ranks.				
	Killed.	Wounded.	Missing.	Gassed.	Total.	Killed.	Wounded.	Missing.	Gassed.	Total.
H.Q., 44th Brigade	—	—	1	—	1	—	—	—	—	—
9th Black Watch	9	11	1	—	21	68	314	292	5	679
8th Seaforth Highlanders	5	9	4	—	18	44	362	294	—	700
10th Gordon Highlanders	—	5	2	—	7	23	221	114	—	358
7th Cameron Highlanders	6	6	1	—	13	64	255	215	—	534
13th Royal Scots	6	9	1	—	16	37	224	105	4	370
7th Royal Scots Fusiliers	7	12	—	—	19	63	246	83	—	392
11th A. & S. Highlanders	7	4	1	—	12	36	211	64	—	311
6th Cameron Highlanders	8	8	—	1	17	30	270	70	—	370
7th K.O.S.B.	12	6	1	—	19	86	410	160	—	656
8th K.O.S.B.	7	4	2	—	13	23	124	228	4	379
10th Scottish Rifles	16	5	—	—	21	68	318	239	—	625
12th H.L.I.	9	9	1	—	19	59	184	315	—	558
9th Gordon Hrs. (Pioneers)	5	4	—	—	9	30	179	70	4	283
70th Brigade, R.F.A.	—	2	—	—	2	1	12	—	—	13
71st Brigade, R.F.A.	—	—	—	—	—	1	14	2	2	19
72nd Brigade, R.F.A.	—	1	—	—	1	—	2	—	—	2
73rd Brigade, R.F.A.	—	—	—	—	—	2	8	—	—	10
11th M.M.G. Battery	—	2	—	—	2	—	3	—	—	3
Fifteenth Divisional Cyclists	—	—	—	—	—	1	6	—	—	7
73rd Field Company, R.E.	2	2	1	—	5	14	22	11	—	47
74th Field Company, R.E.	—	—	—	—	—	3	9	1	10	23
91st Field Company, R.E.	1	—	—	—	1	13	30	10	—	53
45th Field Amb., R.A.M.C.	—	—	—	—	—	—	4	—	—	4
46th Field Amb., R.A.M.C.	—	1	—	—	1	—	1	—	4	5
47th Field Amb., R.A.M.C.	—	—	—	—	—	—	3	—	—	3
Totals	100	100	16	1	217	666	3432	2273	33	6404
Attached Units—										
180th Company, R.E.	—	—	—	—	—	1	22	2	—	25
187th Company, R.E	—	—	—	—	—	—	1	1	4	6

Note.—An analysis of the casualties of the 7th R.S.F. and 10th Scottish Rifles, recorded in the official lists of men who died in the war, shows that 78 out of 83 of the former, and 192 out of 239 of the latter unit reported "missing" above, were actually killed. Other units would doubtless show similar results.

APPENDIX H.

DIAGRAM SHOWING METHOD OF COLLECTION AND EVACUATION OF WOUNDED.

YPRES, JULY 31, 1917.

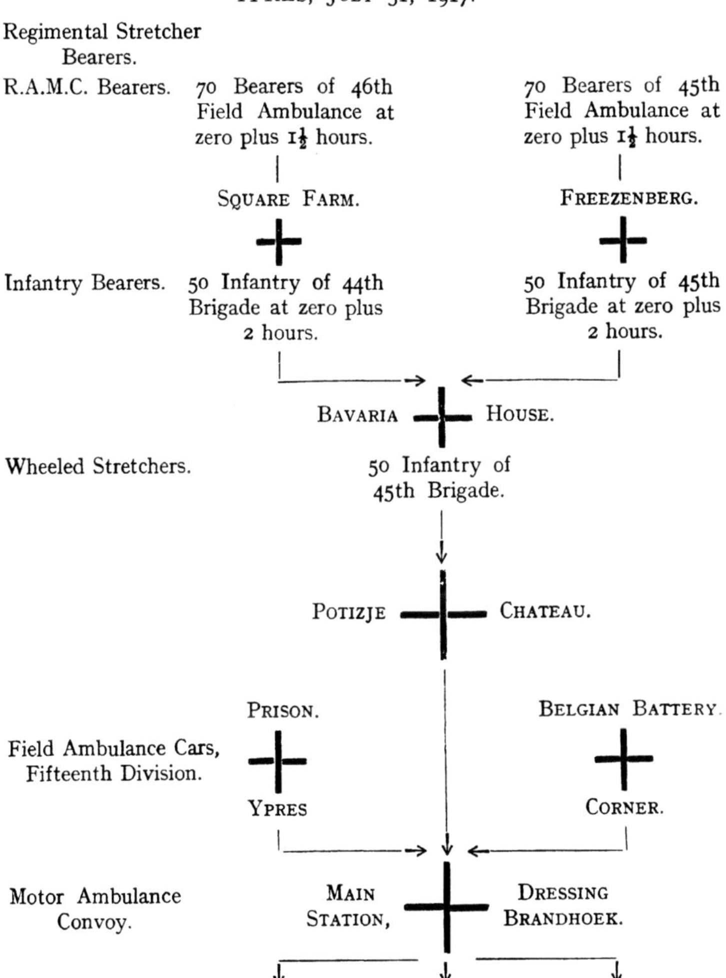

APPENDIX I.

CASUALTIES.

To compile a complete return of casualties of all units from the information given in the War Diaries is impossible. Every care has been taken, and every page (some 65,000 sheets) of the whole of the records of the Division has been read. The resulting lists have been checked, and added to materially, by Regimental Record Offices and by private individuals, who have devoted much time to the work. The compiler claims indulgence for obvious omissions and for errors, which are inevitable in such a list, as detailed information regarding some units was found to be very scanty, and in other cases entirely lacking.

44TH INFANTRY BRIGADE CASUALTIES.

9TH BLACK WATCH.

BATTLE OF LOOS.

OFFICERS.

Killed.	*Wounded.*	*Wounded and Missing.*
2nd Lieut. H. A. Sharpe.	Capt. A. K. M'Leod.	Lieut. J. H. Cameron.
Capt. J. Gilchrist (died of wounds, Sept. 28).	Lieut. R. Andrew.	
Major W. M. Henderson.	Lieut. A. O. Denniston.	
Capt. J. M. Bell.	Lieut. E. R. Wilson.	
Capt. D. H. M. Hamilton.	2nd Lt. H. D. J. Glenny.	
Lieut. J. Crighton.	2nd Lt. M. J. Campbell.	
Lieut. J. C. Henderson-Hamilton.	2nd Lt. R. Sterling.	
	2nd Lt. W. J. Leslie.	
2nd Lieut. J. Miller.	2nd Lt. F. R. Wilson.	
Capt. R. E. Harvey.	Capt. F. A. Bearne (R.A.M.C.)	
	2nd Lt. G. Scott-Pearce.	

Missing (believed killed).

Capt. C. S. Tuke (B.M.G.O.)

1915.

Nov. 4.	2nd Lieut. F. H. Harper	Wounded.
Nov. 5.	2nd Lieut. M. Mackenzie	Killed.
Nov. 14.	Lieut. J. D. D. Miller	Died of wounds.

OTHER RANKS.

	Killed.	*Wounded.*	*Missing*
Battle of Loos.	68	319	292
Aug.-Dec. 1915.	13	43	1

OFFICERS.

1916.

Feb. 27.	Lieut. Macgregor	Killed.
March 17.	2nd Lieut. G. R. Clow	Killed.
March 17.	2nd Lieut. R. G. Howard	Killed.
April 27.	2nd Lieut. Read	Wounded.
April 29.	Lieut. J. Small	Killed.
April 29.	2nd Lieut. Drummond	Wounded.
April 29.	2nd Lieut. Dewar	Wounded.
May 22.	2nd Lieut. T. M'Gregor	Wounded.
May 29.	2nd Lieut. H. M'William	Killed.
June 23.	2nd Lieut. J. Allan	Wounded.
June 27.	Capt. W. Storey Wilson	Wounded.
July 9.	Capt. G. A. Rusk	Wounded.
July 10.	2nd Lieut. N. Bartmen	Wounded.
July 14.	2nd Lieut. D. M. Wilson	Wounded.
Aug. 25.	2nd Lieut. D. O. Tweedie	Wounded.
Aug. 26.	2nd Lieut. H. B. Johnstone	Wounded.
Aug. 18.	2nd Lieut. R. B. A. Macdonald	Killed.
Aug. 18.	Capt. F. A. Bearn (R.A.M.C.)	Wounded.
Aug. 18.	Lieut. D. C. Eglinton	Wounded.
Aug. 18.	2nd Lieut. J. F. N. Macrae	Wounded.
Aug. 18.	2nd Lieut. A. F. Watson	Wounded.
Aug. 18.	2nd Lieut. R. J. M'Murray	Wounded.
Aug. 18.	2nd Lieut. J. S. Strang	Wounded.
Sept. 7.	Capt. J. B. Robertson	Wounded.
Sept. 8.	2nd Lieut. J. E. Drummond	Wounded.
Sept. 9.	Capt. W. B. Binnie	Wounded.
Sept. 9.	Capt. R. Stirling	Wounded.
Sept. 9.	2nd Lieut. J. N. Humble	Wounded.
Sept. 9.	2nd Lieut. J. B. Ireland	Killed.
Sept. 13.	2nd Lieut. J. F. N. Macrae	Wounded (Gas).
Oct. 11.	2nd Lieut. T. R. Turnbull	Killed.
Oct. 11.	Lieut. F. R. Wilson	Wounded.
Dec. 23.	2nd Lieut. J. M. Brown	Wounded.

OTHER RANKS.

1916.	*Killed.*	*Wounded.*	*Missing.*
January . . . . . . } February . . . . . }	11	33	3
March	3	27	nil
April	22	85	nil
May	8	42	nil
June	3	46	nil
July	7	35	12
August	34	171	24
September	9	123	30
October	10	66	13
November	nil	1	nil
December	nil	2	nil
	96	631	82

OFFICERS.

1917.		
Jan. 6.	2nd Lieut. G. H. Gordon	Wounded.
Jan. 24.	2nd Lieut. W. Dow	Wounded.
Feb. 2.	2nd Lieut. W. Dow	Died of wounds.
April 9-11.	Capt. H. T. Collins, C.F.	Killed.
	2nd Lieut. O. C. Fraser	Killed.
	Capt. W. Storey Wilson	Wounded.
	2nd Lieut. W. Anderson	Wounded.
	2nd Lieut. D. W. H. Cuthbert . . .	Died of wounds.
	2nd Lieut. R. W. Hunter	Wounded.
	2nd Lieut. E. M'C. Reid	Wounded.
	2nd Lieut. J. Callan	Wounded.
	2nd Lieut. R. K. MacRoberts . . .	Wounded.
	2nd Lieut. A. Marshall	Wounded.
	2nd Lieut. F. Proudfoot	Wounded.
	2nd Lieut. J. W. Barr	Wounded.
	2nd Lieut. H. S. Muir	Wounded.
	2nd Lieut. R. M. Dinwiddie (Lanarkshire Yeomanry, attached)	Wounded.
	Capt. S. Norrie Miller	Wounded.
	2nd Lieut. E. M. Reid	Wounded.
April 12.	2nd Lieut. T. E. Reid	Died of wounds.
April 23-28.	Capt. L. G. Morrison	Killed

Date	Name	Casualty
1917.		
April 23-28.	Lieut. O. L. Bearn	Killed.
	2nd Lieut. A. F. Watson	Killed.
	2nd Lieut. J. Wilson	Killed.
	2nd Lieut. W. Anderson	Died of wounds.
	2nd Lieut. C. K. Young	Wounded.
	2nd Lieut. J. N. Humble	Wounded.
	2nd Lieut. J. B. Third	Wounded.
	2nd Lieut. R. A. M. Hastings	Wounded.
	2nd Lieut. A. D. M'Diarmid	Wounded.
	2nd Lieut. T. B. Allison	Wounded.
	2nd Lieut. J. L. Burton	Killed.
	2nd Lieut. A. F. Watson	Killed.
	2nd Lieut. E. E. Dale	Wounded.
	2nd Lieut. M. Duggan	Wounded.
July 7.	2nd Lieut. W. K. Macgregor	Wounded.
July 8.	2nd Lieut. T. Edwards	Wounded.
July 31.	2nd Lieut. J. Taylor	Killed.
	Capt. N. A. Grant	Wounded.
	2nd Lieut. E. M. Drummond	Wounded.
	2nd Lieut. J. H. Fraser	Wounded.
	2nd Lieut. C. F. J. Neish	Wounded.
	2nd Lieut. W. R. Tovani	Wounded.
	2nd Lieut. W. Marchbank	Wounded.
	2nd Lieut. Macgregor	Wounded.
	2nd Lieut. R. B. Anderson	Wounded.
	Lieut.-Colonel S. A. Innes, D.S.O.	Wounded.
Aug. 2.	2nd Lieut. J. E. Drummond	Wounded.
	Capt. S. Norie Miller	Wounded.
Aug. 15.	2nd Lieut. G. C. Leslie	Died of wounds.
Aug 23.	Major H. F. F. Murray	Killed.
	2nd Lieut. R. Stevenson	Killed.
	2nd Lieut. G. E. R. Young	Wounded.
	Capt. J. Donaldson	Killed.
	2nd Lieut. G. R. M. Kerr	Wounded.
Aug. 26.	Capt. J. S. Strang	Wounded.
	Capt. G. F. Young	Wounded.
	2nd Lieut. S. Graham	Wounded.
	2nd Lieut. C. J. B. Ritchie	Wounded.
Sept. 28.	Lieut. Viscount Drumlanrig	Wounded.
Dec. 10.	2nd Lieut. A. B. Sinclair	Missing.
Dec. 24.	Lieut. Viscount Drumlanrig	Wounded.
Dec. 30.	Capt. N. G. Johnstone	Killed.
	Lieut. A. Graham	Killed.

OTHER RANKS.

	1917.	Killed.	Wounded.	Missing.
	January	4	26	2
	February	nil	nil	nil
	March	2	14	nil
	April	2	10	2
Battles of Arras	April 9-11	42	190	24
	April 23-28	28	175	27
	July 1-28	nil	15	2
Battles of Ypres	July 29 to Aug. 4	26	207	22
	Aug. 5-31	44	101	23
	September	13	20	nil
	October	5	12	nil
	November	1	15	12
	December	2	18	4
		169	803	118

Attached to 46TH BRIGADE *from 8th February* 1918.

OFFICERS.

1918.		
March 28.	2nd Lieut. J. M'Veigh	Killed.
March 28.	2nd Lieut. A. Forrest	Wounded and Missing.
March 28.	2nd Lieut. E. P. McWalcott	Wounded and Missing.
March 28.	Lieut. J. W. Morris	Missing.
March 28.	Major W. B. Binnie, M.C.	Wounded.
March 28.	Capt. J. S. Strang	Wounded.
March 28.	2nd Lieut. G. E. M. Govan	Wounded
March 28.	2nd Lieut. A. S. G. Loxton	Wounded.
March 28.	Capt. T. Calvert, M.C.	Wounded.
April 4.	Lieut. L. M'Kenzie	Died of Wounds.
Sept. 2.	2nd Lieut. C. R. Belford	Killed.
Sept. 14.	2nd Lieut. A. L. Robertson	Wounded.
Sept. 15.	Lieut. J. H. Lauder	Wounded.
	2nd Lieut. E. R. C. Walker	Wounded.
	2nd Lieut. W. D. G. Reid	Wounded.
Sept. 16.	2nd Lieut. J. R. M'Callum	Wounded.
Nov. 16.	2nd Lieut. M. Lambroughton	Died.

OTHER RANKS.

	Killed.	*Wounded.*	*Missing.*
February . .	4	5	nil
March . . .	46	87	99
April . . .	nil	nil	nil
	50	92	99

In May 1918 this Battalion was reduced to Training Cadre.

4/5TH BLACK WATCH.

OFFICERS.

1918.		
May 21.	2nd Lieut. W. F. Dundas . . .	Wounded.
May 31.	2nd Lieut. F. Edwards . . .	Wounded.
July 3.	2nd Lieut. D. Syme . . .	Wounded (died 4/7).
July 28.	2nd Lieut. J. Stuart . . .	Killed.
July 28.	2nd Lieut. R. G. Tait . . .	Wounded.
July 28.	2nd Lieut. W. K. M'Gregor . .	Missing.
Aug. 1.	2nd Lieut. J. H. Barnett . .	Killed.
Aug. 1.	Capt. D. Maxwell, M.C. . . .	Wounded (died of wounds).
Aug. 1.	2nd Lieut. J. A. Ritchie . . .	Wounded (died of wounds).
Aug. 1.	2nd Lieut. G. Herbert . . .	Wounded.
Aug. 1.	2nd Lieut. J. Vint	Wounded.
Aug. 1.	2nd Lieut. A. Scott . . .	Wounded.
Aug. 1.	2nd Lieut. F. A. Brown . . .	Wounded.
Aug. 1.	2nd Lieut. W. Malcolm . . .	Wounded.
Sept. 15.	Lieut. J. N. Duncan . . .	Wounded.
Sept. 15.	2nd Lieut. C. C. Culross . . .	Gassed.
Oct. 5.	Lieut. J. Baldwin, M.O. . . .	Gassed.
Oct. 21.	2nd Lieut. C. C. Culross . . .	Wounded.

OTHER RANKS.

1918.	*Killed.*	*Wounded.*	*Missing.*	*Gassed.*	*Died of Wounds.*
May . . .	6	7	nil	nil	nil
June . . .	1	27	1	11	nil
July . . .	24	133	27	nil	1
August . . .	25	123	6	nil	nil
September . .	12	52	5	nil	3
October . . .	6	13	15	54	nil
November . .	nil	nil	nil	nil	nil
	74	355	54	65	4

8th Seaforth Highlanders.

Battle of Loos.

Officers.

Killed.	*Wounded.*	*Missing.*
Major A. J. H. Tremearne.	Lieut.-Colonel N. A. Thompson.	Lieut. J. E. Kennedy.
Capt. A. G. Ravenhill.	Major U. P. Swinburne.	2nd Lieut. W. C. Tremearne.
Lieut. A. Miller.	Lieut. D. M. Dunlop.	2nd Lieut. G. Macgregor.
Lieut. J. V. Stanford.	2nd Lieut. A. W. Turnbull.	2nd Lieut. F. L. MacCrae.
2nd Lieut. G. M. Calder.	2nd Lieut. J. M. L. Nicholson.	
	Capt. R. M. Powell.	
	Lieut. D. B. Macaulay.	
	Capt. H. F. Munro (died of wounds).	
	2nd Lieut. W. Heath.	

Officers.

1915.		
Oct. 30.	2nd Lieut. J. Mackenzie	Killed.
Nov. 1.	Lieut. I. H. S. Jameson	Wounded.
Nov. 6.	2nd Lieut. G. G. Blackwood	Accidentally wounded.
	2nd Lieut. F. H. Harper	Wounded.

Other Ranks.

	Killed.	*Wounded.*	*Missing.*
Battle of Loos, 1915 .	44	362	294
Aug.-Dec. 1915 . .	16	61	nil

Officers.

1916.		
Jan. 26.	Capt. Ferguson	Killed.
Feb. 25.	Lieut. R. W. Straw	Wounded.
March 17.	Capt. J. F. Myles	Wounded.
March 17.	Lieut. J. Keith	Wounded.

1916.		
March 17.	2nd Lieut. C. Macmillan	Wounded.
May 3.	2nd Lieut. O. J. Beaton	Wounded.
May 3.	2nd Lieut. T. Milne	Wounded.
May 3.	2nd Lieut. T. M. Darling	Wounded.
May 18.	Lieut. R. F. M. Scholefield	Wounded.
May 22.	Lieut. B. Murray	Killed.
July 7.	Lieut. S. J. Morrell	Wounded.
July 10.	Capt. F. G. Hart	Wounded.
July 10.	Capt. F. Holmes	Wounded.
July 10.	Lieut. J. E. Smith	Wounded.
July 10.	2nd Lieut. F. M. M'Callion	Wounded.
July 10.	2nd Lieut. K. MacKenzie	Wounded.
July 12.	2nd Lieut. J. M. L. Nicholson	Killed.
Aug. 18.	2nd Lieut. J. B. Ross	Wounded.
Aug. 19.	2nd Lieut. E. A. Maule	Wounded.
Aug. 19.	2nd Lieut. D. Macdonald Cameron	Wounded.
Aug. 19.	2nd Lieut. E. M. Fraser	Wounded.
Aug. 20.	2nd Lieut. R. P. Smith	Wounded.
Aug. 27.	2nd Lieut. K. H. Grant	Killed.
Aug. 27.	2nd Lieut. J. Kirkwood	Wounded.
July 19.	2nd Lieut. H. J. R. Kilpatrick	Wounded.
Sept. 10.	2nd Lieut. A. Browning	Wounded.
Sept. 12.	2nd Lieut. E. M. Fraser	Gassed.
Sept. 21	2nd Lieut. J. E. Wink	Killed.
Oct. 9.	2nd Lieut. C. L. B. Davie	Wounded.
Oct. 10.	2nd Lieut. A. Browning	Wounded.
Oct. 13.	2nd Lieut. W. M. Potter	Gassed.

OTHER RANKS.

1916.	*Killed.*	*Wounded.*	*Missing.*
January, February	10	50	1
March	3	27	nil
April	nil	4	nil
May	16	39	19
June	8	32	nil
July	8	116	nil
August	34	191	24
September	6	91	2
October	14	87	20
November	nil	2	nil
December	1	10	3
	90	649	68

OFFICERS.

1917.		
Jan. 15.	2nd Lieut C. Forrest	Wounded.
Jan. 29.	2nd Lieut. J. T. Wilson	Killed.
April 11.	Capt. W. Murray	Wounded.
April 22.	2nd Lieut. Reginald Vance Cuthbert (Died of wounds on 28/4/17.)	Wounded.
April 23.	Capt. Ian Herbert Sydney Jameson	Killed.
	2nd Lieut. William Blair	Killed.
	2nd Lieut. Albert Abercrombie Gardner	Killed.
	2nd Lieut. Richard Forsyth M'Gibbon	Killed.
	2nd Lieut. James Hector Ross	Killed.
	Capt. William John Taylor (Died on 1/8/17.)	Wounded.
	2nd Lieut. A. J. M. D. Miller	Wounded.
	2nd Lieut. D. E. Lothian	Wounded.
	2nd Lieut. J. R. Wardrope	Wounded.
	2nd Lieut. W. M. Wishart	Wounded.
	2nd Lieut. H. C. Duncan	Wounded.
	2nd Lieut. R. A. Berry Hart	Wounded.
	Lieut. F. C. G. Haynes	Wounded.
	Lieut. D. E. F. C. Hervey	Wounded.
July 2.	2nd Lieut. R. D. S. Mackenzie	Died of wounds.
July 6.	Capt. H. L. Fraser, M.C.	Wounded.
July 8.	2nd Lieut. Æ. Mackenzie	Missing.
July 9.	Lieut.-Colonel R. G. Buchanan, D.S.O.	Wounded.
	Capt. J. F. Myles	Wounded.
	2nd Lieut. J. Hamilton	Wounded.
July 31.	2nd Lieut. F. Burns	Killed.
	2nd Lieut. G. Brodie	Killed.
	2nd Lieut. J. L. Turing, M.C.	Wounded.
	2nd Lieut. T. C. Irvine, M.C.	Wounded.
	2nd Lieut. A. H. Grove	Wounded.
	2nd Lieut. J. V. Fraser	Wounded.
	2nd Lieut. T. L. Christie	Wounded.
Aug. 1.	Capt. J. B. Smith, M.C.	Wounded.
Aug. 1.	2nd Lieut. P. Chapman	Wounded.
Aug. 2.	2nd Lieut. R. P. Smith, M.C.	Died of wounds.
Aug. 22.	Capt. G. M. Thornton	Killed.
	Capt. C. Macmillan	Killed.
	2nd Lieut. W. M. Gardner	Died of wounds.
	Capt. G. Murray	Wounded.
	2nd Lieut. J. Moodie	Wounded (died).
	2nd Lieut. K. Mackenzie	Wounded.

1917.		
Aug. 22	2nd Lieut. J. P. Key	Wounded.
	2nd Lieut. H. H. Fraser	Died of wounds.
	2nd Lieut. K. B. Murchison	Killed.
	2nd Lieut. D. A. Macadie	Killed.
	2nd Lieut. T. W. Horne	Killed.
Nov. 17.	2nd Lieut. G. Syme, M.C.	Wounded.

OTHER RANKS.

	1917.	*Killed.*	*Wounded.*	*Missing.*
	January . .	6	18	3
	March . . .	5	16	nil
	April . . .	nil	2	nil
Battles of Arras	April 9-11 . .	16	84	54
Battles of Arras	April 21-28 . .	85	203	16
	July 1-28 . .	7	36	12
Battles of Ypres	July 29 to Aug. 4 .	26	153	13
Battles of Ypres	Aug. 5-31 . .	37	223	122
	September . .	1	12	nil
	October . .	4	8	nil
	November . .	3	5	nil
	December . .	4	16	nil
		194	776	220

OFFICERS.

1918.		
Feb. 19.	"1 officer wounded."	
March 9	Capt. D. G. Georgeson	Killed.
March 9.	Capt. P. W. Shaw, M.C.	Wounded.
March 22.	2nd Lieutenant A. M. Campbell . .	Killed.
March 23.	Capt. S. A. Munro, R.A.M.C. . .	Wounded.
April 20.	2nd Lieut. J. Mackinnon	Killed.
April 21.	2nd Lieut. W. A. Dixon	Killed.
June 4.	Lieut.-Col. Hon. E. D. Campbell, D.S.O. .	Died.
June 17.	2nd Lieut. Christie	Wounded.
July 20.	Lieut. F. M. M'Callion, M.C. . .	Killed.
July 21.	2nd Lieut. J. Christie	Killed.
July 21.	Lieut. T. M. Darling	Wounded.
July 21.	2nd Lieut. D. K. M'Morran . . .	Wounded.
July 22.	Capt. G. Murray, M.C.	Wounded.

1918.

July 23.	2nd Lieut. A. Hutchison . . .	Wounded.
July 27.	Lieut.-Col. H. H. Kennedy . . .	Killed.
July 28.	2nd Lieut. T. T. Pettigrew . . .	Killed.
July 28.	2nd Lieut. E. C. Curtis . . .	Killed.
July 28.	2nd Lieut. D. R. Tran	Wounded and missing.
July 28.	2nd Lieut. R. F. Patrick . . .	Wounded.
July 28.	2nd Lieut. J. M. Mitchell . . .	Wounded.
July 28.	Lieut. J. P. Kirk	Wounded.
July 28.	2nd Lieut. A. M. Ford	Wounded.
July 28.	2nd Lieut. J. D. Reid	Wounded.
July 29.	Capt. G. Murray, M.C. . . .	Wounded.
Sept. 30.	Lieut. A. J. Macrae	Died of wounds (4/10).
Sept. 30.	2nd Lieut. W. Leckie	Wounded.
Oct. 9.	Major J. D. Simpson, Brigade-Major .	Wounded.
Oct.	2nd Lieut. W. R. Sutherland . .	Killed.
Oct. 30.	2nd Lieut. J. D. Reid	Wounded.
Oct. 31.	Major A. W. Turnbull, M.C. . . .	Gassed.

OTHER RANKS.

1918.	*Killed.*	*Wounded.*	*Missing.*	*Gassed.*
January . . .	1	3	nil	nil
February . . .	2	8	nil	nil
March 1-21 . . .	6	27	3	nil
March 21-28 . . .	16	106	16	nil
April	12	60	nil	nil
May	5	23	nil	nil
June	1	30	nil	nil
July	43	235	99	nil
August . . .	1	24	2	nil
September . . .	7	27	nil	5
October . . .	2	39	nil	4
November . . .	nil	nil	nil	nil
	96	591	120	9

10TH GORDON HIGHLANDERS.

BATTLE OF LOOS.

OFFICERS.

Killed.	*Wounded.*	*Wounded and Missing.*
Nil	Lieut. R. L. Watson.	Major C. S. M. Makgill-Crichton.
	Lieut. A. R. Roche (R.A.M.C.)	Lieut. R. C. Christison.
	2nd Lieut. G. S. Lumsden.	
	2nd Lieut. G. W. Syme.	
	2nd Lieut. L. G. Robertson.	

1915.		
July 21.	Lieut.-Colonel S. Macdougall	Killed.
Aug. 28.	Captain R. G. Longman	Wounded.
Sept. 20.	Lieut. H. B. Vade-Walpole	Killed.
Nov. 17.	2nd Lieut. Gordon Robertson	Killed.
Nov. 28.	2nd Lieut. A. F. Sprott	Wounded.
Dec. 3.	Capt. N. G. Pearson	Wounded.
Dec. 4.	Lieut. J. G. Paterson	Wounded.

OTHER RANKS.

	Killed.	*Wounded.*	*Wounded and Missing.*
Battle of Loos, 1915	23	221	114
Aug.-Dec. 1915	20	103	nil

OFFICERS.

1916.		
April 27.	Capt. H. B. St de Vine, C.F.	Killed.
May 10.	2nd Lieut. J. Collier	Wounded
May 19.	2nd Lieut. A. N. Bain	Killed.
June 28.	Lieut. D. M'Cullum	Wounded.
June 28.	2nd Lieut. A. C. S. Buist	Wounded.
June 29.	Capt. M. L. Gordon	Wounded.
July 1.	2nd Lieut. R. M. Riddell	Killed.
July 18.	2nd Lieut. W. J. G. Birnie	Wounded.
Aug. 20.	Capt. F. J. C. Moffat	Wounded.
Aug. 20.	2nd Lieut. A. F. Sprott	Wounded.
Sept. 17.	2nd Lieut. H. L. Knowles	Wounded.
Sept. 20.	Capt. H. K. Cornish, C.F.	Wounded.
Oct. 15.	2nd Lieut. O. F. C. Elliot	Killed.
Nov. 1.	2nd Lieut. A. D. Sutherland	Wounded.
Nov. 2.	2nd Lieut. T. Cornford	Wounded.
Nov. 12.	2nd Lieut. H. L. Knowles	Wounded (accidentally).

Other Ranks.

1916.	*Killed.*	*Wounded.*	*Missing.*
January . . . . } February . . . . }	5	32	nil
April	nil	5	nil
	5	37	

8/10th Gordon Highlanders.

Other Ranks.

1916.	*Killed.*	*Wounded.*	*Missing.*
May	11	40	nil
June	10	29	nil
July	6	43	nil
August	12	67	nil
September . . .	35	112	1
October	7	73	nil
November . . .	6	30	nil
December	4	11	nil
	91	405	1

Officers.

1917.		
Jan. 16.	2nd Lieut. C. M'Gregor	Accidentally wounded.
Jan. 30.	2nd Lieut. H. L. Knowles	Killed.
	2nd Lieut. T. E. Forster	Wounded.
April 9-11.	Capt. J. Martin, M.C.	Killed.
	2nd Lieut. A. C. Hay	Killed.
	2nd Lieut. J. Smith	Killed.
	Lieut. A. Inglis	Killed.
	Lieut. D. Booth	Wounded.
	2nd Lieut. B. Burnett	Wounded.
	2nd Lieut. R. H. Blair	Wounded.
	2nd Lieut. R. A. M. Black	Wounded.

1917.		
April 23.	2nd Lieut. G. Hotchkis	Killed.
April 24.	2nd Lieut. G. R. Brooke	Killed.
April 24.	2nd Lieut. J. Little	Killed.
April 24.	2nd Lieut. H. Logan	Missing.
April 25.	2nd Lieut. A. Scott	Killed.
May 2.	Capt. A. K. Priday	Wounded.
May 4.	2nd Lieut. J. Robertson	Wounded.
May 4.	2nd Lieut. V. M. J. Stewart	Wounded.
May 5.	2nd Lieut. P. F. Rennie	Wounded.
July 31.	2nd Lieut. F. S. Howell	Killed.
July 31.	2nd Lieut. J. H. C. Grierson	Killed.
July 31.	2nd Lieut. A. C. Spark	Killed.
Aug. 18.	2nd Lieut. W. S. Kemp	Wounded.
Aug. 22.	2nd Lieut. A. J. E. Carey	Killed.
Aug. 23.	2nd Lieut. G. B. L. Price	Died of wounds.
Aug. 26.	2nd Lieut. R. S. Raitt	Wounded.
Aug. 30.	2nd Lieut J. Napier	Wounded.
Aug. 30.	2nd Lieut. A. W. Robertson	Wounded.
Oct. 14.	2nd Lieut. A. S. Williams	Wounded.
Oct. 14.	Lieut. G. S. Milne	Killed.
Oct. 14.	2nd Lieut. J. B. Simpson	Wounded.
Dec. 19.	Lieut.-Colonel D. Macleod	Died.

OTHER RANKS.

	1917.	*Killed.*	*Wounded.*	*Missing.*
	January	1	28	5
	March	3	10	nil
	April	2	12	nil
Battles of Arras	April 9-11	51	196	37
Battles of Arras	April 23	11	131	nil
	July	2	10	nil
Battles of Ypres	July 29 to Aug. 4	38	245	51
Battles of Ypres	Aug. 5-31	24	161	13
	September	5	18	nil
	October	2	7	nil
	November	1	8	1
	December	5	10	nil
		145	836	107

OFFICERS.

1918.		
Feb. 6.	Lieut. C. B. M'Farlane	Wounded.
March 24.	2nd Lieut. F. M'Ewan	Died of wounds.
March 28.	2nd Lieut. R. S. Knox	Missing.
March 28.	2nd Lieut. G. R. M'Gechan . .	Killed.
March 28.	Lieut. K. A. Robertson	Wounded
March 28.	Lieut. T. F. Forster	Wounded.
March 28.	2nd Lieut. J. T. Leith	Wounded.
March 28.	2nd Lieut. A. J. F. Duncan . .	Wounded.
March 31.	2nd Lieut. R. Buntine	Died of wounds.
March 31.	2nd Lieut. A. J. F. Duncan . .	Died of wounds.
April 13.	Capt. and Q.M. W. Drummond, M.C. .	Missing.
April 21.	Lieut. E. G. Wishart	Died of wounds.
May 15.	2nd Lieut. J. R. Bruce	Wounded.
May 15.	2nd Lieut. J. M. Mackenzie . .	Wounded.
May 24.	2nd Lieut. A. Cantlay	Missing, believed killed.
May 24.	Capt. W. J. P. Beveridge	Wounded.
June 2.	2nd Lieut. R. A. B. Allan	Wounded.

OTHER RANKS.

	Killed.	*Wounded.*	*Missing.*
February	1	6	nil
March 21-28	25	193	79
April	nil	2	nil
May	nil	22	1
June	nil	6	nil
	26	229	80

To Training Cadre, June 1918.

5TH GORDON HIGHLANDERS.

OFFICERS.

July 24.	Lieut. J. M'Hardy	Killed.
July 27.	Capt. R. A. M. Black	Killed.
July 28.	Lieut.-Colonel G. A. Smith, D.S.O. .	Killed.
July 28.	Capt. W. T. Currie	Died of wounds.
July 28.	Lieut. F. W. Lovie	Wounded.
July 30.	Lieut. J. B. Eliott	Wounded.
July 30.	2nd Lieut. R. A Cameron	Gassed.
Aug. 1.	2nd Lieut. A. Brown	Wounded.

1918.		
Aug. 1.	Lieut. T. L. Warrack, M.C.	Wounded.
Aug. 1.	Lieut. J. T. Reid	Wounded.
Aug. 1.	Lieut. G. M. Berry	Wounded.
Aug. 1.	Lieut. J. E. Adam	Wounded.
Aug. 3.	Capt. W. S. Kemp, M.C.	Gassed.
Aug. 3.	Lieut. D. A. D. Fraser	Gassed.
Aug. 3.	2nd Lieut. J. M. Gill	Gassed.
Aug. 3.	2nd Lieut. J. G. Insch, M.M.	Gassed.
Aug. 3.	2nd Lieut. J. F. Martin	Gassed.
Aug. 6.	2nd Lieut. G. A. Middleton	Wounded.
Aug. 18.	2nd Lieut. J. Currie	Gassed.
Sept. 13.	Lieut. G. Dian	Killed.
Oct. 6.	2nd Lieut. A. H. Buchanan	Killed.
Oct. 8.	2nd Lieut. A. G. Tindall	Killed.
Oct. 16.	2nd Lieut. A. W. Haig	Wounded (died 17/10).
Oct. 19.	2nd Lieut. W. J. Hadden	Wounded.
1919.		
Feb. 2.	Capt. G. Cowper	Died.

OTHER RANKS.

1918.	*Killed.*	*Wounded.*	*Missing.*	*Gassed.*	*Wounded and Missing.*	*Died of Wounds.*
July	39	187	19	5	12	nil
August	15	61	6	72	nil	nil
September	1	15	nil	nil	nil	nil
October	5	39	nil	nil	nil	1
November	nil	nil	nil	nil	nil	nil
	60	302	25	77	12	1

7TH CAMERON HIGHLANDERS.

BATTLE OF LOOS.

OFFICERS.

Killed.	*Wounded.*	*Missing.*
2nd Lieut. S. E. Chapman.	Capt. N. Macleod.	Capt. E. K. Cameron.
2nd Lieut. R. A. Stuart.	Capt. L. R. Douglas Hamilton.	Capt. W. N. Kirkland.
2nd Lieut. E. G. Taylor.	Capt. G. A. C. Davy.	
2nd Lieut. S. M'Donald.	2nd Lieut. D. A. Stuart.	
2nd Lieut. B. Watt.	2nd Lieut. A. M'Niven.	
	Lieut. W. G. S. Stuart.	

Died of Wounds.

Major J. Barron.

AUGUST TO DECEMBER 1915. (As apart from Battle of Loos.)

OFFICERS.

Aug. 19.	Lieut. A. R. Chapman	Accidentally wounded.
Sept. 9.	Lieut. W. G. Stuart	Wounded.
Sept. 9.	Lieut. K. C. MacDonell	Wounded.
Sept. 9.	Lieut. K. Macrae	Wounded.
Nov. 19.	2nd Lieut. D. Forbes	Wounded.
Nov. 23.	Lieut. M. C. Pearson	Killed.

OTHER RANKS.

	Killed.	*Wounded.*	*Missing.*
Battle of Loos	64	253	217
Aug.-Dec. 1915	19	52	nil

OFFICERS.

1916.

Feb. 10.	Lieut. J. C. Cattanach	Wounded.
Feb. 27.	Lieut. M. N. Maclean	Wounded
April 29.	2nd Lieut. S. C. Welch	Killed.
May 21.	Lieut. J. S. Robertson	Killed.
July 12.	2nd Lieut. J. H. Mauchlin, M.C.	Wounded.
July 18.	2nd Lieut. M. D. MacDonald	Killed.
July 18.	2nd Lieut. D. Taylor	Missing.
July 19.	Major T. L. Cunningham, D.S.O.	Wounded.
July 19.	2nd Lieut. A. Macniven	Wounded.
July 19.	2nd Lieut. T. Orr	Wounded.
July 19.	2nd Lieut. G. C. Macleay	Wounded.
Aug. 16.	2nd Lieut. J. W. MacKay	Wounded.
Aug. 18.	Lieut. and Adjutant H. B. Hardman	Killed.
Aug. 18.	Lieut. F. B. Cameron	Killed.
Aug. 17.	2nd Lieut. H. B. Goudie	Killed.
Aug. 17.	2nd Lieut. J. W. Anderson	Killed.
Aug. 17.	2nd Lieut. G. C. Macleay	Killed.
Aug. 17.	Capt. H. B. Johnstone	Wounded.
Aug. 17.	Capt. A. Ogilvy	Wounded.
Aug. 17.	Lieut. M. Murchison	Wounded.
Aug. 17.	2nd Lieut. A. Luen	Wounded.
Aug. 17.	2nd Lieut. C. R. G. Scott	Wounded.

1916.

Aug. 17.	2nd Lieut. R. B. Purdon	Wounded.
Aug. 17.	2nd Lieut. C. W. D. Mackay	Wounded.
Aug. 18.	2nd Lieut. D. Moir	Wounded.
Aug. 18.	2nd Lieut. W. Mill	Wounded.
Sept. 12.	2nd Lieut. R. Jardine	Wounded.
Oct. 8.	2nd Lieut. G. L. B. Davie, D.C.M.	Wounded.
Oct. 11.	2nd Lieut. J. R. Steele	Wounded.
Oct. 11.	2nd Lieut. E. D. Hosken	Wounded.
Oct. 13.	2nd Lieut. G. R. Morton	Wounded.
Nov. 2.	2nd Lieut. W. Black	Wounded (accidentally).
Dec. 24.	2nd Lieut. A. C. M'Cuish	Missing.
Dec. 24.	2nd Lieut. J. D. W. M'Cracken	Wounded.

OTHER RANKS.

	Killed.	*Wounded.*	*Missing.*
January, February	8	30	nil
March	3	4	nil
April	9	19	nil
May	8	111	nil
June	17	71	nil
July	13	72	nil
August	22	171	71
September	5	34	5
October	22	109	nil
November	nil	2	1
December	nil	2	1
	99	625	78

OFFICERS.

1917.

Jan. 2.	2nd Lieut. T. G. Brown	Accidentally wounded.
Jan. 19.	2nd Lieut. J. Dunn	Wounded.
Jan. 26.	2nd Lieut. J. A. Symon	Wounded.
Jan. 26.	2nd Lieut. T. Orr	Suffering from burns.
March 16.	2nd Lieut. D. F. Suttie	Wounded.
April 4.	2nd Lieut. T. D. G. Watt	Wounded.
April 8.	2nd Lieut. D. Moir, M.C.	Wounded.
April 9-11.	2nd Lieut. R. W. B. Semple, M.C.	Killed.
	2nd Lieut. G. R. Morton, M.C.	Killed.
	2nd Lieut. D. G. Jenkins	Killed.

1917.

April 9-11.	2nd Lieut. J. S. Ronaldson	Killed.
	2nd Lieut. J. F. Smith	Killed.
	2nd Lieut. D. F. Suttie	Wounded.
	2nd Lieut. T. D. G. Watt	Wounded.
	Capt. G. A. C. Davy	Wounded.
	Lieut. S. C. Russell	Wounded.
	2nd Lieut. J. A. Symon	Wounded.
	2nd Lieut. T. G. Brown	Wounded.
	2nd Lieut. J. K. M'Millan	Wounded.
	2nd Lieut. E. W. Forrest	Wounded.
	2nd Lieut. C. J. Coventry	Wounded.
April 23-28.	Capt. W. G. S. Stuart, M.C.	Killed.
	2nd Lieut. G. Lambert	Killed.
	2nd Lieut. H. P. W. Walker	Killed.
	2nd Lieut. M. S. Mackay	Killed.
	Lieut. J. Finlay	Wounded.
	2nd Lieut. A. Macniven	Died of wounds.
	2nd Lieut. W. L. M. Kay	Wounded.
	2nd Lieut. A. Fraser	Wounded.
July 6.	Capt. T. C. Boyd	Wounded.
July 6.	2nd Lieut. T. A. Begbie	Wounded.
Aug. 1.	2nd Lieut. H. S. Deans	Wounded.
Aug. 1.	2nd Lieut. T. A. Begbie	Wounded.
Aug. 1.	2nd Lieut. J. Miller	Wounded.
Aug. 1.	2nd Lieut. J. W. MacKay	Wounded (died of wounds, 20th).
Aug. 1.	2nd Lieut. J. Moran	Wounded.
Aug. 1.	Capt. J. A. Symon	Wounded.
Aug. 2.	2nd Lieut. J. Lamont	Wounded.
Aug. 6.	2nd Lieut. T. A. S. Elliot	Died of wounds.
Aug. 13.	Major A. Irving	Accidentally wounded.
Aug. 22.	Capt. Rev. W. B. T. Black, C.F.	Killed.
Aug. 22.	Capt. J. M'Culloch	Killed.
Aug. 22.	Lieut. W. Young	Killed.
Aug. 22.	2nd Lieut. J. A. Sabiston	Killed.
Aug. 22.	Capt. J. L. C. Jenkins	Wounded.
Aug. 22.	2nd Lieut. C. R. G. Scott	Wounded.
Aug. 22.	2nd Lieut. J. T. Macdonald	Wounded.
Aug. 22.	2nd Lieut. R. Jardine	Wounded.
Aug. 22.	2nd Lieut. C. Courtney	Wounded.
Oct. 17.	2nd Lieut. A. Chisholm	Killed.
Oct. 17.	2nd Lieut. E. D. Hoskin	Killed.

OTHER RANKS.

	1917.	*Killed.*	*Wounded.*	*Missing.*
	January . .	6	22*	3
	February . .	nil	nil	nil
	March . . .	10	57	1
	April . . .	3	17	1
Battles of Arras	April 9-11 . .	44	240	52
Battles of Arras	April 23-28 . .	78	252†	42
	July 1-28 . .	9	37	2
Battles of Ypres	July 31 to Aug. 4	16	251	47
Battles of Ypres	Aug. 5-31 . .	8	134	59
	September . .	4	6	nil
	October . .	4	10	7
	November . .	1	12	nil
	December . .	1	7	nil
		184	1045	214

* Includes 4 "suffering from burns."

† No other figures in Battalion, Brigade, Divisional, or "Q" Diaries.

OFFICERS.

1918.		
March 8.	2nd Lieut. T. Gidden	Wounded.
March 21.	2nd Lieut. S. S. Gemmell . .	Killed.
March 28.	2nd Lieut. J. N. Finlay . .	Killed.
March 28.	2nd Lieut. T. S. Denholm . .	Killed.
March 28.	2nd Lieut. H. R. Rennie . .	Killed.
March 28.	2nd Lieut. M. N. M'Indeor . .	Wounded.
March 28.	2nd Lieut. J. M'Murray . .	Wounded.
March 28.	2nd Lieut. A. R. Macdonald, M.C.	Wounded and missing.
March 28.	2nd Lieut. W. J. Grieve . .	Wounded and missing.
March 28.	2nd Lieut. J. A. Donald . .	Wounded and missing.
March 28.	Capt. A. C. Bateman, M.C., R.A.M.C.	Wounded and missing.
March 28.	Capt. D. T. Milne	Wounded and missing.
March 28.	2nd Lieut. J. S. M'Nab . .	Wounded and missing.
March 28.	2nd Lieut. P. Drummond . .	Wounded and missing.
March 28.	2nd Lieut. R. Smith . . .	Wounded and missing.
March 28.	2nd Lieut. W. Muirhead . .	Wounded and missing.
March 28.	2nd Lieut. L. Macleod . . .	Wounded, believed prisoner.
March 28.	Lieut. E. J. G. Gibb, M.C. . .	Wounded.
April 8.	Capt. J. D. E. M'Cracken . .	Wounded.
May 3.	2nd Lieut. D. M. B. White . .	Wounded.
June 1.	Lieut. G. Wedderspoon . .	Wounded.
June 1.	Capt. R. B. Purdon, M.C. . .	Wounded.
June 5.	Lieut. N. S. Sim, M.C. . .	Wounded.

OTHER RANKS.

1918.	Killed.	Wounded.	Missing.
February	nil	7	nil
March 1-21	3	20	nil
March 21-28	10	154	352
April	nil	7	nil
May	nil	8	nil
	13	196	352

44TH MACHINE-GUN COMPANY.

OFFICERS.

1916.

July 7. 2nd Lieut. A. T. Rayner . . . . Died of wounds.
Aug. 19. 2nd Lieut. A. V. L. Hadaway . . Wounded.
Nov. 25. 2nd Lieut. F. C. Gibb . . . . Wounded (accidentally).

OTHER RANKS.

1916.	Killed.	Wounded.	Missing.
April	nil	7	nil
May	1	1	nil
June	nil	1	nil
July	nil	1	nil
August	11	44	nil
September	1	10	1
October	1	10	2
December	nil	1	nil
	3	75	3

OFFICERS.

1917.

Jan. 19. 2nd Lieut. C. J. Swatbridge . . . . . . Wounded.

Battles of Arras.

April 9-11. Major C. King . . . . Killed.
April 25. 2nd Lieut. Ground . . . . Killed.

Battles of Ypres.

July 29 to Aug. 4. 2nd Lieut. Schloss . . . . . Killed (July 31).
July 29 to Aug. 4. 2nd Lieut. Brown . . . . . Killed (July 31).
Aug. 21. 2nd Lieut. Erskine . . . . . Wounded.

OTHER RANKS.

1917.		Killed.	Wounded.	Missing.
Battles of Arras	April	nil	nil	1
		1	8	nil
	July	1	5	nil
Battles of Ypres	July 29 to Aug. 4	8	26	nil
	Aug. 5-31	3	22	4
		13	61	5

44TH INFANTRY BRIGADE SIGNAL SECTION HEADQUARTERS.

Battles of Arras, April 9-11.

	Killed.	Wounded.
Other ranks	2	3

44TH INFANTRY BRIGADE TRENCH-MORTAR BATTERY.

1915.	Killed.	Wounded.	Missing.
	nil	1	nil
1916.			
June	nil	1	nil
August	1	nil	nil
	1	1	nil

1918.

2nd Lieut. N. S. Knox . . . . Missing.
Lieut. E. J. G. Gibb . . . . Missing.

OTHER RANKS.

	Killed.	Wounded.	Missing.
March 28	2	14	49

44TH INFANTRY BRIGADE HEADQUARTERS.

1916.

Sept. 18. Interpreter A. Bonsergent . . . . . . Wounded.

45TH INFANTRY BRIGADE CASUALTIES.

13TH ROYAL SCOTS.

BATTLE OF LOOS.

OFFICERS.

Killed.	*Wounded.*	*Wounded and Missing.*
Major G. D. Macpherson.	Lt.-Col. Maclear, D.S.O.	Lt. R. A. Macfarlane.
Capt. I. C. Penney.	Capt. J. H. Glover.	
Capt. G. S. Robertson.	Capt. and Adjutant K. G. Buchanan.	
Capt. B. D. Bruce.	Lt. R. J. M. Christie.	
Lt. C. B. Munro.	Lt. H. J. Underwood.	
2nd Lt. D. D. Brown.	2nd Lt. H. M. Scott.	
	2nd Lt. G. V. Faithfull Davies.	
	2nd Lt. H. G. Crowden.	
	2nd Lt. K. G. M'L. Bramwell.	

OFFICERS.

1915.

Sept. 14.	Capt. M. Halcrow	Wounded.
Sept. 14.	Lieut. A. E. Considine	Wounded.
Nov. 3.	2nd Lieut. G. Barnett	Killed.

OTHER RANKS.

	Killed.	*Wounded.*	*Missing.*
Battle of Loos	37	228	105
Aug.-Dec. 1915	18	98	1

OFFICERS.

1916.

Jan. 26.	2nd Lieut. J. W. F. Neill	Wounded.
Mar. 16.	Lieut.-Colonel H. Maclear	Killed.
May 4.	2nd Lieut. W. M. Martin	Wounded.
May 6	2nd Lieut. J. Crabbe	Died of wounds.
May 11.	Lieut.-Colonel R. B. C. Raban	Killed.

1916.

May 11.	Major H. F. M. Worthington-Wilmer	Killed.
May 11.	Capt. C. W. Yule	Killed.
May 11.	Capt. A. M. Macdonald	Killed.
May 11.	Capt. A. C. A. Jekyll, R.A.M.C.	Killed.
May 11.	Capt. I. A. G. Ferguson	Killed.
May 11.	Capt. and Adjutant C. T. Francis	Wounded.
May 11.	Lieut. M. Halcrow	Wounded.
May 11.	2nd Lieut. A. Wemyss	Wounded.
May 11.	2nd Lieut. A. Linton	Wounded.
May 11.	2nd Lieut. L. D. K. Collins	Missing.
May 12.	2nd Lieut. A. Taylor Sim	Killed.
May 13.	Major D. M. Tomlinson	Died of wounds.
May 31.	2nd Lieut. D. M. Miller	Wounded.
June 27.	2nd Lieut. J. K. Wylie	Wounded.
June 28.	Lieut. R. C. A. Appleby	Died of wounds.
June 28.	2nd Lieut. L. R. C. Ferguson	Wounded.
June 28.	2nd Lieut. F. Tingle	Wounded.
June 28.	2nd Lieut. J. R. M'Lennan	Wounded.
June 28.	2nd Lieut. J. T. Glover	Wounded.
July 1.	Capt. H. S. E. Stevens	Wounded.
July 2.	2nd Lieut. J. R. Mitchell	Wounded.
July 12.	2nd Lieut. R. Armstrong	Wounded.
Aug. 12.	2nd Lieut. S. Burrows	Wounded.
Aug. 19.	2nd Lieut. A. Fulton	Killed.
Aug. 21.	2nd Lieut. Smith	Wounded.
Aug. 27.	Capt. P. Tanner	Wounded.
Aug. 27.	2nd Lieut. Buchanan	Wounded.
Aug. 29.	Lieut. C. H. Jardine	Wounded.
Sept. 2.	2nd Lieut. R. F. Scott	Wounded.
Sept. 15.	Capt. R. J. M. Christie	Wounded.
Sept. 15.	Lieut. C. H. Jardine	Wounded.
Sept. 15.	Capt. M. C. Fitch	Wounded.
Sept. 15.	2nd Lieut. T. Smith	Wounded.
Sept. 15.	2nd Lieut. W. Cowie	Wounded.
Sept. 15.	2nd Lieut. J. Ogston	Wounded.
Sept. 15.	2nd Lieut. R. Gellatly	Wounded.
Sept. 15.	2nd Lieut. W. R. Lawrie	Wounded.
Sept. 15.	2nd Lieut. G. H. Berry	Wounded.
Sept. 16.	2nd Lieut. J. J. Fenwick	Missing.
Sept. 17.	2nd Lieut. J. F. G. Turner	Wounded.
Sept. 17.	2nd Lieut. A. Brown	Wounded.
Oct. 9.	2nd Lieut. A. Brown	Shell shock.
Oct. 16.	2nd Lieut. W. D. Howat	Accidentally wounded.
Dec. 28.	2nd Lieut. A. Young	Killed.

OTHER RANKS.

1916.	Killed.	Wounded.	Missing.	Died of Wounds.
January	5	29	nil	nil
February	nil	17	nil	nil
March	5	18	nil	nil
April	nil	2	nil	nil
May	29	133	161	nil
June	10	74	nil	nil
July	4	35	1	nil
August	26	85	3	nil
September	33	171	95	nil
October	12	58	nil	nil
November	nil	2	nil	nil
December	nil	10	nil	1
	225	634	260	1

OFFICERS.

1917.		
Jan. 22.	2nd Lieut. H. F. S. Lowery	Wounded.
April 9-11.	2nd Lieut. F. C. Buchanan	Killed.
	2nd Lieut. G. L. Stewart	Killed.
	2nd Lieut. D. S. Fraser	Wounded.
	Capt. J. A. Turner	Wounded.
	Capt. A. J. Simpson	Wounded.
	Capt. T. Brydone	Wounded.
	2nd Lieut. H. F. S. Lowery	Wounded.
	2nd Lieut. N. Fyfe	Wounded.
	2nd Lieut. C. M. Coutts	Wounded.
	2nd Lieut. W. B. Easton	Wounded.
	2nd Lieut. J. C. Howie	Wounded.
April 21-30.	Lieut. J. C. Kincaid	Killed.
	Lieut. R. T. Adamson	Killed.
	2nd Lieut. W. K. M. Spense	Killed.
	2nd Lieut. J. F. Scott	Killed.
	2nd Lieut. D. R. Cromb	Killed.
	2nd Lieut. A. A. Farquharson	Wounded.
	2nd Lieut. E. W. Fleming	Wounded.
	2nd Lieut. W. D. Woodrow	Wounded.
	2nd Lieut. G. M. Kydd	Wounded.
	Lieut. G. V. F. Davies	Missing.
	2nd Lieut. R. Mungall	Missing.
	2nd Lieut. K. G. Maclachan	Missing.

1917.		
April 21-30.	2nd Lieut. C. Hoyle Smith	Missing.
	2nd Lieut. E. T. Salveson	Missing.
	2nd Lieut. R. Gellatly	Missing.
July 31.	2nd Lieut. D. Robertson	Killed.
July 31.	Capt. J. F. G. Turner	Wounded
July 31.	2nd Lieut. G. M. Kydd	Wounded.
July 31.	2nd Lieut. J. R. Gall	Wounded.
July 31.	2nd Lieut. G. E. Curry	Wounded.
Aug. 1.	Capt. J. Hastie Logan	Killed.
Aug. 1.	Capt. R. J. M. Christie	Wounded
Aug. 1.	2nd Lieut. J. S. Aitken	Wounded and missing
Aug. 1.	2nd Lieut. G. Dobbie	Missing.
Aug. 1.	2nd Lieut. C. W. Guthrie	Missing.
Aug. 1.	2nd Lieut. W. T. Low	Missing.
Aug. 1.	2nd Lieut. J. Gibson	Missing.
Aug. 1.	Lieut. J. Rickards, M.C.	Missing.
Aug. 22.	Lieut. A. T. Long	Killed.
Aug. 22.	2nd Lieut. B. Hanley	Killed.
Aug. 22.	2nd Lieut. R. C. Hutton	Killed.
Aug. 22.	2nd Lieut. W. A. Henderson, M.C.	Wounded.
Aug. 22.	2nd Lieut. F. A. Baker	Wounded.
Aug. 22.	2nd Lieut. J. Cavers	Wounded.
Aug. 22.	2nd Lieut. G. A. F. Renwick	Wounded.
Aug. 22.	2nd Lieut. T. W. Benson	Missing.
Aug. 22.	2nd Lieut. W. M. Martin	Missing.
Aug. 23.	Capt. A. H. Hargreaves (R.A.M.C.)	Wounded.
Aug. 27.	2nd Lieut. J. H. Byres	Killed.

OTHER RANKS.

	1917.	*Killed.*	*Wounded.*	*Missing.*	*Wounded and Missing.*
	January	nil	16	nil	nil
	April	1	16	nil	nil
Battles of Arras	April 9-11	29	191	8	nil
	April 19-25	21	160	71	nil
	July	7	41	nil	nil
Battles of Ypres	July 29 to Aug. 4	14	149	183	6
	August 5-31	18	167	125	nil
	September	1	3	nil	nil
	October	nil	nil	nil	nil
	November	8	12	nil	nil
	December	2	13	nil	nil
		101	768	387	6

OFFICERS.

1918.		
March 25.	2nd Lieut. C. G. L. Hodgson	Wounded
March 28.	2nd Lieut. D. Forbes	Killed.
March 28.	2nd Lieut. K. Maclean	Killed.
March 28.	2nd Lieut. J. R. Mitchell	Wounded and missing.
March 28.	2nd Lieut. A. A. Farquharson	Missing.
March 28.	2nd Lieut. H. Higgins	Missing.
March 28.	2nd Lieut. J. S. M'Gregor	Missing.
March 28.	2nd Lieut. L. W. Guthrie	Missing.
March 28.	2nd Lieut. J. Hobbs	Missing.
March 28.	2nd Lieut. S. C. Cumming	Missing.
March 28.	2nd Lieut. W. A. Mathieson	Missing.
May 11.	Lieut. J. Davie, M.C.	Killed.
May 16.	2nd Lieut. T. Smith	Missing.
June 9.	Capt. J. Kelly, M.C.	Wounded.
June 21.	2nd Lieut. W. A. West, M.C.	Killed.
June 21.	2nd Lieut. J. E. Fearby	Wounded.
June 21.	2nd Lieut. K. Paterson	Wounded.
July 22.	Capt. A. H. Craig, D.S.O., M.C.	Wounded.
July 26.	Lieut.-Colonel J. A. Turner, D.S.O., M.C.	Killed.
July 26.	Lieut. J. D. Shaw	Killed.
Aug. 1	2nd Lieut. A. Lindsay	Wounded.
Sept. 13.	2nd Lieut. R. Louden	Killed.
Sept. 15.	2nd Lieut. W. F. Forsyth	Killed.
Sept. 15.	2nd Lieut. H. Watson	Wounded.
Oct. 6.	2nd Lieut. N. P. Manning	Killed.

OTHER RANKS.

1918.	*Killed.*	*Wounded.*	*Missing.*	*Died of Wounds.*
January	nil	nil	nil	nil
February	nil	11	nil	nil
March	2	26	nil	1
March 28	5	140	230	1
April	nil	23	nil	nil
May	9	33	1	nil
June	5	30	4	nil
July	6	50	nil	nil
August	26	71	9	3
September	23	113	7	nil
October	5	30	13	nil
November	nil	nil	nil	nil
	81	527	264	5

7TH ROYAL SCOTS FUSILIERS.

BATTLE OF LOOS.

OFFICERS.

Killed.	*Wounded.*
Capt. F. G. Burr.	Major W. L. Campbell.
Capt. E. G. Moyna.	Capt. A. W. Ferguson.
Lt. F. T. Hay.	Capt. A. V. Baker, M.C.
2nd Lt. G. S. Sharer.	Capt. G. H. M. Mair.
2nd Lt. J. E. Watson.	Capt. and Adjutant J. W. Nesbitt.
Major F. P. Skipwith.	Lt. P. R. N. Carleton.
2nd Lt. R. T. Stewart.	Lt. N. J. A. L. Prinsep.
	Lt. J. C. Glanville.
	Capt. J. Gardner, M.C.
	Lt. R. R. M'Queen.
	2nd Lt. C. M'K. M'Gavin.
	2nd Lt. W. J. Cuthbert.

1915.		
Aug. 7.	Lieut.-Colonel A. H. Allenby	Killed.
Aug. 10.	Lieut. Harris (R.A.M.C.)	Died of wounds.
Aug. 17.	Capt. W. Stavers	Wounded.
Aug. 15.	Lieut. L. C. Powell	Wounded.
Sept. 7.	Lieut. Garvin	Wounded.
Nov. 11.	2nd Lieut. R. H. Lockhart	Killed.
Nov. 22.	2nd Lieut. E. C. Black	Killed.
Nov. 26.	2nd Lieut. J. D. Purdie	Wounded.

OTHER RANKS.

	Killed.	*Wounded.*	*Missing.*
Aug.-Dec. 1915	19	39	nil
Battle of Loos	63	246	83

OFFICERS.

1916.		
Mar.	Capt. W. K. Kelso	Wounded.
May 12.	2nd Lieut. R. T. Steedman	Wounded.
May 12.	2nd Lieut. T. Watson	Wounded.
May 12.	2nd Lieut. J. B. Cooper	Wounded.
May 12.	2nd Lieut. A. Allan	Wounded.
May 15.	Capt. R. R. Macqueen	Killed.
May 15.	2nd Lieut. J. J. Scandrett	Killed.

1916.		
May 29.	Lieut. A. C. M. Gordon	Wounded.
June 4.	Lieut. A. C. M. Gordon	Wounded.
June 28.	2nd Lieut. J. Laurie	Wounded.
June.	2nd Lieut. A. W. Mackenzie	Wounded.
July 4.	2nd Lieut. W. B. Hodge	Wounded.
Aug. 12.	2nd Lieut. R. Warnock	Killed.
Aug. 12.	2nd Lieut. D. Kerr	Killed.
Aug. 12.	Capt. J. B. Foulkes	Killed.
Aug. 12.	2nd Lieut. W. Nicolson	Wounded.
Aug. 12.	Lieut. A. Dingwall	Wounded.
Aug. 12.	2nd Lieut. M. H. Jones	Wounded.
Aug. 12.	2nd Lieut. A. D. Austen	Wounded.
Aug. 12.	2nd Lieut. R. B. Strang	Died of wounds.
Aug. 12.	2nd Lieut. R. C. Hackstoun	Wounded.
Aug. 12.	Lieut. Fairlie	Wounded.
Aug. 13.	2nd Lieut. A. L. Carr	Wounded and missing.
Aug. 13.	2nd Lieut. R. E. Jackston	Wounded.
Aug. 13.	2nd Lieut. J. F. Mackie	Wounded.
Aug. 13.	2nd Lieut. T. Hutcheon	Died of wounds.
Aug. 14.	2nd Lieut. E. E. Griffin	Wounded.
Aug. 31.	2nd Lieut. T. Watson	Wounded.
Sept. 2.	2nd Lieut. J. H. Stubbs	Wounded.
Sept. 15.	2nd Lieut. M. Wallace	Wounded.
Sept. 15.	Lieut. J. D. Purdie (att. 45th M.G.C.)	Wounded.
Sept. 15.	2nd Lieut. J. Fenwick	Missing.
Sept. 16.	2nd Lieut. J. T. Wotherspoon	Wounded.
Sept. 16.	Lieut. J. I. Morrison (att. 45th M.G.C.)	Wounded.
Oct. 13.	2nd Lieut. W. D. Goodall	Wounded.

OTHER RANKS.

1916.	*Killed.*	*Wounded.*	*Missing.*
January	2	16	nil
February	16	21	nil
March	3	23	nil
April	nil	nil	nil
May	22	244	21
June	10	84	nil
July	3	56	2
August	54	218	nil
September	7	150	22
October	10	54	10
November	nil	nil	nil
December	4	26	nil
	131	892	55

OFFICERS.

1917.		
Jan. 23.	Major T. Smith	Died of wounds.
Jan. 23.	2nd Lieut. R. A. Clark	Wounded.
Jan. 24.	2nd Lieut. A. Stiven	Killed.
Jan. 28.	2nd Lieut. T. K. Stevenson (att. 45th T.-M.B.)	Killed.
Jan. 31.	2nd Lieut. J. Carnan	Wounded.
Feb. 1.	2nd Lieut. W. S. Hamilton	Wounded.
March 1.	2nd Lieut. A. C. M. Gordon	Died of wounds.
March 17	2nd Lieut. A. G. Moore	Died of wounds.
April 5.	2nd Lieut. A. J. Johnstone	Killed.
April 7.	2nd Lieut. D. Scott	Killed.
April 8.	2nd Lieut. W. G. Austin	Wounded.
April 8.	2nd Lieut. J. P. Seward	Wounded.
April 9.	Lieut. A. E. Buchan	Died of wounds.
April 9.	2nd Lieut. W. M'Ghee	Killed.
April 9.	Capt. A. P. Skeil, M.C.	Wounded.
April 9.	Lieut. J. M'Cosh	Wounded.
April 9.	Lieut. L. A. Wheatley	Wounded.
April 9.	Lieut. Traunson	Wounded.
April 11.	Capt. T. Watson	Killed.
April 11.	2nd Lieut. J. W. Whitelaw	Killed.
April 13.	2nd Lieut. A. D. Monro	Wounded.
April 23.	2nd Lieut. J. S. Smith	Wounded.
May 6.	Capt. J. F. Fisher	Died of wounds.
July 15.	2nd Lieut. N. W. Robertson	Wounded.
July 18.	2nd Lieut. T. J. Ronald	Wounded.
July 20.	Lieut. and Q.M. E. W. Carpenter	Wounded.
July 31.	Capt. W. E. Paul	Killed.
July 31.	2nd Lieut. E. B. Sykes	Killed.
Aug. 22.	2nd Lieut. D. Simpson	Wounded.
August.	Lieut. G. Coghill	Wounded.
	Lieut. F. Coghill	Wounded.
	Lieut. Fraser	Wounded.
	Lieut. Blain	Wounded.
	Lieut. Cunningham	Wounded.
	Lieut. A. Nimmo	Wounded.
Sept. 27.	Capt. J. Gardner, M.C.	Died of wounds.

6/7TH ROYAL SCOTS FUSILIERS.

1917.	*Killed.*	*Wounded.*	*Missing.*
April 9-11—			
Officers	3	11	1
Other ranks	26	238	32

1917.	Killed.	Wounded.	Missing.
April 19-25—			
Officers	nil	4	nil
Other ranks	23	99	26
July 29 to August 1—			
Officers	2	10	nil
Other ranks	43	205	28
August 5-31—			
Officers	nil	6	1
Other ranks	27	159	33
Other Ranks—			
September	4	16	nil
October	2	6	7
November	3	24	nil
December	1	18	nil

OFFICERS.

1918.

March 21.	Capt. A. S. Dixon	Wounded.
March 21.	2nd Lieut. H. M. Muir	Wounded.
March 21.	2nd Lieut. N. W. Robertson	Wounded.
March 21.	2nd Lieut. C. P. Crockett	Wounded.
March 22.	Capt. W. R. Hutchison	Killed.
March 22.	2nd Lieut. W. T. Gooding	Killed.
March 22.	2nd Lieut. A. Weir	Killed.
April 11.	Lieut. W. H. Phimister	Wounded.

6TH CAMERON HIGHLANDERS.

BATTLE OF LOOS.

OFFICERS.

1915.

Killed.	*Wounded.*	*Gassed.*
Lt.-Col. A. F. Douglas Hamilton.	Capt. A. J. Campbell Colquhoun.	2nd Lt. H. Leitch
Capt. and Adj. H. W. Milne (74th Punjabis).	Lt. A. F. P. Christison.	
Capt. H. Antrobus.	Lt. D. C. Heron Watson.	
Capt. E. G. Macdougall.	Lt. T. H. Macdonald.	
Capt. F. J. Maccunn.	2nd Lt. G. F. Cameron.	
Lt. D. C. D. Macmaster.	2nd Lt. J. M. Mackintosh.	
Lt. R. D. Cameron.	2nd Lt. J. Pringle Thomson.	
2nd Lt. K. Biggar.	2nd Lt. P. M'Diarmid	

OTHER RANKS.

	Killed.	*Died of Wounds.*	*Wounded.*	*Missing.*
Battle of Loos, 1915 .	30	nil	270	70
Aug.-Dec. 1915 . .	15	1	48	nil

OFFICERS.

1916.		
Jan.	Lieut. Sir A. A. Ava Campbell, Bart. . .	Wounded.
Feb. 9.	2nd Lieut. Robinson	Wounded (at duty).
Feb. 28.	Capt. H. S. Walker	Missing.
March 3.	Capt. H. B. Rowan	Wounded.
March 6.	2nd Lieut. J. Keir, 12th Scottish Rifles (attached)	Wounded.
March 15.	Lieut.-Col. H. Maclear	Killed.
May 9.	Lieut. Sir A. A. Ava Campbell, Bart. . .	Killed.
May 12.	2nd Lieut. H. A. Young	Wounded.
June 28.	2nd Lieut. J. W. Borthwick	Wounded.
June 30.	2nd Lieut. L. M'Kinnon	Killed.
June.	2nd Lieut. H. T. R. Kerr	Died.
July 1.	2nd Lieut. J. M'Callum	Wounded.
July 17.	2nd Lieut. W. T. Mackie	Wounded.
July 19.	2nd Lieut. J. Crawford	Killed.
July 20.	2nd Lieut. A. H. Kinnear	Wounded.
Aug. 11.	2nd Lieut. M. M'Intyre	Wounded.
Aug. 11.	2nd Lieut. H. G. Gerry	Wounded.
Aug. 13.	2nd Lieut. T. J. C. Crawford	Wounded.
Aug. 13.	2nd Lieut. J. Morrison	Wounded.
Aug. 15.	Lieut. J. Pringle Thomson	Died of wounds.
Aug. 24.	2nd Lieut. R. D. Marshall	Wounded.
Aug. 31.	2nd Lieut. W. D. Hay	Wounded.
Sept. 2.	Major J. E. M. Farquhar	Wounded.
Sept. 4.	Lieut. J. Garrick	Wounded.
Sept. 15.	Major J. E. M. Farquhar	Killed.
Sept. 15.	2nd Lieut. C. Newton	Killed.
Sept. 15.	2nd Lieut. J. M'Callum	Killed.
Sept. 15.	Capt. A. R. Lovelock	Wounded.
Sept. 15.	Lieut. D. M'D. Currie	Wounded.
Sept. 15.	2nd Lieut. T. M. M'Leod	Wounded.
Sept. 15.	2nd Lieut. A. D. M'Phee	Wounded.
Sept. 15.	2nd Lieut. T. Ness	Wounded.
Sept. 16.	2nd Lieut. R. Simpson	Wounded.
Sept. 21.	2nd Lieut. M. M'Intyre	Died of wounds.
Oct. 13.	2nd Lieut. D. Maclean	Died of wounds.
Oct. 31.	2nd Lieut. G. Hamilton . . .	Wounded (at duty).

OTHER RANKS.

1916.	*Killed.*	*Wounded.*	*Missing.*
January	3	35	nil
February	2	6	nil
March	1	19	nil
April	nil	16	nil
May	4	14	nil
June	18	94	nil
July	10	31	nil
August	37	125	11
September	34	213	21
October	22	83	2
November	nil	nil	nil
December	1	4	nil
	132	640	34

OFFICERS.

1917.		
Jan. 19.	2nd Lieut. Guthrie	Wounded.
March 11.	2nd Lieut. W. Cameron	Wounded.
March 13.	2nd Lieut. J. W. Thorburn	Died of wounds.
April 3.	2nd Lieut. M'Gregor	Wounded.
April 9-11.	2nd Lieut. W. M. Cameron	Killed.
	2nd Lieut. C. S. Cameron	Killed.
	2nd Lieut. A. Carmichael	Killed.
	2nd Lieut. D. Ross	Killed.
	2nd Lieut. V. Begbie	Killed.
	Capt. N. Morrison	Wounded.
	2nd Lieut. Jones	Wounded.
	2nd Lieut. J. Cleland	Wounded.
	2nd Lieut. W. D. Hay	Wounded.
	2nd Lieut. C. C. Paterson	Killed.
	2nd Lieut. S. S. Cameron	Wounded.
	2nd Lieut. J. G. Ferguson	Wounded.
	2nd Lieut. F. S. Sandeman	Wounded.
April 23-28.	Capt. Mackie	Wounded.
	Lieut. Moffatt	Wounded.
	2nd Lieut. Alexander	Wounded.
	2nd Lieut. Guthrie	Wounded.

1917.		
April 23-28	2nd Lieut. Mitchell	Wounded.
	2nd Lieut. M'Glennan	Wounded.
July 13.	Capt. Baird	Gassed.
July 13.	Capt. Ruthven	Gassed.
July 13.	2nd Lieut. Hunt	Gassed.
July 13.	2nd Lieut. A. H. Kinnear	Died of wounds.
July 13.	2nd Lieut. M'Kinnon	Gassed.
July 16.	2nd Lieut. M'Leod	Wounded.
July 31 to Aug. 1.	Lieut.-Col. J. C. Russell, D.S.O.	Killed.
	Lieut. and Adjutant J. Carrick	Killed.
	Capt. J. Hislop, M.C.	Killed.
	Capt. C. K. Carruthers	Killed.
	2nd Lieut. W. C. Donald	Killed.
	2nd Lieut A. L. Baxter	Killed.
	Capt. R. W. S. Kellie, C.F.	Killed.
	Capt. W. E. David	Wounded.
	2nd Lieut. F. Turner	Wounded.
	2nd Lieut. H. M. M'Corquodale	Wounded.
	2nd Lieut. M. M'Lean	Wounded.
	2nd Lieut. A. C. M'Kair	Wounded.
	2nd Lieut. J. R. M'Kay	Missing.
	2nd Lieut. F. S. Sandeman, M.C.	Missing.
	2nd Lieut. A. G. M'Gruer, M.C.	Missing.
	2nd Lieut. G. Hamilton	Wounded and missing.
Aug. 22-29.	Capt. R. D. Wylie	Killed.
	Lieut. D. G. Macpherson	Wounded.
	2nd Lieut. A. Snaddon	Wounded.
	2nd Lieut. J. Cameron	Wounded.
Aug. 31.	2nd Lieut. J. C. Watson	Died of wounds.
Oct. 12.	2nd Lieut. J. G. Gibson	Killed.
Oct. 27	2nd Lieut. R. Murray	Died of wounds.
Oct. 30.	2nd Lieut. W. J. Patterson	Died of wounds.
Nov. 19.	2nd Lieut. W. P. M'Gregor	Wounded.
Nov. 30.	Capt. J. Wilson, M.C.	Killed.
Nov. 30.	2nd Lieut. T. W. M'Callum	Wounded.
Dec. 18.	2nd Lieut. C. G. Reid	Wounded.

OTHER RANKS.

	1917.	Killed.	Wounded.	Missing.	Gassed.
	January	8	17	nil	nil
	February	3	36	nil	nil
	March	2	10	nil	nil
	April	8	5	nil	nil
Battles of Arras	April 9-11	37	187	34	nil
	April 21-30	21	79	34	nil
	July	1	29	nil	114
Battles of Ypres	July 1 to Aug. 4	19	145	108	nil
	Aug. 22-29	11	99	nil	nil
	September	7	13	nil	nil
	October	nil	10	7	nil
	November	3	31	1	nil
	December	nil	16	nil	nil
		120	677	184	114

1918. OFFICERS.

March 11.	2nd Lieut. J. Miller, M.C.	Killed.
March 28.	Capt. I. Mackay	Killed.
March 28.	2nd Lieut. J. W. Docherty	Missing.
March 28.	2nd Lieut. A. Milligan	Wounded and missing.
March 28.	Capt. D. T. Milne	Killed.
April 19.	Capt. A. Fraser, M.C.	Died of wounds.
May 25.	2nd Lieut. Coutts	Wounded.
July 23.	Lieut. D. Noble	Wounded.
July 23.	Lieut. J. R. Macmillan	Wounded.
July 23.	2nd Lieut. R. C. Mitchell	Wounded.
July 23.	2nd Lieut. A. N. Blair	Wounded.
July 23.	Capt. R. K. Drummond, M.C.	Wounded.
July 23.	Lieut. G. O. Grein, R.A.M.C.	Wounded.
July 24.	2nd Lieut. R. C. Mitchell	Died of wounds.
July 25.	Capt. J. B. Park, M.C.	Wounded.
July 26.	Capt. H. C. Gundall, M.C.	Gassed.
July 26.	Capt. R. P. Fraser	Gassed.
July 26.	Lieut. R. L. Hamilton	Gassed.
July 26.	Lieut. M. G. Shaw	Gassed.
July 26.	Lieut. J. G. Telford	Gassed.
July 26.	Lieut. E. P. B. Cameron	Gassed.
July 26.	2nd Lieut. F. Turner	Gassed.
July 26.	2nd Lieut. A. King	Gassed.
July 26.	2nd Lieut. S. E. Smith, M.C.	Gassed.

1918.		
July 29.	2nd Lieut. J. M. T. Taylor	Gassed.
July 31.	2nd Lieut. M. J. H. Wilson	Gassed.
Aug 1.	2nd Lieut. J. L. Grey	Killed.
Sept. 3.	2nd Lieut. J. P. Cran	Gassed.
Sept. 3.	Lieut. R. R. Marshall	Gassed.
Sept. 3.	Lieut. R. R. Anderson	Gassed.
Sept. 15.	2nd Lieut. J. Turnbull	Wounded.
Sept. 16.	2nd Lieut. A. P. C. Hannay	Gassed.
Sept. 18.	2nd Lieut. D. H. M. Jack	Wounded.
Sept. 30.	2nd Lieut. F. H. Macbeth	Wounded.
Oct. 4.	Lieut. S. A. Luen	Wounded.

OTHER RANKS.

	Killed.	*Wounded.*	*Missing.*	*Gassed.*
January	nil	nil	nil	nil
February	2	3	nil	nil
March	8	61	30	nil
March 28-31	nil	nil	278 casualties	
March 28	nil	nil	272 casualties	
April	5	25	nil	nil
May	6	37	37	nil
June	nil	3	nil	13
July	25	108	22	37
August	14	32	nil	nil
September	10	55	3	71
October	6	31	1	1
November	nil	nil	nil	nil
	76	355	93	112

11TH A. & S. HIGHLANDERS.

BATTLE OF LOOS.

OFFICERS.

Killed.	*Wounded.*	*Wounded and Missing.*
Capt. W. M'L. M'Millan.	Maj. W. Macalister Hall.	2nd Lt. A. A. Richardson.
Capt. M. M'Lennan.	Capt. W. H. Alston.	
Lt. W. D. Deas.	Lt. D. E. O. Jackson.	
Lt. G. Jackson.	Lt. R. R. Langtry (died of wounds).	
Lt. A. C. Frost.	2nd Lt. A. H. St Clair.	
2nd Lt. W. M. Dickson.		

OFFICERS

1915.		
Nov. 9.	Lieut. F. C. Wilkinson	" Shock."
Nov. 24.	2nd Lieut. D. M. Sutthery	Wounded.
Nov. 25.	2nd Lieut. Sieber	Wounded.

OTHER RANKS.

	Killed.	*Wounded.*	*Wounded and Missing.*
Battle of Loos, 1915	36	211	64
Aug.-Dec. 1915	33	110	3

OFFICERS.

1916.		
May 6.	2nd Lieut. A. M. Gardiner	Died of wounds.
May 12.	2nd Lieut. W. M'Bean	Killed.
May 12.	2nd Lieut. D. P. M'Iver	Wounded.
May 16.	Capt. R. D. Stevenson	Killed.
May 30.	2nd Lieut. D. A. Forbes	Wounded.
June.	2nd Lieut. F. T. D. Matthews	Wounded.
June.	2nd Lieut. T. C. Jameson	Wounded.
July 5.	2nd Lieut. J. T. D. Matthews	Wounded.
July 5.	2nd Lieut. A. R. Muirhead	Wounded.
Aug. 13.	Lieut. J. G. Mitchell	Wounded.
Aug. 20.	Lieut. J. H. Hutcheson	Wounded.
Aug. 21.	Lieut. A. K. Alport	Killed
Aug. 26.	2nd Lieut. J. M. M'Crone	Killed.
Aug. 27.	2nd Lieut. W. C. F. Macfarlane	Killed.
Aug. 31.	2nd Lieut. R. Shedden-Dobbie	Wounded.
Sept. 15.	2nd Lieut. J. Cullen	Killed.
Sept. 15.	2nd Lieut. W. D. Todd	Killed.
Sept. 15.	Capt. A. D. Shewan	Killed.
Sept. 15.	2nd Lieut. C. T. Henry	Wounded.
Sept. 15.	Lieut. J. G. Mitchell	Wounded.
Sept. 15.	Lieut. W. F. C. M'Clure	Wounded.
Sept. 15.	2nd Lieut. W. Miller	Wounded (died of wounds).
Sept. 15.	2nd Lieut. A. S. Gilmour	Killed.
Sept. 15.	Capt. B. S. Wilson, C.F.	Wounded.
Sept. 16.	Capt. G. L. Wilson	Wounded.
Sept. 19.	2nd Lieut. R. M. Scott	Wounded.
Sept. 19.	2nd Lieut. R. M. Scott	Died of wounds.
Sept. 31.	2nd Lieut. A. S. Gilmour	Killed.
Oct. 13.	Capt. and Adjutant A. S. Campbell	Wounded.
Oct. 13.	2nd Lieut. D. W. Fyfe	Wounded.
Oct. 16.	2nd Lieut. W. Henderson	Wounded.

OTHER RANKS.

1916.	*Killed.*	*Wounded.*	*Missing.*
January	2	13	nil
February	5	13	nil
March	5	23	nil
April	nil	nil	nil
May	19	30	nil
June	7	49	nil
July	8	16	nil
August	43	128	2
September	45	245	30
October	10	51	1
November and December	nil	nil	nil
	144	468	33

OFFICERS.

1917.		
April 9-12.	2nd Lieut. A. H. Whyte	Killed.
	2nd Lieut. D. C. Morrison	Killed.
	2nd Lieut. R. Shedden-Dobbie	Died of wounds.
	2nd Lieut. J. L. Stewart	Wounded.
	2nd Lieut. E. F. Duncan	Wounded.
	2nd Lieut. T. M. Weir	Wounded.
	2nd Lieut. W. S. Shankland	Wounded.
April 24.	2nd Lieut. J. Farquharson	Killed.
April 24.	2nd Lieut. G. Beattie, M.C.	Killed.
April 24	2nd Lieut. E. W. Wilson	Killed.
April 24.	2nd Lieut. M'Intyre	Wounded.
April 30.	2nd Lieut. C. D. Miller	Wounded.
April 30.	Capt. T. Healy	Wounded.
May 2.	Lieut. D. M Sutthery	Died of wounds.
May 4.	2nd Lieut. S. F. Baillie	Wounded.
May 4.	2nd Lieut. T. F. Heyworth	Wounded.
May 6.	2nd Lieut. C. M. Bateman	Wounded.
May 11.	2nd Lieut. R. G. Miller	Died of wounds.
May 12.	2nd Lieut. W. P. Mitchell	Wounded.
May 12.	2nd Lieut. A. Ferguson	Wounded.
June 3.	Lieut.-Col. M. M'Neill, C.M.G., D.S.O.	Died.
July 9.	2nd Lieut. R. P. Blyth	Killed.
July 9.	2nd Lieut. W. R. Haldane	Wounded.

1917.		
July 9.	2nd Lieut. A. Mills	Wounded.
July 30.	Lieut. A. B. Ruthven	Wounded.
July 31 to Aug. 1.	Capt. E. Leitch	Killed.
	2nd Lieut. D. R. Cameron	Killed.
	2nd Lieut. N. M'Callum	Killed.
	2nd Lieut. J. A. Ewing	Killed.
	2nd Lieut. G. N. D. Sinclair	Wounded.
	2nd Lieut. A. S. Miller	Wounded.
	Capt. M. Wilson	Wounded.
	Lieut. Prosser	Wounded.
	2nd Lieut. Robertson	Wounded.
Aug. 22.	Capt. J. H. Porteous	Killed.
Aug. 22.	2nd Lieut. W. J. Dow	Killed.
Aug. 22.	Capt. W. F. C. M'Clure	Wounded.
Aug. 22.	Lieut. A. R. Muirhead	Wounded.
Aug. 22.	2nd Lieut. R. H. Bates	Wounded.
Aug. 22.	2nd Lieut. F. C. Stewart	Wounded.
Aug. 22.	2nd Lieut. A. R. Chesney	Wounded.
Aug. 22.	2nd Lieut. W. J. Denholm	Wounded.
Aug. 22.	Lieut. G. H. Mitchell	Killed.
Aug. 22.	2nd Lieut. C. L. Jamieson	Killed.
Aug. 22.	Lieut. C. W. Hewer	Killed.
Aug. 22.	2nd Lieut. K. J. Niven	Killed.
Aug. 22.	2nd Lieut. A. H. D. Richmond	Missing.
Oct. 7.	2nd Lieut. G. B. Black	Killed.
Oct. 18.	Lieut. A. R. Muirhead	Wounded
Oct. 24.	2nd Lieut. H. R. Emslie	Killed.

OTHER RANKS.

	1917.	*Killed.*	*Wounded.*	*Missing.*
	January	5	7	nil
	April	7	28	nil
Battles of Arras	April 9-11	42	127	7
	April 21-30	50	178	40
	July	25	63	nil
Battles of Ypres	July 31 to August 1	15	110	21
	August 22	26	157	22 (approximate)
	October	5	4	16
		175	674	106

OFFICERS.

1918.		
March 23.	Lieut.-Colonel J. T. R. Mitchell, D.S.O.	Wounded (died April 1)
March 28.	Capt. M. Wilson, M.C.	Wounded.
March 28.	Lieut. J. L. Stewart	Wounded.
March 28.	Lieut. T. Bertram	Wounded.
March 31.	2nd Lieut. M. Mackay	Deid of wounds.
April 17.	2nd Lieut. J. G. L. Christie	Wounded.
April 20.	2nd Lieut. D. H. Stewart	Killed.
April 20.	2nd Lieut. A. Brown	Killed.
April 21.	2nd Lieut. H. W. Robertson	Died of wounds.
April 26.	2nd Lieut. V. A. Smith	Wounded.
April 26.	Lieut. D. Kerr	Wounded.
May 26.	2nd Lieut. R. B. Burbidge	Wounded.
May 26.	2nd Lieut. Roberts	Gassed.

1/8TH A. & S. HIGHLANDERS.

July 28.	Lieut. G. R. Swan	Wounded.
July 28.	2nd Lieut. F. MacElwer	Wounded.
July 28.	Capt. A. M. Pollock	Wounded.
Aug. 28.	Lieut. G. Stratford	Wounded.
Sept. 8.	2nd Lieut. H. C. Tolliday	Wounded.
Oct. 29.	2nd Lieut. A. Bruce Forbes	Died of wounds

1919.		
Feb. 16.	Lieut.-Colonel G. L. Wilson, D.S.O., M.C.	Died.

OTHER RANKS.

1918.	*Killed.*	*Wounded.*	*Missing.*	*Buried.*
January	nil	nil	nil	nil
February	3	2	nil	nil
March 28	nil	nil	80 casualties	
April	5	5	nil	nil
May	5	16	nil	9
	13	23	80	9

1/8th A. & S. Highlanders (absorbing 11th Battalion).

Other Ranks.

1918.	*Killed.*	*Wounded.*	*Missing.*	*Gassed.*
June	nil	5	nil	22
July	11	57	13	nil
July 23 (all ranks)	26	95	24	nil
August	nil	26	nil	nil
September	10	94	nil	nil
October	5	16	nil	nil
November	nil	nil	nil	nil
	52	293	37	22

45th Infantry Brigade Headquarters.

1916.

Jan.	3 other ranks	Wounded.
Sept. 15.	Capt. H. G. Fowler, Staff Captain	Wounded.

45th Machine-Gun Company

Officers.

1916.

July 22.	Lieut. J. A. M'Ferran	Wounded.
Aug. 20.	Lieut. A. E. Pescod	Wounded.
Sept. 16.	2nd Lieut. P. Wilson	Wounded.

Other Ranks.

1916.	*Killed.*	*Wounded.*
February	nil	1
March	nil	2
April	nil	1
June	nil	1
July	nil	9
August	9	11
September	13	32
October	nil	9
	22	66

1917.	Killed.	Wounded.	Missing.
Battles of Ypres—			
July 29 to August 4—			
Officers	1	1	1
Other ranks	6	32	8
August 5-31—			
Officers	nil	2	nil
Other ranks	10	32	nil
Other Ranks—			
September	3	1	nil
October	nil	3	nil
November	1	4	nil
December	1	nil	nil

45TH TRENCH-MORTAR BATTERY.

1916.	Killed.	Wounded.	Missing.
February	nil	3	nil
March	nil	1	nil
1917.			
July 29 to August 4—			
Officers	nil	nil	nil
Other ranks	1	6	3
August 5-31—			
Officers	nil	nil	nil
Other ranks	8	10	1

45TH BRIGADE SIGNAL COMPANY.

1916.

January . . . . . 2 other ranks wounded.

ATTACHED BATTALIONS.

OTHER RANKS.

1916.	Killed.	Wounded.
February (8th Dublin Fusiliers)	5	13
March (8th Royal Irish Fusiliers)	nil	4
June (14th H.L.I.)	3	3
	8	20

46TH INFANTRY BRIGADE CASUALTIES.

9TH BATTALION (HIGHLANDERS) THE ROYAL SCOTS.

(Joined 15th (Scottish) Division on 1st June 1918.)

OFFICERS.

Killed or Died of Wounds.

Lieut. J. D. Willesen	July.
2nd Lieut. T. H. Lawrie	July.
Lieut. F. M. Ross, M.C.	August.
Lieut. T. Stevenson	August.
Lieut. D. A. Bannatyne	August.
Lieut. J. C. Jackson	August.
2nd Lieut. J. M. Black	August.
2nd Lieut. W. M. Robertson	August.
2nd Lieut. B. Webster	September.
2nd Lieut. A. A. Forsyth	October.

Wounded.

2nd Lieut. A. M. Kirkwood	July.
Lieut. J. A. MacDonald	July.
Lieut. A. S. Black	July.
2nd Lieut. T. Moffat	July.
2nd Lieut. L. K. Reid	August.
2nd Lieut. H. D. MacGregor	August.
Capt. E. S. Fiddes	September.
Lieut. A. J. Hughson	September.
Lieut. J. G. Steel	September.
2nd Lieut. H. Williamson	September.
2nd Lieut. T. J. E. Barclay	September.

OTHER RANKS.

	Killed.	*Wounded.*	*Missing.*
June	2	13	nil
July	23	152	6
August	94	147	5
September	1	39	11
October	8	78	2
November	nil	nil	nil
	128	429	24

7TH KING'S OWN SCOTTISH BORDERERS.

(July 1915 to amalgamation, May 28, 1916.)

OFFICERS.

(Before Battle of Loos.)

Major G. S. D. Forbes . . . . . . Died of Wounds.

(Battle of Loos.)

Major T. A. Glenny . . . . . . Killed.
Capt. F. R. Hutt . . . . . . Killed.
Capt. P. Newton . . . . . . Killed.
Capt. P. L. Lethbridge (Adj.) . . . . Killed.
Lieut. J. M. Sellar . . . . . . Killed.
Lieut. J. Scott . . . . . . Killed.
Lieut. W. Jarvis . . . . . . Killed.
2nd Lieut. J. L. S. Allan . . . . . Killed.
2nd Lieut. W. Haddon . . . . . Killed.
2nd Lieut. F. M. C. Tod . . . . . Killed.
2nd Lieut. M. C. de B. Young . . . . Killed.
Lieut. J. R. G. Garbutt (R.A.M.C.) . . . Killed.
Lieut.-Colonel G. de W. Verner . . . . Died of Wounds.
Capt. M. F. B. Dennis . . . . . Wounded.
Lieut. J. D. Denniston . . . . . Wounded.
Lieut. A. K. Gilmour . . . . . Wounded.
Lieut. J. Frew . . . . . . Wounded.
2nd Lieut. A. J. M. Tuck . . . . . Wounded.
2nd Lieut. W. G. Kerr . . . . . Wounded.
Capt. T. Blackburn . . . . . . Wounded and Prisoner.

(From Battle of Loos until amalgamation.)

Capt. C. H. M. Horne . . . . . Killed.
Lieut. A. Booth (R.A.M.C.) . . . . Killed.
2nd Lieut. J. Lamont . . . . . Killed.
2nd Lieut. J. B. Penfold . . . . . Killed.
2nd Lieut. E. F. Ranken . . . . . Killed.
2nd Lieut. Miller . . . . . . Killed.
Capt. C. B. Bird . . . . . . Wounded.
Capt. J. D. Denniston . . . . . Wounded.
2nd Lieut. C. Hanbury . . . . . Wounded.
2nd Lieut. T. J. Glover . . . . . Wounded.
2nd Lieut. A. E. O. Crombie . . . . Wounded.
2nd Lieut. G. P. Randall . . . . . Wounded.
2nd Lieut. I. D. Scott . . . . . Wounded.

OTHER RANKS.

	Killed.	Died of Wounds.	Wounded.	Missing.	Gassed.
Battle of Loos till amalgamation .	40	nil	193	nil	4
Battle of Loos .	72	14	410	160	nil

8TH KING'S OWN SCOTTISH BORDERERS.

BATTLE OF LOOS.

OFFICERS.

Capt. H. T. Cruickshank	Killed.
Capt. H. H. Smith	Killed.
2nd Lieut. P. C. Drummond	Killed.
2nd Lieut. W. G. Herbertson	Killed.
2nd Lieut. I. R. Ardill	Killed.
2nd Lieut. S. G. M'Clelland	Killed.
Major H. M. Forster	Died of Wounds.
Capt. H. P. Hart	Wounded.
Capt. W. W. Home	Wounded.
Capt. S. S. Lang	Wounded.
2nd Lieut. C. K. Thursby-Pelham . . .	Wounded.
2nd Lieut. P. M. Ross	Wounded and Prisoner.
2nd Lieut. H. G. Mitchell	Wounded and Prisoner.

(July 1915 to amalgamation, May 28, 1916.)

OFFICERS.

2nd Lieut. R. Clark	Killed.
2nd Lieut. K. M. Hamilton	Killed.
Major H. P. Hart	Wounded.
Capt. C. H. Crawshaw	Wounded.
Capt. J. S. M'Arthur	Wounded.
Lieut. J. D. Brown	Wounded.
2nd Lieut. J. H. Patrick	Wounded.
2nd Lieut. W. Thomson	Wounded.
2nd Lieut. D. Chalmers	Wounded.
2nd Lieut. A. M. Little	Wounded.
2nd Lieut. A. M'Intosh	Wounded.
2nd Lieut. W W. Henderson	Wounded.
2nd Lieut. W. W. Barton	Wounded.
2nd Lieut N. Lee	Wounded.
2nd Lieut. J. Cragg	Wounded.

OTHER RANKS.

	Killed.	Wounded.	Missing.
Battle of Loos	23	124	228
To April 1916	31	71	nil

May 14, 1916—85 casualties.
May 14-28, 1916—16 casualties.

7/8TH KING'S OWN SCOTTISH BORDERERS.

As from June 1916.

OFFICERS.

Hohenzollern Sector.

Major M. F. B. Dennis	Wounded.
Capt. H. W. Sutherland	Wounded.
Capt. S. S. Lang	Wounded.
Capt. A. R. Brown	Wounded.
Lieut. J. H. N. Macleod	Killed.
2nd Lieut. A. B. Lawson	Wounded.
2nd Lieut. B. Thursby-Pelham	Wounded.

Somme, before Martinpuich.

Capt. A. K. Gilmour	Killed.
Capt. A. R. Brown	Killed.
Lieut. A. W. Murray	Wounded.
Lieut. G. A. Fraser	Wounded.
Lieut. F. L. Hamilton	Wounded.
2nd Lieut. J. H. Lawrie	Killed.
2nd Lieut. J. B. Walmsley	Killed.
2nd Lieut. A. M'Intosh	Wounded.
2nd Lieut. J. M. Ure	Killed.
2nd Lieut. J. M. M'Alpin	Wounded.
2nd Lieut. C. K. Thursby-Pelham	Wounded.
2nd Lieut. G. J. Mitchell	Wounded.
2nd Lieut. D. T. Holmes	Wounded.
2nd Lieut. A. B. Lawson	Wounded.
2nd Lieut. J. H. Patrick	Wounded.
Lieut. J. Wyper	Died of Wounds.

Martinpuich, to December 31, 1916.

Lieut.-Colonel T. B. Sellar	Wounded.
Lieut. H. F. Brigstocke	Killed.
2nd Lieut. G. Snowie	Killed.
2nd Lieut. Farquhar	Killed.
2nd Lieut. Murray	Killed.
2nd Lieut. C. C. Mahood	Killed.
2nd Lieut. R. R. Harkus	Wounded.
2nd Lieut. C. M. Holme	Wounded.
2nd Lieut. Middlemas	Wounded.
2nd Lieut. J. C. Wilson	Wounded.
2nd Lieut. W. H. Allan	Wounded.

OTHER RANKS.

	Killed.	*Wounded.*	*Missing.*
June	7	31	nil
July	24*	41	nil
August	19	102	nil
August 17-18	31	163	27
September 12-17	22	129	90
October	9	20	1
November	nil	nil	nil
December	4	12	nil
	116	498	118

* On July 9, 11 Other Ranks were buried under sap (bodies not recovered) owing to explosion of enemy mine.

Casualties during fighting on the Somme.

	Killed.	*Wounded.*	*Died of Wounds.*	*Missing.*
Officers	9	16	1	nil
Other Ranks	86	490	24	118
	95	506	25	118

7/8TH KING'S OWN SCOTTISH BORDERERS.

OFFICERS.

January 1 *to April* 11, 1917.

2nd Lieut. J. W. M'Intyre	Died.
Capt. W. Parker (R.A.M.C.)	Wounded.
Lieut. W. W. Henderson	Wounded.
2nd Lieut. G. Sutherland	Killed.
2nd Lieut. J. M. M'Alpin	Killed.
2nd Lieut. J. Jarvie	Died of Wounds.
2nd Lieut. G. G. Lang	Killed.
2nd Lieut. W. Irving	Wounded.
2nd Lieut. G. O. D. Watson	Wounded.
2nd Lieut. A. B. Davidson	Wounded.
2nd Lieut. J. H. Strachan	Wounded.
2nd Lieut. E. O. Rodger	Wounded.
2nd Lieut. E. C. I. Crofts	Wounded.

April 23-25, 1917.

Lieut.-Colonel M. F. B. Dennis	Wounded.
Lieut. W. Thomson	Wounded.
2nd Lieut. W. A. Howard	Killed.
2nd Lieut. P. Reay	Wounded.
2nd Lieut. N. D. Kennedy	Wounded.

Battle of Ypres, July 31, 1917.

Lieut.-Colonel M. F. B. Dennis	Wounded.
Capt. A. B. Lawson	Wounded.
Capt. H. W. Sutherland	Wounded.
Capt. D. Elder	Wounded.
Capt. F. G. Causley	Killed.
2nd Lieut. W. Connochie	Killed.
2nd Lieut. A. M'Call	Died of Wounds.
2nd Lieut. A. H. Allan	Killed.
2nd Lieut. C. T. Tod	Wounded.
2nd Lieut. A. B. Dickson	Wounded.
2nd Lieut. J. G. Dickie	Wounded.
2nd Lieut. Bryson	Killed.
2nd Lieut. T. A. Skinner	Died of Wounds.
Capt. G. O. D. Watson	Wounded.

2nd Lieut. W. M. Douglas	Killed.
2nd Lieut. J. Black	Died of Wounds.
2nd Lieut. A. R. Templeton	Wounded.
2nd Lieut. N. D. Kennedy	Wounded.
2nd Lieut. R. M'George	Wounded.
2nd Lieut. J. D. Scott	Wounded.
2nd Lieut. J. Rae	Wounded.
2nd Lieut. R. R. Douglas	Died of Wounds.

Arras Front, September 1917 *to July* 10, 1918.

Lieut.-Colonel M. F. B. Dennis	Killed.
Capt. G. A. White	Wounded.
Capt. H. B. Morgan (R.A.M.C.)	Wounded.
Lieut. A. E. Forbes-Dennis	Wounded.
Lieut. J. F. Irving	Wounded.
Lieut. G. J. Mitchell	Wounded.
Lieut. W. G. Douglas	Wounded.
2nd Lieut. T. M'Quade	Wounded.
2nd Lieut. T. G. Menzies	Wounded.
2nd Lieut. G. Jackson	Wounded.
2nd Lieut. J. Laird	Killed.
2nd Lieut. T. Gormley	Killed.
2nd Lieut. J. Dryburgh	Died of Wounds.
2nd Lieut. G. A. Haining	Wounded.

OTHER RANKS.

	1917.	*Killed*	*Wounded.*	*Missing.*
	January	5	21	nil
	February	1	8	nil
	March	nil	14	nil
Battles of Arras	April	28	370	50
	May	nil	nil	nil
	June	7	39	nil
	July (to 30th)	nil	10	nil
	July 31 to Aug. 31	50	292	19
	September	nil	7	nil
	October	4	20	nil
	November	nil	nil	nil
	December	2	14	nil
		97	795	69

OFFICERS.

July 22 to August 3, 1918.

Lieut.-Colonel H. P. Hart	Wounded.
Capt. I. Taylor	Wounded.
Capt. A. B. Paton	Wounded.
Lieut. V. Cowley	Killed.
Lieut. S. Wilson	Wounded.
Lieut. E. M. S. Houstoun	Wounded.
Lieut. J. C. Wilson	Wounded.
Lieut. J. M'Millan	Killed.
2nd Lieut. J. B. Sloan	Killed.
2nd Lieut. A. B. White	Killed.
2nd Lieut. J. Wyper	Killed.
2nd Lieut. M. Fenwick	Wounded.
2nd Lieut. J. M'Cauley	Wounded.
2nd Lieut. K. Lidster	Wounded.
2nd Lieut. W. M. Honeyman	Wounded and Prisoner.
2nd Lieut. J. Shannon	Killed.
2nd Lieut. A. J. Lewis	Killed.

August 15 to Armistice.

Capt. H. M. Deans	Killed.
Capt. G. A. White	Wounded.
Lieut. G. B. Hopkins	Killed.
Lieut. J. Gracie	Killed.
Lieut. C. T. Tod	Wounded.
Lieut. S. R. Irvine	Wounded.
2nd Lieut. R. T. Pritchard	Wounded.

OTHER RANKS.

1918.	*Killed.*	*Wounded.*	*Missing.*
January	nil	nil	nil
February	2	7	nil
March	12	92	2
April	nil	24	nil
May	5	29	nil
June	8	44	4
July	41	217	60
August	5	69	5
September	10	51	11
October	8	24	nil
November	nil	1	nil
	91	548	82

10TH THE CAMERONIANS (SCOTTISH RIFLES).

BATTLE OF LOOS.

OFFICERS.

Major J. H. Scott	Killed.
Capt. E. H. Baillie	Killed.
Capt. J. F. Duncan	Killed.
Capt. W. H. Robertson-Durham	Killed.
Capt. A. S. Pringle	Killed.
Capt. F. E. Trouton	Killed.
Lieut. W. Anderson	Killed.
Lieut. A. D. C. Moll	Killed.
Lieut. R. G. C. Robb	Killed.
Lieut. A. Stenhouse	Killed.
Lieut. D. G. Young	Killed.
2nd Lieut. J. J. Carswell	Killed.
2nd Lieut. G. A. W. Flynn	Killed.
2nd Lieut. D. A. B. Lindsay	Killed.
2nd Lieut. D. M'Callum	Killed.
2nd Lieut. T. Paisley	Killed.
Lieut.-Colonel A. Vesey Ussher	Wounded.
Major F. L. Grant	Wounded.
Lieut. W. G. Paton	Wounded.
2nd Lieut. J. C. Lovell	Wounded.
2nd Lieut. L. C. Paton	Wounded.

1915.

Oct. 25.	2nd Lieut. G. Morrison	Killed.
Oct. 29.	Capt. A. La T. Baillie	Killed.
Nov. 23.	2nd Lieut. J. Brown	Accidentally injured.
Nov. 23.	2nd Lieut. D. A. Foulis	Wounded.

OTHER RANKS.

	Killed.	*Wounded.*	*Missing.*
Battle of Loos, 1915	68	318	239

OFFICERS.

1916.

Jan. 27.	Capt. J. C. Grant	Killed.
Jan. 27.	2nd Lieut. R. A. Peacock	Killed.
March 24.	Capt. J. A. Callen, M.C.	Wounded.

1916.

May 11.	2nd Lieut. J. M. Smith	Killed.
May 19.	Capt. C. K. Glegg	Killed.
May 19.	2nd Lieut. W. J. Warden	Wounded.
May 24.	2nd Lieut. A. R. Erskine	Wounded.
May 27.	2nd Lieut. J. B. Stewart	Wounded.
May 27.	Capt. M. W. Robertson	Wounded.
June 8.	2nd Lieut. J. Bilsland, M.C.	Killed.
June 8.	2nd Lieut. A. Ronaldson	Killed.
June 15.	Capt. W. G. Paton	Killed.
June 16.	2nd Lieut. J. Mallinson	Wounded.
June 17.	Major P. R. Hardinge, M.C.	Died of Wounds.
July 3.	Lieut. R. Worton	Wounded.
Aug. 10.	2nd Lieut. A. M. Stevenson	Wounded.
Aug. 12.	Capt. J. Main	Died of Wounds.
Aug. 28.	2nd Lieut. G. Ross	Wounded.
Aug. 31.	Capt. L. M. R. Gordon	Wounded.
Aug. 31.	2nd Lieut. H. F. Tait	Killed.
Sep. 14-15.	2nd Lieut. H. M. Brickman	Killed.
Sep. 14-15.	2nd Lieut. W. W. Myles	Killed.
Sep. 14-15.	2nd Lieut. A. C. Struthers	Killed.
Sep. 14-15.	2nd Lieut. H. A. A. Spring	Killed.
Sep. 14-15.	2nd Lieut. F. A. Shearburn	Killed.
Sep. 14-15.	Capt. D. A. Foulis	Wounded.
Sep. 14-15.	Capt. H. H. M'Gregor	Wounded.
Sep. 14-15.	Capt. C. C. Scott	Wounded.
Sep. 14-15.	Lieut. W. S. Gulloch	Wounded.
Sep. 14-15.	Lieut. J. C. Lovell	Wounded.
Sep. 14-15.	Lieut. D. A. Seath	Wounded.
Sep. 14-15.	2nd Lieut. A. W. Buttar	Wounded.
Sep. 14-15.	2nd Lieut. R. Caldwell	Wounded.
Sep. 14-15.	2nd Lieut. A. K. Campbell	Wounded.
Sep. 14-15.	2nd Lieut. G. M. Ferguson	Wounded.
Sep. 14-15.	2nd Lieut. J. W. Jack	Wounded.
Sep. 14-15.	2nd Lieut. J. H. D. Lawrie	Wounded.
Sep. 14-15.	2nd Lieut. G. W. R. M'Connachie	Wounded.
Sep. 14-15.	2nd Lieut. I. S. Torrance	Wounded.
Sep. 14-15.	2nd Lieut. J. L. Walker	Wounded.
Oct. 16.	Lieut. E. W. Waddy	Wounded.
Oct. 17.	Capt. J. B. W. Dewar	Wounded.
Oct. 17.	Lieut. A. R. Prentice	Wounded.
Nov. 5.	2nd Lieut. A. Munro	Killed.
Dec. 30.	2nd Lieut. S. H. Dow	Killed.

OTHER RANKS.

Jan. 27.—78 killed and wounded.
Feb. and March.—No figures given.
April.—4 wounded.
May 11-15.—72 killed and wounded.
June.—12 killed, 55 wounded.
July.—49 killed and wounded.

	Killed.	*Wounded.*	*Missing.*
August . . .	34	240	14
September . .	12	172	63
October . .	1	8	nil
November . .	nil	nil	nil
December . .	2	8	nil

OFFICERS.

1917.

Jan. 1.	Capt. Hamilton	Killed.
March 24.	2nd Lieut. A. S. Pratt	Killed.
March 24.	2nd Lieut. Stewart	Killed.
March 24.	Capt. A. H. Steedman	Died of Wounds.
March 24.	Capt. A. R. Prentice	Wounded.
March 29.	2nd Lieut. I. G. Kennedy	Wounded.
March 30.	Capt. D. J. Robertson, C.F. . . .	Wounded.

Battles of Arras.

April 9.	2nd Lieut. F. W. Turner	Killed.
April 9.	2nd Lieut. W. G. Benzie	Killed.
April 9.	Lieut. G. Menary	Wounded.
April 9.	Lieut. J. S. Munro	Wounded.
April 9.	2nd Lieut. C. H. Whitelaw . . .	Wounded.
April 24.	2nd Lieut. A. M. Fisher	Killed.
April 24.	Lieut. D. A. Seath	Killed.
April 24.	2nd Lieut. C. W. Gemmell	Killed.
April 24.	2nd Lieut. E. J. Rodgers	Killed.
April 24.	2nd Lieut. A. T. Gray	Killed.
Ap. 23-25.	Lieut. R. Miller	Died of Wounds.
Ap. 23-25.	2nd Lieut. J. Mallinson	Wounded.
Ap. 23-25.	2nd Lieut. W. D. Roger	Wounded.
Ap. 23-25.	2nd Lieut. A. G. K. Allison . . .	Wounded.
Ap. 23-25.	2nd Lieut. W. M'L. Moffat . . .	Wounded.
Ap. 23-25.	2nd Lieut. H. G. S. Douglas . . .	Wounded.
Ap. 23-25.	2nd Lieut. J. W. G. Tomkin . . .	Wounded.
June 23.	2nd Lieut. J. H. Saunders	Killed.
June 23.	2nd Lieut. A. S. Low	Killed.

1917.			
June	28.	2nd Lieut. W. M'Kenzie	Wounded.
June	28.	2nd Lieut. A. B. Smith	Wounded.
July	21.	2nd Lieut. A. Nicol	Wounded.
July	28.	Capt. G. Menary	Wounded.
July	28.	2nd Lieut. J. B. Maxwell	Wounded.

Battles of Ypres—July 31 *to August* 31.

		Lieut. J. C. Lovell	Killed.
		2nd Lieut. A. C. Neale	Killed.
		2nd Lieut. D. Pitt	Killed.
		2nd Lieut. W. S. Hunter	Killed.
		2nd Lieut. H. M. Currie	Killed.
		Lieut. C. H. H. Slater	Killed.
		2nd Lieut. K. S. Miller	Killed.
		Capt. G. Kermack	Wounded.
		Capt. W. K. Knott	Wounded.
		Lieut. R. P. H. Maxwell	Wounded.
		2nd Lieut. H. Campbell	Wounded.
		2nd Lieut. G. D. Killeen	Wounded.
		2nd Lieut. J. F. Cameron	Wounded.
		2nd Lieut. A. Fleming	Wounded and Missing.
Aug.	16.	2nd Lieut. I. G. Kennedy	Wounded.
Sept.	2.	2nd Lieut. J. Steele	Wounded.
Oct.	16.	2nd Lieut. T. P. White	Died of Wounds.
Nov.	9.	Capt. A. R. Prentice, M.C.	Killed.
Dec.	12.	2nd Lieut. J. Wallace	Wounded.
Dec.	21.	2nd Lieut. L. M. Ewen	Wounded and Missing.

OTHER RANKS.

	1917.	*Killed.*	*Wounded.*	*Missing.*
	January	2	7	nil
	February	nil	8	nil
	March	20	77	7
Battles of Arras	April	51	232	15
	May	nil	nil	nil
	June	18	81	nil
	July (to 30th)	10	54	nil
Battles of Ypres	July 31 to Aug. 31	42	261	79
	September	2	3	nil
	October	1	1	nil
	November	2	22	nil
	December	2	23	1
		150	869	102

OFFICERS.

1918.		
March 21.	Lieut. and Q.M. G. Maskell	Killed.
March 27.	Capt. G. M'Call	Killed.
March 27.	Lieut. G. W. Jamieson	Killed.
March 27.	2nd Lieut. J. Kerr	Killed.
March 27.	Lieut. J. Mackenzie	Wounded.
March 27.	2nd Lieut. J. R. Robb	Wounded.
May 27.	2nd Lieut. W. Scott	Wounded.
May 27.	2nd Lieut. W. S. Drever	Wounded.
May 27.	2nd Lieut. A. M. Alexander	Wounded.
June 11.	2nd Lieut. J. Blair	Died of Wounds.
July 23.	Lieut. W. Scott	Wounded.
July 23.	2nd Lieut. R. C. Philips	Wounded.
July 23.	2nd Lieut. A. M. Crawford	Wounded.
July 23.	Capt. A. M. M'George	Wounded.
July 23.	2nd Lieut. W. Henderson	Wounded.
July 23.	2nd Lieut. F. Keir	Wounded.
July 23.	Lieut. R. H. P. Maxwell	Killed.
July 23.	2nd Lieut. Delarue	Killed.
July 23.	Lieut. G. C. Collier	Killed.
July 23.	2nd Lieut. J. Campbell	Killed.
July 29.	2nd Lieut. G. F. Simpson	Killed.
Aug. 1.	Lieut. A. B. Smith	Killed.
Aug. 1.	Capt. G. P. Simpson	Died of Wounds.
Aug. 1.	2nd Lieut. S. Mathieson	Died of Wounds.
Aug. 1.	2nd Lieut. J. S. Kelt	Wounded.
Aug. 1.	2nd Lieut. H. Penman	Wounded.
Aug. 18.	Lieut. H. J. Robison	Missing.
Aug. 18.	2nd Lieut. G. M. Drew	Missing.
Aug. 18.	2nd Lieut. D. C. Caldwell	Missing.
Sept. 20.	2nd Lieut. E. M. H. Galbraith	Wounded.
Sept. 29.	2nd Lieut. W. F. Ross	Wounded
Oct. 11.	2nd Lieut. W. B. Semple	Wounded.
Oct. 11.	2nd Lieut. J. W. Carrick	Wounded.
Oct. 21.	2nd Lieut. W. Misell	Killed.

OTHER RANKS.

1918	Killed.	Wounded.	Missing.
January . .	nil	nil	nil
February . .	nil	5	nil
March . . .	34	142	29
April . . .	6	34	8
May . . .	5	73	nil
June . . .	3	32	nil
July . . .	39	214	29
August . . .	10	59	40
September . .	6	46	1
October . .	8	24	nil
November . .	nil	2	nil
	111	636	107

10/11TH BATTALION THE HIGHLAND LIGHT INFANTRY.

Joined Division May 16, 1916.

OFFICERS.

1916.		
2nd Lieut. W. S. Maxwell	Wounded,	24/5/16.
2nd Lieut. C. T. Brown	Death presumed,	13/7/15.
2nd Lieut. H. G. Hendry	Wounded,	17/6/16.
2nd Lieut. N. Newman	Killed in action,	27/6/16.
Capt. R. W. Reid	Killed in action,	13/8/16.
2nd Lieut. A. Frazer	Killed in action,	13/8/16.
2nd Lieut. D. A. Anderson . . .	Killed in action,	17/8/16.
Capt. J. D. Russell	Wounded,	12/8/16.
Lieut. C. H. T. Alston	Wounded,	12/8/16.
Lieut. A. Cathcart-Bruce	Wounded,	14/8/16.
Lieut. D. R. Keith	Wounded,	14/8/16.
2nd Lieut. W. S. Maxwell	Wounded,	12/8/16.
2nd Lieut. A. Craig	Wounded,	14/8/16.
2nd Lieut. J. J. Lean	Wounded,	14/8/16.
2nd Lieut. D. D. Pratt	Wounded,	17/8/16.
2nd Lieut. J. F. J. Yeo	Wounded,	17/8/16.
2nd Lieut. R. M. Dingwall	Wounded,	17/8/16.
2nd Lieut. R. E. Baxter	Wounded,	17/8/16.
2nd Lieut. R. M'L. Crawford	Killed in action,	14/8/16.
2nd Lieut. A. W. Bell	Wounded,	27/8/16.

1916.

Lieut.-Colonel R. F. Forbes	Wounded,	30/8/16.
Capt. W. B. M'Culloch	Wounded,	30/8/16.
2nd Lieut. J. R. Young . . .	Wounded,	27/8/16.
2nd Lieut. A. B. Meikle . . .	Wounded,	29/8/16.
2nd Lieut. S. H. Barnett . . .	Wounded,	30/8/16.
Capt. D. M'D. Cowie	Died of wounds,	17/9/16.
Capt. J. Harrower	Died of wounds,	15/9/16.
2nd Lieut. D. Thom	Killed in action,	14/9/16.
2nd Lieut. J. A. M'Kinlay . . .	Wounded,	15/9/16.
2nd Lieut. N. St C. Johnston . .	Wounded,	15/9/16.
2nd Lieut. W. D. White . . .	Wounded,	15/9/16.
2nd Lieut. R. G. Hugo	Wounded,	15/9/16.
2nd Lieut. W. Holmes	Killed in action,	16/9/16.
2nd Lieut. R. J. Burns	Killed in action,	16/9/16.
Lieut. C. M'Nab	Wounded,	16/9/16.
2nd Lieut. A. B. Rodgers . . .	Wounded,	16/9/16.
2nd Lieut. C. E. T. Stafford . . .	Wounded,	16/9/16.
Capt. Rev. J. R. Forgan . . .	Wounded,	15/9/16.
2nd Lieut. D. D. Beaton . . .	Wounded,	18/10/16.
2nd Lieut. A. J. Smith	Wounded,	19/10/16.
2nd Lieut. W. Gemmell . . .	Wounded,	19/10/16.
Major C. E. Andrews	Killed in action,	25/10/16.
2nd Lieut. A. Ganson	Killed in action,	14/10/16.
2nd Lieut. T. M. Sibold . . .	Death presumed,	25/9/15.

OTHER RANKS.

1916.	*Killed.*	*Wounded.*	*Missing.*
May . . .	No figures given in War Diaries.		
June . . .	8	27	nil
July . . .	96 casualties.		
August * . .	30	185	26
September * . .	26	125	46
October 15-20 * .	nil	24	2
October 21-31 * .	5	25	nil
December . . .	9	14	nil
	78	400	74

* These figures are from Brigade and "Q" Diaries.

OFFICERS.

1917.

2nd Lieut. D. C. Ferguson	Wounded,	14/1/17.
2nd Lieut. D. C. Ferguson	Died of wounds,	26/1/17.
2nd Lieut. G. Ross	Wounded,	9/4/17.
2nd Lieut. A. Gilchrist	Wounded,	9/4/17.
2nd Lieut. J. Matheson	Killed in action,	9/4/17.
Capt. W. B. MacCulloch	Killed in action,	11/4/17.
Lieut. W. Rose	Killed in action,	11/4/17.
2nd Lieut. A. L. Hay	Died of wounds,	26/4/17.
2nd Lieut. D. K. Webster	Died of wounds,	3/5/17.
Lieut. J. L. Fowlie	Killed in action,	23/4/17.
2nd Lieut. J. M. Bell	Killed in action,	24/4/17.
2nd Lieut. J. H. Campbell	Killed in action,	24/4/17.
2nd Lieut. A. Scott	Missing,	24/4/17.
2nd Lieut. J. Miller	Wounded,	23/4/17.
2nd Lieut. W. W. C. Miller	Wounded,	23/4/17.
2nd Lieut. A. B. Stewart	Wounded,	23/4/17.
2nd Lieut. R. J. Law	Wounded,	23/4/17.
2nd Lieut. J. A. Smith	Wounded,	24/4/17.
2nd Lieut. A. L. Hay	Wounded,	23/4/17.
2nd Lieut. W. S. Reid	Wounded,	23/4/17.
Capt. J. Johnston	Wounded,	24/4/17.
2nd Lieut. G. E. Oliver	Died of wounds,	31/7/17.
2nd Lieut. D. D. Beaton	Wounded,	31/7/17.
2nd Lieut. R. Aitken	Wounded,	31/7/17.
Lieut. J. Y. Milne-Henderson . . .	Killed in action,	31/7/17.
Lieut. J. Duncan	Killed in action,	31/7/17.
2nd Lieut. C. E. T. Stafford	Killed in action,	31/7/17.
2nd Lieut. W. S. Calderwood	Killed in action,	31/7/17.
2nd Lieut. J. Miller	Killed in action,	1/8/17.
2nd Lieut. C. D. Thomson	Missing,	1/8/17.
2nd Lieut. J. C. Whyte	Missing,	1/8/17.
2nd Lieut. A. W. Gill	Missing,	1/8/17.
2nd Lieut. J. F. J. Yeo	Missing,	1/8/17.
2nd Lieut. K. D. M'Neill	Wounded and missing,	1/8/17.
2nd Lieut. N. M. Campbell	Wounded,	18/8/17.
2nd Lieut. J. Drysdale	Wounded,	2/8/17.
Capt. R. Robertson	Died on leave,	13/9/17.
2nd Lieut. W. M. Robertson	Wounded (accident),	24/10/17.
2nd Lieut. J. A. Smith	Wounded,	21/11/17.

OTHER RANKS.

	1917.	*Killed.*	*Wounded.*	*Missing.*
	January . .	nil	14	nil
	February . .	1	2	nil
	March . . .	4	31	2
Battles of Arras	April . . .	33	366	65
	May . . .	nil	nil	nil
	June . . .	2	12	nil
	July (to 30th) . .	1	8	nil
Battles of Ypres	July 31 to Aug. 31 .	37	233	99
	September . .	nil	2	nil
	October . . .	3	12	nil
	November . .	6	29	nil
	December . .	2	4	nil
		89	713	166

12TH BATTALION THE HIGHLAND LIGHT INFANTRY.

OFFICERS.

1915.

Lieut. J. E. A. Alexander	Killed in action,	16/8/15.
2nd Lieut. J. D. Lavelle	Killed in action,	19/8/15.
2nd Lieut. J. Reid	Wounded,	27/8/15.
Lieut. M. Shaw	Died of wounds,	30/9/15.
Capt. G. M. Harley	Killed in action,	25-26/9/15.
Capt. J. Gemmell	Killed in action,	25-26/9/15.
Lieut. K. G. Campbell	Killed in action,	25-26/9/15.
Lieut. F. J. Nicoll	Killed in action,	25-26/9/15.
2nd Lieut. D. Brown	Killed in action,	25-26/9/15.
2nd Lieut. G. Adamson	Killed in action,	25-26/9/15.
2nd Lieut. H. M. Porteous	Killed in action,	25-26/9/15.
Capt. A. L. Young	Wounded,	25-26/9/15.
Capt. R. S. Dixon	Wounded,	25-26/9/15.
Lieut. and Adjutant E. A. M'Lellan . .	Wounded,	25-26/9/15.
Lieut. and Q.M. J. Carpenter	Wounded,	25-26/9/15.
Lieut. H. M. Linton	Wounded,	25-26/9/15.
2nd Lieut. H. C. Jonas	Wounded,	25-26/9/15.
2nd Lieut. N. H. M'Neil	Wounded,	25-26/9/15.
2nd Lieut. L. Lucas	Wounded,	25-26/9/15.
2nd Lieut. D. G. Campbell	Wounded,	25-26/9/15.
Capt. P. W. Torrance	Wounded (gassed),	25-26/9/15.
Lieut. H. M. Linton	Died of wounds,	28/9/15.
2nd Lieut. W. J. Aitchison	Killed in action,	23/10/15.

OTHER RANKS.

	Killed.	Wounded.	Missing.
Battle of Loos, 1915 .	63	228	214
July-Dec. 1915 . .	16	38	nil

OFFICERS.

1916.

Capt. J. W. Hawley	Wounded,	14/1/16.
2nd Lieut. J. E. Smith	Killed in action,	15/1/16.
2nd Lieut. T. D. Adie	Wounded,	20/3/16.
2nd Lieut. W. M'Hardie	Wounded,	20/3/16.
2nd Lieut. R. M'P. Cowper	Killed in action,	27/4/16.
Capt. N. Leitch	Killed in action,	20/5/16.
2nd Lieut. T. A. J. Aitchison	Died of wounds,	9/6/16.
2nd Lieut. R. F. Shiel	Wounded,	9/6/16.
2nd Lieut. J. M'Lellan	Wounded,	9/6/16.
2nd Lieut. E. H. Wuensch	Wounded,	1/7/16.
2nd Lieut. J. M'Lellan	Wounded,	6/7/16.
2nd Lieut. T. Christie	Wounded,	6/7/16.
2nd Lieut. J. Cossar	Died of wounds,	16/8/16.
2nd Lieut. D. Drury-Lowe	Wounded,	9/7/16.
2nd Lieut. R. B. O. Moir	Wounded,	12/8/16.
2nd Lieut. W. G. Notman	Missing,	13/8/16.
Capt. D. G. Campbell	Killed in action,	13/8/16.
2nd Lieut. A. R. Jeff	Killed in action,	13/8/16.
2nd Lieut. H. M. Austin	Killed in action,	13/8/16.
Capt. J. E. Sloan	Wounded,	13/8/16.
Capt. C. F. G. Humphries	Wounded,	13/8/16.
Lieut. H. A. Martin	Wounded,	13/8/16.
Lieut. P. B. Milligan	Wounded,	13/8/16.
2nd Lieut. T. Christie	Wounded,	13/8/16.
2nd Lieut. R. E. Sander	Wounded,	13/8/16.
2nd Lieut. F. J. Adamson	Wounded,	13/8/16.
2nd Lieut. E. V. H. Toovey	Wounded,	13/8/16.
2nd Lieut. T. D. Adie	Wounded,	13/8/16.
2nd Lieut. A. Bryan	Wounded,	13/8/16.
2nd Lieut. L. Lucas	Wounded,	16/8/16.
2nd Lieut. W. M. Crawford	Wounded,	23/8/16.
2nd Lieut. J. G. Hamilton	Wounded,	28/8/16.
2nd Lieut. A. Stewart	Wounded,	1/9/16.
2nd Lieut. S. W. Hutcheon	Died of wounds,	4/9/16.

1916.

2nd Lieut. G. H. Moore	Wounded,	15/9/16.
2nd Lieut. G. H. Leiper	Wounded,	16/9/16.
2nd Lieut. J. A. M'Farlane	Killed in action,	16/9/16.
2nd Lieut. J. L. Frew	Wounded,	16/9/16.
2nd Lieut. J. Scott	Wounded,	16/9/16.
2nd Lieut. R. R. Marshall	Wounded,	15/9/16.
2nd Lieut. J. H. Leiper	Wounded,	16/9/16.
Lieut.-Colonel The Earl of Rothes	Wounded,	7/10/16.
Major R. S. Dixon	Wounded,	7/10/16.
Capt. W. D. Shaw	Wounded,	7/10/16.
Capt. D. G. Watson	Wounded,	7/10/16.
Capt. Rev. J. Stratton	Wounded,	7/10/16.
2nd Lieut. H. P. MacDougald	Wounded,	7/10/16.
2nd Lieut. H. H. Guille	Wounded,	16/12/16.

OTHER RANKS.

(No details given in the War Diaries.)

OFFICERS.

1917.

2nd Lieut. D. W. Haldane	Died of wounds,	9/4/17.
Capt. W. M'Hardie	Wounded,	9/4/17.
Lieut. H. F. Martin	Wounded,	9/4/17.
2nd Lieut. N. M'Lean	Wounded,	9/4/17.
2nd Lieut. J. R. Prentice	Wounded,	9/4/17.
2nd Lieut. S. I. Murdoch	Wounded,	9/4/17.
2nd Lieut. M. Wallace	Wounded,	10/4/17.
2nd Lieut. J. A. Penman	Wounded,	10/4/17.
2nd Lieut. J. M'Kie	Wounded,	10/4/17
2nd Lieut. D. R. Sillars	Wounded,	9/4/17.
2nd Lieut. D. Wood	Wounded,	9/4/17.
2nd Lieut. G. Taylor	Wounded,	14/4/17.
Lieut. A. R. J. Chislett	Killed in action,	24/4/17.
2nd Lieut. N. C. Watson	Killed in action,	24/4/17.
2nd Lieut. J. M'Queen	Killed in action,	24/4/17.
2nd Lieut. W. D. M. M'Caul	Wounded,	25/4/17.
2nd Lieut. W. Nelson	Wounded,	24/4/17.
2nd Lieut. D. Donley	Wounded,	24/4/17.
2nd Lieut. W. G. Notman	Killed in action,	13/8/16.
2nd Lieut. J. M. Bannatyne	Died of wounds,	2/8/17.
2nd Lieut. N. M'Lean	Wounded,	31/7/17.

1917.

2nd Lieut. J. Trotter	Wounded,	31/7/17.
2nd Lieut. J. W. Hardie	Wounded,	31/7/17.
2nd Lieut. F. S. Sutherland	Wounded,	31/7/17.
Capt. T. B. Myles	Killed in action,	28/8/17.
2nd Lieut. F. T. Gardiner	Killed in action,	31/7/17.
2nd Lieut. L. S. Graham	Died of wounds,	29/8/17.
2nd Lieut. W. Dunsmoor	Wounded,	12/10/17.
Lieut. P. B. Milligan	Wounded,	3/11/17.
2nd Lieut. R. Crawford	Wounded,	3/11/17.

OTHER RANKS.

	1917.	*Killed.*	*Wounded.*	*Missing.*
	January	3	27	nil
	February	2	1	nil
	March	5	16	nil
Battles of Arras	April	53	304	22
	May	nil	nil	nil
	June	3	22	nil
	July (to 30th)	16	76	9
Battles of Ypres	July 31 to Aug. 31	22	136	21
	September	nil	10	nil
	October	nil	2	nil
	November	nil	8	nil
	December	12	45	nil
		116	647	52

46TH MACHINE-GUN COMPANY.

OFFICERS.

Battles of Arras, April 1917.

April.	3 officers wounded (no names given).	
June 21.	Lieut. A. H. K. Berry	Gassed.
July.	Lieut. H. Beavis	Wounded (date not given).

Battles of Ypres—July 31 *to August* 31.

2 officers wounded (no names given).

OTHER RANKS.

		Killed.	*Wounded.*	*Missing.*
	January . .	nil	5	nil
	February . .	nil	1	nil
	March . . .	1	nil	nil
Battles of Arras	April . . .	6	40	4
	May . . .	nil	nil	nil
	June . . .	2	8	nil
	July (to 30th) .	1	5	nil
Battles of Ypres	July 31 to Aug. 31 .	15	34	16
	September . .	1	4	nil
	October . . .	nil	nil	nil
	November . .	nil	nil	nil
	December . .	nil	1	nil
		26	98	20

46TH TRENCH-MORTAR BATTERY.

1917. OFFICERS.

Jan.-Dec. Casualties nil.

OTHER RANKS.

		Killed.	*Wounded.*	*Missing.*
	January-March .	nil	nil	nil
Battles of Arras	April . . .	2	17	3
	May . . .	nil	nil	nil
	June . . .	nil	2	nil
	July (to 30th) .	nil	1	nil
Battles of Ypres	July 31 to Aug. 31 .	2	11	1
	September . .	1	3	nil
	October . . .	nil	nil	nil
	November . .	nil	2	nil
	December . .	nil	nil	nil
		5	36	4

46TH MACHINE-GUN COMPANY.

Jan. and Feb. Casualties nil. Company transferred to Machine-Gun Corps, March 1918.

1/4TH DORSETSHIRE REGIMENT.

1916.
Jan. 20. Lieut.-Colonel Cruddas . . . . Killed.
Jan. and Feb.—Casualties in Other Ranks, 15.

(To 33rd Division, February 27.)

9TH GORDON HIGHLANDERS (PIONEER BATTALION).

Battle of Loos—25th-27th *September* 1915.

OFFICERS.

1915.
Sept. 25. Lieut. J. G. Allan . . . . Killed.
Sept. 25. Lieut. K. B. Kershaw . . . . Killed.
Sept. 25. 2nd Lieut. J. M. Usher . . . . Killed.
Sept. 25. 2nd Lieut. G. A. Macgregor . . . Killed.
Sept. 25-27. Capt. E. G. Macgregor . . . Wounded.
Sept. 25-27. Capt. T. Macwhirter . . . Wounded.
Sept. 25-27. 2nd Lieut. W. T. Murray . . . Wounded.
Sept. 25-27. 2nd Lieut. G. D. Pitcairn . . . Wounded.
Sept. 25-27. 2nd Lieut. W. F. Errington-Bisset . Wounded and Missing.

OTHER RANKS.

	Killed.	*Wounded.*	*Missing.*	*Wounded and Missing.*
Battle of Loos . .	30	179	44	16
Aug.-Dec. 1915 . .	3	12	nil	nil
	33	191	44	16

OFFICERS.

1916.
Jan. 30. Capt. R. D. Robertson . . . . . . Wounded.
Feb. 16. Lieut. G. B. Gourlay . . . . . . Wounded.
May 13. 2nd Lieut. M'Kean . . . . . . Wounded.
May 22. 2nd Lieut. R. Reid . . . . . . Killed.
May 23. 2nd Lieut. H. R. Lyle . . . . . . Killed.
July 20. 2nd Lieut. J. A. W. Robertson . . . . Wounded.
Aug. 8. Capt. G. B. Gourlay . . . . . . Wounded.

1916.

Aug. 12.	2nd Lieut. Macgregor	Wounded.
Aug. 12.	2nd Lieut. Harvie	Wounded.
Aug. 26.	2nd Lieut. J. D. Robertson	Wounded.
Aug. 31.	2nd Lieut. D. A. Wright	Wounded.
Sept. 2.	Lieut. Livingstone	Wounded.
Sept. 5.	2nd Lieut. Figgis	Wounded.
Sept. 12.	Capt. J. A. Robertson-Durham	Wounded.
Sept. 17.	Lieut. G. D. Pitcairn	Wounded.
Sept. 19.	Capt. T. Macwhirter	Wounded.
Sept. 19.	Major Lord Dudley Gordon	Wounded.
Sept. 19.	2nd Lieut. W. M. Allan	Wounded.
Oct. 18.	2nd Lieut. W. W. Smith	Wounded.
Oct. 25.	2nd Lieut. Hutchinson	Killed.
Dec. 22.	Lieut. W. Belleny	Wounded.
Dec. 29.	2nd Lieut. J. Webster	Wounded.

OTHER RANKS.

	Killed.	*Wounded.*	*Missing.*
January / February	3	14	nil
March	1	8	nil
April	nil	2	nil
May	8	18	nil
June	nil	13	nil
July	3	19	nil
August	16	123	nil
September	10	125	1
October	8	38	nil
November	nil	6	nil
December	5	8	1
	54	374	2

OFFICERS.

1917.

Jan. 6.	2nd Lieut. D. G. Shepstone	Wounded.
Jan. 22.	2nd Lieut. J. Robb	Wounded.
March 16.	2nd Lieut. R. F. Simpson	Wounded.
April 7.	Capt. D. E. Burnett	Wounded.
April 7.	2nd Lieut. J. T. Pope	Wounded.
April 9.	2nd Lieut. J. D. Blakely	Killed.

1917.		
April 20.	2nd Lieut. G. S. M'Kay	Wounded.
April 27.	Major T. Macwhirter	Missing.
July 13.	2nd Lieut. J. D. Y. Stewart	Wounded.
July 13.	2nd Lieut. P. C. Garson	Wounded.
July 17.	2nd Lieut. J. B. Butchart	Wounded.
July 27.	2nd Lieut. Milne	Wounded.
July 27.	Capt. G. Cowper	Wounded.
July 31.	2nd Lieut. A. Johnstone	Wounded
July 31.	Capt. R. Lumsden	Wounded.
Aug. 2.	Lieut. J. Scobie	Died of wounds.
Aug. 2.	2nd Lieut. A. C. Richardson	Wounded.
Aug. 3.	2nd Lieut. G. Stephen	Wounded.
Aug. 15.	2nd Lieut. G. M'Gaw	Wounded.
Aug. 22.	2nd Lieut. A. J. B. Milne	Killed.
Aug. 22.	2nd Lieut. R. G. A. Crowe	Wounded.
Aug. 22.	2nd Lieut. G. M. Cantlay	Wounded.
Aug. 22.	2nd Lieut. N. I. Angus	Died of wounds.
Aug. 22.	2nd Lieut. G. A. M'Laren	Wounded.
Aug. 25.	2nd Lieut. J. N. M'Iver	Killed.
Aug. 26.	Lieut. J. D. Robertson, M.C.	Killed.
Aug. 26.	2nd Lieut. G. A. Maclean	Wounded.
Aug. 26.	2nd Lieut. J. D. Leslie	Wounded.
Nov. 4.	2nd Lieut. G. S. M'Kay	Wounded.

OTHER RANKS.

	1917.	*Killed.*	*Wounded.*	*Missing.*	*Gassed.*
	January	3	12	nil	nil
	February	nil	nil	nil	nil
	March	3	38	nil	nil
	April	14	73	6	nil
	May	nil	nil	nil	nil
	June	9	55	nil	nil
Battles of Ypres	July 29 to Aug. 4	3	230*	3	nil
Battles of Ypres	Aug. 5 to 31	25	106	2	nil
	September	nil	2	nil	nil
	October	nil	2	nil	nil
	November	9	17	2	nil
	December	nil	3	nil	nil
		66	538	13	nil

* Including Gassed.

OFFICERS.

1918.		
March 21.	2nd Lieut. S. M'Kechnie	Wounded.
March 28.	2nd Lieut. A. F. Murray	Wounded.
April 4.	Lieut.-Colonel T. G. Taylor, D.S.O.	Wounded.
April 22.	Lieut. R. J. M. Gordon	Wounded.
June 8.	2nd Lieut. S. Forrest	Wounded.
July 21.	Lieut. F. J. Jolly	Wounded.
Aug. 3.	2nd Lieut. W. Gray	Wounded.
Sept. 16.	Lieut. J. S. Westwood	Wounded.
Oct. 31.	2nd Lieut. N. M'Cormack	Killed.

OTHER RANKS.

	Killed.	*Wounded.*	*Missing.*	*Gassed.*
January	nil	nil	nil	nil
February	1	5	nil	nil
March	16	45	nil	nil
April	6	48	nil	nil
May	2	12	nil	nil
June	2	15	nil	nil
July	6	29	1	nil
August	3	142	nil	nil
September	6	6	nil	nil
October	1	10	nil	nil
November	1	nil	nil	nil
	44	312	1	nil

ATTACHED BATTALIONS.

OTHER RANKS.

1915.	*Killed.*	*Wounded.*	*Missing.*
1/4th Black Watch	2	10	nil
1916.			
June. 13th East Surrey Regiment	3	24	nil
June. 11th King's Own	1	11	nil
	4	35	nil

FIFTEENTH DIVISIONAL ARTILLERY.

70TH BRIGADE R.F.A.

OFFICERS.

1915.

Sept. 22.	2nd Lieut. T. E. Chambalayne	Wounded.
Sept. 27.	Major M. R. Courage	Wounded.

1916.

Aug. 9.	2nd Lieut. H. F. Metson	Died of Wounds.	
Aug. 17.	2nd Lieut. Hugh St Pierre Banbury	Died of Wounds.	
Aug. 19.	2nd Lieut. C. B. R. Evans	Wounded.	
Sept. 26.	Major G. E. Kidd	Killed.	Shell through roof A/70 Mess.
Sept. 26.	2nd Lieut. J. B. C. Capper	Died of Wounds.	
Sept. 26.	2nd Lieut. G. Nairn	Wounded.	

OTHER RANKS.

1916.	*Killed.*	*Wounded.*
August	9	12
September	nil	6
	9	18

OFFICERS.

1917.

Apr. 8-14. 1 officer wounded (no name given).

July 3.	2nd Lieut. C. L. C. Marshall	Wounded.
July 14.	Captain T. E. K. Cross	Killed.
July 14.	2nd Lieut. W. Donald	Wounded.
July 15.	2nd Lieut. S. B. Lane	Wounded.
July 28.	Major G. R. Briggs	Wounded.
July 31.	2nd Lieut. S. N. Willoughby	Killed.
July 31.	2nd Lieut. T. F. Rennie	Missing, believed killed.
Aug. 16.	2nd Lieut. J. H. Price	Wounded.
Aug. 25.	Capt. J. H. Bampton, R.A.M.C.	Wounded.
Aug. 22.	2nd Lieut. L. Tudsbury	Killed.

OTHER RANKS.

	Killed.	Wounded.	Missing.
January-March .	nil	nil	nil
April . . .	3	18	nil
May-June . .	nil	nil	nil
July . . .	5	49	1
August . . .	10	20	2
	18	87	3

OFFICERS.

1918.

March 21. 2 officers wounded (no names given).
March 28. Lieut. Going . . . . Killed.
March 28. Lieut. A. C. Strachan . . . . Killed.
March 28. Lieut. Rowe-Evans . . . . Missing.
March 28. Lieut. Wilkie . . . . Missing.
March 28. Lieut. Frater . . . . Wounded.
Sept. 17. 2nd Lieut. P. F. Aspinall . . . . . . Killed.

OTHER RANKS.

1918.	Killed.	Wounded.	Missing.
March . . .	7	28	6
September . .	7 killed, wounded, and missing.		

71ST BRIGADE R.F.A.

OFFICERS.

1915.

No details available.

OTHER RANKS.

1915.	Killed.	Wounded.	Missing.
September 26 .	1	11	2
October . .	nil	9	nil
	1	20	2

OFFICERS.

1916.

Feb. 23.	2nd Lieut. D. J. K. Geere	Killed.
Feb. 23.	2nd Lieut. M. Thompson	Wounded.
Feb. 24.	Lieut. K. R. F. Denniston	Wounded.
March 14.	Capt. Alan Patterson	Killed.
Aug. 18.	2nd Lieut. B. M. Stockley	Wounded.
Aug. 20.	2nd Lieut. H. S. Dewey	Killed.
Sept. 25.	2nd Lieut. R. S. Pearse	Killed.
Sept. 29.	Lieut. J. K. Dacre	Died of Wounds.
Nov. 17.	Capt. C. E. P. Henderson	Killed.

OTHER RANKS.

	Killed.	*Wounded.*	*Missing.*	*Died of Wounds.*
January	2	nil	nil	nil
February	3	6	nil	nil
March	nil	5	nil	1
April	3	12	nil	nil
May	3	12	nil	nil
June-July	nil	nil	nil	nil
August	3	7	nil	nil
September	1	1	nil	nil
October	2	7	1	nil
November	2	nil	nil	nil
	19	50	1	1

OFFICERS.

1917.

April. 5 officers killed (names not given).

July 3.	Capt. A. P. J. Day	Wounded.
July 8.	2nd Lieut. H. J. Day	Killed.
July 11.	2nd Lieut. Jacobs	Wounded.
July 14.	2nd Lieut. H. R. Brassey	Gassed.
July 17.	2nd Lieut. G. P. Lewis	Wounded.
July 27.	Major K. Willet	Wounded.

1917.

July 31. 2nd Lieut. O. W. Stewart . . . . . . Killed.
Aug. 11. 2nd Lieut. C. E. Hughes-Davies . . . . Wounded.
Aug. 25. Capt. S. A. Rowden . . . . Gassed.
Sept.-Dec. No particulars given of casualties.

OTHER RANKS.

	Killed.	Wounded.	Missing.	Gassed.
Jan.-Feb. . . .	No particulars.			
March . .	1	nil	1	nil
April . . .	51	121	nil	nil
May . . .	No particulars.			
June . . .	nil	nil	nil	nil
July . . .	14	52	nil	75
August . .	6	37	nil	nil
September . .	No particulars.			
October . .	No particulars.			
November . .	No particulars.			
December . .	No particulars.			
	72	210	1	75

OFFICERS.

1918.

Jan., Feb., April-June, Aug.-Nov.—No casualties mentioned in the War Diaries.

March. Major F. Graham . . . . Killed.
March. Lieut. Morrison . . . . Killed.
March. Lieut. Roddanachi . . . . Wounded.
March. Lieut. Brown . . . . Wounded.
March. Lieut. Stevens . . . . Wounded.
July 26. 2nd Lieut. R. S. Morris . . . . Wounded.

(No other casualties given in the War Diaries.)

OTHER RANKS.

	Killed.	Wounded.	Missing.
March . . .	4	7	35

72ND BRIGADE R.F.A.

OFFICERS.

1915.

Sept. 25. 2nd Lieut. V. R. Brown . . . . Wounded.

1916.

Jan. 17. 2nd Lieut. L. K. Tweedie . . . . . . Killed.
Feb. 8. 2nd Lieut. J. F. Dyce . . . . Wounded.
July 18. Lieut. L. P. S. Bacon . . . . Wounded.
Aug. 13. Lieut. V. R. Barron . . . . Wounded.
Aug. 14. Capt. W. H. B. Saville . . . . Killed.
Sept. 2nd Lieut. Hacket . . . . Gassed.

OTHER RANKS.

	Killed.	*Wounded.*	*Died of Wounds.*	*Gassed.*
January . .	nil	1	nil	nil
March . .	1	nil	nil	nil
July . . .	nil	2	nil	nil
August . .	5	19	nil	nil
September . .	2	4	nil	4
October . .	5	9	nil	nil
November . .	nil	4	1	nil
December . .	nil	4	1	nil
	13	43	2	4

No particulars available for 1917 and 1918.

73RD BRIGADE R.F.A.

OTHER RANKS.

1915.	*Killed.*	*Wounded.*	*Died of Wounds.*
September 25-27 .	2	7	nil
October . .	nil	nil	1
	2	7	1

OFFICERS.

1916.

Aug. 18. Lieut. Chamberlayne . . . . Killed.
Aug. 25. Lieut. Massey . . . . Shell Shock.

OTHER RANKS.

	Wounded.
August . . .	24
September . . .	2
October . . .	3
Nov.-Dec. . . .	nil

No particulars available for 1917 and 1918.

DIVISIONAL AMMUNITION COLUMN.

OFFICERS.

1917.

Jan.-June.—Nil. Sept.-Dec.—No particulars given.

OTHER RANKS.

	Killed.	*Wounded.*
July . . .	5	25
August . . .	5	5
	10	30

OFFICERS.

1918.

Jan.-Feb.—Nil. March.—Nil. April-Nov.—No particulars given.

OTHER RANKS.

	Killed.	*Wounded.*	*Missing.*
March . . .	5	8	3

15TH TRENCH-MORTAR BATTERY.

OFFICERS.

1917.

March. 1 officer wounded (no name or date given).
July 25. Lieut. Macartney . . . . Wounded.

OTHER RANKS.

	Killed.	Wounded.
Jan.-Feb. . . .	nil	nil
March . . .	15	7
June . . .	nil	nil
July . . .	2	13
August . . .	1	2
	18	22

OFFICERS.

1918.

Jan.-Feb.—Nil. April.—Nil. May-Nov.—No particulars given in the War Diaries.

March 28. Lieut. Urquhart . . . . Missing.

OTHER RANKS.

	Killed.	Wounded.	Missing
March . . .	1	10	8
April . . .	nil	2	nil
	1	12	8

ROYAL ENGINEERS.

DIVISIONAL SIGNAL COMPANY.

OFFICERS.

1915.

Sept., Nov., and Dec.—Nil.

OTHER RANKS.

1915.	Killed.	Wounded.
October . .	4	3

1916.

Officers . . . . Nil.

OTHER RANKS.

1916.	*Killed.*	*Wounded.*
January . .	nil	2
June . . .	1	nil
	1	2

OFFICERS.

1917.

Aug. 20. 2nd Lieut. R. S. Smith . . . . . . Wounded.

OTHER RANKS.

	Killed.	*Wounded.*
April . . .	3	1
July . . .	nil	4
August . . .	nil	3
	3	8

OFFICERS.

1918.

March 28. Lieut. J. Morrison . . . . Killed.
July 26. 2nd Lieut. N. C. D. Brown . . . . . Wounded.

OTHER RANKS.

	Killed.	*Wounded.*
March . . .	1	5
July . . .	nil	20
	1	25

73RD FIELD COMPANY, R.E.

OFFICERS.

Battle of Loos, September 1915.

1915.

Sept. 25.	Lieut. Inglis	Killed.
Sept. 25.	2nd Lieut. Nolan	Killed.
Sept. 25.	Capt. Carden	Wounded and Missing.
Sept. 25.	2nd Lieut. Ryan	Wounded.
Sept. 25.	2nd Lieut. Johnson	Wounded.

OTHER RANKS.

Killed.	*Wounded.*	*Missing.*
14	22	11

OFFICERS.

1916.

April 28.	2nd Lieut. F. P. Lefroy	Killed.
Oct. 22.	2nd Lieut. F. Craig	Wounded.
Aug. 18.	Lieut. H. J. Howie	Wounded.

OTHER RANKS.

	Killed.	*Wounded.*
April	nil	1
August	4	16
October	1	2
	5	19

OFFICERS.

1917.

July 21.	2nd Lieut. Burrows	Wounded.
July 21.	2nd Lieut. Adams	Wounded.
Aug. 22.	2nd Lieut. Poole	Died of Wounds.

Sept.-Dec.—No casualties given in War Diaries of unit, C.R.E., or "Q" of Division.

Jan.-Feb., May and June.—Nil.

OTHER RANKS.

1917.	*Killed.*	*Wounded.*	*Missing.*
March . . .	2	8	nil
April . . .	6	7	nil
July . . .	2	22	1
	10	37	1

OFFICERS.

1918.

March 28. Lieut. Andrews . . . . . . Died of Wounds.
July 30. 2nd Lieut. J. F. S. Jack . . . . Wounded.

OTHER RANKS.

	Killed.	*Wounded.*	*Gassed.*
March . . .	nil	2	nil
April . . .	nil	1	nil
June . . .	1	nil	nil
July . . .	nil	2	nil
August . . .	1	nil	6
September . .	1	4	nil
October . .	nil	1	nil
	3	10	6

74TH FIELD COMPANY, R.E.

1915.

Officers . . . . . . Nil.

OTHER RANKS.

	Killed.	*Wounded.*	*Gassed.*
September . .	3	9	1
October . .	nil	1	nil
	3	10	1

OFFICERS.

1916.

July 10.	Lieut. J. W. Ware	Killed.
Sept. 3.	2nd Lieut. S. W. Irwin	Wounded.
Sept. 7.	Lieut. R. E. Deane Oliver	Killed.
Sept.	Lieut. W. R. Frecheville	Wounded.
Dec. 14.	Lieut. Bartrum	Wounded.

OTHER RANKS.

	Killed.	*Wounded.*
January	nil	4
February	nil	2
May	nil	1
July	nil	4
August	nil	1
September	2	20
November	1	2
December	1	8
	4	42

OFFICERS.

1917.

April 8.	Lieut. T. H. Upton	Wounded.
April 27.	Lieut. W. H. Close	Wounded.
July 22.	2nd Lieut. H. H. Bradshaw	Killed.

Sept.-Dec.—No casualties given in War Diaries of unit, C.R.E., or "Q" of Division.

OTHER RANKS.

	Killed.	*Wounded.*
March	1	2
April	2	18
August	4	10
	7	30

OFFICERS.

1918.

Oct. 30.	Lieut. T. F. H. White	Wounded.

OTHER RANKS.

	Killed.	Wounded.
March . . .	2	6
June . . .	1	2
July . . .	nil	1
October . .	1	1
	4	10

91ST FIELD COMPANY, R.E.

1915.

OFFICERS.

Sept. 27. Lieut. F. C. MacNaught . . . . . . Killed.

OTHER RANKS.

	Killed.	Wounded.	Missing.
September . .	13	30	10

1916.

OFFICERS.

Jan. 25. 2nd Lieut. Dyer . . . . Wounded.
March 19. Capt. A. P. Sayer . . . . . . Wounded.
Sept. 3. 2nd Lieut. P. Hamilton Davies . . . . Wounded.
Sept. 19. 2nd Lieut. O'Brien . . . . . . Wounded.

OTHER RANKS.

	Killed.	Wounded.
February . .	2	2
March . . .	nil	1
June . . .	6	nil
August . . .	nil	5
Sept.-Dec. . .	nil	nil
	8	8

1917.

OFFICERS.

Jan. 11. 2nd Lieut. A. C. Kerr . . . . . . Killed.
Jan. 12. 2nd Lieut. Y. La Montagne . . . . . Wounded.
March 28. 2nd Lieut. G. F. Heaney . . . . . Wounded.
Aug. 20. Lieut. G. R. Pim . . . . Wounded.
Dec. 18. Lieut. A. O. Day . . . . Wounded.

OTHER RANKS.

	Killed.	Wounded.
January . .	3	nil
March . . .	nil	2
April . . .	nil	2
July . . .	1	1
August . . .	nil	5
	4	10

OFFICERS.

1918.

March 22. 2nd Lieut. R. W. Kenley . . . . . . Wounded.
July 26. Major A. H. Davenport . . . . . . Wounded.
July 26. Lieut. Milligan . . . . Wounded.
July 28. 2nd Lieut. Arbuthnott . . . . . . Wounded.

OTHER RANKS.

	Killed.	Wounded.	Missing.
February . .	nil	3	nil
March . . .	nil	4	nil
June . . .	nil	2	nil
July . . .	2	6	2
October . .	nil	3	nil
	2	18	2

HEADQUARTERS, R.E.

1917.

Aug. 17. Capt. C. de L. Gaussen (Adjt.) . . . . . Wounded.

DIVISIONAL CAVALRY (B Squadron, 1/1 Westmorland and Cumberland Yeomanry).

Casualties, 1915 to April 1916—nil.

(To XI. Corps, May 1916.)

15TH DIVISIONAL CYCLISTS.

1915.

Officers . . . . . Nil.

OTHER RANKS.

	Killed.	Wounded.
October . . .	1	6
December . .	nil	1
	1	7

Casualties, January to May 1916—nil.

(To XIV. Corps Cyclist Battalion, May 1916.)

225TH MACHINE-GUN COMPANY (joined July 1917).

OFFICERS.

1917.

July 26.	2nd Lieut. Grove	Wounded.
Aug. 1.	2nd Lieut. E. B. Davis	Killed.
Aug. 1.	2nd Lieut. Grove	Wounded.
Aug. 12.	2nd Lieut. Howells	Wounded.
Sept. 17.	2nd Lieut. L. E. Gill	Killed.
Oct. 24.	2nd Lieut. Dyke	Wounded.

OTHER RANKS.

	Killed.	Wounded.	Gassed.
July . . .	1	7	3
August . . .	2	14	nil
September . .	nil	1	nil
October . . .	nil	nil	nil
November . .	1	1	nil
December . .	nil	3	nil
	4	26	3

15TH BATTALION MACHINE-GUN COMPANY (formed March 1918).

OFFICERS.

March 28.	2nd Lieut. W. J. Finnigan	Killed.
March 28.	2nd Lieut. S. A. Parrott	Wounded.
March 28.	2nd Lieut. A. R. Littlejohn	Wounded.
March 28.	2nd Lieut. E. A. Smith	Wounded.
March 28.	2nd Lieut. H. W. Stagg	Missing.
March 28.	2nd Lieut. J. C. Ashburner	Missing.

1918.

March 28. 2nd Lieut. J. T. Kirk . . . . Missing.
March 28. 2nd Lieut. W. J. Taylor . . . . . . Missing.
March 28. Lieut. L. S. Winn . . . . Missing.
March 28. Lieut. E. Rogers . . . . Gassed.
March 28. 2nd Lieut. A. F. Poole . . . . Gassed.
July 23. Lieut. Lunn . . . . Wounded.
Aug. 1. 2nd Lieut. De Vere . . . . Wounded.
Aug. 1. 2nd Lieut. Stevens . . . . Wounded.
Oct. 16. 2nd Lieut. R. B. Mason . . . . . . Killed.

OTHER RANKS.

	Killed.	*Wounded.*	*Missing.*
March . . .	142 casualties.		
April-June . .	nil	nil	nil
July . . .	4	19	nil
August . . .	1	12	nil
Sept.-Nov. . .	nil	nil	nil

ROYAL ARMY SERVICE CORPS.

DIVISIONAL TRAIN.

Casualties, 1915 }
Casualties, 1916 } None given in War Diaries.

OFFICERS.

1917.

April 4. Capt. C. S. M. Hutchinson . . . . . Wounded.

OTHER RANKS.

	Wounded.
April . . .	1
July . . .	1
	2

OFFICERS.

1918.

March 22. Capt. F. D. Livingstone . . . . . . Wounded.
March 26. Lieut. G. A. G. Godley . . . . . . Killed.

D.A.D.O.S.

Casualties, 1915 to 1918—nil (except March 1918, 1 killed, 1 wounded).

D.A.D.V.S.

Casualties, 1915 to 1918—nil (except Jan. 1917, 1 killed, 4 wounded, bombed).

15TH DIVISIONAL "A" AND "Q" DIARY.

"Q" Diary starts 1st February 1916 (February numbered Vol. I).
No monthly figures given for February and March.

	Officers.			*Other Ranks.*		
1916.	*Killed.*	*Wounded.*	*Missing.*	*Killed.*	*Wounded.*	*Missing.*
April .	6	13	—	59	320	2
May .	28	43	1	234	1224	267
June .	9	26	1	131	746	9
July .	6	42	1	98	696	30
Aug. .	25	126	8	478	2613	294
Sept. .	25	123	—	379	2257	405
Oct. .	7	37	1	161	1017	39
Nov. .	2	9	—	19	90	4
Dec. .	3	11	1	44	188	6

	Officers.			*Other Ranks.*		
1917.	*Killed.*	*Wounded.*	*Missing.*	*Killed.*	*Wounded.*	*Missing.*
Jan. .	7	21	1	63	319	15
Feb. .	—	2	—	14	87	1
March .	3	17	—	85	372	10
April .	80	203	10	887	4410	723
May . June .	Division training.					

Casualties as given in "Q" War Diary :—

	Killed.	*Wounded.*	*Missing.*
July—			
Officers . . .	—	63	—
Other Ranks . .	—	1545	—
August 5-25—			
Officers . . .	26	77	11
Other Ranks . .	330	1935	509

	Killed.	Wounded.	Missing.
September—			
Officers . . .	—	2	—
Other Ranks . .	—	197	—
October—			
Officers . . .	—	14	—
Other Ranks . .	—	202	—
November—			
Officers . . .	—	12	—
Other Ranks . .	—	290	—
December—			
Officers . . .	—	8	—
Other Ranks . .	—	208	—

	Officers.			Other Ranks.		
1918.	Killed.	Wounded.	Missing.	Killed.	Wounded.	Missing.
Jan. .	Division out of the line.					
Feb. .	—	7	—	35	103	—
March .	25	65	36	299	1418	1112
April .	No figures given.					
May .	3	23	2	66	439	2
June .	5	25	1	55	454	16
July .	22	87	7	323	2940	177
Aug. .	9	53	7	191	999	268
Sept. .	9	34	1	84	733	41
Oct. . / Nov. .	No figures given in the War Diaries.					

The following are the total casualties as given in the Divisional H.Q. Diaries, which show certain discrepancies with the figures given above :—

	Officers.			Other Ranks.		
	K.	W.	M.	K.	W.	M.
44th Brigade .	129	323	24	1569	9227	2505
45th Brigade .	126	313	41	1701	8248	1836
46th Brigade .	151	246	23*	1481	8784	1921*
15th Div. Art. .	28	36	4	183	650	58
R.E. and Pioneers	21	50	2	233	1120	90
15th Div. Troops .	5	14	5	11	211	—
	460	982	99	5178	28,240	6410

* These are casualties from battalions of the 46th Brigade. They were not classified in any way.—J.S.

Or—

	Officers.	*Other Ranks.*
	1541	39,828
To which add	20*	628*
	B	
	1561	40,456

Or—

Total casualties . . . . 42,017†

TOTAL CASUALTIES AS SHOWN IN G.H.Q. DIARIES.

	Officers.			*Other Ranks.*		
	Killed.	*Wounded.*	*Missing.*	*Killed.*	*Wounded.*	*Missing.*
Totals .	300	1136	89	4035	25,802	3930

Or—

Officers.	*Other Ranks.*
1525	33,767

Or—

Total casualties 35,292

* These are casualties from battalions of the 46th Brigade. They were not classified in any way.—J.S.

† These numbers are as nearly correct as it is possible to get them.—J.S.

APPENDIX J.

AWARDS OF THE VICTORIA CROSS

MAJOR (TEMP. LIEUT.-COLONEL) A. F. DOUGLAS HAMILTON, R. OF O., COMMANDING 6TH CAMERON HIGHLANDERS.

For most conspicuous bravery and devotion to duty when commanding his battalion during operations on September 25 and 26, 1915, on Hill 70.

On the 26th, when the battalions on his right and left had retired, he rallied his own battalion again and again, and led his men forward four times. The last time he led all that remained, consisting of about fifty men, in a most gallant manner, and was killed at their head. It was mainly due to his bravery, untiring energy, and splendid leadership that the line at this point was enabled to check the enemy's advance.

TEMP. 2ND LIEUTENANT F. H. JOHNSON, 73RD FIELD COMPANY, R.E.

For most conspicuous bravery and devotion to duty in the attack on Hill 70 on September 25, 1915.

2nd Lieutenant Johnson was with a section of his company of the Royal Engineers. Although wounded in the leg he stuck to his duty throughout the attack, led several charges on the German redoubt, and at a very critical time under very heavy fire repeatedly rallied the men who were near him. By his splendid example and cool courage he was mainly instrumental in saving the situation, and establishing firmly his part of the position which had been taken. He remained at his post until relieved in the evening.

36830 A/SERGEANT J. C. RAYNES, "A" BATTERY, 71ST BRIGADE, R.F.A., FOSSE 7 DE BETHUNE, OCTOBER 11, 1915.

On October 11, 1915, at Fosse 7 de Bethune, his battery was being heavily bombarded by armour-piercing and gas shells. On "Cease fire" being ordered, Sergeant Raynes went out under an intense shell fire to assist Sergeant Ayres, who was lying wounded forty yards away. He bandaged him, and returned to his gun when it was again ordered into action. A few minutes later "Cease fire" was again ordered owing to the intensity of the enemy's fire. Sergeant Raynes, calling on two gunners to help him—both of whom were killed shortly afterwards,—went out and carried Sergeant Ayres into a dug-out. A gas shell burst at the mouth of the dug-out, and Sergeant Raynes once more ran across the open, fetched his own smoke helmet, put it on Sergeant Ayres, and then, himself badly gassed, staggered back to serve his gun. On October 12, 1915, at Quality Street, a house was knocked down by a heavy shell, four men being buried in the house and four in the cellar. The first man rescued was Sergeant Raynes, but he insisted on remaining under heavy shell fire to assist in the rescue of all the others. Then after having his wounds dressed, he reported himself immediately for duty with his battery, which was being heavily shelled.

15851 Piper D. Laidlaw, 7th King's Own Scottish Borderers.

For most conspicuous bravery prior to an assault on German trenches near Loos and Hill 70 on September 25, 1915.

During the worst of the bombardment, when the attack was about to commence, Piper Laidlaw, seeing that his company was somewhat shaken from the effects of gas, with absolute coolness and disregard of danger, mounted the parapet, marched up and down, and played his company out of the trench. The effect of his splendid example was immediate, and the company dashed out to the assault. Piper Laidlaw continued playing his pipes till he was wounded.

18274 Private R. Dunsire, 13th Royal Scots.

For most conspicuous bravery on Hill 70 on September 26, 1915.

Private Dunsire went out under very heavy fire, and rescued a wounded man from between the firing lines. Later, when another man considerably nearer the German lines was heard shouting for help, he crawled out again with utter disregard to the enemy's fire and carried him in also. Shortly afterwards the Germans attacked over this ground.

APPENDIX K.

HONOURS AND AWARDS.

MUCH labour has been expended in compiling the following lists and in making them as complete as possible from information derived from War Diaries, Record Offices, and private sources. The compiler claims indulgence for many obvious omissions, as detailed information regarding some units was found to be very scanty, and in other cases entirely lacking.

44TH INFANTRY BRIGADE.

9TH THE BLACK WATCH.

OFFICERS.

1916.

Jan. 5. *Mentioned in Despatches* ('London Gazette,' January 1, 1916) :—
Major (T/Lt.-Col.) T. O. Lloyd. Capt. (T/Major) J. Stewart.
T/Capt. C. S. Tuke. T/Lieut. E. R. Wilson.
Capt. F. A. Bearn, R.A.M.C.

Sept. 27. *Military Cross* (for services, August 17, 1916) :—
Capt. W. B. Binnie.

Nov. 28. *Military Cross :* Lieut. and Q.M. W. Clark.

1917.

Jan. 5. *D.S.O. :*
Major (T/Lt.-Col.) S. A. Innes. Capt. F. A. Bearn, R.A.M.C.
Mentioned in Despatches :
Major (T/Lt.-Col.) S. A. Innes. T/Major A. D. Carmichael.
T/Capt. S. Norie Miller. T/Lieut. J. F. N. Macrae.
T/Lieut. G. Mackie. T/Q.M. and Hon. Lieut. W. Clark.

March 19. *Italian Silver Medal* (for military valour) : Capt. Storey-Wilson.

May 10. *Military Cross :* 2/Lieut. F. Proudfoot.

May 25. *Mentioned in Despatches :*
Lt.-Col. S. A. Innes, D.S.O. Capt. W. Storey-Wilson.

May 31. *Bar to D.S.O. :* Major (T/Lt.-Col.) S. A. Innes, D.S.O.
Military Crosses :
2/Lieut. T. Byers. 2/Lieut. T. B. Allison.

Aug. 31. *Bar to Military Cross :* 2/Lieut. F. Proudfoot, M.C.

1917.

Aug. 31. *Military Crosses:*
2/Lieut. J. E. Drummond. 2/Lieut. W. R. Tovani.

Oct. 4. *Bar to Military Cross:* A/Major W. B. Binnie.
Military Crosses:
T/Capt. J. S. Strang. T/Lieut. S. Graham.
T/Lieut. N. G. Johnstone. 2/Lieut. J. Addison.
2/Lieut. T. Calvert.

Dec. 18. *Mentioned in Despatches:*
Lt.-Col. S. A. Innes, D.S.O. Major A. H. O. Dennistoun.
Capt. and Q.M. W. Clark, M.C.

1918.

Jan. 1. *Military Cross:* Capt. S. Norie Miller.

April 22. *Military Crosses:*
Lieut. A. K. Hamilton. Lieut. A. Marshall.
Lieut. E. W. D. Wilkinson.

May 21. *Mentioned in Despatches:*
Lt.-Col. S. A. Innes, D.S.O. 2/Lieut. A. G. Loxton.

May 31. *Military Cross:* Capt. W. Storey Wilson.

June 23. *Military Cross:* Lieut. E. W. D. Wilson.

June 26. *Military Crosses:*
Lieut. A. K. Hamilton. Lieut. A. Marshall.

4/5th The Black Watch.

Officers.

1918.

June . *Bar to Military Cross:* Lieut. (A/Capt.) D. Maxwell, M.C.
Military Cross: 2/Lieut. G. R. Farrar.

June 3. *Military Cross:*
Lieut. (A/Capt.) J. R. Philip. Lt. (A/Capt.) C. H. C. R. Penn
2/Lieut. A. C. Skinner.

June 11. *Mentioned in Despatches:*
Major (T/Lt.-Col.) S. A. Innes, D.S.O. 2/Lieut. A. G. Loxton.

Aug. . *Chevalier de la Legion d'Honneur et Croix de Guerre:*
Lt.-Col. R. A. Bulloch, D.S.O.
Croix de Guerre:
Major J. S. Y. Robers, D.S.O. Capt. J. I. Buchan, D.S.O.

Aug. 31. *Military Cross:*
Capt. R. E. Badenoch. Lieut. R. Inch.
2/Lieut. G. Fullerton. 2/Lieut. A. Scott.

9TH THE BLACK WATCH.

OTHER RANKS.

(From July 1915 to June 1918.)

No.	Rank.	Name.	Award.	Date of London Gazette.
S/4294	L/Cpl.	Ledlie, R.	Ment. in Des.	1/1/16
6323	Sergt.	Henderson, J.	,, ,,	5/1/16
7977	Pte.	Boak, G.	,, ,,	,,
S/4291	L/Cpl.	Bell, W.	D.C.M.	14/1/16
S/4855	Sergt.	Green, I.	,,	,,
S/4560	L/Sergt.	M'Kellar, D. R.	Croix de Guerre	24/2/16
S/3982	Sergt.	Bayne, A. E.	D.C.M.	15/3/16
S/6660	L/Cpl.	Thomson, A.	,,	,,
4416	Cpl.	Cashmore	Military Medal	21/5/16
7979	A/C.S.M.	Jack, A.	,, ,,	,,
3/3731	C.S.M.	Munro, J.	Ment. in Des.	15/6/16
S/7979	Sergt.	Jack, A.	,, ,,	,,
3/3831	Q.M.S.	Hampton, T.	D.C.M.	21/6/16
S/4295	L/Sergt.	Brown, A.	Military Medal	29/7/16
			Ment. in Des.	1/1/16
S/4333	Pte.	Hailstones, T.	Military Medal	29/7/16
			Bar to M.M.	28/1/18
S/4094	Sergt.	Millar, J.	Military Medal	3/6/16
S/4902	L/Cpl.	Brown, R.	,, ,,	14/9/16
S/6628	Sergt.	Foster, T.	,, ,,	,,
S/5360	Pte.	Robertson, W.	,, ,,	14/9/16
			Bar to M.M.	16/11/16
S/6829	Sergt.	Sanders, J.	Military Medal	14/9/16
S/6603	Pte.	Thomson, H.	,, ,,	,,
3/3653	Sergt.	M'Cann, P.	Mer. Ser. Medal	18/10/16
S/43294	Pte.	Cobban, W. L.	D.C.M.	14/11/16
S/11458	Sergt.	Booth, J. W.	Military Medal	16/11/16
S/4571	Cpl.	Christie, W.	,, ,,	,,
S/9197	Pte.	Dickson, A. D.	,, ,,	,,
S/4779	Pte.	Fletcher, W.	,, ,,	,,
S/9947	A/Cpl.	Macaulay, J. W.	,, ,,	,,
S/10001	Pte.	M'Kay, F.	,, ,,	,,
S/4343	Pte.	M'Queen, R.	,, ,,	,,
S/9461	Pte.	Milne, R.	,, ,,	,,

No.	Rank.	Name.	Award.	Date of London Gazette.
S/5167	Pte.	Murray, W.	Military Medal	16/11/16
S/9394	Pte.	Pullar, J.	" "	"
S/9617	Sergt.	Simpson, G.	" "	"
S/9813	Pte.	Smith, C.	" "	"
S/4754	Pte.	Sullivan, D.	" "	"
S/4362	Pte.	Wallace, D.	" "	"
S/9995	Pte.	Ward, T.	" "	"
S/4794	Pte.	Beattie, T.	" "	14/9/16
			Bar to M.M.	16/11/16
3999	Cpl.	M'Cluskie, W.	Military Medal	"
3/3849	S.M.	Bedson, G. D.	Military Cross	1/1/17
S/11214	Sergt.	Goward, W.	Military Medal	22/1/17
S/11888	A/Cpl.	Mullen, J.	" "	26/3/17
S/6560	Pte.	Robin, W.	Croix de Guerre	1/5/17
5337	Pte.	Mechan, W.	Military Medal	18/5/17
9344	Pte.	Murray, W.	Ment. in Des.	25/5/17
S/9338	Pte.	Wotherspoon, J.	" "	25/5/17
3/3731	Q.M.S.	Munro, J.	D.C.M.	4/6/17
S/16877	Pte.	Black, A.	"	18/6/17
1994	Sergt.	Crisp, A.	Military Medal	"
S/15995	Pte.	Isles, S.	" "	"
S/40387	L/Cpl.	Lindsay, W. E.	" "	"
S/7308	Pte.	Logan, W.	" "	"
S/5351	Cpl.	Dick, W.	" "	3/7/17
240046	Sergt.	Gibb, J.	" "	"
1490	Sergt.	Wilson, E.	" "	"
S/4701	Cpl.	Park, J. T.	Croix de Guerre	12/7/17
S/9883	C.S.M.	M'Kerchar, J.	Military Cross	18/7/17
S/4926	C.S.M.	Price, J. W.	" "	"
S/43174	L/Cpl.	Sandilands, J.	D.C.M.	"
7979	Pte.	Jack, A.	Bar to M.M.	24/8/17
9937	Sergt.	Cody, C.	Military Medal	"
8435	A/Sergt.	Wright, G.	" "	"
17082	Pte.	Moffat, W.	" "	"
16555	A/Sergt.	Johnstone, A.	D.C.M.	1/9/17
3814	A/Cpl.	Ross, R.	Bar to M.M.	6/10/17
240240	A/Cpl.	Gouk, G.	Military Medal	4/9/17
9499	Pte.	Brown, W.	" "	"
S/6618	Pte.	Black, A.	" "	17/9/17
S/9458	Pte.	Keatings, J.	" "	"
S/4539	C.S.M.	M'Call, J.	Military Cross	26/9/17

No.	Rank.	Name.	Award.	Date of London Gazette.
265339	Pte.	Ross, T.	Military Medal	6/10/17
8639	Pte.	Somerville, J.	,, ,,	,,
40822	Pte.	Kennedy, W.	,, ,,	,,
9397	L/Cpl.	MacIsaac, G.	,, ,,	,,
9678	L/Cpl.	Smith, J.	,, ,,	,,
267234	A/Sergt.	Rankin, W.	,, ,,	,,
9399	A/Sergt.	Murphy, W.	,, ,,	,,
2694	Pte.	Duffy, R.	,, ,,	,,
9937	Pte.	Cockett, H. E.	,, ,,	18/10/17
S/4109	Cpl.	Davidson, J.	,, ,,	,,
S/11798	Cpl.	Duncan, J. A.	,, ,,	,,
S/4246	Pte.	Grant, J.	,, ,,	,,
3/3759	Sergt.	Ogilvie, C.	,, ,,	,,
S/43427	Cpl.	Sharples, W.	,, ,,	,,
S/12320	Pte.	Stone, A.	,, ,,	,,
240171	L/Cpl.	Brown, H. R.	,, ,,	2/11/17
S/40820	Pte.	Johnston, J.	,, ,,	,,
S/3814	L/Cpl.	Ross, R.	,, ,,	,,
200397	Pte.	Scott, J.	,, ,,	,,
S/4750	Pte.	Beveridge, J.	,, ,,	19/11/17
11256	C.Q.M.S.	Naesmith, A.	Ment. in Des.	18/12/17
6319	Sergt.	Steele, A.	,, ,,	,,
S/3681	Sergt.	Gray, G.	Mer. Ser. Medal	1/1/18
S/7197	Cpl.	Scobie, W.	,, ,,	1/1/18
S/18249	Pte.	Greig, R. A.	Military Medal	13/3/18
9678	Cpl.	Smith, J.	Bar to M.M.	17/4/18
351149	L/Cpl.	Callaghan, J.	Military Medal	,,
18731	Pte.	Robertson, A. R.	,, ,,	,,
290695	L/Cpl.	Clink, J.	,, ,,	,,
8976	C.S.M.	Barclay, D.	Military Cross	31/5/18
4682	R.Q.M.S.	Ramage, A.	Mer. Ser. Medal	14/6/18
S/11160	Cpl. (A/S.)	Buchan, A.	Ment. in Des.	24/5/18
S/5133	Pte. (A/S.)	Robertson, A.	,, ,,	11/6/18
S/43489	Pte.	Rowley, A.	Military Medal	27/6/18
202280	Pte.	Grieve, R.	Croix de Guerre	12/7/18
3/3652	Sergt.	Monkley, J.	,, ,,	,,
S/19494	Pte.	Funkie, R. D.	Military Medal	29/8/18
43730	R.S.M.	Hutton, A. J.	Ment. in Des.	28/8/18
1709	Pte.	Duncan, F.	Military Medal	11/2/19

4/5TH THE BLACK WATCH.

OTHER RANKS.

(From June 1918 to Finish.)

No.	Rank.	Name.	Award.	Date of London Gazette.
240991	C.S.M.	Stewart, W.	Bar to D.C.M.	3/6/18
11160	L/Sergt.	Buchan, A.	Ment. in Des.	11/6/18
201211	C.S.M.	Anderson, A.	Mer. Ser. Medal	17/6/18
240225	L/Cpl.	Ramsay, W.	Military Medal	27/6/18
18731	Pte.	Robertson, A.	,, ,,	,,
240345	Pte.	Hutcheson	,, ,,	16/7/18
—	Pte.	Graham, J.	Croix de Guerre	10/8/18
350226	Sergt.	Malcolm, S.	,, ,,	,,
			D.C.M.	31/8/18
201211	C.S.M.	Anderson, A.	,,	3/9/18
201115	Sergt.	Hedley, D.	,,	,,
200501	Sergt.	Keith, J. J.	,,	,,
202339	Pte.	Petrie, D.	,,	,,
203186	Pte.	South, H. S.	,,	,,
200288	Cpl.	Anderson, W.	,,	13/9/18
200315	Pte.	Croll, W. M.	,,	,,
S/12927	Cpl.	Durie, A.	,,	,,
241094	Pte.	Easton, S.	,,	,,
200241	Sergt.	Griffen, W. H.	Military Medal	,,
201163	Pte.	M'Gregor, A.	,, ,,	,,
200001	C.Q.M.S.	M'Kenzie, W. F.	,, ,,	,,
202267	Pte.	Morrison, J.	,, ,,	,,
202288	Pte.	M'Connell, J.	Bar to M.M.	,,
202283	Sergt.	Wallace, A.	,, ,,	,,
S/40340	Sergt.	Dickson, A.	D.C.M.	30/10/18
			Med. Militaire	22/11/18
3/1368	L/Cpl.	Somerville, W. W.	D.C.M.	30/10/18
240948	Sergt.	Stephen, J.	Military Medal	13/11/18
291706	L/Cpl.	Brough, A.	,, ,,	,,
350376	L/Cpl.	Mill, H.	,, ,,	,,
12369	Pte.	Sayle, F. A.	,, ,,	,,
S/16521	Pte.	Stewart, W.	,, ,,	,,
S/9822	Pte.	Willetts, F.	,, ,,	,,

No.	Rank.	Name.	Award.	Date of London Gazette.
202386	Sergt.	Cairns, J. C.	Croix de Guerre	22/11/18
	C.S.M.	Cairns, J.	D.C.M.	3/6/19
S/4109	Cpl.	Davidson, J.	Croix de Guerre	22/11/18
S/40340	Sergt.	Dickson, A.	,, ,,	,,
292132	Pte.	Kidd, M.	,, ,,	,,
15943	Cpl.	Moffat, J.	,, ,,	,,
S/9317	Pte.	Robertson, A.	,, ,,	,,
265339	Pte.	Rose, T.	,, ,,	,,
202613	Pte.	Robertson, W.	Military Medal	11/12/18
202476	C.Q.M.S.	Campbell, D.	Mer. Ser. Medal	18/1/19
200029	Sergt. Piper	M'Leod, D.	Bar to M.M.	2/11/19
291706	L/Cpl.	Brough, A.	,, ,,	27/10/18
3958	C.Q.M.S.	Smith, W.	Military Medal	7/11/18
—	L/Cpl.	Hill, W. F.	Bar to M.M.	19/12/18
9866	C.S.M.	Duff, R. H.	Ment. in Des.	27/3/19
3/4315	Sergt.	Paton, G.	Military Medal	14/5/19
S/13453	Pte.	Reid, J.	,, ,,	,,
S/24147	Pte. (L/C.)	Sutherland, R.	,, ,,	,,
290034	Sergt.	Ballingall, G.	Mer. Ser. Medal	3/6/19
291669	Cpl. (A/S.)	Jack, A.D.	,, ,,	,,
S/6735	Sergt.	Higgins, J.	Military Medal	17/6/19
S/4458	Cpl.	Davidson, J.	,, ,,	,,
S/4750	Cpl.	Beveridge, J.	Ment. in Des.	9/7/19
13	Pte.	M'Pherson, H.	,, ,,	,,
S/3111	Sergt. (A/Q.M.S.)	Pollock, J.	,, ,,	,,
S/4682	R.Q.M.S.	Ramage, A.	,, ,,	,,
			Méd. d'Honneur Avec Glaives (en Argent)	5/12/19
S/40844	Pte. (A/C.Q.M.S.)	Wood, J. A.	Ment. in Des.	9/7/19
240228	L/Cpl.	Dalgetty, W.	Military Medal	23/7/19
201262	Pte.	Rankine, T.	,, ,,	,,
S/4271	Pte.	Scott, C.	,, ,,	,,
200421	Pte.	Tolmie, D.	,, ,,	,,
200735	Cpl. (A/S.)	Cargill, J.	,, ,,	20/8/19
S/12172	C.S.M.	Land, H. D. B.	D.C.M.	3/9/19
S/4371	Cpl. (A/S.)	Craig, J.	Military Medal	20/10/19

8th Seaforth Highlanders.

Officers.

C.M.G.

Colonel N. A. Thomson, D.S.O. (with Brigade Headquarters).

D.S.O.

Lieut.-Colonel F. Anderson	January 1919.
Major A. Macmillan	August 1918.
Lieut.-Colonel N. A. Thomson	May 1916.

Bar to the D.S.O.

Lieut.-Colonel the Hon. E. O. Campbell . . .	May 1918.

Military Cross.

Capt. F. W. Ashard	January 1919.
Capt. G. G. Blackwood	August 1917.
Lieut. F. Burns	August 1917.
Lieut. T. L. Christie	August 1917.
The Rev. W. Crawford (Royal Army Chaplain's Dept.)	
Capt. G. W. Duncan	January 1917.
Lieut. J. Graham	March 1918.
Lieut. T. C. Irvine	August 1917.
Lieut. D. A. Macadie	August 1917.
Capt. D. B. Macaulay	August 1917.
Lieut. D. W. Mackenzie	August 1917.
Lieut. F. M. M'Callion	July 1916.
Lieut. H. L. M'Kinlay (with 6th Camerons)	
Lieut. T. Milne	May 1916.
Capt. S. A. W. Munro (R.A.M.C.)	
Capt. T. G. Muir	April 1918.
Capt. G. Murray	July 1918.
Capt. G. D. K. Murray	July 1918.
Lieut. R. W. Paulden	July 1918.
Capt J. E. Smith	July 1916.
Lieut. R. P. Smith	May 1917.
Major D. W. P. Strang	September 1915.

Capt. P. W. Straw	August 1917.
Lieut. G. Syme	November 1917.
Lieut. A. Thomson	August 1918.
Lieut. J. L. Turing	August 1917.
Lieut.-Colonel A. W. Turnbull	August 1916.
Lieut. J. R. Wardrope	April 1917.

Croix de Chevalier Legion d'Honneur.

Colonel N. A. Thomson, C.M.G., D.S.O.	
Major A. Macmillan	July 1918.
Major D. W. P. Strang	September 1915.

Croix de Guerre avec Palmes.

Colonel N. A. Thomson, C.M.G., D.S.O.	
Major A. Macmillan	July 1918.
Lieut. A. J. Marr	July 1918.
Capt. S. A. W. Munro (R.A.M.C.)	July 1918.
Capt. G. D. K. Murray	July 1918.

Belgian Croix de Guerre.

Lieut. M. Jackson	November 1918.

Order of St Stanislaus.

Colonel N. A. Thomson, C.M.G., D.S.O.

Mentioned in Despatches.

(The 8th Battalion Seaforth Highlanders was one of the units mentioned in Sir Douglas Haig's despatch of 19th May 1916.)

Lieut.-Colonel F. Anderson, M.C.	21/12/18.
Capt. F. W. Ashard, M.C.	23/12/16 and 25/12/17.
2/Lieut. T. Beatson	21/12/18.
Lieut.-Colonel K. G. Buchanan, D.S.O.	25/12/17.
Lieut.-Colonel the Hon. E. O. Campbell, D.S.O.	20/6/18.
Capt. G. W. Duncan, M.C.	23/12/16.
Capt. H. C. Duncan	25/12/17.
Capt. E. K. O. Ferguson	30/11/15.

Capt. E. M. Fraser	25/12/17.
Capt. D. H. Georgeson (twice).	
Lieut.-Colonel H. H. Kennedy, M.C.	21/12/18.
Capt. J. Kirkwood	23/12/16.
Major A. Macmillan, D.S.O., M.C.	21/12/18.
2/Lieut. A. J. Marr	21/12/18.
Lieut. S. J. Morrell	19/5/16
Capt. T. G. Muir, M.C.	20/6/18.
Capt. G. Murray, M.C.	19/5/16 and 25/12/17.
Capt. J. E. Smith, M.C.	23/12/16.
2/Lieut. R. F. W. Patrick	21/12/18.
Major D. W. P. Strang, M.C.	30/11/15.
Major J. E. Thornhill, D.S.O.	19/5/16.
Brig.-General N. A. Thomson, C.M.G., D.S.O. (seven times with Battalion and Brigade).	
Lieut.-Colonel A. W. Turnbull, M.C.	7/11/17.

OTHER RANKS.

	D.C.M. with Bar.	*D.C.M.*	*Bar.*
2946	C.S.M. R. Burns	4/6/17.	16/8/17.

	D.C.M. and Military Medal.	*D.C.M.*	*M.M.*
9725	L/Cpl. R. C. Cotton	3/6/18.	27/6/18.
7544	Cpl. J. Dalziel	3/6/19.	23/7/19.
9045	Sergt. J. Hogg	22/10/17.	23/8/16.
2700	Pte. F. M'Glone	14/1/16.	18/6/17.

Distinguished Conduct Medal.

8901	Pte. M. Barrie	19/8/16.
7595	L/Cpl. A. J. Bell	31/5/16.
238096	Cpl. G. Bullimore	1/1/19.
3926	R.S.M. W. A. Currie	14/1/16.
8870	Sergt. D. J. Duff	18/2/19.
2264	R.S.M. W. Forbes	21/1/16.
2793	Pte. D. Holligan	16/11/15.
40865	Sergt. R. Hunter	30/10/18.
6931	Sergt. D. Macarthur	3/6/18.

8121	Sergt. Piper A. Mackenzie	1/1/17.
1515	C.S.M. R. M'Phail	14/1/16.
200372	Pte. W. Munro	18/2/19.
3043	Sergt. J. Noble	1/1/19.
427	C.S.M. R. Paterson	3/6/19.
6327	Pte. T. Taylor	3/3/17.
2971	Cpl. J. Tinsley	29/11/15.
11153	Cpl. W. Turnbull	22/10/17.
3172	C.S.M. W. C. White	3/6/19.
12866	Sergt. D. Williams	
9894	Sergt. J. Wigtson	30/10/18.

Military Medal with Bar.

		M.M.	*Bar.*
12602	Sergt. G. Bethune	12/12/17.	25/4/18.
3302	Sergt. M. Coleman	23/8/16.	3/7/17.
40676	Pte. R. Dingwall	3/7/17.	18/10/17.
2626	Sergt. M. Eaglesham	14/9/16.	17/6/19.
9558	Pte. S. Ealing	2/11/17.	27/6/18.
12594	Pte. W. Lyall	2/11/17.	13/11/18.
12175	Sergt. D. Macrae	9/12/16.	19/11/17.
6737	L/Cpl. J. O'Brien	2/11/17.	13/11/18.
7217	Sergt. W. Taylor	10/10/16.	18/10/17.

Military Medal and French Croix de Guerre (Étoiles).

		M.M.	*C. de. G.*
40088	L/Cpl. I. Bremner	13/11/18.	22/11/18.
12501	L/Cpl. D. Calder	11/12/18.	22/11/18.
6069	Pte. J. R. Hay	11/12/18.	22/11/18.
203034	Cpl. D. M'Phee	13/11/18.	22/11/18.

Military Medal.

3615	Pte. T. Alexander	23/8/16.
1323	L/Cpl. S. Allen	29/8/17.
240436	L/Cpl. D. Baikie	27/6/18.
6813	Pte. W. Beveridge	16/11/18.
43068	Pte. T. Broadbent	
8556	Pte. A. Brown	27/6/18.
8876	L/Cpl. A. Caldwell	18/10/17.
3855	Pte. A. Campbell	
7160	L/Cpl. M. Campbell	29/8/17.
12624	Pte. D. Chalmers	
10260	Sergt. A. Clark	29/8/17.

40669	L/Cpl. D. Coghill	
3038	Pte. J. Cummings	18/10/17.
2783	L/Cpl. F. Edwards	14/9/16.
40678	Pte. W. Elliott	3/7/17.
9302	Pte. J. Enright	23/8/16.
6268	L/Cpl. R. Ewart	23/8/16.
6734	Sergt. G. Farries	3/7/17.
12714	Sergt. A. Forbes	13/11/18.
9294	C.S.M. A. H. Fraser	14/9/16.
8196	C.S.M. D. Fraser	18/10/17.
12819	Sergt. G. Gechie	25/4/18.
22837	Pte. T. B. Gellatly	7/10/18.
203493	L/Cpl. D. V. Grundy	20/8/19.
9628	Pte. W. Hamilton	16/11/16.
12661	L/Cpl. F. Hiddersley	13/11/18.
13069	Pte. T. M. Huggins	29/8/18.
8143	L/Cpl. R. Hunter	13/11/18.
12186	Pte. F. Hurst	18/10/17.
10307	Cpl. H. Innes	
10285	Cpl. T. Jamieson	
8863	Pte. J. Johnston	23/8/16.
17441	Pte. G. J. Jones	
6379	Sergt. W. J. Killin	14/5/19.
1229	L/Cpl. L. King	29/8/17.
5597	Sergt. A. Leahy	16/11/16.
9641	Pte. R. Low	23/8/16.
6038	Pte. J. M'Avoy	29/8/18.
6558	Sergt. G. A. M'Beth	3/7/17.
40643	C.S.M. G. M'Donald	3/7/17.
241473	Pte. K. M'Donald	27/6/18.
25934	Sergt. T. M'Donald	13/9/18.
2901	L/Cpl. J. M'Dougall	
8770	Pte. M. M'Ghie	22/1/17.
7484	Cpl. R. M'Gowan	18/10/17.
40037	Pte. J. Mackay	23/2/18.
6561	Sergt. J. Mackenzie	11/2/20.
10166	L/Cpl. W. Mackenzie	
9551	Pte. A. M'Lean	18/10/17.
9007	L/Cpl. M. Macleod	29/8/17.
2766	Sergt. R. T. Macleod	18/10/17.
3832	Pte. R. M'Nab	3/6/16.
8162	Pte. C. J. Martin	16/11/16.
5531	Pte. J. Martin	25/4/18.
9300	Sergt. T. Martin	18/6/17.
3124	Pte. I. Maxwell	

7368	Sergt. W. S. Meikle	17/6/19.
5742	L/Cpl. D. Millar	14/9/16.
204075	Pte. A. Miller	30/1/20.
40645	L/Cpl. J. Mitten	3/7/17.
9236	L/Cpl. D. Montgomery	16/7/18.
6896	Pte. J. Morrison	
2036	Pte. J. Nicholson	2/11/17.
3633	Sergt. J. O'Donnell	14/9/16.
10967	Pte. G. P. Peace	23/2/18.
6755	Pte. I. Robertson	
9089	Pte. I. Robinson	20/8/19.
9090	L/Cpl. J. Ross	18/10/17.
3826	Pte. J. Rowley	18/6/17.
8824	Pte. G. Roy	
1089	L/Cpl. J. Russell	18/10/17.
3709	Sergt. P. Russell	3/7/17.
3560	Cpl. J. Shanks	14/9/16.
8559	Cpl. J. Shearer	27/6/18.
6740	Pte. W. Shearer	3/7/17.
43173	L/Cpl. G. Smith	18/10/17.
4699	L/Cpl. P. Smith	2/11/17.
21842	Pte. J. G. Stephen	25/4/18.
7096	L/Cpl. A. Stitt	18/10/17.
15483	Pte. D. Stoddart	
241122	Sergt. A. Sutherland	18/10/17.
3461	Pte. W. Sutherland	14/9/16.
21663	L/Cpl. D. J. Thomas	13/11/18.
7339	Pte. D. Urquhart	27/6/18.
6611	Cpl. L. Urquhart	
1929	Pte. J. Wallace	16/11/16.
44504	L/Cpl. J. Watson	20/8/19.
8922	L/Cpl. A. Williams	
3252	Cpl. J. Wilson	
3407	Cpl. J. Wilson	

Meritorious Service Medal.

3216	Cpl. A. Braes	18/10/16.
6404	R.Q.M.S. J. H. Fraser	17/6/18.
690	Sergt. G. Kirkwood	1/1/18.
6023	C.Q.M.S. H. Rule	3/6/19.

Médaille Militaire and Croix de Guerre (*Palmes*).

10700	C.S.M. Du Fen	22/11/18.
6176	Sergt. B. Malcolm	22/11/18.

Croix de Guerre (Étoiles).

238005	L/Cpl. W. Bain	22/11/18.
203034	Sergt. D. Baneford	
1515	Sergt. R. D. M'Phail	24/2/16.
17889	L/Cpl. A. Thomson	22/11/18.

Belgian Croix de Guerre.

8329	L/Cpl. H. Casson	

Italian Medaille Barbarite si Credinta.

7299	Sergt. J. Murray	20/9/19.

Mentioned in Despatches.

9294	C.S.M. A. H. Fraser	30/11/15.
2626	Sergt. M. Eaglesham	30/11/15.
3216	Cpl. A. Braes	30/11/15.
2783	L/Cpl. F. Edwards	30/11/15.
3633	L/Cpl. J. O'Donnell	30/11/15.
9294	C.S.M. A. H. Fraser	19/5/16.
8273	C.Q.M.S. J. Colclough	19/5/16.
7884	C.S.M. C. R. Strickland	23/12/16.
690	Sergt. G. Kirkwood	23/12/16.
2764	Sergt. A. Simpson	23/12/16.
5562	Sergt. J. A. M'D. Sharp	23/12/16.
6830	L/Cpl. W. Ruth	23/12/16
3701	C.Q.M.S. W. Fisken	25/12/17.
241731	Pte. W. Nicol	20/6/18.
9090	L/Cpl. J. Ross	20/6/18.
9666	Sergt. A. Paterson	21/3/19.
5986	Sergt. J. Thomson	21/3/19.
12866	Sergt. D. Williams	21/3/19.
18035	Cpl. F. Whitton	21/3/19.
8825	Pte. H. Wright	21/3/19.
18068	Pte. P. Robertson	21/3/19.

10TH GORDON HIGHLANDERS.

OFFICERS.

1916.

Jan. 1. *Mentioned in Despatches :*
Lt.-Col. R. H. Wallace. Major H. K. Longman.
Lieut. F. W. Gordon. 2/Lieut. P. B. Boyd.
2/Lieut. T. S. Husband. 2/Lieut. L. G. Robertson.

Jan. 14. *Military Crosses :*
Major H. K. Longman. 2/Lieut. L. G. Robertson.

8/10TH GORDON HIGHLANDERS.

OFFICERS.

1916.

June 15. *Mentioned in Despatches :*
Lt.-Col. A. D. Greenhill-Gardyne. Major A. W. Angus.
Capt. J. G. Thom. Capt. and Q.M. Drummond.

Dec. 8 *Military Cross :* 2/Lieut. A. C. S. Buist.

1917.

Jan. 4. *Mentioned in Despatches :*
Lt.-Col. D. M'Leod, D.S.O. Major H. K. Longman.
Capt. W. G. Maxwell.

Jan. 4. *Military Cross :* Capt. J. G. Thom.

March 12. *D.S.O. :* Lieut. G. Mutch.

March 12. *Military Cross :* Capt. J. Martin.

May 9. *Military Crosses :*
Capt. W. M'Call. 2/Lieut. J. W. T. Leith.

May 29. *Mentioned in Despatches* (' London Gazette,' May 25, 1917) :
Major J. G. Thom, D.S.O., M.C. Capt. A. K. Priday.

June 4. *Military Cross :* Capt. A. P. L. Bethell.

June 8. *Military Cross :* Capt. W. Drummond.

July 18. *D.S.O. :* Major J. G. Thom, M.C.

Aug. 30. *D.S.O. :* Capt. F. J. C. Moffat. Capt. G. P. Geddes.
Military Crosses :
Capt. J. A. Smith. 2/Lieut. K. C. Davidson.

Sept. 1. *Military Cross :* Capt. J. A. Smith, R.A.M.C. (att. battalion).

1917.

Oct. 2. *Military Crosses* (for bravery east of Ypres, August 22-26, 1917):
Capt. J. Lynn. 2/Lieut. R. J. Watson.

Dec. 22. *Mentioned in Despatches* ('London Gazette,' December 21, 1917):
Maj. Lord Dudley Gordon, D.S.O. Major J. G. Thom, D.S.O., M.C
Major C. Reid. Capt. F. J. C. Moffat, D.S.O.
Capt. G. P. Geddes, D.S.O. Lieut. A. W. Boyce.
2/Lieut. F. C. Penberthy.

1918.

Jan. 1. *Military Cross:* 2/Lieut. K. C. Davidson.

Jan. 31. *D.S.O.:* Major Charles Reid.
Military Cross: Lieut. B. L. Keyes, M.O.R. (*sic*), C.Q.S.R. (att.)

April 7. *Mentioned in Despatches:*
Major Charles Reid, D.S.O. Capt. N. G. Pearson.
Lieut. A. W. Boyce. Lieut. J. Doull.

July 12. *D.S.O.:* Capt. J. B. Wood.

July 12. *Military Cross:* Lieut. W. S. Kemp.

5th Gordon Highlanders.

Officers.

For gallantry, March 21 to April 2, 1918.

Bar to Military Cross: Capt. Thomas Macnaughten Dacre, M.C.
Military Crosses:
2/Lieut. Magnus H. Irvine. Capt. and Q.M. J. Marr.

1918.

May 21. *Mentioned in Despatches:*
Capt. J. L. Low. Capt. U. T. A. Robertson.

Aug. 12. *Legion d'Honneur et Croix de Guerre avec Palmes:*
Capt. G. P. Geddes, D.S.O.
Groix de Guerre avec Palmes:
Major J. B. Wood, M.C. 2/Lieut. I. M. Gill.

Aug. 22. *Military Crosses:*
Lieut. R. W. Youngson. 2/Lieut. F. W. Lovie.

Aug. 29. *Military Cross:* Lieut. J. T. Reid.

Nov. 8. *Mentioned in Despatches:*
Lt.-Col. G. A. Smith, D.S.O. Major J. B. Wood, D.S.O., M.C
Capt. & Adjt. G. P. Geddes, D.S.O. Capt. J. M. Stewart.

10TH GORDON HIGHLANDERS.

OTHER RANKS.

(From July 1915 to May 1916.)

No.	Rank.	Name.	Award.	Date of London Gazette.
S/5249	Pte.	Allan, T.	D.C.M.	16/11/15
S/8460	Sergt.	Masson, W.	,,	14/1/16
S/5092	Sergt.	Shaw, G.	,,	,,
S/4358	Cpl.	Kerr, J.	,,	22/1/16
S/5658	C.S.M.	Young, J.	Ment. in Des.	1/1/16
	R.S.M.	Young, J.	,, ,,	15/6/16
S/5323	Sergt.	Forgan, D.	,, ,,	,,
S/5109	Sergt.	Meins, H.	,, ,,	,,
S/4840	Sergt.	Arbuckle, F. S.	D.C.M.	27/7/16
S/12201	Pte.	Ross, A.	Military Medal	29/7/16
S/5350	Sergt.	Young, A. J.	Ment. in Des.	1/1/16
S/4926	Sergt.	Aitken, H.	Military Medal	3/6/16
7202	C.S.M.	Rodgers, J.	Ment. in Des.	1/1/16
5350	Sergt.	Young, A. J.	,, ,,	,,
5092	Sergt.	Shaw, G.	D.C.M.	14/1/16

8/10TH GORDON HIGHLANDERS.

OTHER RANKS.

(From May 1916 to June 1918.)

No.	Rank.	Name.	Award.	Date of London Gazette.
12201	Pte.	Ross, A.	Military Medal	25/5/16
4926	Sergt.	Aitken, H.	,, ,,	3/6/16
2069	Cpl.	M'Gough, A.	,, ,,	,,
5658	A/R.S.M.	Young, J.	Ment. in Des.	15/6/16
3158	C.Q.M.S.	Clark, J.	,, ,,	,,
3882	Sergt.	Ash, P.	,, ,,	,,
5323	Sergt.	Forgan, D.	,, ,,	,,
5109	Sergt.	Meins, H.	,, ,,	,,
6441	L/Cpl.	Hoops, D.	Military Medal	5/7/16

No.	Rank.	Name.	Award.	Date of London Gazette.
1748	Sergt.	Morris, J.	D.C.M.	12/7/16
10306	L/Cpl.	Skelton, F.	,,	,,
1673	Sergt.	Paxton, R.	Military Medal	,,
6441	L/Cpl.	Hooper, D.	,, ,,	,,
9229	Pte.	Marshall, D.	D.C.M.	,,
10483	C.S.M.	Maclean, A.	Military Cross	19/8/16
S/3158	C.Q.M.S.	Clark, J.	Mer. Ser. Medal	18/10/16
170	Sergt.	Rolls, J. K.	Military Medal	27/10/16
10306	L/Cpl.	Skelton, F.	,, ,,	,,
S/7598	Pte.	Gentleman, J.	D.C.M.	14/11/16
S/10075	Pte.	Moreland, J.	,,	,,
			Bar to D.C.M.	18/6/17
S/9697	Pte.	Calder, A.	Military Medal	9/12/16
S/10316	Pte.	Collin, A.	,, ,,	,,
S/9230	Sergt.	M'Cue, H.	,, ,,	,,
S/7101	L/Sergt.	Murray, A.	,, ,,	,,
S/9549	Pte.	Phillips, D.	,, ,,	,,
8844	C.S.M.	Gordon, W.	Ment. in Des.	29/12/16
607	Cpl.	Rettie, J.	Military Medal	9/12/16
10681	L/Cpl.	Hepburn, T.	,, ,,	14/12/16
8844	C.M.S.	Gordon, W.	Ment. in Des.	4/1/17
3/5675	L/Cpl.	MacArthur, J. M.	Military Medal	22/1/17
S/7622	Sergt.	Matthew, A. R.	D.C.M.	26/1/17
S/5634	Sergt.	Duncan, R.	,,	26/3/17
S/15380	Pte.	Mathieson, J.	,,	,,
S/1732	A/C.S.M.	Wilkie, D.	,,	,,
2178	Sergt.	Donnelly, P.	Military Medal	,,
S/10571	Pte.	M'Lellan, J.	,, ,,	,,
10071	C.S.M.	Henderson, W.	Croix de Guerre	1/5/17
3/7182	C.S.M.	Ross, D.	Ital. Bronze Med.	24/5/17
			Ment. in Des.	25/5/17
S/7423	Sergt.	Spence, C.	,, ,,	,,
S/5405	L/Sergt.	Garnett, A.	,, ,,	,,
S/5712	Pte. (A/C.)	Sinclair, T.	,, ,,	,,
7459	Pte.	Kelly, J.	,, ,,	,,
S/1799	Q.M.S.	Milne, R.	Mer. Ser. Medal	14/6/17
S/4936	Cpl. (A/S.)	Duncan, J.	D.C.M.	18/6/17
S/5242	Pte.	Taylor, R.	,,	,,
6705	Cpl.	Baillie, C.	Military Medal	,,
S/12428	Pte.	Campbell, J.	,, ,,	,,
S/4384	Pte.	Cook, J.	,, ,,	,,
S/5548	L/Cpl.	Dunsmore, J.	,, ,,	,,

No.	Rank.	Name.	Award.	Date of London Gazette.
S/10961	Sergt.	Hines, J. C.	Military Medal	18/6/17
	C.S.M.	Hines, J. C.	Military Cross	26/9/17
S/13337	Pte.	Kelly, G. W.	Military Medal	18/6/17
3/6678	Sergt.	Leith, H.	,, ,,	,,
S/1833	L/Cpl.	Lindsay, J.	,, ,,	,,
S/7819	Sergt.	Mackinnon, M. A.	,, ,,	,,
S/5585	Cpl.	M'Niven, H.	,, ,,	,,
S/7084	Cpl.	Neilson, A.	,, ,,	,,
S/3250	Pte.	Orr, J.	,, ,,	,,
S/7070	L/Cpl.	Peaston, R.	,, ,,	,,
S/5963	Pte.	Sim, A.	,, ,,	,,
S/3873	Sergt.	Thomson, R. M.	,, ,,	,,
S/5650	L/Cpl.	Tolerton, J.	,, ,,	,,
S/7557	Pte.	Wilson, A.	,, ,,	,,
S/10399	Pte.	Buchanan, D.	,, ,,	3/7/17
S/13859	L/Cpl.	Kennard, L. G.	,, ,,	,,
S/5201	C.S.M.	Ritchie, J.	Military Cross	18/7/17
3/6341	Sergt.	Cruden, A.	Military Medal	18/10/17
S/4328	Pte.	Dunn, R.	,, ,,	,,
			Bar to M.M.	17/6/19
S/12932	Cpl.	Gass, J.	Military Medal	18/10/17
3/6352	Pte.	Gordon, J. R.	,, ,,	,,
S/8758	Sergt.	Inglis, R.	,, ,,	,,
S/40440	Pte. (L/C.)	Kearney, R.	,, ,,	,,
S/40423	Sergt.	M'Dougall, R.	,, ,,	,,
7648	Pte. (L/C.)	M'Intosh, J.	,, ,,	,,
S/3193	Pte.	Peattie, W.	,, ,,	,,
374	Pte.	Shaw, A.	,, ,,	,,
S/5644	Pte.	Stewart, J.	,, ,,	,,
S/40531	Pte.	Todd, W.	,, ,,	,,
S/4649	Pte.	Graham, W.	D.C.M.	22/10/17
S/8512	Pte.	Greig, H.	,,	,,
S/7972	Sergt.	Martin, W. J.	,,	,,
5674	Pte.	Condie.	Military Medal	2/11/17
17162	Pte.	Craik.	,, ,,	,,
4762	Cpl.	M'Clusky.	,, ,,	12/11/17
6426	Cpl.	M'Donald.	,, ,,	,,
10576	L/Cpl.	Hunter.	,, ,,	,,
1454	Pte.	Henry.	,, ,,	,,
S/1970	L/Cpl.	Hendry, T. L.	D.C.M.	19/11/17
3/6535	A/Sergt.	M'Gregor, F.	,,	,,
S/7084	Cpl.	Neilson, A.	,,	,,

No.	Rank.	Name.	Award.	Date of London Gazette.
S/16536	Sergt.	D. H. M'Gibb.	Military Medal	4/11/16
S/16738	Pte.	W. Train	" "	"
S/5712	Cpl.	Sinclair, T.	D.C.M.	19/11/17
S/13862	Cpl.	Whitehead, W.	"	"
1705	C.Q.M.S.	Keir, J. F.	Ment. in Des.	21/12/17
6943	C.Q.M.S.	Hannigan, J.	" "	"
1863	Sergt.	Bryce, J.	" "	"
3884	Cpl.	M'Bryde, D. H.	" "	"
5504	Cpl.	Marshall, J.	" "	"
10827	Pte.	Shorthose, G. O.	D.C.M.	26/11/17
1651	Pte.	M'Ewen, J.	"	1/1/18
7529	C.S.M.	Smith, W.	"	"
S/5607	Sergt.	Fletcher, T. H.	Mer. Ser. Medal	"
1863	Sergt.	Bryce, J.	Military Medal	27/6/18
10941	Cpl.	Crook, W.	" "	"
7523	Sergt.	Bishop, A. T.	Mer. Ser. Medal	12/6/18
	C.S.M.	Fletcher, T. H.	Croix de Guerre	12/7/18
3/6963	Cpl.	Pirie, J.	Mer. Ser. Medal	1/1/18
9646	R.Q.M.S.	Gray, J.	Ment. in Des.	24/5/18
S/5504	Cpl. (L/S.)	Marshall, J.	" "	"
S/5708	Pte.	Barclay, J. S.	Military Medal	12/6/18
S/1703	C.Q.M.S.	Keir, J. F.	Mer. Ser. Medal	17/6/18
S/4913	Sergt.	Reoch, J.	" "	"
S/4252	Pte.	Hutchison, J.	Military Medal	27/6/18
6671	Pte.	Little, A.	" "	"
S/40929	Pte.	Logan, F.	" "	"
S/40501	Cpl.	Paterson, A.	" "	"
S/6677	Pte.	Robertson, W.	" "	"
235409	Sergt.	Hunter, W. V.	D.C.M.	3/9/18

5TH GORDON HIGHLANDERS.

OTHER RANKS.

(From June 1918 to Finish.)

No.	Rank.	Name.	Award.	Date of London Gazette.
14630	Pte.	Thornley, W.	Military Medal	27/6/18
265349	Pte.	Wilson, A.	" "	3/6/18
242077	Pte.	Duffins, N.	" "	27/6/18
240010	R.Q.M.S.	Chalmers, J.	Mer. Ser. Medal	17/6/18
240063	C.Q.M.S.	Taylor, J.	" "	"
240041	Cpl.	Neilson, R.	" "	"
240444	C.Q.M.S.	Johnston, J.	Military Medal	16/7/18
242321	Sergt.	M'Allister, R.	" "	"
240964	L/Cpl.	Milne, W.	" "	"
242465	L/Cpl.	Smith, J.	" "	"
241311	Pte.	Watson, J.	" "	"
6678	Sergt.	Leith, H.	Croix de Guerre	20/8/18
240225	Cpl.	Henderson, A.	" "	12/7/18
240573	Sergt.	M'Intosh, A.	" "	"
242456	Pte.	Thomson, D.	Bar to M.M.	29/8/18
9838	Sergt.	Gordon, W.	" "	"
240164	R.S.M.	Park, W.	Military Cross	16/9/18
241468	Sergt.	Annand, T.	D.C.M.	3/9/18
265349	Pte.	Wilson, A.	"	21/10/18
40512	A/Cpl.	Rule, J.	Croix de Guerre	22/11/18
S/13186	Sergt.	Iveson, J. C.	" "	30/10/18
			" "	22/11/18
			Méd. Militaire	"
2120	Sergt.	Raphael, W.	D.C.M.	30/10/18
			Croix de Guerre	22/11/18
			Méd. Militaire	"
S/5140	Cpl.	Peart, J.	Military Medal	13/11/18
S/8390	Pte.	Ballantyne, W.	" "	"
S/7065	L/Cpl.	Clague, R.	" "	"
S/41090	Pte.	Fraser, A.	" "	"
202484	L/Cpl.	Harrison, F.	" "	"
241229	Pte.	Sutherland, J.	" "	"
266529	Pte.	Will, W.	" "	"
2033	Pte.	Lloyd, J.	" "	"
242305	Cpl.	Easton, A.	Croix de Guerre	22/11/18

No.	Rank.	Name.	Award.	Date of London Gazette.
240341	L/Cpl.	Greig, C.	Croix de Guerre	22/11/18
292655	L/Cpl.	Inkster, W.	,, ,,	,,
3/6678	Sergt.	Leith, H.	,, ,,	,,
S/13308	Cpl.	Mercer, J.	,, ,,	,,
S/13391	L/Cpl.	Scorgie, W.	,, ,,	,,
3/6583	Sergt.	Urquhart, J.	,, ,,	,,
265908	Pte.	Watt, G.	Military Medal	11/12/18
240263	Sergt.	Duthie, J. S.	Ment. in Des.	28/12/18
S/5504	Cpl. (L/S.)	Marshall, J.	Mer. Ser. Medal	18/1/19
241967	L/Cpl.	Barron, W.	Military Medal	14/5/19
6876	Sergt.	Murray, J.	D.C.M.	3/6/19
S/3884	Cpl.	M'Bryde, D. H.	Mer. Ser. Medal	,,
S/40524	Cpl.	Simpson, A.	,, ,,	,,
240088	L/Cpl.	Gordon, D. R.	,, ,,	,,
240321	Sergt.	M'Gillivray, A. B.	Military Medal	17/6/19
S/5391	Pte.	Cowan, J.	Ment. in Des.	9/7/19
S/40543	Pte.	Fraser, D.	,, ,,	,,
240716	Cpl.	Henderson, W. H.	,, ,,	,,
266304	Cpl.	M'Ewan, A.	,, ,,	,,
241006	Sergt.	Simpson, J.	,, ,,	,,
3/6679	Sergt.	Stuart, E. B.	,, ,,	,,
S/4448	Pte.	Boyle, W.	Military Medal	20/8/19
242115	Pte. (A/C.)	Tough, G.	D.C.M.	30/1/20
240523	Sergt.	Bisset, T.	Military Medal	,,
242198	Cpl. (L/S.)	Gerrard, G.	,, ,,	,,
263900	Cpl.	Steele, J. B.	,, ,,	,, (New No. 292109)
240956	Pte.	Thomson, R.	,, ,,	30/1/20
S/8758	C.S.M. (A/R.S.M.)	Inglis, R.	D.C.M.	25/2/20
6876	Sergt.	Murray, J.	,,	11/3/20

7th Queen's Own Cameron Highlanders.

Officers.

1916.

Jan. 1. *Mentioned in Despatches :*

Lt.-Col. J. W. Sandilands, D.S.O. Lieut. W. G. S. Stuart.
2/Lieut. R. R. Anderson.

1916.

Jan. 14. *C.M.G.:* Lt.-Col. J. W. Sandilands, D.S.O.
Military Cross: 2/Lieut. R. R. Anderson.

June 4. *D.S.O.:* Major T. L. Cunningham.

June 13. *Mentioned in Despatches:* Lieut. J. S. Robertson.

Oct. 16. *Military Cross:* 2/Lieut. D. Moir.

Oct. 20. *Military Crosses:*
2/Lieut. T. Orr. 2/Lieut. W. Black.

1917.

Jan. 1. *Military Cross:* Capt. W. G. S. Stuart.

Jan. 4. *Mentioned in Despatches* ('London Gazette,' January 4):
Capt. K. Macrae. Capt. A. Ogilvie.

April 13. *Military Cross:*
2/Lieut. C. R. Morton. 2/Lieut. R. W. B. Semple.

May 10. *Military Cross:* Lieut. J. Findlay.

June 6. *Military Crosses:*
2/Lieut. W. L. Muir Kay. 2/Lieut. N. S. Sim.
2/Lieut. J. W. Graham.

June 11. *Mentioned in Despatches* ('London Gazette,' April 9, 1917):
Major N. MacLeod. Capt. A. R. Chapman.
Lieut. G. J. S. Lumsden.

July 6. *D.S.O.:* Major Norman MacLeod.

July 27. *Military Cross:* 2/Lieut. H. B. Goudie.

Sept. 4. *D.S.O.:* Capt. J. A. Symon.
Military Crosses:
Capt. J. L. C. Jenkins. Capt. A. C. Bateman, R.A.M.C.
2/Lieut. R. Jardine. 2/Lieut. J. Miller.
2/Lieut. R. B. Purdon.

Oct. 4. *Military Crosses:*
2/Lieut. J. T. Bookless (4th Camerons).
2/Lieut. J. I. Macdonald (7th Argyll & Sutherland).

1918.

Jan. 29. *Mentioned in Despatches* ('London Gazette,' December 21, 1917):
Lt.-Col. N. MacLeod, D.S.O. Capt. J. A. Symon, D.S.O.
Lieut. J. H. Mauchlin.

Feb. 27. *Military Cross:* Capt. G. J. S. Lumsden.

March 13. *Military Cross:* 2/Lieut. A. R. Macdonald.

1918.

April 29. *Military Crosses:*
Lieut. E. J. G. Gibb.
2/Lieut. J. M'Murray.
2/Lieut. P. Austin.

May 24. *Mentioned in Despatches:*
Major P. M'F. Cram.
Lieut. J. D. W. M'Cracken.

June 3. *Military Cross:* Lieut. J. H. Mauchlin.

OTHER RANKS.

1916.

Jan. 1. *Mentioned in Despatches:* 13321 S.M. D. Adam.

Jan. 14. *D.C.M.:*
13537 L/Sergt. W. C. Lamb.
13840 L/Sergt. H. Winning.

June 4. *D.C.M.:*
S/12647 B.S.M. A. K. Scott.
S/13635 C.S.M. C. L. B. Davie.

Military Medals:
S/16957 L/C. J. M'Dougall.
S/13204 L/C. G. S. Sutherland.
S/16816 L/C. R. Gardner.

June 13. *Mentioned in Despatches:*
5651 C.S.M. J. B. Cranston.
13603 Q.M.S. T. F. Watson.
13901 Cpl. P. M'Donald.
15814 L/Cpl. J. M'Callum.
13088 Pte. A. E. Morgan.

Aug. 8. *Military Medals:*
12824 Sergt. R. F. J. Small.
13024 L/Sergt. G. S. Sutherland.
16957 L/Cpl. J. M'Dougall.
16816 L/Cpl. R. Gardner.
20039 Pte. J. Healy.

Oct. 11. *Military Medals:*
16536 Sergt. D. H. M'Gill.
16738 Pte. W. Train.

Nov. 14. *Military Medals:*
16973 Cpl. W. Ramage.
21669 L/Cpl. E. B. Thomson.
13888 L/Cpl. J. M'Gowan.
17792 Pte. J. Boyle.
14002 Pte. W. Johnson.
18578 Pte. A. Craig.

D.C.M.:
15245 L/Cpl. J. Drysdale.
13428 Sergt. J. Montgomerie.

Dec. 9. *Military Medal:* 13466 Pte. J. MacLean.

1917.

Jan. 1. *Military Cross:* 13232 C.S.M. A. Kidd.

D.C.M.: 15857 C.S.M. J. Little.

1917.

Jan. 4. *Mentioned in Despatches:* S/14241 Sergt. J. D. M'Gill.

Jan. 28. *Military Medal:* 9260 Sergt. M. Grant.

Feb. 24. *Mentioned in Despatches:* 12229 R.S.M. A. Anderson.

April 13. *Military Medals:*
S/16841 L/C. J. Kelly.
S/14069 Pte. G. M'Lean.

April 15. *Military Medal:* R/6765 Sergt. Macdonald ("D" Coy.)

May 1. *Military Medals:*
S/18323 Sergt. R. J. Cameron.
S/15513 L/C. J. Fulton.
S/22946 Pte. J. B. Keillor.
S/14140 L/C. R. Young.
S/25532 Sergt. D. Maxwell.
S/15565 Pte. J. MacLeod.
S/19197 Sergt. M. Morrison.

May 10. *D.C.M.:*
S/14241 C.S.M. J. D. M'Gill.
R/5074 Sergt. F. Fleming.

May 19. *Military Medals:*
S/18170 Cpl. J. Spiers.
S/18090 Pte. R. Bell.
S/13686 L/C. W. Miller.
S/23439 Pte. T. M'Govern.
S/16086 Pte. J. M'Lellan.
R/5563 A/C.S.M. D. Anderson.

June 11. *Mentioned in Despatches:*
S/15620 Sergt. J. Torrance.
S/16137 L/C. J. O'Rourke.
S/13264 R.Q.M.S. J. Wilson.
S/13184 L/C. A. Bell.
S/13241 Pte. W. M'Intosh.

Aug. 25. *Bar to Military Medal:* Sergt. A. Macdonald.

Military Medals:
200334 A/Sergt. M. P. King.
200204 L/C. T. Nicolson.
14032 L/C. T. Shumacker.
23246 Pte. J. Rose.
10501 Sergt. J. Morgan.
22930 Cpl. W. Taylor.
40965 Pte. G. W. Allan.
8900 Cpl. A. Donegan.
16391 J. Tulloch ("C" Coy.)
26863 L/C. W. Rose.

Sept. 30. *Military Medals:*
R/8983 L/Sergt. C. Smith.
S/43231 L/C. J. Forsyth.
S/14297 Cpl. A. Simpson.
S/359184 L/C. J. Anderson.

Nov. 2. *Military Medal:* 9035 Pte. J. Spence.

Nov. 19. *Bar to Military Medal:* 15565 Pte. J. M'Leod.

Dec. 12. *Mentioned in Despatches:* 13866 Pte. J. Oliphant.

1918.

Jan. 1. *M.S.M.:* 16824 Sergt. R. Burton.

Feb. 5. *Belgian Croix de Guerre:*
R/3871 R.S.M. W. Vass.
S/13264 R.Q.M.S. J. P. Wilson.

1918.

March 13. *Military Medals:*

S/10391 L/Sergt. W. Mackay.
S/200142 L/C. J. Stoddart.
S/41016 Pte. H. Finlay.

April 29. *D.C.M.:* R/9708 Sergt. (A/C.S.M.) T. Yates.

Bar to Military Medal: S/14297 L/Sergt. A. Simpson.

Military Medals:

S/10495 L/Sergt A. M'Innes.
S/14064 Sergt. R. Grierson.
S/48993 L/Sergt. T. Wright.
S/17962 L/C. B. Logan.
S/14322 Pte. S. Hill.

May 13. *Military Medal:* S/18231 Pte. J. Vickers.

May 24. *Mentioned in Despatches:*

21667 L/Cpl. H. Fleming.
13436 Pte. A. C. Campbell.

45TH INFANTRY BRIGADE.

HONOURS AND AWARDS.

13TH THE ROYAL SCOTS.

1915.

Oct. *Victoria Cross:* 18274 Pte. R. Dunsire.

Military Cross: 2/Lieut. A. Linton.

For operations, May 11-12, 1916.

Military Crosses:

Capt. H. S. E. Stevens.
2/Lieut. W. A. Henderson.
2/Lieut. J. R. M'Lennan.

Military Medals:

L/C. M'Kinley.
L/C. Parker.

1917.

May 1. *Military Medals:*

16611 Sergt. D. Glen (killed 9/4/17).
13793 Cpl. A. Wilson.
41114 Pte. A. Rutherford.
31133 Pte. A. Rattray.
30465 L/Sergt. F. Dennistoun.
14362 L/Sergt. J. Allan.
38214 Pte. G. Chalmers.
39203 Pte. R. Wallace.

1917.

May 18. *Military Medals :*

15398 Cpl. G. Chirray.
23198 Pte. M. Higgins.
16472 Pte. H. Cowe.
16894 Pte. M. Doyle.
14440 Cpl. R. M'Intosh.
26531 Pte. P. Spence.
16151 Pte. J. G. Baxter.

May 31. *Military Crosses :*

Lieut. J. Rickards, R.A.M.C.
2/Lieut. J. K. Ogilvie.
2/Lieut. W. A. Henderson.
2/Lieut. J. Kelly (Black Watch, attached to battalion).

June 2. *D.C.M. :* 16355 Sergt. John M'Millan.

June 17. *Military Medals :*

41260 Pte. D. Laing.
38098 Pte. A. M'Kirmell.
47873 Pte. J. R. Smith.
14977 Sergt. J. Connell.
16381 L/Sergt. B. Solomon.
17735 Pte. J. Robertson.
9292 Cpl. A. Anderson.
18531 Pte. P. Balloch.
43137 Pte. R. Purdie.
16485 Pte. J. Ritchie.

Aug. 30. *D.S.O. :* Lt.-Col. G. M. Hannay.

Bar to Military Cross :

Capt. J. F. G. Turner, M.C.
2/Lieut. J. K. Ogilvie, M.C.
2/Lieut. W. A. Henderson, M.C.

Military Crosses :

Capt. R. J. M. Christie.
2/Lieut. J. Cavers.
Capt. A. H. Craig.

D.C.M. : 30710 Pte. A. Michie.

Oct. 1. *D.S.O. :* Capt. A. H. Craig, M.C.

Bar to M.C. : Lieut. J. Cavers, M.C.

Military Crosses :

Major J. A. Turner, D.S.O.
Capt. J. R. Henderson.

D.C.M. :

15223 C.S.M. R. Orr.
23390 Pte. M. Higgins.
7538 Sergt. T. Shenton.

Military Medal : 31424 Sergt. S. Cownie.

1918.

Jan. 1. *Military Cross :* 2/Lieut. J. Davie.

Mentioned in Despatches (' London Gazette,' December 14, 1917) :

Lt.-Col. G. M. Hannay, D.S.O.
Major J. A. Turner, D.S.O., M.C.
Capt. A. H. Craig.
2/Lieut. F. A. Baker.
2/Lieut. G. L. Stewart.
Major J. T. R. Mitchell, D.S.O.
Capt. E. A. Aldridge, R.A.M.C.
Hon. Lt. and Q.M.R. W. Price.
2/Lieut. W. B. L. Easton.

1918.

Feb. 2. *Belgian Croix de Guerre:*
2/Lieut. W. B. Easton. C.S.M. G. Stern.

April 22. *Bar to Military Cross:* Capt. J. Kelly, M.C.

Military Crosses:
Capt. A. E. Considine. 2/Lieut. R. D. Brown.
2/Lieut. H. A. Pattullo. 2/Lieut. W. A. West.

D.C.M.: 14529 Sergt. W. Dick.

Military Medals:
50510 Sergt. G. Barbour.
23263 Pte. D. Campbell.
16660 Cpl. A. Macdonald.
16668 Sergt. J. C. Johnstone.
38847 L/C. J. Galloway.
14551 Sergt. W. Watson.
20680 Pte. R. Gale.
27060 Pte. S. Smith.
15153 Sergt. R. Vage.

April 26. *Military Cross:* Capt. E. A. Aldridge, R.A.M.C.

May 23. *Mentioned in Despatches:*
Capt. H. S. E. Stevens, M.C.
7791 R.Q.M.S. C. M'Evoy.
Capt. F. Barnett.

May 31. *D.C.M.:* 16660 Cpl. A. Macdonald, M.M.

June 4. *Military Cross:* 2/Lieut. J. S. Ross.

June 12. *Military Medals:*
23056 Cpl. W. Quinton.
302571 L/C. A. Merriman.
28010 Pte. H. Wright.

June 30. *Military Medals:*
9843 Sergt. W. Mone.
7838 C.S.M. T. Shenton, D.C.M.
27470 Cpl. J. Salmond.
330064 Pte. J. Young.
53200 Pte. T. Quinn.
10697 L/Sergt. C. Jaggard.
250850 Pte. J. Johnstone.
16234 Sergt. D. Young.
15132 Pte. M. Cullen.
37774 Pte. R. Titterington.
30722 Pte. D. Williamson.

July 10. *Bar to Military Cross:* Capt. J. R. Henderson, M.C.

Military Crosses:
2/Lieut. P. Y. M'Niven.
2/Lieut. K. Paterson.
2/Lieut. A. Gordon.

Sept. 1. *Bar to Military Cross:* Capt. A. E. Considine, M.C.

Military Cross: Capt. F. Barnett.

7TH AND 6/7TH ROYAL SCOTS FUSILIERS.

OFFICERS.

1915.

Oct. 1. *Military Cross:* 2/Lieut. G. D. Begg.

Nov. 30. *Mentioned in Despatches:*
Lt.-Col. H. H. Northey.
Major G. O. Turnbull.
Capt. A. W. Baker.
Capt. J. Brodie.
Capt. G. G. B. Purves.
2/Lieut. C. M'K. M'Gavin.
Major N. M'D. Teacher.
Major C. M. S. Henning.
Capt. J. W. Nesbitt.
Capt. G. D. Begg.
Lieut. R. C. Galloway.

1916.

Jan. 11. *C.M.G.:* Lt.-Col. H. H. Northey.
D.S.O.: Major N. M'D. Teacher.
Military Cross: Capt. A. W. Baker.

April 30. *Mentioned in Despatches:*
Capt. J. Gardner.
2/Lieut. W. W. Kelso.
Capt. G. L. Ritchie.

June 20. *Military Cross:* 2/Lieut. R. Warnock.

June 23. *Military Cross:*
Capt. J. Gardner.
2/Lieut. D. Kerr.

Nov. 13. *Mentioned in Despatches:*
Major N. M'D. Teacher.
2/Lieut. W. Pettigrew.
Capt. J. Y. Scott.
2/Lieut. T. K. Stevenson.

Dec. 29. *Military Cross:* 2/Lieut. A. P. Skeil.

1917.

May 23. *Mentioned in Despatches:* 2/Lieut. J. Boag.

July 17. *Military Cross:*
Capt. W. M'Indoe.
Capt. F. K. Kerr (R.A.M.C.), (att.)
2/Lieut. J. Carnan.

July 24. *Military Cross:* 2/Lieut. J. S. Smith.

Sept. 25. *Military Cross:*
Capt. W. Jope.
Lieut. A. Dingwall.

Oct. 18. *Military Cross:* 2/Lieut. T. Shanks.

Dec. 7. *Mentioned in Despatches:* Major E. A. Beck.

Dec. 14. *Mentioned in Despatches:*
Lt.-Col. E. I. D. Gordon.
Capt. C. J. L. MacDonald.
Major T. L. De Havilland.
Lieut. and Q.M. E. W. Carpenter.

1918.

April 7. *Mentioned in Despatches :*
Lieut. A. M. Whyte. Lieut. W. Haddon.
Lieut. A. Mair.

May 31. *Military Cross :* 2/Lieut. J. Boag.

July 23. *Military Cross :*
Capt. W. Pettigrew. Lieut. G. A. Massie.

July 23. *Bar to Military Cross :* 2/Lieut. T. Shanks, M.C.

OTHER RANKS.

No.	Rank.	Name.	Award.	Date of London Gazette.
11487	Sergt.	Quinn, W.	D.C.M.	16/11/15
11866	Pte.	Barton, J. H.	,,	,,
16206	Pte.	MacDonald, J.	,,	11/3/16
13409	L/Cpl.	M'Haffie, J.	,,	,,
7360	R.Q.M.S.	Graham, F.	,,	,,
7408	Sergt.	M'Neil, T.	,,	,,
7512	Sergt.	Willstrop, G. T.	,,	20/6/16
8011	A/R.S.M.	Brass, J.	,,	,,
6897	C.S.M.	Boyle, A.	,,	,,
9918	C.S.M.	Goble, V.	,,	,,
10145	Sergt.	Moffatt, J.	,,	,,
15438	Cpl.	Mackay, J.	,,	23/6/16
16270	Pte.	Agnew, W.	,,	,,
11976	Sergt.	Connell, M.	Military Medal	20/10/16
19875	Pte.	Connelly, P.	,, ,,	,,
19179	Pte.	Cowe, T.	,, ,,	,,
14794	Pte.	Crossan, R.	,, ,,	,,
15278	L/Sergt.	Hart, A.	,, ,,	,,
16695	Pte.	Long, C.	,, ,,	,,
13193	Pte.	Luke, J.	,, ,,	,,
12332	Sergt.	M'Ghie, S.	,, ,,	,,
13005	Sergt.	M'Lenaghan, C.	,, ,,	,,
13456	Sergt.	Petrie, E.	,, ,,	,,
7512	Sergt.	Willstropp, G. T.	Ment. in Des.	30/11/15
8801	C.S.M.	Bentley, J. W.	,, ,,	,,
7795	C.Q.M.S.	Williams, J.	,, ,,	,,
7041	Sergt.	Wilson, J.	,, ,,	,,
15328	Pte.	Kino, J.	,, ,,	,,

No.	Rank.	Name.	Award.	Date of London Gazette.
13058	Cpl.	Thomson, W.	Ment. in Des.	30/4/16
13172	Sergt.	Pettigrew, J.	,, ,,	,,
15278	L/Sergt.	Hart, A.	,, ,,	,,
16339	C.Q.M.S.	Adie, A.	,, ,,	,,
14764	Pte.	Chesney, W.	,, ,,	,,
17121	Pte.	Reid, W.	,, ,,	,,
6940	Sergt.	Aird, S.	Military Medal	8/8/16
11366	L/Sergt.	Halliday, J.	,, ,,	,,
12949	Pte.	M'Cabe, R.	,, ,,	,,
12473	Sergt.	Todd, A.	,, ,,	,,
13618	Pte.	Kean, C.	,, ,,	,,
19472	Pte.	Hamilton, H.	,, ,,	,,
10145	Sergt.	Moffat, J.	,, ,,	12/9/16
11048	Pte.	Morrison, J.	,, ,,	,,
12982	Pte.	Dobson, W.	,, ,,	,,
13477	C.S.M.	Pollard, A. E.	,, ,,	,,
14882	Pte.	Wells, G. E.	,, ,,	,,
15711	Sergt.	Collyer, A. J.	,, ,,	,,
10518	A/C.S.M.	North, W. J. E.	D.C.M.	26/9/16
14764	Pte.	Chesney, W.	Military Medal	11/10/16
13005	L/Cpl.	M'Lenaghan, C., M.M.	Bar to M.M.	12/10/16
11187	Pte.	Murray, G.	Ment. in Des.	13/11/16
11470	Pte.	Waters, W.	,, ,,	,,
13316	Pte.	Stewart, G.	,, ,,	,,
16339	C.Q.M.S.	Addie, A.	,, ,,	,,
11232	Pte.	Rae, M.	D.C.M.	14/11/16
13287	Cpl.	Noble, J.	,,	,,
11187	Pte.	Murray, G.	Military Medal	8/12/16
16257	Pte.	Robertson, H.	,, ,,	,,
12475	Cpl.	Alexander, T.	,, ,,	19/1/17
12984	L/Cpl.	Fanning, J.	Ment. in Des.	22/5/17
13290	Pte.	Quinn, J.	,, ,,	,,
15780	Pte.	Rolfe, F.	,, ,,	,,
16131	Pte.	Belcher, A.	,, ,,	,,
16968	L/Cpl.	Lister, S.	,, ,,	,,
43203	Pte.	Houston, P.	,, ,,	,,
13340	C.S.M.	Burns, J.	D.C.M.	1/6/17
15273	Cpl.	Pollock, P.	Military Medal	18/6/17
16136	L/Cpl.	M'Lelland, W.	,, ,,	,,
16123	L/Cpl.	Riley, J.	,, ,,	,,
43256	Cpl.	Wilson, W.	,, ,,	,,

No.	Rank.	Name.	Award.	Date of London Gazette.
11349	Pte.	M'Lennon, A.	Military Medal	6/7/17
11895	L/Sergt.	Tonner, T.	" "	"
13590	Sergt.	Houston, C.	" "	"
14715	Pte.	Garrigan, M.	" "	"
15287	Pte.	M'Laughlin, J.	" "	"
34890	Pte.	Campbell, J.	" "	"
34903	Pte.	Dunn, W.	" "	"
11895	Sergt.	Tonner, J., M.M.	Bar to M.M.	18/10/17
12288	Sergt.	Orr, J., M.M.	" "	"
31972	Pte.	Martin, W., M.M.	" "	"
7934	Sergt.	Young, E.	Military Medal	"
15780	Pte.	Rolfe, E.	" "	"
40147	A/Cpl.	Reed, W. T.	" "	"
9951	L/Cpl.	Barker, J. W.	D.C.M.	22/10/17
14439	L/Cpl.	Briggs, G.	Military Medal	16/11/17
16229	Pte.	M'Cutcheon, A.	" "	11/12/17
20386	Pte.	Cox, I. H.	" "	"
13287	Sergt.	Noble, J.	Ment. in Des.	14/12/17
12782	Cpl.	Kerr, A.	D.C.M.	1/1/18
34926	Pte.	Duncan, D.	"	"
12932	Sergt.	Dodson, W.	Mer. Ser. Medal	14/6/18
13099	A/Sergt.	Laidlaw, G. R.	" "	"
20188	Pte.	Buchan, J.	" "	"
29114	Pte.	Duncan, C.	" "	"
12085	C.S.M.	Williams, G.	Belgian Croix de Guerre	9/7/18

6th Cameron Highlanders.

Officers.

1915.

Sept. 26. *Victoria Cross:* Lt.-Col. A. F. Douglas-Hamilton.

1916.

Jan. 1. *Mentioned in Despatches:*

Capt. H. W. Milne.
Lieut. H. B. Rowan.
2/Lieut. J. Wilson.
Lieut. A. F. P. Christison.
2/Lieut. D. C. H. Watson.

1916.

Jan. 14. *Military Cross:* Lieut. A. F. P. Christison.

June 15. *Mentioned in Despatches:*
Capt. A. J. Campbell-Colquhoun. 2/Lieut. J. Garrick.

July 27. *Military Cross:* Lieut. A. Gardner.

Aug. 25. *Military Cross:* 2/Lieut. W. T. M'Kie.

Oct. 26. *Military Cross:* 2/Lieut. R. K. Drummond.

Nov. 14. *D.S.O.:* Capt. A. Gow.

Military Cross:
2/Lieut. A. David. 2/Lieut. T. Ness.
2/Lieut. F. S. Sandeman.

Bar to Military Cross: 2/Lieut. R. K. Drummond.

1917.

Jan. *D.S.O.:* Lt.-Col. J. C. Russell.

Military Cross: Capt. W. E. David (R.A.M.C.)

Jan. 4. *Mentioned in Despatches:*
2/Lieut. G. P. Riach. Capt. A. Gow.
Capt. D. L. Macintyre. Lieut. D. M'D. Currie.
Capt. A. R. Lovelock.

May 25. *Mentioned in Despatches:* Lieut. and Q.M. E. J. Wilkins.

July 14. *Croix de Guerre:* 2/Lieut. W. D. Hay.

July 18. *Bar to Military Cross:* Capt. A. F. P. Christison, M.C.

Military Cross:
2/Lieut. H. D. Dalrymple. 2/Lieut. H. Grindell.
2/Lieut. J. Hislop. 2/Lieut. N. Jones.
2/Lieut. A. G. M'Gruer. Capt. H. B. Rowan.
2/Lieut. A. R. Watts.

Oct. 26. *Military Cross:*
2/Lieut. A. Donaldson. 2/Lieut. H. M'Corquodale.

Dec. 21. *Mentioned in Despatches:* Capt. D. L. Macintyre.

1918.

Jan. 18. *Military Cross:* 2/Lieut. J. M. T. Thomson.

March 3. *Military Cross:* Capt. M. G. F. Moffat.

OTHER RANKS.

1916.

Jan. 1. *Mentioned in Despatches:*
12861 Sergt. T. Clapperton. 6077 Sergt. J. Porter.

1916.

Jan. 14. *D.C.M.:*
12617 C.S.M. W. Cowans. 6025 R.S.M. P. N. Scotland.

Feb. 24. *Croix de Guerre:* 16551 Pte. J. Campbell.

June 3. *D.C.M.:* 10978 Sergt. P. Brown.

June 15. *Mentioned in Despatches:*
13923 C.S.M. C. S. Robertson. 16774 Sergt. T. B. Hyslop.
12358 C.Q.M.S. J. G. Tollerton.

July 12. *Military Medal:* 11495 Pte. W. Carson.

Aug. 10. *Military Medals:*
11493 Pte. W. Carson. 11616 Pte. J. M'Bride.
16245 Pte. A. M'Diarmid. 11951 Sergt. R. M'Grath.
11179 Cpl. J. Stevenson.

Aug. 19. *D.C.M.*
13804 Cpl. J. Cardwell. 9107 Cpl. A. West.

Aug. 23. *Military Medals:*
13332 L/Cpl. L. MacGillivray. 10191 Pte. R. M'Arthur.
15483 Pte. D. T. Stoddart.

Sept. 1. *Military Medals:*
10546 Pte. W. Bovell. 10599 Cpl. D. Glen.

Sept. 26. *D.C.M.:* 7920 Sergt. H. C. Ernst.
Military Cross: 6297 C.S.M. W. Aitken.

Oct. 11. *Military Medals:*
10976 C.Q.M.S. H. M. Adams. 11139 Pte. D. M'Kay.
11946 C.Q.M.S. T. M'Allister.

Oct. 21. *Military Medals:*
18115 Pte. A. Anderson. 13175 Pte. A. K. Blackburn.
16483 Pte. J. Laidlaw. 13260 Pte. A. D. Mason.
21648 Pte. W. H. Rickard. 14134 Pte. J. Ward.
13612 L/Cpl. H. Weatherhead.

Nov. 14. *D.C.M.:*
15993 Cpl. J. M'Callum. 21641 Pte. W. Logan.
16045 Pte. A. Farquharson. 13403 L/Cpl. G. Dunlop.
21907 Pte. T. Crate. 8292 L/Cpl. T. Clarke.
Military Cross: C.S.M. Clelland.

Nov. 16. *Military Medals:*
11570 Pte. F. G. Hanna. 12760 Cpl. G. Murray.
16781 Sergt. W. Paterson.

Dec. 9. *Military Medals:*
16551 Cpl. J. Campbell. 11064 Pte. T. Isaac.
6053 Sergt. C. M'Lean. 16017 Pte. W. Searle.

1917.

Jan. 1. *D C.M.:* 16802 Sergt. J. Jamieson.

Jan. 4. *Mentioned in Despatches:* 16551 L/Cpl. J. Campbell.

May 1. *Croix de Guerre:* 18817 Pte. M. Kay.

May 25. *Mentioned in Despatches:*
13429 A/Sergt. C. Hutchinson. 18871 L/Cpl. H. Heggie.

June 4. *D.C.M.:* 18846 Pte. D. Galt.

June 18. *Military Medals:*
16439 L/Cpl. H. Forrester. 40484 L/Cpl. W. Fraser.

July 9. *Bar to Military Medal:* 16245 L/Sergt. A. M'Diarmid.

Military Medals:
18846 Pte. D. Galt. 13038 Pte. E. W. Geyer.
18871 Cpl. H. G. Heggie. 40716 Pte. D. Mackenzie.

July 14. *Médaille Militaire:* 13175 L/Cpl. A. K. Blackburn.

July 18. *Military Cross:* 10978 C.S.M. P. Brown.

Oct. 18. *Bar to Military Medal:* 11139 Pte. D. Mackay.

Military Medals:
40590 A/Cpl. J. Gilfillan. 40593 Pte. P. Grant.
10619 Pte. D. M'Neil.

Oct. 22. *D.C.M.:* 8280 Cpl. Hyslop.

Nov. 19. *Military Medals:*
40486 Cpl. A. S. Bennie. 21971 Pte. G. Crockett.
26311 Pte. M. Hilton. 18721 Cpl. E. M'Kenna.
8982 Pte. H. Reid.

Dec. 21. *Mentioned in Despatches:*
12965 L/Cpl. J. Campbell. 12241 R.Q.M.S. J. Duff.
17916 A/Sergt. H. S. Wilson.

1918.

Jan. 1. *D.C.M.:* 40685 Sergt. W. Mitchell.

Feb. 23. *Military Medals:*
21100 Cpl. J. Amos. 7874 Pte. S. Hannah.
203285 Pte. W. Lennox.

March 28. *D.C.M.:* L/Cpl. D. M'Kenzie.

May 24. *Mentioned in Despatches:*
12354 Cpl. W. Blaikie. 13429 A/Sergt. C. Hutchinson.
11915 L/Cpl. A. Mackay.

June 3. *D.C.M.:* 21354 L/Cpl. T. Flannigan.

1918.

June 12. *Military Medals :*

12965 Pte. J. Campbell.
16822 Cpl. A. F. David.
40992 Pte. F. Medcalf.
13266 Sergt. D. Nicol.
24820 Sergt. W. Sadler.
29662 Pte. J. Sorley.
12871 Sergt. G. Spence.
21663 Pte. M. Thompson.
43302 Pte. W. Thomson.

June 17. *M.S.M. :*

16003 Sergt. T. P. Bennet.
9380 A/C.S.M. J. Dennison.
40104 L/Sergt. E. Fenn.

June 27. *Military Medal :* 203195 Pte. J. Docherty.

July 12. *Belgian Croix de Guerre :*

200031 C.S.M. D. F. Fraser.
4861 C.S.M. W. Falconer.

Oct. 3. *D.C.M. :* 4861 C.S.M. W. Falconer.

11th Argyll & Sutherland Highlanders

Officers.

1916.

Jan. 14. *Military Crosses :*

Capt. N. C. Bennett.
2/Lieut. J. F. C. Cameron.

June 15. *Mentioned in Despatches :*

Lt.-Col. M. M'Neill, D.S.O., C.M.G.
Capt. A. H. Cook.
2/Lieut. J. M. M'Crone.

June 16. *C.M.G. :* Lt.-Col. M. M'Neill, D.S.O.

June 23. *Military Crosses :*

2/Lieut. M. Wilson.
2/Lieut. D. P. M'Ivor.

July 10. *Military Cross :* Capt. N. Black (R.A.M.C.)

July 12. *Military Crosses :*

2/Lieut. F. T. D. Mathews.
2/Lieut. C. B. Alexander.

Sept. 9. *Military Crosses :*

2/Lieut. G. Beattie.
2/Lieut. W. Irvine.

Nov. 14. *Military Crosses :*

Capt. C. F. Henry.
Lieut. W. F. C. M'Clure.
Rev. B. S. Wilson.

1917.

Jan. 1. *Military Cross :* Capt. G. L. Wilson.

1917.

Jan. 4. *Mentioned in Despatches :*
Capt. H. G. Fowler. Lieut. A. S. Campbell.
Lieut. and Q.M. A. E. Bennett.

May 25. *Mentioned in Despatches :*
2/Lieut. D. Sorley. 2/Lieut. J. D. Stewart.

July 18. *Military Crosses :*
Capt. C. H. Bateman. Capt. A. G. Cameron.
Lieut. D. G. H. Hood.

Oct. 2. *D.S.O. :*
Major G. L. Wilson, M.C. Lieut. J. F. C. Cameron, M.C.

Oct. 18. *Military Crosses ;*
2/Lieut. R. L. Mackay. Lieut. G. F. MacLeod.

Oct. 26. *Bar to Military Crosses :*
Lieut. J. F. C. Cameron, M.C. Capt. W. F. C. M'Clure, M.C.
Capt. M. Wilson, M.C.

Military Crosses :
2/Lieut. C. Mitchell. 2/Lieut. D. Sorley.

Nov. 26. *Military Cross :* Lieut. A. R. Muirhead.

1918.

Jan. 1. *D.S.O. :* Lt.-Col. H. A. Duncan.

Mentioned in Despatches (' London Gazette,' November 7, 1917) :
Lt.-Col. H. A. Duncan. Capt. C. A. MacLean.
Lt. G. L. Wilson, D.S.O., M.C. Lt. J. F. C. Cameron, D.S.O., M.C.
Q.M. Lieut. A. E. Bennett. Capt. A. J. MacArthur.
Lieut. W. Irvine, M.C. 2/Lieut. W. A. Hollins.

Jan. 9. *Military Crosses :*
2/Lieut. C. Mitchell. 2/Lieut. D. G. Prosser.

April 6. *Military Crosses :*
2/Lieut. J. G. L. Christie. Lieut. A. B. Muirhead.

June 3. *Military Crosses :*
Capt. C. A. MacLean. Lieut. J. L. Stewart.

June 22. *Bar to Military Cross :* Capt. W. Irvine, M.C.

Croix de Guerre : Lt.-Col. J. T. R. Mitchell, D.S.O.

Legion of Honour and Croix de Guerre : Lt.-Col. G. L. Wilson, D.S.O., M.C.

Croix de Guerre :
Lieut. D. Barbour, M.C. Capt. & Adjt. G. F. MacLeod, M.C.
Lieut. T. W. Bradshaw.

OTHER RANKS.

(From July 1915 to June 1918.)

No.	Rank.	Name.	Award.	Date of London Gazette.
S/5093	Sergt.	Campbell, M.	Ment. in Des.	1/1/16
3573	C.S.M.	Esoon, D. S.	D.C.M.	1/1/16
7943	Sergt.	M'Millan, J.	,,	14/1/16
4008	Pte.	Watson, T.	Military Medal	3/6/16
S/1789	Sergt.	M'Lean, D.	D.C.M.	3/6/16
4018	Sergt.	Strang, J.	Ment. in Des.	15/6/16
S/5147	Cpl.	Westlake, W.	,, ,,	,,
4865	S.M.	Bertram, R.	,, ,,	,,
			D.C.M.	3/6/16
S/4763	Sergt.	Balloch, A.	D.C.M.	27/7/16
S/4774	Pte.	Deacons, J.	Military Medal	29/7/16
S/5025	Sergt.	Forker, W. G.	,, ,,	,,
S/5003	Pte.	Steel, W.	,, ,,	,,
S/7185	Pte.	Blackie, J.	,, ,,	14/9/16
S/4868	Pte.	Dalgleish, J.	,, ,,	,,
S/3670	Pte.	Grant, A.	,, ,,	,,
			Bar to M.M.	9/12/16
	L/Cpl.	Grant, A.	D.C.M.	18/7/17
S/3907	L/Cpl.	Hughes, D.	Military Medal	14/9/16
S/6640	Pte.	Joss, J.	,, ,,	,,
S/7288	Pte.	Stewart, J.	,, ,,	,,
S/7360	Sergt.	Thomson, R.	,, ,,	,,
S/7099	Sergt.	Thomson, D.	,, ,,	,,
5828	Cpl.	Westlake, W.	,, ,,	,,
S/7515	Cpl.	Ferguson, J.	D.C.M.	14/11/16
S/6512	L/Cpl.	Hunter, C.	,,	,,
S/6048	Pte.	Mackay, M.	,,	,,
			Cross of St George, 3rd Cl.	15/2/17
S/7658	Pte.	Tait, P.	D.C.M.	14/11/16
6321	Pte.	Ferguson, H. C.	Military Medal	16/11/16
10439	L/Sergt.	Dunn, A.	,, ,,	9/12/16
S/6330	Pte.	Bratchie, H.	,, ,,	,,
S/4094	Sergt.	Lyon, J.	,, ,,	,,
			Bar to M.M.	20/8/19
S/5032	Cpl.	Maxwell, J.	Military Medal	9/12/16

No.	Rank.	Name.	Award.	Date of London Gazette.
S/3817	L/Cpl.	M'Ilroy, J.	Military Medal	9/12/16
			Bar to M.M.	12/3/17
S/5034	Sergt.	M'Quarrie, W.	Military Medal	9/12/16
S/7230	Pte.	Meek, W.	,, ,,	,,
S/3773	Sergt.	Mitchell, J.	,, ,,	,,
3/3893	C.S.M.	Stanton, P.	,, ,,	,,
S/4131	Pte.	Clarkson, C.	D.C.M.	11/12/16
S/4851	Pte.	Millar, J.	,,	20/12/16
3/7848	Sergt.	Robertson, J. F. W. G.	Ment. in Des.	29/12/16
S/7304	Cpl.	Wilson, J.	,, ,,	,,
S/43042	Pte.	Newman, G.	Military Medal	22/1/17
S/7269	Cpl.	Wallace, J. S.	,, ,,	,,
S/4125	L/Cpl.	Mitchell, J.	,, ,,	19/2/17
S/13001	Pte.	Gibson, J.	,, ,,	12/3/17
3/7952	Cpl. (A/Sergt.)	Crawley, D.	Ment. in Des.	25/5/17
3/7774	Sergt.	Telfer, D.	,, ,,	,,
S/40267	Pte. (A/L/Cpl.)	M'Clymont, W.	,, ,,	,,
S/4051	Pte.	Renfrew, W.	,, ,,	,,
—	Pte.	Sutton.	Military Medal	17/5/17
S/4017	Pte.	Stirton, A.	,, ,,	18/6/17
S/16213	L/Cpl.	Ramsay, A.	,, ,,	3/7/17
S/4696	Pte.	Woodburn, D. C.	,, ,,	,,
637	Sergt.	Pollock, A.	D.C.M.	18/7/17
3623	L/Cpl.	Lindsay, W.	Military Medal	21/8/17
4015	L/Cpl.	Scott, J.	,, ,,	28/9/17
5977	Pte.	Mayes, J.	,, ,,	,,
S/16136	Pte.	Gillan, A.	,, ,,	,,
S/6397	Sergt.	Wilson, H.	,, ,,	,,
S/3598	L/Cpl.	Wilson, R.	,, ,,	,,
S/3855	Sergt.	Flynn, W. S.	D.C.M.	19/11/17
S/14335	Sergt.	Leitch, N.	,,	,,
S/16029	Pte.	Macaulay, A.	,,	,,
S/10413	Pte.	Baxter, D.	Military Medal	,,
S/7689	Pte.	Dorrington, P.	,, ,,	,,
S/7821	Sergt.	Hutton, A.	,, ,,	,,
8660	Pte.	Welsh, P.	,, ,,	,,
S/9846	Pte.	MacTaggart, H.	,, ,,	28/1/18
S/3123	Pte.	Provan, J.	,, ,,	23/2/18
S/12093	Cpl.	Best, J. W.	,, ,,	13/3/18
S/8992	L/Cpl.	Gordon, G.	,, ,,	,,

No.	Rank.	Name.	Award.	Date of London Gazette.
S/3886	Pte.	Peacock, W.	Military Medal	13/3/18
S/4032	Sergt.	Dower, W.	Mer. Ser. Medal	1/1/18
S/40001	Cpl.	Foy, W.	Military Medal	28/1/18
298006	L/Cpl.	Cox, G.	,, ,,	—/4/18
3647	L/Cpl.	Simpson, A.	,, ,,	—/4/18
9262	C.S.M. (A/R.S.M.)	Gilchrist, D.	D.C.M.	3/6/18 (Army No. 2966369)
275717	L/Cpl.	Fulton, W.	Military Medal	12/6/18
276059	Pte.	Gardner, W.	,, ,,	,,
S/11343	Pte.	Grant, N.	,, ,,	,,
S/16131	L/Sergt.	Honeyman, A.	,, ,,	,,
S/7367	Pte.	Rodger, J.	,, ,,	,,
276356	Pte.	Russell, E.	,, ,,	,,
S/11836	Pte.	Mason, F.	,, ,,	,,
			Bar to M.M.	13/3/19
S/7481	Sergt.	Scott, G.	Military Medal	12/6/18
40503	Cpl.	M'Kinlay, G.	,, ,,	,,
19854	Pte.	May, T. J.	,, ,,	,,
4183	Sergt.	M'Farlane, J.	,, ,,	,,
4349	C.Q.M.S.	Chaplin, T.	Mer. Ser. Medal	17/16/18
S/6698	Sergt.	Donaghy, F.	,, ,,	17/6/18
S/4873	Cpl.	Palmer, W.	,, ,,	,,
S/14659	Sergt.	Conly, J. B.	Croix de Guerre	12/7/18
S/17475	Cpl.	Porteous, A.	Méd. Militaire	17/8/18
7000	Pte.	Macleod, J.	Military Medal	29/8/18
S/3993	Sergt.	M'Ewan, J.	,, ,,	,,

8th Argyll & Sutherland Highlanders.

Other Ranks.

(From June 1918 to Finish.)

No.	Rank.	Name.	Award.	Date of London Gazette.
300032	C.S.M.	M'Donald, J.	D.C.M.	1/1/18
300616	Cpl.	Lamont, J.	,,	4/3/18
300171	L/Cpl.	M'Lean, D.	Ment. in Des.	24/5/18
300057	Q.M.S.	M'Lennan, A.	Military Cross	3/6/18

No.	Rank.	Name.	Award.	Date of London Gazette.
300628	Pte.	Clark, S.	Military Medal	16/7/18
303279	Pte.	Kinsella, H., M.M.	Méd. Militaire	17/8/18
17475	Cpl.	Porteous, A.	,, ,,	,,
9368	L/Cpl.	Brogan, P.	Mer. Ser. Medal	14/6/18
4498	Pte.	Christie, R.	Bar to M.M.	16/7/18
10837	Pte.	Haldane, J.	Military Medal	,,
20312	Pte.	Bond, A. T.	,, ,,	,,
9368	Cpl.	Brogan, P.	,, ,,	6/8/18
24	Pte.	Crawford, J.	,, ,,	,,
3725	Pte.	M'Craw, P.	,, ,,	,,
9198	C.S.M.	M'Ilwham, T.	Croix de Guerre	12/7/18
9156	Pte.	Richardson, A.	Military Medal	29/8/18
19421	Pte.	Parkinson, E.	,, ,,	,,
14231	Cpl.	Robertson, J.	D.C.M.	3/9/18
22469	Pte.	Jackson, J.	,,	,,
300597	Cpl.	Ferguson, A.	,,	,,
350580	A/Sergt.	Gillies, L.	,,	,,
300070	Cpl.	Kennedy, A.	,,	,,
303279	Cpl. (A/S.)	Kinsella, H.	,,	,,
300212	Sergt.	Logan, N.	,,	,,
300246	Sergt.	Reid, T.	,,	,,
301801	L/Cpl.	Sinclair, N.	,,	,,
298006	Pte.	Cox, G.	Military Medal	13/9/18
303356	Sergt.	Travers, P.	D.C.M.	3/10/18
13227	Pte.	M'Robbie, J.	Military Medal	7/10/18
8981	L/Cpl.	M'Kinlay, R.	,, ,,	,,
301383	Pte.	Anderson, J.	,, ,,	,,
303199	Pte.	Godfrey, R.	,, ,,	,,
301250	Pte.	Grubb, T.	,, ,,	,,
300797	Cpl.	Jennings, P. S.	,, ,,	,,
S/4817	Pte.	Kilpatrick, S.	,, ,,	,,
300525	L/Cpl.	MacDougall, D.	,, ,,	,,
303341	Pte.	M'Cadden, D.	,, ,,	,,
300111	L/Sergt.	M'Neil, D.	,, ,,	,,
300593	L/Cpl.	M'Tavish, A.	,, ,,	,,
303356	L/Sergt.	Travers, P.	,, ,,	,,
300813	Pte.	M'Farland, T.	D.C.M.	30/10/18
303326	Sergt.	Wilson, G.	Military Medal	13/11/18
S/7817	Cpl.	Clark, A.	,, ,,	,,
S/8232	Cpl.	M'Groarty, D.	,, ,,	,,
327121	Pte.	Bowie, C. L.	,, ,,	,,
S/4668	Pte.	Frame, G.	,, ,,	,,

No.	Rank.	Name.	Award.	Date of London Gazette.
S/7789	Pte. (A/C.)	Hunter, M.	Military Medal	13/11/18
303157	Pte.	M'Kinnon, A.	" "	"
3725	Pte.	M'Graw, P.	Bar to M.M.	"
S/10294	Pte.	Gardner, W.	Croix de Guerre	22/11/18
S/40758	Cpl.	Langridge, W. T.	" "	"
			Méd. Militaire	"
300135	Pte.	Mitchell, D.	Croix de Guerre	"
S/19666	Cpl.	Robertson, S. M.	" "	"
S/1748	A/C.S.M.	Russell, H.	" "	"
S/7812	Cpl.	Shoebridge, G. S.	" "	"
			Méd. Militaire	"
S/20351	Pte.	Thain, J.	Croix de Guerre	"
S/4166	Sergt.	Gray, J.	D.C.M.	5/12/18
303335	Pte.	MacGregor, P.	"	"
301329	Pte.	M'Coll, J.	Military Medal	11/12/18
8825	Q.M.S.	Kidd, J.	Mer. Ser. Medal	16/1/19
300076	C.Q.M.S.	MacLaurin, A.	" "	"
300228	Sergt.	Buie, N.	" "	"
251766	Sergt.	Prow, A. A.	Military Medal	11/2/19
10416	Sergt.	Stevenson, J.	" "	"
S/14368	Cpl.	Martin, W. M.	" "	"
24787	Pte.	Tempest, A.	" "	"
11493	Cpl.	Spowart, S.	" "	" (Army No. 2966469)
S/9402	Pte.	Bunting, C. W.	" "	11/2/19
S/40190	Pte.	Gardiner, R.	" "	"
S/9064	Pte.	Kohler, L. J.	" "	"
276103	Pte.	Liddle, A. R.	" "	"
201058	Pte.	Melville, R.	" "	"
10014	Pte. (A/C.)	Stewart, W.	" "	" (Army No. 2966413)
300616	Sergt.	MacEwan, A.	" "	13/3/19
300176	Sergt.	M'Gougan, J.	" "	"
300172	Cpl.	Ellis, W. B.	" "	"
302183	Pte.	Blanchflower, P. R.	" "	"
S/6973	Pte.	Buchan, D.	" "	"
S/20340	Pte.	Sorrie, A. L.	" "	"
S/15335	L/Cpl.	Thomson, A. R.	" "	"
S/43130	Cpl.	Sitch, V.	" "	14/5/19
S/17615	Pte.	Cummings, J.	" "	"

No.	Rank.	Name.	Award.	Date of London Gazette.
300261	Pte.	Munro, J.	Military Medal	14/5/19
S/9674	Sergt.	Paterson, A. G.	D.C.M.	3/6/19
300028	Sergt.	Logan, N.	Mer. Ser. Medal	,,
S/10594	Cpl. (L/S.)	Bowie, W.	,, ,,	,,
300013	Cpl.	M'Farlane, R.	,, ,,	,,
275371	L/Cpl.	Hunter, A.	Military Medal	17/6/19
303108	Pte.	Cuthbertson, R.	Ment. in Des.	9/7/19
300585	Sergt.	Dixon, E. H.	,, ,,	,,
326011	Pte.	Gray, K. C.	,, ,,	,,
S/5045	Pte. (A/C.)	Seel, H.	,, ,,	,,
300097	A/C.Q.M.S.	Sinclair, D.	,, ,,	,,
201823	Pte.	Smith, R.	,, ,,	,,
301403	Pte.	Carmichael, J.	Military Medal	23/7/19
301085	Pte. (A/L/C.)	Crowe, R.	,, ,,	,,
300728	Pte.	M'Callum, D. L.	,, ,,	,,
S/9142	Sergt.	Robb, A.	,, ,,	20/8/19
9694	C.S.M.	Waters, C. J.	Croix de Virtute Militara, 1st Cl. (Rumanian)	20/9/19 (Army No. 2966397)
300802	Sergt. (A/C.S.M.	Nimmo, W.	Croix de Guerre	7/10/19
300381	C.Q.M.S.	Taylor, F. H.	D.C.M.	11/3/20

45TH COMPANY MACHINE-GUN CORPS.

1917.

May 2. *Military Medals:* 22632 L/C. Lees. Cpl. N. Hornby. 16894 Pte. M. Doyle.

46TH INFANTRY BRIGADE.

HONOURS AND AWARDS.

9TH THE ROYAL SCOTS.

OFFICERS.

1918.

Aug. 12. *Legion d'Honneur, Chevalier:* Lt.-Col. J. B. Muir, D.S.O.

Croix de Guerre: Lieut. J. S. Thompson. Lieut. A. J. Hughson.

1918.

Aug. *Military Cross:* Capt. R. M. Murray.

Oct. Lieut. W. S. Leslie.

1919.

Jan. 1. *Military Cross:* 2/Lieut. J. Haig.

C.M.G.: Lt.-Col. A. Stephenson, D.S.O., M.C.

OTHER RANKS.

D.C.M.

351055	Sergt. J. Fraser	August 1918.
352379	Sergt. J. Hynds, M.M.	October 1918.
51885	Pte. S. G. Salberg	October 1918.
350106	Cpl. A. Squair	January 1919.
350566	Pte. A. Simpson	January 1919.
351176	Pte. A. Haig	January 1919.

Bar to M.M.

350314	Sergt. K. M. Baird, M.M.	August 1918.
352321	Pte. W. Dobbin, M.M.	August 1918.

M.M.

352379	L/Cpl. J. Hynds	August 1918.
44189	L/Cpl. G. Pringle	August 1918.
352247	Pte. M. Clougherty	August 1918.
44398	Pte. A. J. Campbell	August 1918.
352207	Pte. D. J. Brown	August 1918.
51889	Pte. J. Boyne	August 1918.
352017	Pte. H. Macdonald	August 1918.
350787	Pte. H. Salmon	August 1918.
5195	Pte. J. S. Smart	August 1918.
376054	Pte. H. Wilson	August 1918.
352461	Sergt. W. Allan	October 1918.
30229	L/Cpl. W. F. Clarke	October 1918.
202425	Pte. G. Briggs	October 1918.
352285	Pte. J. M'Gregor	October 1918.
352508	Cpl. J. Todd	October 1918.
353151	Sergt. T. Macdonald	January 1919.
351110	Sergt. C. Haig	January 1919.
350180	L/Cpl. L. M'Lellan	January 1919.

M.S.M.

350446	C.Q.M.S. G. S. Bruce	January 1919.
350520	C.Q.M.S. S. T. Wilson	January 1919.

Médaille Militaire.

351055	Sergt. J. Fraser, D.C.M.	January 1919.
350314	Sergt. K. M. Baird, M.M.	January 1919.

Croix de Guerre.

352321	Pte. W. Dobbin, M.M.	January 1919.
351191	Sergt. A. Lockie	January 1919.
42525	Pte. E. J. M'Whirter	January 1919.
352558	Pte. W. Pennie	January 1919.
350579	Pte. W. Blythe	January 1919.
202667	Pte. A. Cope	January 1919.

7/8TH KING'S OWN SCOTTISH BORDERERS.

(The 7th and 8th Battalions were amalgamated on May 27, 1916.)

OFFICERS.

1915.

Nov. *D.S.O.:* Capt. M. F. B. Dennis.

1916.

Jan. *Military Crosses:*

Capt. T. K. Newbigging.
Lieut. S. Grant.
2/Lieut. C. K. Thursby-Pelham.

Mentioned in Despatches:

Lt.-Col. G. de W. Verner.
Lt.-Col. T. B. Sellar.
Major G. M. Hannay.
Capt. M. F. B. Dennis, D.S.O.
Capt. T. K. Newbigging.
2/Lieut. C. K. Thursby-Pelham.
2/Lieut. W. G. Herbertson.

June. *C.M.G.:* Lt.-Col. T. B. Sellar.

Military Crosses:

Capt. C. H. Crawshaw.
2/Lieut. Kennedy.
2/Lieut. G. P. Randall.

1916.

June. *Mentioned in Despatches:*
Lt.-Col. T. B. Sellar, C.M.G.
Capt. J. P. Larkin.
2/Lieut. H. Kennedy.
Capt. H. W. Sutherland.
Lieut. A. R. Brown.

Sept. *Military Cross:* Lieut. F. L. Hamilton.

Dec. *Mentioned in Despatches:*
Lt.-Col. T. B. Sellar, C.M.G.
Major H. P. Hart.
Major M. F. B. Dennis, D.S.O.

1917.

Jan. *D.S.O.:* Major H. P. Hart.
Military Crosses:
Capt. W. Parker, R.A.M.C. (attd.)
2/Lieut. J. H. Patrick.
2/Lieut. R. R. Harkus.

May. *Mentioned in Despatches:*
Capt. T. K. Newbigging, M.C.
Lieut. and Q.M. J. Goss.
Lieut. J. D. Brown.

June. *D.S.O.:* Capt. (Acting Major) J. P. Larkin.
Military Crosses:
Capt. W. W. Home.
Capt. J. S. M'Arthur.

July. *Military Crosses:*
Capt. A. B. Lawson.
2/Lieut. J. H. Strachan.

Oct. *Military Cross:* Lieut. J. Weir.

Dec. *D.S.O.:* Lt.-Col. T. B. Sellar, C.M.G.
Mentioned in Despatches:
Lt.-Col. T. B. Sellar, C.M.G., D.S.O.
Major H. P. Hart, D.S.O.
Lieut. J. E. Thomson.
Lt.-Col. M. F. B. Dennis, D.S.O.
Capt. and Q.M. J. Goss.
Lieut. E. M. S. Houston.

1918.

Jan. *Bar to D.S.O.:* Lt.-Col. M. F. B. Dennis, D.S.O.
Bar to Military Cross: Capt. C. K. Thursby-Pelham, M.C.
Military Crosses:
2/Lieut. A. B. Dickson.
2/Lieut. A. M'Call.
2/Lieut. J. F. Irving.
2/Lieut. H. K. M'Kee.

May. *Military Cross:* Capt. W. W. Henderson.

July. *Bar to Military Cross:* Capt. J. H. Patrick, M.C.
Military Cross: Capt. G. A. Whyte.

Aug. *Bar to Military Cross:* Capt. J. Weir, M.C.
Military Crosses:
Capt. A. B. Paton.
2/Lieut. G. A. Haining.
Lieut. P. Reay.

1918.

Oct. *Military Crosses:*
2/Lieut. S. R. Irvine. 2/Lieut. W. Mellalieu.

1919.

Jan. *Mentioned in Despatches:*
Lieut. M. Fenwick. Lieut. W Torrance.

Feb. *Military Cross:* Capt. J. A. Pretty, M.O.R.C., U.S.A. (attd.)

March. *D.S.O.:* Capt. (Acting Lt.-Col.) H. W. Sutherland.

March. *Military Cross:* Capt. Q.M. J. Goss.

Mentioned in Despatches:
Lt.-Col. H. P. Hart, D.S.O. Capt. (Acting Lt.-Col.) H. W. Sutherland.
Lieut. J. D. Scott.

June. *O.B.E.:* Major T. Blackburn.

Oct. *Bar to Military Cross:* Capt. H. M'Kee, M.C.

Foreign Decorations.

Chevalier of the Order of St Maurice and St Lazarus:
Lt.-Col. T. B. Sellar, C.M.G., D.S.O.

Croix de Guerre:
Lt.-Col. H. P. Hart, D.S.O. Lt.-Col. B. J. B. Coulson.

Chevalier of the Legion of Honour and Croix de Guerre (with Palm):
Major F. L. Hamilton, M.C.

Croix de Guerre (with Palm): 2/Lieut. W. D. Jamie.

OTHER RANKS.

V.C.: 15851 Piper Daniel Laidlaw.

Military Cross: 10537 C.S.M. (Acting R.S.M.) J. A. Munro.

D.C.M.:

13964 Sergt. J. Adamson, M.M.
14397 Pte. J. Bould.
16985 Cpl. J. Bulloch.
15612 Sergt. J. Carmichael.
7529 Sergt. J. Colthart.
5012 C.S.M. R. Douglas.
16713 L/C. J. Findlay.
13145 Pte. R. Hardman.
13384 L/C. S. Hargreaves, M.M.
44013 Sergt. C. Hawthorn.
17068 L/C. V. Kempshall.
14712 Sergt. D. M'Farlane.
13120 Pte. J. M'Vinnie.
14248 Pte. J. Mooney.
13367 Pte. N. Morrison.
21980 Sergt. J. Murfin, M.M.
13645 Cpl. J. Rae.
25156 Pte. W. Reid.
13699 L/C. J. M. Rooney, M.M.
200202 Sergt. J. S. Waugh.
40336 Pte. T. Wright, M.M.

Military Medals:

13964 Cpl. J. Adamson, D.C.M.
6195 Pte. R. Aitken.
22129 Pte. J. Aitken.
16629 Pte. A. Aldred.
16187 Sergt. J. E. W. Alderson.
40115 L/C. D. S. Anderson.
15781 L/C. G. Ashton.
29909 L/C. G. Bacon.
200734 Pte. W. Baillie.
15529 Cpl. H. Beddall.
27810 Pte. T. C. Bell.
9917 L/C. J. Brannon.
14173 Sergt. H. T. Brown.
19197 Sergt. J. Brown.
16528 Sergt. T. Buckshaw.
11874 Pte. R. Bulloch.
12003 L/C. G. Carmichael.
27413 Pte. R. Clark.
17153 Sergt. C. S. Crampton.
18710 Cpl. A. Cruickshanks.
40943 Pte. A. Cruickshanks.
25578 Pte. F. M. Cullen.
14634 Pte. D. Davies.
22465 L/C. D. Dover.
27737 Sergt. A. Duncan.
14315 Sergt. H. Eccles.
40139 Cpl. H. B. Edwards.
11825 Pte. J. Fitzpatrick.
21973 Pte. J. Gavanagh.
16795 L/C. W. Gracie.
40286 Pte. P Gray.
14140 Sergt. J. Hamilton.
15205 L/C. G. Hampson.
13384 L/C. S. Hargreaves, D.C.M.
14021 Pte. A. Harris.
15480 Pte. T. Harper.
15121 L/C. H. Harvey.
13767 Pte. J. Hazlehurst.
15006 Cpl. F. Healey.
27785 Pte. J. Henderson.
8648 Pte. G. Henderson.
8344 Sergt. J. M. Hume.
17740 Pte. W. Hunter.
13579 Pte. H. Irving.
7611 C.Q.M.S. D. Jackson.
14777 Pte. J. Jamieson.
43137 Cpl. J. E. W. Johnston.
17003 Sergt. W. Kent.
13888 Pte. R. Kenyon.
13457 Sergt. D. Kerr.
21345 Pte. A. Leishman.
17506 Pte. W. Lockwood.
21164 Pte. J. M'Bride.
15013 Pte. D. M'Clure (M.M. and 2 Bars).
9798 Sergt. A. G. M'Cormack.
10317 Sergt. J. M'Dermott.
13522 Pte. J. M'Gowan.
29506 Pte. T. D. Mackay.
15823 Sergt. W. M'Quillan.
14277 Sergt. A. M'Vittie.
20317 Sergt. J. Mack.
27425 Pte. H. Matheson.
40861 Pte. P. Mathieson.
17950 Pte. G. H. May.
18125 Pte. F. Maybury.
33178 Cpl. W. Melrose.
14992 Pte. W. Montgomery (M.M. and Bar).
15376 Pte. R. Montgomery.
14248 Cpl. J. Mooney, D.C.M.
44016 Pte. C. H. Morrison.
27801 Pte. F. W. Moseley.
21491 Cpl. J. J. Moss.
18161 L/C. A. Muff.
17954 L/C. J. Muirhead.
21980 Sergt. J. Murfin, D.C.M.
11388 Sergt. S. Murray.
12164 Cpl. J. Murray.
12293 Sergt. S. B. Nivison, M.S.M.
15125 Pte. T. Parker.
14271 Pte. W. Paton.
19958 Pte. D. Pepper.
15124 Sergt. W. Price.
15458 Pte. F. J. Quinn.
22398 Pte. J. W. Rankin.

Military Medals:

7498 L/C. E. Reilly.
17093 Sergt. G. Robinson.
10922 Sergt. P. Rowan.
15941 Cpl. J. Slater.
10556 Cpl. J. W. Smith.
14242 L/C. P. Syme.
28814 Pte. J. Taylor.
11782 Sergt. J. Thornton.
29310 Sergt. W. Tully.
16507 Sergt. J. Urquhart.
15955 L/C. H. Waring.
19909 Sergt. J. F. West.
15961 Sergt. J. H. Wilby.
13007 Cpl. T. Williamson.
40336 Pte. T. Wright, D.C.M.
15631 Cpl. E. Ridley (M.M. and Bar).
13699 L/C. J. M. Rooney, D.C.M.
14270 Cpl. J. Shaw.
14471 Sergt. J. Smart.
13874 Cpl. T. Stephenson.
11042 Pte. D. Taylor.
28838 L/C. S. Thomas.
15931 L/C. R. Tinkler.
40217 Sergt. J. Tweedie.
17846 Cpl. W. Ward.
40196 L/C. J. Waugh.
22117 Cpl. J. Wiggan.
40845 Pte. E. D. Wilkie.
12888 Sergt. J. Worthington.

M.S.M.:

14617 Sergt. T. Agar.
7704 Sergt. J. Hay.
14858 Sergt. J. W. Kippen.
14172 Sergt. A. Morris.
14497 Sergt. J. Osborne.
8352 Sergt.-Piper J. Balloch.
14535 Sergt. R. Jackson.
13528 Sergt. L. Mills.
12295 Sergt. S. B. Nivison, M.M.

Mentioned in Despatches:

13964 L/C. J. Adamson, D.C.M., M.M.
12003 L/C. G. Carmichael, M.M.
8062 R.S.M. C. Cowper.
8159 Sergt. J. T. Dillon.
14013 Pte. W. Hanratty.
13635 C.S.M. J. Hilton.
10317 C.S.M. J. M'Dermott.
14172 Sergt. J. Morris.
10537 R.S.M. J. A. Munro.
13699 Pte. J. M. Rooney, D.C.M., M.M.
17203 Cpl. J. Stephenson.
10473 Pte. S. Webb.
14397 Pte. S. Bould, D.C.M.
20415 Pte. B. Chapman.
17153 Sergt. C. S. Crampton, M.M.
15089 Sergt. J. Gill.
13384 Pte. S. Hargreaves, D.C.M., M.M.
13888 Pte. R. Kenyon, M.M.
10810 Sergt. S. Melville.
14384 L/C. D. Mulholland.
44106 Pte. M. O'Neill.
17094 Cpl. H. Sherrocks.
16507 Sergt. J. Urquhart, M.M.
22117 Pte. J. Wiggan, M.M.

Foreign Decorations.

French Médaille Militaire:

27755 Cpl. A. Blake.
18698 Pte. N. M'Kinnon.

French Croix de Guerre:

27755 Cpl. A. Blake.
17938 Pte. J. Forrester.
14248 Sergt. J. Mooney, D.C.M., M.M.
14288 Sergt. J. Ralston.
11806 Pte. H. Wood.
40943 Pte. A. F. Cruickshanks.
18698 Pte. N. M'Kinnon.
13973 Pte. R. Pow.
14471 Sergt. J. Smart, M.M.

Belgian Croix de Guerre:

13596 C.S.M. H. Gilliver.
10317 C.S.M. J. M'Dermott, M.M.

10th The Cameronians (Scottish Rifles).

Officers.

C.M.G.:

1/1/17....Lt.-Col. A. V. Ussher.

Bar to D.S.O.:

27/7/18....Lt.-Col. A. C. L. Stanley Clarke.

D.S.O.:

1/8/17....Capt. D. A. Foulis.
1/1/18....Lt.-Col. A. C. L. Stanley Clarke.
1/3/19....Major W. H. Murray.

Military Crosses:

1/1/19....Major H. E. C. Bacon.
3/6/16....2/Lieut. J. Bilsland.
3/6/18....Lieut. S. Cranston.
1/1/17....Capt. D. B. Keith.
30/8/17....Capt. G. M'Call, D.C.M., M.M.
18/7/17....Lieut. R. Miller.
2/11/15....Lieut. L. C. Paton.
1/1/18....Capt. C. M. Power.
26/7/18....2/Lieut. J. R. Robb.
11/1/16....Capt. J. A. Callen.
11/1/16....Capt. J. C. Grant.
3/6/16....Major P. R. Hardinge.
30/8/17....2/Lieut. G. D. Killeen.
18/7/17....2/Lieut. G. Menary.
26/7/17....Capt. J. S. Munro.
27/7/17....Capt. A. R. Prentice.
27/12/18....Capt. G. Pride.
25/11/16....Lieut. A. D. Roberts.

Mentioned in Despatches:

25/9/15....Capt. J. A. Callen.
11/1/16....Capt. J. F. Duncan.
25/9/15....Capt. J. C. Grant.
21/5/18....Lieut. H. J. Gunn.
21/7/17....Capt. J. S. Munro.
13/6/16, 27/12/18 } Lieut. and Q.M. F. R. Needham.
21/5/18....Capt. G. Pride.
23/5/17, 1/1/18, 27/7/18 } Lt.-Col. A. C. L. Stanley Clarke.
1/1/17....2/Lieut. J. W. Walker.
27/12/18....Lieut. A. M'L. Crawford
1/1/17, 17/12/17 } Capt. D. A. Foulis.
21/5/18....Capt. E. Grindlay.
27/12/18....Capt. W. K. Knott.
17/12/17....Major W. H. Murray.
23/5/17 Capt. C. M. Power.
11/1/16....Capt. A. S. Pringle.
1/1/16, 1/1/17, 13/3/18 } Lt.-Col. A. V. Ussher, C.M.G.
21/5/18....Lieut. T. Young.

Legion of Honour :

22/11/18....Lt.-Col. A. C. L. Stanley Clarke, D.S.O.

Croix de Guerre :

22/11/18....Lt.-Col. A. C. L. Stanley Clarke, D.S.O.

22/11/18....Capt. G. Gibson.

OTHER RANKS.

Bar to Military Cross :

26/9/17....8859 R.S.M. H. Grant.

Military Crosses :

1/7/16....8859 R.S.M. H. Grant.

9/10/16....13585 C.S.M. J. Baxenden.

D.C.M. :

25/8/17.... 13830 Pte. G. F. Baldwin.
11/1/16.... 8915 Sergt. A. Bigg.
3/6/16.... 8095 Sergt. Cowan.
3/6/19.... 26684 Cpl. A. Dott.
12/4/17.... 26158 Pte. T. Flatt.
18/7/17.... 11372 Sergt. M'Millan.
26/9/17.... 14105 Sergt. S. Moore.
30/10/18.... 23529 Pte. R. Owenson.
11/1/16.... 14272 Pte. P. Richardson.
1/1/18.... 10530 C.S.M. W. Thomas.
22/4/18.... 8500 Sergt. W. Barlow.
30/10/18.... 7058 C.S.M. C. C. Bull.
1/1/16.... 14180 Sergt. H. Dixon.
11/1/17.... 14182 Pte. J. Dunlop.
20/10/18.... 25661 Sergt. T. Goodall.
23/5/17.... 12565 R.Q.M.S. B. Marmion.
3/6/19.... 39331 Pte. J. Morrison.
3/6/19....202348 Pte. G. Paton.
11/1/16.... 13770 Cpl. R. E. Smith.
26/5/17.... 7377 C.S.M. P. Timoney.

Bar to Military Medal :

25/9/16, 12/11/17 } 13442 Sergt. J. Hutchison.
26/7/18.... 18609 Sergt. J. Pearson.
19/7/17.... 18524 Sergt. G. Payne.
13/10/18.... 40689 Pte. J. Thomson.

Military Medal :

25/9/16.... 13830 Pte. G. F. Baldwin.
16/10/16.... 13339 Sergt. T. Barnes.
13/10/18.... 40118 Sergt. H. G. Berry.
18/6/17.... 13359 Cpl. W. Budge.
13/10/18.... 27337 Sergt. D. Campbell.
19/11/17.... 13611 Cpl. A. Clayton.
26/5/17.... 14164 Cpl. M. Cockfield.
19/7/17.... 13385 L/C. J. Crook.
14/9/16.... 14173 Pte. P. Daly.
16/10/16.... 20744 L/C. G. Deans.
25/9/16.... 14078 Pte. G. Doughty.
16/10/16.... 13403 Sergt. T. Eaglesham.
27/6/18.... 26043 L/C. T. Espin.
27/9/16....265372 Cpl. W. Fleming.
13/10/18....235186 Sergt. B. Hay.
30/9/16.... 7759 Pte. C. Innes.
3/6/16.... 15475 L/C. T. Barbour.
18/6/17.... 17631 Cpl. Barnett.
14/9/16.... 13353 Sergt. F. A. Brook.
14/9/16.... 16908 Pte. C. Barton.
13/10/18.... 40289 Pte. R. Clarke.
14/9/16.... 17021 Pte. W. Clelland.
3/6/16.... 8095 Sergt. T. Cowan.
19/7/17.... 13858 C.S.M. J. Curry.
26/7/18....240096 Sergt. J. Davidson.
19/7/17.... 23064 Pte. J. Donnelly.
19/11/17.... 22120 Pte. E. Dronfield.
14/9/16.... 18883 Sergt. E. Ellis.
30/9/16.... 16066 Pte. R. Fenwick.
18/6/17.... 13409 Pte. D. Foster.
3/6/16.... 13442 Cpl. J. Hutchison.
19/11/17.... 14220 Pte. W. Jardine.

Military Medal:

25/9/16.... 14226 Pte. J. Lamb.
25/9/16.... 8551 L/Sergt. A. M. Lane.
9/7/17.... 18396 Pte. M. Lawson.
19/11/17.... 14229 Cpl. J. Lindsay.
25/9/16.... 13478 Pte. S. M'Donald.
26/5/17.... 43339 Pte. J. M'Ginty.
19/11/17.... 11372 Sergt. M'Millan.
13/10/18....266285 Pte. J. Matthew.
19/11/17.... 16913 Pte. L. Mulvey.
20/10/18.... 16206 Pte. W. Oddie.
8/8/16.... 17145 Cpl. W. Pollard.
13/10/18.... 20605 L/C. S. Preston.
14/9/16.... 16098 Sgt. J. R. Robinson.
19/11/17.... 13759 C.S.M. A. Sawers.
18/6/17.... 19593 L/C. Skoulding.
16/10/16.... 14286 Cpl. J. Smith.
19/11/17.... 22234 Pte. J. Stirling.
19/11/17.... 40884 L/Sergt. J. Swan.
27/6/18.... 40689 Pte. J. Thomson.
28/11/18.... 14306 Sgt. J. Waddington.
13/10/18.... 18869 Sergt. T. Watson.
27/6/18.... 14391 Pte. H. Westmacott.
31/12/17.... 43385 Sergt. J. Wilson.
29/8/18.... 9408 Pte. J. Wood.
19/7/17.... 18260 Pte. Langham.
13/10/18.... 30447 Pte. W. Law.
18/6/17.... 25689 Pte. Lee.
14/9/16.... 16062 Sergt.-Piper J. M'Coll.
21/10/16.... 6909 Sergt. J. M'Donough.
18/6/17.... 40109 L/C. J. M'Intyre.
16/10/18.... 41453 Cpl. J. E. Martin.
16/8/18.... 18263 Pte. J. Meahan.
27/9/17....235130 Cpl. T. Murdoch.
18/6/17.... 18524 Sergt. G. Payne.
19/11/17.... 16513 Pte. W. Porteous.
19/11/17.... 8894 Sergt. H. Reid.
18/6/17.... 16645 Pte. J. Roe.
7/11/18.... 40245 Sergt. J. Scott.
18/6/17.... 17814 Cpl. D. Smith.
14/9/16.... 13485 Pte. J. Stevenson.
18/6/17.... 13070 L/C. G. Suter.
31/12/17.... 33810 L/C. J. Thomson.
16/10/18.... 23014 Pte. A. Urquhart.
14/6/17.... Pte. Walker.
27/6/18.... 8714 Pte. J. Watson.
19/11/17.... 40773 Pte. G. Wheatley.
27/9/16....203642 Cpl. G. Wiseman.
19/11/17.... 16091 Pte. E. Wray.

Meritorious Service Medal:

17/6/18.... 20764 Cpl. R. Adair.
18/1/19.... 40160 Sergt. T. Hunter.
17/6/18....240099 Sergt. J. Potter.
17/6/18.... 18869 Sergt. T. Watson.
3/6/19.... 78763 Sergt. W. Bain.
18/1/19.... 13472 Sergt. J. M'Crossan.
17/6/18.... 14126 C.Q.M.S. E. Smithson.

Mentioned in Despatches:

18/3/18.... 18637 Sergt. W. Bain.
13/6/16.... 17021 Pte. W. Clelland.
23/5/17.... 20737 Pte. W. Gallacher.
13/6/16.... 14229 Cpl. J. Lindsay.
23/5/17.... 12565 R.Q.M.S. B. Marmion.
18/3/18.... 18263 Pte. J. Meahan.
13/6/16.... 13360 Cpl. C. Burgess.
23/5/17.... 13636 Pte. Elgin.
1/1/17.... 18359 L/C. J. Jacques.
27/12/18.... 14242 L/C. R. M'Dowall.
1/1/17.... 9587 C.S.M. J. Mason.
7/4/18.... 20668 Cpl. J. Warren.

Médaille Militaire:

24/2/16.... 8915 Sergt. A. Bigg.
22/11/18.... 23529 Pte. R. Owenson.

Croix de Guerre:

12/7/17.... 13830 Pte. G. F. Baldwin.
17/2/17.... 18359 L/C. J. Jacques.
22/11/18....235246 Pte. J. M'Blane.
22/11/18.... 34140 Pte. J. Clanachan.
22/11/18.... 18260 Pte. Langham.
28/11/18.... 13505 Sergt. G. Marshall.

Croix de Guerre:

9/12/16.... 16137 Pte. C. Martin.
21/11/18.... 23529 Pte. R. Owenson.
22/11/18.... 37745 L/C. J. Pullen.
22/11/18.... 34435 Pte. H. Scobbie.
22/11/18.... 14391 Pte. H. Westmacott.
12/7/17.... 14105 Sgt. S. Moore (*Belgian*).
22/11/18.... 18524 C.S.M. G. Payne.
22/11/18....240363 Pte. J. Robertson.
18/6/17.... 13485 Pte. J. Stevenson.

10/11TH HIGHLAND LIGHT INFANTRY.

OFFICERS.

1916.

April 30. *Mentioned in Despatches:*
Capt. C. B. Campbell.
2/Lieut. A. A. Easton.
Lieut. J. A. Campbell.
Lieut. and Q.M. J. Drawbell.
Capt. L. M. Paterson.
2/Lieut. F. M. Sibold.
Lieut. J. Y. Milne-Henderson.

June 3. *Military Cross:* Capt. P. Stewart.

July 27. *Military Cross:* 2/Lieut. A. Fraser.

Nov. 13. *Mentioned in Despatches:*
Lt.-Col. R. F. Forbes.
Capt. R. P. Easton.
2/Lieut. D. D. Pratt.
Major H. C. Stuart.
2/Lieut. A. Christie.
Lieut. and Q.M. J. Drawbell.

Nov. 14. *Military Cross:* Lieut. D. R. Keith.

1917.

May 9. *Mentioned in Despatches:*
Major H. C. Stewart, D.S.O.
Lieut. and Q.M. J. Drawbell.
2/Lieut. A. Christie.

July 17. *Military Crosses:*
2/Lieut. T. Allan.
2/Lieut. J. H. Campbell.
2/Lieut. J. A. Smith.
Lieut. J. F. F. Bowers.
2/Lieut. J. Miller.

Sept. 25. *Military Crosses:*
Lieut. J. A. M'Kinlay.
2/Lieut. J. W. E. Smith.

Oct. 16. *Military Cross:* Capt. J. A. Campbell.

Nov. 7. *Mentioned in Despatches:*
Lt.-Col. R. F. Forbes, D.S.O.
Lieut. and Q.M. J. Drawbell.
Capt. J. F. Marshall.

Dec. 28. *Bar to D.S.O.:* Lt.-Col. R. F. Forbes, D.S.O.

1918.

Jan. 1. *Military Cross:* 2/Lieut. J. Grant.

OTHER RANKS.

1916.

April 30. *Mentioned in Despatches :*
196 Sergt. J. Cunningham. 420 L/Cpl. A. Dobbie.

June 3. *Military Medal :* 17335 A/C.S.M. G. Lovatt.

Oct. 14. *Military Medals :*
465 Cpl. P. Croal. 196 Sergt. J. Cunningham.
215 L/Cpl. J. Ellingham. 24930 Pte. A. Boyle.

Nov. 14. *Military Cross :* 10930 C.S.M. D. Sheridan.

D.C.M. :
8512 Cpl. H. M'Donald. 1918 L/Cpl. H. Davies.

Nov. 16. *Military Medals :*
21433 L/Cpl. H. Blackburn. 452 Pte. W. Birnie.
19826 Pte. A. M'Neill.

Dec. 9. *Military Medals :*
19391 Pte. J. Davies. 108 Pte. G. Lennon.
17268 Pte. R. M'Garva. 18513 Pte. J. M'Kay.
9470 Sergt. J. M'Vey.

1917.

Jan. 1. *D.C.M. :* 10325 C.S.M. A. Freeborn.

March 14. *Italian Bronze Medal :* 10930 C.S.M. D. Sheridan.

May 9. *Mentioned in Despatches :*
19900 R.S.M. J. Donnelly. 19625 Sergt. E. Elliott.
9676 Sergt. A. Fleming. 21093 L/Cpl. S. French.
589 Pte. J. M'Kenzie.

June 18. *Military Medals :*
10571 Sergt. E. Swain. 3882 A/Sergt. A. Cormack.
19514 Cpl. G. Arthur. 19528 L/Cpl. J. M'Davitt.
14925 L/Cpl. J. M'Donald. 23007 Pte. M. Black.
17218 Pte. J. M'Ginlay. 8648 Pte. W. Spowart.

July 6. *Military Medal :* 12900 Pte. J. M'Laren.

July 17. *D.C.M. :* 8874 C.S.M. W. Turner.
Military Medal : 21291 Pte. J. Nicholson.

Oct. 16. *Military Medals :*
17189 Pte. J. Cupples. 42464 Cpl. W. Dingwall.
32490 Pte. J. Harvey. 8805 Sergt. J. Leggate.
41629 Pte. J. Morrison. 8629 Cpl. J. Stewart.

Nov. 16. *Military Medal :* 40186 Cpl. W. Wilson.

1917.

Nov. 19. *Military Medals :*

19644 Pte. F. Beaton.
19432 Sergt. W. Hogg.

Dec. 12. *Military Medals :*

21727 Pte. W. Campion.
12364 L/Cpl. J. Somerville.
38366 Pte. W. Wilson.

Dec. 21. *Mentioned in Despatches :*

11090 Cr./Sergt. G. M'Cord.
17393 C.S.M. W Mowatt.
631 Sergt. J. O'Neill.

Dec. 28. *D.C.M. :* 669 C.Q.M.S. M. Searle.

12TH HIGHLAND LIGHT INFANTRY.

OFFICERS.

1915.

Oct. 25. *D.S.O. :* Lieut. N. H. M'Neil.

Nov. 30. *Mentioned in Despatches :*

Lt.-Col. J. H. Purvis.
Capt. P. W. Torrance.
2/Lieut. G. S. Laird.
2/Lieut. N. H. M'Neil.
2/Lieut. D. G. Watson.

1916.

Jan. 14. *Military Crosses :*

Capt. P. W. Torrance.
2/Lieut. D. G. Watson.

May 31. *Military Cross :* 2/Lieut. L. Lucas.

June 15. *Mentioned in Despatches :*

Lt.-Col. J. H. Purvis.
Capt. D. G. Watson.
2/Lieut. W. J. Aitchison.

Oct. 31. *Military Crosses :*

Capt. J. Shatton (R.C. Padre).
2/Lieut. A. Bryan.

1917.

Jan. 4. *Mentioned in Despatches :*

Lt.-Col. A. A. J. Heyman.
Capt. C. F. G. Humphries.

April 3. *Mentioned in Despatches :*

Capt. W. M'Hardie.
2/Lieut. R. R. Marshall.
Q.M. and Lieut. J. Carpenter.

July 17. *Military Cross :* 2/Lieut. D. A. M. Main.

Aug. 10. *Military Cross :* Capt. T. B. Myles.

Sept. 3. *Military Cross :* Capt. R. L. Hannah.

Oct. 25. *Military Cross :* Lieut. R. R. Marshall.

1917.

Dec. 31. *Mentioned in Despatches:*

2/Lieut. J. M. Bannatyne.
2/Lieut. W. Dunsmore.
2/Lieut. J. Trotter.
Q.M. and Capt. J. Carpenter.
Capt. R. L. Hannah.
2/Lieut. O. V. Harland.

OTHER RANKS.

1915.

Oct. 26. *D.C.M.:* 17538 Sergt. M. Bain.

Nov. 30. *Mentioned in Despatches:* 18973 Cpl. A. M'Nicol.

1916.

Jan. 14. *D.C.M.:*

19160 C.M.S. A. Bruce.
18831 Cpl. C. S. Flower.

June 15. *Mentioned in Despatches:*

9394 C.S.M. E. Campbell.
19164 Sergt. W. M'Nab.

Oct. 31. *Military Medals:*

17641 Sergt. A. Ramage.
19164 Sergt. Wm. M'Nab.
23156 L/Sergt. E. Breazley.
19541 Pte. J. M'Henry.
17569 Sergt. A. M'Alpine.
19976 Sergt. E. Feather.
1921 Pte. W. Young.
18675 Pte. John M'Lean.

1917.

Jan. 4. *Mentioned in Despatches:*

6291 C.S.M. A. Brown.
18666 Pte. R. Sadler.
17649 Pte. J. Lawson.

March 9. *Military Medals:*

18793 Cpl. A. M'Nicol.
18643 Pte. D. Robertson.

April 30. *Military Medals:*

40233 Sergt. J. Dockery.
17879 Sergt. H. Robinson.
32541 Pte. H. M'Donald.
18823 Pte. A. Doyle.
23068 Pte. D. Rose.
18553 Pte. R. Robertson.
8264 Sergt. T. Gardner.
17833 Sergt. G. M. Henry.
22353 Pte. W. Ross.
12460 Pte. J. M'Lellan.
18426 Pte. A. Cassells.

Mentioned in Despatches:

17833 Sergt. G. M. Henry.
23149 Pte. T. Porter.
17796 Sergt. C. M'Garry.

June 6. *D.C.M.:* 11712 C.S.M. D. Wood.

July 6. *Military Medal:* 40352 Pte. T. O. Stewart.

July 17. *D.C.M.:*

17641 Sergt. A. Ramage.
11312 C.S.M. J. H. Warrington.

1917.

July 17. *Military Medal:* 43497 Cpl. J. Lawler.

July 28. *Military Medal:* 7826 Pte. R. Humphries.

Aug. 5. *Military Medals:*

17910 Sergt. P. M'Brearty. 9287 Sergt. H Cook.
42633 Pte. S. Dunnett. 42604 Pte. E. Ormsby.

Sept. 3. *D.C.M.:*

6923 C.S.M. J. W. M'Donald. 9287 Sergt. H. Cook.

Bar to Military Medal:

12460 Pte. J. M'Lellan, M.M. 17833 Sergt. G. M. Henry, M.M.

Military Medals:

40231 Sergt. D. C. Armour 21634 Sergt. J. Maxwell.
41851 Sergt. T. P. Brown. 22264 Cpl. D. O'Hea.
41862 Cpl. J. W. Whenham. 43140 L/Cpl. W. Jack.
18031 Pte. H. Eddowes. 25137 Pte. R. Wilson.
19525 Pte. W. M'Cart.

Sept. 10. *Bar to Military Medal:* 23068 Pte. D. Rose, M.M.

Military Medals:

18885 Cpl. J. M'Master. 8743 Pte. F. Fox.
25305 Pte. W. Sandison. 42548 Pte. J. Duffy.
25318 Pte. A. Robinson.

Sept. 30. *Military Medals:*

17988 Sergt. H. Muir. 27479 Cpl. G. Brian.
40234 Pte. V. W. Agnew. 24561 Pte. J. Jess.

Oct. 2. *Military Medal:* 9678 Sergt. T. Moore.

Oct. 16. *2nd Bar to M.M.:* 12460 Pte. J. M'Lellan.

Military Medal: 41765 L/Cpl. J. Campbell.

Oct. 24. *Military Medal:* 9086 Sergt. J. Turner.

Dec. 15. *Military Medals:*

17 Pte. George Beagrie. 36148 Pte. J. Graham.

Dec. 31. *Mentioned in Despatches:*

18389 Cpl. W. Duffy. 1970 R.Q.M.S. J. Stevenson.

1918.

Jan. 10. *M.S.M.:* 17796 Sergt. C. M'Garry.

46TH BRIGADE MACHINE-GUN COMPANY.

1917.

Aug. 5. *Military Medals:*

Sergt. A. Hawkins. L/C. R. Stansfield.
Pte. A. Doyle. Pte. P. Doherty.

9TH GORDON HIGHLANDERS (PIONEERS).

OFFICERS.

1915.

Oct. 21. *D.S.O.:* Major W. W. Macgregor.

1916.

June 4. *D.S.O.:* Lt.-Col. E. H. H. Gordon.

June 12. *Military Cross:* Lieut. G. Figgis.

June 25. *Mentioned in Despatches:*
Lt.-Col. E. H. H. Gordon, D.S.O. Major T. G. Taylor.
Capt. T. Smith. Capt. A. B. Gourlay.

1917.

Jan. 3. *D.S.O.:* Lt.-Col. T. G. Taylor.
Military Cross: Capt. G. B. Gourlay.

Jan. 7. *Mentioned in Despatches:*
Lt.-Col. E. H. H. Gordon. Lt.-Col. T. G. Taylor, D.S.O.
2/Lieut. R. Kynoch.

April *Military Cross:* Lieut. J. D. Robertson.

May *Mentioned in Despatches:*
Lt.-Col. T G. Taylor, D.S.O. Lieut. C. F. M. MacLachan.

June *Military Crosses:*
Capt. R. Lumsden. Capt. D. E. Burnett.

Aug. 16. *Military Cross:* 2/Lieut. R. Kynoch.

Sept. 6. *Military Crosses:*
Major Lord Dudley Gordon (afterwards altered to D.S.O.)
Rev. G. M. Fairweather.

Oct. 2. *Military Cross:* Capt. W. N. Allan.

Dec. 25. *Mentioned in Despatches:*
Lt.-Col. T. G. Taylor, D.S.O. Major Lord Dudley Gordon, D.S.O.
Capt. R. M. Maclean. Capt. D. F. Burnett, M.C.

1918.

May 27. *Mentioned in Despatches:*
Capt. A. E. O. Black. Capt. E. G. Mackean.

June 6. *Military Cross:* Capt. H. Wright.

Aug. 10. *Croix de Guerre avec Palmes:*
Major G. B. Gourlay, M.C. Capt. R. Lumsden, M.C.
Capt. A. E. O. Black.

1919.

June 3. *Military Cross:* Capt. J. D. Leslie.

OTHER RANKS.

(From July 1915 to Finish.)

No.	Rank.	Name.	Award.	Date of London Gazette.
6868	Pte.	Smith, G.	Ment. in Des.	1/1/16
S/2953	Sergt.	Robson, W.	D.C.M.	14/1/16
	C.S.M. (T/R.S.M.)	Robson, W.	Mer. Ser. Medal	1/1/18
9486	Pte.	Evans, W.	Military Medal	12/6/16
6794	C.S.M.	Merry, R.	Ment. in Des.	,,
4751	Pte.	Blencow, J.	,, ,,	,,
S/7746	Sergt.	Keith, S.	D.C.M.	21/6/16
S/3935	Sergt.	Finlay, G. W.	Military Medal	3/6/16
S/2880	Cpl.	Black, J.	,, ,,	14/9/16
S/4751	Pte.	Blencow, J.	,, ,,	,,
S/6381	Sergt.	Burgess, F.	,, ,,	,,
			Bar to M.M.	16/11/16
S/3808	C.S.M.	Donaldson, J.	Military Medal	14/9/16
S/4797	Pte.	Lees, P. H.	,, ,,	,,
S/3704	L/Cpl.	Macaulay, H.	,, ,,	,,
S/3145	L/Sergt.	Meikle, A.	,, ,,	,,
S/4093	Sergt.	Naismith, J.	,, ,,	,,
			Bar to M.M.	16/11/16
S/6746	L/Cpl.	Taylor, C. H.	Military Medal	14/9/16
S/5775	L/Cpl.	Wemyss, W.	,, ,,	,,
S/3149	L/Sergt.	Craig, J.	,, ,,	21/9/16
S/6414	Sergt.	Henderson, G.	,, ,,	,,
			Ital. Bronze Med.	24/5/17
S/8092	Pte.	Ball, W.	Military Medal	21/10/16
S/4233	Pte.	Brown, W.	,, ,,	9/12/16
S/8742	Pte.	Fairgrieve, R.	,, ,,	,,
3/6785	C.S.M.	Coles, H. T.	Ment. in Des.	29/12/16
S/8035	L/Cpl.	M'Lellan, S.	,, ,,	,,
			Military Medal	25/5/17
S/2959	Sergt.	Smith, J.	,, ,,	6/1/17
S/8696	Cpl.	Wood, J.	,, ,,	,,
3/7165	C.S.M.	Owens, J.	Méd. Militaire	1/5/17
S/3053	Pte.	Elliott, G.	Military Medal	25/5/17
S/3072	Cpl.	Gibson, W.	,, ,,	,,
S/6385	L/Sergt.	Gray, N.	,, ,,	,,

No.	Rank.	Name.	Award.	Date of London Gazette.
S/4302	R.Q.M.S.	Binnie, J. B.	Military Medal	25/5/17
S/2930	Sergt.	M'Conville, P.	Ment. in Des.	,,
S/3072	Cpl.	Gibson, W.	,, ,,	,,
S/8023	L/Cpl.	Runciman, G. C.	,, ,,	,,
S/5665	L/Cpl.	Clinton, T.	Military Medal	3/7/17
S/2876	Sergt.	Fox, J.	Méd. Militaire	12/7/17
	C.S.M.	Fox, J.	D.C.M.	19/11/17
3647	Pte.	Davidson, J.	Military Medal	4/8/17
17363	Pte.	Cameron, H.	,, ,,	/7/17
S/2849	Pte.	Pirrie, J.	,, ,,	16/8/17
			Croix de Guerre	12/7/18
5665	Cpl.	Clinton, T.	Bar to M.M.	7/10/17
12392	Sergt.	Peat, Q.	Military Medal	,,
8044	Cpl.	Cochrane, W.	,, ,,	,,
3955	L/Cpl.	Stevenson, A.	,, ,,	,,
14607	L/Sergt.	Macdonald, W.	,, ,,	,,
3073	L/Cpl.	Mawer, P.	,, ,,	,,
3864	Sergt.	Bruce, R.	,, ,,	,,
54	L/Sergt.	Jennings.	,, ,,	,,
17383	Pte.	Ramsey, W.	,, ,,	,,
S/3079	L/Cpl.	M'Leod, J.	,, ,,	28/9/17
S/5399	L/Cpl.	Smith, A	,, ,,	,,
S/6383	Pte.	Brandis, W.	,, ,,	18/10/17
S/4033	Cpl. (L/S.)	Gorman, J. H.	,, ,,	,,
S/6374	Pte.	Hay, W.	,, ,,	,,
S/3792	Pte. (L/C.)	King, H.	,, ,,	,,
			Croix de Guerre	22/11/18
10310	Cpl.	M'Phail, F.	Military Medal	18/10/17
S/6413	Sergt.	Rae, A.	,, ,,	,,
S/14182	Pte.	Candy, W.	,, ,,	2/11/17
S/3814	Sergt.	Cranston, M.	,, ,,	,,
S/4326	Pte.	Marnock, F.	,, ,,	,,
3/6125	Pte.	M'Kay, A.	,, ,,	,,
3810	Sergt.	Campbell, W.	Ment. in Des.	25/12/17
10488	Pte.	Thomson, W.	,, ,,	,,
S/6369	Sergt.	Cooper, J.	D.C.M.	1/1/18
S/12035	Cpl.	Campbell, A.	Military Medal	28/1/18
223	Sergt.	Wallace, C.	D.C.M.	28/3/18
S/18832	Pte.	Wileman, E.	Military Medal	2/4/18
S/3946	Cpl. (L/S.)	Macpherson, J.	Ment. in Des.	24/5/18
4558	Pte.	Farmer, J.	Military Medal	15/4/18

No.	Rank.	Name.	Award.	Date of London Gazette.
June 6.	S/14386 L/C.	A. M'Leod.	(Record to be made in conduct sheet in accordance with K.R., para. 1919/XIV.: gave 800 c.c. of blood for transfusion to another soldier.)	
7046	C.S.M.	Gardner, J.	D.C.M.	8/6/18
S/3203	Cpl.	Barr, W.	Mer. Ser. Medal	17/6/18
S/7523	Sergt.	Bishop, A. T.	,, ,,	,,
S/3800	Sergt.	Scott, R.	,, ,,	,,
S/6751	L/Cpl.	Kain, H.	Military Medal	27/6/18
S/3169	Pte.	Kelly, M.	,, ,,	,,
S/26781	Pte.	M'Kinnon, D. J.	,, ,,	,,
S/4857	Sergt.	Folkes, J.	Croix de Guerre	12/7/18
4148	Pte.	Taylor, A.	,, ,,	10/8/18
3792	L/Cpl.	King, H.	,, ,,	,,
S/2033	L/Cpl.	Lloyd, J.	Military Medal	13/11/18
S/7748	Pte.	Ferguson, A.	Croix de Guerre	22/11/18
S/2928	Sergt.	Ferguson, P.	,, ,,	,,
S/6739	L/Cpl.	Hossack, C.	,, ,,	,,
S/4167	L/Sergt.	Neill, J.	,, ,,	,,
S/14936	C.Q.M.S.	Thomson, J.	,, ,,	,,
S/6814	Cpl.	Duncan, J. C.	Ment. in Des.	28/12/18
			Mer. Ser. Medal	3/6/19
238116	Sergt.	Cameron, N.	Ment. in Des.	28/12/18
			D.C.M.	3/9/19
S/6137	Sergt.	Strachan, C.	Mer. Ser. Medal	18/1/19
S/6718	C.Q.M.S.	Campbell, A. L.	,, ,,	3/6/19
S/6408	Pte.	Gray, A.	Military Medal	17/6/19
S/14620	Pte.	Miller, E.	,, ,,	11/2/19
S/14632	Pte.	Walker, C.	,, ,,	,,
S/5441	Pte.	Gow, T.	Ment. in Des.	9/7/19
S/3086	Pte. (A/C.)	Ramsay, A.	,, ,,	,,
S/10488	Pte.	Thomson, W.	,, ,,	,,
S/10398	Cpl.	Reid, J.	Military Medal	20/8/19
S/2938	Pte.	Cowe, W.	,, ,,	,,

FIFTEENTH DIVISIONAL ARTILLERY.

1915.

Oct. 11. *V.C.:* 36830 Sergt. J. C. Raynes (71st Brigade).

Nov. 5. *D.C.M. and Médaille Militaire:*
11029 Cpl. J. R. Handyside (71st Brigade).
9178 Bdr. J. Veitch („).
22189 Gnr. G. Armitt („).

1916.

Jan. *D.S.O.:*
Major J. Berkeley (71st Brigade).
Major A. C. L. Theobald (73rd Brigade).

Military Cross:
Capt. E. St C. Gray (Staff Captain).
Lieut. R. H. Bingham (72nd Brigade).

D.C.M.:
14986 Cpl. A. E. Galvin (73rd Brigade).
9277 Bdr. J. Gray (72nd Brigade).
90279 Gnr. A. Revell (70th Brigade).

Mentioned in Despatches:
Brig.-Gen. E. W. Alexander, V.C., C.M.G. (C.R.A.)
Bt.-Col. J. W. Stirling (72nd Brigade).
Lt.-Col. H. W. A. Christie (70th Brigade).
Major L. H. C. Sherbrooke (Brigade Major).
Major E. W. T. Elam (72nd Brigade).
Capt. A. T. C. Gardner („).
Lieut. H. W. Deacon (71st Brigade).
Lieut. J. W. Mason („).
2/Lieut. H. G. Dewey (73rd Brigade).
2/Lieut. H. M. Pearse („).
2/Lieut. I. A. W. Grant (72nd Brigade).
5163 B.S.M. J. Shann (73rd Brigade).
61297 B.S.M. Franklin, S.G. (70th Brigade).
55152 Cpl. T. Rees („).
36682 Gnr. A. W. Tucker (Not stated).

June *Mentioned in Despatches* (' London Gazette,' June 3, 1916):
Lt.-Col. J. W. Stirling.

Military Cross: Lieut. J. C. Russel (72nd Brigade).

Aug. *Military Medals* (72nd Brigade):
58663 Sergt. E. J. Hewitt. 86671 Bdr. E. Eggins.
9043 Bdr. C. Blunden.

1916.

Sept. *D.C.M.:* Sergt. F. Miles (72nd Brigade).

Military Medals (72nd Brigade):

Gnr. Silvester. Gnr. Nicholson.
Sergt. R. Williams. Sergt. A. E. Dewkins.
Bdr. C. Holmes. Gnr. Nuttall.
Gnr. J. Thompson. Gnr. F. A. Middleton.

Sept. 73rd Brigade, R.F.A. "During month of September 1916 the following distinctions were won in Brigade:—
1 D.C.M., 21 M.M.'s." (No names given.)

73rd Brigade, R.F.A.—4 Military Crosses:—
Capts. Kane and Graham. Lieuts. Hatton and Mason.

1 M.M. and 2 M.S.M.'s. (No names given.)

Oct. *Military Cross:* Capt. J. Fairgrieve (72nd Brigade).

1 D.C.M. and 16 M.M.'s and 1 Bar to M.M. (72nd Brigade).

Nov. *Military Medal:* B.S.M. Fulmann (72nd Brigade).

Nov. 6. *Bar to Military Cross:* 2/Lieut. H. T. Vizard.

No particulars available for the years 1917 *and* 1918.

DIVISIONAL AMMUNITION COLUMN.

1916.

Sept. 25. *Military Medals:*
19059 Sergt. J. J. Nolan. 41696 Dvr. J. D. Vasey.
18922 Dvr. N. Kemp.

1917.

April 28. 18161 Sergt. A. T. Hodgetts. 9937 Cpl. J. Parker.
97904 Gnr. B. Owen.

Mentioned in Despatches ('London Gazette,' May 21, 1918):
Lt.-Col. J. Fergus Duncan. 43404 B.S.M. W. E. Perry, D.C.M.

June 23. *M.S.M.:*
6080 R.S.M. C. Chatfield. 51479 B.S.M. A. Hodge.

Aug. 10. *Croix de Guerre:*
51479 B.S.M. A. Hodge, M.S.M. 43404 B.S.M. W. E. Perry, D.C.M.

Dec. 12. *D.C.M.:* 78109 Sergt. E. Piercy.

No particulars available for 1918.

FIFTEENTH DIVISIONAL ROYAL ENGINEERS.

OFFICERS.

1916.

June 3. *D.S.O.:*
Majors R. S. Walker and H. Pollard Lowsley, C.I.E.
Military Crosses:
Capt. A. P. Scott. Capt. L. R. Guthrie.

June *Mentioned in Despatches:*
Lt.-Col. R. S. Walker, D.S.O. Maj. H. Pollard Lowsley, C.I.E.
Capt. J. W. T. Palmer. Capt. A. H. Davenport.
C.M.G.: Lt.-Col. J. M. Arthur, D.S.O.
Military Cross: Capt. P. J. Mackesey.

73RD FIELD COMPANY, R.E.

OFFICERS.

1915. *V.C.:* Capt. F. H. Johnson.
1918. *D.S.O.:* Major S. Mildred.
1918. *Croix de Guerre:* Major E. W. Nesham.
1919. *Military Cross:* Capt. R. Swire.

74TH FIELD COMPANY, R.E.

OFFICERS.

1917.

Sept. 9. *D.S.O.:* Major J. A. Graeme.
Military Crosses:
Lieut. D. L. Middlemass. Lieut. D. B. Brow.
Lieut. J. Scott. Lieut. W. R. Frecheville.
Lieut. V. F. Craig.

91ST FIELD COMPANY, R.E.

OFFICERS.

D.S.O.: Capt. A. P. Sayer.
Military Crosses:
Lieut. H. W. Coales. Lieut. R. L. Withington.
Lieut. G. R. Pim.

1918. *Military Cross:* Major A. H. Davenport.
Croix de Guerre: Lieut. R. G. Lamb.

Fifteenth Divisional Royal Engineers.

1916. Other Ranks.

June 3. *D.C.M.:*

42656 Sergt. W. Hephen. 52891 Sergt. T. Oates.

June *Mentioned in Despatches:*

42580 Cpl. F. T. Gibson. 52275 C.S.M. F. Fell.
57052 R.S.M. J. Paley.

73rd Field Company, R.E.

1916. Other Ranks.

Military Medals:

42315 Cpl. H. W. Cunningham. 90190 Dvr. H. Semmens.
60414 L/C. A. Beesley. 61163 Dvr. D. N. Owens.
154086 Spr. A G. Milton.

74th Field Company, R.E.

1918. Other Ranks.

Sept. 17. *Military Medals:*

42758 Cpl. M. H. Cassin. 44216 Cpl. F. Lamb.
Sept. 25. 42654 Sergt. W. Duffin.
Oct. 5. 51009 Sergt. J. Petty.
Oct. 18. 44237 Cpl. J. H. Hammond. 44208 Sergt. W. T. S. Woodger.

91st Field Company, R.E.

1917. Other Ranks.

July 25. *Military Medal:*

92330 Dvr. J. Sked. Cpl. Dodd.

1918.

Sept. 8. *D.C.M.:*

Sergt. Coleman, M.M. Cpl. Brazier.
Sergt. Crichton. Cpl. Young.

Divisional Signal Company.

1916.

Sept. 8. *Military Medal :* Spr. W. L. Wallace.

Sept. 18. *Military Medals :*

44466 Sergt. A. B. Rorke.
42788 Sergt. J. R. Clarke.
42666 Cpl. N. Bottwood.
43357 Spr. J. R. Rowland.
42632 Spr. S. G. Barnes.
62255 Spr. W. King.
43518 Sergt. F. J. Lewis.
56208 Sergt. H. J. Hoare.
63432 L/C. R. Hume.
42855 Cpl. C. Ketley.
44384 Spr. H. Jackson.
63690 Spr. T. J. Mays.

Sept. 19. 62254 Spr. W. Bunce. 63494 Spr. C. Prosser.

Sept. 20. *Bar to Military Medal :* 44466 Sergt. A. B. Rorke, M.M.

Sept. 26. *Military Medal :* 49128 L/C. R. Iley.
Bar to M.M. : 42788 Sergt. J. R. Clarke.

Sept. 30. *Military Medal :*

49773 Cpl. F. Barrett.
43219 Spr. T. Davies.

1917.

May 1.

43407 Cpl. Andrews.
42421 Cpl. Cleverly.
63537 Cpl. J. Davis.
42798 Spr. H. L. Bazley.
56133 Spr. H. Smither.
42558 Spr. G. Cousins.
45047 Spr. J. Jacobs.
53077 Sergt. J. Ellis.
46082 Cpl. R. G. Coates.
71184 Spr. J. T. Brough.
42589 Spr. D. J. Maclean.

Second Bar to M.M. : 42902 Sergt. J. M'Creath.
Bar to M.M. : 44384 Spr. H. J. Jackson.

June 1. *Mentioned in Despatches* (' London Gazette,' May 18, 1917) :

56679 Sergt. C. R. Callaway.
56132 Spr. R. R. Butler.
44135 Sergt. L. Smith.

June 12. *Military Cross :* Capt. J. F. Chadwick.

Oct. 7. *Bar to Military Medal :* 63537 Sergt. J. Davis.

Nov. 26. *Bar to Military Medal :* 18255 Spr. F. C. Flight.
Military Medal : 424140 Pioneer R. Lorraine.

1918.

Jan. 1. *D.S.O. :* Major A. R. Marshall, M.C.
Military Cross : Lieut. N. C. D. Brownjohn.
M.S.M. : 43061 Sergt. F. Hills.
Mentioned in Despatches :

Lieut. J. G. Heslop.
43516 Spr. A. R. Tylor.
62345 L/C. D. W. Barth.

1918.

Aug. 9. *Croix de Guerre (Palmes) :*

Major J. F. Ormsby. Lieut. J. B. le Gros.
74994 Cpl. H. A. Lewis.

Médaille Militaire :

53077 Sergt. J. T. Ellis. 182255 Spr. F. C. Flight.

Croix de Guerre (Étoile) :

54287 Cpl. F. Hobson. 126834 L/C. P. C. Begent.
53651 L/C. E. H. Daborn. 63529 Spr. W. R. Thompson.
62974 Dvr. T. Maddy.

Sept. 9. *Military Medal :*

254940 Cpl. J. Quinn. 42539 Spr. H. Robinson.
246482 Spr. J. Rae.

Fifteenth Divisional Train.

141st Company, A.S.C.

1916.

Aug. 29. *Military Medals :*

T/17102 Sergt. A. Coulson. T/086949 Dvr. A. Stott.

139th Company, A.S.C.

Nov. 6. *M.S.M. :* Shoeing-Smith Epsom.

141st Company, A.S.C.

Nov. 10. *Military Medal :* T/016215 Cpl. W. H. Jones.

15th Battalion Machine-Gun Corps.

1918.

Aug. 9. "The Divisional General presented French honours gained during recent operations. In all 11 Croix de Guerre were presented. Among the recipients were :—

Lt.-Col. Nasmith, M.C.
2/Lieuts. Harbottle, Wallington, Ward.
Pte. D. Roper, Sergts. D. Budge, Smith, Tucker, and Key."

INDEX.

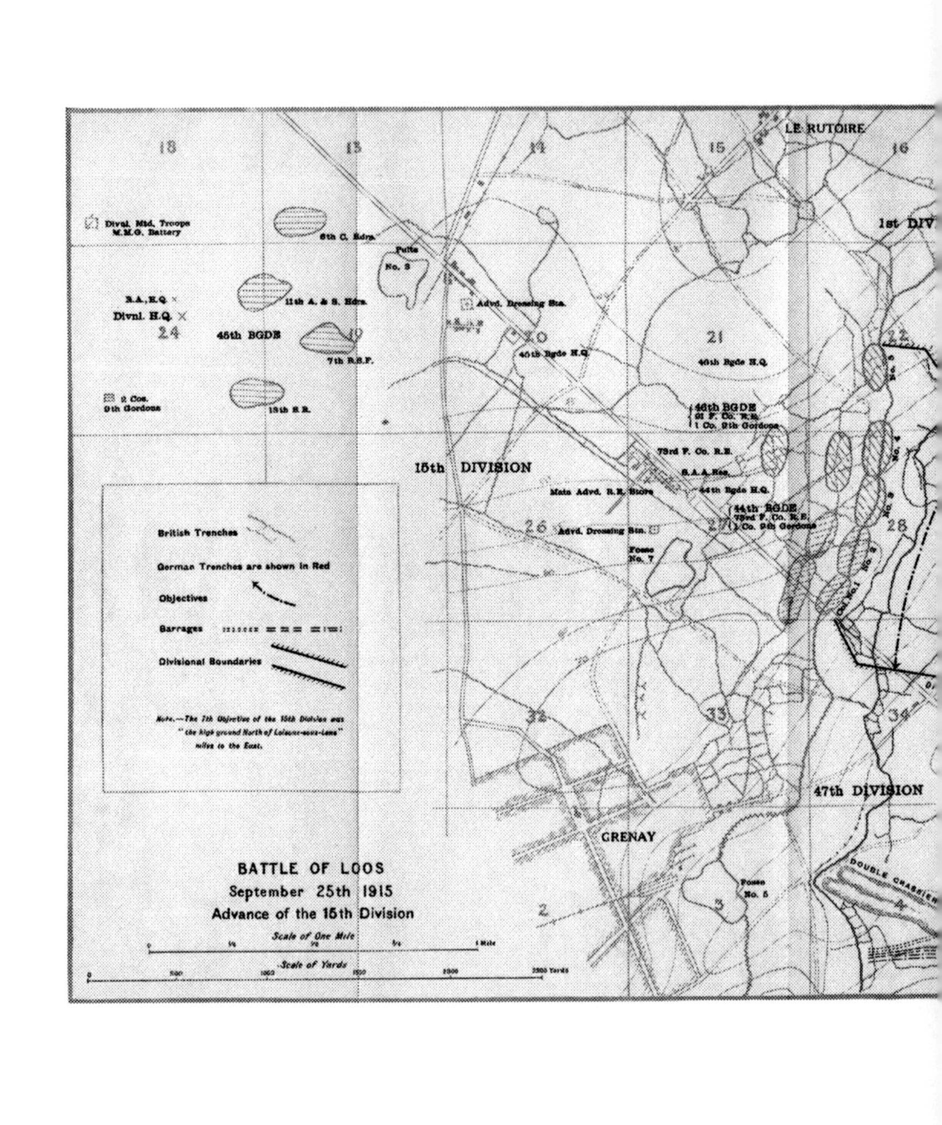

LE RUTOIRE
1st DIV
Divnl. Mtd. Troops
M.M.G. Battery
6th C. Hdrs.
Puits
No. 3
11th A. & S. Hdrs.
Advd. Dressing Sta.
Divnl. H.Q.
45th BGDE
7th R.S.F.
46th Bgde H.Q.
2 Cos.
9th Gordons
13th R.S.
46th BGDE
1 Co. 9th Gordons
73rd F. Co. R.E.
S.A.A. Res.
15th DIVISION
Main Advd. R.E. Store
44th Bgde H.Q.
44th BGDE
73rd F. Co. R.E.
1 Co. 9th Gordons
Advd. Dressing Stn.
Fosse
No. 7
British Trenches
German Trenches are shown in Red
Objectives
Barrages
Divisional Boundaries
47th DIVISION
GRENAY
Fosse
No. 5
DOUBLE CRASSIER
BATTLE OF LOOS
September 25th 1915
Advance of the 15th Division
Scale of One Mile
Scale of Yards

MAP 1

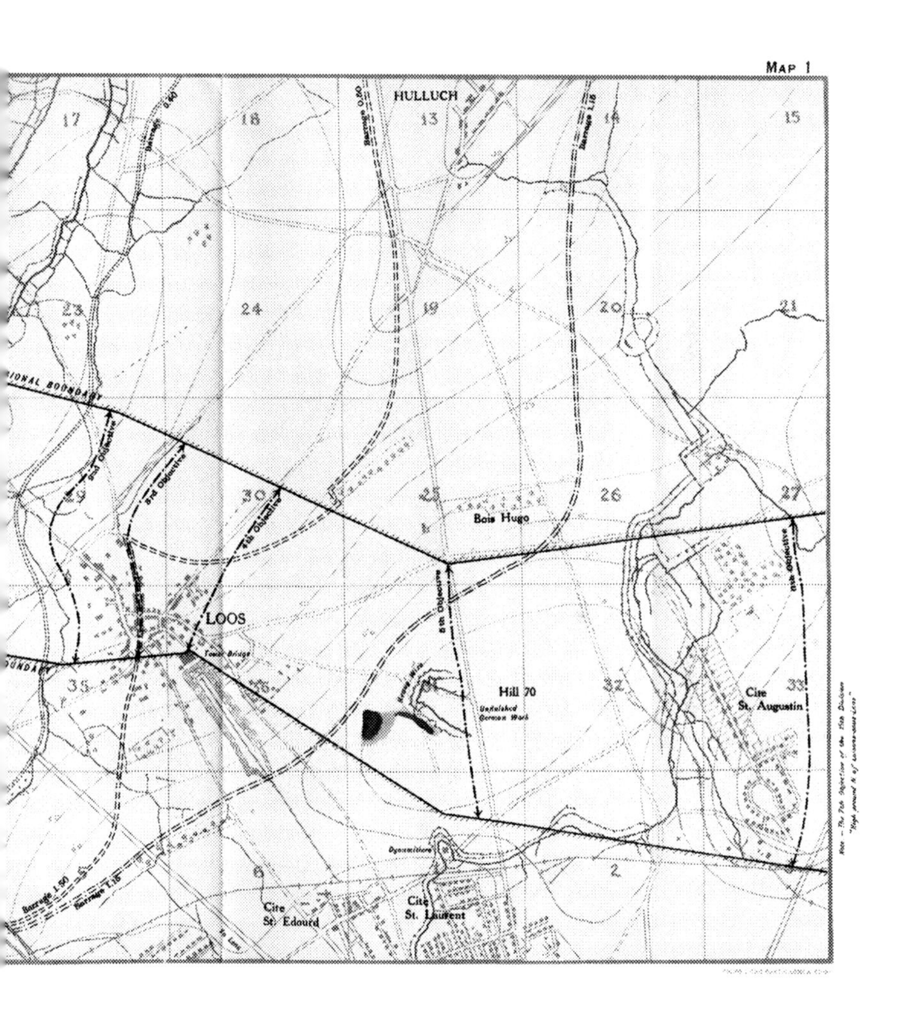

HULLUCH
Barrage 0.40
Barrage 0.50
Barrage 1.15
17
18
13
14
15
23
24
19
20
21
DIVISIONAL BOUNDARY
2nd Objective
3rd Objective
4th Objective
29
30
25
26
27
Bois Hugo
5th Objective
6th Objective
LOOS
Tower Bridge
35
36
Hill 70
Unfinished German Work
32
33
Cite
St. Augustin
Dynamitière
Barrage 1.50
Barrage 1.15
6
2
Cite
St. Edourd
Cite
St. Laurent

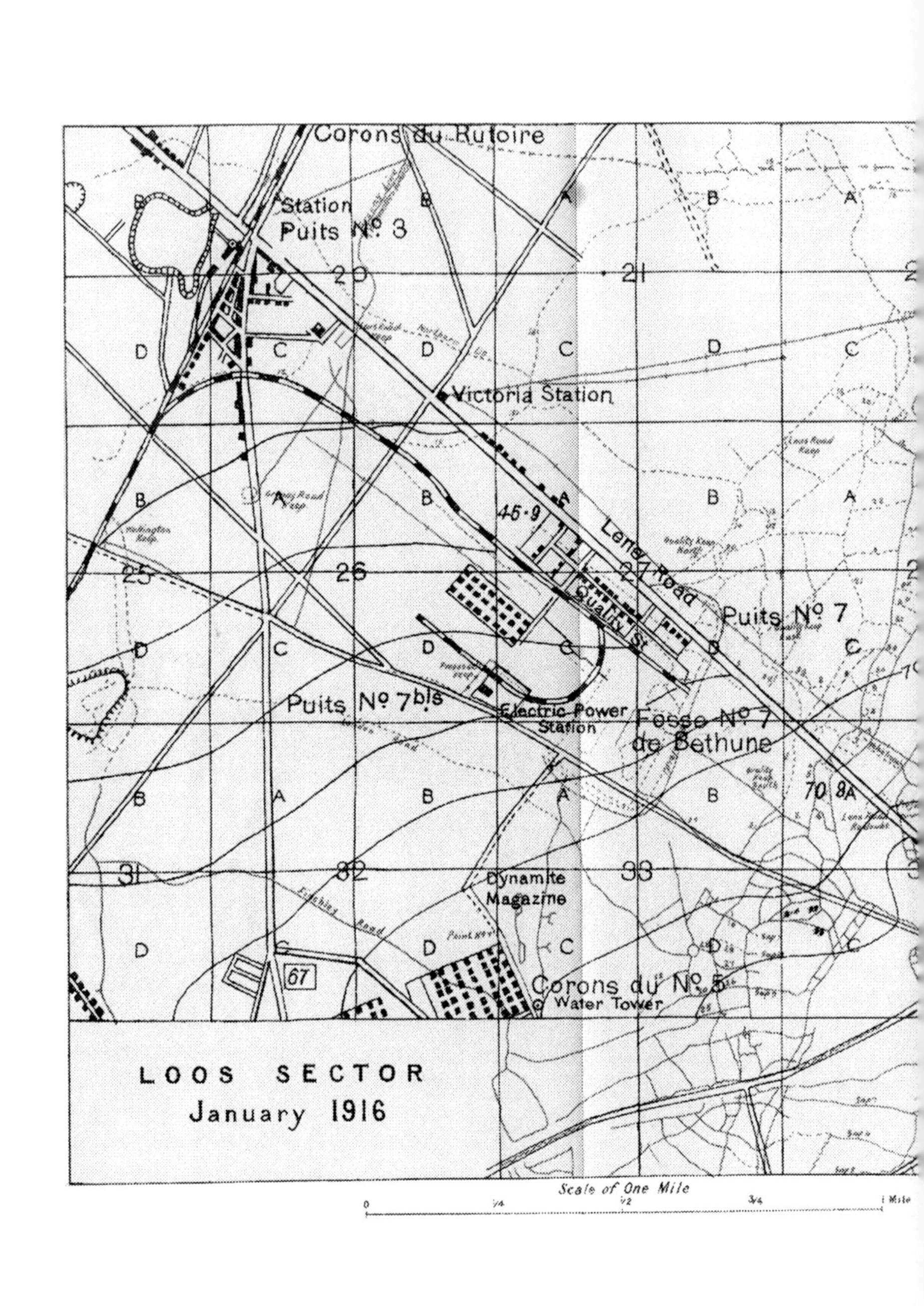

Corons du Rutoire
Station
Puits Nº 3
Victoria Station
Lens Road
Quality St
Puits Nº 7
Puits Nº 7bis
Electric Power Station
Fosse Nº 7 de Bethune
Dynamite Magazine
Corons du Nº 5
Water Tower
LOOS SECTOR
January 1916
Scale of One Mile

MAP 2

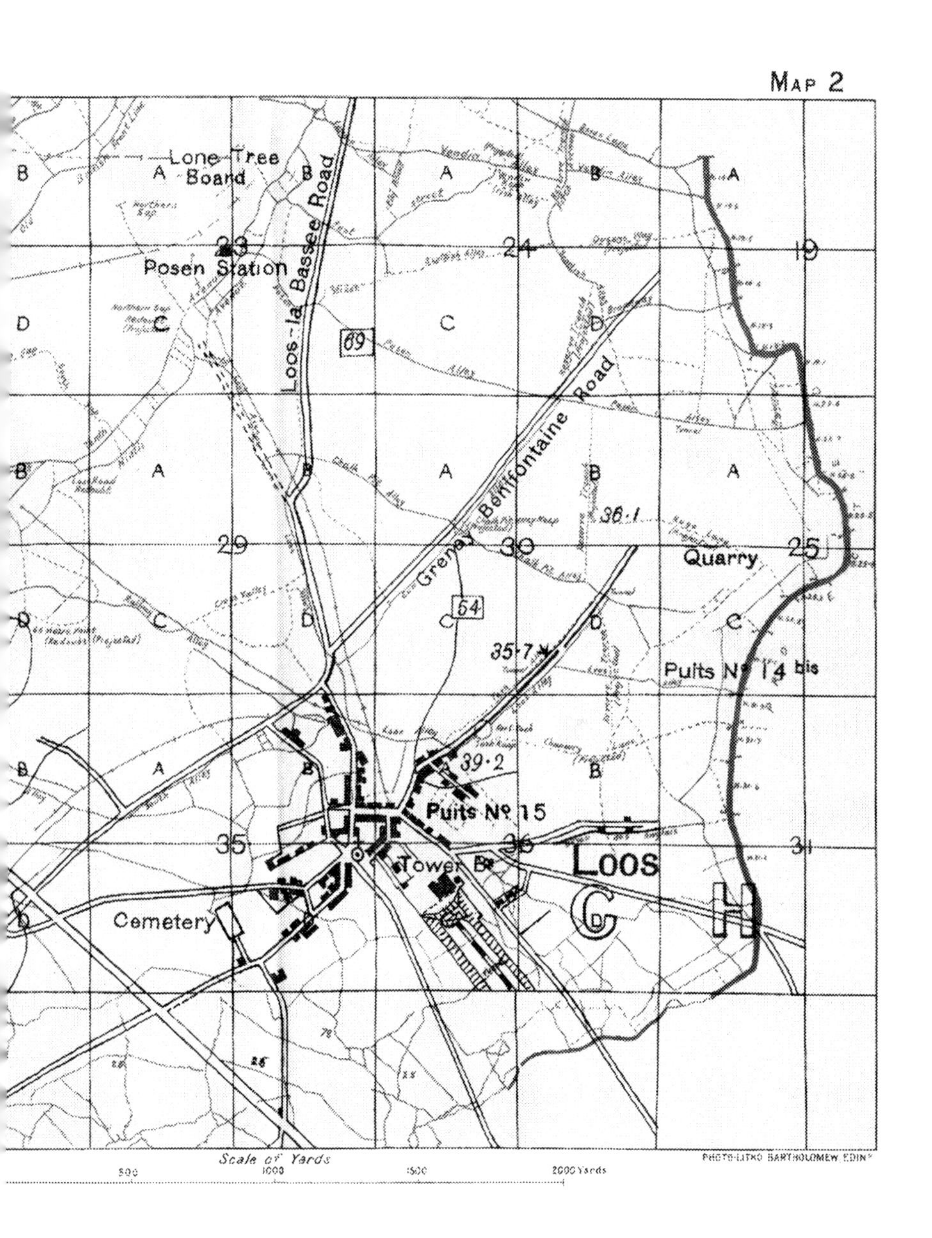
Lone Tree
Board
Posen Station
Loos-la Bassée Road
Grenay Benifontaine Road
Quarry
Pults Nº 14 bis
Puits Nº 15
Tower Br.
Loos
Cemetery
36·1
35·7
39·2
Scale of Yards
500
1000
1500
2000 Yards
PHOTO-LITHO BARTHOLOMEW EDINR

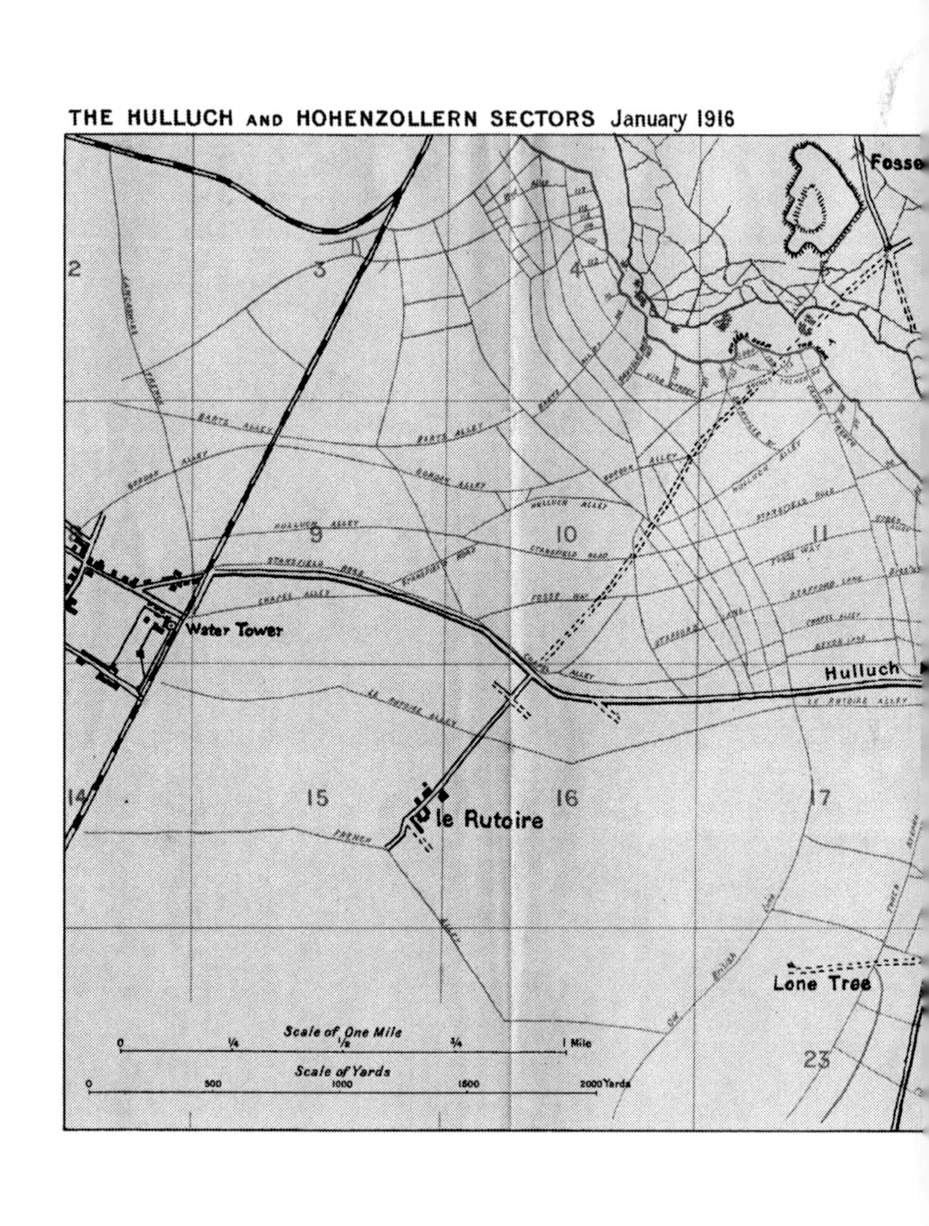

THE HULLUCH AND HOHENZOLLERN SECTORS January 1916

MAP 3

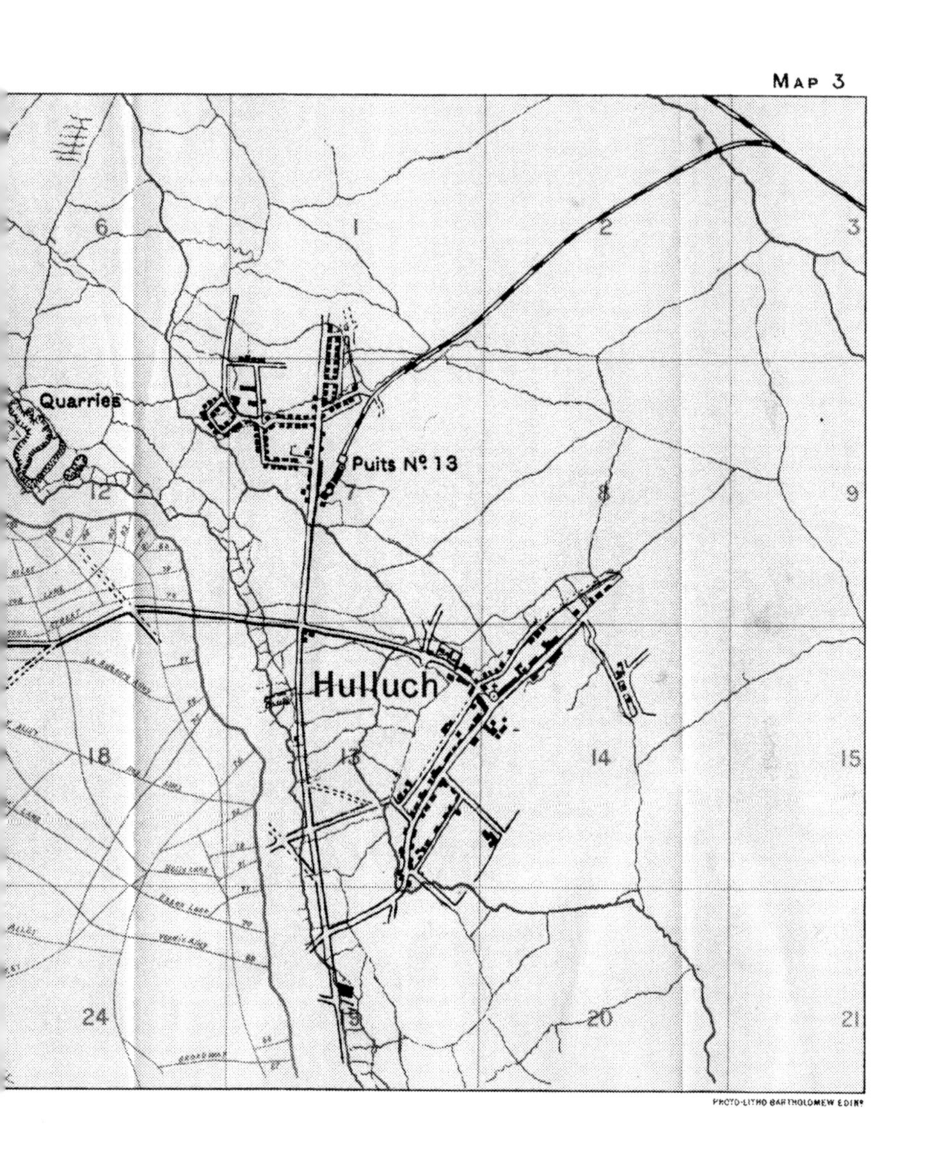

PHOTO-LITHO BARTHOLOMEW EDINR

THE SOMME BATTLE (Bazentin Area) August-September 1916

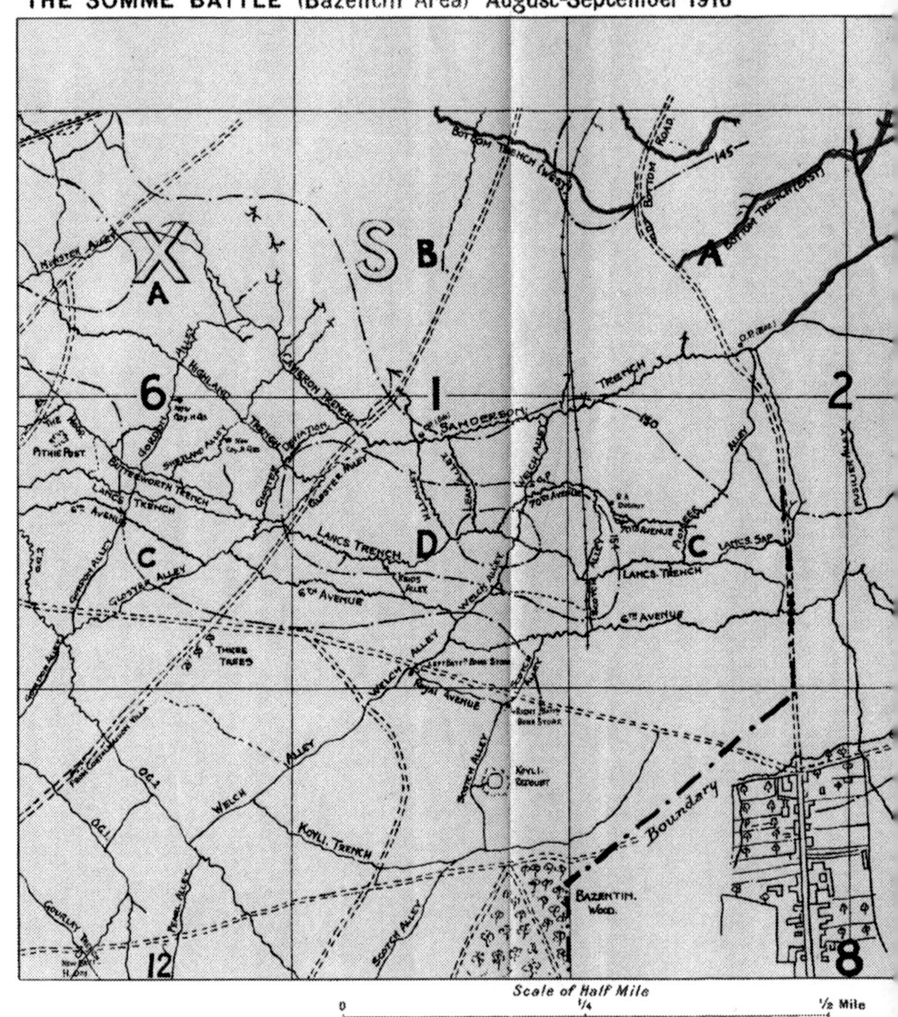

MAP 4

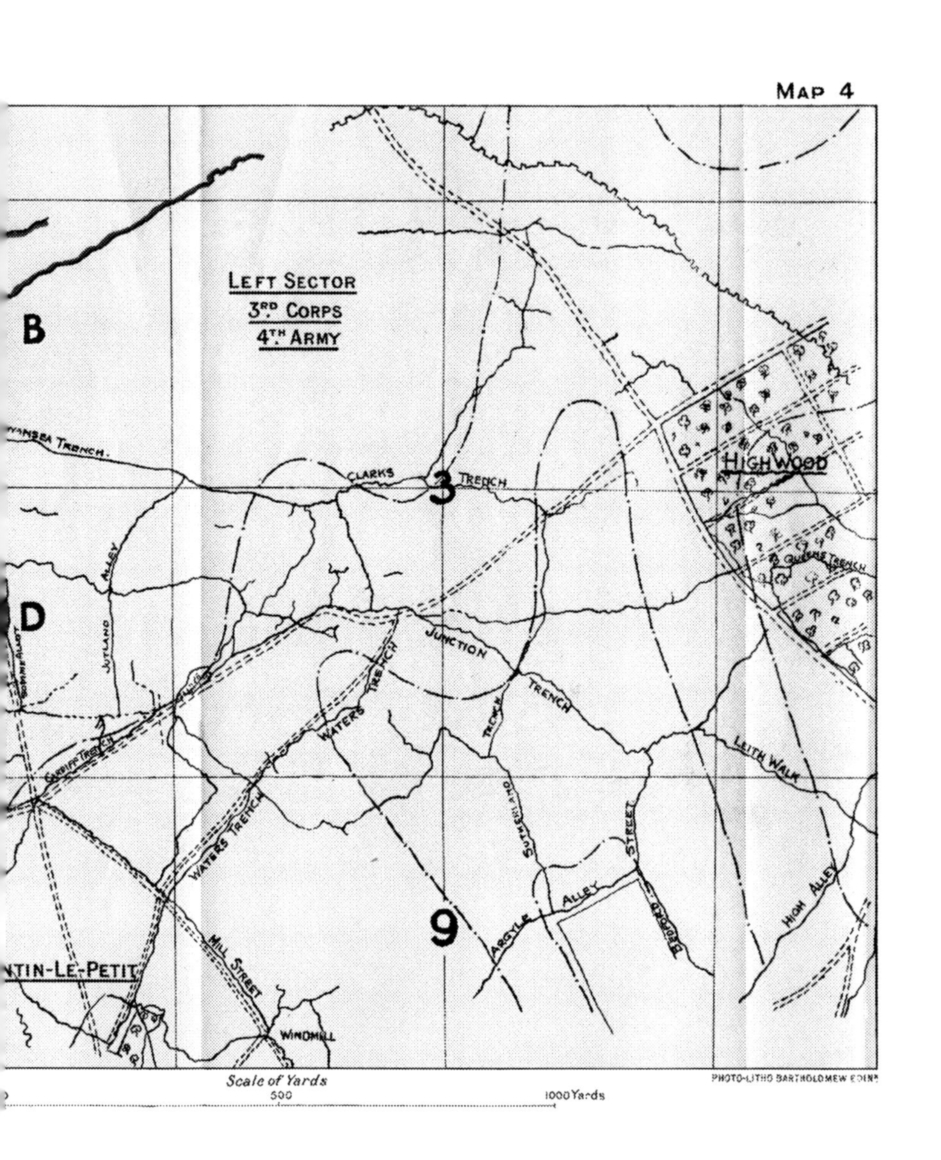
LEFT SECTOR
3RD CORPS
4TH ARMY
B
D
3
9
CLARKS
TRENCH
HIGHWOOD
JUNCTION
TRENCH
WATERS TRENCH
WATERS TRENCH
CARDIFF TRENCH
JUTLAND
ALLEY
LEITH WALK
SUTHERLAND
STREET
ARGYLE
ALLEY
HIGH ALLEY
MILL STREET
WINDMILL
NTIN-LE-PETIT
Scale of Yards
500
1000 Yards
PHOTO-LITHO BARTHOLOMEW EDINR

PANORAMA FROM JUNCTION OF WELCH ALLEY & LANCS TRENCH (S.I.D.6

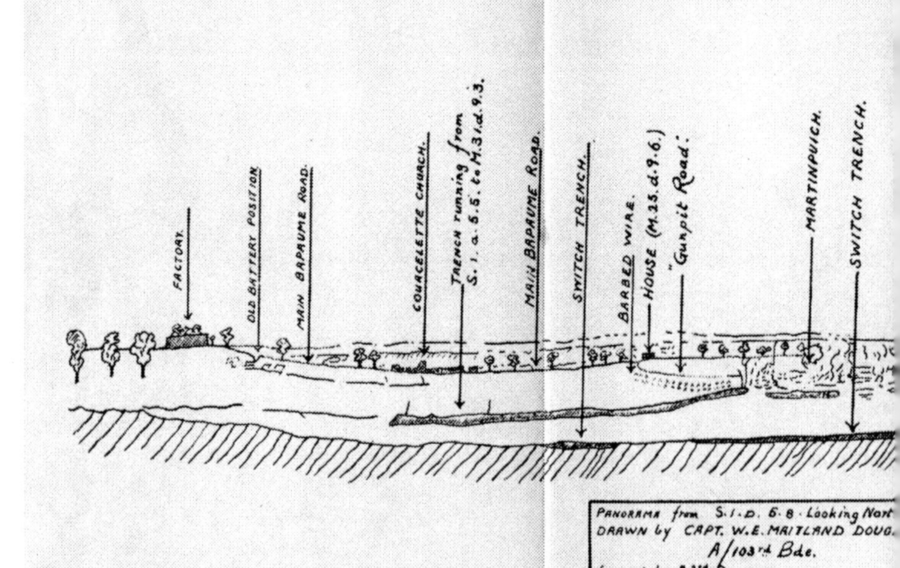

See Map 4

MAP 4A

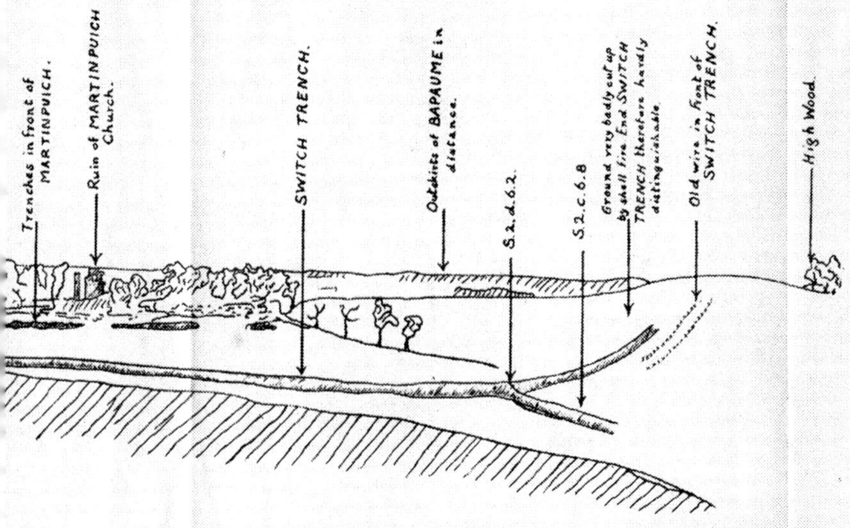

Trenches in front of MARTINPUICH.
Ruin of MARTINPUICH Church.
SWITCH TRENCH.
Outskirts of BAPAUME in distance.
S.2.d.6.2.
S.2.c.6.8
Ground very badly cut up by shell fire. End SWITCH TRENCH therefore hardly distinguishable.
Old wire in front of SWITCH TRENCH.
High Wood.

PHOTO-LITHO BARTHOLOMEW EDINR

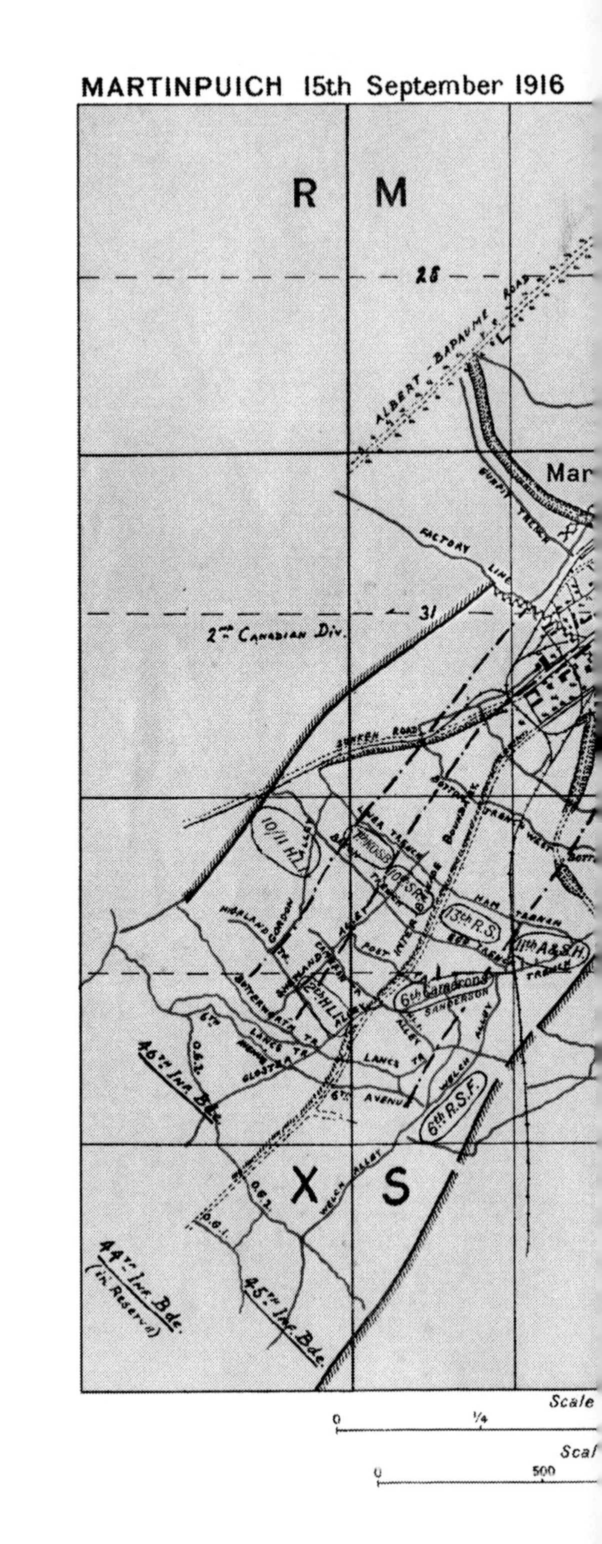

MARTINPUICH 15th September 1916

MAP 5

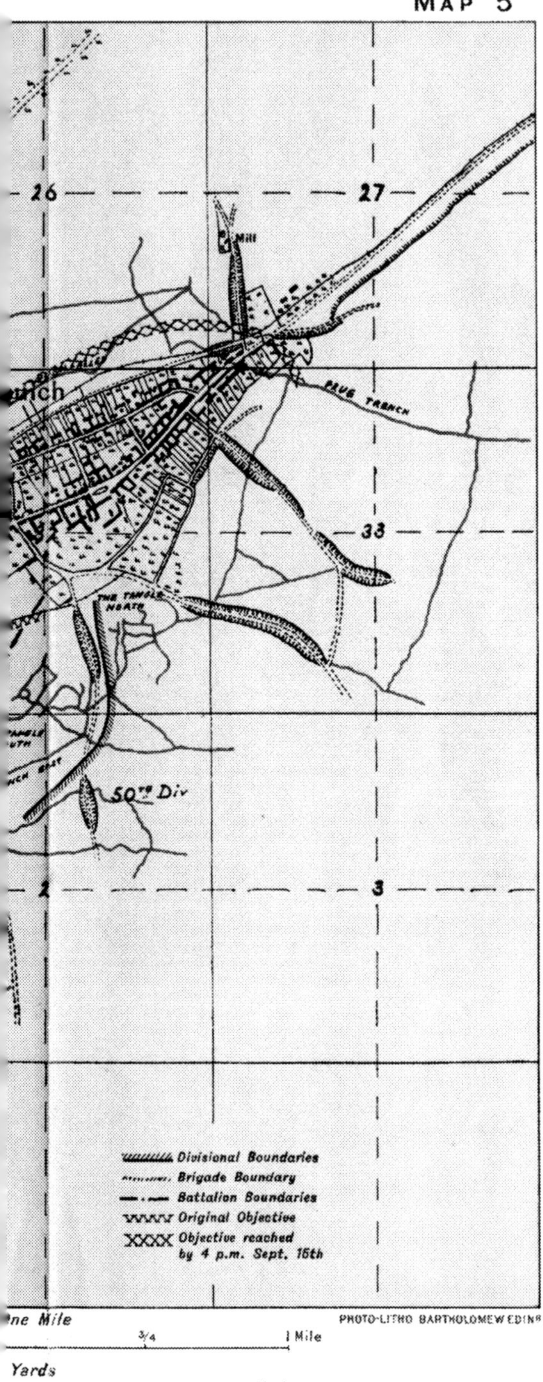
26
27
33
2
3
Mill
FLUG TRENCH
50TH Div
Divisional Boundaries
Brigade Boundary
Battalion Boundaries
Original Objective
Objective reached
by 4 p.m. Sept. 15th
One Mile
3/4
1 Mile
Yards
1000
1500 Yards
PHOTO-LITHO BARTHOLOMEW EDINR

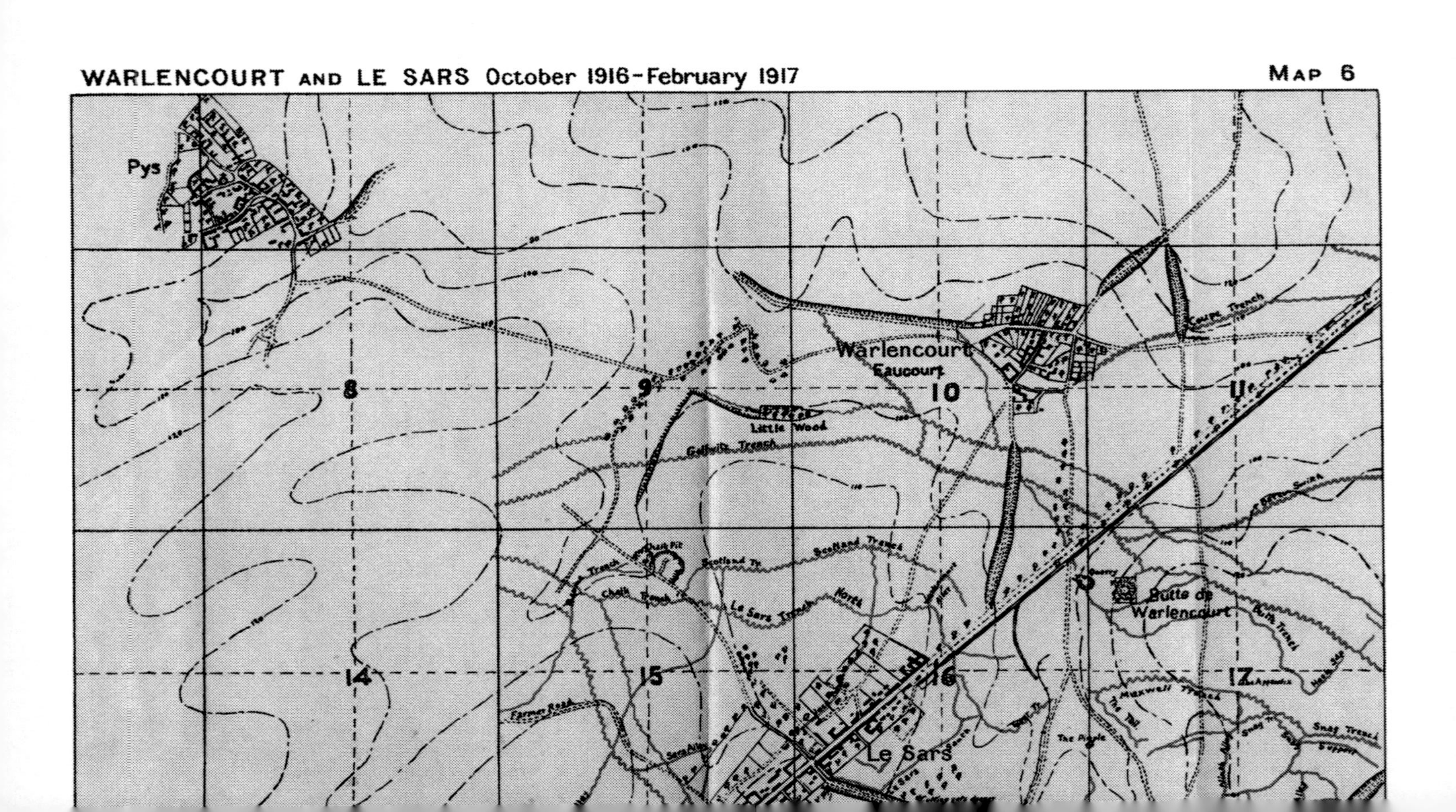
WARLENCOURT AND LE SARS October 1916–February 1917
MAP 6
Pys
Warlencourt
Eaucourt
Little Wood
Gallwitz Trench
Scotland Trench
Scotland Tr.
Chalk Pit
Chalk Trench
Le Sars Trench
Butte de Warlencourt
Quarry
Le Sars
Maxwell Trench
The Tail
The Apple
Snag Trench
Farmer Road
8
9
10
11
14
15
16
17

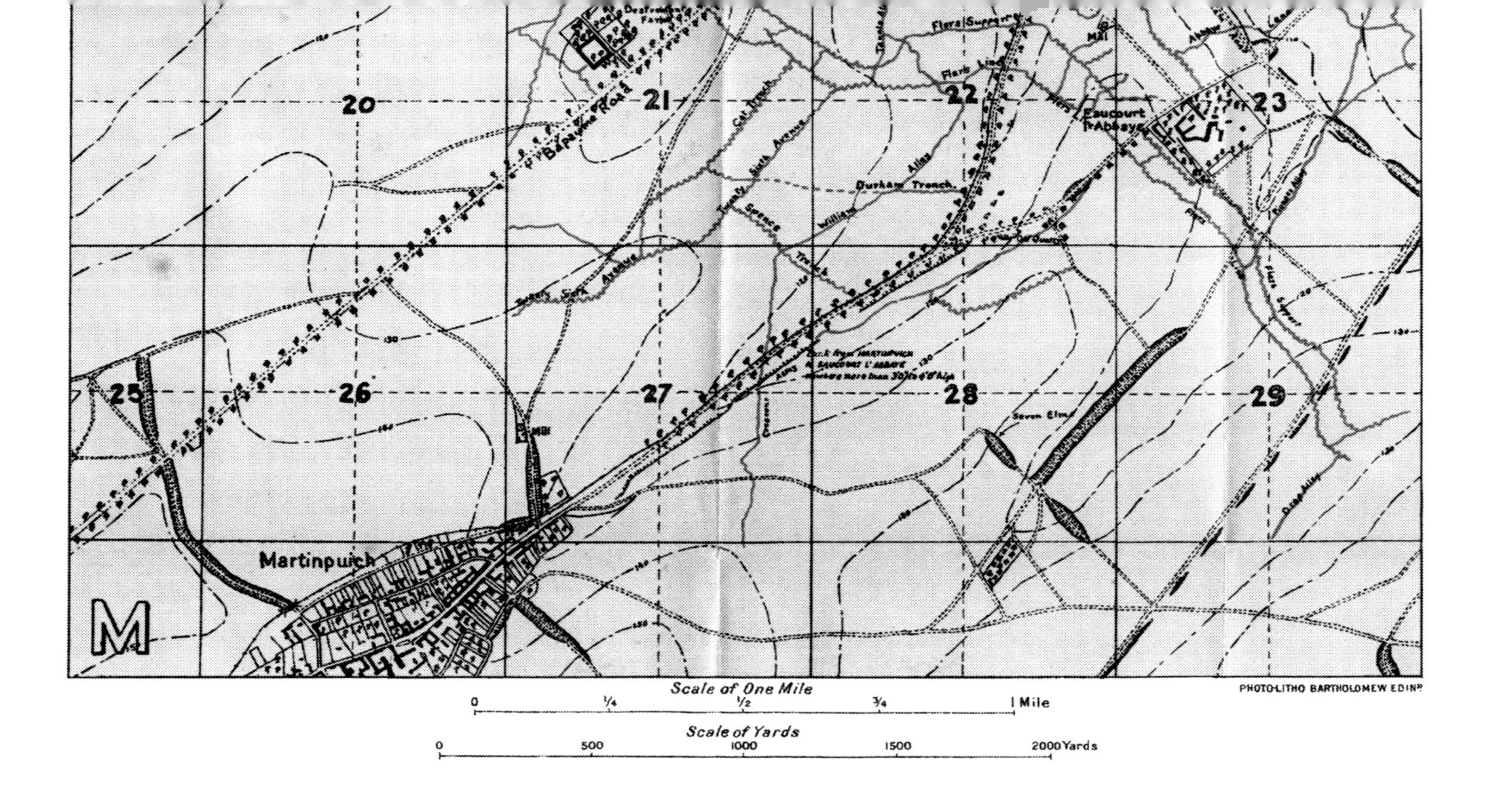
20
21
22
23
25
26
27
28
29
M
Martinpuich
Bapaume Road
Durham Trench
Cut Trench
Flers Support
Flers Line
Eaucourt l'Abbaye
Mill
Seven Elms
Twenty Sixth Avenue
Spence
William
Alley
Scale of One Mile
0
1/4
1/2
3/4
1 Mile
Scale of Yards
0
500
1000
1500
2000 Yards
PHOTO-LITHO BARTHOLOMEW EDIN^R

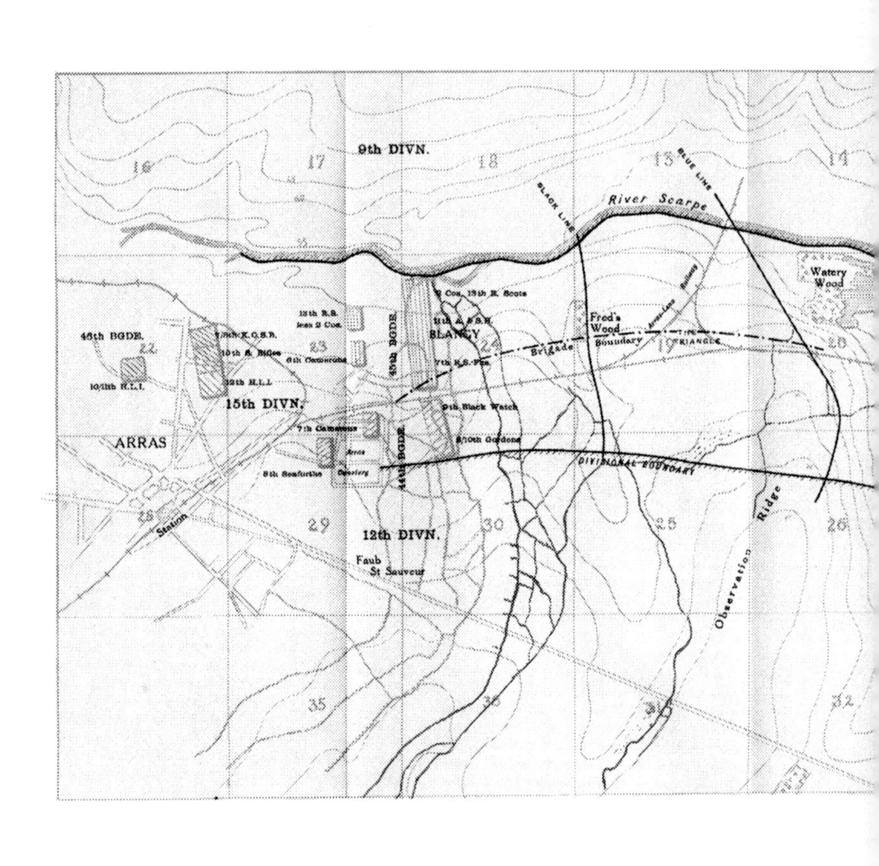
9th DIVN.
River Scarpe
BLACK LINE
BLUE LINE
Watery Wood
Fred's Wood
Brigade Boundary
DIVISIONAL BOUNDARY
46th BGDE.
10/11th H.L.I.
12th H.L.I.
15th DIVN.
ARRAS
Station
2 Cos. 13th R. Scots
13th R.S. less 2 Cos.
11th A. & S.H.
BLANGY
45th BGDE.
7th R.S. Fus.
9th Black Watch
8/10th Gordons
44th BGDE.
12th DIVN.
Faub St Sauveur
Observation Ridge

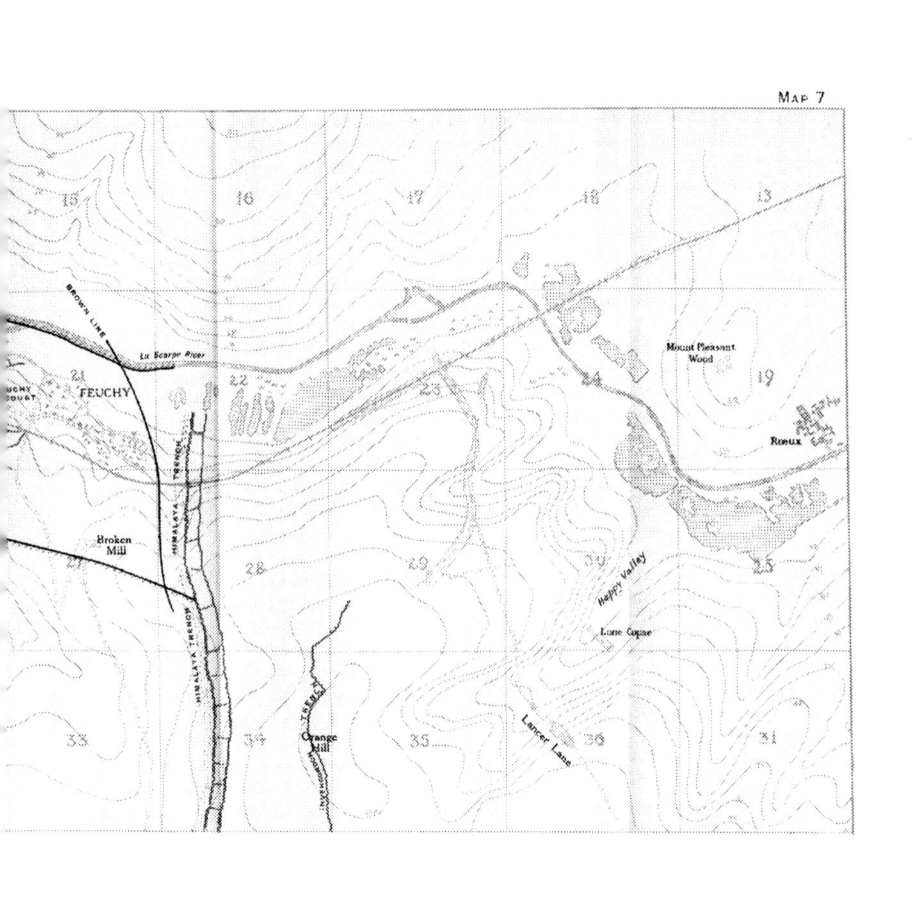
BROWN LINE
La Scarpe River
FEUCHY
Broken Mill
HIMALAYA TRENCH
Orange Hill
Mount Pleasant Wood
Roeux
Happy Valley
Lone Copse
Lancer Lane

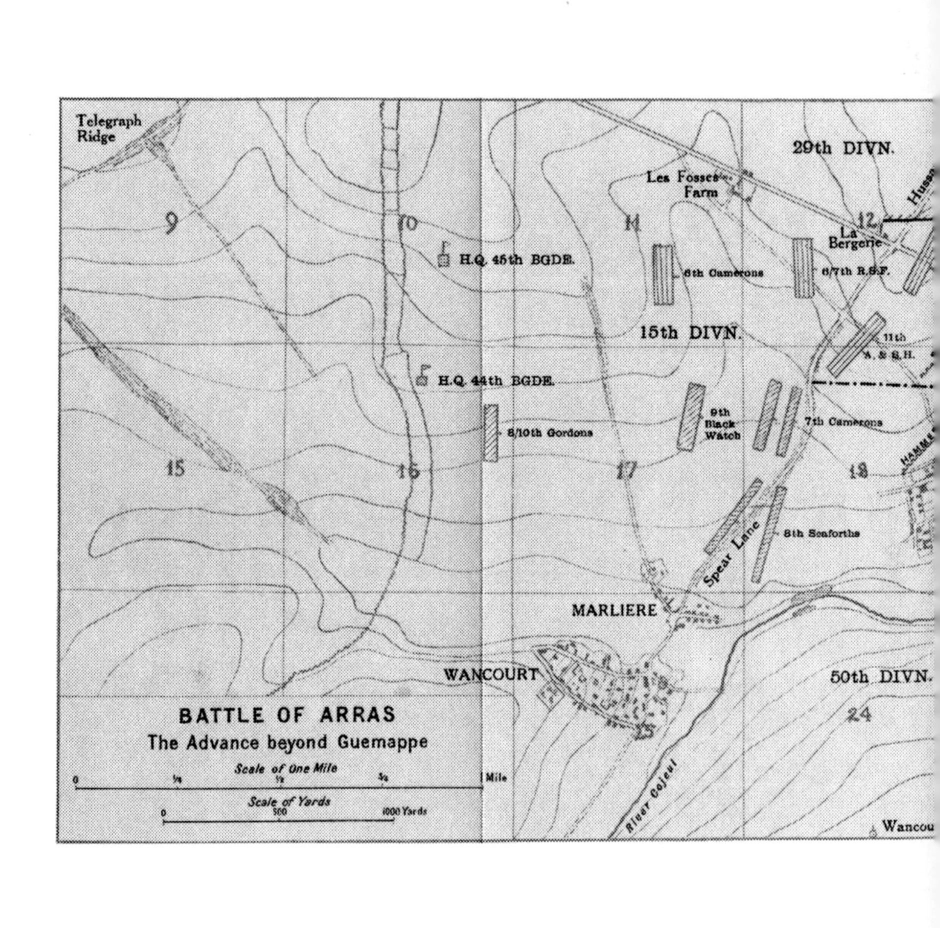

Telegraph Ridge
29th DIVN.
Les Fosses Farm
La Bergerie
H.Q. 45th BGDE.
6th Camerons
6/7th R.S.F.
15th DIVN.
11th A. & S.H.
H.Q. 44th BGDE.
8/10th Gordons
9th Black Watch
7th Camerons
8th Seaforths
Spear Lane
MARLIERE
WANCOURT
50th DIVN.
River Cojeul
BATTLE OF ARRAS
The Advance beyond Guemappe
Scale of One Mile
Scale of Yards

Map 8

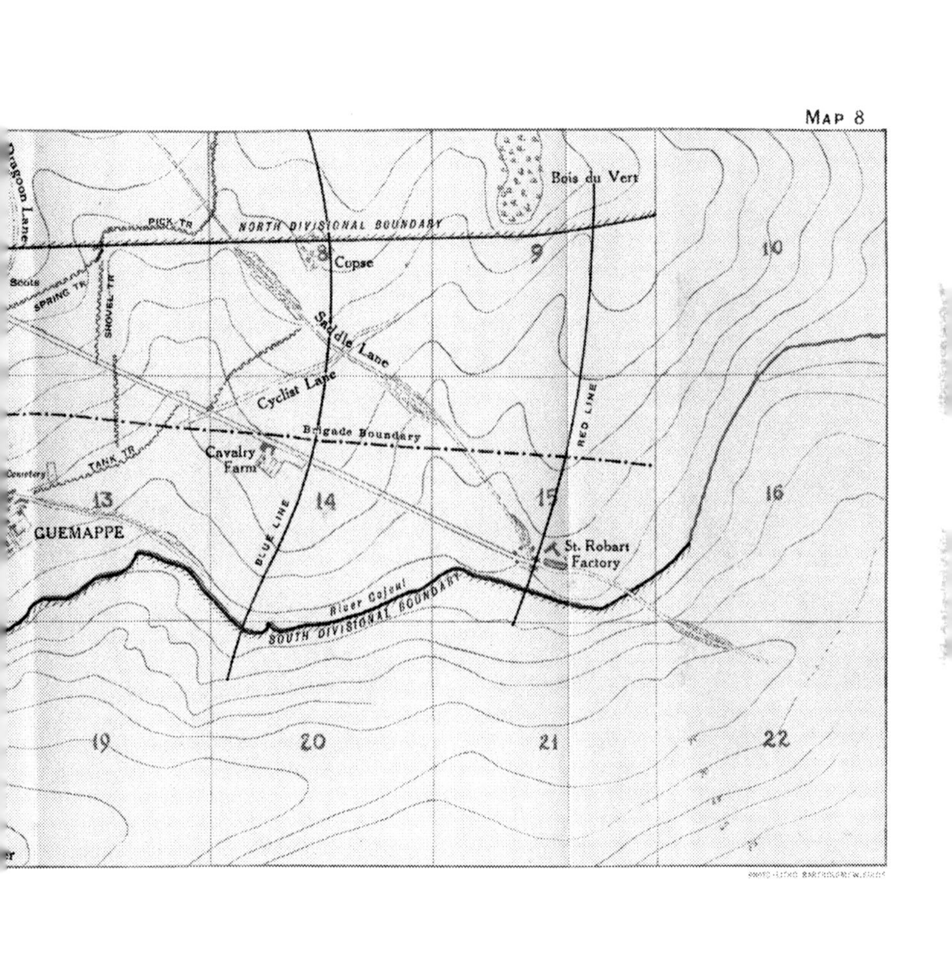

Dragoon Lane
Bois du Vert
PICK TR
NORTH DIVISIONAL BOUNDARY
8
Cupse
9
10
Scots
SPRING TR
SHOVEL TR
Saddle Lane
Cyclist Lane
RED LINE
Brigade Boundary
Cavalry Farm
TANK TR
Cemetery
13
14
15
16
GUEMAPPE
BLUE LINE
St. Robart Factory
River Cojeul
SOUTH DIVISIONAL BOUNDARY
19
20
21
22

THIRD BATTLE OF YPRES.– Operations of 31st July–August 4th, 1917

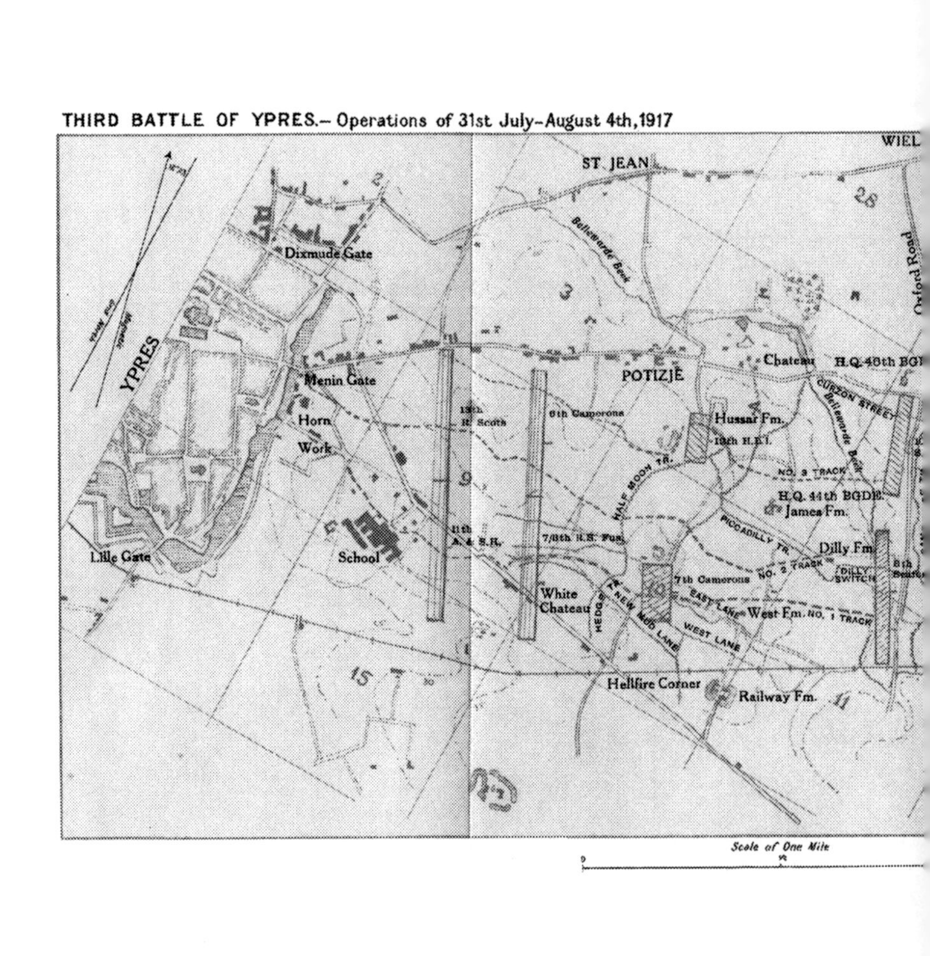

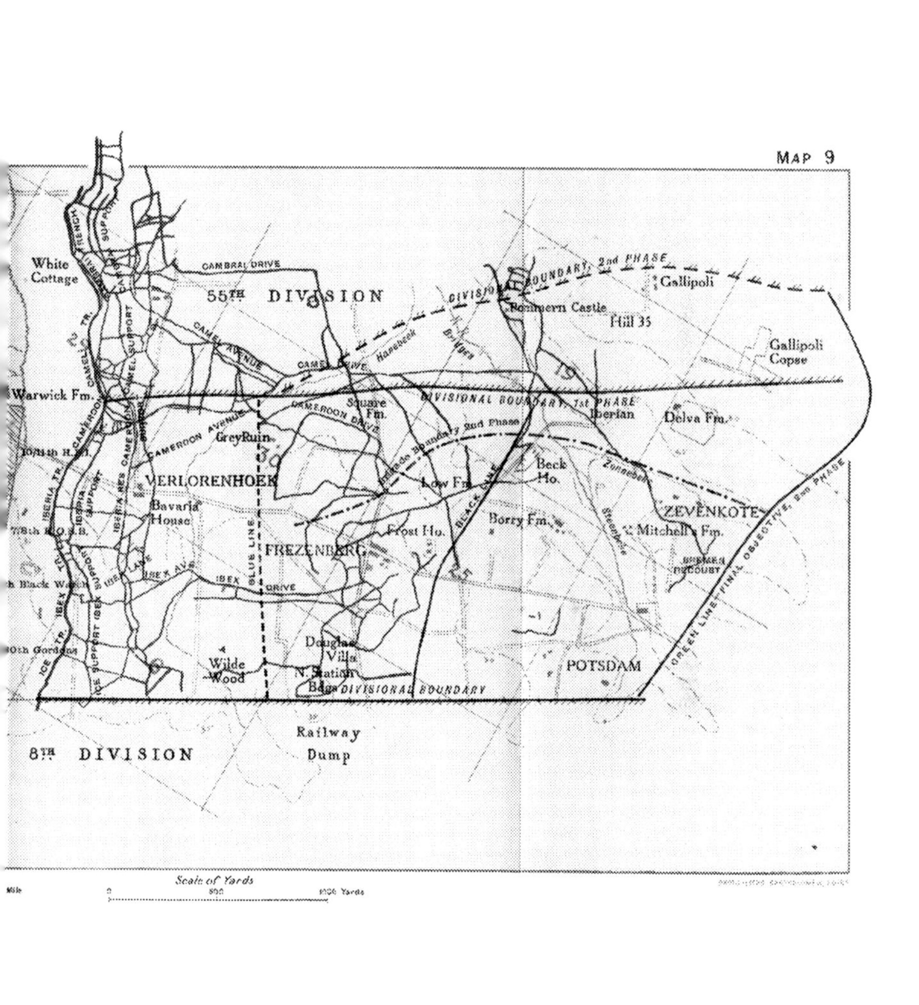
MAP 9
White Cottage
55TH DIVISION
CAMBRAI DRIVE
Gallipoli
Frezenberg Castle
Hill 35
Gallipoli Copse
Warwick Fm.
Square Fm.
DIVISIONAL BOUNDARY 1st PHASE
DIVISIONAL BOUNDARY 2nd PHASE
Iberian
Delva Fm.
Grey Ruin
CAMERON DRIVE
CAMERON AVENUE
VERLORENHOEK
Low Fm.
Beck Ho.
Bavaria House
ZEVENKOTE
Frost Ho.
Borry Fm.
Mitchell's Fm.
FREZENBERG
BLUE LINE
BLACK LINE
IBEX DRIVE
Douglas Villa
Wilde Wood
N. Station Bdgs
DIVISIONAL BOUNDARY
POTSDAM
GREEN LINE FINAL OBJECTIVE, 2nd PHASE
Railway Dump
8TH DIVISION
Scale of Yards
1000 Yards

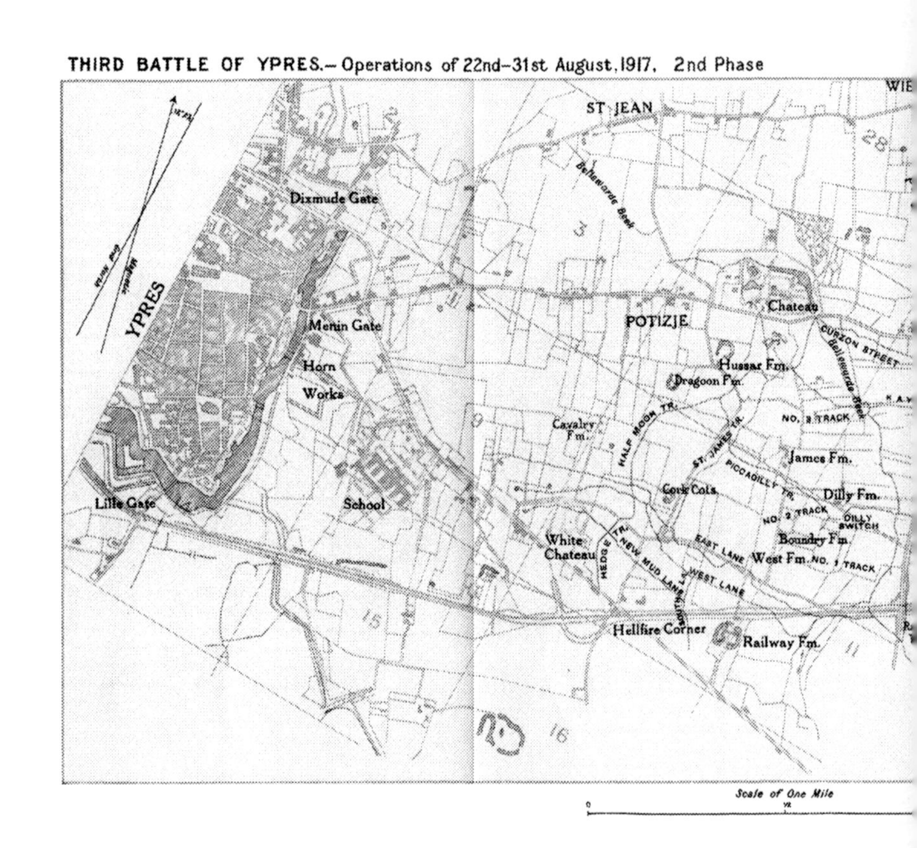

THIRD BATTLE OF YPRES.– Operations of 22nd–31st August, 1917. 2nd Phase

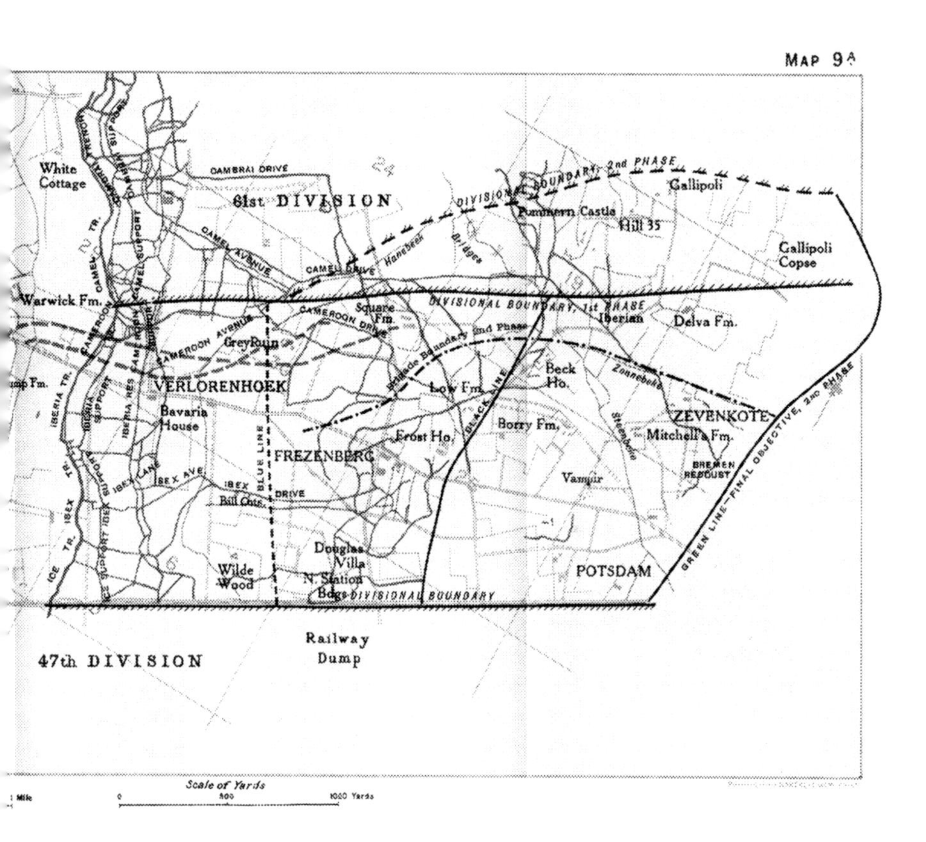
61st. DIVISION
47th DIVISION
White Cottage
Warwick Fm.
CAMBRAI DRIVE
CAMEL AVENUE
CAMEL DRIVE
Hanebeek
Bridges
DIVISIONAL BOUNDARY, 2nd PHASE
Pommern Castle
Hill 35
Gallipoli
Gallipoli Copse
DIVISIONAL BOUNDARY, 1st PHASE
Iberian
Delva Fm.
Square Fm.
CAMEROON DRIVE
CAMEROON AVENUE
Grey Ruin
Brigade Boundary 2nd Phase
VERLORENHOEK
Beck Ho.
Zonnebeke
Low Fm.
BLACK LINE
ZEVENKOTE
Bavaria House
Borry Fm.
Mitchell's Fm.
Frost Ho.
FREZENBERG
BLUE LINE
BREMEN REDOUBT
Vampir
GREEN LINE—FINAL OBJECTIVE, 2ND PHASE
IBEX DRIVE
Bill Cots.
Douglas Villa
N. Station Bdgs.
DIVISIONAL BOUNDARY
Wilde Wood
POTSDAM
Railway Dump
IBERIA TR.
IBERIA SUPPORT
IBEX TR.
ICE TR.
IBEX LANE
IBEX AVE
Scale of Yards
1 Mile
0
500
1000 Yards

OPERATIONS EAST OF ARRAS, March 1918.

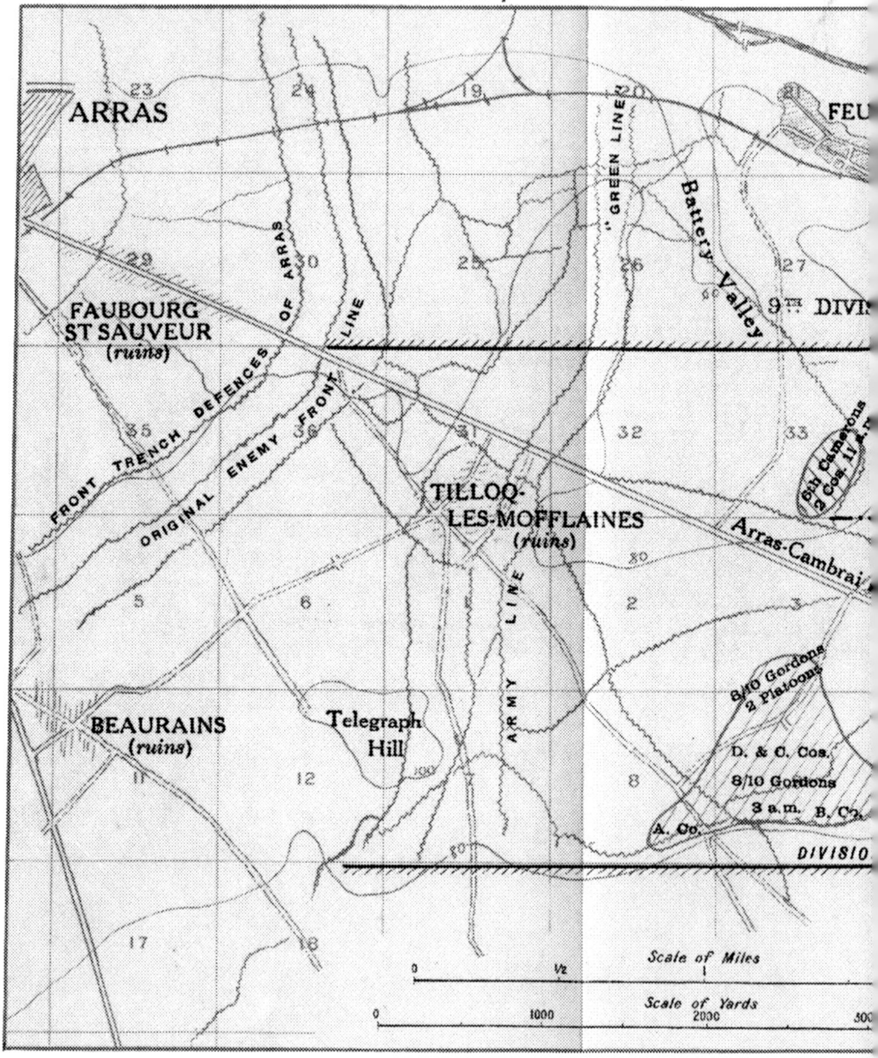

ARRAS
FEU
"GREEN LINE"
Battery Valley
9TH DIVI
FAUBOURG ST SAUVEUR (ruins)
FRONT TRENCH DEFENCES OF ARRAS
ORIGINAL ENEMY FRONT LINE
TILLOQ-LES-MOFFLAINES (ruins)
6th Camerons 2 Cos. II &
Arras-Cambrai
ARMY LINE
BEAURAINS (ruins)
Telegraph Hill
8/10 Gordons 2 Platoons
D. & C. Cos.
8/10 Gordons
3 a.m. B. Co.
A. Co.
DIVISIO
23 24 19 20 21
29 30 25 26 27
35 36 31 32 33
5 6 2 3
11 12 8
17 18
Scale of Miles
0 1/2 1
Scale of Yards
0 1000 2000 300

Map 10

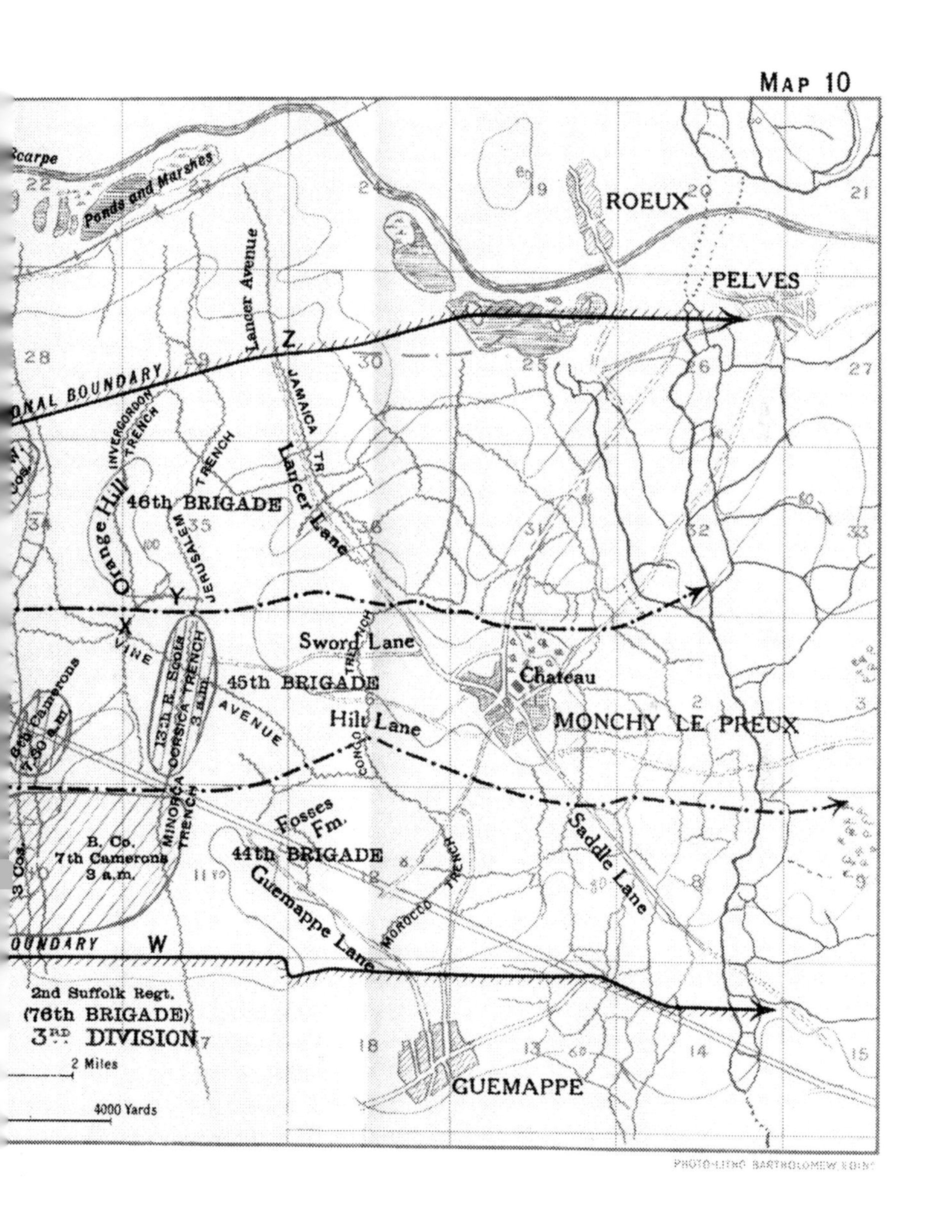

Scarpe
Ponds and Marshes
ROEUX
PELVES
Lancer Avenue
Z
ONAL BOUNDARY
JAMAICA TR
INVERGORDON TRENCH
TRENCH
Lancer Lane
Orange Hill
46th BRIGADE
JERUSALEM
Y
X
VINE
Sword Lane
TRENCH
13th R. Scots CORSICA TRENCH 3 a.m.
6th Camerons 7.30 a.m.
45th BRIGADE
AVENUE
Chateau
Hill Lane
MONCHY LE PREUX
CONGO
MINORCA TRENCH
Fosses Fm.
Saddle Lane
B. Co. 7th Camerons 3 a.m.
44th BRIGADE
Guemappe Lane
MOROCCO TRENCH
OUNDARY
W
2nd Suffolk Regt.
(76th BRIGADE)
3RD DIVISION
2 Miles
4000 Yards
GUEMAPPE
PHOTO-LITHO BARTHOLOMEW EDIN

OPERATIONS EAST OF ARRAS, March 1918.

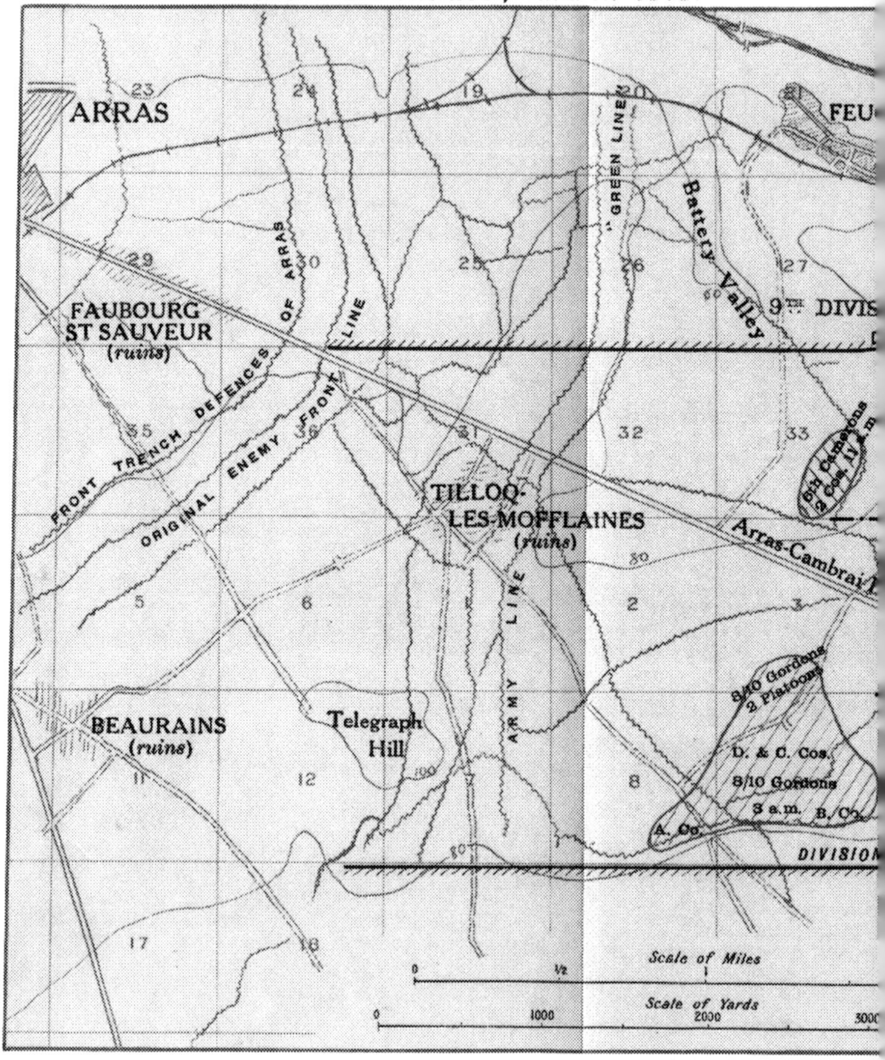

ARRAS

FAUBOURG ST SAUVEUR (ruins)

FRONT TRENCH DEFENCES OF ARRAS

ORIGINAL ENEMY FRONT LINE

GREEN LINE

Battery Valley

9TH DIVIS

TILLOQ-LES-MOFFLAINES (ruins)

Arras-Cambrai

ARMY LINE

BEAURAINS (ruins)

Telegraph Hill

8/10 Gordons 2 Platoons

D. & C. Cos.

8/10 Gordons 3 a.m. B. Co.

A. Co.

DIVISION

FEU

Scale of Miles

0 ½ 1

Scale of Yards

0 1000 2000 3000

MAP 10

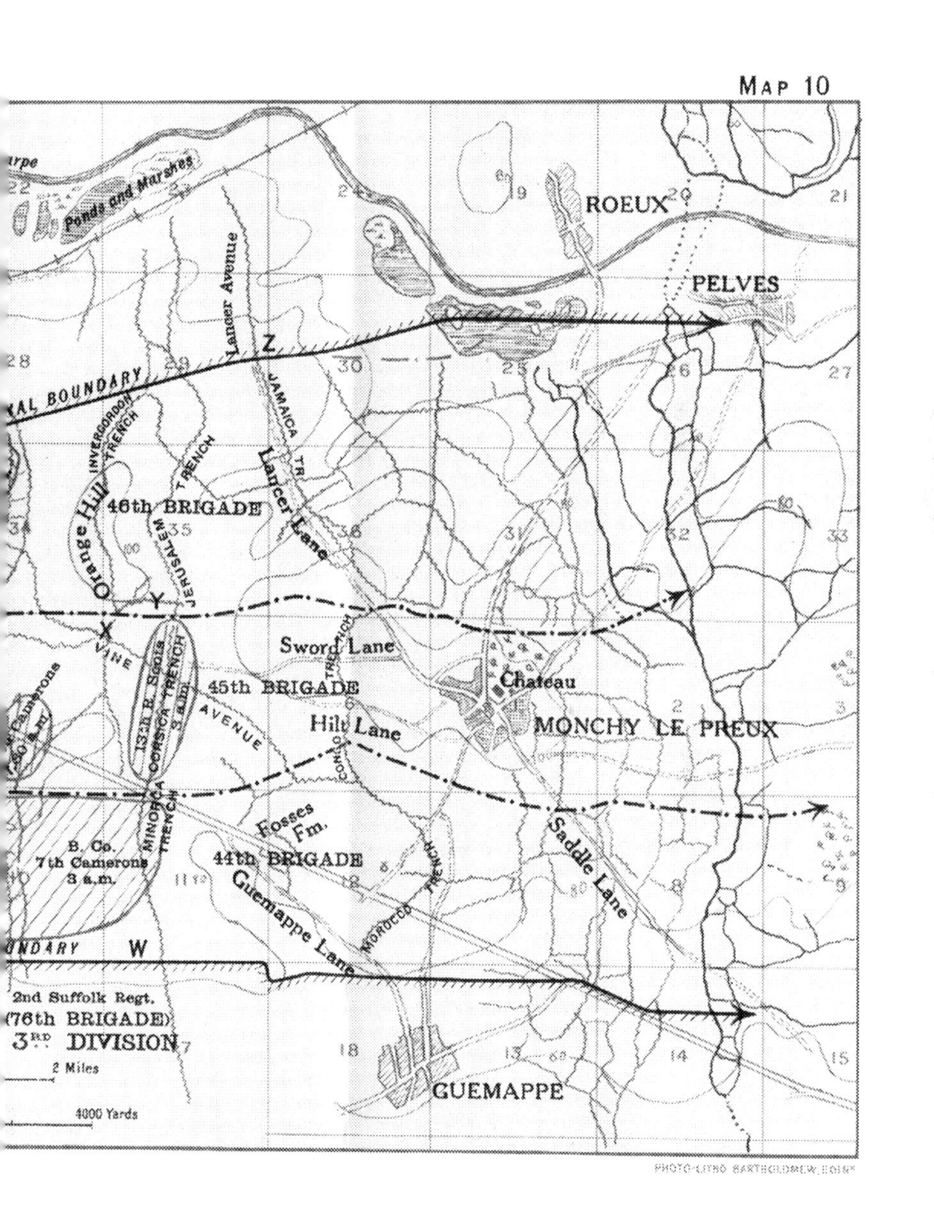

PHOTO-LITHO BARTHOLOMEW, EDINR

OPERATIONS EAST OF ARRAS, March 1918.

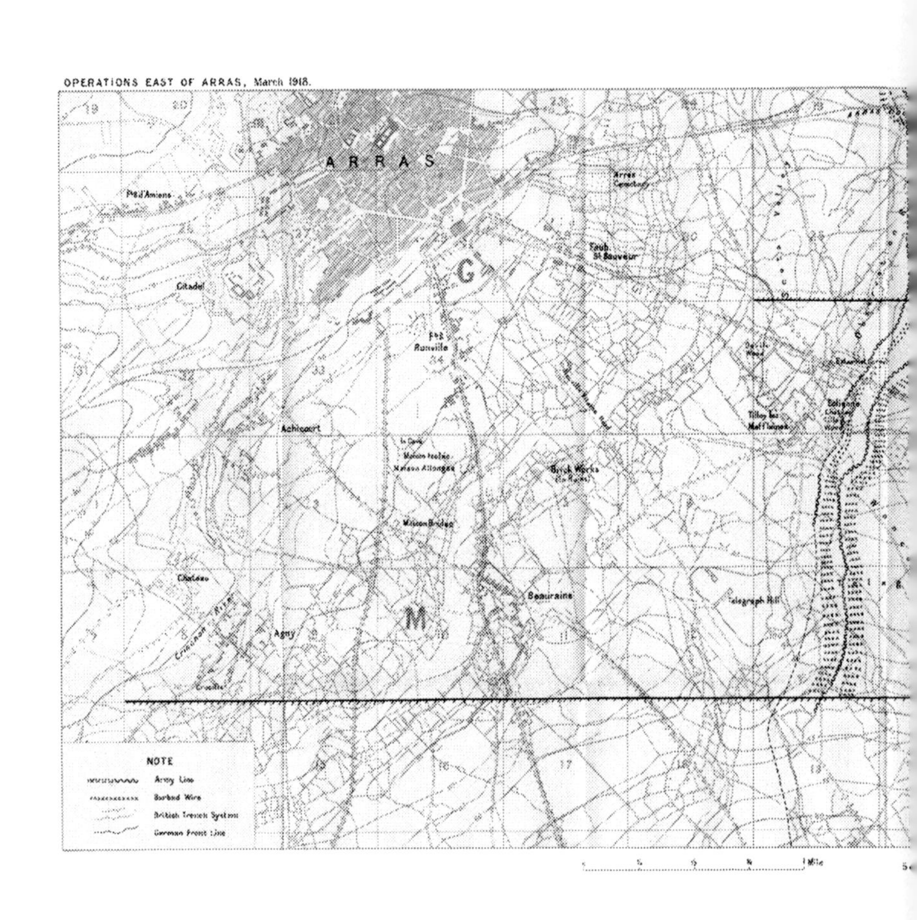

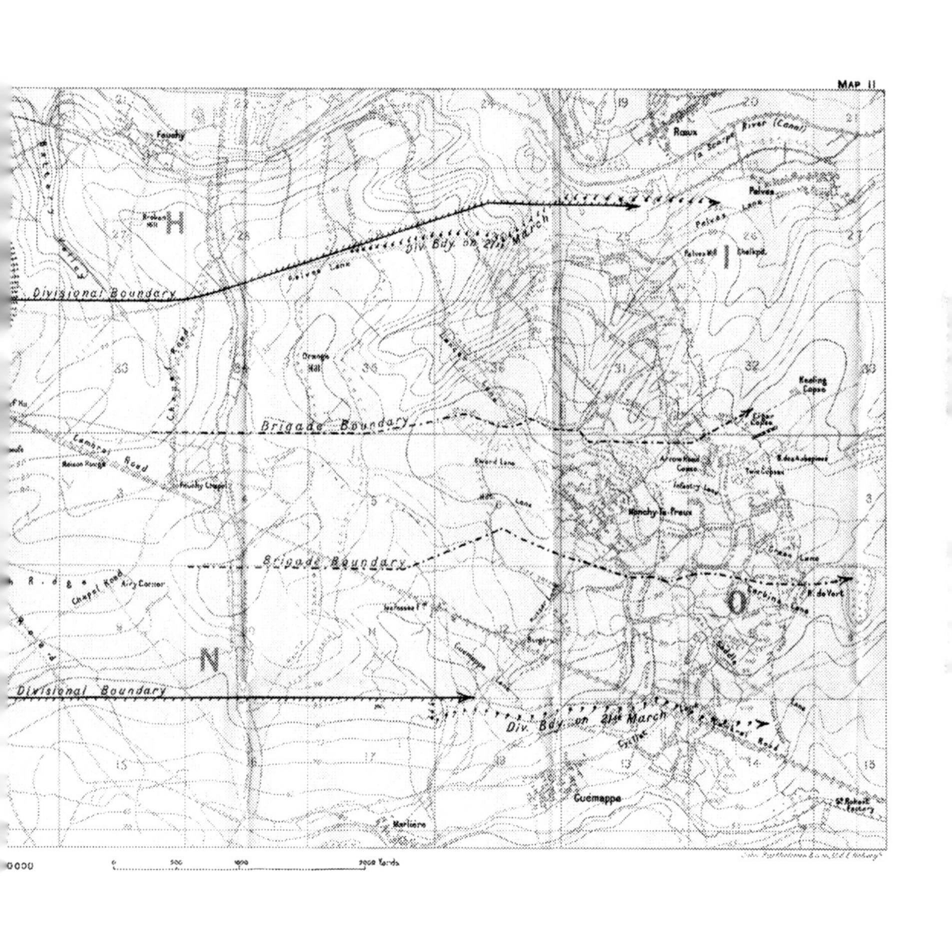
MAP 11
Divisional Boundary
Div. Bdy. on 21st March
Brigade Boundary
Brigade Boundary
Divisional Boundary
Div. Bdy. on 21st March
Fampoux
Roeux
River (Canal)
Pelves
Pelves Lane
Pelves Mill
Chalk pit
Keeling Copse
Orange Hill
Cambrai Road
Feuchy Chapel
Chapel Road
Airy Corner
Arrow Head Copse
Infantry Lane
Twin Copses
Monchy-le-Preux
Green Lane
Carbine Lane
Bois du Vert
Guemappe
Cavalry Farm
St Rohart Factory
Marliere
H
N
O
2000 Yards

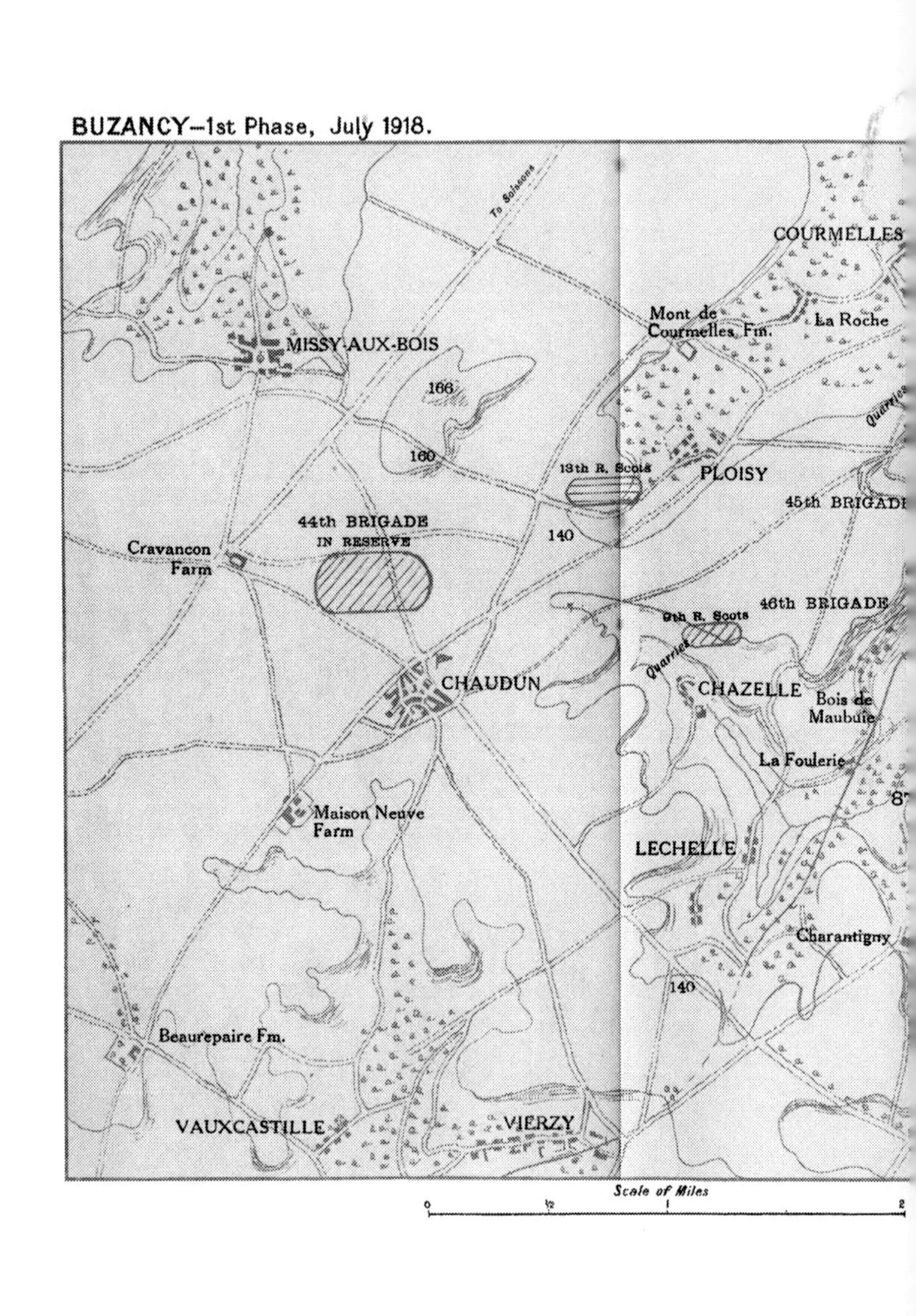

BUZANCY—1st Phase, July 1918.

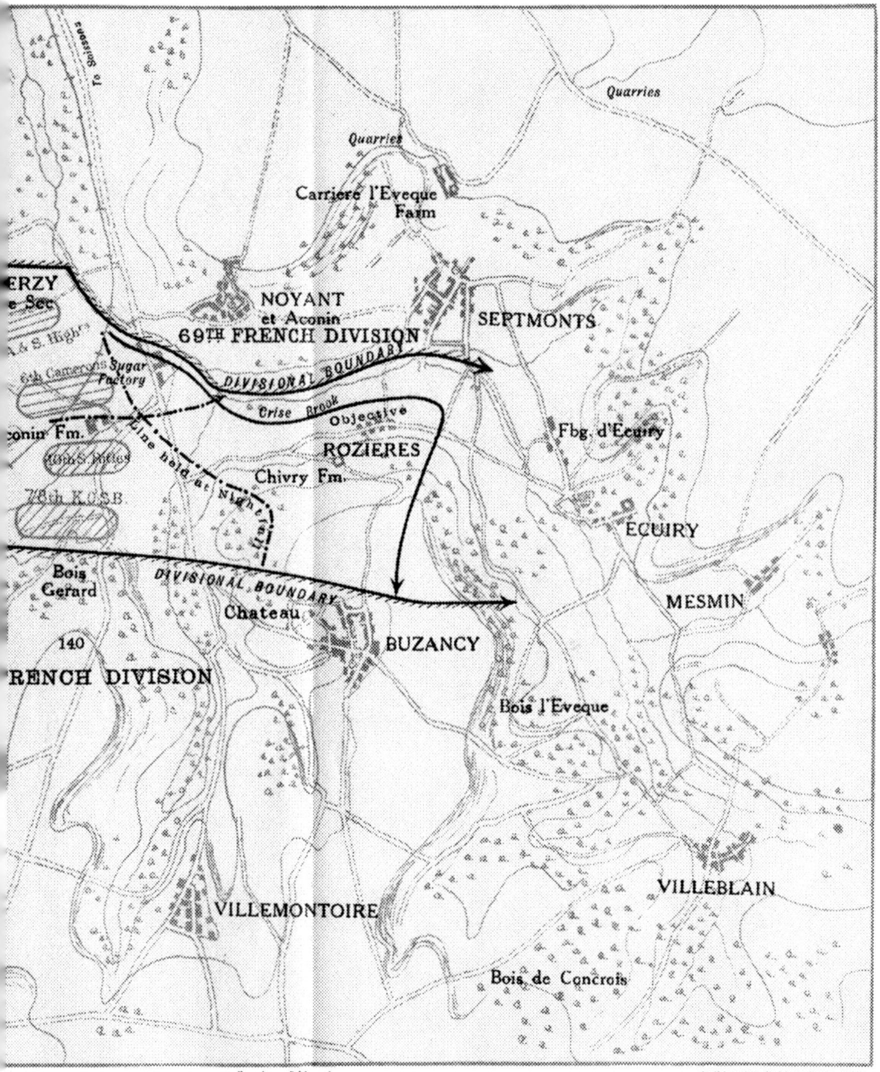

MAP 12

To Soissons
Quarries
Quarries
Carriere l'Eveque Farm
ERZY
e Sec
NOYANT et Aconin
69TH FRENCH DIVISION
SEPTMONTS
A. & S. Highrs
6th Camerons
Sugar Factory
DIVISIONAL BOUNDARY
Crise Brook
Objective
conin Fm.
ROZIERES
Chivry Fm.
Fbg. d'Ecuiry
78th K.O.S.B.
Line held at Night
ECUIRY
Bois Gerard
DIVISIONAL BOUNDARY
Chateau
MESMIN
140
BUZANCY
RENCH DIVISION
Bois l'Eveque
VILLEBLAIN
VILLEMONTOIRE
Bois de Concrois

Scale of Yards
0 1000 2000 3000 Yards

PHOTO-LITHO BARTHOLOMEW EDIN^R

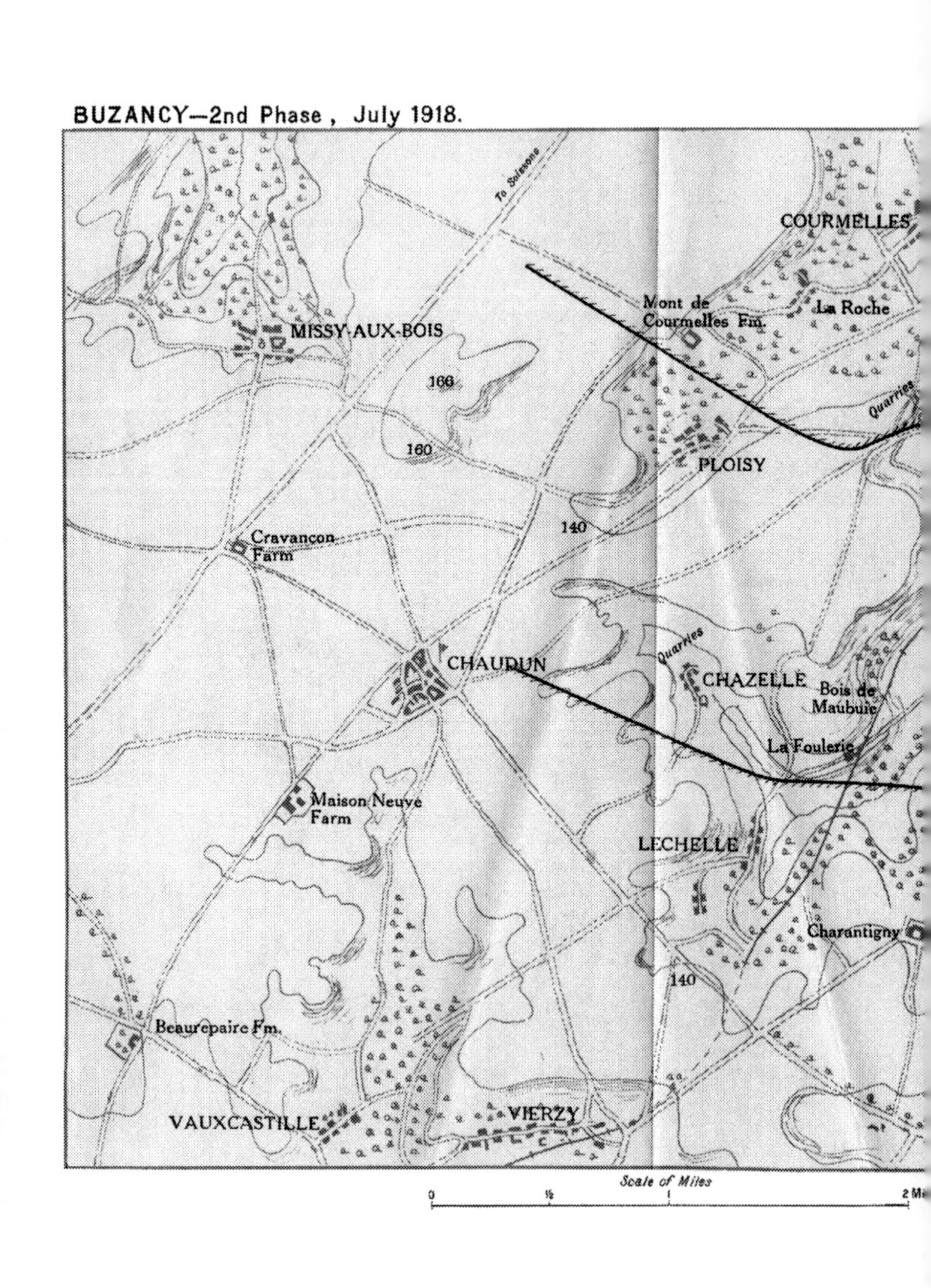
To Soissons
COURMELLES
MISSY-AUX-BOIS
Mont de Courmelles Fm.
La Roche
Quarries
160
PLOISY
140
Cravançon Farm
CHAUDUN
Quarries
CHAZELLE
Bois de Maubuic
La Foulerie
Maison Neuve Farm
LECHELLE
Charantigny
140
Beaurepaire Fm.
VAUXCASTILLE
VIERZY
Scale of Miles
0
½
1
2 Mi

BUZANCY—2nd Phase, July 1918.

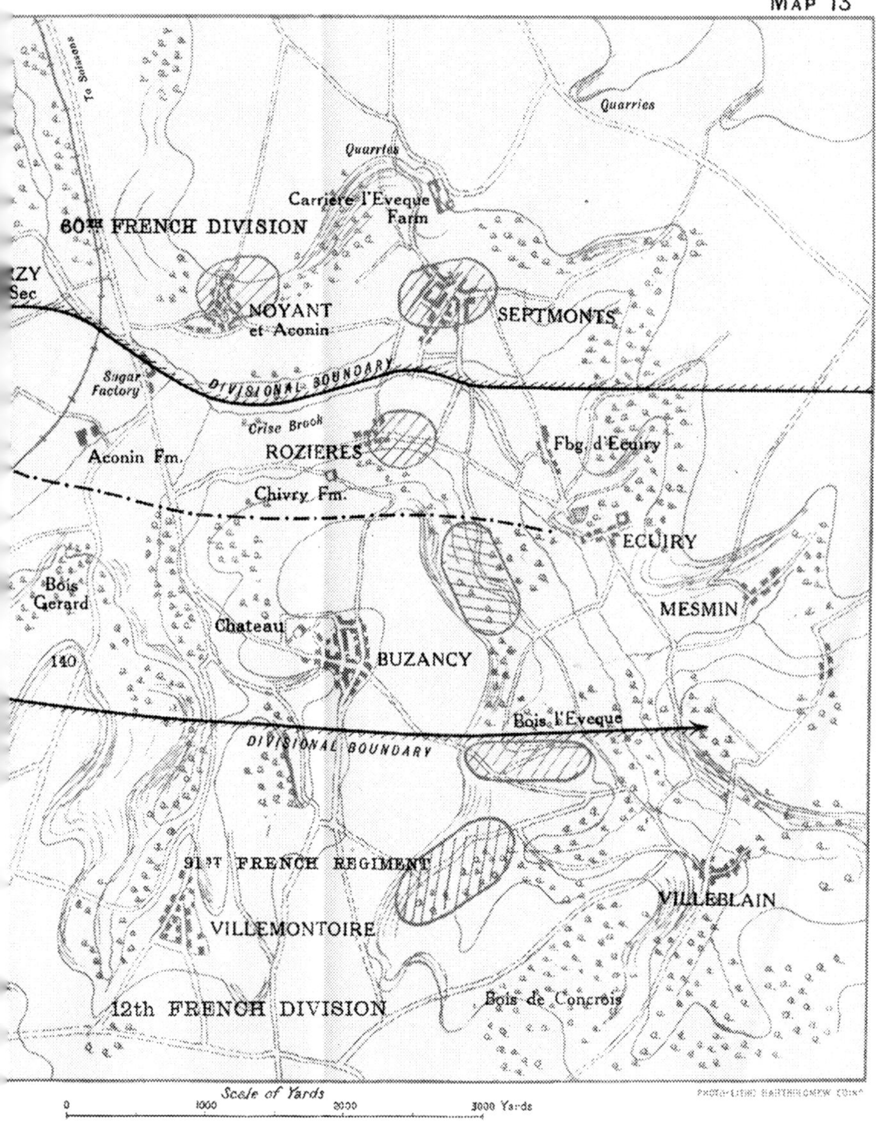

To Soissons
Quarries
Quarries
Carrière l'Eveque Farm
60TH FRENCH DIVISION
NOYANT et Aconin
SEPTMONTS
Sec
Sugar Factory
DIVISIONAL BOUNDARY
Crise Brook
Aconin Fm.
ROZIERES
Fbg. d'Ecuiry
Chivry Fm.
ECUIRY
Bois Gerard
MESMIN
Chateau
140
BUZANCY
Bois l'Eveque
DIVISIONAL BOUNDARY
91ST FRENCH REGIMENT
VILLEBLAIN
VILLEMONTOIRE
12th FRENCH DIVISION
Bois de Concrois
Scale of Yards
0
1000
2000
3000 Yards

BUZANCY – 3rd Phase, July 1918.

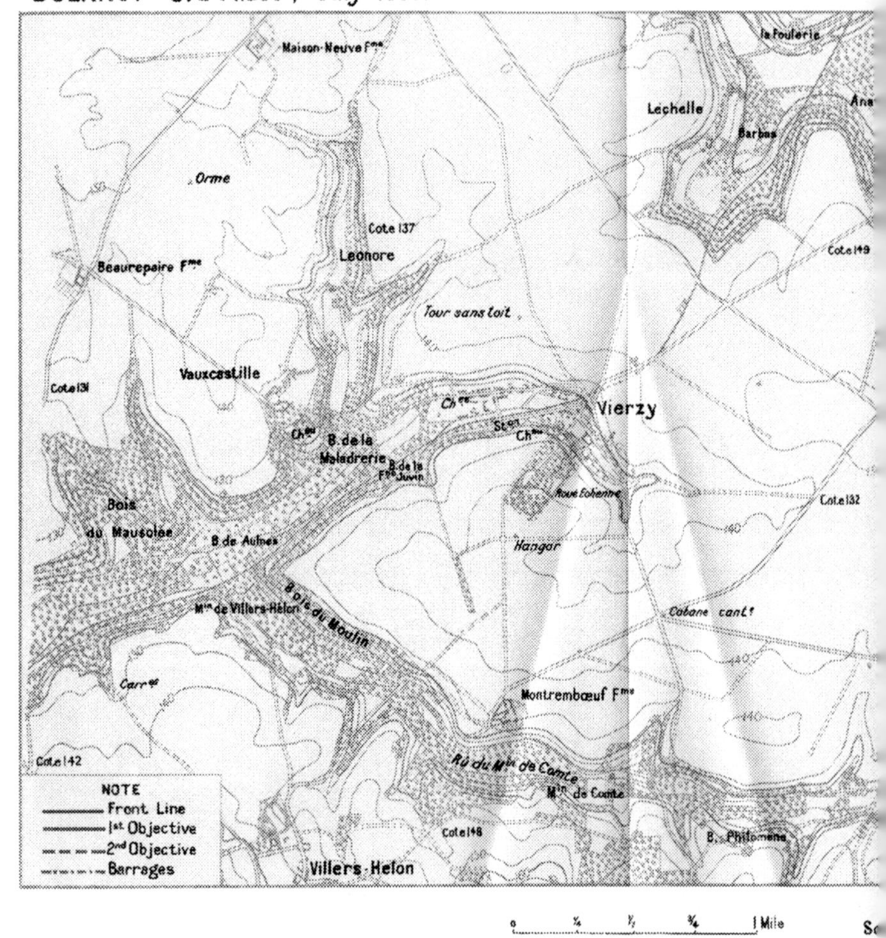

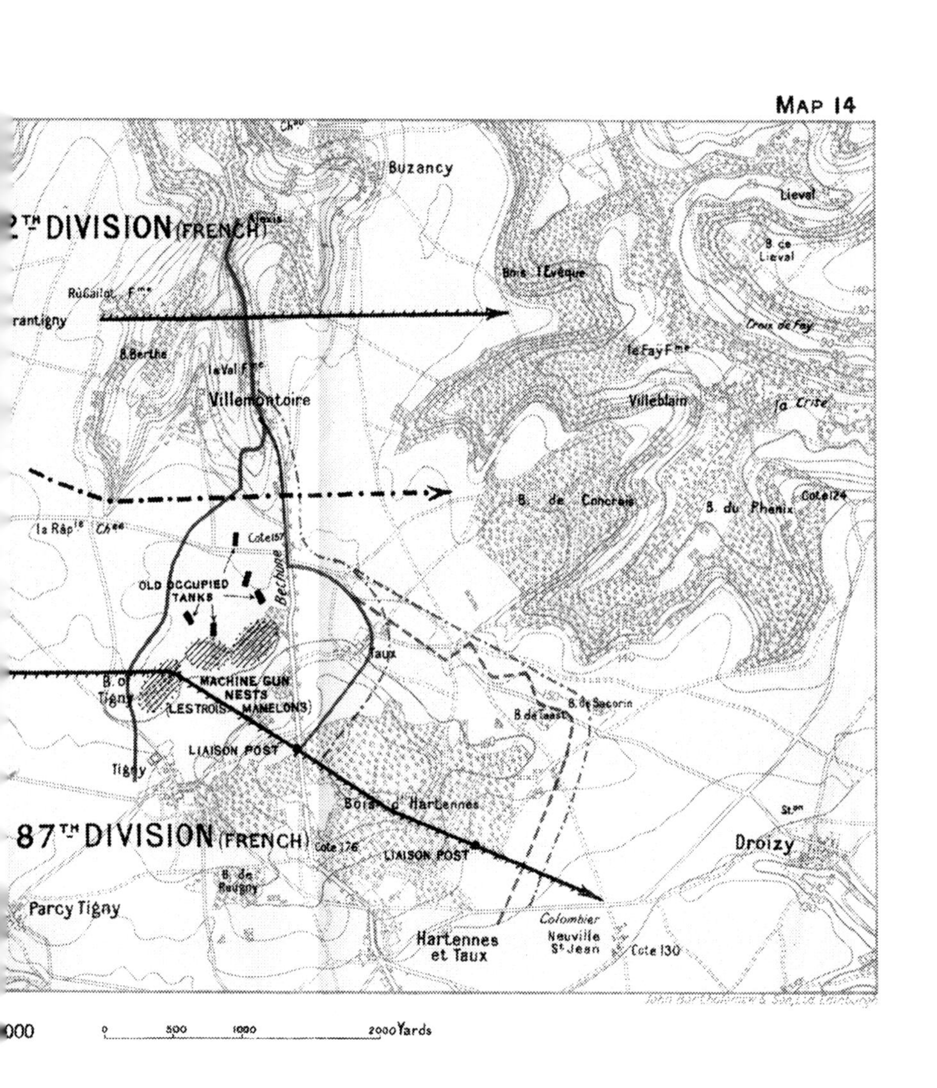

MAP 14
Buzancy
Lieval
B. de Lieval
2TH DIVISION (FRENCH)
Bois l'Evêque
Rûgailot Fme
rantigny
Croix de Fay
B.Berthe
le Fay Fme
le Val Fme
Villemontoire
Villeblain
la Crise
B. de Concrois
B. du Phenix
Cote 124
la Râp'ie Chee
Cote 157
OLD OCCUPIED TANKS
Bethune
Taux
MACHINE GUN NESTS (LES TROIS MANELONS)
B. de Tigny
B. de Sacorin
B. de Taast
LIAISON POST
Tigny
Bois d'Hartennes
87TH DIVISION (FRENCH)
Cote 176
LIAISON POST
Droizy
B. de Raugny
Parcy Tigny
Colombier
Hartennes et Taux
Neuville St Jean
Cote 130
0 500 1000 2000 Yards

ADVANCE OF THE 15th DIVISION N.E. OF LENS, October 1918

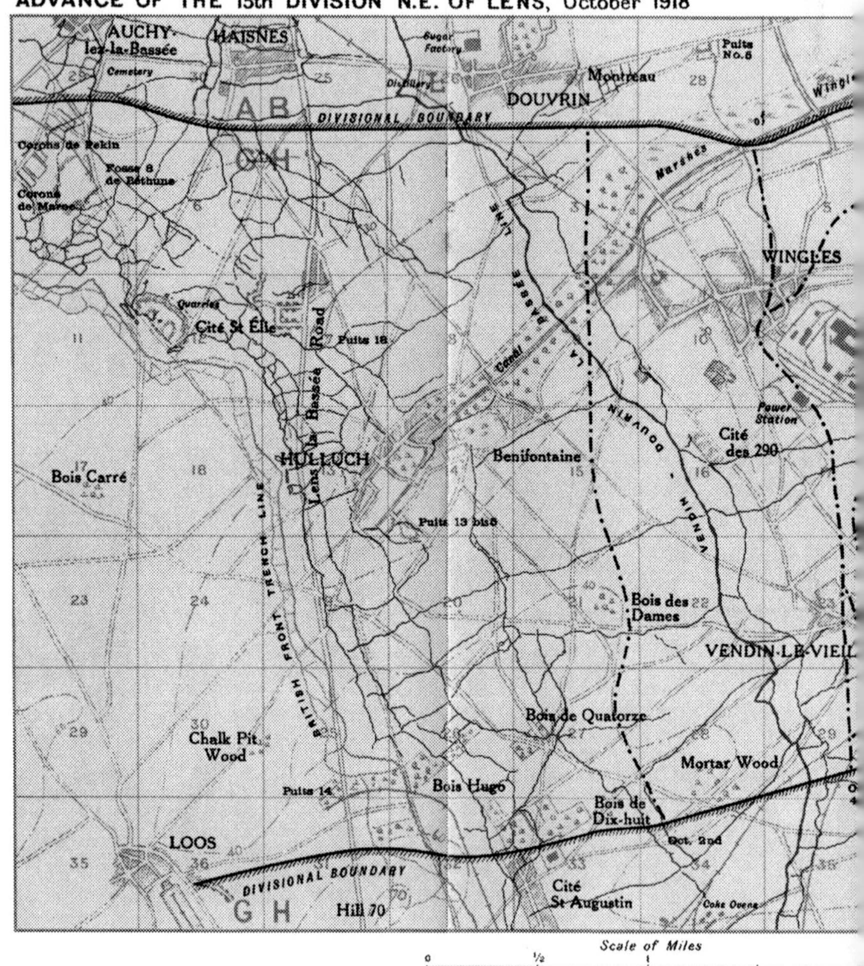

MAP 15

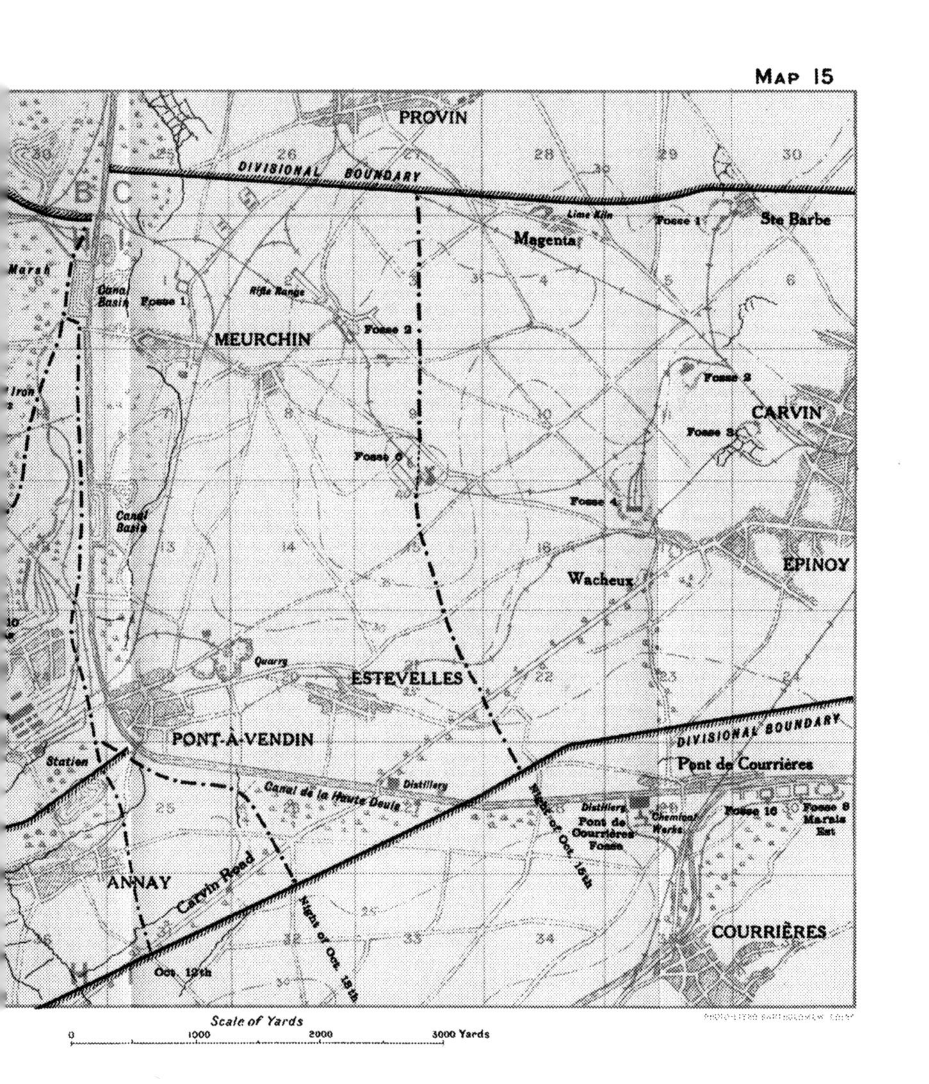

PROVIN
DIVISIONAL BOUNDARY
Lime Kiln
Fosse 1
Ste Barbe
Magenta
Marsh
Canal Basin
Fosse 1
Rifle Range
Fosse 2
MEURCHIN
Fosse 2
CARVIN
Fosse 3
Fosse 6
Fosse 4
Canal Basin
EPINOY
Wacheux
Quarry
ESTEVELLES
DIVISIONAL BOUNDARY
PONT-A-VENDIN
Station
Pont de Courrières
Distillery
Canal de la Haute Deule
Distillery
Chemical Works
Fosse 16
Fosse 8 Marais Est
Pont de Courrières Fosse
Night of Oct. 16th
ANNAY
Carvin Road
Night of Oct. 15th
Oct. 12th
COURRIÈRES
Scale of Yards
0
1000
2000
3000 Yards

SCHELDT AREA November 1918

0 ¼ ½ ¾ 1 2 Miles

Sca

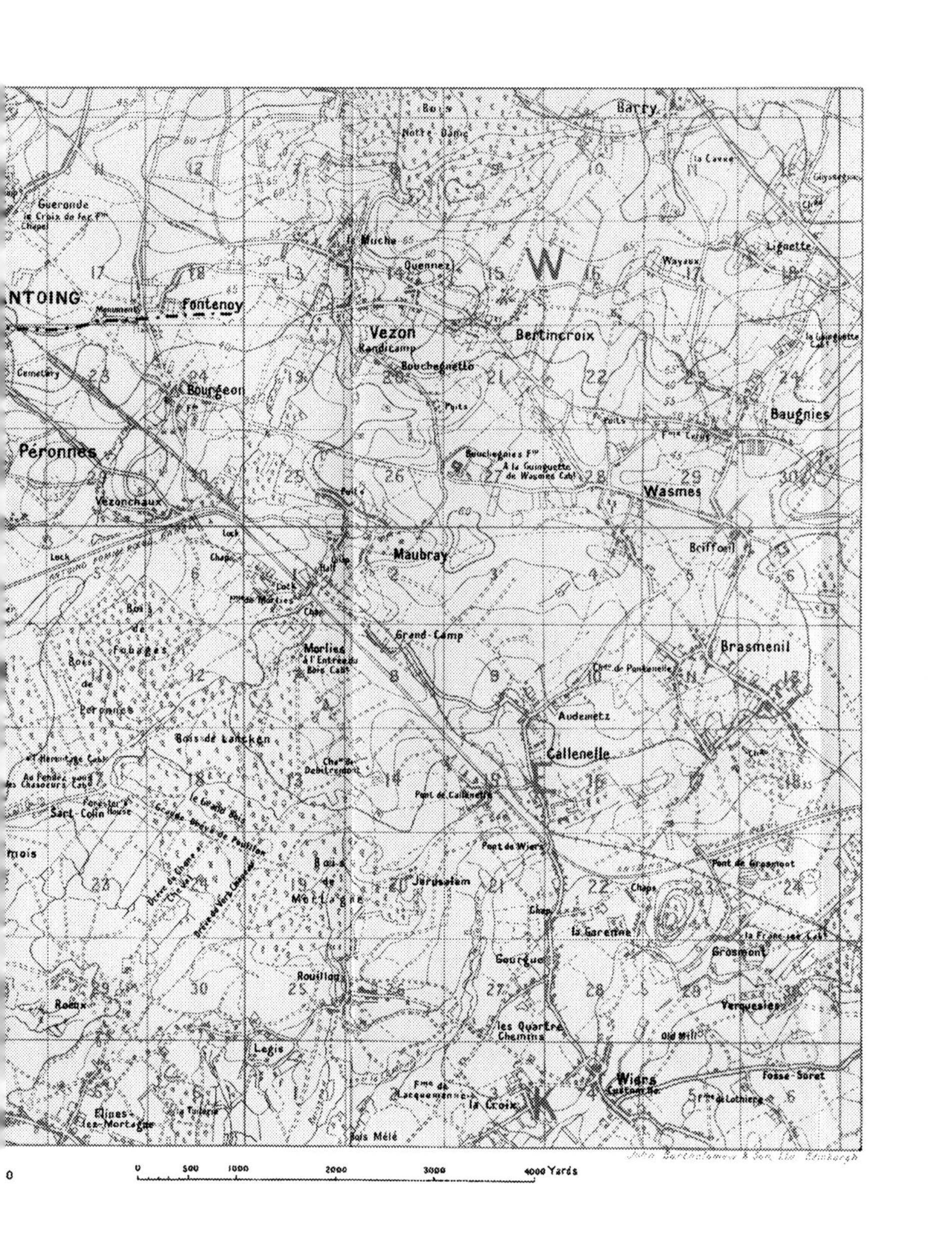

Barry
Notre Dame
la Cavée
Guerande
la Croix de fer Fme
Chapel
le Muche
Quennez
W
Wayaux
Lignette
ANTOING
Monument
Fontenoy
Vezon
Randicamp
Bertincroix
Bouchegnette
Cemetery
Bourgeon
Baugnies
Péronnes
Bouchegnies Fme
Vezonchaux
Wasmes
Lock
Maubray
Briffoeil
Bois de Fouages
Morlies
Grand Camp
Brasmenil
Bois de Péronnes
Audemetz
Bois de Lancken
Callenelle
Pont de Callenelle
Sart-Colin
Pont de Wiers
Pont de Grosmont
Jerusalem
Bois de Mortagne
la Garenne
Grosmont
Gourgue
Rouillon
Verquesies
Roeux
les Quartre Chemins
Old Mill
Legis
Wiers
Fosse-Soret
la Croix
Elines-les-Mortagne
Bois Mélé
0 500 1000 2000 3000 4000 Yards
John Bartholomew & Son Ltd. Edinburgh

Lightning Source UK Ltd.
Milton Keynes UK
18 March 2011

169480UK00001B/65/A